17th Linguistic Annotation Workshop (LAW-XVII)

Toronto, Canada
13 July 2023

ISBN: 978-1-7138-8228-2

Printed from e-media with permission by:

Curran Associates, Inc.
57 Morehouse Lane
Red Hook, NY 12571

Some format issues inherent in the e-media version may also appear in this print version.

Printed with permission by Curran Associates, Inc. (2024)

Association for Computational Linguistics
209 N. Eighth Street
Stroudsburg, Pennsylvania 18360

Phone: 1-570-476-8006
Fax: 1-570-476-0860

acl@aclweb.org

Additional copies of this publication are available from:

Curran Associates, Inc.
57 Morehouse Lane
Red Hook, NY 12571 USA
Phone: 845-758-0400
Fax: 845-758-2633
Email: curran@proceedings.com
Web: www.proceedings.com

LAW 2023

The 17th Linguistic Annotation Workshop (LAW-XVII) @ ACL 2023

Proceedings of the Workshop

July 13, 2023

The LAW organizers gratefully acknowledge the support from the following sponsors.

Introduction

Linguistic annotation of natural language corpora is the backbone of supervised methods of statistical natural language processing. The Linguistic Annotation Workshop (LAW) is the annual workshop of the ACL Special Interest Group on Annotation (SIGANN), and it provides a forum for the presentation and discussion of innovative research on all aspects of linguistic annotation, including the creation and evaluation of annotation schemes, methods for automatic and manual annotation, use and evaluation of annotation software and frameworks, representation of linguistic data and annotations, semi-supervised "human in the loop" methods of annotation, crowd-sourcing approaches, and more. As in the past, this year's LAW provides a forum for annotation researchers to work towards standardization, best practices, and interoperability of annotation information and software. These proceedings include papers that were presented at the 17th Linguistic Annotation Workshop (LAW-XVII), co-located with ACL 2023 in Toronto, Canada, on July 13, 2023.

This edition of the workshop is the seventeenth meeting of the ACL Special Interest Group for Annotation. The first workshop took place in 2007 at the ACL in Prague. Since then, the LAW has been held every year, consistently drawing substantial participation (both in terms of paper/poster submissions and participation in the actual workshop) providing evidence that the LAW's overall focus continues to be an important area of interest in the field, a substantial part of which relies on supervised learning from gold standard data sets. This year, we received 51 submissions, out of which 26 papers have been accepted to be presented at the workshop. In addition, 9 papers accepted to the Findings of ACL 2023 have been invited to be presented at the LAW.

The papers presented at LAW-XVII cover phenomena in a diverse range of 23 languages: Ancient Greek, English, Turkish, German, Czech, Spanish, Bengali, Italian, Hungarian, French, Chinese, Arapaho, Arabic, Gujarati, Hebrew, Hausa, Hindi, Indonesian, Javanese, Kannada, Sundanese, Swahili, and Yoruba.

The special theme of LAW-XVII is *Ethics and Annotation*. The workshop includes a discussion session about various aspects of ethics related to annotation work, e.g., the treatment of annotators, psychological health of annotators, bias, ethics in crowd-sourcing annotation scenarios, or annotation of information regarding ethics in text. LAW-XVII also features invited talks by Emily Bender (University of Washington, USA), Anne Lauscher (University of Hamburg, Germany), and Lilian Wanzare (Maseno University, Kenya).

Our thanks go to SIGANN, our organizing committee, for their continuing organization of the LAW workshops, and to the ACL 2023 workshop chairs, Eduardo Blanco, Yang Feng, and Annie Louis, for their support. Most of all, we would like to thank all the authors for submitting their papers to the workshop and our program committee members for their dedication and their extremely thoughtful reviews.

The LAW-XVII Program Co-Chairs:
Jakob Prange and Annemarie Friedrich

Organizing Committee

Program Chairs

Jakob Prange, The Hong Kong Polytechnic University
Annemarie Friedrich, University of Augsburg

SIGANN President

Amir Zeldes, Georgetown University

SIGANN Secretary

Ines Rehbein, Mannheim University

Remote Session Chairs

Heike Zinsmeister, Universität Hamburg
Djamé Seddah, Inria

SIGANN Officers

Claire Bonial, US Army Research Laboratory
Stefanie Dipper, Ruhr-Universität Bochum
Chu-Ren Huang, The Hong Kong Polytechnic University
Jena D. Hwang, Allen Institute for AI
Sandra Kübler, Indiana University
Lori Levin, Carnegie-Mellon University
Adam Meyers, New York University
Antonio Pareja-Lora, Universidad de Alcalá (UAH) / FITISPos (UAH) / ATLAS (UNED) / DMEG (UdG)
Massimo Poesio, Queen Mary University of London
Sameer Pradhan, LDC, Cemantix
Nancy Ide, Vassar College
Nathan Schneider, Georgetown University
Manfred Stede, Universität Potsdam
Katrin Tomanek, Google
Fei Xia, University of Washington
Nianwen Xue, Brandeis University
Deniz Zeyrek, Middle East Technical University

Invited Speakers

Emily M. Bender, University of Washington
Lilian D. A. Wanzare, Maseno University
Anne Lauscher, University of Hamburg

Program Committee

Program Committee

Omri Abend, The Hebrew University of Jerusalem
Melanie Andresen, Universität Stuttgart
Aditya Bhargava, University of Toronto
Claire Bonial, US Army Research Lab
Miriam Butt, University of Konstanz
Emmanuele Chersoni, The Hong Kong Polytechnic University
Christian Chiarcos, Goethe-Universität Frankfurt am Main
Kathryn Conger, Universitiy of Colorado, Boulder
Daniel Dakota, Indiana University
Marie-Catherine De Marneffe, The Ohio State University
Stefanie Dipper, Ruhr-Universität Bochum
Lucia Donatelli, Vrije Universiteit Amsterdam
Jonathan Dunn, University of Canterbury
Markus Egg, Humboldt-Universität zu Berlin
Kim Gerdes, Paris-Saclay University
Luke Gessler, Georgetown University
Jinghang Gu, The Hong Kong Polytechnic University
Udo Hahn, Friedrich-Schiller-Universitaet Jena
Andrea Horbach, Universität Hildesheim
Jena D. Hwang, Allen Institute for AI
Nancy Ide, Vassar College/Brandeis University
Michael Kranzlein, Georgetown University
Sandra Kübler, Indiana University
Ekaterina Lapshinova-Koltunski, Stiftung Universität Hildesheim
Katja Markert, Heidelberg University
Adam Meyers, New York University
Philippe Muller, IRIT, University of Toulouse
Anna Nedoluzhko, Charles University in Prague
Simon Ostermann, German Research Center for Artificial Intelligence (DFKI)
Alexis Palmer, University of Colorado Boulder
Antonio Pareja-Lora, Universidad de Alcalá (UAH) / FITISPos (UAH) / ATLAS (UNED) / DMEG (UdG)
Siyao Peng, Georgetown University
Miriam R. L. Petruck, FrameNet
Barbara Plank, LMU Munich
Massimo Poesio, Queen Mary University of London
James Pustejovsky, Brandeis University
Ines Rehbein, University of Mannheim
Michael Roth, University of Stuttgart
Josef Ruppenhofer, FernUniversität in Hagen
Nathan Schneider, Georgetown University
Djamé Seddah, Inria
Ludovic Tanguy, CLLE: University of Toulouse & CNRS
Joel Tetreault, Dataminr
Lilian Diana Awuor Wanzare, Maseno University
Bonnie Webber, University of Edinburgh

Michael Wiegand, Alpen-Adria-Universitaet Klagenfurt
Fei Xia, University of Washington
Nianwen Xue, Brandeis University
Amir Zeldes, Georgetown University
Winnie Huiheng Zeng, The Hong Kong Polytechnic University
Deniz Zeyrek, Middle East Technical University
Heike Zinsmeister, Universität Hamburg

Table of Contents

Program

Thursday, July 13, 2023

08:45 - 09:00	*Opening Remarks*
09:00 - 09:45	*Invited Talk 1*
09:45 - 11:15	*Onsite/remote Poster Sessions 1 (Coffee served from 10:30 to 11:00)*
11:15 - 12:00	*Invited Talk 2*
12:00 - 14:00	*Lunch Break*
14:00 - 15:00	*Invited Talk 3*
15:00 - 15:30	*Theme Paper Highlights Session*
15:30 - 17:00	*Onsite/remote Poster Sessions 2 (Coffee served from 15:30 to 16:00)*
17:00 - 17:45	*Discussion Session*
17:45 - 18:00	*Closing Remarks*

Medieval Social Media: Manual and Automatic Annotation of Byzantine Greek Marginal Writing

Colin Swaelens[1], **Ilse De Vos**[2] and **Els Lefever**[1]
[1] LT3, Language and Translation Technology Team
Department of Translation, Interpreting and Communication
[2] Department of Linguistics Ghent University, 9000 Ghent, Belgium
{colin.swaelens, i.devos, els.lefever}@ugent.be

Abstract

In this paper, we present the interim results of a transformer-based annotation pipeline for Ancient and Medieval Greek. As the texts in the Database of Byzantine Book Epigrams have not been normalised, they pose more challenges for manual and automatic annotation than Ancient Greek, normalised texts do. As a result, the existing annotation tools perform poorly. We compiled three data sets for the development of an automatic annotation tool and carried out an inter-annotator agreement study, with a promising agreement score. The experimental results show that our part-of-speech tagger yields accuracy scores that are almost 50 percentage points higher than the widely used rule-based system Morpheus. In addition, error analysis revealed problems related to phenomena also occurring in current social media language.

1 Introduction

Despite the nonexistence of the world wide web in the Middle Ages, Byzantine book epigrams bear some resemblance to current social media, such as Twitter.[1] Just like a tweet, a book epigram is usually a rather short, personal statement of an author, who expresses themselves on their daily occupation, i.e. copying manuscripts. Furthermore, the typeface of both tweets and book epigrams displays a lot of *orthographic inconsistencies* as the content is often written phonetically. However, the big difference between social media and Byzantine book epigrams is the amount of text available for NLP: 575,000 tweets are sent every minute, while the Database of Byzantine book epigrams (DBBE) (Ricceri et al., 2023) counts 12,000 epigrams in total.

The Byzantine book epigrams that make up the DBBE, can be defined as metrical paratexts, i.e. poems standing next to (para, from the Greek word παρά) another text or figure. They often appear in the margins of manuscripts or as scribblings between two paragraphs. Concerning content, these epigrams, among other things, comment on the main text of the manuscript, give some insight in the life of the scribe or show off the scribe's knowledge. DBBE Occurrence 32143 serves as an example, provided with the authors' translation:

(1) ὥσπερ ξένοι χαίρουσιν ἰδεῖν πατρίδα
οὕτω καὶ οἱ γράφοντες βιβλίου τέλος
Just like travellers rejoice upon seeing their homeland,
so do writers upon reaching the end of a book.[2]

The orthographic idiosyncrasies these book epigrams display are mainly due to a phonetic evolution, called *itacism*, which indicates the shift of the classical Athenian pronunciation of the vowels ι [i], η [ɛ], υ [y] and the diphthongs ει [ɛj], οι [oj] to the pronunciation [i]. The scribe of the book epigram – who may or may not have authored it – did not always know (or care?) which of the five [i]'s needed to be written. The disyllabic word ἰδεῖν (to look), for example, is present in 19 different forms in DBBE. Exactly that is the added value of DBBE compared to other pre-Modern Greek corpora: these corpora generally provide Greek that is normalised to an Ancient Greek model, while DBBE provides both the original transcription of the manuscript and an edited, normalised version. The former is called *occurrence*, the latter *type*.

[1] *Byzantine* and *Medieval* will be used as synonyms, covering the period between ca. 500 and 1500 AD

[2] Translations are made by the authors, unless stated otherwise.

Proceedings of the 17th Linguistic Annotation Workshop (LAW-XVII), pages 1–9
July 13, 2023 ©2023 Association for Computational Linguistics

The texts of the DBBE will be subject of further linguistic and literary research, for which these texts are ideally all annotated. Since manual annotation is not feasible for all words, we opted for an automatic way to do so. Preliminary tests showed that existing systems for morphological analysis do not perform well on the text of the occurrences. To overcome the shortcomings of current systems for morphological analysis, we developed a novel transformer-based part-of-speech tagger for Ancient and Medieval Greek.[3] To evaluate the performance of the tagger, a novel gold standard for Byzantine Greek was developed, where all tokens were provided with a coarse-grained part-of-speech tag and full morphological analysis. In addition, we also performed an error analysis, which revealed several problems that are very typical to this kind of texts, i.e. texts where the material context (the manuscript) strongly affects the language.

2 Related Research

The interest in NLP for pre-Modern Greek has increased over the last few years, thanks to – among other things – the availability of open-source corpora. The first corpus initiative for Greek texts was the Thesaurus Linguae Graecae (TLG) (Pantelia, 2022), a comprehensive digital library of Greek texts written between 800 BC and 1453 AD (viz. the fall of Byzantium), that sums up to more than 110M tokens, covering 10,000 works and 4,000 authors. The TLG, however, is not freely available. An open-source alternative is the Open Greek and Latin Project[4], that consists of the Perseus Digital Library (Crane, 2022), a collection of more than 13,5M tokens of mostly classical Greek prose and poetry, on the one hand, and the First1K Project, a complementary part to Perseus summing up to 25,5M tokens of classical and post-classical Greek prose and poetry[5].

In addition to these two text corpora, several treebanks were developed. The Ancient Greek Dependency Treebank (AGDT) (Bamman and Crane, 2011; Celano, 2019) stores 560,000 tokens from both classical prose and poetry, that were manually provided with a part-of-speech tag, morphological analysis, lemma and syntactic relation. PROIEL (Haug and Jøhndal, 2008) has a more specific content: the treebank stores the New Testament in Greek and four other languages, counting 277,000 tokens. The Gorman treebank (Gorman, 2020) is a treebank of around 550,000 tokens of exclusively classical Greek prose. As a last example, the Pedalion Trees (Keersmaekers et al., 2019) are almost completely complementary to the AGDT (apart from some texts) and count some 320,000 tokens. The Pedalion Trees contain annotated texts from Trismegistos (Depauw and Gheldof, 2014), a database of papyrus texts, that displays the original text with all its idiosyncrasies and even *errors*, just like the occurrences in DBBE. All of the above mentioned treebanks make use of or have extended the Universal Dependencies (Nivre et al., 2017).

Since the development of Morpheus (Crane, 1991), a rule- and dictionary-based system to perform part-of-speech tagging (or morphological analysis) of Greek tokens, multiple part-of-speech taggers have been developed to cope with Morpheus' two main pitfalls: it does not disambiguate ambiguous forms and it cannot deal with out-of-vocabulary words. Celano et al. (2016) did a comparative study, which showed that MateTagger (Bohnet and Nivre, 2012) outperformed Hunpos tagger (Halácsy et al., 2007), RFTagger (Schmid and Laws, 2008), the OpenNLP part-of-speech tagger[6] and NLTK Unigram tagger (Bird, 2006) on Ancient, normalised Greek data. When Keersmaekers (2019) repeated that experiment with Mate tagger, RFTagger and MarMot tagger (Mueller et al., 2013) to find out which is best suited for papyrological data, RFTagger outperformed the other two. Schmid (2019) also developed RNN tagger, the neural counterpart of RFTagger. Singh et al. (2021) explored the possibilities of a transformer-based part-of-speech tagger on DBBE types, the normalised text of the book epigrams, which yielded promising results.

[3] As Greek is a highly inflectional language, we use part-of-speech tag to cover both the part-of-speech and the full morphological analysis of a word in the rest of the paper.

[4] https://opengreekandlatin.org

[5] https://opengreekandlatin.github.io/First1KGreek/

[6] https://opennlp.apache.org

3 Data Compilation and Annotation

Our aim is not to annotate the DBBE *types*, the normalised poems, but the DBBE *occurrences*. To achieve this, we trained a transformer-based language model, of which the embeddings are used to train a part-of-speech tagger. Section 3.1 describes the data sets used for training the language model and fine-tuning it for part-of-speech tagging, while Section 3.2 describes the manual annotation and validation of the Byzantine Greek evaluation set.

3.1 Training Data Compilation

Since transformer-based language models are very greedy and the Greek data available is rather scarce, we complemented all corpora described in Section 2, except for the TLG, with the Modern Greek Wikipedia data, shown in Figure 1. This is done, because Byzantine Greek is situated in time between Ancient Greek and Modern Greek, and because Byzantine Greek displays already quite some Modern Greek characteristics (Holton et al., 2019). Data labelled as *incerta* could not be situated in any time period, *varia* treats anthologies. From now on, we call this the LM data set. In addition to this data set, we compiled a training set for the part-of-speech tagger, consisting of all above described treebanks, summing up to 1,132,120 Ancient Greek tokens.

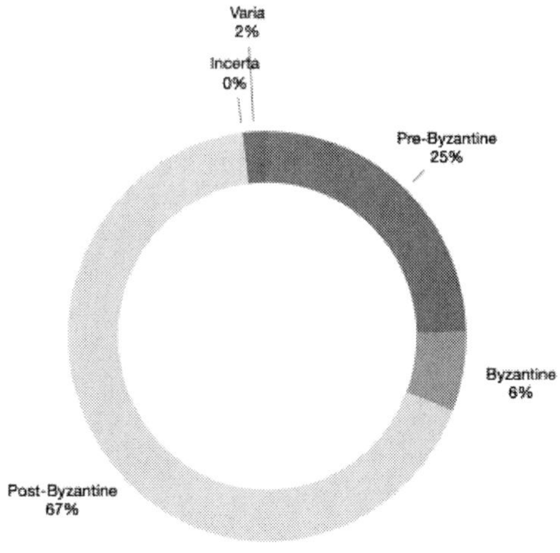

Figure 1: BERT training data

3.2 Evaluation Data Annotation

We compiled a test set of 10,000 tokens from the DBBE *occurrences* to evaluate whether the part-of-speech model is able to analyse the Byzantine data given its training on Ancient Greek data. This evaluation set has been manually annotated, following the AGDT annotation guidelines (Celano, 2018), so that the DBBE, when eventually annotated, is complementary to the existing resources. However, we first carried out an inter-annotator agreement experiment (IAA), which has – to the best of our knowledge – not yet been conducted for either Ancient or Byzantine Greek. The aim of this IAA study is twofold: firstly to evaluate whether the label set shown in Table 1 is suitable for this corpus of Byzantine book epigrams; secondly to evaluate whether the manual annotations are reliable and consistent across annotators, which is a prerequisite to use the resulting corpus for evaluating and – in the near future – training our part-of-speech tagger.

Given the nature of our data, we saw it necessary to add one label to the AGDT label set, namely *missing*. As mentioned above, our corpus consists of faithful manuscript transcriptions. As shown in Example 2, words or word groups that are illegible are marked with (...). These so-called lacunae are rather rare in Greek text editions. This is why pre-existing corpora – which consist only of text editions – do not need any label for them. For easy reference, we decided to name this label *missing*.

(2) *(...) χρόνον τε και λόγους καὶ τὴν φύσιν*
(...) χronon te kje logus kje tin fisin

(...) time and also words and the nature

DBBE Occurrence 30520

The IAA experiment was carried out by three annotators, linguists with profound knowledge of Ancient Greek. They were asked to annotate some 1,000 tokens we extracted from the epigrams shown in Table 3 with the features shown in Table 1. Because of the highly inflectional nature of the Greek language, the annotation consisted of both the assignment of a part-of-speech and the token's morphological analysis. Since the part-of-speech tag and the morphological analysis of a token are aggregated in one label, our tag set sums up to more than 1,200 labels. The eventual tag consists of nine slots, corresponding to the nine columns in Table 1. This label set follows, just like the treebanks in Section 2, the Universal Dependencies label set. To relieve the annotators, we bootstrapped the tokens making use of Singh et al.'s part-of-speech tagger to already suggest a morphological analysis. However, this was a difficult assessment, as we know that the annotators might be influenced by the result of the bootstrapping. The annotators were asked to annotate no more than two hours a day to assure that they could stay focused. Upon completion, we calculated the IAA scores with Fleiss' Kappa.

The IAA experiment resulted in an agreement of 92.72% for the part-of-speech and 89.83% for the complete morphological analysis. The agreement scores are very high, showing *almost perfect* agreement (>90%) for the part-of-speech tagging and morphological analysis in isolation, and very *strong* agreement (80-90%) for the combined label. These scores are very encouraging, especially because we perform part-of-speech tagging on Greek data, for which different tags are often possible and arguments can be made for different analyses of the same word.

This can be illustrated with the word χάριν (*on behalf of*) followed by a genitive. One can argue that its part-of-speech is a noun, χάρις, since its accusative is used in an adverbial way. It is just as valid, however, to state that χάριν is an adverb *an sich*. In our test set, not once is there an agreement between the three annotators about the token χάριν. One of the annotators consistently tags χάριν as a preposition, while the other two annotators tagged two occurrences of χάριν as noun, and the other four as preposition. For the eventual annotation, χάριν is tagged as adverb when followed by a genitive; otherwise it is tagged as a noun.

While further investigating cases of disagreement, some tendencies caught the eye. About 50% of the disagreement is attributed to the part-of-speech tag, especially the difference between *noun* and *adjective*. According to the dictionary LSJ (Liddell et al., 1966), the last word of Example 3, φίλον (friend), is an adjective. This adjective, however, can be substantivised by putting an article in front, as is the case in Example 3. Two of our annotators tagged φίλον as an adjective, one as a noun. For the eventual annotation of the gold standard, these substantivised adjectives were annotated as a noun.

(3) χείρας ἐκτείνας δεξιοῦται τον φίλον
with extended hands, he greets his friend
DBBE Occurrence 21375

The next category of disagreement is related to the gender of words. Quite some Greek words have the same morphology for both masculine and feminine, e.g. the adjective ἄπιστος (*untrue*), or for both masculine and neutral, e.g. the genitive singular ἀγαθοῦ (*good*), or even for the three genders, e.g. the article in the genitive plural τῶν (the). The article τῶν is twelve times attested in our IAA study and caused disagreement four times. In our view, this is due to fatigue or negligence of the annotators, as the gender can be deducted from the agreeing noun, as shown in Example 4. Two annotators tagged this τῶν as masculine, notwithstanding its agreement with the neutral word βουλευμάτων (*decisions*).

(4) ἐπήβολος φρὴν τῶν σοφῶν βουλευμάτων
the intelligence, partaking in wise decisions
DBBE Occurrence 30520

For future annotations we explicitly pointed out to not assign a tag before the whole constituent was read, in the hope to prevent this type of inaccuracies.

Nevertheless, we dare say that the label set is well suited for this annotation task, given the high agreement scores.

4 A Novel Part-of-Speech Tagger for Byzantine Greek

4.1 BERT Language Model

As we desire our part-of-speech tagger copes with all idiosyncrasies of our Medieval Greek corpus, the need emerged to include context

PoS	Person	Number	Tense	Mood	Voice	Gender	Case	Degree
adjective	1	singular	aorist	imperative	active	common	nom	comp
adverb	2	plural	future	indicative	medial	feminine	acc	super
article	3	dual	fut. perf.	infinitive	med-pass	masculine	gen	-
conjunction	-		imperfect	optative	passive	neutral	dat	
exclamation			perfect	participle	-	-	voc	
interjection			pluperfect	subjunctive			-	
punctuation			present	-				
noun			-					
numeral								
particle								
preposition								
pronoun								
verb								
missing								

Table 1: Overview of the nine slots that make up the part-of-speech tag of each token. That tag is a combination of the part-of-speech and the morphological analysis of the token.

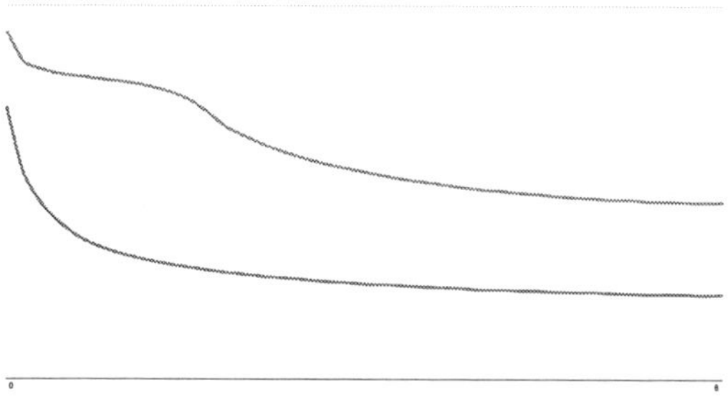

Figure 2: Convergence of loss on held out test set. The blue graph is the pre-Byzantine and Byzantine data set, the red one is complemented with post-Byzantine greek.

into the model. Firstly, we developed two BERT (Devlin et al., 2018) language models: one that has been trained on the LM data set *without* Modern Greek, described in Section 3.1, and a second that has been trained on the complete LM data set, including Modern Greek. This LM data set consists of 31,467,014 pre-Byzantine tokens, 7,952,719 Byzantine tokens, 85,575,140 post-Byzantine tokens and 2,418,672 tokens that could not be classified in one of the previous classes, counting 127,413,536 tokens in total, as shown in Figure 1. This data served as input for the BERT model, optimised for Masked Language Modelling, with the following parameters: 15% of the input tokens are replaced by [MASK] tokens, the maximum sequence length per sentence was limited to 512 sub-words and 12 hidden layers were used. The validation loss convergence as a function of time of both language models is shown in Figure 2.

As illustrated by the loss functions in Figure 2, it is clear that the language model trained on all pre-Byzantine, Byzantine and post-Byzantine Greek data performs best. We call this language model DBBErt, and made it available for the research community[7]. This model will be the basis for the fine-tuning for part-of-speech tagging.

4.2 Part-of-Speech Fine-tuning

As a second step, the DBBErt language model is incorporated into our part-of-speech tagger, that, as mentioned in Section 1, also provides the full morphological analysis.

As a training set, we used the treebanks described in Section 2 and extracted the part-of-speech tags and morphological information. In addition we extended the training set with 2,000 manually annotated tokens from DBBE occurrences. To train the part-of-speech tagger, we made use of the FLAIR framework (Akbik et al., 2019). The contextual token embeddings from DBBErt (cf. Section 4.1) are stacked with randomly initialised character embeddings. These are processed by a bi-directional long short-term memory (LSTM) encoder and a conditional random field (CRF) decoder: a combination commonly used for sequential tagging tasks. The LSTM has a hidden size of 256 and starts with a learning rate of 0.1 that is linearly decreased during training.

4.3 Evaluation of the Part-of-Speech Tagger

For the evaluation of our part-of-speech tagger, we have to keep in mind that the training was

[7]This model is available at https://huggingface.co/colinswaelens/DBBErt

Model	Accuracy	Precision	Recall	F1
RNN Tagger	63.04%	65.27%	63.04%	61.92%
fine-tuned pre-Byzantine and Byzantine LM	63.29%	69.19%	63.29%	62.14%
fine-tuned DBBErt LM	69.89%	73.22%	68.57%	67.32%

Table 2: Evaluation scores for the full morphological analysis for (1) RNN Tagger, (2) the tagger fine-tuned on the LM containing pre-Byzantine and Byzantine data, and (3) the tagger fine-tuned on DBBErt (containing all Greek data).

done with mostly Ancient, normalised Greek data, while the evaluation set existed of not-normalised Byzantine Greek epigrams. As an intermediate step, we first evaluated the performance of our part-of-speech tagger on a test set consisting of manually annotated tokens from DBBE types. Our model yielded an accuracy score of 83.64%, a score competitive to Singh et al.'s 86.66% on that same test set. The slight difference in performance might be attributed to the fact that Singh et al. retrained a Modern Greek language model that stripped off all diacritics of both training and test data. Our model, however, did take into account all diacritics present in Medieval Greek.

The final evaluation, however, is performed on 8,000 tokens from DBBE occurrences and resulted in 69,89% accuracy. The drop in accuracy is not surprising, given the very challenging nature of the Byzantine poems, which is also illustrated by the performance of Morpheus (cf. Section 2) on our test set of occurrences. Morpheus could not process 44% of the test set (out-of-vocabulary tokens), 30% of the tokens were ambiguous and not disambiguated, while only 24% of the test set was disambiguated. In the end did Morpheus yield an accuracy score of 19%. We also compared our results with RNN Tagger (Schmid, 2019), a neural model that displayed state-of-the-art results for Ancient Greek. As shown in Table 2, our novel part-of-speech model outperforms RNN tagger, which obtains an accuracy score of 63%, with more than 6 percentage points. For completion, we also trained a model fed with the word embeddings from the smaller pre-Byzantine and Byzantine model. This model, which was not trained on post-Byzantine data, clearly performs worse that the tagger fine-tuned on the full language model. In addition to this quantitative analysis, we also performed a qualitative analysis of the results of our part-of-speech tagger with a special focus on two phenomena that also appear in current social media posts.

5 Error Analysis and Discussion

As mentioned in Section 1, the book epigrams bear some resemblance to modern social media posts. Exactly those similarities are an interesting starting point for our error analysis.

Let us begin with the appearance of a social media comment, which can accompany a picture, an opinion on someone's message, or just a retweet of another tweet. Those social media comments could be categorised as paratexts: a text standing next to (para, from the Greek παρά) another text, just as our book epigrams. They are mostly to be found in the margins around the main text of a manuscript, a material property of this corpus that determines the first category of errors. To illustrate this error type, we will discuss the following verse (English translation in italics):

(5) + X(ριστὸ)ν ἀεὶ ζῶοντα θεβροτὸν αὐτὸν ὄντα :·
Christ, the always living God, being mortal as well.
DBBE Occurrence 20483

The word *θεβροτὸν* is not an existing word but a mistake made by the scribe, who erroneously combined the abbreviation of θεόν (God) with the next word, βροτόν (mortal). Although it was standard practice to abbreviate θεόν as θε with a dash above it, it is clear that the scribe of this manuscript did not intend to write an abbreviation. 146 related occurrences show that our scribe did not realise this was an abbreviation, and thus wrote the two words as a compound. The performance of the part-of-speech tagger, however, was not affected too much by these irregularities: θεβροτὸν was analysed as a noun, accusative masculine singular, which is the correct analysis of βροτὸν. Most of the other erroneous compounds are analysed correctly, what might be attributed to the sub-word tokenizer used to train DBBErt. The opposite phenomenon, erroneously split words, occurs as well in DBBE:

(6) νυκτα δι' ἀμβροσίην τὴν οὐ θέμις ἔξον ὀμῆναι ·
Through the immortal night that should not rightfully be called by its name
DBBE Occurrence 31488

The last two words of this verse are the result of an incorrect split of the word ἐξονομῆναι. This error might have been caused by confusion with the future participle of "to have", the existing word ἔξον, the second part, however, does not make any sense at all. Although not correctly analysed, the part-of-speech tagger made a reasonable attempt. It tagged ἔξον and ὀμῆναι as a verb, the former as active indicative aorist 3 singular, the latter as active infinitive aorist. Both analyses are, to our opinion, based on the suffixes of the words. Most of these split words are analysed incorrectly.

The second category of mistakes can be attributed to an even more salient characteristic of present social media posts, namely the writing mistakes due to a phonetic way of writing. The English word *because*, for instance, can be found on twitter as *becuz*, as both are pronounced identically. The same principle applies to a lot of words in DBBE, which are written incorrectly, as shown in the following examples:

(7) εἱρμώσας ἐζόφωσεν ἧρεν μετείχους
Being in tune, he threw it into darkness, he made an end to it with his sound [8]
DBBE Occurrence 17374

(8) ὤπο(ς) μοναστὴς νεόφυτο(ς) οἰκέτ(ης)
Thy servant the monk Neophytos[9]
DBBE Occurrence 17594

The examples above contain several spelling mistakes that were made because of a phonetic way of writing. The words εἱρμώσας and μετείχους of Example 7 are incorrect because of the itacism (See Section 1). Although the stem is completely incorrect, εἱρμώσας was analysed correctly as a verb, active participle aorist nominative masculine singular. As for μετείχους, there might be two reasons for it not being analysed correctly: the spelling mistake and the fact that it is an incorrect contraction of μετ`ἤχους. The first word of Example 8 should have been ὅπως instead of ὤπος, yet both the spiritus and the length of the vowels have lost their distinctive value after the classical period. We noticed that if the orthographic mistake happens at the ultimate and/or penultimate syllable, the algorithm outputs an incorrect morphological analysis. This is in line with our conclusion about the compound words (cf. supra): the embeddings are sub-word based, so if the sub-words are nonsensical, the part-of-speech tagger will not provide a correct morphological analysis.

6 Conclusion and Future research

The Database of Byzantine Book Epigrams stores a very challenging corpus with its own peculiarities and problems for automatic processing. This automatic processing is necessary since manual annotation is not feasible for the complete DBBE corpus. To develop a more flexible approach that is able to cope with lots of orthographic variety and out-of-vocabulary words, we trained a novel language model for Greek, the DBBErt, and fine-tuned it for part-of-speech tagging. To evaluate this part-of-speech-tagger on Byzantine Greek, we developed a novel gold standard, which was manually annotated using the AGDT annotation guidelines. This label set was first subject of an IAA study, that showed very high agreement scores.

Although the evaluation showed promising results, the error analysis exposed once more the inherent problems of the book epigrams, which philologists still agonise over.

An important next step in our research is the development of a lemmatizer, which will make the annotation of our corpus complete. Once this annotation is done, we will research how similarity can be measured between hemistichs, verses and epigrams in the DBBE, in order

[8] translation by Bentein et al. (2010)
[9] translation by Marava-Chatzēnikolaou et al. (1978)

to link similar texts copied (and sometimes altered) by different scribes.

Limitations

The main limitation of our research, is the limited amount of data available. Transformer-based language models are very data-greedy, which made us add Modern Greek data to our model for Ancient and Medieval Greek to have a substantial amount of data. The nature of the data is a second limitation. We want to process the Greek texts as they are found in manuscripts, in their original form. That entails that the texts not only contain orthographic irregularities but, as mentioned in Section 5, also words that are either erroneously split or glued together. As a result, the non-existing words in the corpus considerably impact the system performance for the task of morphological analysis.

References

Alan Akbik, Tanja Bergmann, Duncan Blythe, Kashif Rasul, Stefan Schweter, and Roland Vollgraf. 2019. FLAIR: An easy-to-use framework for state-of-the-art NLP. In *Proceedings of the 2019 Conference of the North American Chapter of the Association for Computational Linguistics (Demonstrations)*, pages 54–59, Minneapolis, Minnesota. Association for Computational Linguistics.

David Bamman and Gregory Crane. 2011. The ancient greek and latin dependency treebanks. In *Language Technology for Cultural Heritage*, pages 79–98, Berlin, Heidelberg. Springer Berlin Heidelberg.

Klaas Bentein, Floris Bernard, Kristoffel Demoen, and Marc de Groote. 2010. New testament book epigrams. some new evidence from the eleventh century. *Byzantinische Zeitschrift*, 103(1):13–23.

Steven Bird. 2006. Nltk: the natural language toolkit. In *Proceedings of the COLING/ACL 2006 Interactive Presentation Sessions*, pages 69–72.

Bernd Bohnet and Joakim Nivre. 2012. A transition-based system for joint part-of-speech tagging and labeled non-projective dependency parsing. In *Proceedings of the 2012 Joint Conference on Empirical Methods in Natural Language Processing and Computational Natural Language Learning*, pages 1455–1465, Jeju Island, Korea. Association for Computational Linguistics.

Giuseppe G. A. Celano. 2018. Guidelines for the ancient greek dependency treebank 2.0. Last consulted December 2022.

Giuseppe G. A. Celano, Gregory Crane, and Saeed Majidi. 2016. Part of speech tagging for ancient greek. *Open Linguistics*, 2(1).

Giuseppe GA Celano. 2019. The dependency treebanks for ancient greek and latin. *Digital Classical Philology*, page 279.

Gregory R. Crane. 1991. Generating and Parsing Classical Greek. *Literary and Linguistic Computing*, 6(4):243–245.

Gregory R. Crane. 2022. Perseus digital library. Last accessed 10 February 2023.

Mark Depauw and Tom Gheldof. 2014. Trismegistos: An interdisciplinary platform for ancient world texts and related information. In *Theory and Practice of Digital Libraries – TPDL 2013 Selected Workshops*, pages 40–52, Cham. Springer International Publishing.

Jacob Devlin, Ming-Wei Chang, Kenton Lee, and Kristina Toutanova. 2018. Bert: Pre-training of deep bidirectional transformers for language understanding. *arXiv preprint arXiv:1810.04805*.

Vanessa B Gorman. 2020. Dependency treebanks of ancient greek prose. *Journal of Open Humanities Data*, 6(1).

Péter Halácsy, Andras Kornai, and Csaba Oravecz. 2007. Hunpos: an open source trigram tagger. *Proceedings of the 45th Annual Meeting of the Association for Computational Linguistics Companion Volume Proceedings of the Demo and Poster Sessions*, pages 209–212.

Dag TT Haug and Marius Jøhndal. 2008. Creating a parallel treebank of the old indo-european bible translations. In *Proceedings of the second workshop on language technology for cultural heritage data (LaTeCH 2008)*, pages 27–34.

David Holton, Geoffrey Horrocks, Marjolijne Janssen, Tina Lendari, Io Manolessou, and Notis Toufexis. 2019. *Phonology*, page 1–238. Cambridge University Press.

Alek Keersmaekers. 2019. Creating a richly annotated corpus of papyrological Greek: The possibilities of natural language processing approaches to a highly inflected historical language. *Digital Scholarship in the Humanities*, 35(1):67–82.

Alek Keersmaekers, Wouter Mercelis, Colin Swaelens, and Toon Van Hal. 2019. Creating, enriching and valorizing treebanks of Ancient Greek. In *Proceedings of the 18th International Workshop on Treebanks and Linguistic Theories (TLT, SyntaxFest 2019)*, pages 109–117, Paris, France. Association for Computational Linguistics.

Henry George Liddell, Robert Scott, Henry Stuart Jones, and Roderick McKenzie. 1966. *A Greek-English Lexicon*. Clarendon press.

A. Marava-Chatzēnikolaou, Ethnikē Vivliothēkē tēs Hellados, C. Touphexē-Paschou, and Akadēmia Athēnōn. 1978. *Catalogue of the Illuminated Byzantine Manuscripts of the National Library of Greece: Manuscripts of New Testament texts 10th-12th century*. Catalogue of the Illuminated Byzantine Manuscripts of the National Library of Greece. Publications Bureau of the Academy of Athens.

Thomas Mueller, Helmut Schmid, and Hinrich Schütze. 2013. Efficient higher-order CRFs for morphological tagging. In *Proceedings of the 2013 Conference on Empirical Methods in Natural Language Processing*, pages 322–332, Seattle, Washington, USA. Association for Computational Linguistics.

Joakim Nivre, Daniel Zeman, Filip Ginter, and Francis Tyers. 2017. Universal Dependencies. In *Proceedings of the 15th Conference of the European Chapter of the Association for Computational Linguistics: Tutorial Abstracts*, Valencia, Spain. Association for Computational Linguistics.

M.C. Pantelia. 2022. *Thesaurus Linguae Graecae: A Bibliographic Guide to the Canon of Greek Authors and Works*. University of California Press.

Rachele Ricceri, Klaas Bentein, Floris Bernard, Antoon Bronselaer, Els De Paermentier, Pieterjan De Potter, Guy De Tré, Ilse De Vos, Maxime Deforche, Kristoffel Demoen, Els Lefever, Anne-Sophie Rouckhout, and Colin Swaelens. 2023. The database of byzantine book epigrams project: Principles, challenges, opportunities. Working paper or preprint.

Helmut Schmid. 2019. Deep learning-based morphological taggers and lemmatizers for annotating historical texts. In *Proceedings of the 3rd international conference on digital access to textual cultural heritage*, pages 133–137.

Helmut Schmid and Florian Laws. 2008. Estimation of conditional probabilities with decision trees and an application to fine-grained pos tagging. In *Proceedings of the 22nd International Conference on Computational Linguistics - Volume 1*, COLING '08, page 777–784, USA. Association for Computational Linguistics.

Pranaydeep Singh, Gorik Rutten, and Els Lefever. 2021. A pilot study for BERT language modelling and morphological analysis for ancient and medieval Greek. In *Proceedings of the 5th Joint SIGHUM Workshop on Computational Linguistics for Cultural Heritage, Social Sciences, Humanities and Literature*, pages 128–137, Punta Cana, Dominican Republic (online). Association for Computational Linguistics.

A Appendix A

This table shows all occurrences used in the inter-annotator agreement study.

Occ. id	Tokens
17368	50
18180	33
18446	9
19604	101
20167	60
21375	43
22487	91
22734	75
23607	10
23615	12
23631	16
23632	19
25463	52
26551	66
30520	354
30844	31

Table 3: The set of epigrams used for the inter-annotator agreement study, summing up to 1,022 tokens.

'Orpheus Came to His End by Being Struck by a Thunderbolt'[1]: Annotating Events in Mythological Sequences

Franziska Pannach
Institute of Computer Science
University of Göttingen
franziska.pannach@uni-goettingen.de

Abstract

The mythological domain has various ways of expressing events and background knowledge. Using data extracted according to the hylistic approach (Zgoll, 2019), we annotated a data set of 6315 German sentences from various mythological contexts and geographical origins, like Ancient Greece and Rome or Mesopotamia, into four categories: *single-point* events (e.g. actions), *durative-constant* (background knowledge, continuous states), *durative-initial*, and *durative-resultative*. This data is used to train a classifier, which is able to reliably distinguish event types.

1 Introduction

In narratological terms, *events* have been defined as "constitutive features of narrativity" (Hühn, 2014), the atomic building blocks of a story. An utterance is an event if it communicates a change of state, a "transformation", which is a fundamental property of any event. In order to produce a plot or a story, events need to follow a chronological or diegetical order, with events being subject to a change in time. *Succession* and *transformation* are therefore key principles in a narrative (Todorov, 1971).

Pustejovsky (2021) distinguished two types of event structures in texts: the surface structure, represented by verbal predicates, and the latent event structure, which refers to sub-events and their representations.

According to Herman (2005), events are often conjoined with *states*, in the sense that a source state S occurs before the transition into a target state S', triggered by an event (or series of events) E.

In narrative annotation studies, distinctions between events and states are most commonly attributed to the eventfulness of the predicate. The focus on the question what constitutes an event is very much on the question "Who does what to whom?"

This works presents the annotation efforts to classify different types of events in the mythological and religious domain. Textual sources from those domains often do not narrate plots in a straightforward manner. Instead, they use stylistic devices, like prolepses, to transport their narrative, which can make automatic extraction and event labelling challenging.

For this study, different types of events and their chronological order have been extracted by domain experts from the fields of Ancient Near Eastern Studies, Religious Studies and Classics from a large variety of sources.

For each source, a sequence of events and background information was manually extracted based on the original, e.g. in ancient Greek or Sumerian, where available. Those sequences were derived according to the hylistic approach (Zgoll, 2019) from the narrative domains of mythological and religous studies (Zgoll and Zgoll, 2020; Gabriel et al., 2021). Each sequence corresponds to one variant of a (mythological) plot in the respective source.

The context window of the myth variant, i.e. which passages of the source refer to a mythological plot, is identified by the domain expert. Hence, the text passages that correspond to the sequences, as well as the sequences themselves, differ in length. The sequences can be used for comparatistic tasks, such as the comparison of narrative plots or background information, e.g. the characterization of entities. The distribution of disciplines from which the sources are taken are presented in Figure 2.

The narrative sequences contain practically no discourse markers, and are comprised of individual statements (*hylemes*) which are strictly in present tense. The hylemes contain events, including stative events or states in the chronological (narrative) order, not the diegetic order.

As an example, we use the quote 'Orpheus

Proceedings of the 17th Linguistic Annotation Workshop (LAW-XVII), pages 10–18
July 13, 2023 ©2023 Association for Computational Linguistics

came to his end by being struck by a thunderbolt'[1]. From this sentence, the following short sequence of statements (*hyleme sequence*) can be manually extracted:

1. 'Orpheus is struck by a thunderbolt.'
2. 'Orpheus dies.'
3. 'Orpheus is dead.'

The task of this work is to annotate the *event* types of each individual statement (*hyleme*). The data is in German, examples have been translated by the author for this paper, where necessary.

This paper is structured as follows: Section 2 frames the work into context of similar annotation efforts. Section 3 compares the categorisation of events used in this work with previous annotation efforts by Gius and Vauth (2022). The data set used for this study is described in Section 4. In Section 5, we describe the annotation effort and its results. We present a simple classifier to determine the event types, which we describe in Section 6. Finally, the paper ends in a discussion in Section 7.

2 Related Works

Our work is situated in the context of mythological research, but has potential for application in other domains. On the linguistic level, it is related to the study of lexical aspect (or *Aktionsart*) and the situation entity (SE) annotation task. Friedrich et al. (2016) label SE types from clauses in a supervised sequence modelling task using features of the main verb, its main referent, and the clause itself. They report good results across different genres. In an earlier study, Friedrich and Pinkal (2015) annotated clausal aspect for automatically recognising whether a clause describes a *habitual*, *episodic*, or *static* phenomenon.

Metheniti et al. (2022) sucessfully identified temporal aspect (*telicity* and *duration*) in English and French data sets using a transformer approach.

Furthermore, there are a number of practical approaches which attempt to define and narrow the narrative concept of *events* and their representation.

Chambers and Jurafsky (2008) introduce an approach to use unsupervised learning of event chains centered around an event protagonist. They train a temporal classifier to produce a temporally ordered narrative chain. In a subsequent study, they present the concept of narrative schemas, as "coherent sequences or sets of events" (Chambers and Jurafsky, 2009). By applying an unsupervised learning approach, they add semantic roles to the argument structure of their event chains. Multiple events chains are then combined into a narrative schema.

TimeML (Pustejovsky et al., 2005a,b) is a markup language designed based on XML which provides a standardized way of annotating temporal expressions and events in text, including the temporal relationships between events. It is used for the annotation of temporal and event information. Four automatic TimeML annotation systems have been evaluated by Ocal et al. (2022).

Reiter (2015) compared the annotation of narrative segments performed through crowd-sourcing, by student annotators and summary annotations. Kwong (2011) annotated a corpus of fables regarding their structural and semantic properties, including temporal information. Events that are part of a script, such as 'baking a cake', have been automatically mapped to narrative texts by Ostermann et al. (2017).

Events and event types in narrative plots have been studied by Gius and Vauth (2022). They operationalize the concepts of narrativity and tellability as discourse phenomena. They use spans of text defined by finite verbs as annotation units. Guis' and Vauth's concepts of states and events are probably closest to those of the hylistic theory presented by (Zgoll, 2019). Therefore, we will compare the two annotation approaches in more detail in the next section.

3 Event Categories

The narrative event model of Gius and Vauth (2022) and Vauth and Gius (2021) uses four categories of events: *change of state*, *process events*, *stative events*, and *non-events*. The basis of their event representation is the finite verb in 'minimal sentences', i.e. all tokens that are assigned to the verb.

In contrast, the categories used for hylistic analysis are: *single-point* (punctual), *durative-constant*, *durative-initial* and *durative-resultative*. We classify a statement (*hyleme*) into one of these four categories, but the value is of course mainly associated with the verb. In both theories, each annotation unit has one finite verb. Figure 1 illustrates the difference between four hyleme types.

Single-point hylemes are true at one point during the narrative sequence extracted from the source. This includes active actions, passive experiences,

[1]Pausanias, Description of Greece

reactions, perceptions or feelings. The *single-point* event has its beginning and end during the sequence. However, that does not necessarily indicate an event with a short duration.

Durative hylemes hold true for a part of the sequence or over the course of the entire sequence. There are three sub-types: *Durative-constant*, *durative-initial*, and *durative-resultative*. *Durative-constant* hylemes are always true, e.g. "Orpheus is the son of Oeagrus." They often communicate background knowledge about the narrative. Additionally, certain 1N/nS statements[2] (Genette, 1983), e.g. "Hades works the sails" are also considered *durative-constant*.

There are two types of states which are true over a part of the sequence, but change their value at some point. *Durative-initial* hylemes are true at the beginning of the sequence. *Durative-resultative* hylemes are statements that become true at some point during the sequence (e.g. 'Orpheus is dead.') and remain true for the rest of the sequence. In the mythological domain, these context-sensitive hylemes often connect contexts and plots. Hyleme sequences follow a relative temporal order, without discourse markers.

Table 1 shows how different example sentences from Kafka's *Metamorphosis* are annotated according to both theories.

Guis and Vauth's category 'change of state', used for the first example sentence in Table 1, corresponds widely to the *single-point* category that is used for the annotations presented in this work. However, the category 'change of state' can be realised with different properties (Gius and Vauth, 2022). One of those properties is *iterative*. In most cases where this property would be applied, the hylistic theory would dictate the annotation of *durative-constant* (resp. *-initial* or *-resultative*), e.g. "Charon works the sails". This statement refers to an action that is characteristic for a character. It can be either ongoing, continuous, or characteristic in the sense that *Charon* is someone who is capable of performing this action.

The second example sentence "found he himself in his bed into a monstrous insect-like creature transformed" would be annotated as *single-point* statement according to hylistic theory, because the predicate "found" implies that he realises he has been transformed into a bug exactly once[3] during the course of the narrative. However, a hylistic analysis of the plot would necessarily include a statement like "Gregor Samsa is a human transformed into a bug", which would be annotated as *durative-constant*. This statement does not need to be explicitly stated in the text, it can be implied. The sentence "His room lay quietly between the four well-known walls" demonstrates where the main difference between the two theories lie:

According to Gius and Vauth (2022), this sentence is annotated as a *stative-event*. While the hylistic theory (Zgoll, 2019) also recognises that this is an ongoing state, it distinguishes between types of ongoing states. Hylemes that are valid at the beginning, but change during the course of the narrative are categorised as *durative-initial*, e.g. *Eurydice is alive*. Hylemes that are the result of an event, e.g. *A snake bites Eurydice* $\rightarrow$ *Eurydice is dead*, are *durative-resultative*. Thirdly, there are hylemes that are true over the entire course of the narrative, e.g. *Eurydice is Orpheus' wife*. Those statements are *durative-constant*. They communicate the background knowledge that is the basis of a narrative, e.g. information about characters, their relations between each other and properties of the world in which a (mythological) story takes place. In order to determine the hylistic event category of the third sentence, therefore, we need to establish if the quietness of the room is a) the result of something that happened previously, or b) the initial state that is changed later-on, e.g. by someone barging in, or c) a general characterisation of the room. *Durative-resultative* statements are often preceded by a *single-point* statement, which corresponds to a *change of state* event according to Gius and Vauth (2022). However, occasionally *durative-resultative* statements are the result of the entire narrative, e.g. "No one can solve this incantation" is the result of the entire narrative of the invocation MS 2353 (CUSAS 32, 19a) (George, 2016; Rudik, 2011).

Non-events are not represented in hylistic theory, because they do not contain plot relevant information. Non-events contain mainly conditional, subjunctive, or modalised statements (Vauth and Gius, 2021).

4 Data

As explained in the previous section, the event definition used in this paper is different from the ones mentioned in Section 2. Furthermore, event

[2] "narrating one time what happened n times"

[3] Afterwards he knows that he is a bug. (*durative-constant*)

Table 1: Comparison of Event and State Categories

Sentence	Guis and Vauth, 2022	Hylistic Class
"Gregor Samsa one morning from uneasy dreams awoke"	Change of state	single-point
"found he himself in his bed into a monstrous insect-like creature transformed"	Process Events	single-point
"His room lay quietly between the four well-known walls"	Stative Events	durative(-constant, -initial, or -resultative dependent on context)
"She would have closed the door to the apartment"	Non-events	*NA*

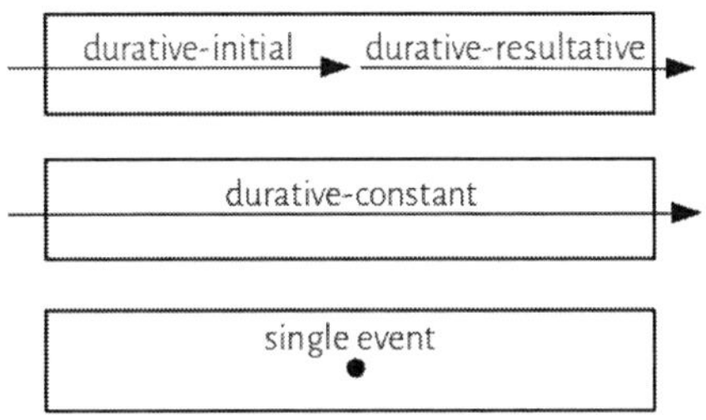

Figure 1: Types of Hylemes

statements (hylemes) are not derived directly from the textual representation in a source. Mythological plots and descriptions of background knowledge are often not told in a straightforward manner. Rather, they allude to related aspects of similar myths, and use comparisons, context and intertextuality in ways that makes the interpretation of what exactly happens in a myth variant hard to understand for laymen and even harder to process using NLP tools. Even the order of events is sometimes difficult to establish, as the following example illustrates:

> (1) "But Orpheus, son of Oeagrus, [they sent back$_4$ with failure from Hades], [showing$_3$ him only a wraith] [of the woman for whom he came$_2$]; [her real self they would not bestow$_3$], [for he was accounted to have gone upon a coward's quest$_1$], ..."[4]

We can see that the sequential order of events is different from the order presented in the source. Chronologically, *Orpheus* first goes on a coward's quests (1), in order to rescue his wife (2), but they (= the inhabitants of the netherworld) do not give him his real wife (= Euydice), but show him only a wraith of her (3). As a result, they send him back with failure (4). Fictional texts often follow their own order or use non-linear narrative, in order to create tension or highlight certain aspects of the plot. In-text annotations can rarely account for the discrepancy, especially if the events are presented without discourse markers or temporal expressions. The hylistic theory distinguishes between the order in the source and the chronological order.

The next example will illustrate how main plot events in classical sources are communicated merely by allusion.

> (2) "If Orpheus, arm'd with his enchanting lyre,
> The ruthless king with pity could inspire,
> And from the shades below redeem his wife;"[5]

In this variant of the myth *Orpheus and Eurydice*, we know that *Orpheus* has a lyre, which has some enchanting properties. He successfully inspires some unnamed ruthless king (possibly *Dis* through *Proserpina* (Bowra, 1952)). Exactly how he achieves this is left out, because this passage might allude to other variants of the myth, where this is discussed in more detail. Then *Orpheus* redeems his wife from the shadows below, alluding to the netherworld (*Hades*). This information alone does not tell us much about what exactly takes place. In Georgics, 4, 453–527, Vergil himself tells a more detailed story of how the events took place. This includes how exactly *Eurydice* dies, and the

[4]Plato Symp. 179d `http://data.perseus.org/citations/urn:cts:greekLit:tlg0059.tlg011.perseus-eng1:179d`

[5]Vergil. Aeneid. 6, L.98-123 `http://data.perseus.org/citations/urn:cts:latinLit:phi0690.phi003.perseus-eng1:6.98-6.123`

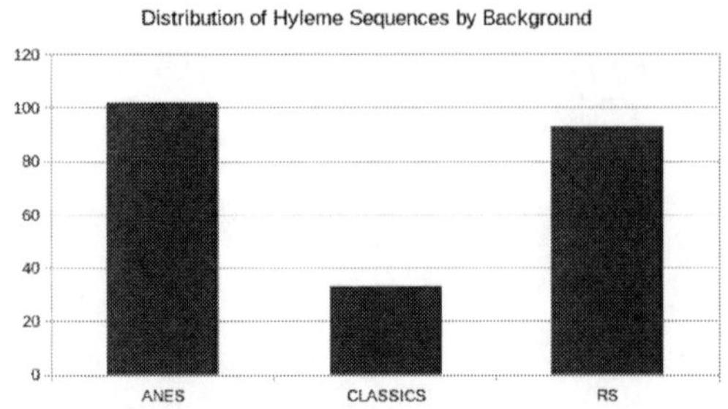

Figure 2: Distribution of narrative sequences (*hyleme sequences*) by topic, Ancient Near Eastern Studies (ANES): 102, Classics: 33, Religious Studies: (RS) 93

fact that *Orpheus* is presented with conditions for bringing his wife back from the netherworld (i.e. he is not allowed to look at her).

Both examples show that extracting information from the texts is a challenging task that needs to be guided by informed scholars. This issue severely magnifies if we do not consider the well documented Classical domain, but extend studies to fields like Ancient Near Eastern Studies, where sources are often scarce, and their supporting material (e.g. cuneiform on stone tablets) can be damaged or difficult to read.

Therefore, the context-window, the plot inherent events and background knowledge presented in the 228 sources have been extracted manually. Each source is presented in one sequence of event statements, so called *hyleme sequence* (Zgoll, 2019). The hylemes were originally not annotated with their state or event types. However, in order to process the sequences for further study using NLP methods, e.g. measuring the similarity of plots or aligning variants of the same myth, the annotation of *single-point* events, and *durative* statements was needed.

Each hyleme sequence describes the plot of one myth variant and related background information. The statements usually do not contain fixed or relative temporal expressions, or relations such as *before* or *after*. Instead, the succession of events is expressed through the sequential order.

The annotated data is a set of 6315 hylemes and their assigned category. It is not, as discussed above, an annotation of concurrent text from the sources, but sequences describing the plot that were extracted manually.

The statements themselves are usually short, concise sentences in German, consisting of only main clauses, containing one finite verb in present tense and active voice (where possible). Co-references are widely avoided. Instead, each statements contains the resolved arguments, which are repeated in the subsequent statements, even if they are only communicated by co-references in the text. One sentence in a source can translate to multiple statements, e.g. "Orpheus is the son of Oeagrus.", "The gods send Orpheus back from Hades as a failure.",... Aspects which are alluded but can be safely determined by the informed scholar (e.g. Orpheus' wife's name is Eurydice) are added in square brackets. Those implications can be part of the statement, e.g. a name, or an entire statement. For instance, in the example sentences from Kafka's *Metamorphosis*, the first statement "Gregor Samsa one morning from uneasy dreams awoke" would be preceded by a statement like "Gregor Samsa is sleeping" in a hylistic analysis.

5 Annotation

The data set was annotated by six annotators. Since *durative-initial* and *durative-resultative* statements are context-sensitive, annotators always processed the entire sequence. Each narrative sequence was annotated twice. Table 2 gives an overview of the annotators' disciplines, and level of education.

Annotator	Background	Level of Education
A1	ANES	B.A.
A2	CS/CL	M.Sc.
A3	Classical Studies	B.A.
A4	ANES/DH	Doctoral Deg.
A5	ANES	B.A.
A6	ANES	M.A.

Table 2: Annotators' backgrounds

All annotators had previous experience with the hylistic theory. Additionally, they were trained in an initial annotation meeting. Each annotator was given a set of sequences, which were annotated individually and discussed by the group afterwards. Annotators were also given a set of guiding questions and example statements to help them chose the right event category where in doubt. The guiding questions were presented in a flowchart. Additionally, annotators with explicit knowledge in the field, e.g. Classics, were also asked to check the original sources for guidance where in doubt. For example, the English statement "Orpheus brings back the dead (from the netherworld)" can be interpreted as *single-point* or *durative-constant*. Through the original Greek source, it can be determined that it should be annotated as *durative-constant*, because the imperfect form (ἀνῆγεν) is used (Bowra, 1952). In a second meeting, questions that arose during the annotation process were discussed.

Items were annotated in 11 different pairings, with varying first and second annotators. In all but one cases, the inter-annotator agreement for the annotation task ranges from substantial (κ 0.61-0.80) to almost perfect agreement (κ 0.81-0.99). The agreement is reported in Table 3. Annotator pairs A2-A4 and A4-A5 have perfect agreement over the shared annotations. Pair A2-A5 has a relatively low value of $\kappa = 0.4$. This is due to one particularly long sequence containing 114 hylemes. Many statements in this sequence contain descriptions of a mythical house, e.g. "The vault of the house is a rainbow". These were annotated as *durative-constant* by one annotator, while the other interpreted these descriptions as results of some action in the sequence, and therefore annotated them as *durative-resultative*. Consequently, event type annotations of all descriptions of the house in that sequence are mismatching (consequential error). This results in a low overall κ for the annotator pair A2-A5.

Pair	No. of items	Cohen's κ
A1-A2	4552	0.848930
A1-A3	398	0.874665
A1-A4	299	0.929306
A1-A5	149	0.733025
A1-A6	96	0.631285
A2-A3	187	0.918325
A2-A4	90	1
A2-A5	127	0.402008
A3-A4	136	0.866710
A3-A5	239	0.811959
A4-A5	42	1

Table 3: Inter-annotator agreement (Cohen's κ) between pairs of annotators

In cases where the first and second annotator disagreed, the gold standard was derived by discussion in a separate meeting, or following the judgement of the annotator whose discipline the sequence belongs to. Performance of annotators against gold standard, and total number of annotated items are

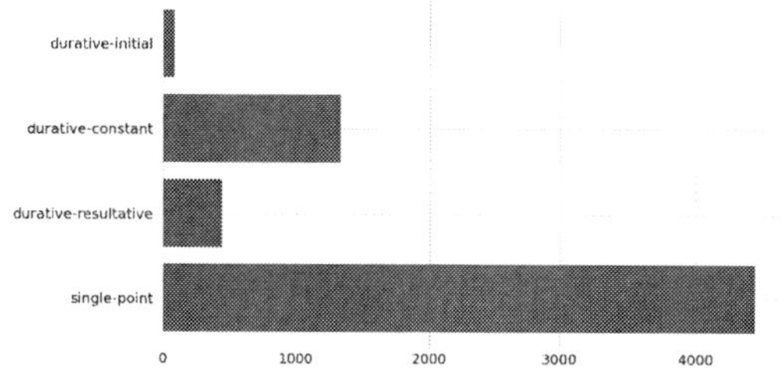

Figure 3: Distribution of the event types in the final data set (gold standard annotation)

reported in Table 4.

Annotator	Gold	No. of items
A1	0.939978	5494
A2	0.914271	4956
A3	0.951389	960
A4	0.953625	567
A5	0.705362	557
A6	0.631285	96

Table 4: Cohen's κ of annotators against Gold standard

The final gold labels are an important foundation for the next analyses, e.g. plot comparison and alignment or the comparison of background information in the individual sources. The distribution of the gold-standard labels is shown in Figure 3. The majority of the data consists of *single-point* statements, of the *durative* statements, the *durative-constant* hylemes are the largest group. Three hylemes had to be excluded from the data, because their types could not be determined (e.g. the statement "The *kur-ĝara* and *gala-tur* ...?" has a missing predicate due to the source not being properly readable).

6 Classifier

Based on the gold labels of the annotation as described in the previous section, two event type classifiers were trained.[6] The resulting models can be used to pre-classify new statements, and to classify statements in future data sets that can be used for comparison, e.g. including movie adaptations of mythological narratives.

The separation of the data into *durative* and *single-point* statements is an important first step for the subsequent analyses of the narrative sequences,

[6]The classifiers and an excerpt of the annotated data can be found under: `https://gitlab.gwdg.de/franziska.pannach/hylva_event_types` For access to the full data, kindly contact the author.

since *single-point* statements correspond to events, whereas *durative* hylemes correspond to descriptions of background knowledge.

The task to automatically classify event types is not trivial. Especially, automatically distinguishing the three types of *durative* hylemes is challenging. This is due to multiple reasons. Firstly, the three classes are unbalanced, with more *durative-constant* hylemes, and very few *durative-initial* hylemes. Additionally, *durative-initial* or *-resultative* hylemes can be quite similar to *durative-constant* hylemes in terms of vocabulary and grammatical structure. As discussed above, their value is often context-sensitive.

For the classification task, a multinomial naive bayes model was selected. For that purpose, the data set was split into a training and test set with a split of 75 %-25 %. The hyper-parameters were selected by performing a grid search. In particular, the grid search established whether the feature vector is best constructed using a bag-of-words or TF-IDF vectorizer.

As a result, the hyper-parameters were set as: Laplace smoothing parameter $\alpha = 0.01$, bag-of-words features, and an n-gram range of 3.

Firstly, we analyze the results for binary classes *single-point* and *durative*, which combines *durative-initial*, *durative-constant*, and *durative-resultative* statements. For that purpose, all three labels were subsumed under the coarse class *durative* for training. The binary classifier performs well on *single-point* hylemes, and reasonably on *durative* hylemes. The performance of the classifier is reported in Table 5.

Secondly, we investigate how the classifier performs if trained on just the different types *durative* hylemes. For that purpose, all *single-point* hylemes were removed from the training and test set. The majority of the test set consists of *durative-constant* hylemes (69 %) and *durative-resultative* hylemes (24 %). The results are reported in Table 6.

Lastly, we present the classifier for the classification of fine-grained classes. It was trained on the entire training and test set including fine-grained *durative* classes. A second classifier combining the first two models (binary and durative-only) in two steps was trained but did not improve results.

Table 7 shows the performance of the fine-grained classifier. The confusion matrix for the classifier is shown in Figure 4. We can see that the classifier favours the *single-point* class. This is most apparent in the case of *durative-constant* statements, which were misclassified as *single-point* in 70 cases.

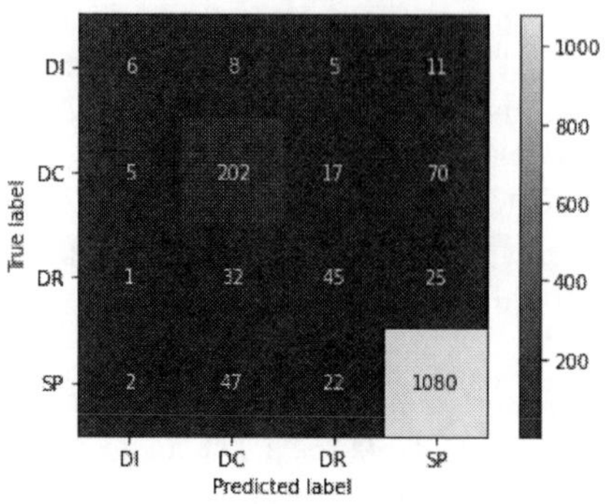

Figure 4: Confusion matrix for the classifier trained on the gold labels, DI = *durative-initial*, *durative-constant*, DR = *durative-resultative*, SP = *single-point*

	Precision	Recall	F1
durative	0.83	0.75	0.79
single-point	0.91	0.94	0.92

Table 5: Performance of the binary classifier

	Precision	Recall	F1
dur.-initial	0.50	0.23	0.32
dur.-constant	0.81	0.90	0.85
dur.-resultative	0.62	0.51	0.56

Table 6: Performance of the durative classifier

7 Discussion

In order to annotate event types for the mythological and religious domains from the source, the sequence of events and background information has to be extracted. Automatically extracting these events from can be challenging, as demonstrated in the examples in Section 4. Therefore, the sequences of statements describing events and states from the sources was achieved manually. Subsequently, we present annotations based on the hylistic theory (Zgoll, 2019), which was developed specifically for the mythological domain, but can be easily applied to other types of narrative as well. The data includes over 6300 statements from 228 narrative sequences. The statements have been annotated into four categories. *Single-point* statements, communicating events, *durative-constant* (background information), *durative-initial*

	Prec.	Recall	F1	Support
d.-initial	0.50	0.17	0.25	30
d.-constant	0.72	0.67	0.69	294
d.-resultative	0.55	0.45	0.49	103
single-point	0.90	0.95	0.93	1151

Table 7: Performance of the fine-grained classifier

and *durative-resultative*, which hylemes indicate that their truth value changes during the course of the sequence. After training the annotators, an overall satisfying inter-annotator agreement κ was reached.

The main weakness of the presented approach is that the event categories are not assigned directly to the text. This is due to the original source material being extremely diverse in form, language, and genre. Instead, the labels are assigned to the *hyleme sequences* which require significant manual effort and knowledge of the original material.

Durative labels, especially *durative-initial* and *durative-resultative*, are context-sensitive. The value of a statement has to be assessed within the context of the narrative sequence. Since two identical statements can have different labels in different contexts, the classification task is particularly challenging. This is the case especially if the label depends not only on a single preceding statement (e.g. *Eurydice dies.* $\rightarrow$ *Eurydice is dead.*), but on the entire sequence (e.g. *Nobody can solve this invocation.*)

When hyleme sequences are extracted from modern texts in well-resourced languages, such as German or English, the manual effort could be alleviated by employing NLP methods, such as named entity recognition or semantic role labelling. With a larger number of texts and corresponding sequences, it would also be possible to automatically identify candidate statements from text.

The gold standard data represents the actual distribution of labels, i.e. *single-point* statements (actions) are more prevalent than *durative* statements. Hence, the final data set is skewed which explains the performance of the classifier. In this work, a simple Naive Bayes classifier was implemented for demonstration purposes. A more sophisticated model, e.g. following a multi-lingual transformer approach (Conneau et al., 2020), would potentially deliver better results.

In future studies, the plots of mythological and religious narrative can now be studied and compared using NLP and alignment techniques on sequences of *single-point* statements. The background information in *durative-constant* can be included, or processed separately to represent the narrative-inherent background knowledge.

References

C. M. Bowra. 1952. Orpheus and Eurydice. *The Classical Quarterly*, 2(3-4):113–126.

Nathanael Chambers and Dan Jurafsky. 2008. Unsupervised learning of narrative event chains. In *Proceedings of ACL-08: HLT*, pages 789–797, Columbus, Ohio. Association for Computational Linguistics.

Nathanael Chambers and Dan Jurafsky. 2009. Unsupervised learning of narrative schemas and their participants. In *Proceedings of the Joint Conference of the 47th Annual Meeting of the ACL and the 4th International Joint Conference on Natural Language Processing of the AFNLP*, pages 602–610.

Alexis Conneau, Kartikay Khandelwal, Naman Goyal, Vishrav Chaudhary, Guillaume Wenzek, Francisco Guzmán, Edouard Grave, Myle Ott, Luke Zettlemoyer, and Veselin Stoyanov. 2020. Unsupervised cross-lingual representation learning at scale. In *Proceedings of the 58th Annual Meeting of the Association for Computational Linguistics*, pages 8440–8451, Online. Association for Computational Linguistics.

Annemarie Friedrich, Alexis Palmer, and Manfred Pinkal. 2016. Situation entity types: automatic classification of clause-level aspect. In *Proceedings of the 54th Annual Meeting of the Association for Computational Linguistics (Volume 1: Long Papers)*, pages 1757–1768, Berlin, Germany. Association for Computational Linguistics.

Annemarie Friedrich and Manfred Pinkal. 2015. Automatic recognition of habituals: a three-way classification of clausal aspect. In *Proceedings of the 2015 Conference on Empirical Methods in Natural Language Processing*, pages 2471–2481, Lisbon, Portugal. Association for Computational Linguistics.

Gösta Ingvar Gabriel, Brit Kärger, Annette Zgoll, and Christian Zgoll, editors. 2021. *Was vom Himmel kommt:Stoffanalytische Zugänge zu antiken Mythen aus Mesopotamien, Ägypten, Griechenland und Rom.* De Gruyter, Berlin, Boston.

Gérard Genette. 1983. *Narrative discourse: An essay in method*, volume 3. Cornell University Press.

Andrew R George. 2016. *Mesopotamian incantations and related texts in the Schøyen Collection.* CUSAS: Cornell University Studies in Assyriology and Sumerology 32.

Evelyn Gius and Michael Vauth. 2022. Towards an event based plot model. a computational narratology approach. *Journal of Computational Literary Studies*, 1(1).

David Herman. 2005. Events and event-types. *Routledge Encyclopedia of Narrative Theory. London: Routledge*, pages 151–52.

Peter Hühn. 2014. Event and eventfulness. In Peter Hühn, John Pier, Wolf Schmid, and Jörg Schönert, editors, *the living handbook of narratology*. Hamburg University, Hamburg.

Olivia OY Kwong. 2011. Annotating the structure and semantics of fables. In *Proceedings of the 25th Pacific Asia Conference on Language, Information and Computation*, pages 275–282.

Eleni Metheniti, Tim Van De Cruys, and Nabil Hathout. 2022. About time: Do transformers learn temporal verbal aspect? In *Proceedings of the Workshop on Cognitive Modeling and Computational Linguistics*, pages 88–101, Dublin, Ireland. Association for Computational Linguistics.

Mustafa Ocal, Adrian Perez, Antonela Radas, and Mark Finlayson. 2022. Holistic evaluation of automatic timeML annotators. In *Proceedings of the Thirteenth Language Resources and Evaluation Conference*, pages 1444–1453.

Simon Ostermann, Michael Roth, Stefan Thater, and Manfred Pinkal. 2017. Aligning script events with narrative texts. In *Proceedings of the 6th Joint Conference on Lexical and Computational Semantics (*SEM 2017)*, pages 128–134, Vancouver, Canada. Association for Computational Linguistics.

James Pustejovsky. 2021. The role of event-based representations and reasoning in language. In Tommaso Caselli, Eduard Hovy, Martha Palmer, and Piek Vossen, editors, *Computational Analysis of Storylines: Making Sense of Events*, chapter 1, pages 23–46. Cambridge University Press.

James Pustejovsky, Robert Ingria, Roser Saurí, José M. Castaño, Jessica Littman, Robert J. Gaizauskas, Andrea Setzer, Graham Katz, and Inderjeet Mani. 2005a. The specification language timeml. In *The Language of Time - A Reader*.

James Pustejovsky, Robert Knippen, Jessica Littman, and Roser Saurí. 2005b. Temporal and event information in natural language text. *Language resources and evaluation*, 39:123–164.

Nils Reiter. 2015. Towards annotating narrative segments. In *Proceedings of the 9th SIGHUM Workshop on Language Technology for Cultural Heritage, Social Sciences, and Humanities (LaTeCH)*, pages 34–38, Beijing, China. Association for Computational Linguistics.

Nadezda Rudik. 2011. *Die Entwicklung der keilschriftlichen sumerischen Beschwörungsliteratur von den Anfängen bis zur Ur III-Zeit*. Ph.D. thesis, Friedrich-Schiller-Universität Jena.

Tzvetan Todorov. 1971. The 2 principles of narrative. *Diacritics*, pages 37–44.

Michael Vauth and Evelyn Gius. 2021. Richtlinien für die Annotation narratologischer Ereigniskonzepte.

Annette Zgoll and Christian Zgoll, editors. 2020. *Mythische Sphärenwechsel: Methodisch neue Zugänge zu antiken Mythen in Orient und Okzident*. De Gruyter, Berlin, Boston.

Christian Zgoll. 2019. *Tractatus mythologicus: Theorie und Methodik zur Erforschung von Mythen als Grundlegung einer allgemeinen, transmedialen und komparatistischen Stoffwissenschaft*. De Gruyter, Berlin, Boston.

Difficulties in Handling Mathematical Expressions in Universal Dependencies

Lauren Levine
Georgetown University
lel76@georgetown.edu

Abstract

In this paper, we give a brief survey of the difficulties in handling the syntax of mathematical expressions in Universal Dependencies, focusing on examples from English language corpora. We first examine the prevalence and current handling of mathematical expressions in UD corpora. We then examine several strategies for how to approach the handling of syntactic dependencies for such expressions: as multi-word expressions, as a domain appropriate for code-switching, or as approximate to other types of natural language. Ultimately, we argue that mathematical expressions should primarily be analyzed as natural language, and we offer recommendations for the treatment of basic mathematical expressions as analogous to English natural language.

1 Introduction

Universal Dependencies (UD, Nivre et al. 2016, 2020; de Marneffe et al. 2021) is a project that aims to develop cross-linguistically consistent guidelines for multiple annotation layers, including syntactic dependency relations. Mathematical and numerical expressions comprise a particularly challenging class of cases, which require special attention to handle. Thus far, work on how to handle numerical expressions in UD has included analysis on annotating date and time cross-linguistically (Zeman, 2021), discussion of numbered entities in nominal expressions (Schneider and Zeldes, 2021), and discussion of different types of numeral related expressions in UD corpora of Uralic languages (Rueter et al., 2021).

However, there has been little discussion of how mathematical expressions, such as equations and other language which includes mathematical symbols and operators, should be handled in UD. As mathematical expressions are likely to appear as little more than edge cases in many corpus genres, this is understandable, but mathematical expressions can also feature prominently in corpora related to academic and scientific domains, such as the ACL Anthology Corpus (Rohatgi, 2022) and the academic section of the Corpus of Contemporary American English (COCA) (Davies, 2010). Unfortunately, the amount of corpora built for technical domains is limited, and the specialized nature of the language in such corpora has been a barrier in annotating them with more complex schemas, such as dependency relations. This means that there is a large gap in availability for annotated texts containing mathematical expressions that can be leveraged by NLP systems.[1]

As a result, technical texts with mathematical expressions can be viewed as a low-resource domain, and state-of-the-art systems trained on standard language will inevitably face a large drop in performance when handling such out of domain texts (Plank, 2016; Joshi et al., 2018). This is particularly an issue for real world applications of NLP technologies in technical domains, such as text mining or document processing in industrial engineering, where copious amounts of technical documents are generated by industry systems (Dima et al., 2021).

Pushing for the annotation of domain specific technical corpora will help to address this gap and provide more resources for NLP systems attempting to handle technical language. This will first require discussions on how to handle the annotation of such technical language, including standards for the handling of mathematical expressions. In this paper, we will first examine the current state of mathematical expressions in UD corpora, and then we will consider several possible approaches for handling such expressions. We

[1] While resources remain limited, we do note the release of a genre diverse UD test corpus, GENTLE, which contains dependency annotations and has a genre section for mathematical proofs: https://github.com/UniversalDependencies/UD_English-GENTLE/

Proceedings of the 17th Linguistic Annotation Workshop (LAW-XVII), pages 19–30
July 13, 2023 ©2023 Association for Computational Linguistics

will then give recommendations on how to handle the dependency relations for basic mathematical expressions, which we hope will encourage the inclusion of more mathematical texts in future annotation work.

It should be noted that while many arguments about syntactic analysis of mathematical expressions apply cross-linguistically, the focus of this paper is on mathematical expressions in English corpora, as mathematical English is the basis of most academic and professional STEM discourse, making it a logical place to start.

2 Prevalence and Existing Treatment of Mathematical Expressions in UD Data

In this section we will examine the prevalence of mathematical expressions in Universal Dependencies corpora (version 2.11),[2] as well as the distribution of dependency relations used to handle such expressions. We will also compare the prevalence of mathematical expressions in UD corpora with the prevalence of mathematical expressions in a subsection of the ACL Anthology Corpus, illustrating that expanding UD coverage more broadly into academic and technical domains would require a meaningful treatment of such expressions.

2.1 Prevalence in UD and ACL Data

In order to estimate the prevalence of mathematical expressions in UD corpora, we created a regular expression to query sentences containing combinations of numerical values and Unicode mathematical operators and symbols (a more detailed description of this query is provided in Appendix A). To determine the accuracy of this query, its performance was evaluated on a subsection of the ACL Anthology Corpus (which provides the full-text and metadata for papers and abstracts in the ACL (Association of Computational Linguistics) Anthology).[3]

From the 2021 papers in the ACL Anthology Corpus, 125 documents were randomly selected to be analyzed. The documents were sentence split and tokenized using Trankit (Nguyen et al., 2021),[4] and "gold" mathematical expressions where identified using the "formula" tag annotations included in the xml format of the corpus. After running our query on the ACL documents, the results were compared to the "gold" from the "formula" tag annotations. The resulting false positives and false negatives were then manually adjudicated for the actual presence/absence of mathematical expressions.

The performance of our query on this data sample was found to have a precision of 0.93, a recall of 0.88, and an f-score of 0.90, which we believe is accurate enough to give an estimate of the prevalence of mathematical expressions in UD corpora. However, it is worth noting that because many of the genres in the UD corpora are substantially different from the technical language in ACL papers, there is likely to be a somewhat higher proportion of false positives when we apply our query to the UD data.

Applying our query to all of the available UD corpora, we found 886 instances of sentences containing mathematical expressions, which corresponds of 0.05% of sentences in the UD corpora. These instances are spread over a total of 51 different corpora in 43 different languages, meaning that 20% of corpora and 31% of languages within UD contain some type of mathematical expression. While this may still seem like a marginal phenomenon, if we examine the prevalence of mathematical expressions by genre, as shown in Figure 1, we see that the proportion of sentences containing mathematical expressions rises to over 0.1% for several genres, including academic, legal, and medical. As data selected for UD coprora may purposely avoid difficult to annotate non-standard language such as mathematical expressions, it stands to reason that the typical proportion of mathematical expressions in these genres is likely even higher.

In order to further illustrate the genre dependent nature of the prevalence of mathematical expressions, we examined another subset of the ACL Anthology Corpus. We again used Trankit to sentence split and tokenize the 5847 paper documents from 2021 (those with both abstracts and paper bodies). Again using the "formula" tag annotations from the xml format of the corpus to identify sentences and tokens with mathematical expressions, we calculated the frequency of mathematical expressions in the data.

We found that 68% of the documents contained

[2] https://lindat.mff.cuni.cz/repository/xmlui/handle/11234/1-4923

[3] https://github.com/shauryr/ACL-anthology-corpus

[4] https://github.com/nlp-uoregon/trankit

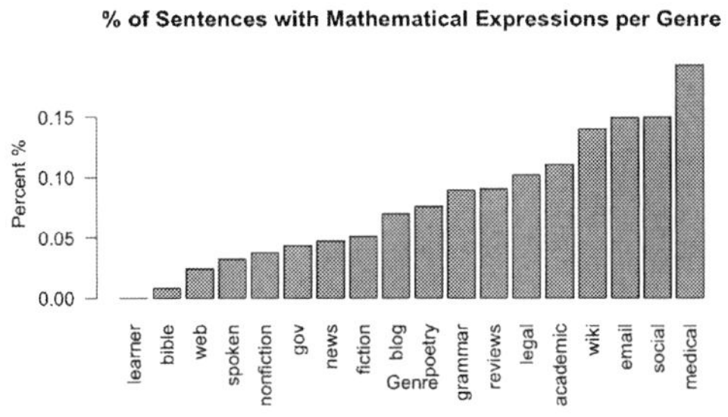

Figure 1: Proportion of sentences containing mathematical expressions for each genre category in UD.

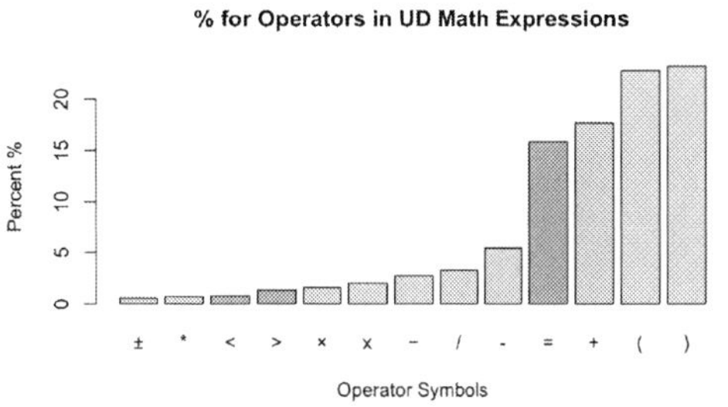

Figure 2: Frequency proportions (> 0.5%) for operators in UD mathematical expressions. (Green: Arithmetic operators, Purple: Predicate operators, Blue: Brackets.)

some kind of mathematical expression, that 3.7% of the sentences contained a mathematical expression, and that 4.5% of all tokens were contained within mathematical expressions. The prevalence of mathematical expressions in this data sample shows that we will need a standardized method of handling mathematical expressions if we want to expand UD corpora to cover such academic, scientific, and technical domains.

2.2 Frequencies for Mathematical Operators and Dependency Relations

We will now turn our attention to how the mathematical expressions we have identified in the UD data are currently being handled in terms of dependency relations. Searching the UD sentences we previously determined to contain mathematical expressions, we found that the expressions contained 33 unique mathematical symbols/operators, and we calculated the relative frequency of each of these symbols. The relative frequencies of some of these operators (those with relative frequency > 0.5%) are shown in Figure 2. In this Figure, we see that these operators are primarily those for basic arithmetic ("+", "-", "/", "*"), basic predicate relations ("=", "<", ">"), and parentheses ("(", ")").

Figure 3 shows the proportions of the dependency relations from all of the mathematical operators we observed in the previously identified mathematical expressions. We see that by far the most prominent relation is `punct` (punctuation), with a proportion of approximately 72%, and that `cc` (coordinating conjunction) is the next most frequent relation at 7.5%. Though `punct` is a generally uninformative dependency relation, this may not immediately strike us as an inappropriate handling of the operators we observed, considering that about 46% of them were parentheses.

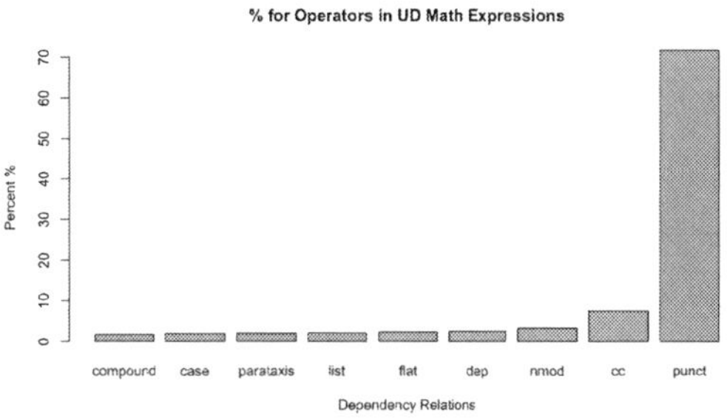

Figure 3: Dependency relation proportions (> 1%) for operators in UD mathematical expressions.

However, looking at the relative frequencies of the dependency relations for the individual operators, we found that the conjoining operator "+" and the predicate operator "=" have `punct` at proportions of 32% and 41% respectively (the full cross table of mathematical operators and their dependency relation proportions is included in Appendix B). This demonstrates that in the current handling of mathematical expressions in UD, informative operators, such as "=", are frequently not analyzed meaningfully, instead being dismissed as syntactically uninformative punctuation.

3 Difficulties Presented by Mathematical Expressions

In this section, we will examine several types of mathematical expressions that present difficulties for analysis with Universal Dependencies.[5] Examples of these types of expressions were taken

[5]A list of the Universal Dependency relations discussed in this paper and their abbreviations can be found in Appendix C. A full list of UD relations can be found here: `https://universaldependencies.org/u/dep/index.html`

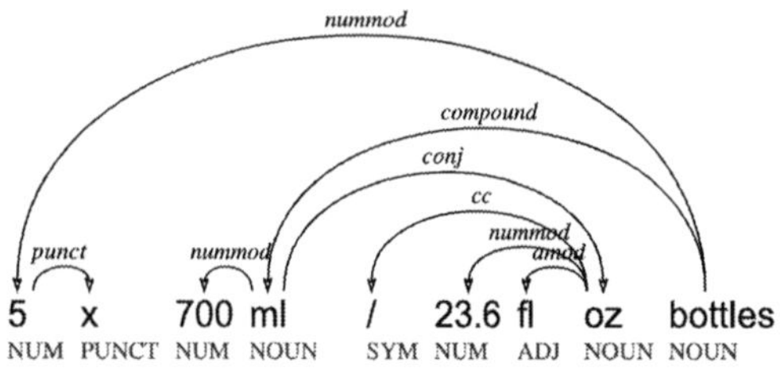

Figure 4: Mathematical Expression without Predication *(Source: GUM)*

from The Georgetown University Multilayer Corpus (GUM) (Zeldes, 2017).[6] Additional examples taken from the ACL Anthology Corpus, and the academic section of COCA[7] for each of the expression types discussed can be found in Appendix D.

3.1 Expressions without Predication

First, we will discuss mathematical expressions which lack predication. By this we mean expressions that lack a relational operator like "=" or "→", and as such could theoretically be evaluated down to a single mathematical term. Such expressions may be as simple as "3*5", but they can also become substantially more complicated (see additional examples in Appendix D.1). We single out this type of expression for discussion because it is a class of expression that can be thought of as a constituent unit, functioning essentially as a complex noun phrase. Such expressions may appear within a larger phrase of natural language, in which case they frequently occupy a syntactic position similar to that of a noun phrase.

They may also appear as individual units that can be combined to create more complicated mathematical expressions, such as equations. Because these expressions seem to act as individual units, it can be debated to what extent their internal structure should be represented. The headedness of an expression such as "8 - 6 / 2" is dubious, but it is clear that the order of operations which readers use to interpret the expression carries an understanding of hierarchy that we would want to include in a syntactic representation. Just as complex noun phrases receive internal syntactic analysis, we should also strive to provide an analysis to the internal structure of mathematical expressions without predication.

[6]https://github.com/amir-zeldes/gum
[7]https://www.english-corpora.org/coca/

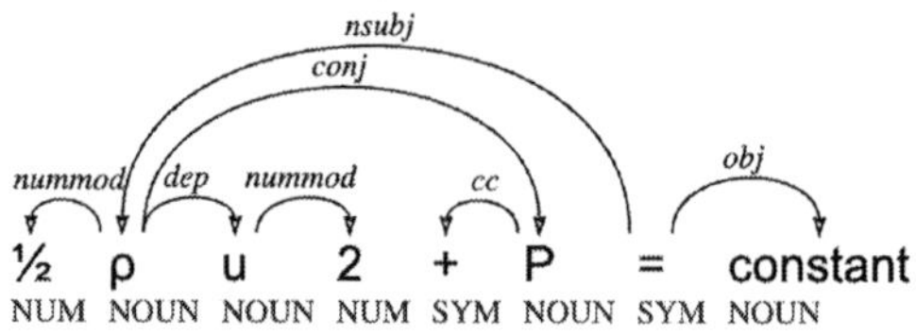

Figure 5: Mathematical Equation *(Source: GUM)*

Keeping these points in mind, we consider Figure 4, which includes an example of a mathematical "unit" expression and accompanying UD annotation taken from the GUM corpus. We see that this "unit" expression is used as a modifier to the noun "bottles", and that there is a mix of numbers, mathematical operators, and unit abbreviations. The main relation in the mathematical expression is handled with `conj` (which is reasonable), but it is the units that serve as the conjoined elements in the analysis rather than the numbers. The expression serves as an example of how in corpora we may find mathematical expressions with internal elements that we may not consider to be truly mathematical (such as units) and how they may create complications, as it is not immediately clear whether the numbers or the units should be preferred as the head in this example. Additionally, in this analysis, the mathematical operator "x" is dismissed as punctuation (in both POS and deprel) and "5" is treated as a regular counting determiner, which fails to capture how multiplication is overtly indicated in the expression.

3.2 Equations

The second type of mathematical expression we will consider is equations (see additional examples in Appendix D.2). While equations are largely composed of the sorts of predication lacking expressions that we discussed in the last section, they also contain mathematical operators, such as "<", ">", and "=", which define relationships between different expressions, and introduce a predicate structure to the main expression.

We see an example of an equation and accompanying UD annotation in Figure 5. In this example, the "=" operator is taken to be the root of the expression, which makes sense as it is proposing a relation between the elements to its left and to its right, just as the verb "equals" does in natural language. However, it is questionable whether or not the `nsubj` and `obj` relations are appropriate for

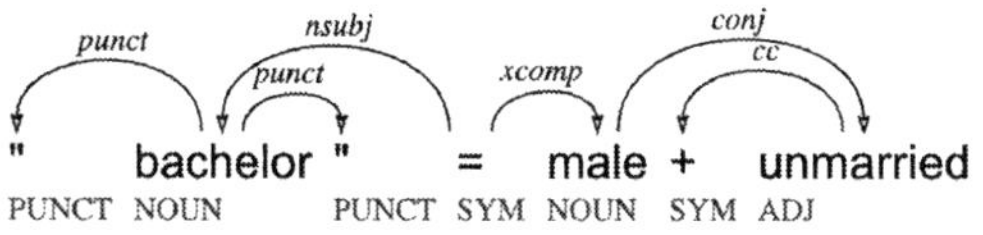

Figure 6: Math and Natural Language Mixed Equation *(Source: GUM)*

the equals operator. We may consider the equals relation in mathematics to be similar to that of the verb "equals", which typically takes the `xcomp` relation in UD analysis rather than `obj`. In fact, we see an example of "=" being modeled in such a manner in Figure 6, which we will discuss below.

Another point worth noting in this example is that there is a tokenization issue where "u^2" is separated as "u" and "2" without any indication of how the two tokens were originally related, which creates an ambiguity which was not present in the original expression. Even knowing the intended relation, it is unclear what single dependency relation could be used to express the "to the power of" relation. While not directly part of the syntactic analysis, tokenization is a task that will inevitably have consequences on what options are available during the syntactic analysis. It is particularly important to keep in mind for equations and other mathematical expressions, which frequently have nonstandard formatting which could prompt many tokenization ambiguities and errors (further discussion of such issues can be found in Appendix E).

3.3 Math and Natural Language Mixed Expressions

Within corpora which are primarily natural language, it is possible that mathematical expressions may appear as an isolated block, entirely divorced and alien from the rest of the text. However, it is more frequent for such expressions to be integrated into the natural language of the rest of the document to various degrees. In fact, there are many instances where segments of mathematical expressions are so deeply integrated into the natural language of the surrounding text that the decision of whether or not to call them mathematical expressions at all becomes uncertain. We will refer to such instances as mixed expressions (see additional examples in Appendix D.3).

One such example is shown in Figure 6. In this example, we see mathematical operators being used convey a definition, where all of the units being related are natural language terms. Again, we see the addition operator being treated as a coordinating conjunction, though, as previously noted, this time the equals operation is treated in a syntactically different manner than we saw in the example in Figure 5. It is worth questioning whether the equals operation in these two cases is the same, in which case they should have the same analysis.

We also may question whether the units example in Figure 4 is also an example of a mixed expression. The involvement of natural language elements in both of these expressions illustrates that the line between mathematical expressions and natural language can be blurry.

4 Approaches for Handling Mathematical Expressions

Now that we've examined several examples of the types of mathematical expressions that can appear in scientific and academically oriented corpora, we will discuss various approaches we can take to analyze these expressions with dependency relations.

4.1 Multi-word Expressions

Multi-word expressions (MWEs) are expressions that are made up of multiple tokens that are considered to be syntactically idiosyncratic and can be analyzed as a single unit (Sag et al., 2002). At first glance, this may seem like a reasonable way to consider mathematical expressions, which frequently appear as analogous to a single nominal unit when they are integrated with natural language. However, simply deciding to treat mathematical expressions as analogous to MWEs would not give an immediate solution. Previous work on the handling of multi-word expressions in UD has indicated that MWEs are not treated uniformly across UD corpora, but are frequently analyzed with the relations `compound`, `fixed`, and `flat` (Kahane et al., 2017).

First, `compound` would be difficult to apply to any complicated expression consisting of more than a few terms. Additionally, `compound` implies a right headedness (in English) that is not representative of the structure of most mathematical expressions, many of which are composed of relations such as multiplication and addition, which are commutative in nature, defying the notion of headedness.

Next, `fixed` is an analysis that works for MWEs which are idiomatic set phrases that are not open to general extension. However, mathematical expressions have endless variation through the use of established operations. In short, the general notion of a mathematical expression is productive, so the application of `fixed` seems misguided. While some internal parts of a mathematical expressions could still independently be considered to be `fixed`, this would need to be considered at the level of individual languages, since many UD languages independently keep a closed list of expressions that can make use of the `fixed` relation.

Finally, `flat` completely gives up on the intent to represent the internal complexities of mathematical expressions. It it an unsatisfying simplification, but it is not without its merits. First, it requires minimal effort to implement and apply to isolated mathematical expressions, and can work as a hold over while more in depth standards for analysis are developed. However, it will not be able to account for grey areas where mathematical expressions or symbols are integrated into the surrounding natural language.

4.2 Code-Switching

Code-switching refers to a process in which two or more languages are switched between over the course of a single communication (Myers-Scotton, 2017). In Universal Dependencies, when an instance of code-switching is identified, the methods of analysis can be completely switched over from the standards of the first language to the standards of a second language using the `Foreign` feature and the `Lang` MISC attribute. As such, we could consider math to be its own completely independent language, like English or French, which deserves its own separate analysis, rather than trying to incorporate its analysis into the scope of the natural language that surrounds it.

However, if the syntax of the language is unknown, as would currently be the case with mathematical expressions, the UD guidelines recommend that the `flat` or `flat:foreign` label be used for all dependency relations in the code-switched segment (Sanguinetti et al., 2022). Such an analysis would be syntactically uninformative and would still leave open the need for developing UD standards to handle mathematical expressions.

Additionally, while there are some contexts where prolonged use of mathematical expressions may more strongly suggest that code-switching is warranted, such as multi-line proofs or derivations, we would still need a way to handle the use of mathematical operators and symbols integrated with natural language. Such instances could be considered as intra-sentential code-switching, where the switching happens within a clause or phrase, and the individual symbols could be marked with `Foreign`, but we would still need a means of determining the dependency relations needed to connect these tokens with the rest of the sentence.

Furthermore, treating math as a separate language would open up questions of when a niche domain can be considered independent enough to merit being handled though code-switching. If math can be its own language in UD, we might also extend the same consideration to domains like chemistry or computer programming which are rife with specialized jargon.

4.3 Natural Language

To treat a mathematical expression as natural language means to represent its internal structure as completely as possible with the existing relations of UD. We see evidence that mathematical expressions should be treated as analogous to natural language through the existence of mixed math and natural language expressions, such as the example in Figure 6, and through examples of mathematical expressions being integrated into passages of natural language. These examples show us that the line of what should and should not be considered a mathematical expression is not always clear. Because this line is not clear, code-switching or MWEs alone would not be sufficient to handle mathematical expressions or elements that are integrated with natural language. As such, it is worthwhile to develop standards of how to treat mathematical expressions in a manner analogous to natural language.

The most intuitive strategy for analyzing mathematical expressions as natural language is to treat the written expression the same as its spoken form. As most mathematical expressions can be verbalized in conversation, it stands to reason that we should be able to syntactically analyze them as language as well. Of course, when we verbalize mathematical expressions there may be instances where the words in the verbalized expression do not map neatly onto the written symbols, or where different speakers (particularly speakers of different languages) may not verbalize things in same way. Additionally, even once the expressions are considered in their spoken forms, it may still not be obvious which dependency relations should apply, as is often the case with technical, jargon filled natural language. As such, it is worthwhile to develop additional guidelines for the treatment of mathematical expressions as natural language.

5 Preliminary Recommendations for Analysis of Mathematical Operators as Natural Language

In this section we offer some brief guidelines on how to treat mathematical operators as analogous to English natural language in the application of dependency relations. As previously shown in Figure 2, mathematical operators present in UD corpora are primarily those for basic arithmetic, predicate relations, and parentheses. As such, these operators will be the focus of our recommendations. Since functions are a fundamental means of expressing relations in mathematics, we also give brief recommendations for the treatment of function application.

In these guidelines, we follow the view put forward by Schneider and Zeldes, 2021 that the relation `nummod` should be strictly used for quantity modification, as opposed to being a more general modifier to be used in any situation involving numbers. As such, we generally treat free standing numbers in mathematical expressions (e.g., "4" in "x + 4") syntactically the same as we treat variables like "x": as nominal terms.

5.1 Predicate Operators (e.g., =, <, >)

If we want to handle mathematical operators in a manner analogous to handling natural language, we may start by considering how the operators would be realized in spoken language. The predicate operator "=" is pronounced as the verb "equals" in spoken language, and it seems reasonable to treat "=" similarly. As discussed in Section 3.2, the verb "equals", is generally analyzed with arguments taking the `nsubj` relation and the `xcomp` relation. An example of such an analysis is shown below in (1) for the expression "x = 1":

(1)

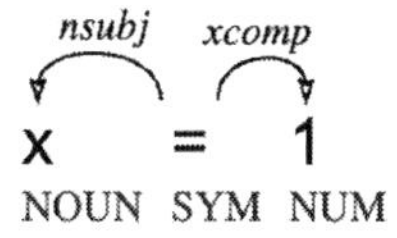

Similarly, we may consider that "<" is generally pronounced as "less than" when spoken aloud. However, we must additionally take into account that the natural language context surrounding the operator will influence what syntactic analysis we want to apply to it. For instance, in the example "Let us consider x < 5", "x < 5" is itself a term where "x" is the head and "< 5" is a modifying expression for the type of "x". In this example, we can analyze "< 5" as an adnominal clause headed by "5". The clause then functions as a modifier to the leftmost term "x", and we give its head the relation `acl`. "<" is then an extent modifer for the nominal term "5", so we give it the relation `obl`. The analysis for this example is shown in (2) below:

(2)

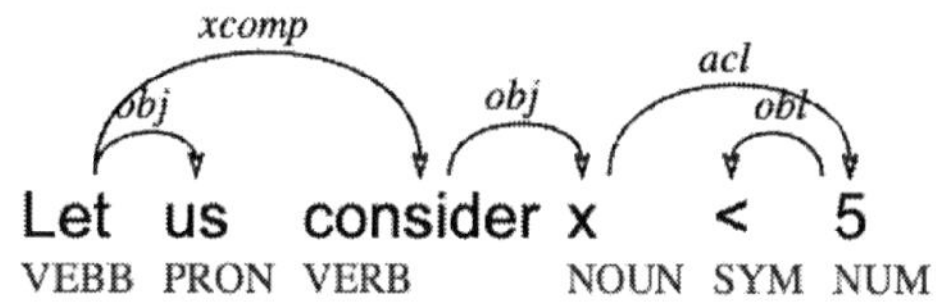

We may also consider the example "We will prove that x < 5", where "x < 5" is itself an equation with predication. In this instance, "<" must be the predicate and serve as the head of "x < 5". It follows that we may treat "x" as the `nsubj` of the predicate, and because the predicate relation is that of a comparative adjective, we may treat "5" as an `obl` argument to "<". The analysis for this example is shown in (3) below:

(3)

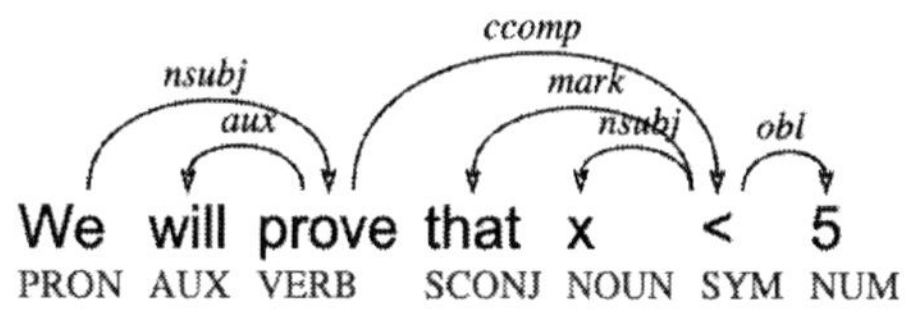

The ">" operator can be analyzed in a manner analogous to the above examples.

5.2 Conjoining Operators (e.g., +, -, *, /)

Next, we will consider the operators for the mathematical operations of addition ("+"), subtraction ("-"), multiplication ("*"), and division ("/"). It is worth noting here that some of these operations may be represented in multiple forms, not all of which will have the same syntactic analysis (e.g., in mathematical expressions, multiplication can be implied by the adjacency of terms, as well as by the use of the "*" or "x" operators). We primarily consider these operations to be conjoining relations, and as such, we link the terms to the left and right of the operator with the `conj` relation, and the operator itself can be labeled with the `cc` relation. An example of this analysis is shown in (4) for the expression "x + y":

(4)

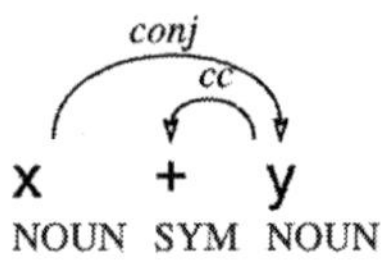

One benefit of this analysis is that it allows us to distinguish the scope of certain operations. For instance, consider the expression "8 - 6 / 2", which evaluates to 5. In accordance with the order of operations for mathematical expressions, in which division occurs before subtraction, the division by 2 should just be applied to the 6. We can express that by making "2" a dependent of "6". This analysis is show below:

(5)

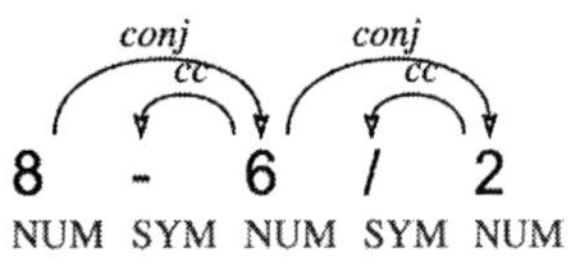

In contrast, consider the expression "(8 - 6) / 2", which used parentheses to force the subtraction to occur first so the expression evaluates to 1 rather than 5. We can express this difference by making "2" a dependent of "8" rather than "6". The added parentheses are treated as punctuation to the head. This analysis is show below:

(6)

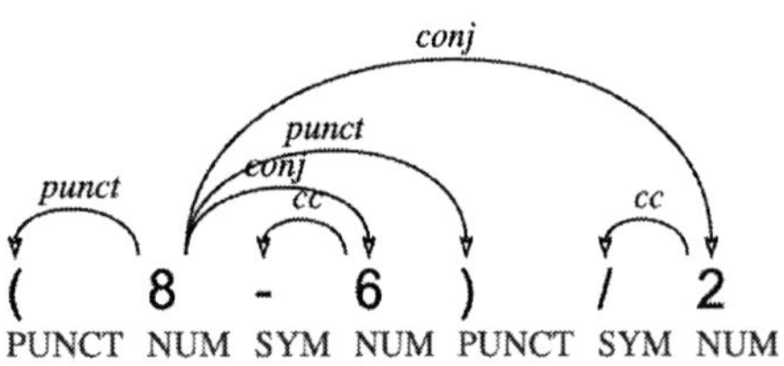

As previously mentioned, multiplication can be implied by the adjacency of terms, and in such cases, there is no operator to assign the `cc` relation. Even so, if it is two adjacent variable terms (such as "xy"), we believe it is still appropriate to apply the relation `conj`. However, if it is a coefficient adjacent to a variable, as in "2x", then we believe the coefficient can be treated as `nummod` to the variable. This is because "2x" (pronounced "two x") is generally interpreted as quantity modification on the number of "x", similar to how "5 bottles" is quantity modification on the number of bottles.

While in this section we have treated basic mathematical operators as conjoining relations, we also note that it is possible to view them as instances of more general function application (for which we offer a recommended treatment in the next section). While this is reasonable from a semantic perspective, we believe that in the formulation of mathematical expressions the verbalizations of these basic operators typically occupy syntactic positions more similar to natural language conjunctions (which themselves could be modeled as simple functions if desired), and as such can be handled using the `conj` and `cc` relations in most instances.

5.3 Function Application

We will now consider how to analyze function application in expressions such as "f(x)". This expression can be pronounced as "F of X", and so we may analyze "f" as the head of the expression, and "x" as a nominal extent modifier to the function using the `nmod:npmod` relation. The parentheses are treated as punctuation attached to "x". This analysis is show below:

(7)

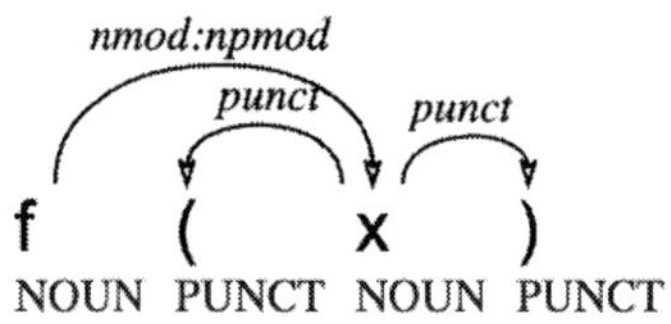

6 Conclusion

In this paper, we gave an high level overview of the current treatment of mathematical expressions in UD corpora, and considered various difficulties that arise when attempting to handle mathematical expressions with dependency relations by examining different types expressions attested in corpora related to academic and scientific domains. We argued that in most cases mathematical expressions should be treated in a manner analogous to natural language, rather than being treated as multi-word expressions with minimal internal structure, or as instances of an entirely separate "language" that would be handled via code-switching. As a part of this argument, we provided guidelines for using dependency relations to analyze basic mathematical expressions as natural language.

The main purpose of this paper is to raise awareness of the problems presented by mathematical expressions, and present various alternative philosophies for how to address them. We also wish to highlight the current lack of UD resources containing mathematical and technical texts. We believe that the adoption of the philosophy to treat mathematical expressions as natural language and the further development of such guidelines will help to facilitate the inclusion of such technical texts in future UD corpora and expand the resources available for the under resourced domain of technical language.

Limitations

As previously mentioned, while many of our arguments regarding syntactic analysis of mathematical expressions can apply cross-linguistically, this paper has primarily discussed how to analyze mathematical expressions as analogous to English natural language. As we argue that mathematical expressions should be treated as natural language in general (not just English), mathematical expressions in non-English texts should be analyzed as analogous to the primary natural language used in that document. However, the recommendations in this paper focus only on English language verbalization of mathematical expressions.

Additionally, the guidelines offered here only cover basic mathematical expressions, and more substantial guidelines will need to be developed in order to inform the annotation of texts containing more complicated mathematical expressions. This paper also does not include annotations for a significant amount of data, which would be useful in demonstrating the validity of analyzing mathematical expressions as natural language. Future work will need to include the further development of guidelines and a demonstration of their application on a substantial amount of data.

References

Mark Davies. 2010. The Corpus of Contemporary American English as the first reliable monitor corpus of English. *Literary and Linguistic Computing*, 25(4):447–464.

Marie-Catherine de Marneffe, Christopher D. Manning, Joakim Nivre, and Daniel Zeman. 2021. Universal Dependencies. *Computational Linguistics*, 47(2):255–308.

Alden Dima, Sarah Lukens, Melinda Hodkiewicz, Thurston Sexton, and Michael P Brundage. 2021. Adapting natural language processing for technical text. *Applied AI Letters*, 2(3):e33.

Vidur Joshi, Matthew Peters, and Mark Hopkins. 2018. Extending a parser to distant domains using a few dozen partially annotated examples. *arXiv preprint arXiv:1805.06556*.

Sylvain Kahane, Marine Courtin, and Kim Gerdes. 2017. Multi-word annotation in syntactic treebanks - propositions for Universal Dependencies. In *Proceedings of the 16th International Workshop on Treebanks and Linguistic Theories*, pages 181–189, Prague, Czech Republic.

Carol Myers-Scotton. 2017. Code-switching. *The handbook of sociolinguistics*, pages 217–237.

Minh Van Nguyen, Viet Dac Lai, Amir Pouran Ben Veyseh, and Thien Huu Nguyen. 2021. Trankit: A light-weight transformer-based toolkit for multilingual natural language processing. In *Proceedings of the 16th Conference of the European Chapter of the Association for Computational Linguistics: System Demonstrations*.

Joakim Nivre, Marie-Catherine de Marneffe, Filip Ginter, Yoav Goldberg, Jan Hajič, Christopher D. Manning, Ryan McDonald, Slav Petrov, Sampo Pyysalo, Natalia Silveira, Reut Tsarfaty, and Daniel Zeman. 2016. Universal Dependencies v1: A multilingual treebank collection. In *Proceedings of the Tenth International Conference on Language Resources and Evaluation (LREC'16)*, pages 1659–1666, Portorož, Slovenia. European Language Resources Association (ELRA).

Joakim Nivre, Marie-Catherine de Marneffe, Filip Ginter, Jan Hajič, Christopher D. Manning, Sampo Pyysalo, Sebastian Schuster, Francis Tyers, and Daniel Zeman. 2020. Universal Dependencies v2: An evergrowing multilingual treebank collection. In *Proceedings of the Twelfth Language Resources and Evaluation Conference*, pages 4034–4043, Marseille, France. European Language Resources Association.

Barbara Plank. 2016. What to do about non-standard (or non-canonical) language in NLP. *arXiv preprint arXiv:1608.07836*.

Shaurya Rohatgi. 2022. Acl anthology corpus with full text. Github.

Jack Rueter, Niko Partanen, and Flammie A. Pirinen. 2021. Numerals and what counts. In *Proceedings of the Fifth Workshop on Universal Dependencies (UDW, SyntaxFest 2021)*, pages 151–159, Sofia, Bulgaria. Association for Computational Linguistics.

Ivan A Sag, Timothy Baldwin, Francis Bond, Ann Copestake, and Dan Flickinger. 2002. Multiword expressions: A pain in the neck for NLP. In *International conference on intelligent text processing and computational linguistics*, pages 1–15. Springer.

Manuela Sanguinetti, Cristina Bosco, Lauren Cassidy, Özlem Çetinoğlu, Alessandra Teresa Cignarella, Teresa Lynn, Ines Rehbein, Josef Ruppenhofer, Djamé Seddah, and Amir Zeldes. 2022. Treebanking user-generated content: a UD based overview of guidelines, corpora and unified recommendations. *Language Resources and Evaluation*, pages 1–52.

Nathan Schneider and Amir Zeldes. 2021. Mischievous nominal constructions in Universal Dependencies. In *Proceedings of the Fifth Workshop on Universal Dependencies (UDW, SyntaxFest 2021)*, pages 160–172, Sofia, Bulgaria. Association for Computational Linguistics.

Amir Zeldes. 2017. The GUM corpus: creating multilayer resources in the classroom. *Language Resources and Evaluation*, 51(3):581–612.

Daniel Zeman. 2021. Date and time in Universal Dependencies. In *Proceedings of the Fifth Workshop on Universal Dependencies (UDW, SyntaxFest 2021)*, pages 173–193, Sofia, Bulgaria. Association for Computational Linguistics.

A Query to Identify Mathematical Expressions

This section gives a description of the search criteria in the query we used to identify mathematical expression in UD corpora. Our query identified sentences containing the at least one of following combinations of numerical values and Unicode mathematical operators and symbols:

1. At least 1 token that is included in one of the following Unicode blocks:
   - Mathematical Operators
   - Supplemental Mathematical Operators
   - Mathematical Alphanumeric Symbol
2. Or, at least 2 basic mathematical operators
3. Or, at least 1 number, 1 basic mathematical operator, and 1 ambiguous mathematical operator

where "basic mathematical operators" are defined as the following set of symbols: +, ×, ÷, =, ±, >=, <=, and "ambiguous mathematical operators" are defined as the following set of symbols: -, /, <, >, x, *, ^, (,).

Abbreviation	Relation
`acl`	clausal modifier of noun
`cc`	coordinating conjunction
`compound`	compound
`conj`	conjunct
`fixed`	fixed multiword expression
`flat:foreign`	foreign words
`nmod:npmod`	NP as adverbial modifier
`nsubj`	nominal subject
`nummod`	numeric modifier
`obj`	object
`obl`	oblique nominal
`punct`	punctuation
`xcomp`	open clausal complement

Table 1: Abbreviations of dependency relations discussed in this paper.

B Dependency Relation Proportions for Mathematical Operators

	-	(	)	*	/	^	+	±	×	<	=	>	−	≤	≥	x
acl	0	0	0	0	0	0	0	0	0	0	0.2	0	0	0	0	0
advcl	0	0	0	0	0	0	0	0	0	0	1	0	0	0	0	0
advmod	0	0	0	0	0	0	2.6	0	0	0	0.6	0	0	0	0	0
amod	0	0	0	0	0	0	0.2	0	0	0	0	0	0	0	0	0
appos	0.6	0	0	0	0	0	1.9	0	3.9	4	1	0	0	0	0	4.6
case	1.1	0	0	0	12.3	0	2.6	23.5	37.3	0	0.2	0	0	0	0	12.3
cc	0	0	0	0	2.8	0	31.1	5.9	11.8	0	10.8	0	0	0	0	1.5
compound	1.7	0	0	0	0	0	4.9	0	3.9	0	3.7	0	2.3	0	0	0
conj	0	0	0	0	0	0	0.7	0	9.8	0	3.1	0	0	0	0	0
dep	0	0	0	0	0	20	5.4	0	2	20	6.7	4.7	8	0	0	0
discourse	0	0	0	0	0	0	0.4	0	0	0	1	0	0	0	0	0
fixed	1.7	0	0	0	0	0	0.2	0	0	0	0.2	0	0	0	0	0
flat	0	0	0	4.5	0	13.3	7.4	0	0	0	5.1	0	0	0	0	9.2
flat:foreign	0	0	0	0	0	0	0	0	0	0	0.6	0	0	0	0	0
flat:name	0	0	0	0	0.9	0	1.2	0	7.8	0	0.4	0	0	0	0	0
list	1.1	0	0	18.2	0	0	3.5	0	15.7	0	4.1	25.6	0	0	0	0
nmod	0	0	0	0	0.9	0	3	5.9	0	4	8.4	0	0	33.3	7.1	47.7
nsubj	0	0	0	0	0	0	0.2	0	5.9	0	0	0	0	0	0	0
nsubj:pass	0	0	0	0	0	0	0	0	2	0	0	0	0	0	0	0
obj	0	0	0	0	0	0	0.2	0	0	0	1	0	0	0	0	0
obl	0	0	0	4.5	0	0	0.9	0	0	0	0.4	0	0	0	0	0
parataxis	0	0	0	0	0	0	1.4	0	0	4	7.6	27.9	0	0	0	0
punct	93.7	100	100	72.7	83	66.7	31.9	64.7	0	68	40.5	41.9	89.8	66.7	92.9	24.6
root	0	0	0	0	0	0	0.2	0	0	0	3.5	0	0	0	0	0
xcomp	0	0	0	0	0	0	0.2	0	0	0	0	0	0	0	0	0

Table 2: Dependency relation proportions for the most frequent mathematical operators in Universal Dependencies corpora (UD version 2.11, contains 243 treebanks, 138 languages).

C Dependency Relation Abbreviations

Table 1 lists the UD dependency relations discussed in this paper. The left column lists the deprel abbreviation used in the paper and the right column gives a short description of the relation.

D Examples of Mathematical Expressions in Corpora

This section gives additional examples of mathematical expressions in corpora and includes discussion on notable aspects of each example.

D.1 Expressions Lacking Predication

Examples taken from COCA:

(1)

(n + 1)

(2)

Square root of 37

(3)

1 + 2 + 4 + 8 + 16 + 32 + 64 cents

Examples (1) and (2) above may function as independent nominal phrases, while the mathematical expression in example (3) acts as a modifier to the word "cents". Example (2) also includes an expression composed primarily of word tokens rather than symbols, which provides additional motivation for a natural language based analysis.

D.2 Equations

Examples taken from the ACL Anthology Corpus:

(1)

λ v = log (D / D(v))

(2)

β = 1 + β 2 × C × E β 2 × C + E

(3)

γ = 1/1.3 = 0.77

While examples (1) and (2) show expressions with a single predicate operator, example (3) shows that it is possible to have multiple predicate operators in a single expression. Also, we note that because "x" indicates multiplication in example (2), it is likely that "β" is squared rather than multiplied by "2", but the formatting has introduced ambiguity into the expression.

D.3 Mixed Expressions

Examples (1) and (2) taken from COCA. Example (3) taken from the ACL Corpus:

(1)

The total number of productions (unintelligible + simplified + correct)

(2)

Global fee = hospital costs + hospital profits + physician fees

(3)

king - man + woman = queen

The above examples show expressions that mix mathematical operators and words to convey various kinds of definitions. Notably, in example (1) we see parentheses serving a similar function to the equals signs in the other two examples.

E Expressions Unfit for Syntactic Analysis

We would also like to highlight that there are issues regarding how mathematical expressions are represented and tokenized in corpora, which need to be figured out before syntactic analysis can be applied. While searching for example mathematical expressions to use in this paper, we came across numerous examples where the reformatting done to import the equation into the corpus leaves it mangled and unintelligible to the extent that attempting to apply a syntactic analysis would be meaningless.

Here are example equations taken from the the ACL Anthology Corpus, which were heavily altered upon being imported into the corpus. For the sake of comparison, the original equations from the corresponding ACL papers are included directly below each equation:

(1)

) , cos(1 2 1 2 1 Σ Σ Σ = = = × × = n i
n i n i bi ai bi ai B A

$$\cos(A,B) = \frac{\sum_{i=1}^{n} ai \times bi}{\sqrt{\sum_{i=1}^{n} ai^2} \times \sqrt{\sum_{i=1}^{n} bi^2}}$$

(2)

0 H : (|) (|) i i P t R p P t R = = 1 1 2
H : (|) (|) i i P t R p p P t R = ≠ =

$$\begin{aligned} &\mathrm{H}_0: \; P(t_i \mid R) = p = P(t_i \mid \tilde{R}) \\ &\mathrm{H}_1: \; P(t_i \mid R) = p_1 \neq p_2 = P(t_i \mid \tilde{R}) \end{aligned}$$

The examples above illustrate that importing complex mathematical expressions into corpora without taking into account how the formatting should be represented and how the expressions should be tokenized can result in expressions that cannot be interpreted and thus cannot be syntactically analyzed. While it is essential to have some means of handling ambiguous or mangled expressions in an analysis of mathematical expressions, it will also be important to consider representation and tokenization issues separately.

A Dataset for Physical and Abstract Plausibility and Sources of Human Disagreement

Annerose Eichel, Sabine Schulte im Walde
Institute for Natural Language Processing, University of Stuttgart
{annerose.eichel,schulte}@ims.uni-stuttgart.de

Abstract

We present a novel dataset for physical and abstract plausibility of events in English. Based on naturally occurring sentences extracted from Wikipedia, we infiltrate degrees of abstractness, and automatically generate perturbed pseudo-implausible events. We annotate a filtered and balanced subset for plausibility using crowd-sourcing, and perform extensive cleansing to ensure annotation quality. In-depth quantitative analyses indicate that annotators favor plausibility over implausibility and disagree more on implausible events. Furthermore, our plausibility dataset is the first to capture abstractness in events to the same extent as concreteness, and we find that event abstractness has an impact on plausibility ratings: more concrete event participants trigger a perception of implausibility.

1 Introduction

The ability to discern plausible from implausible events is a crucial building block for natural language processing (NLP). Most previous work on modelling plausibility however focuses on the kinds of semantic knowledge necessary for distinguishing a *physically* plausible event from an implausible one (Wang et al., 2018; Porada et al., 2019). As illustrated in Fig. 1, the current study extends the traditional focus to discern physically plausible events such as *cat-eat-sardine* from physically implausible ones such as *rain-break-belly*. Furthermore, while recent datasets include some events with conceptually *abstract* participants (Emami et al., 2021; Pyatkin et al., 2021), as to our knowledge no dataset nor model up to date has paid attention to the interaction of event plausibility and abstractness of the involved concepts. We propose to systematically examine plausibility across levels of abstractness, and distinguish between abstractly plausible events such as *law-prohibit-discrimination* and abstractly implausible ones such as *humour-require-merger*. We hypothesize that (i) plausible vs. implausible events can be captured through physical vs. abstract levels, and that (ii) integrating degrees of abstractness into events fosters the understanding and modelling of plausibility (cf. Fig. 1).

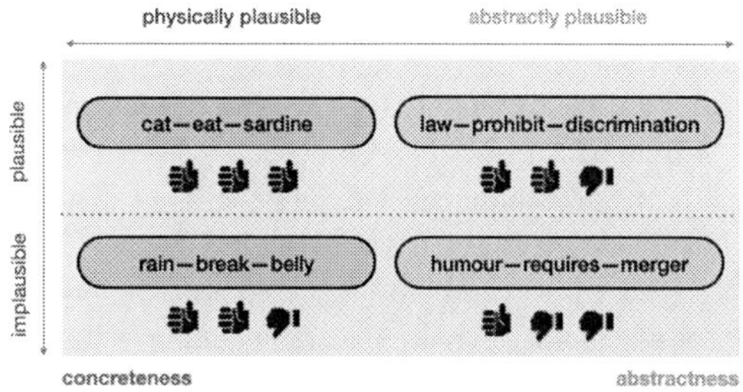

Figure 1: Plausible and implausible example events integrating degrees of concreteness/abstractness, cf. physical (green) and abstract (pink) levels. Annotators might agree (thumbs up) or disagree (thumbs down) on the (im)plausibility of the events.

We start out with a set of attested, i.e., *plausible*, natural language events in form of *s-v-o* triples from the English Wikipedia, assign abstractness ratings to event participants, and partition the triples into bins with varying degrees of abstractness. We then automatically generate pseudo-*implausible* event triples and assign degrees of abstractness in a similar way. To obtain human plausibility ratings for each event triple, we conduct a crowd-sourcing annotation study. We collect and validate a total of 15,571 judgements amounting to an average of 8.9 ratings for 1,733 event triples.

Human intuition regarding the assessment of plausibility is, however, incredibly multi-faceted, highly individual, and not easily reproducible automatically (Resnik, 1993). In particular, boundaries between categories to be annotated or predicted might not necessarily be strictly true *or* false, i.e., either plausible or implausible, thus reflecting the true underlying distribution of non-deterministic human judgements with inherent disagreement about labels (Baan et al., 2022). Over

Proceedings of the 17th Linguistic Annotation Workshop (LAW-XVII), pages 31–45
July 13, 2023 ©2023 Association for Computational Linguistics

the past decade, a growing body of work has emphasized the need to incorporate such disagreement in NLP datasets to reflect a more realistic and holistic picture across NLP tasks (Plank et al., 2014; Aroyo and Welty, 2015; Jamison and Gurevych, 2015; Basile et al., 2021b; Uma et al., 2021a). Accordingly, we argue for the necessity to preserve and examine disagreement when annotating and modelling plausibility, and represent inherent disagreement in annotation in order to devise a range of silver standards for analysis and modelling. More specifically, we disentangle subjectivity from annotation error, limitations of the annotation scheme, and interface (Pradhan et al., 2012; Poesio et al., 2019), and examine disagreements in physical and abstract plausibility annotation.

Overall, we find that our annotators tend to favor plausibility over implausibility, and we observe stronger disagreements for implausible in comparison to plausible events. Second, we explore the impact of abstractness on plausibility ratings. Here, our results reveal a positive relation between plausibility and events consisting of more abstract words, while implausibility is mostly found in predominantly concrete events.

2 Background and Related Work

2.1 Capturing (Semantic) Plausibility

The notion of plausibility has been approached from many perspectives. Inspired by the overview in Porada et al. (2021), we present distinctions and discuss viewpoints from previous work. Similarly to related notions such as *selectional preference* (Wilks, 1975; Resnik, 1993; Erk et al., 2010; Van de Cruys, 2014; Zhang et al., 2019; Metheniti et al., 2020) and *thematic fit* (Chersoni et al., 2016; Sayeed et al., 2016; Pedinotti et al., 2021), plausibility estimations capture non-surprisal in a given context. For example, the event *kid-sleep* with the agent *kid* is less surprising than *tree-sleep* and therefore considered more plausible. Within the context of (semantic) plausibility, however, plausible events are not necessarily assumed to be the most typical or preferred events. This stands in contrast with selectional preference or thematic fit, where whatever is not preferred is considered atypical albeit, in principle, a given event might be plausible. Wilks (1975) also discusses naturally occurring cases where the most preferred option does not yield the only correct interpretation: "[t]he point is to prefer the normal, but to *accept* the unusual."

In this vein, Wang et al. (2018) propose the task of semantic plausibility as "recognizing plausible but possibly novel events", where a "novel" event might be an unusual but nevertheless plausible event. Porada et al. (2021) further point out that "[p]lausibility is dictated by likelihood of occurrence on the world rather than text", and attribute this discrepancy to reporting bias (Gordon and Van Durme, 2013; Shwartz and Choi, 2020). For example, it is much more likely that the event *human-dying* is attested than the event of *human-breathing*. The sum of all plausible events in a given world thus encompasses not only the sum of all attested events in a corpus (including modalities other than text), but also possibly plausible events which are *not* necessarily attested in a corpus.

In our definition what is *preferred* is considered the *most plausible*, but what is *unusual* might still be highly *plausible*. Plausibility therefore (i) **exceeds the boundaries of (selectional) preference**. Further, plausibility (ii) is **a matter of degree** as the preferred is considered *more* plausible. In turn, what is unusual is still considered plausible albeit to a lesser degree. Moreover, plausibility (iii) captures **non-surprisal in a given context**, and (iv) denotes what is generally **likely, but not necessarily attested in a given corpus**.

2.2 Measuring Semantic Plausibility

There are various positions on how to model, measure, and evaluate whether an event triple is plausible. In this study, we model plausibility as the proportion of what is considered plausible, requiring a minimal label set of {implausible, plausible} (Wang et al., 2018). Note that a value regarding what is "true" is not involved in measuring plausibility. Consider the examples *eat-strawberry*, *eat-pebble*, and *eat-skyscraper*. Given our label set, the first two events would be considered plausible (even though they strongly vary in their degree of plausibility and likelihood to be attested in text with eating a strawberry considered more plausible than the less, but still plausible process of eating a pebble)[1], while the last event is physically implausible. Derived label sets such as {implausible, neutral, plausible} may include a "neutral" label which is considered to not carry plausibility information, as it does not provide insight into whether an expression is (im)plausible (Anthonio et al., 2022).

[1]Using e.g., Google n-grams, *eat-strawberry* is clearly attested more often than *eat-pebble*, while *eat-skyscraper* is not attested at all.

When annotating plausibility, drawing hard lines between labels is difficult and increases in complexity when considering words and concepts that are more abstract than concrete. This is especially true when considering free-standing events where no information on limiting factors regarding interpretation can be inferred. An example would be *human-breathe* which is plausible unless the human in question is dead. A more complex example would be *human-have-human_rights*, which is likely to be considered plausible by the majority of people and mirrored by corresponding laws in many countries, but (a) not universally accepted by each individual, and (b) not formalized as such by all countries.

2.3 Physical and Abstract Plausibility

Concepts can be described in accordance with the way people perceive them. While concepts that can be seen, heard, touched, smelled, or tasted are described as *concrete*, those that cannot be perceived with the five senses are referred to as *abstract* (Barsalou and Wiemer-Hastings, 2005; Brysbaert et al., 2014). Examples of concrete concepts include *apple, house* and *trampoline*, abstract examples encompass *absurdity, luck*, and *realism*. While instances at each extreme of abstractness occur, the notion is not binary but rather continuous, including many concepts between each extreme. Mid-range examples include concepts such as *inflation, punctuality* and *espionage*.

The grounding theory of cognition argues that humans process abstract concepts by creating a perceptual representation that is inherently concrete as it is generated through exposure to real world situations using our five senses (Van Dam et al., 2010; Brysbaert et al., 2014). However, more recent work brings forth evidence suggesting that such representations incorporate both perceptual and non-perceptual features (Dove, 2009; Naumann et al., 2018; Frassinelli and Schulte im Walde, 2019).

Regarding suitable abstractness ratings, we find a variety of datasets of growing size and diversity for many languages.[2] A widely used collection are the concreteness norms devised by Brysbaert et al. (2014), who collected ratings for approx. 40K "generally known" English words such as *sled* and *dream*, referring to strength of sense perception.

[2]See for a detailed overview, e.g., Schulte im Walde and Frassinelli (2022); Charbonnier and Wartena (2019).

2.4 Disagreement in Dataset Construction

While humans excel at assessing plausibility, they might naturally disagree regarding the plausibility of an event such as *law-prohibit-discrimination*. In the course of the last decade, a growing line of research argues for the preservation and integration of disagreement in dataset construction, modelling, and evaluation (Aroyo and Welty, 2015; Pavlick and Kwiatkowski, 2019; Basile et al., 2021b; Fornaciari et al., 2021; Uma et al., 2021a)[3]. While highly subjective tasks such as sentiment analysis (Yin et al., 2012; Kenyon-Dean et al., 2018) and offensive language detection (Leonardelli et al., 2021; Almanea and Poesio, 2022) have gathered particular attention, prior work has also presented evidence for seemingly objective tasks requiring linguistic knowledge such as PoS tagging (Gimpel et al., 2011; Hovy et al., 2014; Plank et al., 2014). We thus argue for the necessity to disentangle, devise, and examine disagreement when annotating and modelling plausibility. In contrast to previous work on plausibility assessments, we represent inherent disagreement in annotation and devise a range of silver standards for analysis and modelling.

3 Construction of Event Targets

Our first goal is to create a dataset[4] that systematically (a) covers both plausible event triples that are selectionally preferred or unusual, (b) captures events attested in the real world, i.e., extracted from triples produced in natural language, (c) measures plausibility on a degree scale from plausible to implausible, and (d) puts equal emphasis on both abstractly and physically plausible events. We visualize the dataset construction process in Fig. 2.

3.1 Extracting Natural Language Triples

To compile a set of natural language triples, we first extract all text from an English Wikipedia dump using `gensim` (Řehůřek and Sojka, 2010). We then randomly sample k articles[5] with k=50,000 and syntactically parse the articles using `stanza` (Qi et al., 2020). Next, we extract a triple (s, v, o) whenever the following conditions are satisfied: s

[3]For an overview we refer to, e.g., Basile et al. (2021a); Uma et al. (2021b).

[4]The dataset including event triples, ratings, and aggregated labels is available at `https://github.com/AnneroseEichel/PAP`.

[5]We only store the section texts and discard (section) titles as they tend to not contain 3-tuples of the desired form.

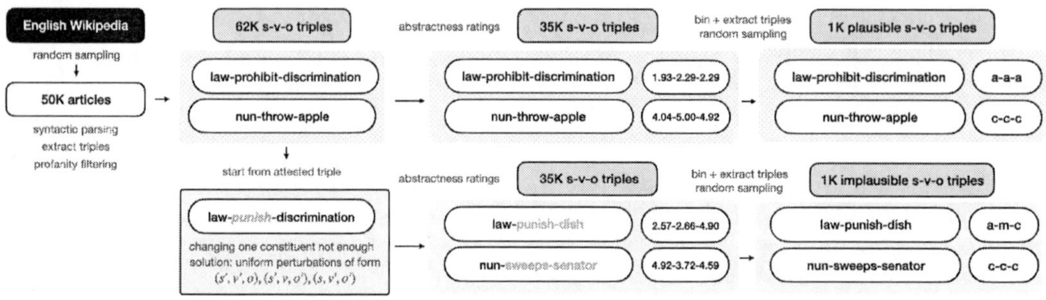

Figure 2: Simplified illustration of dataset construction starting with the extraction of attested event triples from a sample of the English Wikipedia. We filter triples, assign abstractness ratings, bin, and sample 1,080 plausible event triples for 27 abstractness combinations (marked in blue). Based on attested triples, we automatically generate pseudo-implausible triples and similarly filter triples, assign abstractness ratings, perform bining, and sample 1,080 implausible event triples (marked in yellow).

is the lemma of the head of `nsubj`, o is the lemma of the head of `obj`, and v is the lemma of the head of the root verb. We only allow nouns in subject and object positions and disregard proper names and pronouns as well as nouns and verbs that are part of a compound, yielding 62,843 triples. We extract each triple once, keeping track of frequency w.r.t sampled text data. Triples containing nouns or verbs that are explicit or have offensive connotations are filtered out using existing tools.[6] In total, this leaves us with 62,473 triples.

3.2 Creating Physically and Abstractly Plausible Triples

To discern triples containing highly concrete words from triples which encompass more abstract words, we assign abstractness scores to all nouns and verbs in a triple, drawing on the concreteness ratings by Brysbaert et al. (2014). We use a reduced collection[7] encompassing 12,880 noun and 2,522 verb targets to assign concreteness ratings to all 62,473 triples where a rating r exists for each word $w \in \{s, v, o\}$. Instances with nouns or verbs for which no rating exists are discarded. Overall, the assignment step yields 35,602 triples[8] with ratings. As we are specifically interested in distinctive features of abstractness vs. concreteness and cases which can be found in the middle of the continuous scale, we partition each constituent and each triple into 5 bins [*highly abstract, abstract, mid-range, concrete, highly concrete*]. To construct our dataset, we then only consider the bins at each extreme as well as the mid-range bin. Each constituent of a triple t can be either *highly abstract* (a), *mid-range* (m), or *highly concrete* (c). Taking the Cartesian product, we thus define 27 possible triple combinations, e.g., triples consisting of words with very high concrete ratings only, e.g., (c, c, c) or fully mixed triples, e.g., (c, m, a). To extract triples satisfying the conditions of each of the 27 possible triple combination, we carry out the following steps:

(a) Partition each constituent in s, v, o in each $triple_{1...n}$ into 5 bins of equal size, ranging from very abstract to very concrete. Whenever the relative threshold θ between bins prohibits perfectly equal sizes, we trade perfect bin size for perfectly separated abstractness ratings.

(b) Extract all triples satisfying the conditions of a combination e.g., (c, c, c) from our set of 35,602 triples.

The distribution of all naturally occurring triples for each triple combination $\in \{(a, a, a), ...(c, c, c)\}$ is presented in Fig. 6, App. A.2. To select plausible triples for annotation, we randomly sample 40 triples for each combination, yielding a total of 1,080 plausible triples.

3.3 Constructing Physically and Abstractly Implausible Triples

To construct implausible triples, we use the 35,602 cleaned triples for which an abstractness rating as provided by Brysbaert et al. (2014) exists. This restriction makes the task of implausible triple generation non-trivial as the set of possible constituents in each function is now limited to subjects,

[6] filter-profanity, alt-profanity-check

[7] For details on the filtering process, cf. App. A.1.

[8] Subject and object types amount to 4,140 and 4,551 unique words, respectively, while verb types are significantly less diverse (1,218 unique words).

verbs and objects that are attested to be plausible in their given function. Generating perturbations of attested triples as used by Porada et al. (2021) –where only one constituent, e.g., the subject, is perturbed while verb and object are kept– also results in disproportionally many plausible triples, e.g., *jurisdiction-evaluate-reaction*.

We thus use only the following perturbations: For each $t \in$ attested triples, we obtain a randomly perturbed t' serving as a pseudo-implausible natural language triple. We uniformly generate perturbations of the form (s', v', o), (s', v, o') and (s, v', o'), where s', v', and o' are arguments randomly sampled from the plausible triple collection taking into account corresponding functions, e.g., only words for which the use as object is attested in the corpus are randomly sampled as an object perturbation. We discard all triples that exist in the plausible triple collection and only keep unique instances, thus yielding 35,600 pseudo-implausible triples. After profanity filtering, we are left with 35,447 triples. We assign abstractness ratings and apply the binning method as described in the previous section 3.2.

The distribution of physically and abstractly pseudo-implausible triples per combination is shown in Fig. 6 (b), App. A.2. In analogy to plausible triple construction, we sample 40 triples for each abstractness combination to obtain 1,080 implausible triples.

4 Human Annotation

Our second goal targets the annotation of the collected event triples with respect to subjective assessments of plausibility on a degree scale (1–5) ranging from implausible to plausible. For this, we perform a human annotation study.

4.1 Collecting Ratings for (Im)Plausibility

Task We collect plausibility judgements on Amazon Mechanical Turk[9] for our 2,160 plausible and implausible triples. Each triple is annotated by 10 annotators. In particular, we ask annotators to indicate whether a given sentence is implausible or plausible using a sliding bar (corresponding to a scale from 1 to 5). An example of the task with full instructions as presented to annotators in our Human Intelligence Task (HIT) is illustrated in Fig 7, App. B.1. To avoid bias, the slider is by default set to the middle of the bar. Annotators are required to move the slider and thereby make a decision for either plausible or implausible. Task instructions clearly inform about the possibility of submission rejections if the slider remains in the middle position.

Annotators Participation is limited to annotators based in the United States and the United Kingdom. We further require annotators to have a HIT Approval Rate $> 98\%$ and a number of $\geqslant 1{,}000$ approved HITs from previous work.

Quality Checks To track annotation quality, we use an initial set of 20 manually produced check instances (cf. App. B.2) that were judged clearly plausible/implausible by the authors and an additional English native speaker. Annotators are presented batches of 24 randomly shuffled plausible or implausible triples, plus one randomly sampled check instance. In case of failed check instances, we discard all annotations submitted by the corresponding worker.

4.2 Annotation Post-Processing

After discarding submissions where the slider is set to the default (rating=3) as well as submission from workers who failed a check instance, we collect a total of 21,317 plausibility ratings.[10] We further perform the following post-processing steps in order to minimise the impact of spam and low-quality annotations regarding the plausibility of a given event (Roller et al., 2013; Rodrigues et al., 2017; Leonardelli et al., 2021), with datasets statistics at every processing step shown in Table 3, App. B.3. We first filter out ratings from workers who submitted annotations for $<$10 instances. Assuming that events observed in Wikipedia represent plausible events, we then exclude ratings from workers whose annotations disagree with the original label *plausible* in more than 75% of their corresponding submissions.

After these steps, our number n of annotators A still amounts to a large set of nA > 500 annotators. To ensure sufficient agreement between annotators, we calculate a *soft* pairwise Jaccard Coefficient J (Jaccard, 1902)[11] for all annotator combinations, and only keep annotations from workers whose submissions yield an average $J > 0.4$, following

[9]https://www.mturk.com/

[10]After our main collection round, we experiment with basic post-processing steps and perform a small second collection round to collect 5 ratings for 84 triples with <8 ratings.

[11]See App. B.3 for details on the calculation.

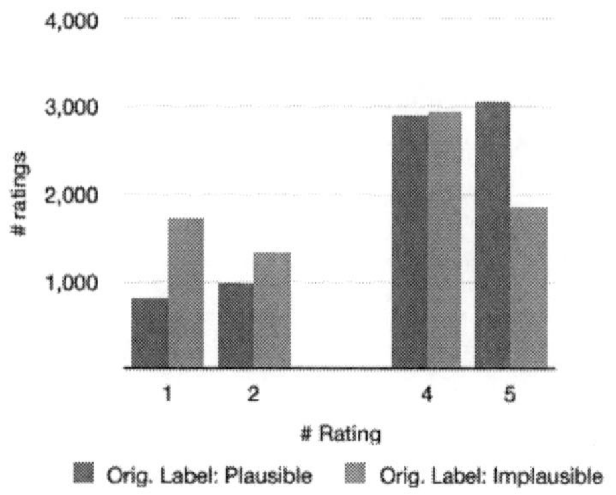

(a) Number of ratings per rating option.

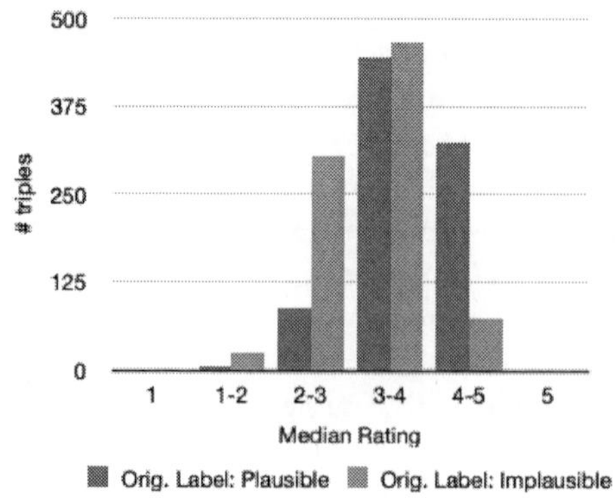

(b) Number of triples per average median rating bin.

Figure 3: (a) Number of plausibility ratings per rating option where ratings below 3 denote implausibility and ratings above 3 denote plausibility. (b) Number of triples across ratings aggregated as averaged median ratings. Ratings range from implausible $\{1, 2\}$ to plausible $\{4, 5\}$.

Bettinger et al. (2020). Finally, we keep only triples in the dataset if they received at least 8 ratings.

4.3 Dataset Statistics

After post-processing, we are left with 15,571 plausibility ratings for 1,733 triples (80% of the original triple set). With respect to instance coverage per abstractness combination, we have an average number of 32 triples per combination for both plausible and implausible triples with a minimum of 27 triples for the combinations (a, a, m) and (m, c, c) for plausible and implausible triples, respectively. Triples receive between 8 and 12 ratings, with an average of 8.9 ratings.

Estimated average Inter-Annotator Agreement (IAA) across our post-processed dataset using the previously introduced soft pairwise Jaccard Coefficient reaches 0.64. This indicates reasonable agreement among annotators; cases of disagreement we will explore in the next section.

5 Analysis of Human Judgements and Disagreement

5.1 Examining Rating Distributions

Fig. 3 (a) shows the distribution of ratings across the four rating options, with green and pink bars indicating originally plausible and implausible label, respectively. The distribution is skewed towards plausibility with 68.98% ratings $\in \{4, 5\}$. We aggregate all individual ratings as average median rating per triple and show the resulting distribution in Fig. 3 (b). While the distribution for originally plausible triples (green bars) evens out as expected with a peak number of average median rating for average plausibility (avg. median ratings $\in (3; 4]$), a similar peak can be observed given the distribution for originally implausibly triples (pink bars). The graph also shows differences, namely substantially more triples with a median rating indicating weak implausibility (avg. median rating $\in (2; 3]$) for originally implausible triples. On the other hand, high plausibility (rating $\in (4; 5]$) is annotated for mostly originally plausible triples.

To further investigate the skew towards plausibility, we visualize the average median rating for originally plausible and implausible triples in Fig. 4. The plot also illustrates the standard deviation of the values as a cloud. We observe that annotator ratings tend to show more overlap for plausible triples, with standard deviation decreasing with higher plausibility. In contrast, rating triples labeled as implausible result in greater deviation from the average mean rating decreasing only with implausibility. Taking into account the black horizontal line at a median rating of 3, we clearly see that median ratings for originally plausible triples are mostly above the cut line, thus indicating an overlap with the original label. On the other hand, median ratings for originally implausible triples are mostly below the cut line, thus indicating a clash with the original label.

These observations suggest (i) that **humans favor plausibility over implausibility**, while avoiding the extreme on the plausibility end of the scale, and (ii) that **implausibility yields higher disagreement**, as annotators disagree more when rating triples that were originally labeled as implausible.

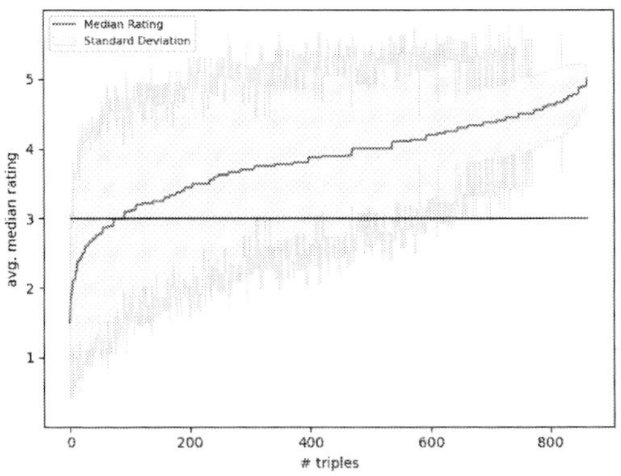

(a) Average median rating across plausible triples.

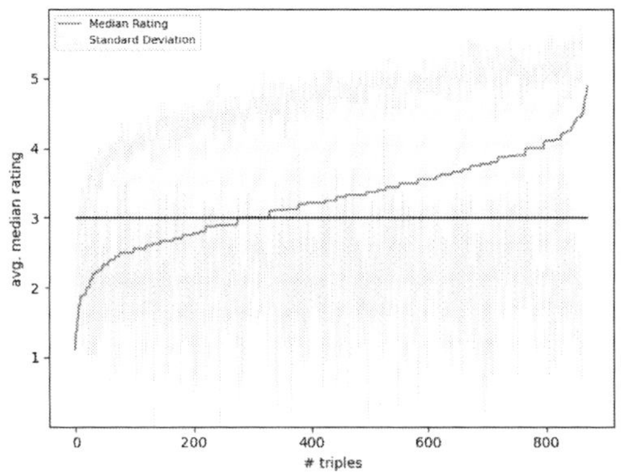

(b) Average median rating across implausible triples.

Figure 4: Average median ratings across originally plausible (a) and implausible (b) triples with standard deviation visualized as cloud around average rating lines. Triples are represented numerically on the x-axis. The black horizontal line denotes a median rating of 3. Average median ratings for *plausible* triples *below* the line disagree with the original label, while the opposite is true for average median ratings for *implausible* triples. Here, ratings *above* the line disagree with the original label.

5.2 Exploring the Impact of Abstractness on Plausibility Ratings

Abstractness at Event Level To assess the relation between degrees of abstractness for combinations of words and plausibility on physical and abstract levels, we first examine the proportion of plausibility ratings across triples from each of our 27 abstractness combinations. For this, we calculate a *strict* majority ($\geqslant$70%) for each triple. Whenever ratings do not point to a majority, i.e., *50% plausible* vs. *50% implausible*, we mark the triple as *unsure*. We present a visualization in Fig. 5 where green bars denote a strict majority of plausible ratings $\in \{4, 5\}$, pink bars refer to a strict majority of implausible ratings $\in \{1, 2\}$, and orange bars illustrate the lack of clear majorities.

For attested plausible triples, original label and proportional majority rating overlap in all cases. In only three cases we observe majority ratings proportions below 50%, namely for the mostly concrete combinations (c, c, m), (a, c, c), and (a, c, m). In contrast, majority rating proportions are generally higher for more abstract combinations, e.g., (a, a, a), (m, a, a). While a very low average of majority ratings for implausibility (1.3) can be observed, an average of 26.2 is obtained for triples with no majority. These observations suggest that (i) implausibility is most likely assigned to triples with concrete words, inducing higher disagreement among annotators, (ii) plausibility is most likely assigned given more abstract words.

For perturbed implausible triples, the picture looks different with only one abstractness combination for which original and majority rating proportions overlap, namely (a, c, c). For four highly abstract combinations (a, m, a), (m, a, a), (m, m, a), (m, m, a), a plausible majority is observed. However, in comparison with attested plausible triples, disagreement and uncertainty is much higher with no clear majority for 80% of abstractness combinations. These findings underline the observations for attested plausible triples with (i) implausibility being easier to catch given concrete words, and (ii) plausibility connected to more abstract words.

Abstractness at Event Constituent Level We further examine abstractness at constituent level, i.e., we explore whether abstractness degrees of individual constituents play a role. For this, we again calculate strict majority ratings across triples for each abstractness combination in a binary label setup (cf. 5.2). We focus on triples with a $\geqslant$ 70% majority for either plausible or implausible and calculate the proportion of concrete, mid-range, and abstract constituents $\in \{s, v, o\} \in t$.

Results are presented in Table 1. For constituents of triples receiving plausible majority votings, no particular pattern stands out: we find relatively equal shares for all constituents across abstractness levels. For originally implausible triples rated plausible, we observe a slightly higher share of mid-range and abstract constituents. In contrast, abstractness levels seem to play a more important

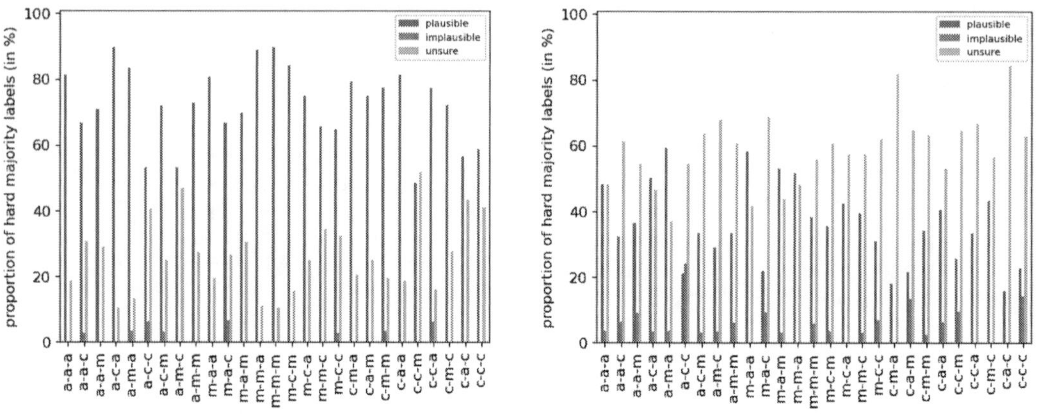

(a) Attested plausible triples.

(b) Perturbed implausible triples.

Figure 5: Proportion of strict majority ratings (⩾70%) across abstractness combinations for attested plausible triples (a) and perturbed implausible triples (b). Green bars denote a majority of plausible ratings $\in \{4, 5\}$, pink bars refer to a majority of implausible ratings $\in \{1, 2\}$, and orange bars capture cases of no clear majority.

role for constituents of triples with implausible majority votings. For both originally plausible and implausible triples, percentage shares clearly increase for concrete subjects and objects as compared to triples with plausible majorities. We also observe more abstract verbs, while shares of concrete and mid-range verbs decrease. In addition, a decrease in abstract subjects and objects as well as mid-range subjects can be observed. Regarding verb constituents, the line seems to be clear-cut between verbs as we find an increase in abstract, a decrease in mid-range, and relatively equal shares for concrete verbs.

These examinations suggest that abstractness levels of event constituents are especially important when assessing the absence of plausibility. Generally, events with a majority voting for implausible tend to include more concrete subjects and objects. However, the picture gets more diverse with clear increases in abstract verbs. Interestingly, these observations hold irrespective of the original label.

The exploration of abstractness at event constituents underlines our findings from the previous analysis focusing on abstractness at event level. We again find that the majority of human annotators tend to agree on what is plausible, while implausibility seems to be harder to catch and introduces more disagreement. Moreover, assignment **likelihood of plausibility increases with abstractness** of triple constituents, whereas assignment **likelihood of implausibility increases with concreteness** of triple constituents – no matter the underlying original label.

6 Final Dataset: Aggregations

To foster learning with and from disagreement, we release not only (i) the raw annotator ratings, but also (ii) provide the following standard aggregations to enable various perspectives for interpretation and modelling; for further aggregation options see e.g., Uma et al. (2021b). We account for both multi-class (label $\in \{1, 2, 4, 5\}$) and binary (label either plausible $\in \{4, 5\}$ or implausible $\in \{1, 2\}$) categorizations. The dataset is available at `https://github.com/AnneroseEichel/PAP`.

(a) **Strict Majority with Disagreement**
Classes are assigned based on a 70% majority for a multi-class or binary setup. In case of no clear majority, a label denoting disagreement is assigned to reflect conflicting perspectives of annotators.

(b) **Distribution**
To account for fine-grained disagreement and uncertainty, we calculate class distributions for a multi-class or binary setup.

(c) **Probabilistic Aggregation**
As we work with crowd workers, we also provide probabilistic label aggregations using Multi-Annotator Competence Estimation (MACE)[12] (Hovy et al., 2013). MACE leverages an unsupervised item-response model that learns to identify trustworthy crowd annotators and predicts the correct underlying label. We

[12] `https://github.com/dirkhovy/MACE`

among 1,733 valid triples	originally plausible			originally implausible		
	maj. plausible	maj. implausible	no maj.	maj. plausible	maj. implausible	no maj.
# triples	622	11	229	309	46	516
constituent	constituent proportion (in %)					
concrete subjects	0.106	**0.182**	**0.158**	0.100	**0.152**	0.144
concrete verbs	0.109	0.091	**0.162**	0.093	0.116	**0.172**
concrete objects	0.100	**0.182**	0.070	0.088	**0.159**	0.060
mid-range subjects	**0.115**	0.061	0.129	0.118	0.058	0.144
mid-range verbs	**0.115**	0.091	0.034	**0.128**	0.072	0.132
mid-range objects	0.111	0.061	0.125	0.111	0.138	0.042
abstract subjects	0.113	0.091	0.148	0.115	0.123	**0.146**
abstract verbs	0.109	0.152	0.148	0.112	0.145	0.129
abstract objects	**0.122**	0.091	0.025	**0.134**	0.036	0.031

Table 1: Overview of constituent analysis focusing on triples with a $\geqslant 70\%$ majority (maj.) for either plausible or implausible triples (# triples). We present the proportion of concrete, mid-range, and abstract constituents $\in \{s, v, o\} \in t$ for each abstractness level (concrete, mid-range, abstract) and constituent (subject, verb, object), in %. For completeness, we also show constituent proportions for triples with no strict majority (no maj.).

provide both predicted silver labels and class distributions for a multi-class and binary setup.

7 Discussion

We formulated the task of automatically distinguishing *abstract* plausible events from implausible ones as an extension of Wang et al. (2018) who focused specifically on *physical* plausible events. Based on the presented findings, we affirm our hypothesis as to (i) whether plausible and implausible events can be systematically captured on physical and abstract levels by (ii) integrating degrees of abstractness for combinations of words.

We further note differences in collected annotations with assignment likelihood of plausible ratings increasing with abstractness of events' constituents, while concreteness seems to facilitate the detection of more implausible events. We hypothesize that more concrete words evoke a more stable mental image grounded in the real world. Events like our introductory example *rain-breaks-belly* that represent a violation of quite fixed mental images are thus more often recognized as implausible. In contrast, more abstract words that lack a tangible reference object seem to open up a greater space of potentially plausible interpretations. This possibly invites annotators to cooperate and use their imagination resulting in more plausible ratings for more abstract triples.

Our findings further suggest that it is the recipient who comes up with an interpretation, thus making sense of the seemingly implausible. Moreover, generating fully implausible events is not trivial, which should be taken into account when using automatically generated implausible triples.

Lastly, while events based on *s-v-o* triples or comparably simple constructions have been successfully leveraged for exploring selection preference and thematic fit (Erk et al., 2010; Zhang et al., 2019; Pedinotti et al., 2021), the addition of context exceeding sentences constructed from *s-v-o* triples could potentially resolve present ambiguity and possibly reduce disagreement. We thus encourage future work extending this work by collecting and analyzing plausibility ratings for more complex constructions within broader contexts.

8 Conclusion

We presented a novel dataset for physical and abstract plausibility for events in English. Based on naturally occurring sentences extracted from Wikipedia, we infiltrated degrees of abstractness, and automatically generated perturbed pseudo-implausible events. We annotated a filtered and balanced dataset for plausibility using crowd-sourcing and performed extensive cleaning steps to ensure annotation quality. We provided in-depth analyses to explore the relationship between abstractness and plausibility and examined annotator disagreement. We hope that the presented dataset is used for both analyzing and modelling the notion of plausibility as well as the exploration of closely related tasks such as selectional preference and thematic fit and relevant downstream tasks including commonsense reasoning, NLI, and coreference resolution. Moreover, we make both raw annotations and a range of aggregations publicly available to foster research on disagreement and enable interpretation from various perspectives.

Limitations

In this paper, we present a collection of plausibility ratings for simple sentences in English that are automatically constructed from *s-v-o* triples that are extracted from natural language. We are aware that, for example, events such as *eat-skyscraper* might have a plausible interpretation in a given fictional world. When constructing our dataset, we do not explicitly account for triples which might originate from Wikipedia articles with content where other possible worlds are assumed.

As we conduct a relatively large annotation experiment via AMT crowd-sourcing, we aim to apply post-processing methods minimising the impact of unreliable annotations on our analyses. With more than 500 different final annotators and a very subjective annotation task, we however note the possibility of potentially wrong annotations due to errors, limitations of task instructions, or the interface (Pradhan et al., 2012; Poesio et al., 2019; Uma et al., 2022). This is especially true for the implausible portion of the dataset where no comparison with an attested triple label is possible. Approaches of mitigation could be concentrating on triples with high (im)plausibility ratings or use e.g., probabilistic methods to aggregate labels. We thus provide a dataset version with labels aggregated using MACE (Hovy et al., 2013).

As far as the transfer of the suggested approach of dataset construction to languages other than English is concerned, we call attention to the potential need to adapt the event extraction. Further, abstractness ratings might not readily be available in every language. In addition, AMT annotation for languages other than English potentially requires more time and resources, as annotator population is heavily skewed towards speakers of English.

Ethics Statement

To generate our dataset of events, we use a portion of the English Wikipedia which has been shown to exhibit a range of biases (Olteanu et al., 2019; Schmahl et al., 2020; Falenska and Çetinoğlu, 2021; Sun and Peng, 2021). While our goal is to enable others to explore plausibility on physical and abstract levels as well as sources of potential disagreement, users of this dataset should acknowledge potential biases and should not use to to make deployment decisions or rule out failures.

In the context of our annotation task, we collected plausibility ratings from crowd-workers using Amazon Mechanical Turk between January, 20 and March 7, 2023. Crowd-workers were compensated 0.02$ per instance. Although we aimed for strict quality control during data collection, we mostly compensated completed hits also when annotations were finally discarded because they did fail a check instance or, sometimes, did not move the slider. To this end, we engaged in email conversations with crowd-workers in case they reached out to clarify issues. We invested time to answer all requests and made our decision-making transparent to the annotators.

Acknowledgements

We are grateful to Prisca Piccirilli, Neele Falk, and the whole SemRel group for helpful suggestions and feedback regarding this work. We would also like to thank the anonymous reviewers for their nuanced comments and constructive suggestions. Annerose Eichel received funding by the Hanns Seidel Foundation's Talent Program.

References

Dina Almanea and Massimo Poesio. 2022. ArMIS - the Arabic misogyny and sexism corpus with annotator subjective disagreements. In *Proceedings of the Thirteenth Language Resources and Evaluation Conference*, pages 2282–2291, Marseille, France. European Language Resources Association.

Talita Anthonio, Anna Sauer, and Michael Roth. 2022. Clarifying Implicit and Underspecified Phrases in Instructional Text. In *Proceedings of the Thirteenth Language Resources and Evaluation Conference*, pages 3319–3330, Marseille, France. European Language Resources Association.

Lora Aroyo and Chris Welty. 2015. Truth is a lie: Crowd truth and the seven myths of human annotation. *AI Magazine*, 36(1):15–24.

Joris Baan, Wilker Aziz, Barbara Plank, and Raquel Fernandez. 2022. Stop measuring calibration when humans disagree. In *Proceedings of the 2022 Conference on Empirical Methods in Natural Language Processing*, pages 1892–1915, Abu Dhabi, United Arab Emirates. Association for Computational Linguistics.

Lawrence W Barsalou and Katja Wiemer-Hastings. 2005. Situating Abstract Concepts. *Grounding cognition: The role of perception and action in memory, language, and thought*, pages 129–163.

Valerio Basile, Federico Cabitza, Andrea Campagner, and Michael Fell. 2021a. Toward a perspectivist turn in ground truthing for predictive computing.

Valerio Basile, Michael Fell, Tommaso Fornaciari, Dirk Hovy, Silviu Paun, Barbara Plank, Massimo Poesio, and Alexandra Uma. 2021b. We need to consider disagreement in evaluation. In *Proceedings of the 1st Workshop on Benchmarking: Past, Present and Future*, pages 15–21, Online. Association for Computational Linguistics.

Julia Bettinger, Anna Hätty, Michael Dorna, and Sabine Schulte im Walde. 2020. A domain-specific dataset of difficulty ratings for German noun compounds in the domains DIY, cooking and automotive. In *Proceedings of the Twelfth Language Resources and Evaluation Conference*, pages 4359–4367, Marseille, France. European Language Resources Association.

Marc Brysbaert, Boris New, and Emmanuel Keuleers. 2012. Adding part-of-speech information to the SUBTLEX-US word frequencies. *Behavior research methods*, 44(4):991–997.

Marc Brysbaert, Amy Beth Warriner, and Victor Kuperman. 2014. Concreteness ratings for 40 thousand generally known English word lemmas. *Behavior research methods*, 46(3):904–911.

Jean Charbonnier and Christian Wartena. 2019. Predicting word concreteness and imagery. In *Proceedings of the 13th International Conference on Computational Semantics - Long Papers*, pages 176–187, Gothenburg, Sweden. Association for Computational Linguistics.

Emmanuele Chersoni, Philippe Blache, and Alessandro Lenci. 2016. Towards a distributional model of semantic complexity. In *Proceedings of the Workshop on Computational Linguistics for Linguistic Complexity (CL4LC)*, pages 12–22, Osaka, Japan. The COLING 2016 Organizing Committee.

Guy Dove. 2009. Beyond perceptual symbols: A call for representational pluralism. *Cognition*, 110(3):412–431.

Ali Emami, Ian Porada, Alexandra Olteanu, Kaheer Suleman, Adam Trischler, and Jackie Chi Kit Cheung. 2021. ADEPT: An Adjective-Dependent Plausibility Task. In *Proceedings of the 59th Annual Meeting of the Association for Computational Linguistics and the 11th International Joint Conference on Natural Language Processing (Volume 1: Long Papers)*, pages 7117–7128, Online.

Katrin Erk, Sebastian Padó, and Ulrike Padó. 2010. A flexible, corpus-driven model of regular and inverse selectional preferences. *Computational Linguistics*, 36(4):723–763.

Agnieszka Falenska and Özlem Çetinoğlu. 2021. Assessing gender bias in Wikipedia: Inequalities in article titles. In *Proceedings of the 3rd Workshop on Gender Bias in Natural Language Processing*, pages 75–85, Online. Association for Computational Linguistics.

Tommaso Fornaciari, Alexandra Uma, Silviu Paun, Barbara Plank, Dirk Hovy, and Massimo Poesio. 2021. Beyond black & white: Leveraging annotator disagreement via soft-label multi-task learning. In *Proceedings of the 2021 Conference of the North American Chapter of the Association for Computational Linguistics: Human Language Technologies*, pages 2591–2597, Online. Association for Computational Linguistics.

Diego Frassinelli and Sabine Schulte im Walde. 2019. Distributional interaction of concreteness and abstractness in verb–noun subcategorisation. In *Proceedings of the 13th International Conference on Computational Semantics - Short Papers*, pages 38–43, Gothenburg, Sweden. Association for Computational Linguistics.

Kevin Gimpel, Nathan Schneider, Brendan O'Connor, Dipanjan Das, Daniel Mills, Jacob Eisenstein, Michael Heilman, Dani Yogatama, Jeffrey Flanigan, and Noah A. Smith. 2011. Part-of-speech tagging for Twitter: Annotation, features, and experiments. In *Proceedings of the 49th Annual Meeting of the Association for Computational Linguistics: Human Language Technologies*, pages 42–47, Portland, Oregon, USA. Association for Computational Linguistics.

Jonathan Gordon and Benjamin Van Durme. 2013. Reporting bias and knowledge acquisition. In *Proceedings of the 2013 Workshop on Automated Knowledge Base Construction*, page 25–30, New York, NY, USA. Association for Computing Machinery.

Dirk Hovy, Taylor Berg-Kirkpatrick, Ashish Vaswani, and Eduard Hovy. 2013. Learning whom to trust with MACE. In *Proceedings of the 2013 Conference of the North American Chapter of the Association for Computational Linguistics: Human Language Technologies*, pages 1120–1130, Atlanta, Georgia. Association for Computational Linguistics.

Dirk Hovy, Barbara Plank, and Anders Søgaard. 2014. Experiments with crowdsourced re-annotation of a POS tagging data set. In *Proceedings of the 52nd Annual Meeting of the Association for Computational Linguistics (Volume 2: Short Papers)*, pages 377–382, Baltimore, Maryland. Association for Computational Linguistics.

Paul Jaccard. 1902. Lois de distribution florale dans la zone alpine. *Bulletin de la Société vaudoise des sciences naturelles*, 38:69–130.

Emily Jamison and Iryna Gurevych. 2015. Noise or additional information? Leveraging crowdsource annotation item agreement for natural language tasks. In *Proceedings of the 2015 Conference on Empirical Methods in Natural Language Processing*, pages 291–297, Lisbon, Portugal. Association for Computational Linguistics.

Kian Kenyon-Dean, Eisha Ahmed, Scott Fujimoto, Jeremy Georges-Filteau, Christopher Glasz, Barleen Kaur, Auguste Lalande, Shruti Bhanderi, Robert

Belfer, Nirmal Kanagasabai, Roman Sarrazingendron, Rohit Verma, and Derek Ruths. 2018. Sentiment analysis: It's complicated! In *Proceedings of the 2018 Conference of the North American Chapter of the Association for Computational Linguistics: Human Language Technologies, Volume 1 (Long Papers)*, pages 1886–1895, New Orleans, Louisiana. Association for Computational Linguistics.

Elisa Leonardelli, Stefano Menini, Alessio Palmero Aprosio, Marco Guerini, and Sara Tonelli. 2021. Agreeing to disagree: Annotating offensive language datasets with annotators' disagreement. In *Proceedings of the 2021 Conference on Empirical Methods in Natural Language Processing*, pages 10528–10539, Online and Punta Cana, Dominican Republic. Association for Computational Linguistics.

Eleni Metheniti, Tim Van de Cruys, and Nabil Hathout. 2020. How relevant are selectional preferences for transformer-based language models? In *Proceedings of the 28th International Conference on Computational Linguistics*, pages 1266–1278, Barcelona, Spain (Online). International Committee on Computational Linguistics.

Daniela Naumann, Diego Frassinelli, and Sabine Schulte im Walde. 2018. Quantitative semantic variation in the contexts of concrete and abstract words. In *Proceedings of the Seventh Joint Conference on Lexical and Computational Semantics*, pages 76–85, New Orleans, Louisiana. Association for Computational Linguistics.

Alexandra Olteanu, Carlos Castillo, Fernando Diaz, and Emre Kıcıman. 2019. Social data: Biases, methodological pitfalls, and ethical boundaries. *Frontiers in Big Data*, 2.

Ellie Pavlick and Tom Kwiatkowski. 2019. Inherent disagreements in human textual inferences. *Transactions of the Association for Computational Linguistics*, 7:677–694.

Paolo Pedinotti, Giulia Rambelli, Emmanuele Chersoni, Enrico Santus, Alessandro Lenci, and Philippe Blache. 2021. Did the cat drink the coffee? Challenging transformers with generalized event knowledge. In *Proceedings of *SEM 2021: The Tenth Joint Conference on Lexical and Computational Semantics*, pages 1–11, Online. Association for Computational Linguistics.

Barbara Plank, Dirk Hovy, and Anders Søgaard. 2014. Linguistically debatable or just plain wrong? In *Proceedings of the 52nd Annual Meeting of the Association for Computational Linguistics (Volume 2: Short Papers)*, pages 507–511, Baltimore, Maryland. Association for Computational Linguistics.

Massimo Poesio, Jon Chamberlain, Silviu Paun, Juntao Yu, Alexandra Uma, and Udo Kruschwitz. 2019. A crowdsourced corpus of multiple judgments and disagreement on anaphoric interpretation. In *Proceedings of the 2019 Conference of the North American Chapter of the Association for Computational Linguistics: Human Language Technologies, Volume 1 (Long and Short Papers)*, pages 1778–1789, Minneapolis, Minnesota. Association for Computational Linguistics.

Ian Porada, Kaheer Suleman, and Jackie Chi Kit Cheung. 2019. Can a gorilla ride a camel? Learning semantic plausibility from text. In *Proceedings of the First Workshop on Commonsense Inference in Natural Language Processing*, pages 123–129, Hong Kong, China.

Ian Porada, Kaheer Suleman, Adam Trischler, and Jackie Chi Kit Cheung. 2021. Modeling event plausibility with consistent conceptual abstraction. In *Proceedings of the 2021 Conference of the North American Chapter of the Association for Computational Linguistics: Human Language Technologies*, pages 1732–1743, Online.

Sameer Pradhan, Alessandro Moschitti, Nianwen Xue, Olga Uryupina, and Yuchen Zhang. 2012. CoNLL-2012 Shared Task: Modeling multilingual unrestricted coreference in OntoNotes. In *Joint Conference on EMNLP and CoNLL - Shared Task*, pages 1–40, Jeju Island, Korea. Association for Computational Linguistics.

Valentina Pyatkin, Shoval Sadde, Aynat Rubinstein, Paul Portner, and Reut Tsarfaty. 2021. The possible, the plausible, and the desirable: Event-based modality detection for language processing. In *Proceedings of the 59th Annual Meeting of the Association for Computational Linguistics and the 11th International Joint Conference on Natural Language Processing (Volume 1: Long Papers)*, pages 953–965, Online. Association for Computational Linguistics.

Peng Qi, Yuhao Zhang, Yuhui Zhang, Jason Bolton, and Christopher D. Manning. 2020. Stanza: A Python natural language processing toolkit for many human languages. In *Proceedings of the 58th Annual Meeting of the Association for Computational Linguistics: System Demonstrations*.

Radim Řehůřek and Petr Sojka. 2010. Software Framework for Topic Modelling with Large Corpora. In *Proceedings of the LREC 2010 Workshop on New Challenges for NLP Frameworks*, pages 45–50, Valletta, Malta. ELRA. `http://is.muni.cz/publication/884893/en`.

Philip Stuart Resnik. 1993. *Selection and information: A class-based approach to lexical relationships*. Ph.D. thesis, University of Pennsylvania.

Filipe Rodrigues, Mariana Lourenço, Bernardete Ribeiro, and Francisco C. Pereira. 2017. Learning supervised topic models for classification and regression from crowds. *IEEE Transactions on Pattern Analysis and Machine Intelligence*, 39(12):2409–2422.

Stephen Roller, Sabine Schulte im Walde, and Silke Scheible. 2013. The (un)expected effects of applying standard cleansing models to human ratings on compositionality. In *Proceedings of the 9th Workshop on Multiword Expressions*, pages 32–41, Atlanta, Georgia, USA. Association for Computational Linguistics.

Asad Sayeed, Clayton Greenberg, and Vera Demberg. 2016. Thematic fit evaluation: an aspect of selectional preferences. In *Proceedings of the 1st Workshop on Evaluating Vector-Space Representations for NLP*, pages 99–105, Berlin, Germany. Association for Computational Linguistics.

Roland Schäfer. 2015. Processing and querying large web corpora with the COW14 architecture. Proceedings of the 3rd Workshop on Challenges in the Management of Large Corpora, Lancaster, 20 July 2015, pages 28 – 34, Mannheim.

Katja Geertruida Schmahl, Tom Julian Viering, Stavros Makrodimitris, Arman Naseri Jahfari, David Tax, and Marco Loog. 2020. Is Wikipedia succeeding in reducing gender bias? Assessing changes in gender bias in Wikipedia using word embeddings. In *Proceedings of the Fourth Workshop on Natural Language Processing and Computational Social Science*, pages 94–103, Online. Association for Computational Linguistics.

Sabine Schulte im Walde and Diego Frassinelli. 2022. Distributional Measures of Abstraction. *Frontiers in Artificial Intelligence: Language and Computation 4:796756. Alessandro Lenci and Sebastian Pado (topic editors): "Perspectives for Natural Language Processing between AI, Linguistics and Cognitive Science".*

Vered Shwartz and Yejin Choi. 2020. Do neural language models overcome reporting bias? In *Proceedings of the 28th International Conference on Computational Linguistics*, pages 6863–6870, Barcelona, Spain (Online).

Jiao Sun and Nanyun Peng. 2021. Men are elected, women are married: Events gender bias on Wikipedia. In *Proceedings of the 59th Annual Meeting of the Association for Computational Linguistics and the 11th International Joint Conference on Natural Language Processing (Volume 2: Short Papers)*, pages 350–360, Online. Association for Computational Linguistics.

Tarun Tater, Diego Frassinelli, and Sabine Schulte im Walde. 2022. Concreteness vs. abstractness: A selectional preference perspective. In *Proceedings of the 2nd Conference of the Asia-Pacific Chapter of the Association for Computational Linguistics and the 12th International Joint Conference on Natural Language Processing: Student Research Workshop*, pages 92–98, Online. Association for Computational Linguistics.

Alexandra Uma, Dina Almanea, and Massimo Poesio. 2022. Scaling and Disagreements: Bias, Noise, and Ambiguity. *Frontiers in Artificial Intelligence*, 5.

Alexandra Uma, Tommaso Fornaciari, Anca Dumitrache, Tristan Miller, Jon Chamberlain, Barbara Plank, Edwin Simpson, and Massimo Poesio. 2021a. SemEval-2021 Task 12: Learning with disagreements. In *Proceedings of the 15th International Workshop on Semantic Evaluation (SemEval-2021)*, pages 338–347, Online. Association for Computational Linguistics.

Alexandra Uma, Tommaso Fornaciari, Dirk Hovy, Silviu Paun, Barbara Plank, and Massimo Poesio. 2021b. Learning from disagreement: A survey. *Journal of Artificial Intelligence Research*, 72:1385–1470.

Wessel Van Dam, Shirley-Ann Rueschemeyer, Oliver Lindemann, and Harold Bekkering. 2010. Context effects in embodied lexical-semantic processing. *Frontiers in Psychology*, 1:150.

Tim Van de Cruys. 2014. A neural network approach to selectional preference acquisition. In *Proceedings of the 2014 Conference on Empirical Methods in Natural Language Processing (EMNLP)*, pages 26–35, Doha, Qatar. Association for Computational Linguistics.

Su Wang, Greg Durrett, and Katrin Erk. 2018. Modeling Semantic Plausibility by Injecting World Knowledge. In *Proceedings of the 2018 Conference of the North American Chapter of the Association for Computational Linguistics: Human Language Technologies, Volume 2 (Short Papers)*, pages 303–308, New Orleans, Louisiana.

Yorick Wilks. 1975. A preferential, pattern-seeking, semantics for natural language inference. *Artificial Intelligence*, 6(1):53–74.

Jie Yin, Nalin Narang, Paul Thomas, and Cecile Paris. 2012. Unifying local and global agreement and disagreement classification in online debates. In *Proceedings of the 3rd Workshop in Computational Approaches to Subjectivity and Sentiment Analysis*, pages 61–69, Jeju, Korea. Association for Computational Linguistics.

Hongming Zhang, Hantian Ding, and Yangqiu Song. 2019. SP-10K: A large-scale evaluation set for selectional preference acquisition. In *Proceedings of the 57th Annual Meeting of the Association for Computational Linguistics*, pages 722–731, Florence, Italy. Association for Computational Linguistics.

A Dataset Construction

A.1 Filtering the Brysbaert Norms

To assign abstractness scores to all nouns and verbs in a given event triples, we draw on the concreteness ratings for approximately 40,000 English words devised by Brysbaert et al. (2014). The Brysbaert norms were collected in an out-of-context setting and without providing information about the part-of-speech (POS). POS tags were added in a post-processing step, utilizing the SUBTLEX-US corpus (Brysbaert et al., 2012). To account for this, we follow Schulte im Walde and Frassinelli (2022) and Tater et al. (2022) in adding the most frequent POS tag associated with each target word based on the English web corpus ENCOW16AX (Schäfer, 2015). We then filter for noun and verb target words where the POS tag provided by (Brysbaert et al., 2014) and the POS tag extracted using the ENCOW16AX correspond to each other. We filter out all words with a frequency below 10K to remove infrequent words. This way, we obtain a collection of 12,880 noun and 2,522 verb targets.

A.2 Triple Binning and Distributions

The distribution of all naturally occurring triples for each triple combination $\in \{(a, a, a), ...(c, c, c)\}$ is presented in Fig. 6 (a). While triple numbers accumulate on the extremes highly abstract and highly concrete, the number drops for triples consisting of mid-range constituents. Mixed triple combinations (a, m, c) and (c, m, a) yield minimum numbers of triples as well as triples with highly concrete or abstract subjects and verbs (a, a, c) and (c, c, a).

Similarly, the distribution of all automatically generated pseudo-implausible triples for each triple combination is shown in Fig. 6 (b). Note that a substantially higher number of valid implausible triples is extracted using the binning process with minimum numbers achieved for mostly medium-range abstractness.

B Human Annotation

B.1 HIT Interface

Fig. 7 shows a full example of the HIT interface as presented to HIT workers.

B.2 Check Instances

We list check instances in Table 2. In a post-processing step, we exclude three implausible check instances, e.g., *water cuts ball*, which might be interpreted as plausible in the context of high-pressure water systems which might be able to cut a ball (marked in italics). We use the check instances mainly after the the annotations process to increase annotation quality by filtering out all submissions where annotators failed a valid check instance.

B.3 Annotation Post-Processing

We show an overview of dataset statistics at each post-processing step in Table 3. Specifically, we present changes in number of ratings, validated annotators, and number of triples with >8 ratings across annotation post-processing. Post-processing methods are applied in the order listed. Results in a given row correspond to dataset statistics having applied a given step.

plausible	implausible
grandmother drinks tea	grandmother drinks stone
child eats banana	child eats dream
baker bakes cake	*baker bakes air*
kid plays game	sun beats banana
rabbit eats carrot	baby eats storm
man builds house	man breaks air
man opens window	ant opens window
teenager drinks coke	*sun breaks door*
woman drives car	woman drinks bridge
player throws ball	*water cuts ball*

Table 2: Plausible and implausible check instances. Instances marked in italics are filtered out in a post-processing step due to possible plausible interpretations.

Soft Jaccard Coefficient We estimate Inter-Annotator Agreement (IAA) by calculating the Jaccard Coefficient for all pairwise annotator combinations

$$J(A, B) = \frac{|A \cap B|}{|A \cup B|}$$

where the intersection of A and B captures all cases where annotators agree that a triple is either plausible (ratings $\in \{4, 5\}$) or implausible (ratings $\in \{1, 2\}$), and the union of A and B denotes all cases where both annotators provided a rating for the same sentence regardless of their agreement. As we are not enforcing strict rating agreement, we refer to this way of calculating IAA as *soft* Jaccard Coefficient.

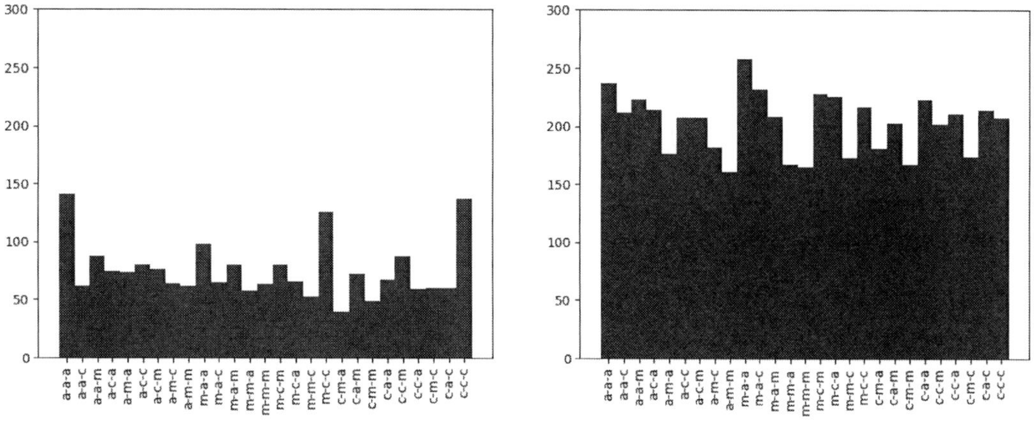

(a) Plausible triples. (b) Implausible triples.

Figure 6: Distribution of attested plausible (left) and perturbed implausible (right) triples per combination.

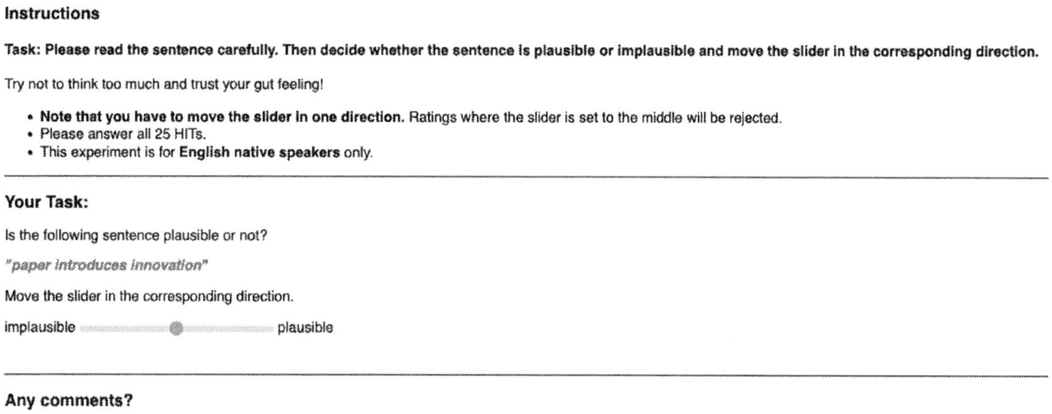

Figure 7: HIT interface including task instruction and requirements for successful answer submission (ratings where the slider is set to the middle can be rejected).

	# annotators		# ratings			# triples
	plausible	implausible	plausible	implausible	total	total
Raw (without check instances)	883	879	11,250	11,343	22,593	2,160
Failed checks/default submission	878	872	10,649	10,668	21,317	2,148
>75% disagreement orig. label	832	838	9,849	10,046	19,895	2,081
<10 ratings submitted	478	479	8,373	8,502	16,875	1,840
AMT approv. rate <80%, incl. 0%	468	471	8,269	8,333	16,602	1,819
Pairwise Jaccard Index <0.4	452	452	7,726	7,845	15,571	1,733

Table 3: Overview of changes in number of ratings, validated annotators, and number of triples with >8 ratings across annotation post-processing. Post-processing methods are applied in the order listed. Results in a given row correspond to dataset statistics having applied a given step, e.g., filtering out submission from annotators who failed check instances as well as all submissions where annotators submitted a default rating of 3 results in the number of 21,317 valid ratings, including both ratings for plausible and implausible triples.

Annotating and Disambiguating the Discourse Usage of the Enclitic *dA* in Turkish

Ebru Ersöyleyen and **Deniz Zeyrek** and **Fırat Öter**
Graduate School of Informatics
Middle East Technical University
Ankara, Türkiye
{ebru.ersoyleyen,dezeyrek,foter}@metu.edu.tr

Abstract

The Turkish particle *dA* is a focus-associated enclitic, and it can act as a discourse connective conveying multiple senses, like additive, contrastive, causal etc. Like many other linguistic expressions, it is subject to usage ambiguity and creates a challenge in natural language automatization tasks. For the first time, we annotate the discourse and non-discourse connnective occurrences of *dA* in Turkish with the PDTB principles. Using a minimal set of linguistic features, we develop binary classifiers to distinguish its discourse connective usage from its other usages. We show that despite its ability to citicize to any syntactic type, variable position in the sentence and having a wide argument span, its discourse/non-discourse connective usage can be annotated reliably and its discourse usage can be disambiguated by exploiting local cues.

1 Introduction

Discourse connectives are one of the most important aspects of discourse structure. They are lexico-syntactic elements that signal a pragmatic or semantic relation (contingency, expansion, contrast, etc.) between two discourse units such as verb phrases, clauses or sentences (Asher, 1993; Prasad et al., 2008). While the most well-known discourse connectives belong to syntactic classes such as coordinating and subordinating conjunctions (*and, but, because*), adverbs (*however*) or prepositional phrases (*in sum*), it is known that clitics can also function similarly as discourse connectives (König, 2002), and may convey additive, contrastive or concessive senses (Forker, 2016; Faller, 2020).

Clitics are particles that are phonologically dependent on the lexical item to which they are attached and in many languages, they play a role in expressing focus. Usually, all types of phrases (noun phrases, verb phrases, etc.) can function as foci of a particle. In Turkish, too, most clitics are attached to phrases. The enclitic *dA* is a special particle, which is both focus- and topic-associated. In this respect, *dA* (orthographically *"de", "da"*) is even more worth investigating.[1]

The focus-sensitive characteristics and the discourse connective role of *dA* have long been noticed in the Turkish linguistics literature (Kerslake, 1992; Ergin, 1975; Erdal, 2000; Göksel and Özsoy, 2003). However, its discourse connective usage has not been annotated in the existing discourse-level Turkish corpora and, to the best of our knowledge, it has not been the topic of a computational discourse analysis so far. The existing experiments are limited to the disambiguation of the orthographic forms *da* (one of the representations of *dA*) and *-da* (one of the representations of the locative suffix, *-DA*) (Arıkan et al., 2019).[2]

It is known that connectives are susceptible to usage ambiguity, that is "whether or not a given token is serving as a discourse connective in its context" (Webber et al., 2019a), and this has initiated usage disambiguation tasks over connectives in many languages. Well-known works that disambiguate English connectives involve Pitler and Nenkova (2009) and Lin et al. (2010). Similar tasks have been carried out in Chinese (Shih and Chen, 2016), French (Laali and Kosseim, 2016), German (Dipper and Stede, 2006; Schneider and Stede, 2012) and Turkish (Başıbüyük and Zeyrek, 2023). To facilitate Natural Language Processing (NLP) tasks such as text summarization, automatic translation, knowledge extraction, etc., usage ambiguity tasks have to involve clitics as well as other types of discourse connectives. Given that there

[1] The upper case letter "A" is used to represent the alteration of vowels ("-e", "-a") with respect to the last syllable of the preceding word.

[2] *da*, one of the representations of the clitic *dA*, can be misspelled and written as a suffix, in which case it becomes a homograph of one of the variants of the locative suffix *-DA*, i.e. *-da*. This motivates the work on the disambiguation of the orthographical forms. In the current work, the upper case letter "D" represents the alternation of the alveolar consonants ("t" and "d") with respect to consonant assimilation rules.

Proceedings of the 17th Linguistic Annotation Workshop (LAW-XVII), pages 46–54
July 13, 2023 ©2023 Association for Computational Linguistics

is a research gap in the usage disambiguation of *dA* in particular and Turkish clitics in general, this paper describes an annotation study followed by a classification task over a corpus where *dA*'s various non-discourse connective roles are distinguished from its discourse connective roles. The summary of our contributions are:

- We construct a reliably annotated dataset of the discourse and non-discourse connective usages of *dA* following the principles of the PDTB (Prasad et al., 2008; Webber et al., 2019b) in terms of discourse connective spotting.
- By using a set of simple linguistic features, we run machine learning experiments to disambiguate the cases where *dA* is used as a discourse connective.
- We show that our basic features can distinguish between *dA* classes to a significant extent.

The outline of the paper is as follows: Section 2 focuses the linguistic behavior of *dA*. It provides a description of its various functions demonstrating its usage ambiguity. In Section 3, the data creation stage of our work is described, the annotation style and inter-annotator agreement results are presented. In Section 4, we describe our experimental setup by introducing the feature set, data processing (e.g. lemmatization, tagging) and the classification algorithms we used. An evaluation of the success of the models and an error analysis are presented. In Section 5, we summarize our work also discussing its limitations and contributions, and offer some ideas for future work.

2 Background

Turkish is a verb-final, agglutinating language, where suffixation plays an important role both in derivation and inflection. It has clitics such as *mI* (the marker of yes/no questions), *(y)DI* and *(y)mIş* (copular markers), and *dA*. An important grammatical fact that teases apart clitics and affixes is that while clitics can attach to material already containing clitics, affixes cannot (Erdal, 2000).

2.1 Basic facts regarding *dA*

As shown by previous researchers, many clitics are multifunctional, and the Turkish *dA* is no different from the clitics in other languages in its multifaceted behaviour. It is basically an additive (akin to English *too, also*, as discussed in the extensive typological study by Forker (2016)). This function goes together with *dA*'s focalizer or intensifier role. Moreover, *dA* has a variable position in the sentence as it can cliticize to any syntactic type and, as it is the case with most of the connectives, it is not easy to demarcate the boundaries of its arguments, i.e. ARG1, ARG2. In the current work, the arguments to *dA* were not annotated.[3]

Syntactically, *dA* is placed at the right outermost boundary of a word to the right of all other case suffixes (Göksel and Özsoy, 2003). Like other clitics mentioned by Zwicky (1977), it cannot be moved independently of its host without change in meaning, but it can be moved with its host as long as the constraints on word order configurations permit. Göksel and Özsoy (2003) show that *dA* can occur with focused or unfocused constituents, but always in a sentence that contains focus. In sentences with *dA*, a set of alternatives is evoked by focus (Rooth, 1992), or by *dA* itself, and *dA* asserts the truth of one of these alternatives. In our work, as also stated by Göksel and Özsoy (2003), we consider *dA* not an additive marker itself; rather, when the presupposition it carries is interpreted together with the rest of the utterance, the additive sense arises.

Throughout the paper, the use of "a" and "b" in the examples denotes the discourse segments linked by a discourse connective. The discourse and non-discourse connective role of the clitic is abbreviated as DC and NDC, respectively. Morpheme-by-morpheme[4] analyses are provided to indicate the variable position of *dA* in the sentence as well as the word to which it clitizes (shown in bold fonts).

2.2 The discourse connective and non-discourse connective usages of *dA*

Following the principles of the PDTB, we consider *dA* a DC when it links two segments that have an "abstract object" interpretation (propositions, eventualities, etc.) (Asher, 1993; Prasad et al., 2008).

[3]In the PDTB framework, the text spans with an abstract object interpretation are legal arguments to a connective; connectives link two text spans with an abstract object interpretation referred to as ARG1 and ARG2.

[4]The morpheme abbreviations we use throughout this article are as follows: ABIL abilitative marker, ACC accusative case, AUX auxiliary, CAUS causative, COND conditional, CV converb marker, DAT dative case, GEN genitive case, MOD modifier, NEG negative, OPT optative, PL plural, POSS possessive, PRES present, PROG progressive, PST past, SG singular, VN verbal noun marker, 1 first person, 2 second person, 3 third person.

In its DC role, it always invites a continuative inference: It allows the extension of information expressed in the first segment by providing further detail in the second segment. The second segment is a "separate but parallel" piece of information (König, 2002) and it is often the host clause for *dA*, as shown in (1) - (2):

(1) a. Sen-i sev-iyor-um de-di,
you-ACC love-PROG-1.SG say-PST

b. **ben** de inan-dı-m.
I *dA* believe-PST-1.SG
'He said 'I love you', <u>and</u> I believed him.' (DC)

(2) a. Halil'in gel-diğ-in-i
Halil-GEN come-VN-2.SG.POSS-ACC
fark et-me-di-ler.
notice do-NEG-PST-3.PL

b. **Halil** de kadınlar-a bir şaka
Halil *dA* ladies-DAT a joke
yap-ma-ya karar ver-di.
do-VN-DAT decide-PST-3.SG
'They did not notice that Halil came, <u>and</u> Halil decided to play a joke on the ladies.' (DC)

dA can also occur in the first segment, attached to the predicate as in examples (3), (4) or an auxiliary, as shown in (5).

(3) a. **Bekle** de,
Wait *dA*,

b. gel-ince konuş.
come-CV speak.
'Wait, <u>and then</u> speak when he comes.' (DC)

(4) a. İyi **güzel** de,
okay nice *dA*

b. bir bak-alım.
have.a look-OPT
'Okay, it's nice, <u>but</u> let's have a look.' (DC)

(5) a. Beni ara-dın **mı** da,
me call-PST.2SG AUX *dA*,

b. yanıt bekli-yor-sun
answer expect-PROG.2SG
'Is it the case that you've called me <u>so</u> you're expecting an answer?' (DC)

In (6), *dA* has a different function, namely, it introduces a new topic rather than conveying a discourse relation. In this excerpt, two friends (A and B) are in an exhibition. Pointing to one of the paintings, A starts the conversation (segment a) and B responds (segment b). We consider *dA* an NDC in this role.

(6) a. Bu **tablo-yu** da Ali al-dı.
This painting-ACC *dA* Ali buy-PST

b. Güzel.
'Nice'.
'A: As for this painting, Ali bought it'.
'B: It's nice'. (NDC)

dA may appear in a discontinous form, acting as a coordinator. In this usage, it often corresponds to the conjunction *both* ... *and* in English. We consider it a DC in its VP coordination role as illustrated in (7), an NDC otherwise, e.g. when adjectives are coordinated, as in (8).

(7) a. Çocuk kedici-ği **okşa-dı** da
child kitty-ACC caress-PST *dA*

b. **öp-tü** de.
kiss-PST *dA*
'The child <u>both</u> caressed <u>and</u> kissed the kitty.' (DC)

(8) Kız- ın saçlar-ı **kızıl** da **kıvırcık** da.
Girl-GEN hair-POSS red *dA* wavy *dA*
'The girl's hair is <u>both</u> **red** <u>and</u> **frizzly**.' (NDC)

In addition to these, *dA* can cliticize to conjunctions and adverbs, yielding the emphatic form of that conjunction or adverb. For example, *ve de* 'and *dA*' is the emphatic form of *ve* 'and' (9). In these cases, the head of the discourse relation (*ve*) is considered the discourse connective and *dA* its modifier (Zeyrek et al., 2013). That is, we do not consider *dA* as the sole discourse connective in such cases and mark it as NDC.

(9) a. Komik ol-malı-yım,
Funny be-ABIL-PRES-1.SG
gül-dür-meli-yim
laugh-CAUS-ABIL-PRES-1.SG

b. **ve** de aşık
and MOD love
ol-malı-yım.
fall.in.love-ABIL-PRES-1.SG
'I should be funny, make [people] laugh; <u>and furthermore</u>, I should fall in love.' (NDC)

On the other hand, *dA* also cliticizes to the conditional, *(y)sA* (10), contributing a concessive sense to the sentence, akin to the role of 'even though'. Thus, we annotate its use with *(y)sA* as DC in examples like (10).

(10) a. Aynı öneri-yi
same suggestion-ACC
sun-du-k-**sa** da,
offer-PST-1.PL-COND *dA*

b. yanaş-ma-dı-lar.
accept-NEG-PST-3.PL
'Even though we made the same suggestion, they didn't accept it.' (DC)

Forbes-Riley et al. (2006) show that there are clausal adverbs (*probably, usually*) and discourse adverbials (*as a result, in addition, consequently*). These are semantically different forms; while clausal adverbs are interpretable with respect to just their matrix clause, discourse adverbials require an abstract object interpretation from prior discourse. So, clausal adverbs are not discourse connectives. *dA* can cliticize to clausal adverbs such as *belki de* 'perhaps *dA*', *gerçekten de* 'indeed *dA*' (11). It can also attach to discourse adverbs (*özellikle de* 'in particular *dA*'), but it is always considered a modifier (hence NDC) when it is cliticized to an adverb.

(11) **Gerçekten** de onun eli açık-tı.
Indeed MOD his hand open-PST
'Indeed *dA*, he was very generous.' (NDC)

3 Data Construction and Reliability Analysis

3.1 Data

To build a corpus for the current study, we started with the TDB 1.1 (Zeyrek and Kurfalı, 2017), an annotated corpus of explicit and non-explicit discourse connectives, their binary arguments and senses in the PDTB 2.0 style (Prasad et al., 2008). Due to having linguistic characteristics quite different than other connectives such as conjunctions and adverbs, *dA* was not systematically annotated in the TDB 1.1; its analysis was postponed until a new annotation study that solely focuses on clitics or *dA* itself could be launched. For the current work, we had initially planned to work on the TDB to extend it with a systematic annotation of *dA*.

A manual inspection of the TDB 1.1 showed that it does not have an adequate number of discourse and non-discourse *dA* occurrences. We decided to create a new dataset, referred to as the *dA Corpus*, by combining selected *dA* samples from the TDB 1.1 with those extracted from another Turkish corpus, namely, the TS Corpus v2 (Sezer and Sezer, 2013; Sezer, 2017).[5] Table 1 shows the distribution of the sources of selected samples in the corpus.[6]

# samples with *dA*	
TDB 1.1	TS Corpus v2
436	438

Table 1: The *dA* corpus.

3.2 Annotation Style and Inter-annotator Agreement (IAA)

Discourse connectives are clear signals that show how discourse units are linked by a pragmatic/semantic relationship. Taking this description and the PDTB 2.0 annotation guidelines as our starting points, we wrote a set of guidelines describing how to recognize the discourse connective and non-discourse connective uses of *dA* mentioned in the current paper. Each sample minimally contained clauses to the immediate right and left context of *dA*, but there were samples that had more than one clause on each side, as they were deemed necessary to infer the meaning of the text. Since a piece of text may have multiple *dA* instances, the tokens to be annotated were highlighted. All the *dA* samples were annotated by two independent, native speaker annotators. They were asked to annotate all the text pieces where the clitic is highlighted.

Although the annotation of *dA*'s discourse senses is out of our scope, we asked our annotators to pay attention to the senses of *dA* when they infer a discourse relation made salient by *dA*. The annotators were told that the basic sense of *dA* is to indicate addition.[7] They were also told that they may infer additional senses such as temporal succession (3), concession (4), result (5).[8] Since *dA* lacks such

[5] The TDB 1.1 is a 40.000-word, multi-genre (research surveys, articles, interviews, news articles, novels), written corpus of modern Turkish. The TS Corpus is based on the BOUN Web Corpus (Sak et al., 2008), containing data from news and other internet websites. It is composed of over 491M units, where all units are marked on the basis of word type (POS tag), morphological structure tag (Morphological Tagging) and root word (Lemma).

[6] The corpus is available at https://github.com/TurkishdA/dA-Corpus.

[7] In the current work, the additive discourse sense corresponds to Expansion.Conjunction or Expansion.Detail.Arg2-as-detail senses in the PDTB 3.0.

[8] In cases like (3) a sense in addition to the additive sense is inferred. These are a type of multiple relations introduced in the PDTB 3.0. In other examples such as (4) and (5), *dA* conveys a single sense. But the annotators are not required to differentiate between single sense versus multiple senses of *dA* tokens, which is left for further work.

additional senses in its non-discourse connective roles, to notice them in the data would further help the annotators while tagging its DC usage.

The annotation cycle involved two steps. First, annotator1 annotated the entire occurrences of *dA* as DC or NDC. In two sessions, which lasted approximately two hours, the guidelines were explained to the independent annotator and a few examples that are not involved in the data were annotated jointly; then annotator2 tagged all the *dA* occurrences highlighted in the corpus.

To measure the inter-annotator agreement, we adopted the method used in Zeyrek et al. (2020) and took one set of annotations (namely those created by annotator1) as the correct annotations since the annotations were created by one of the members of our research team. We calculated the IAA with the standard metrics of Precision, Recall and F1 in formulas[9] 1, 2 and 3, respectively. The results are presented in Table 2.

We also evaluated the IAA with the kappa statistic (Cohen, 1960) to assess base level agreement. The result showed a substantial agreement between annotators with a κ score of 0.74.

$$Precision = \frac{\#\ of\ correct\ DC\ assg.s}{\#\ of\ DC\ assg.s} \quad (1)$$

$$Recall = \frac{\#\ of\ correct\ DC\ assg.s}{\#\ of\ DC\ samples} \quad (2)$$

$$F1 = \frac{2 * Precision * Recall}{Precision + Recall} \quad (3)$$

Precision	Recall	F-score
0.89	0.86	0.87

Table 2: IAA results.

Once we obtained the inter-annotator results, in the second step, we spotted and discussed the disagreed cases in a series of meetings, and reached a unanimous agreement as to whether a disagreed *dA* token is DC or NDC. We thus obtained the gold standard data. Table 3 provides the number of adjudicated DC and NDC tokens in the *dA* corpus. Table 4 lists the different word classes to which *dA* cliticizes and their frequencies (see Appendix A for the distribution of POS tags across DC/NDC instances).

[9] *Assignments* is abbreviated as *assg.s*.

# DC	# NDC
473	401

Table 3: Total number of DC/NDC gold standard annotations.

POS	# of *dA*	POS	# of *dA*
NOUN	307	ADP	22
VERB	263	ADJ	22
PRON	70	NUM	7
CCONJ	67	AUX	3
ADV	59	DET	3
PRN	51	**Total**	874

Table 4: Distribution of grammatical classes that host *dA*.

4 The Machine Learning Approach

4.1 Features Used

We used a canonical set of features provided in Table 5 enabling a simple exploitation of local cues. Earlier work has revealed that the connective's syntactic context is a strong predictor of its DC role ((Lin et al., 2010; Gopalan and Lalitha Devi, 2016), among others). Semantic associations as simple as lexical cohesion manifested on surface through repeating words, or links inferred among propositions pose the harder problem in disambiguation. We observed that these hold for our data as well. The former is addressed by a reduction to parts of speech. The latter is crudely approximated via forms, assuming word-level selection is a signal for relevant constraints. Given that Turkish is a highly inflectional and agglutinating language, morphological variation entails the risk of leading the models to overlearn the declensions over a shared word root and result in the misclassification of *dA*, primarily because semantic information encapsulated in affixes is often tangential to our scope. To alleviate this potential noise, we implemented lemmatization and proceeded with the root forms. Finally, we integrated proper nouns to the feature set so as to capture cases like (2).

To model the context of *dA*, a discrete window size is defined according to standard locality and symmetry assumptions. Preliminary experiments hinted at an inverse relation between performance and text span, outputting a range of (-3, +3). Each line in Table 5 shows how we modeled the relation of three different features with *dA*'s context.

In Table 6, we illustrate what a data point looks like by showing various representation levels of example (2) above (see Table 7 for English glosses).

Features	Range	Definition
POS	(-3,+3)	The POS tags of 3 words before and 3 words after *dA*
LEMMA	(-3,+3)	The lemmas of 3 words before and 3 words after *dA*
ISPROPER	(-3,-1)	Whether one of the 3 words before *dA* is a proper noun or not

Table 5: The feature set for the usage disambiguation of *dA*.

Level	Form
I	Halil'in geldiğini fark etmediler. Halil **de** kadınlara bir şaka yapmaya karar verdi.
II	[*Halil'in geldiğini* *fark* *etmediler*]$_a$ [*Halil* **dA**$_{DC}$ *kadınlara* *bir* *şaka* *yapmaya karar verdi*]$_b$
III	FARK$_{(-3,N)}$ ET$_{(-2,V)}$ HALIL$_{(-1,N)}$ KADIN$_{(+1,N)}$ BIR$_{(+2,DET)}$ ŞAKA$_{(+3,N)}$

Table 6: A demonstrative example of three levels of representation of the data, namely, the *raw*, *annotated* and *encoded* levels of example (2). Level III is a projection of II onto a [-3,+3] window of *dA*'s immediate context. The boxed words in II correspond to the respective tokens in III. Each token is further lemmatized and tagged with POS information, resulting in the forms exploited by the learning model. The tags N, V, DET stand for noun, verb, determiner, respectively. The ISPROPER feature is excluded here for the sake of simplicity.

4.2 Experiments and Results

The *dA* corpus was processed before running ML algorithms over it. Firstly, since the number of DC and NDC samples in the corpus were not evenly distributed (cf. Table 3), we ran a few tests, and noticed a slight performance bias towards the more populated class. So, we pseudo-randomly excluded 72 DC samples and conducted the experiments on 802 data points (401 DC, 401 NDC).

The raw excerpts were processed by the UDPipe 2.0 pipeline (Straka et al., 2016; Straka and Straková, 2017) to obtain tagged and lemmatized discourse segments.

After constructing the final representations over POS tags, lemmas and proper nouns, on the transformed data, three supervised binary classifier models are trained based on Logistic Regression (LogRes) (Fan et al., 2008), Support Vector Machine (SVM) (Cortes and Vapnik, 1995), and Random Forest (RF) (Ho, 1995) algorithms for comparison.

We used the *scikit-learn* (Pedregosa et al., 2011) library in a Python environment, and designed the sessions in 10 epochs all including 5-fold cross validation (CV), as standard test set evaluations may not be consistent about the impact of features when the characteristic variation throughout data is considered (e.g. Shi and Demberg, 2017). Each epoch contains 5 cycles shifting between 5 static

Level	Form
I	They didn't notice Halil came, **and** Halil decided to play a joke on the ladies.
II	[*They didn't notice* *Halil came*]$_a$ **and**$_{DC}$ [*Halil* *decided to play* *a* *joke* *on the* *ladies*]$_b$
III	NOTICE$^{i}_{(-3,N)}$ NOTICE$^{ii}_{(-2,V)}$ HALIL$_{(-1,N)}$ LADY$_{(+1,N)}$ A$_{(+2,DET)}$ JOKE$_{(+3,N)}$

Table 7: English glosses of the example demonstrated in Table 6. Note that *fark et* (*Eng.* 'notice') is a compound verb and taken as two parts tokenwise in the final step, which is denoted by superscripts (*i, ii*) in the gloss.

slices on shuffled (randomly reindexed) data with 1-4, or 20%-80% test-train allocations. Then, the performance rate of the models is calculated by using the standard *classification report* and *confusion matrix* functions to obtain accuracy scores.

The models correctly disambiguated *dA* with the average accuracy of 0.77. Table 8 shows how performance oscillated across CV-cycles and epochs.[10]

4.3 Important Features for Classification

We trained each of our models to examine the predictive strength of each feature (and feature group) we used. Table 9[11] shows that POS is the most

[10] The highest scores achieved are written in **bold**.

[11] *lem* and *prn* are the abbreviations of *lemma* and *proper noun*, respectively.

Parameters	LogRes	SVM	RF
max. cycle	**0.82**	0.80	0.80
min. cycle	0.71	0.70	**0.70**
max. epoch	**0.79**	0.77	0.77
min. epoch	0.75	**0.74**	0.76
sd. (σ)	0.030	0.029	**0.028**
average	**0.77**	0.76	**0.77**

Table 8: Standard deviation, minimum, maximum, and average accuracy rates for classification with 5-fold CV in 10 epoch evaluation.

predictive feature solely achieving a minimum accuracy of 0.76. With all the features combined, the model reached an accuracy of 0.82 in the best case.

Features	LogRes	SVM	RF
pos+lem+prn	**0.82**	0.80	0.80
pos+lem	0.76	0.76	0.77
pos+prn	0.77	0.77	0.76
pos	0.76	0.77	0.76
lem+prn	0.73	0.73	0.74
lem	0.72	0.71	0.71

Table 9: Accuracy of the individual features used in the classification and the best combination.

4.4 Error Analysis

After calculating the success rates, we carried out an analysis to understand the possible causes of classification errors.

The major cause of classification errors is due to wrong POS tag assignment. This either happens when lemmatization is wrong or when the part-of-speech tagger fails to recognize noun-based (nominal or adjectival) predicates. For example, in (3), the verb *bekle* 'wait' at the -1 position, is wrongly lemmatized as 'bek' and assigned NOUN instead of VERB. For our models, being VERB at -1 is an important factor for the DC role of *dA* (e.g. (3), (7)), and mislabeling leads to an error in disambiguation. Logistic Regression and Random Forest sometimes correctly classify such tokens as DC, while SVM has not classified them as DC in any epoch. Hence, the false negative count increases.

Secondly, Turkish has nominal/adjectival predicates (sentences that do not contain an overt verb or auxiliary) such as the following:

(12) Ahmet doktor.
Ahmet doctor
'Ahmet is a doctor.'

Only having access to the surface form of a word, the part-of-speech tagger does not recognize the predicatehood of words like *güzel* '[is] nice' in (4) or *doktor* '[is] a doctor' in (12). These words are straightforwardly labelled as ADJ and NOUN, leading to mislabeling of the discourse connective usage of *dA* (also see Başıbüyük and Zeyrek (2023) for a detailed explanation of this kind of error).

5 Conclusion, Limitations and Further Work

Our work has two main parts; in the first part, we worked on a challenging annotation task not targeted before in Turkish NLP: the task of how the multi-faceted clitic *dA* can be annotated for its discourse and non-discourse connective usage. In the second part, we showed that with an ML approach, we can achieve success rates of an average of 0.77 in disambiguating the usage of *dA*.

However, our work is not without its limitations; for example, it is limited by the size of the corpus. It is assumed that as the dataset grows, more linguistic features of a discourse connective can be attested (Zeldes et al., 2019). Secondly, we are aware that the linguistic features we used in the ML experiments are not novel, but we believe we have shown that with a minimal set of rules, we can reach promising results in disambiguating the usage of *dA*.

Our work not only contributes to Turkish but also to discourse studies in general as we have brought to light the discourse role of a clitic through an annotation study and a computational analysis. It is therefore hoped to set the stage for other languages that have clitics with a discourse function. The results presented here can be used as a benchmark for Turkish clitics, and they can serve as a reference point for other languages that have clitics with a discourse function.

References

Uğurcan Arıkan, Onur Güngör, and Suzan Üsküdarli. 2019. Detecting clitics related orthographic errors in Turkish. In *Proceedings of the International Conference on Recent Advances in Natural Language Processing (RANLP 2019)*, pages 71–76, Varna, Bulgaria. INCOMA Ltd.

Nicholas Asher. 1993. *Reference to abstract objects in discourse*, volume 50. Springer Science & Business Media.

Kezban Başıbüyük and Deniz Zeyrek. 2023. Usage disambiguation of Turkish discourse connectives. *Language Resources and Evaluation*, 57(1):223–256.

Jacob Cohen. 1960. A Coefficient of Agreement for Nominal Scales. *Educational and Psychological Measurement*, 20(1):37–46.

Corinna Cortes and Vladimir Vapnik. 1995. Support-vector networks. *Machine Learning*, 20(3):273–297.

Stefanie Dipper and Manfred Stede. 2006. Disambiguating potential connectives. In *Proceedings of KONVENS 2006 (Konferenz zur Verarbeitung natürlicher Sprache), Universität Konstanz*, pages 167–173, Konstanz.

Marcel Erdal. 2000. Clitics in Turkish. In *Studies on Turkish and Turkic languages : Proceedings of the Ninth International Conference on Turkish Linguistics*, pages 41–55, Wiesbaden. Harrassowitz.

Muharrem Ergin. 1975. *Türk Dil Bilgisi*. Bogazici Universitesi.

Martina Faller. 2020. The many functions of Cuzco Quechua =pas: implications for the semantic map of additivity. *Glossa: a journal of general linguistics*, 5(1):34.

Rong-En Fan, Kai-Wei Chang, Cho-Jui Hsieh, Xiang-Rui Wang, and Chih-Jen Lin. 2008. Liblinear: A library for large linear classification. *Journal of Machine Learning Research*, 9(61):1871–1874.

Katherine Forbes-Riley, Bonnie Webber, and Aravind Joshi. 2006. Computing discourse semantics: The predicate-argument semantics of discourse connectives in D-LTAG. *Journal of Semantics*, 23(1):55–106.

Diana Forker. 2016. Toward a typology for additive markers. *Lingua*, 180:69–100.

Aslı Göksel and A Sumru Özsoy. 2003. *dA*: a focus/topic associated clitic in Turkish. *Lingua*, 113(11):1143–1167.

Sindhuja Gopalan and Sobha Lalitha Devi. 2016. BioDCA identifier: A system for automatic identification of discourse connective and arguments from biomedical text. In *Proceedings of the Fifth Workshop on Building and Evaluating Resources for Biomedical Text Mining (BioTxtM2016)*, pages 89–98, Osaka, Japan. The COLING 2016 Organizing Committee.

Tin Kam Ho. 1995. Random Decision Forests. In *Proceedings of 3rd International Conference on Document Analysis and Recognition*, volume 1, pages 278–282, Montreal, QC, Canada.

Celia Kerslake. 1992. The role of connectives in discourse construction in Turkish. In *Modern studies in Turkish: Proceedings of the 6th International Conference on Turkish Linguistics*, pages 77–104, Eskişehir. Anadolu University, Education Faculty.

Ekkehard König. 2002. *The meaning of focus particles: A comparative perspective*. Routledge.

Majid Laali and Leila Kosseim. 2016. Automatic disambiguation of French discourse connectives. *International Journal of Computational Linguistics and Applications*, 7(1):11–30.

Ziheng Lin, Hwee Tou Ng, and Min-Yen Kan. 2010. A PDTB-styled end-to-end discourse parser. *Natural Language Engineering*, 20(2):151–184.

Fabian Pedregosa, Gaël Varoquaux, Alexandre Gramfort, Vincent Michel, Bertrand Thirion, Olivier Grisel, Mathieu Blondel, Peter Prettenhofer, Ron Weiss, Vincent Dubourg, Jake Vanderplas, Alexandre Passos, David Cournapeau, Matthieu Brucher, Matthieu Perrot, and Édouard Duchesnay. 2011. Scikit-learn: Machine learning in Python. *Journal of Machine Learning Research*, 12:2825–2830.

Emily Pitler and Ani Nenkova. 2009. Using syntax to disambiguate explicit discourse connectives in text. In *Proceedings of the ACL-IJCNLP 2009 Conference Short Papers*, pages 13–16, Suntec, Singapore. Association for Computational Linguistics.

Rashmi Prasad, Nikhil Dinesh, Alan Lee, Eleni Miltsakaki, Livio Robaldo, Aravind K Joshi, and Bonnie L Webber. 2008. The Penn Discourse Treebank 2.0. In *Proceedings of the Sixth International Conference on Language Resources and Evaluation (LREC'08)*, pages 2961–2968, Marrakech, Morocco. European Language Resources Association (ELRA).

Mats Rooth. 1992. A theory of focus interpretation. *Natural Language Semantics*, 1(1):75–116.

Haşim Sak, Tunga Güngör, and Murat Saraçlar. 2008. Turkish language resources: Morphological parser, morphological disambiguator and web corpus. In *Advances in Natural Language Processing*, pages 417–427, Berlin, Heidelberg. Springer Berlin Heidelberg.

Angela Schneider and Manfred Stede. 2012. Ambiguity in German connectives: A corpus study. In *Proceedings of KONVENS (Conference on Natural Language Processing) 2012*, pages 254–258.

Taner Sezer. 2017. TS Corpus project: An online Turkish dictionary and TS DIY Corpus. *European Journal of Language and Literature*, 3:18–24.

Taner Sezer and Bengü Sezer. 2013. TS Corpus: Herkes İçin Türkçe Derlem. In *Proceedings 27th National Linguistics Conference*, pages 217–225.

Wei Shi and Vera Demberg. 2017. On the need of cross validation for discourse relation classification. In *Proceedings of the 15th Conference of the European Chapter of the Association for Computational Linguistics: Volume 2, Short Papers*, pages 150–156, Valencia, Spain. Association for Computational Linguistics.

Yong-Siang Shih and Hsin-Hsi Chen. 2016. Detection, disambiguation and argument identification of discourse connectives in Chinese discourse parsing. In *Proceedings of COLING 2016, the 26th International Conference on Computational Linguistics: Technical Papers*, pages 1891–1902, Osaka, Japan. The COLING 2016 Organizing Committee.

Milan Straka, Jan Hajič, and Jana Straková. 2016. UDPipe: Trainable pipeline for processing CoNLL-U files performing tokenization, morphological analysis, POS tagging and parsing. In *Proceedings of the Tenth International Conference on Language Resources and Evaluation (LREC'16)*, pages 4290–4297, Portorož, Slovenia. European Language Resources Association (ELRA).

Milan Straka and Jana Straková. 2017. Tokenizing, POS tagging, lemmatizing and parsing UD 2.0 with UDPipe. In *Proceedings of the CoNLL 2017 Shared Task: Multilingual Parsing from Raw Text to Universal Dependencies*, pages 88–99, Vancouver, Canada. Association for Computational Linguistics.

Bonnie Webber, Rashmi Prasad, and Alan Lee. 2019a. Ambiguity in explicit discourse connectives. In *Proceedings of the 13th International Conference on Computational Semantics - Long Papers*, pages 134–141, Gothenburg, Sweden. Association for Computational Linguistics.

Bonnie Webber, Rashmi Prasad, Alan Lee, and Aravind Joshi. 2019b. The Penn Discourse Treebank 3.0 Annotation Manual. *Philadelphia, University of Pennsylvania*, 35:108.

Amir Zeldes, Debopam Das, Erick Galani Maziero, Juliano Antonio, and Mikel Iruskieta. 2019. The DISRPT 2019 shared task on elementary discourse unit segmentation and connective detection. In *Proceedings of the Workshop on Discourse Relation Parsing and Treebanking 2019*, pages 97–104, Minneapolis, MN. Association for Computational Linguistics.

Deniz Zeyrek, Işın Demirşahin, AB Sevdik-Çallı, and Ruket Çakıcı. 2013. Turkish Discourse Bank: Porting a discourse annotation style to a morphologically rich language. *Dialogue and Discourse*, 4(2):174–184.

Deniz Zeyrek and Murathan Kurfalı. 2017. TDB 1.1: Extensions on Turkish Discourse Bank. In *Proceedings of the 11th Linguistic Annotation Workshop*, pages 76–81, Valencia, Spain. Association for Computational Linguistics.

Deniz Zeyrek, Amália Mendes, Yulia Grishina, Murathan Kurfalı, Samuel Gibbon, and Maciej Ogrodniczuk. 2020. TED Multilingual Discourse Bank (TED-MDB): a parallel corpus annotated in the PDTB style. *Language Resources and Evaluation*, 54(2):587–613.

Arnold Zwicky. 1977. *On Clitics*. Bloomington: Indiana University Linguistics Club.

A Appendix

In the figures below, we present the distribution of POS types across DC/NDC instances.

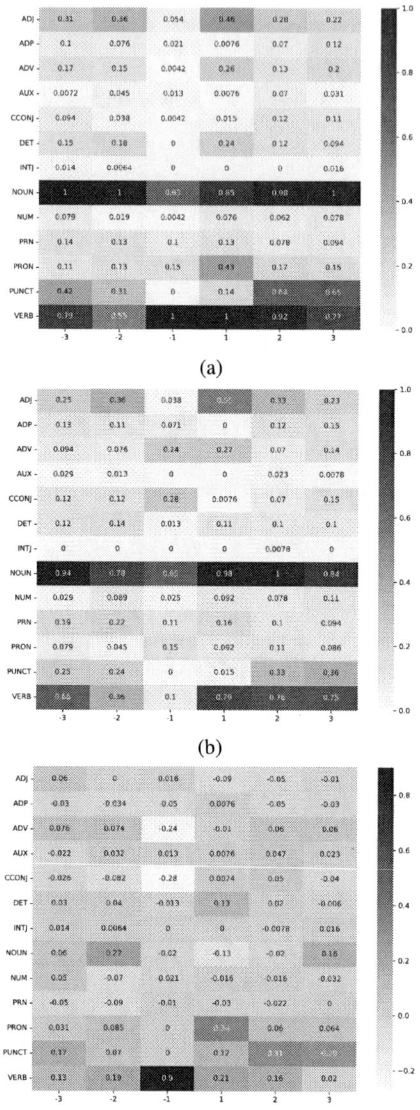

(a)

(b)

(c)

Figure 1: Distribution of POS tags by their relative positions to *dA* within a [-3,+3] window, for DC and NDC samples (Figures 1*a* and 1*b*, respectively). Co-occurrence frequencies are scaled to [0-1] interval. Figure 1*c* represents the *rate of co-occurrence* difference between DC and NDC classes. Each value in the table satisfies the following condition: $c_{i,j} = a_{i,j} - b_{i,j}$. Convergence to 1 means a dominant DC characteristic at that specific position-POS correlation, and convergence to -1 means an NDC dominance.

An Active Learning Pipeline for NLU Error Detection in Conversational Agents

Damián Pascual, Aritz Bercher, Akansha Bhardwaj, Mingbo Cui, Dominic Kohler, Liam van der Poel, Paolo Rosso
Telepathy Labs GmbH
Zürich, Switzerland
{firstname.lastname}@telepathy.ai

Abstract

High-quality labeled data is paramount to the performance of modern machine learning models. However, annotating data is a time-consuming and costly process that requires human experts to examine large collections of raw data. For conversational agents in production settings with access to large amounts of user-agent conversations, the challenge is to decide what data should be annotated first. We consider the Natural Language Understanding (NLU) component of a conversational agent deployed in a real-world setup with limited resources. We present an active learning pipeline for offline detection of classification errors that leverages two strong classifiers. Then, we perform topic modeling on the potentially mis-classified samples to ease data analysis and to reveal error patterns. In our experiments, we show on a real-world dataset that by using our method to prioritize data annotation we reach 100% of the performance annotating only 36% of the data. Finally, we present an analysis of some of the error patterns revealed and argue that our pipeline is a valuable tool to detect critical errors and reduce the workload of annotators.

1 Introduction

Modern machine learning methods rely heavily on the availability of high-quality labeled data (Ouyang et al., 2022; Schuhmann et al., 2022). As a consequence, annotating large volumes of data has become a priority across organizations. However, data annotation is a time-consuming and costly process: it requires, first, to train human experts who, then, have to manually examine large collections of raw data and assign labels. Since assigning labels is often an ambiguous task, it is a standard that each sample is labeled by multiple annotators and labels are assigned based on inter-annotator agreement (Artstein, 2017). The complexity of this process makes data annotation a common bottleneck when it comes to deploying data-driven systems that should operate reliably in production environments.

A relevant example of these data-driven systems are conversational agents that interact directly with human users. These agents typically have at least two components, one for Natural Language Understanding (NLU) and another for Dialogue Management (DM). The NLU component extracts intents and entities from the user utterance at each conversation turn, while the DM component decides on the next action based on the NLU output (Bocklisch et al., 2017). Once deployed, these assistants can have access to large amounts of raw data in the form of user-agent conversations. At scale, the amount of data available for annotation may soon exceed the capacity of the human annotators. The challenge then becomes how to select samples for annotation. On the NLU side, it is desirable to prioritize the annotation of utterances whose intent was misclassified during inference in order to correct existing flaws in the agent. However, automatically finding those utterances is challenging, since intent mis-classifications do not necessarily result in failed conversations and conversations can fail due to the misbehavior of other components of the digital assistant, not only due to the NLU.

In this work, we consider a real-world scenario where an intent classifier needs to run with limited resources, specifically, in CPUs and with low latency. This discards modern Large Language Models (LLMs) as a valid option. Nevertheless, LLMs can be used offline to detect potentially mis-classified data. We present a simple yet effective method based on voting that leverages two LLMs to detect problematic utterances. In particular, we compare the prediction of two LLMs with the intent assigned by the production classifier and if there is no unanimity between the three intents, we mark the utterance as problematic to

Proceedings of the 17th Linguistic Annotation Workshop (LAW-XVII), pages 55–60
July 13, 2023 ©2023 Association for Computational Linguistics

prioritize its annotation and analysis. We embed this method in an active learning pipeline consisting of error detection, clustering and topic modeling, followed by expert annotation. This way, the human expert receives a curated set of problematic utterances clustered by topic, which facilitates the discovery of error patterns and greatly reduces the required workload.

In our experiments, we simulate a real-world environment, where an intent classifier is periodically exposed to new data that can be potentially labeled and incorporated to the training data. We evaluate on a held-out test set and show that on a real-world dataset, an intent classification model trained with data labeled following the priority given by our pipeline can reach with 36% of the train data the same performance as with 100%, which represents a major reduction in annotation costs. Furthermore, we show a qualitative analysis of the error patterns discovered by our method on two public datasets and argue that our pipeline is a valuable tool to early-detect intent classification errors that could be critical for the operation of a conversational agent.

2 Related Work

Error Discovery: Error discovery strategies in machine learning can be categorised into machine-initiated (or, active learning) and human-initiated. While human-initiated approaches put a significant load on humans (Attenberg and Provost, 2010; Attenberg et al., 2015), machine initiated approaches are either based on dialogue failure (Khaziev et al., 2022), disagreement with the expectation (Bhardwaj et al., 2020, 2022), or confidence of the classifier (Lewis and Catlett, 1994). To label individual data instances, existing active learning strategies mainly leverage crowds (Yan et al., 2011; Yang et al., 2018) or components of a machine learning system (Nushi et al., 2017). Detecting feature blindness errors, namely unknown unknowns, with active learning methods is hard, since these methods generally rely on the model's training results (Attenberg et al., 2015; Lakkaraju et al., 2017). To mitigate this limitation, our error prediction workflow involves different machine learning models, diversifying in this way the type of errors discovered.

Interactive machine learning (iML): iML is a growing field in machine learning that has demonstrated its success in building well-performing classifiers using fewer features (Fails and Olsen Jr, 2003; Ware et al., 2001; Chen et al., 2018). Moreover, it improves user's trust and understanding of the system (Stumpf et al., 2009). In this context, our approach stands out as we provide a visualization of topic clusters to the annotators to facilitate their task.

3 Methodology

Our active learning pipeline consists of three stages, intent classification, error detection and topic modeling. The full pipeline is depicted in Figure 1 as a block diagram.

Intent Classification This is the production model that predicts the intent of the user utterance. Due to the scalability constraints in terms of latency and computing resources, this model must have low inference time and run on CPUs. Without loss of generality, in this work we employ the Universal Sentence Encoder (USE) (Cer et al., 2018) as embedder, followed by linear Support Vector Classification (SVC). During live conversations, both the user utterance and the predicted intent are stored and passed to the next stage of the pipeline for offline error detection.

Error Detection We fine-tune two LLMs for intent classification with the same training set used to train the production classifier. Then, for each utterance collected in production, we predict their intent with the two LLMs and compare these results with the intent predicted by the production model. If there is disagreement between the three intents we mark the utterance as problematic. The LLMs used are DistilBERT (Sanh et al., 2019) and DeBERTa-v3-base (He et al., 2021b,a) since they differ significantly in size and pre-training objectives, which diversifies the predictions of hard-to-classify utterances.

Clustering and Topic Modeling We divide the set of utterances marked as problematic in the previous stage by the intent given in production. Then for each intent, we perform clustering and topic modeling following a similar approach to BERTopic (Grootendorst, 2022) but with USE embeddings. We use UMAP (McInnes et al., 2018) for dimensionality reduction, HDBSCAN (McInnes et al., 2017) for clustering and c-TF-IDF for topic modeling i.e. for generating topic keywords that help the annotators to categorize the error type within the cluster. We perform a random search

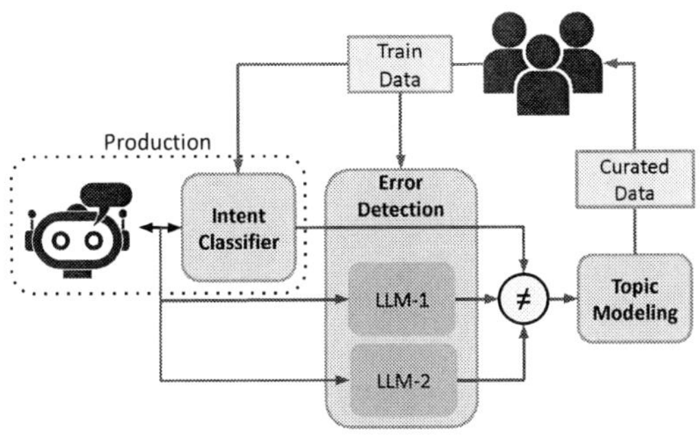

Figure 1: Active learning pipeline: the utterances received by the virtual assistant at production are passed through an intent classifier, error detection and topic modeling to create a curated dataset that is labeled by human experts and integrated in the training data.

to select hyperparameters and pick the combination that minimizes the amount of data points labeled as noise. Formally, we want to minimize the proportion of data clustered with confidence score smaller than 0.05.

For each intent, the topic modeling stage returns a set of clusters of problematic utterances with three topic words describing the cluster. This is the final output of our pipeline which is then given to the human experts for analysis and annotation. This way, the human experts receive a curated and ordered set of potentially critical utterances that can be quickly labeled and integrated in the training set of the production model.

4 Experiments and Results

Here, we conduct a quantitative and a qualitative evaluation. In our quantitative evaluation we assess to what extent our pipeline reduces the amount of labeled data needed to reach certain performance; and in the qualitative evaluation we analyze discovered error patterns. We run our experiments on two public datasets: ATIS (Hemphill et al., 1990) and SNIPS (Coucke et al., 2018); and an internal dataset (AUTO) consisting of real-world data from the automotive domain. ATIS is a dataset of queries about flight information of 4,978 training samples and 893 test samples[1]. SNIPS is a dataset of interactions between users and virtual assistants like Siri or Alexa. We use the version with 26,000 utterances and we set as label the joint fields "intent" and "scenario", which results in 64 classes.

[1]We use: `https://github.com/microsoft/CNTK`

4.1 Data Annotation

We simulate a real-world scenario where a production model f_{prod} classifies the intent of a large number of samples. This prediction is combined with that of two other models f_{err1} and f_{err2} to perform offline error detection. As explained in Section 3, f_{prod} consists of USE for embedding followed by linear SVC, while f_{err1} and f_{err2} are DistilBERT and DeBERTa-base respectively.

To simulate our production setting for a given dataset, we perform a 10-90 split of the training data, where we use the 10% split to train the initial model. This corresponds to the first model deployed in production, trained with a small amount of initially available data. The remaining 90% of the train data simulates the data progressively acquired in production. We follow an iterative process with each iteration corresponding to an annotation campaign where human experts annotate a set of production samples. These samples are incorporated to the training data of f_{prod}, which is then re-trained with the expanded training set. At each iteration i, we denote the training data as D_i^{train} and the rest as D_i^{rest}. Furthermore, we use the held-out test set D^{test} to assess the performance of the intent classification model at each iteration.

In detail, each iteration i starts with training the intent classification model f_{prod} and fine-tuning the error detection models f_{err1} and f_{err2} with D_i^{train}. At this point, to keep track of the evolution of the performance of the model, we evaluate f_{prod} on D^{test} by computing the macro-averaged F1 score. Then, we predict with the three models the intent of 15%[2] of D_i^{rest}. Those samples for which the three models do not agree on the prediction are added with their ground-truth labels to D_{i+1}^{train} and removed from D_{i+1}^{rest}, this simulates the annotation by human experts. The process is repeated until no new data is added to D_{i+1}^{train}.

In Table 2, we report for each dataset the macro F1 score obtained by f_{prod} when training with 100% of the data as well as the percentage of data needed to reach the same performance (within a ±0.005 error) with our active learning pipeline (AL). We also report the maximum F1 attained with our pipeline and the percentage of train data needed to reach it. The results shown are the

[2]15% is an arbitrary amount to simulate incoming data. Proportions like 5% or 10% would serve the same purpose.

Dataset	Topic	Examples	Ground Truth	Predicted Intent
ATIS	flights, flight, Denver	*How much is a flight from Washington to Montreal*	flight	airfare
	flights, flight, Denver	*What is the airfare for flights from Denver to Pittsburgh on Delta airline*	flight	airfare
	flights, flight, Denver	*List airlines that fly from Seattle to Salt Lake City*	flight	airline
	flights, flight, Denver	*Please show me airlines with flights from Denver to Boston with stop in Philadelphia*	flight	airline
SNIPS	events, calendar, today	*When is my next dentist appointment*	query_event_calendar	delete_event_calendar
	events, calendar, today	*Show up the events for me today*	query_event_calendar	delete_event_calendar
	events, calendar, today	*Tell me what is on my calendar for tomorrow*	query_event_calendar	delete_event_calendar
	meeting, hour, remind	*Remind me about the meeting tomorrow at six*	set_reminder	notification_calendar
	meeting, hour, remind	*Schedule a reminder one hour before the meeting*	set_reminder	notification_calendar

Table 1: Examples of error patterns discovered per dataset by our pipeline.

Dataset	100% Data	% Match AL	Max AL	% Max AL
ATIS	0.699	25.6	0.725	26.6
SNIPS	0.745	54.8	0.745	54.8
AUTO	0.784	36.0	0.795	35.7

Table 2: Results of the data annotation experiments; performance numbers are macro F1 scores. *% Match AL* is the amount of data labeled by the active learning (AL) pipeline that matches the *100% Data* score; *Max AL* is the maximum performance reached with AL and *% Match AL* is the amount of data to get that score.

mean across five different splits of the data.

For the three datasets, the amount of data needed to match the performance of the full training set with our pipeline (AL) is much smaller. In particular, for ATIS we need only 25.6% of the data, for SNIPS 54.8% and for AUTO 36.0%. Furthermore, for ATIS and AUTO we outperform the model trained with the full train set with only 26.6% and 35.7% of the data respectively. These results demonstrate the large savings in terms of data annotation that can be obtained with our pipeline, which in turn can represent a major reduction in costs for an organization.

4.2 Error Analysis

Next, we conduct a qualitative analysis of the error patterns discovered by our pipeline, similar to the analysis that would be performed by human experts during error exploration. We report results for the two public datasets, ATIS and SNIPS. For each dataset, we simulate an imperfect production classifier by training f_{prod} on 50% of the data. Then, we run intent classification, error detection and topic modelling on the remaining 50% of the data, as well as, on the test set. We manually analyze the clusters produced to understand where the model is failing and in Table 1 we report some patterns discovered in this way.

For ATIS, some utterances that should be classified as "flight" are mis-classified as "airfare" or "airiline", while for SNIPS, we see that instead of querying the calendar, the model is misunderstanding to delete events, and instead of setting reminders it is adding notifications. We argue that certain intent mis-classifications, such as the ones shown here, can be critical for the operation of a virtual assistant and should be detected as early as possible.

The analysis shown in this section requires little technical knowledge for the human experts, since they only need to look at the generated clusters and assess which ones represent a major risk. This can greatly speed up the error analysis process, helping in the early detection of critical errors and in reducing the amount of time that the annotators need to spend looking at the data.

5 Conclusion

In this work we have presented an active learning pipeline for conversational agents which consists of intent classification, unsupervised error detection and topic modeling. In the experiments, we show that our approach helps in prioritizing data for annotation: in our real-world dataset (AUTO) we reach the same performance with 36% of the data when selected by our pipeline as with 100% without prioritization. Therefore, this method can provide major savings for organizations with limited annotation capabilities. Furthermore, we argue that our approach helps to discover intent classification errors that may be critical for the correct operation of the dialogue agent and which, if not detected on time, could jeopardize the viability of the system. In future work, we plan to extend our proposed pipeline to support also named entity recognition.

References

Ron Artstein. 2017. Inter-annotator agreement. *Handbook of linguistic annotation*, pages 297–313.

Josh Attenberg and Foster Provost. 2010. Why label when you can search? alternatives to active learning for applying human resources to build classification models under extreme class imbalance. In *Proceedings of the 16th ACM SIGKDD international conference on Knowledge discovery and data mining*, pages 423–432.

Joshua Attenberg, Panos Ipeirotis, and Foster Provost. 2015. Beat the machine: Challenging humans to find a predictive model's "unknown unknowns". *Journal of Data and Information Quality (JDIQ)*, 6(1):1–17.

Akansha Bhardwaj, Jie Yang, and Philippe Cudré-Mauroux. 2020. A human-ai loop approach for joint keyword discovery and expectation estimation in micropost event detection. In *Proceedings of the AAAI Conference on Artificial Intelligence*, volume 34, pages 2451–2458.

Akansha Bhardwaj, Jie Yang, and Philippe Cudré-Mauroux. 2022. Human-in-the-loop rule discovery for micropost event detection. *IEEE Transactions on Knowledge and Data Engineering.*

Tom Bocklisch, Joey Faulkner, Nick Pawlowski, and Alan Nichol. 2017. Rasa: Open source language understanding and dialogue management. *arXiv preprint arXiv:1712.05181.*

Daniel Cer, Yinfei Yang, Sheng-yi Kong, Nan Hua, Nicole Limtiaco, Rhomni St John, Noah Constant, Mario Guajardo-Cespedes, Steve Yuan, Chris Tar, et al. 2018. Universal sentence encoder. *arXiv preprint arXiv:1803.11175.*

Nan-Chen Chen, Jina Suh, Johan Verwey, Gonzalo Ramos, Steven Drucker, and Patrice Simard. 2018. Anchorviz: Facilitating classifier error discovery through interactive semantic data exploration. In *23rd International Conference on Intelligent User Interfaces*, pages 269–280.

Alice Coucke, Alaa Saade, Adrien Ball, Théodore Bluche, Alexandre Caulier, David Leroy, Clément Doumouro, Thibault Gisselbrecht, Francesco Caltagirone, Thibaut Lavril, et al. 2018. Snips voice platform: an embedded spoken language understanding system for private-by-design voice interfaces. *arXiv preprint arXiv:1805.10190.*

Jerry Alan Fails and Dan R Olsen Jr. 2003. Interactive machine learning. In *Proceedings of the 8th international conference on Intelligent user interfaces*, pages 39–45.

Maarten Grootendorst. 2022. Bertopic: Neural topic modeling with a class-based tf-idf procedure. *arXiv preprint arXiv:2203.05794.*

Pengcheng He, Jianfeng Gao, and Weizhu Chen. 2021a. Debertav3: Improving deberta using electra-style pre-training with gradient-disentangled embedding sharing.

Pengcheng He, Xiaodong Liu, Jianfeng Gao, and Weizhu Chen. 2021b. Deberta: Decoding-enhanced bert with disentangled attention. In *International Conference on Learning Representations.*

Charles T. Hemphill, John J. Godfrey, and George R. Doddington. 1990. The ATIS spoken language systems pilot corpus. In *Speech and Natural Language: Proceedings of a Workshop Held at Hidden Valley, Pennsylvania, June 24-27,1990.*

Rinat Khaziev, Usman Shahid, Tobias Röding, Rakesh Chada, Emir Kapanci, and Pradeep Natarajan. 2022. Fpi: Failure point isolation in large-scale conversational assistants. In *Proceedings of the 2022 Conference of the North American Chapter of the Association for Computational Linguistics: Human Language Technologies: Industry Track*, pages 141–148.

Himabindu Lakkaraju, Ece Kamar, Rich Caruana, and Eric Horvitz. 2017. Identifying unknown unknowns in the open world: Representations and policies for guided exploration. In *Proceedings of the AAAI Conference on Artificial Intelligence*, volume 31.

David D Lewis and Jason Catlett. 1994. Heterogeneous uncertainty sampling for supervised learning. In *Machine learning proceedings 1994*, pages 148–156. Elsevier.

Leland McInnes, John Healy, and Steve Astels. 2017. hdbscan: Hierarchical density based clustering. *Journal of Open Source Software*, 2(11):205.

Leland McInnes, John Healy, Nathaniel Saul, and Lukas Großberger. 2018. Umap: Uniform manifold approximation and projection. *Journal of Open Source Software*, 3(29).

Besmira Nushi, Ece Kamar, Eric Horvitz, and Donald Kossmann. 2017. On human intellect and machine failures: Troubleshooting integrative machine learning systems. In *Proceedings of the AAAI Conference on Artificial Intelligence*, volume 31.

Long Ouyang, Jeffrey Wu, Xu Jiang, Diogo Almeida, Carroll Wainwright, Pamela Mishkin, Chong Zhang, Sandhini Agarwal, Katarina Slama, Alex Ray, et al. 2022. Training language models to follow instructions with human feedback. *Advances in Neural Information Processing Systems*, 35:27730–27744.

Victor Sanh, Lysandre Debut, Julien Chaumond, and Thomas Wolf. 2019. Distilbert, a distilled version of bert: smaller, faster, cheaper and lighter. *arXiv preprint arXiv:1910.01108.*

Christoph Schuhmann, Romain Beaumont, Richard Vencu, Cade W Gordon, Ross Wightman, Mehdi Cherti, Theo Coombes, Aarush Katta, Clayton Mullis, Mitchell Wortsman, et al. 2022. Laion-5b: An open large-scale dataset for training next generation image-text models. In *Thirty-sixth Conference on Neural Information Processing Systems Datasets and Benchmarks Track*.

Simone Stumpf, Vidya Rajaram, Lida Li, Weng-Keen Wong, Margaret Burnett, Thomas Dietterich, Erin Sullivan, and Jonathan Herlocker. 2009. Interacting meaningfully with machine learning systems: Three experiments. *International journal of human-computer studies*, 67(8):639–662.

Malcolm Ware, Eibe Frank, Geoffrey Holmes, Mark Hall, and Ian H Witten. 2001. Interactive machine learning: letting users build classifiers. *International Journal of Human-Computer Studies*, 55(3):281–292.

Yan Yan, Glenn M Fung, Rómer Rosales, and Jennifer G Dy. 2011. Active learning from crowds. In *Proceedings of the 28th international conference on machine learning (ICML-11)*, pages 1161–1168.

Jie Yang, Thomas Drake, Andreas Damianou, and Yoelle Maarek. 2018. Leveraging crowdsourcing data for deep active learning an application: Learning intents in alexa. In *Proceedings of the 2018 World Wide Web Conference*, pages 23–32.

Multi-layered Annotation of Conversation-like Narratives in German

Magdalena Repp♠, **Petra B. Schumacher**♠, and **Fahime Same**♡
♠Department of German Language and Literature I, Linguistics, University of Cologne
♡Department of Linguistics, University of Cologne
mrepp1, petra.schumacher, f.same@uni-koeln.de

Abstract

This work presents two corpora based on excerpts from two German novels with an informal narration style. We performed fine-grained multi-layer annotations of animate referents, assigning local and global prominence-lending features to the annotated referring expressions. In addition, our corpora include annotations of intra-sentential segments, which can serve as a more reliable unit of length measurement. Furthermore, we present two exemplary studies demonstrating how to use these corpora.

1 Introduction

The rapid development of NLP increases the need for high-quality corpora and corpora of different registers and languages. However, most of the available corpora are in English, and on formal written genres such as Wikipedia (Belz et al., 2010), and newspaper articles (Taylor et al., 2003). But in order to study or generate more naturalistic, colloquial, and spoken language, corpora based on less formal registers must be created and investigated. Due to the high complexity of handling spoken data, spoken corpora are less common than written corpora in NLP studies. Using written corpora that resemble conversational language is one way to reduce the gap between colloquial and formal speech data. In the current work, we present two corpora based on excerpts from the German novel *Tschick*[1] (Herrndorf, 2010) and the Austrian novel *Auferstehung der Toten*[2] [henceforth AdT] (Haas, 1996). These corpora both have a conversation-like narrative style.

We are building a conversation-like corpus to study the choice of Referring Expressions (REs) in naturalistic language use. Our motivation to use a corpus other than the ones using formal language is that the register of a text can influence the choice of REs. For instance, some referential forms are restricted to formal registers, whereas other forms occur more often in informal language. An example are the German demonstrative pronouns *dieser* and *der*, where *dieser* is more likely to occur in formal texts, and *der* in informal texts or spoken language (Patil et al., 2020).

We find the creation of this corpus and the extensive annotations valuable for the following reasons: (1) Most written corpora are based on formal texts such as newspaper or Wikipedia articles. However, in this work, we investigate narrative texts with a conversation-like narration style. (2) In addition to third-person referents, we also include annotations of singular and plural first- and second-person REs, which extends the research of reference to speech act participants. (3) Most available corpora rely on punctuation marks, particularly full stops, for sentence boundary detection. Thus, sentences of widely varying lengths are compared with each other. The current work includes an intra-sentential layer of sentence segment annotations in order to obtain comparable units for sentences. This also allows us to account for insertions in a more precise way. (4) Various corpora have an annotation of coreference (e.g., OntoNotes (Weischedel, Ralph et al.)), but the annotation of RE forms is missing. Few others offer RE form annotation; however, they are majorly limited to coarse-grained annotations such as the distinction between pronouns, proper names, and definite articles. In this work, we offer a fine-grained annotation of RE types in line with the accessibility hierarchy of Ariel (2001).

The structure of this paper is as follows: in section 2, we present an overview of available corpora for the study of reference. Section 3 sets out the motivation for our annotations. In section 4, we introduce the corpora we are developing, followed by a detailed overview of our annotation practice in section 5. In section 6, we demonstrate the application of the annotation by presenting case studies.

[1]The English version of the novel is called *Why we took the car.*

[2]The English version of the novel is called *Resurrection.*

Proceedings of the 17th Linguistic Annotation Workshop (LAW-XVII), pages 61–72
July 13, 2023

Finally, we conclude the paper with discussion and conclusion in sections 7 and 8.

2 Related Work

There are numerous corpora that include annotations of referring expressions. According to Viethen (2012), these corpora can be classified as either collected or found. Collected corpora consist of data gathered in systematically designed experimental settings, whereas found corpora are composed of naturally occurring language data obtained in real-life situations, such as those found in newspapers or telephone conversations.

Most well-known collected corpora that include referring expression annotations are based on elicited language, using giver-director games (e.g. Stoia et al., 2008; Di Eugenio et al., 1998; Gatt et al., 2008; Howcroft et al., 2017). Therefore, they do not include a rich character / protagonist structure. Also, these elicited corpora do not show a consistent, long-lasting narrative structure, but rather short exchanges about mostly inanimate entities. For instance, the SCARE corpus (Stoia et al., 2008) is based on spontaneous instruction-giving dialogues that were collected in a virtual reality game. The corpus, however, only contains annotations of REs referring to inanimate entities such as a door, cabinet, and buttons that are entailed in the virtual reality world. The COCONUT corpus (Di Eugenio et al., 1998) is another corpus including naturalistic language. It is based on computer-mediated dialogues collected in an experiment in which two human subjects collaborated via typed dialogue on the task of buying furniture to decorate two rooms of a house. The corpus includes only annotations of REs that describe task objects. Therefore, it only includes REs referring to inanimate entities. Also, the popular TUNA corpus (van Deemter et al., 2006; Gatt et al., 2008) of elicited spoken English only includes REs referring to inanimate entities. There is also a German pendant, the G-TUNA corpus (Howcroft et al., 2017), which also does not include annotations of animate referents. In addition, there are two other corpora associated with the analysis of German REs, namely the GIVE-2 corpus (Gargett et al., 2010) and the PENTOREF corpus (Zarrieß et al., 2016). Both corpora rely on elicited naturalistic spoken language and only include annotations of REs referring to inanimate entities.

There are also a few narrative corpora that have been elicited through experiments, which offer the advantage of language production in a more "real-life" context. A shortcoming of this approach is that the elicited narratives usually describe a rather random topic (in order to ensure comparability) and are comparatively short and less complex. For instance, the INSCRIPT corpus (Modi et al., 2016) provides simple English narratives that are centered around a specific scenario. The narratives were elicited by asking participants to describe a given scenario in narrative form, pretending to be explaining it to a child (Modi et al., 2016). The corpus includes coreference annotations of REs referring to both inanimate and animate referents. But the corpus does not include detailed annotations of the referential form or additional syntactic and semantic features.

In addition to the above-mentioned corpora that were collected in experiments, there are also various found corpora containing reference annotation. An example is the GNOME corpus that consists of texts describing museum objects and patients' information leaflets (Poesio, 2004a; Poesio et al., 2004). The corpus contains extensive annotation on the sentence and reference level. The annotation of referents contains information such as animacy, referential form, grammatical role, and gender. Two other corpora which have been built specifically for investigating the form of referring expressions in context are GREC-2.0 and GREC-People (Belz et al., 2010). The data in the GREC-2.0 corpus contains the introductory paragraphs of almost 2000 Wikipedia articles classified into five categories: people, city, country, river and mountain. The GREC-People corpus consists of 1,000 introductory sections of Wikipedia articles in the category people, with subcategories chefs, composers and inventors. A limitation of these corpora is that in GREC-2.0, only references to the main subject of the text have been annotated, and in the GREC-People corpus, only references to human referents are marked. Additionally, since the texts consist of only the introductory section of an article, they are relatively short.

The Narrative Corpus (Rühlemann and O'Donnell, 2012) includes conversational narratives, extracted from the demographically-sampled subcorpus of the British National Corpus. However, the corpus does not include annotations of referring expressions, but rather of broader concepts such as speaker (social information on speakers), text (text Ids, title, type of story, type of embedding, etc.), textual components (pre-/post-narrative talk, narrative, and narrative-initial/ final utterances), and utterance (participation roles, quotatives, and reporting modes).

To build annotated reference corpora, various annotation schemes were also developed along the way. The GNOME corpus is annotated using a comprehensive set of guidelines from the MATE/GNOME annotation scheme (Poesio, 2004b). Extensions of this scheme facilitated additional reference annotations, including the annotation of abstract anaphora, i.e., cases where linguistic antecedents are verbal phrases, clauses, and discourse segment (Navarretta and Olsen, 2008). Reflex, as a more recent reference annotation scheme, facilitated the annotation of information status (including coreference and bridging) as well as lexical information status (semantic relations) of referents (Riester and Baumann, 2017).

3 Linguistic motivation for annotations

It is well known that the form of an RE corresponds to the cognitive status of the discourse referent (e.g., Ariel, 2001; Givón, 1983). Psycholinguistic research has shown that so-called prominence-lending features (von Heusinger and Schumacher, 2019) influence the referential form of REs and their interpretation (e.g., pronoun resolution of ambiguous pronouns). It has been shown that multiple local and global prominence-lending features contribute to the interpretation of REs (Bosch et al., 2007; Schumacher et al., 2016; Hinterwimmer, 2019; Givón, 1983). For instance, for pronoun resolution, many cross-linguistic studies have examined the grammatical role of the previous mention as an influential feature (Bosch et al., 2007; Kaiser and Trueswell, 2008). Other studies have highlighted the importance of thematic roles (Schumacher et al., 2016) as well as information structural cues at the discourse level and distance (Givón, 1983). Also, perspectival features have been shown to influence the RE form (Hinterwimmer, 2019).

4 Our corpora

The Tschick corpus was formed from 9 chapters of the novel *Tschick* (Herrndorf, 2010): chapter 28 to 31, and 42 to 46. The novel can be described as a road novel (Krammer, 2021) or a coming-of-age novel (Lorenz, 2019). The AdT corpus was formed from the first four chapters of the crime novel *Auferstehung der Toten* (Haas, 1996). Both novels represent immensely successful contributions to contemporary German literature and have been recognized with awards. Table 1 presents a brief general overview of the corpora's length. Both corpora are stored on the Open Science Framework website (`https://osf.io/bjn5a/`) and are publicly available for educational, research, and non-profit purposes under appropriate attribution.[3]

	Tschick	AdT
Tokenized sentences	723	799
Sentence segments	1633	1823
Mean chapter length (segments)	181.44	455.75
Total REs	1559	1705

Table 1: Overview of the corpora's length.

From a linguistic perspective, the novel *Tschick* is interesting for two main reasons: First, the novel is characterized not only by a naturalistic and conversation-like narration style, but especially by the very authentic and timeless use of youth language. This allows the investigation of the use of REs in a more ecologically valid setting. A side effect of its colloquial language is that *Tschick* includes very explicit swearwords and invective. Further, the novel consists largely of a dialogue structure, which is another factor supporting the naturalistic language of the novel. Second, the novel is written from the point of view of the first-person narrator Maik and is thus characterized by an autodiegetic narrator, i.e. a first-person narrator is at the same time the main character, the narrator in a way tells his own story. The narration style of *Tschick* and its characteristics is illustrated in example (1), where the protagonists try to steal fuel. From the example, the dominant dialogue structure of the novel becomes clear. Square brackets and bold words indicate sentence segments and annotated REs, respectively (cf. section 5 below).

(1) [«Was willst **du mir** erzählen?] [Dass das Wasser von unten nach oben läuft?»]
[«**Du** musst ansaugen.»]
[«Noch nie was von Erdanziehung **gehört** *(zero)*?] [Das läuft nicht nach oben.»]
[«Weil es ja danach nach unten läuft.] [Es läuft ja insgesamt mehr nach unten,] [de-

[3] A dataframe containing only the annotated REs and the additional information is freely accessible for download. The entire corpus is only available via a password-protected link due to copyright restrictions. Please contact us if you would like to access this corpus.

shalb.»]
[«Aber das weiß das Benzin doch nicht,]
[dass es nachher noch runtergeht.»]
"What are you trying to tell me? That the water runs from the bottom to the top?"
"You have to suck it in."
"Never heard of gravity? It doesn't run upwards."
"Because it's going down afterwards. It's running down more overall, that's why."
"But the gasoline doesn't know that it's going down afterward."

In the novel *Auferstehung der Toten* (but also all other Brenner volumes), the events are narrated by an omnipresent, auctorial narrator, who never appears as a protagonist. At the same time, the private detective Brenner is present almost exclusively and his thoughts, impressions, and feelings are described. The narrator always comments and evaluates what is going on. But most importantly, the narrator uses a style strongly reminiscent of oral language. The sentences are usually quite short and contain few embeddings, but they contain numerous left and right shifts, along with repeated omissions and sentence breaks. Additionally, elliptical structures are used with notable frequency. Moreover, the corpus is characterized by a simulated dialogicity (Nindl, 2009), i.e. the narrator repeatedly addresses the reader directly by using the second-person personal pronoun, which reinforces the oral language impression (Hinterwimmer, 2020; Nindl, 2009). By using these stylistic features, the author creates an artificial illustration of oral communication patterns. The following example (2) illustrates the characteristics mentioned.

(2) [Das gehört jetzt eigentlich nicht hierher.] [Aber **dem Brenner** ist es auch nicht anders gegangen.] [**Der** sitzt in seinem heißen Zimmer] [und **soll** *(zero)* über **seine** Arbeit nachdenken,] [aber statt dessen denkt **er** über seine Wohnung nach.] [Und jetzt **paß** *(zero)* auf,] [was **ich dir** sage.] [Zufall ist das keiner gewesen,] [weil Zufall in dem Sinn gibt es keinen,] [das ist erwiesen.]
That doesn't really belong here. But it didn't happen any differently to the Brenner. He sits in his hot room and is supposed to think about his work, but instead he thinks about his apartment. And now pay attention to what I'm telling you. It wasn't a coincidence, because there is no such thing as a coincidence, that's been proven.

5 Annotation practices in current work

In the current work, we present two corpora based on excerpts from two novels with a very conversation-like narration style. Although the two corpora are relatively short, they stand out for their extensive annotations. We annotated all REs that refer to an animate referent and assigned specific grammatical and semantic features to them. Additionally, the sentences were separated into segments to create a comparable sentence equivalent, since the length of the sentences often varied greatly. This approach is not often found in comparable corpora but becomes important when dealing with a text that contains very long sentences due to many insertions.

5.1 Annotation scheme

The annotations were performed with the web-based multi-layer annotation software WebAnno 3.6.7 (Yimam et al., 2013, 2014). A screenshot of the annotation window of WebAnno can be found in the appendix, section 9. Prior to the annotations, the data has been automatically sentence-segmented. Inconsistencies were manually checked and corrected. Sentence boundaries were indicated by sentence-final punctuation (such as period, question mark, and exclamation point). The sentences appeared on separate lines in the WebAnno platform. The annotation process was carried out in parallel by three linguistically trained annotators, all being native German speakers. Both corpora underwent multiple rounds of annotation, during which the annotation scheme was refined gradually. Therefore, no inter-annotator agreement was calculated. First, the Tschick corpus was annotated, followed by the AdT corpus. The chapters were always annotated chronologically. The annotation procedure was as follows: [Step 1] annotation of sentence segments, [Step 2] annotation of all REs that refer to an animate referent, [Step 3] specification of the RE type for each RE annotated in step 2, [Step 4] adding information on grammatical and thematic roles to each annotated RE from step 2, and [Step 5] marking the referential chains between the previous antecedent and RE.

Sentence segments Both corpora are characterized by their colloquial narration style. In colloquial speech, however, syntactic constructions do not usually appear as neatly bounded sentences or clauses, but as unstructured fragments (Hopper, 2004). And indeed, even though the corpora are based on written texts, they both include several instances of non-sentential, fragmented, or elliptical utterances, which are commonly observed in spoken language. First, since sentences varied greatly in length, intra-sentential segments (also called segments in short) were annotated in order to create a comparable sentence equivalent (step 1 of the annotation process). For this purpose, the layer 'segment' was used. For the segmentation, the previously performed sentence segmentation was crucial, in which the sentence boundaries were signaled by punctuation. Our goal was to annotate all clausal elements as segments. For this, we treated all main clauses and subordinate clauses as separate clausal elements. The only exception was restrictive relative clauses, which are dependent on the entity they modify. Also, commas were taken to signal segment boundaries in most cases. See example (1) and (2) for an illustration of the annotated segments.

REs In the current version of the corpus, we have only annotated the REs that refer to animate discourse referents, using the layer 'coreference' for this purpose (cf. (1) and (2) for the annotated REs marked in bold). For each annotated RE, additional features were specified by using different tagsets. The specified features were the type of RE, the grammatical role, and the thematic role. In order to assign the respective RE type to each annotated RE, a selection was made from the following list: personal pronoun (e.g., *sie, er, es*), d-pronoun (*die, der, das*), demonstrative pronoun (*diese, dieser, dieses, jene, jener, jenes*), proper name (*Maik Klingenberg*), definite DP (*die Tänzerin*), indefinite DP (*eine Tänzerin*), coordinated DP (*die Tänzerin und die Pianistin*), relative pronoun (*die, der, das, welche, welcher, welches*), resumptive d-pronoun, resumptive personal pronoun, indefinite pronoun (*beide*), possessive pronoun (*mein, dein*), possessive proper name (*Maiks*), quantifier (*keiner, jeder, alle*), reflexive (*sich*), and zero pronoun.

For each annotated RE, the grammatical role and the thematic role were identified. For grammatical role, it was indicated whether the RE is the subject (nominative), the direct object (accusative), or the indirect object (dative) of the sentence. These annotations were always relative to the predicate. All other forms carry the grammatical role oblique. For the thematic role annotation, not only the verb semantics but also the larger (pragmatic) context was considered. Following the proto-role approach, it was indicated whether the marked RE is the Proto-Agent, Proto-Patient, or Proto-Recipient (Primus, 2012) of the sentence. If none of these thematic roles fitted, no thematic function was annotated in order to reduce annotation efforts. In some cases, grammatical and thematic roles were not annotated, for instance for possessive expressions.

Regarding the annotation of REs, there was some uncertainty among the annotators, especially in the case of predicative constructions, since at first glance these expressions look like normal REs (cf. underlined NPs in (3)). Predicative constructions, however, are not referential, as shown, for example, by the fact that they cannot be referred to with a pronoun. Rather, NPs used predicatively attribute another information to a discourse referent.

(3) Und Anfang März taucht **der Brenner** auf einmal wieder auf. Aber nicht als <u>Polizist</u>, sondern als <u>Privatdetektiv</u>.
And at the beginning of March, the Brenner suddenly reappears. But not as a policeman, but as a private detective.

5.2 Additional (ongoing) annotations

When dealing with longer more naturalistic discourse, investigating the simple antecedent-anaphora relation is not enough to describe the underlying referential behavior of the text. Rather, the dynamically unfolding referential usage must also be described. In addition to the features described above, we, therefore, added further annotations that relate to global discourse properties such as proper referential chains and perspectival features.

Character names Since the referential chains in our corpora were not annotated across chapter boundaries (this was not possible in the WebAnno software), the chain numbers for each referential chain in each chapter start with the number one. Within the context of a novel, however, one can assume that the referential chain of a given referent continues across chapter boundaries. Thus, it is assumed that referents that have been introduced in a certain chapter can be reintroduced by a simple proper name in another chapter and won't be reintroduced by an indefinite description or a modified proper name. To adequately analyze reference chains, chain IDs were mapped to character names to obtain chain information across chapter boundaries. Combined referential chains that consist of at least 15 REs were mapped to character names to indicate recurring characters in the corpus. All referential chains with less than 15 REs were marked by 'other'. The corresponding column in the corpus is called *referent_name*. Therefore, by offering information on the referent names, we not only provide a way to analyze referential chains across chapter boundaries, but also provide information about which (recurring) character a particular RE refers to; this is particularly useful for unspecified REs such as pronouns or generic DPs. Another advantage of having this layer of annotation is that we can later use it to build WebNLG-like reference corpora (Castro Ferreira et al., 2018) that can be used in End-to-End neural modeling of RE generation.

Perspective In a current, ongoing annotation process, we annotate the perspective information of each RE. In doing so, we would like to assign for each RE the character of the story that uttered that expression. So far, we have assigned perspective information for the third-person singular personal and d-pronouns that occur in subject and proto-agent positions. Such information is of particular interest in stories that contain several perspectival shifts. For example, in stories that contain a lot of direct speech, the perspective constantly switches between that of the narrator and that of the character who is uttering the direct speech act.

6 Studies

In the following, we show examples of analyses that can be performed using our corpora.

Together, both corpora contain a total of 3264 REs that refer to an animate referent. Table 2 shows the distribution of the 11 most frequent RE types. The row 'other' summarizes the RE types that have been annotated less than 20 times. For the Tschick corpus, those RE types are quantifier, relative pronoun, coordinated DP, demonstrative DP, possessive proper name, and demonstrative pronoun; and for the AdT corpus, those REs are coordinated DP, possessive proper name, reflexive pronoun, resumptive d-pronoun, and demonstrative DP.

As it becomes clear from Table 2, almost half of the annotated REs are personal pronouns. A striking factor of the current corpus is that it also includes null cases (here referred to by 'zero'), which are typically absent in German formal texts.

RF	Freq	%	% Cum.
PersPron	1390	42.59	42.59
Proper name	390	11.95	54.53
defDP	350	10.72	65.26
zero	306	9.38	74.63
PossPron	250	7.66	82.29
D-Pron	152	4.66	86.95
IndefPron	133	4.07	91.02
indefDP	109	3.34	94.36
other	89	2.73	97.09
Quant	47	1.44	98.53
RelPron	25	0.77	99.30
Reflx	23	0.70	100.00
Total	3264	100.00	100.00

Table 2: Distribution of the annotated referring expressions.

As mentioned earlier, dialogues contain references to speech act participants. For referring to a *participant* of a speech act, other referential forms are used than when referring to referents that do not take part in the conversation, but only occur in the surrounding scene. For instance, second-person pronouns are mainly used to refer to an interlocutor or a future interlocutor, whereas third-person pronouns refer to referents that appear outside the conversational setting or are used by a narrator who is not part of the story. Table 3 shows how 'person' of personal pronouns is distributed. We see that in AdT most personal pronouns occur in third-person singular. Almost equally often we find first-person singular personal pronouns in the Tschick corpus.

Person	Tschick	AdT
1-sg	371 (44.86)	99 (17.58)
2-sg	76 (9.19)	85 (15.10)
3-sg	184 (22.25)	302 (53.64)
1-pl	163 (19.71)	26 (4.62)
2-pl	19 (2.30)	2 (0.36)
3-pl	12 (1.45)	40 (7.10)
Formal	2 (0.24)	9 (1.60)
Total	827 (100.00)	563 (100.00)

Table 3: Distribution of person among all personal pronouns in the two corpora. Percentages of frequencies within a corpus are indicated in parentheses.

To get an overview of the broader distribution of the REs, we grouped the RE types (see Table 2) into three main categories of pronouns, determiner-noun-combinations (henceforth called DP), and names. We see that the largest share belongs to pronouns (69.82 %, N=2279), followed by DPs (14.06 %, N=459), and names (11.95 %, N=11.95). Additionally, REs that cannot be classified within these categories constitute 4.17 % of the total.

Moving on to feature specification, the mosaic

plots in Figure 1 and Figure 2 show the distribution of grammatical roles and thematic roles among the three main groups of RE types. Horizontally, the plots are divided into the three main RE types: name (N=100), DP (N=177), and pronoun (N=1243). Vertically, the plots are divided into different classes of grammatical roles (Figure 1) and thematic roles (Figure 2).

Looking at Figure 1, it becomes clear that pronouns in subject position overall account for the largest share (55.1 %). In addition, when comparing the different grammatical roles (vertically), it can be noted that the grammatical role subject also accounts for the largest share of grammatical roles: 72.5 % of the REs in the three main groups are in the subject position. By a large margin, the grammatical role oblique occurs second most frequently (8.1 %), followed by the grammatical roles direct object (7.6 %), REs with no grammatical role (6.4 %), and indirect object (5.5 %). If we look at the distribution within the grammatical role subject, we see that with 76.0 %, pronouns have the largest share. Vice versa, within the pronoun group, subjects have the largest share (75.6 %).

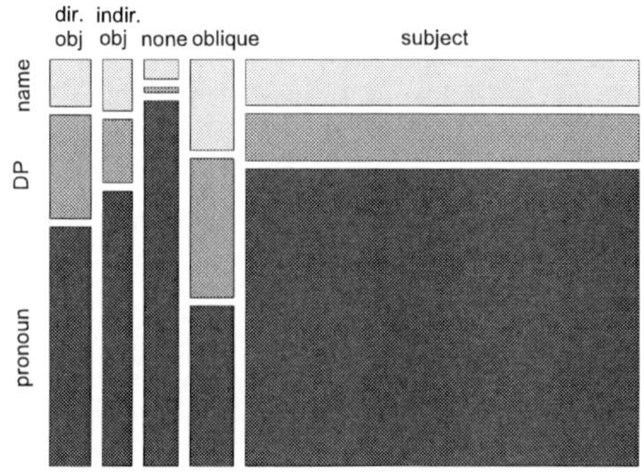

Figure 1: Distribution of grammatical roles of all REs grouped by the categories name, DP, and pronoun.

Looking at Figure 2, we see that pronouns in the proto-agent role comprise the majority of REs (57.0 %) among the three main groups. When comparing the thematic roles, we see that the thematic role proto-agent accounts for the largest share among all thematic roles (75.5 %). The thematic role proto-patient is the second most frequent (12.1 %), followed by REs with no thematic role (11.6 %), and the thematic role recipient (0.8 %). A look at the distribution of the thematic role proto-agent shows that pronouns account for the largest group (75.6 %), and again vice versa, within the pronoun group, the thematic role proto-agent has the largest share (78.3 %).

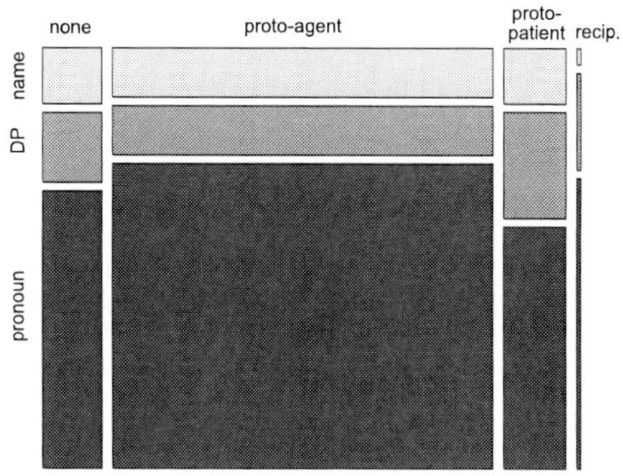

Figure 2: Distribution of thematic roles of all REs grouped by the categories name, DP, and pronoun.

In addition to our corpus analysis, we conducted feature importance analyses to find out (1) which features contribute the most to the choice of the RE form, and (2) how they affect this choice. In this analysis, our focus is solely on third-person anaphoric REs within the AdT corpus[4]. We first trained an XGBoost model from the family of Gradient Boosting trees (Chen and Guestrin, 2016) using the features annotated in our corpus. Concretely, we looked at the following features: the grammatical role of the current RE and its antecedent (`gm` and `prev_gm`), the thematic role of the current RE and its antecedent (`tm` and `prev_tm`), the segment distance between the current RE and its antecedent (`seg_dist`), and the RE form of the antecedent (`prev_ref_type`). To determine the importance ranking of the features, we compute the model-agnostic permutation-based variable importance of the model (Biecek and Burzykowski, 2021). In particular, we measure the extent to which performance changes when a particular feature is removed. Figure 3 shows the change in performance for each feature in the case of a 3-way classification task (pronoun vs. proper name vs. DP). As shown in the figure, the distance calculated in the number of segments and the RE form of the antecedent have the highest contribution.

We then conducted a SHAP (SHapley Additive exPlanations) analysis to evaluate the positive and negative contributions of each feature to the prediction of each class. The SHAP analysis decomposes the predictions of the model into contributions that

[4]As Tschick features a first-person narrator and predominantly includes first- and second-person REs that do not undergo changes in referential form, we exclude them from this analysis.

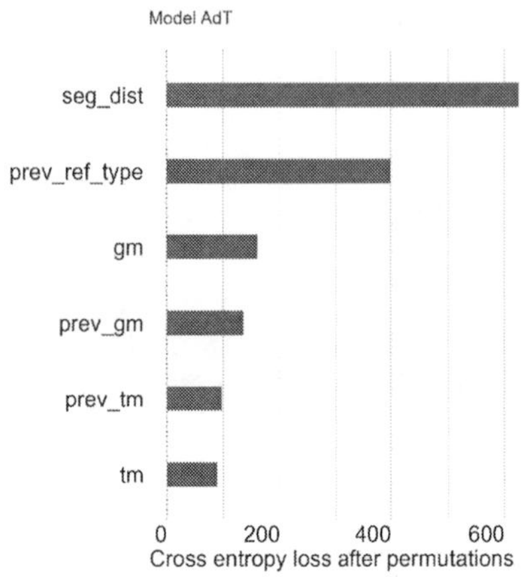

Figure 3: Feature importance analysis of the RE form prediction model. A higher loss indicates the greater importance of a feature.

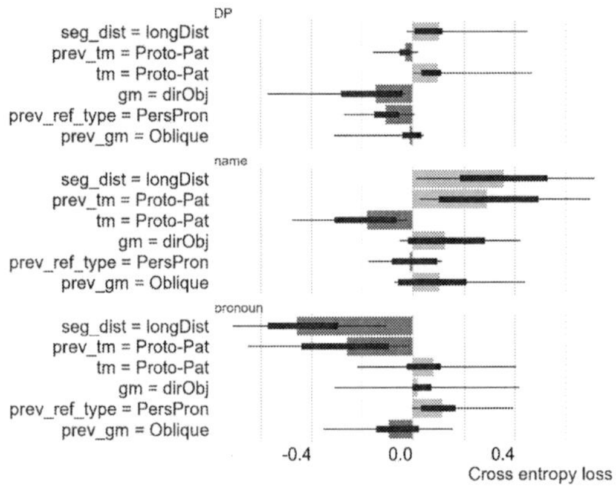

Figure 4: Shapley values with box plots for 100 random orderings of explanatory variables in the XGBoost model. The green and red bars represent positive and negative contributions, respectively.

can be additively attributed to different variables (Lundberg and Lee, 2017). According to Figure 4, the segment distance with the value `longDist` (>6 segments) promotes the use of non-pronominal forms, i.e., name and DP, the most. Interestingly, contrary to the variable importance graph, we see a significant contribution of the thematic role features to the choice of classes.

7 Discussion

The goal of this work was to promote the development of more naturalistic and conversation-like corpora that reflect the nuances of colloquial speech. The analysis of REs in informal language is particularly interesting, since the use of REs may differ from that in formal language (Patil et al., 2020).

Moreover, this work offers fine-grained annotations of the REs on local (referential form, grammatical role, thematic role) and global (referential chains, perspectival features, character name) prominence levels. Although there are several corpora that include coreference annotations (Weischedel, Ralph et al.; Zeldes, 2017), only a few corpora include detailed information on the referential form (Poesio, 2004a); additional annotations of prominence-lending features are even rarer.

We have shown that in our narrative corpora, pronouns make up a very high proportion of the referential forms used. This large count of pronouns, especially personal pronouns, seems to be connected to the informal narrative structure. It appears that in (more) formal registers such as newspaper articles or in mixed collections of texts, the proportion of pronouns is radically lower than what we observed in our corpora. We examined the proportion of pronouns in the training set of two datasets from the CorefUD 1.1 collection: the English GUM corpus (Zeldes, 2017), which includes texts from various genres, and the German Potsdam commentary corpus (Nedoluzhko et al., 2022), which contains commentaries on German newspaper articles. The former had 22% pronouns (7798 out of 35369 REs), while the latter had only 14% pronouns (654 out of 4671 REs). The significant variation in the distribution of RE forms across different corpora highlights the importance of incorporating more diverse text registers, such as the narrative texts analyzed in this study. In addition, we have shown that our corpora can be used for modeling and predicting the referential form of REs. However, since the referential forms in our corpora are unbalanced with a strong tendency towards pronouns, modeling attempts might be biased. As the next step, we will annotate more REs and leverage state-of-the-art models like the German BERT (GBERT) to find out how reliably the RE forms can be predicted.

8 Conclusion

All in all, our two corpora show a comprehensive, diverse picture of the REs that refer to animate referents. By annotating a variety of prominence-lending features, a fine-grained characterization of the use of the REs in the two corpora emerges. It is therefore worthwhile to expand the corpus annotations in the future to create a larger data set.

Limitation

As the current corpora are still work in progress, a number of limitations emerge. The biggest limitation of our corpora is their size. But expanding the corpora for further chapters of the novels is planned. Another limitation is that our corpora only include annotations on animate discourse referents. For future work, annotating inanimate entities and assigning the same features introduced in section 5 would be fruitful. The fact that the perspectival information is only annotated for a subset of REs is another drawback. We intend to expand these annotations for other referential forms.

Acknowledgements

We thank the anonymous reviewers for their fruitful comments. Also, special thanks to Anne Lützeler and Julia Wenzel for their help with annotating the two corpora. This work is supported by the German Research Foundation (DFG)– Project-ID 281511265 – SFB 1252 "Prominence in Language".

References

Mira Ariel. 2001. Accessibility theory: An overview. In Ted Sanders, Joost Schilperoord, and Wilbert Spooren, editors, *Text Representation: Linguistic and psycholinguistic aspects*, volume 8, page 29. John Benjamins Publishing Company.

Anja Belz, Eric Kow, Jette Viethen, and Albert Gatt. 2010. Generating referring expressions in context: The GREC task evaluation challenges. In *Empirical Methods in Natural Language Generation: Data-oriented Methods and Empirical Evaluation*, volume 5790 of *Lecture Notes in Computer Science*, pages 294–327. Springer.

Przemyslaw Biecek and Tomasz Burzykowski. 2021. *Explanatory model analysis: explore, explain, and examine predictive models*. Chapman and Hall/CRC, New York.

Peter Bosch, Graham Katz, and Carla Umbach. 2007. The non-subject bias of German demonstrative pronouns. In Monika Schwarz-Friesel, Manfred Consten, and Mareile Knees, editors, *Studies in Language Companion Series*, volume 86, pages 145–164. John Benjamins Publishing Company, Amsterdam.

Thiago Castro Ferreira, Diego Moussallem, Emiel Krahmer, and Sander Wubben. 2018. Enriching the WebNLG corpus. In *Proceedings of the 11th International Conference on Natural Language Generation*, pages 171–176, Tilburg University, The Netherlands. Association for Computational Linguistics.

Tianqi Chen and Carlos Guestrin. 2016. XGBoost: A scalable tree boosting system. In *Proceedings of the 22nd ACM SIGKDD International Conference on Knowledge Discovery and Data Mining*, KDD '16, page 785–794, New York, NY, USA. Association for Computing Machinery.

Barbara Di Eugenio, Pamela W. Jordan, Johanna D. Moore, and Richmond H. Thomason. 1998. An empirical investigation of proposals in collaborative dialogues. In *COLING 1998 Volume 1: The 17th International Conference on Computational Linguistics*.

Andrew Gargett, Konstantina Garoufi, Alexander Koller, and Kristina Striegnitz. 2010. The GIVE-2 corpus of giving instructions in virtual environments. In *Proceedings of the Seventh International Conference on Language Resources and Evaluation (LREC'10)*, Valletta, Malta. European Language Resources Association (ELRA).

Albert Gatt, Anja Belz, and Eric Kow. 2008. The TUNA challenge 2008: overview and evaluation results. In *Proceedings of the Fifth International Natural Language Generation Conference on - INLG '08*, page 198, Salt Fork, Ohio. Association for Computational Linguistics.

T. Givón. 1983. *Topic Continuity in Discourse: A quantitative cross-language study*. John Benjamins.

Wolf Haas. 1996. *Auferstehung der Toten*. Rowohlt, Reinbek bei Hamburg.

Wolfgang Herrndorf. 2010. *Tschick*. Rowohlt, Reinbek bei Hamburg.

Stefan Hinterwimmer. 2019. Prominent protagonists. *Journal of Pragmatics*, 13(154):79–91.

Stefan Hinterwimmer. 2020. Zum zusammenspiel von erzähler- und protagonistenperspektive in den brenner-romanen von wolf haas. *Zeitschrift für germanistische Linguistik*, 48(3):529–561.

Paul Hopper. 2004. The Openness of Grammatical Constructions. *Proceedings of the Annual Meeting of the Chicago Linguistic Society*, 40:153–175.

David Howcroft, Jorrig Vogels, and Vera Demberg. 2017. G-TUNA: a corpus of referring expressions in German, including duration information. In *Proceedings of the 10th International Conference on Natural Language Generation*, pages 149–153, Santiago de Compostela, Spain. Association for Computational Linguistics.

Elsi Kaiser and John C. Trueswell. 2008. Interpreting pronouns and demonstratives in Finnish: Evidence for a form-specific approach to reference resolution. *Language and Cognitive Processes*, 23(5):709–748.

Stefan Krammer. 2021. Abenteuer Männlichkeit. Adoleszenz in Wolfgang Herrndorfs Roman «Tschick» [Adventure Manhood. Adolescence in Wolfgang Herrndorf's Novel «Tschick»]. *Studia theodisca*, 28:5–24.

Matthias N. Lorenz, editor. 2019. *"Germanistenscheiss": Beiträge zur Werkpolitik Wolfgang Herrndorfs ["Germanistenscheiss": Contributions to the politics of Wolfgang Herrndorf's works]*. Frank et Timme, Berlin. OCLC: on1080642032.

Scott M Lundberg and Su-In Lee. 2017. A Unified Approach to Interpreting Model Predictions. In *Advances in Neural Information Processing Systems*, volume 30. Curran Associates, Inc.

Ashutosh Modi, Tatjana Anikina, Simon Ostermann, and Manfred Pinkal. 2016. InScript: Narrative texts annotated with script information. In *Proceedings of the Tenth International Conference on Language Resources and Evaluation (LREC'16)*, pages 3485–3493, Portorož, Slovenia. European Language Resources Association (ELRA).

Costanza Navarretta and Sussi Olsen. 2008. Annotating abstract pronominal anaphora in the DAD project. In *Proceedings of the Sixth International Conference on Language Resources and Evaluation (LREC'08)*, Marrakech, Morocco. European Language Resources Association (ELRA).

Anna Nedoluzhko, Michal Novák, Martin Popel, Zdeněk Žabokrtský, Amir Zeldes, and Daniel Zeman. 2022. CorefUD 1.0: Coreference meets Universal Dependencies. In *Proceedings of the Thirteenth Language Resources and Evaluation Conference*, pages 4859–4872, Marseille, France. European Language Resources Association.

Sigrid Nindl. 2009. *Wolf Haas und sein kriminalliterarisches Sprachexperiment*. Erich Schmidt Verlag, Berlin.

Umesh Patil, Peter Bosch, and Stefan Hinterwimmer. 2020. Constraints on German diese demonstratives: language formality and subject-avoidance. *Glossa: a journal of general linguistics*, 5(1).

Massimo Poesio. 2004a. Discourse annotation and semantic annotation in the GNOME corpus. In *Proceedings of the Workshop on Discourse Annotation*, pages 72–79.

Massimo Poesio. 2004b. The MATE/GNOME proposals for anaphoric annotation, revisited. In *Proceedings of the 5th SIGdial Workshop on Discourse and Dialogue at HLT-NAACL 2004*, pages 154–162, Cambridge, Massachusetts, USA. Association for Computational Linguistics.

Massimo Poesio, Rosemary Stevenson, Barbara Di Eugenio, and Janet Hitzeman. 2004. Centering: A parametric theory and its instantiations. *Computational linguistics*, 30(3):309–363.

Beatrice Primus. 2012. Animacy, Generalized Semantic Roles, and Differential Object Marking. In Monique Lamers and Peter de Swart, editors, *Case, Word Order and Prominence*, volume 40, pages 65–90. Springer Netherlands, Dordrecht. Series Title: Studies in Theoretical Psycholinguistics.

Arndt Riester and Stefan Baumann. 2017. The reflex scheme-annotation guidelines.

Christoph Rühlemann and Matthew Brook O'Donnell. 2012. Introducing a corpus of conversational stories. Construction and annotation of the Narrative Corpus. *Corpus Linguistics and Linguistic Theory*, 8(2):313–350.

Petra B. Schumacher, Manuel Dangl, and Elyesa Uzun. 2016. Thematic role as prominence cue during pronoun resolution in German. In Anke Holler and Katja Suckow, editors, *Empirical Perspectives on Anaphora Resolution*, pages 121–147. de Gruyter, Berlin.

Laura Stoia, Darla Magdalene Shockley, Donna K. Byron, and Eric Fosler-Lussier. 2008. SCARE: a situated corpus with annotated referring expressions. In *Proceedings of the Sixth International Conference on Language Resources and Evaluation (LREC'08)*, Marrakech, Morocco. European Language Resources Association (ELRA).

Ann Taylor, Mitchell Marcus, and Beatrice Santorini. 2003. The penn treebank: an overview. *Treebanks: Building and using parsed corpora*, pages 5–22.

Kees van Deemter, Ielka van der Sluis, and Albert Gatt. 2006. Building a semantically transparent corpus for the generation of referring expressions. In *Proceedings of the Fourth International Natural Language Generation Conference*, pages 130–132, Sydney, Australia. Association for Computational Linguistics.

Henriette Anna Elisabeth Viethen. 2012. *The generation of natural descriptions: corpus-based investigations of referring expressions in visual domains*. Ph.D. thesis, Macquarie University.

Klaus von Heusinger and Petra B. Schumacher. 2019. Discourse prominence: Definition and application. *Journal of Pragmatics*, 154:117–127.

Weischedel, Ralph, Palmer, Martha, Marcus, Mitchell, Hovy, Eduard, Pradhan, Sameer, Ramshaw, Lance, Xue, Nianwen, Taylor, Ann, Kaufman, Jeff, Franchini, Michelle, El-Bachouti, Mohammed, Belvin, Robert, and Houston, Ann. Ontonotes release 5.0.

Seid Muhie Yimam, Chris Biemann, Richard Eckard de Castilho, and Iryna Gurevych. 2014. Automatic Annotation Suggestions and Custom Annotation Layers in WebAnno. In *Proceedings of 52nd Annual Meeting of the Association for Computational Linguistics: System Demonstrations*, pages 91–96, Baltimore, Maryland. Association for Computational Linguistics.

Seid Muhie Yimam, Iryna Gurevych, Richard Eckart de Castilho, and Chris Biemann. 2013. WebAnno: A flexible, web-based and visually supported system for distributed annotations. In *Proceedings of the 51st Annual Meeting of the Association for Computational Linguistics: System Demonstrations*, pages

1–6, Sofia, Bulgaria. Association for Computational Linguistics.

Sina Zarrieß, Julian Hough, Casey Kennington, Ramesh Manuvinakurike, David DeVault, Raquel Fernández, and David Schlangen. 2016. PentoRef: A corpus of spoken references in task-oriented dialogues. In *Proceedings of the Tenth International Conference on Language Resources and Evaluation (LREC'16)*, pages 125–131, Portorož, Slovenia. European Language Resources Association (ELRA).

Amir Zeldes. 2017. The GUM corpus: Creating multilayer resources in the classroom. *Language Resources and Evaluation*, 51(3):581–612.

9 Appendix

Figure 5 shows the multi-layer annotations in WebAnno. It shows segment annotations, the annotated features grammatical role, thematic role and referential form of the referential expressions referring to an animated referent as well as referential chains of coreferential referents. The translation of the example illustrated in figure 5 is as follows:
We looked around depressed.
Tschick said that we would never get gasoline, and I suggested that we simply open the next car with the tennis ball.
"Way too busy," said Tschick.
"Let's just wait until it's less busy."

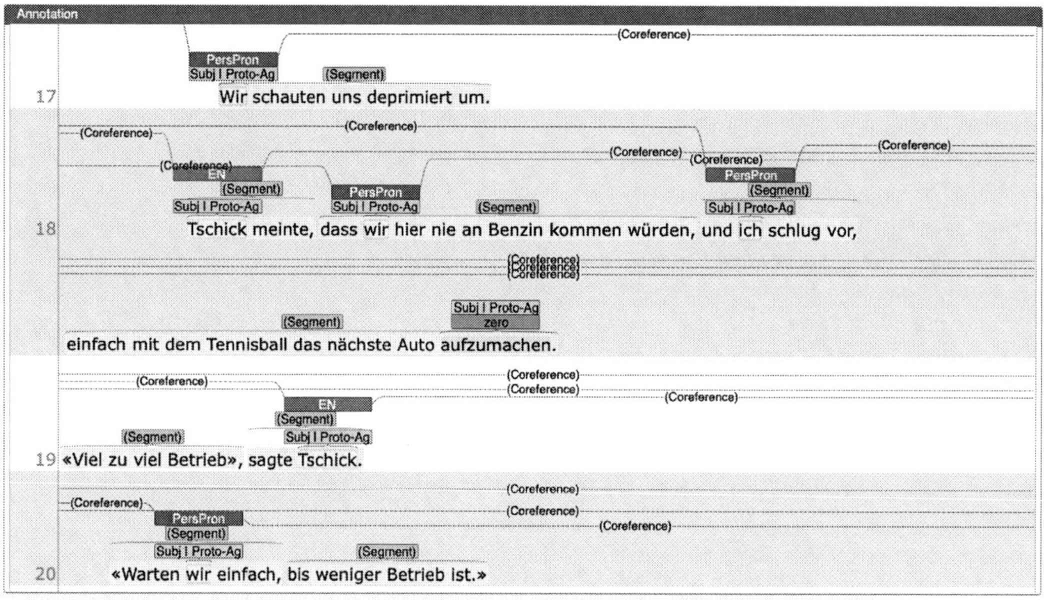

Figure 5: Screenshot of the annotation window of Webanno.

Crowdsourcing on Sensitive Data with Privacy-Preserving Text Rewriting

Nina Mouhammad[a], **Johannes Daxenberger**[b], **Benjamin Schiller**[b] and **Ivan Habernal**[c]
[a]DIPF, Leibniz Institute for Research and Information in Education,
[b]summetix GmbH, [c] Trustworthy Human Language Technologies,
Department of Computer Science, Technical University of Darmstadt
[a]n.mouhammad@dipf.de, [b]{schiller,daxenberger}@summetix.com,
[c] ivan.habernal@tu-darmstadt.de

Abstract

Most tasks in NLP require labeled data. Data labeling is often done on crowdsourcing platforms due to scalability reasons. However, publishing data on public platforms can only be done if no privacy-relevant information is included. Textual data often contains sensitive information like person names or locations. In this work, we investigate how removing personally identifiable information (PII) as well as applying differential privacy (DP) rewriting can enable text with privacy-relevant information to be used for crowdsourcing. We find that DP-rewriting before crowdsourcing can preserve privacy while still leading to good label quality for certain tasks and data. PII-removal led to good label quality in all examined tasks, however, there are no privacy guarantees given.

1 Introduction

For supervised NLP tasks, large amounts of labeled data are needed. In many cases, only unlabeled data is available and labeling is then performed via crowdsourcing/crowdworking platforms like Amazon Mechanical Turk (AMT). These crowdworking platforms are used because they provide a time-efficient way to obtain labels for unlabeled data, making the annotation task easily scalable.

However, data should only be published on crowdsourcing platforms if it contains no privacy-relevant information. Unfortunately, it is not always obvious what is privacy relevant and what is not (Narayanan et al., 2012). As a consequence, most textual datasets cannot be annotated on crowdworking platforms if the privacy of affected persons contained in the data needs to be respected.

A common practice is to automatically replace personally identifiable information (PII) in a text. However, not all privacy-relevant information is contained in PII (Narayanan et al., 2012) and the automatic detection of PII does not work perfectly. Therefore, PII-removal alone is no guarantee that privacy is preserved.

An approach that can actually give privacy guarantees is differential privacy (DP). DP offers formal mathematical guarantees for privacy-preserving data publishing, which has most recently also been applied to textual data (Igamberdiev et al., 2022; Krishna et al., 2021; Bo et al., 2021). The benefit of using differential privacy is that it is possible to set an upper boundary for privacy risks. Therefore, one exactly knows how large the privacy risk is and can set it to a sufficiently low level when using DP.

In this work, we want to explore different privacy preservation techniques for textual data in the context of crowdsourcing. We do this by performing crowdsourcing on data which has been modified by using DP rewriting, PII-removal, or a combination of both. We show that there is a tradeoff between privacy and utility (label quality) when deciding for one of these methods, how this tradeoff is expressed and how it depends on the chosen task and data. Furthermore, we provide recommendations which task properties might lead to the most desirable results.

2 Related work

Privacy leakages can have harmful consequences for individuals. Therefore, privacy protection is regulated by law in some parts of the world, e.g., by the GDPR in Europe (European Commission, 2016) or the HIPAA Act (Centers for Medicare & Medicaid Services, 1996) for medical data in the US. Unfortunately, it is impossible to fully prevent the risk of privacy leakages. Therefore, the ultimate goal is to reduce this risk.

A common practice to reduce the risk of privacy leakages in textual data is to automatically detect and replace personally identifiable information (e.g. Ge et al., 2020; Pilán et al., 2022; Eder et al., 2020). This approach is called PII-removal in the following. However, there are two problems with PII-removal. First, without PII-labeled training data, in most cases named entity recognition or

Proceedings of the 17th Linguistic Annotation Workshop (LAW-XVII), pages 73–84
July 13, 2023 ©2023 Association for Computational Linguistics

regular expressions are used for PII-removal (Ge et al., 2020; Pilán et al., 2022; Eder et al., 2020). This narrows down which kind of PII can be detected. Second, there is no possibility to quantify the remaining privacy risk. Additionally, when using PII-removal the privacy risk is not equally distributed, but often higher for e.g. structurally discriminated parts of the population. Named entity recognition, which is often the basis for PII-removal, is for example better in identifying names commonly given to white people than names commonly given to black, Hispanic or Muslim people (Mishra et al., 2020). Similar problems have been found with commonly female names compared to commonly male names (Mehrabi et al., 2020).

Differential privacy (DP) solves the problem of estimating privacy risks and distributes the privacy risk more equally. It is a mathematical concept, supposed to enable sharing datasets containing private information without giving away this private information (Dwork and Roth, 2014). It has recently been applied in NLP for rewriting texts in a differentially private way (Krishna et al., 2021; Bo et al., 2021; Igamberdiev et al., 2022). The basic idea of 'local' differential privacy rewriting for textual data is to add noise to each data point. As a result, the probability of distinguishing data belonging to one individual from data of any other individual in the dataset is bounded.

Furthermore, we can quantify the amount of differential privacy provided by defining how much two data points are allowed to differ after we added noise to their data. This is commonly done by using the privacy budget $\varepsilon \in \mathbf{R}^+$. However, in (ϵ, δ)-DP this is not a clean cut but we allow the privacy budget ϵ to be overstepped in δ of all data points. A randomized algorithm $M : X- > Z$ is considered as fulfilling (ε, δ)-DP iff for every data point $x, y \in X$ and every possible output $z \in Z$ the following condition holds:

$$Pr[M(x) = z] \leq \exp(\varepsilon) * Pr[M(y) = z] + \delta$$

with $Pr[.]$ being the probability, either defined as a density or a probability mass function.

3 Data

Three corpora were used for the experiments: ATIS (Tur et al., 2010), SNIPS (Coucke et al., 2018) and TripAdvisor (TA) (Li et al., 2013). The ATIS corpus consists of transcriptions of flight information requests and the task is to classify them based on their intent. There are different versions of the ATIS corpus available, we use it in the form provided by Tur et al. (2010). SNIPS (Coucke et al., 2018) is an intent classification dataset as well and consists of instructions for voice assistants. TripAdvisor (Li et al., 2013) (TA) contains hotel reviews. We use only the titles of these hotel reviews because the full review texts were too long.

We chose those datasets based on multiple criteria. First, we had some task-specific criteria. The task should be relevant in real-world use cases, it should not require previous knowledge and it should be simple and quick to solve. Second, we had some text-specific criteria. The texts should contain privacy relevant information, it should be in clear and generally understood language and the text snippets should be short. Furthermore, all datasets should have high-quality gold labels so that we could compare the labels obtained in our experiments with these gold labels. Finally, these datasets have been used in related works on privacy-preserving text rewriting.

To simplify the tasks further, we reduced all of them to binary labelling tasks. This means we chose one class per dataset (e.g. "Airfare" for ATIS) and defined the task as deciding whether a given data point belonged to that class or not. So for the ATIS corpus we then had the two classes "Airfare" and "Not Airfare", for SNIPS we had "Add to playlist" and "Not Add to playlist" and for TripAdvisor we had the classes "Positive" and "Not Positive". For simplification reasons we will call the classes "Airfare", "Add to playlist" and "Positive" the *target classes* in the following, while we will call "Not Airfare", "Not Add to playlist" and "Not Positive" the *not target classes*.

Furthermore, we only included data points which consisted of less than 200 characters for the crowdsourcing, but still used the longer texts for the DP pretraining in order to have enough pretraining data. An overview of the properties of all corpora in the modified versions used in this work can be found in Table 1. Additionally, example sentences are shown in Table 2. More details on the corpora will be explained in more detail in the following.

The ATIS corpus consists of audio recordings of flight information requests and the task is to classify them based on their intent. The privacy-relevant information contained are the information on e.g. when people want to fly, where to and where from which allows us to e.g guess their location

corpus	data points		avg. length	
	target	rest	target	rest
ATIS	403	4100	67.91	66.77
SNIPS	1936	11681	48.24	46.33
TA	19663	9974	181.48	298.96

Table 1: Number of data points ("data points") and average number of characters per data point ("avg length" per corpus in our modified version of the corpora. "target" stands for "target class" and "rest"" for all data points not belonging to the target class.

at specific times. We chose "Airfare" as the target class. An example for the class "Airfare" is the request "cheapest airfare from tacoma to orlando". While requests like "what flights are available from pitsburgh to baltimore on thursday morning", or "what is the arrival time in san francisco for the 755 am flight leaving washington?" do not belong to the target class. There are different versions of the ATIS corpus available, we use it in the form provided by Tur et al. (2010).

SNIPS (Coucke et al., 2018) is an intent classification dataset as well, but instead of flight information requests, it consists of instructions for voice assistants. Those requests contain information about e.g. favorite restaurants, places and persons. We chose the intent category "Add to Playlist" as target class. An example for the class "Add to Playlist" is "add The Crowd to corinne's acoustic soul playlist", while examples for data points that do not belong to the target class are "Play a chant by Mj Cole" or "Book a restaurant in El Salvador for 10 people."

TripAdvisor (Li et al., 2013) is a corpus consisting of hotel reviews from the platform TripAdvisor. Each review consists of a written text as well as additional information, like for example a star based rating. We defined the task as deciding whether a given review title indicates that a review is "Positive" or "Not Positive". The reviews contain information about where the reviewers stayed and when as well as, in some cases, names and personal information about the hotel's staff. An example for the class "Positive" is "Best Hotel in Philly" while "Bugs and terrible housekeeping" is an example for "Not Positive".
The reviews with ratings around three stars often contain positive and negative sentiment. To make the task simpler, we therefore excluded reviews with ratings of two, three and four stars.

4 Model

PII-removal The PII-removal is based on regular expressions and on spacy (Honnibal et al., 2020) which we used for named entity recognition and part of speech tagging. With spacy, we detected names of persons, locations, dates and times. Those were then replaced with the strings "<NAME>", "<LOCATION>", "<DATE>" and "<TIME>". Additionally, we used regular expressions, to replace other personal information like mail addresses and phone numbers.

DP-rewriting For DP-rewriting we used the work of Igamberdiev et al. (2022). They provide an open-source framework for DP rewriting with a trainable model based on the idea behind ADePT (Krishna et al., 2021). This model consists of an auto-encoder which is pretrained first to learn how to compress texts. Afterwards, the texts to be rewritten are transformed into a compressed version, noise according to either a Gaussian or Laplacian distribution is added and then the text is reconstructed based on this vector. We used Gaussian noise and set $\delta = 1 * 10^{-4}$, as this turned out to be the most privacy-preserving setting providing basic utility. For ϵ, different values were used in different experiments. We state which value has been used when explaining each of the experiments. Furthermore, we did not append the class labels (as proposed in (Krishna et al., 2021)), because usually class labels are only crowdsourced if there are none yet.

For each corpus, we split the data into three different subsets, one for pretraining, one for validation of the pretraining and one that will be rewritten for the crowdsourcing. Based on this, we created six differently pretrained models. For each corpus, we had one model pretrained with the unchanged pretraining data and one pretrained with the pretraining data after PII were replaced.

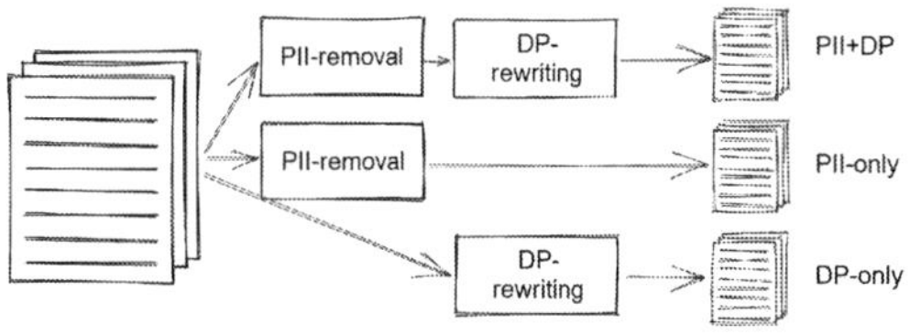

Figure 1: We used three different rewriting pipelines: PII-only, DP-only and PII + DP. They are depicted here.

Rewriting pipelines We created three different

	target class	not target class
ATIS	cheapest airfare from tacoma to orlando	what flights are available from pitsburgh to baltimore on thursday morning
	show me all the one way fares from tacoma to montreal	what is the arrival time in san francisco for the 755 am flight leaving washington?
SNIPS	add The Crowd to corinne's acoustic soul playlist	Book a restaurant in El Salvador for 10 people.
	add this track to krystal's piano 100	Play a chant by Mj Cole
TA	AMAZING Concierge Staff/Eric Sofield is the best	Avoid lower floors... especially room 202
	Best Hotel in Philly	Bugs and terrible housekeeping

Table 2: Examples per corpus and class.

rewriting pipelines so that we can compare the two chosen rewriting methods and the combination of them. For each rewriting method, there is one pipeline where only this rewriting method is applied to privatize the data (PII-only and DP-only). Furthermore, there is one pipeline where we first perform PII-removal and then DP-rewriting (PII + DP). They are visualized in Figure 1. After the data has been rewritten in different ways, we requested annotations based on our binary labeling task on Amazon Mechanical Turk. An example HIT can be found in the Appendix C. All crowdworkers were from the US. Therefore, the payment per HIT was calculated based on the US minimal wage in order to guarantee fair payment.

5 Results

PII-only vs. DP-only vs. PII + DP First, we wanted to explore general differences between the three rewriting pipelines. Therefore, we run the data through all pipelines and requested annotations from 5 crowdworkers per pipeline and data point. For the DP-rewriting in DP-only and PII + DP we set $\epsilon = 10000$. This is a very high choice for ϵ. However, it was the smallest value which ensured that the resulting text still had some very basic utility.

After the annotation, we aggregated the individual annotations per data point by using MACE (Hovy et al., 2013) with a threshold of 1. Then we compared these aggregated labels to the original gold labels by calculating F1-scores (see Table 3).

PII-only performed best for all corpora regarding the F1-score. Furthermore, DP-only led to better F1-scores than PII + DP. However, this depicts only the performance regarding gold label quality.

Pipeline	ATIS	SNIPS	TA
PII + DP	0.377	0.828	0.588
DP-only	0.549	0.935	0.698
PII-only	**0.949**	**0.991**	**0.932**

Table 3: F1-scores of the original gold labels compared to the labels obtained in our experiments. The highest value per column is indicated in bold. Differences per row were statistically significant with $\alpha = 0.05$ for all values.

Regarding privacy, it is the other way around. This will be discussed in more detail in Section 6.

Apart from this, in Table 3 we can see that there are differences between the corpora, especially regarding DP-rewriting. For the SNIPS corpus, the DP-rewriting had a far smaller negative effect on the F1-scores than on the TA corpus or even the ATIS corpus.

The effect of ϵ In DP-rewriting, the ϵ-parameter is the most important parameter, because it represents the privacy guarantee. A high value stands for high privacy risks. To investigate the effects of this ϵ-parameter, we reran the DP-only pipeline in a slightly modified way. We set $\epsilon = 3333$ and requested annotations from three different crowdworkers per pipeline and data point. Then, again, we aggregated the annotations per pipeline and data point by using MACE (Hovy et al., 2013) and calculated the F1-scores in comparison to the original gold labels.

We compared the F1-scores to the F1-scores of the data rewritten with $\epsilon = 10000$. To guarantee a fair comparison, we only used 3 annotations per data point as well and reaggregated them with

MACE (see Table 4). For all corpora, the lower ϵ resulted in statistically significantly lower F1-scores. With the lower ϵ, the performance difference between SNIPS and the other corpora decreased.

Multiple rewritten versions While lower ϵ values increase privacy, they decrease the utility drastically. But what if we rewrite multiple times with the same ϵ, but different random seeds and then aggregate the crowdsourced annotations? Can the differently added noise be counterbalanced by this so that utility is overall increased?

For each data point, we created two other versions rewritten with DP-only and $\epsilon = 3333$. Then we requested three annotations per version from crowdworkers and aggregated the annotations per data point over all versions. This time, we could not use MACE (Hovy et al., 2013) to aggregate the data, because for using MACE the annotations need to be independent when conditioned on the true labels. However, in our case, they are only independent when conditioned on the true labels and the corresponding rewritten version. Therefore, we could only use MACE to aggregate the annotations per version and aggregated the results of this by using majority voting. The whole process is illustrated in Figure 2.

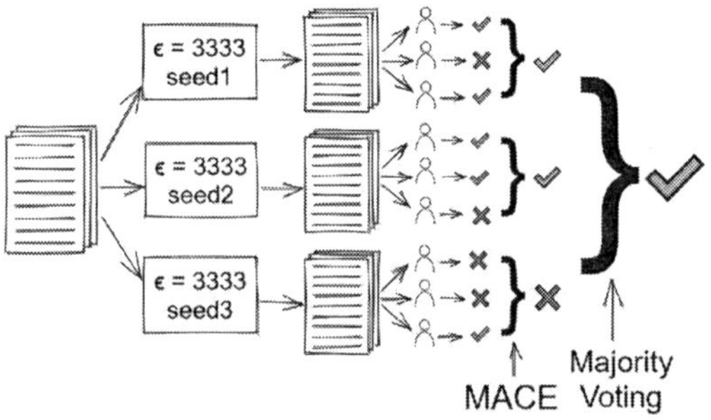

Figure 2: Process of generating multiple differently rewritten versions and aggregating their annotations.

Again, we calculated F1-scores between our aggregated labels and the original gold labels. The results, as well as a comparison to the previous results, can be found in Table 4. Interestingly, using multiple differently rewritten versions did not increase, but decreased the F1-scores for all corpora except SNIPS.

We explored different aggregation methods. They can be divided into two types: two-step-aggregation and one-step-aggregation. The two-step-aggregation methods consist of two steps: In the first, there is an aggregation per rewritten version and in the second step, these aggregations are aggregated again. The aggregation we used for Table 4 and illustrated in Figure 2 is a two-step aggregation method with MACE as the first step and majority voting as the second step. In the one-step-aggregation methods, all annotations of all versions are aggregated in one single step with one aggregation technique.

Corpus	$\epsilon = 3333$	multiple versions	$\epsilon = 10000$
ATIS	0.229	0.180	**0.517**
SNIPS	0.519	0.519	**0.920**
TA	0.426	0.350	**0.687**

Table 4: F1-scores of the same data rewritten with DP-only and different values for ϵ. The highest value per row is highlighted in bold.

The aggregation methods were chosen based on commonly occurring problems in our experiments. In general, it was very noticeable, that there were far more cases where data points that belong to the target class were not recognized as belonging to the target class than the other way around. Therefore, we created a threshold-based aggregation method for this. It is a one-step-aggregation method and the idea is, that the target class is chosen if more than x annotations of one data point are target class annotations. So if we have a threshold of x = 3 and a data point with four target class annotations and five non-target class annotations, the aggregated label will be the target class label. If there were only three target class annotations and six non-target class annotations, the aggregated label would be the non-target class annotation. This method will be abbreviated as tx in the following, where x is replaced with the used threshold.

Based on that threshold idea, we also created a two-step-aggregation method where first, annotations per version were aggregated with MACE and afterwards the aggregated labels were aggregated with a threshold of 0. This method will be abbreviated as MACE_t0. Furthermore, we tried plain majority voting in a one-step-aggregation (MV), majority voting in a two-step-aggregation (MV_MV) and the previously discussed two-step-aggregation with MACE and majority voting (MACE_MV).

Per aggregation method, we calculated the F1-Scores of the resulting labels and the original gold labels (see Table 5). The methods which do not take into consideration that target class data points

Aggregation	ATIS	SNIPS	TA
MV	0.050	0.297	0.260
t0	**0.448**	**0.799**	**0.638**
t1	0.368	0.730	0.581
t2	0.322	0.648	0.503
MV_MV	0.078	0.313	0.269
MACE_MV	0.180	0.519	0.350
MACE_t0	0.431	0.777	0.604

Table 5: Comparison of different aggregation methods for the annotations of multiple rewritten versions. The highest value per column is highlighted in bold.

Corpus	Gold	DP-only
ATIS	29.41%	13.10%
SNIPS	50.00%	42.64%
TA	50.00%	36.86%

Table 6: Percentage of data points in the crowdsourcing set labeled as target class according to the original gold labels ("Gold") and according to the labels gained by crowdsourcing after using DP-only with $\epsilon = 10000$ ("DP-only").

have been mislabeled more often than non-target class points give the worst results. The methods taking this point into consideration lead to a lot better F1-scores. The most extreme method, t0, in which a data point is labeled as target class if only one crowdworker annotated one version as target class, lead to the best F1-scores.

6 Discussion

Corpus differences The negative effect on the utility of DP-rewriting in our experiments has been corpus dependent. In the following, we will explore reasons for this.

As already discussed before, the lower F1-scores can mainly be traced back to data points which belong to the target class but have not been recognized as belonging to the target class. While this problem exists for all corpora, it is least prominent for SNIPS, see Table 6.

To explore potential reasons for the indifference of target class non-recognition, we will use a concept we call *indicator words*. Indicator words are words which do not appear equally often in the target class and the non-target class data. For example, for ATIS the target class is "Airfare", meaning that all requests asking about prices for flights belong to

Corpus	Version	Target	Rest
ATIS	original	232	21
	DP-only	104	24
SNIPS	original	520	2
	DP-only	596	6
TA	original	5	142
	DP-only	48	118

Table 7: Distribution of indicator words for the target class (ATIS and SNIPS) or the non target class (TA) before and after DP-only.

that class. Words that therefore often occur in the target class, but not in the non-target class data are "fare", "airfare", "cost", etc. While it is not possible to correctly identify the class based on only these indicator words in all cases, they are helpful signals in many cases and therefore a useful approximation to explore the indifference in the class recognition further. The used indicator words per class can be found in the appendix A.

For the work at hand, we did not use a structured approach to discover indicator words as we did not expect this phenomenon to have such an impact in the first place. However, while retracing misclassifications in the SNIPS and ATIS data sets, we realized that the task was so easy that only by looking at one of the indicator words, we could guess the class correctly in most cases. We then noticed that, especially for ATIS, most of these indicator words were gone after the DP-rewriting. Therefore, we took a closer look at this phenomenon.

For ATIS and TA, the usefulness of indicator words has been substantially decreased by the DP-rewriting, as we can see in Table 7. Based on the given tasks, indicator words indicate the affiliation to the target class (like in ATIS and SNIPS) or the affiliation to the non-target class (like in TA). After DP-rewriting, we see that in ATIS the target class indicator words occurred only half as often in target class texts as before, while this was not the case in non-target class texts. In TA, the non-target class indicator words appeared less often in the non-target class texts but more often in the target class texts than before. In both cases, the difference between the target class and the non-target class, as approximated by indicator words has been decreased. For SNIPS, however, no such clear effect could be observed.

This assimilation of both classes according to the indicator words in ATIS and TA, but not in SNIPS is due to the relative uncommonness of these indicator words. The basic idea of the version of DP we use is that uncommonness in the dataset is correlated with the probability of being removed. Therefore, uncommon words have a higher probability of being removed than common words. For SNIPS, we had only two indicator words and they occurred 522 times in the original dataset. For ATIS, we had six different indicator words and all of them only occurred 253 times. This is even more extreme in TA, where we used basically all negatively connoted words as indicator words and nevertheless there were only 147 of them in the original corpus. This relative uncommonness of the indicator words in ATIS and TA is the reason why they have often been replaced during DP-rewriting.

However, based on this argumentation, the F1-score as well as the difference between the classes regarding the indicator words should have been higher for ATIS than for TA. Why is this not the case? It can probably be traced back to the pretraining data. For ATIS, the original dataset was very small and imbalanced. Therefore, only 4.28% of the pretraining data (compared to 29.41% of the crowdsourcing data) has been from the target class. This further reduced the uncommonness of the indicator words, especially in comparison to TA where 50% of the pretraining data came from the target class.

Another important factor is the amount of difference between the two classes. If the target class and the non-target class are very similar, changing one word might already change the class. If they are very different, a change of one word does not affect which class a text belongs to. An illustration of the class differences per corpus in the form of wordclouds can be found in the appendix B.

For SNIPS, the indicator words “add” and “playlist” are very prominent in the target class, but not in the non-target class. For ATIS, the used words in the two classes are less different. Furthermore, in ATIS relatively small changes can cause a class change. The sentence “How much is the cheapest flight from Pittsburgh to Baltimore?” belongs to the class “Airfare”, while “What is the cheapest flight from Pittsburgh to Baltimore?” does not belong to the class “Airfare” because the answer to this question would not be a price. There are many more examples like this in ATIS, but not in SNIPS.

For TA, there is less difference between the used words per class than for SNIPS. Additionally, there are also cases where changing one word changes the whole class. For example “Best hotel in Philly” could be changed to “Worst hotel in Philly” and would then belong to the other class. However, there are fewer cases like this in TA than in ATIS.

Corpus	Random	IW	DP-only
ATIS	0.369^-	0.881^+	0.549
SNIPS	0.5^-	0.895	0.935
TA	0.5^-	0.674	0.698

Table 8: F1-Scores for a random classifier ("Random") compared to a classifier based on the indicator words ("IW") and DP-only."+" means that the baseline performed statistically significantly better than DP-only and "-" means that it performed statistically significantly worse than DP-only, both with $\alpha = 0.05$

All in all, there are multiple reasons explaining the corpus differences. First, the balance in the pretraining data is important, especially for very small corpora. Second, the diversity of the corpus, in relation to the corpus size affects the utility. And third, the difference between classes influences how often class distinctions will be removed.

Comparison to baselines Previously we argued that the indicator words were helpful signals for identifying the class of a given text snippet. This leads to the question of how helpful they are exactly and how well a classification based on only the indicator words would perform compared to the manual labeling of the DP-only data. Therefore, we built a baseline classifier using only the indicator words as well as a random classifier and let them label the data. The results can be found in Table 8.

While the F1-scores of the DP-only annotations were significantly better than random annotations for all corpora, the indicator words baseline performed comparably well to DP-only for SNIPS and TA and significantly better than DP-only on the ATIS corpus. These findings, again, underline that the performance of DP is very corpus dependent and that more research on this topic is needed.

Privacy versus utility When comparing PII-removal and DP-rewriting, we saw that the F1-scores approximating the utility have been far better when using PII-removal than when using DP-rewriting. However, this is not the case for privacy. We will discuss this further in the following.

In general, we know that one of the key points of

DP-rewriting is that we can control the privacy risk, while in PII-removal there are no privacy guarantees. By setting the ϵ value in DP-rewriting, we can essentially set an upper boundary for the probability of a privacy leakage. For PII-removal, there are no guarantees at all. If we want to ensure that there are no privacy leakages, we would need to check every rewritten text for potential privacy leakages. Of course, this is unfeasible for larger datasets. Therefore, in practice, one would try to improve the PII-removal as much as possible and then hope that there are no privacy leakages, without knowing how high the risk for such a leakage exactly is.

We will discuss what this means for our data in the following. For this, we will look at how many words of the input text have been changed or replaced. Of course, changing the wording is required but not sufficient to guarantee privacy. However, measuring the exact level of privacy preservation is hard and looking at the number of changed and replaced words is enough to give us a rough impression of how this minimal requirement was fulfilled on our data.

The heatmap in Figure 3 shows the results of this analysis per corpus and rewriting method. For a better understanding of this heatmap, we will explain one row as an example. The first row represents the PII-only version of the ATIS corpus. The value of the first column ("0") is 5.6%. This means, that for 5.6% of all data points of the ATIS corpus, zero ("0") words of the original sentence have been replaced or changed during PII-removal. So all words of the original sentence were copied into the PII-only version. In the next column ("1"), the value is 14%, which means for 14% of all data points of the ATIS corpus there is one word of the original sentence which has been changed or replaced during PII-removal. It continues like this for the next few columns. Then there is a column called "7 - 11", which is an aggregated column. The value 2.9% tells us that for 2.9% of all data points of the ATIS corpus between seven and eleven words of the original sentence have been replaced in the PII-only version of that sentence. The following columns are to be understood the same way.

In general, we see that with PII-only fewer words have been replaced than with DP-only. Especially for the SNIPS and TA data, there were many sentences which have not been changed at all (SNIPS: 48.1%, TA: 36.3%). Privacy preservation completely failed for these data points. Additionally, the amount of sentences where only a few words have been changed is also quite high when using PII-only. The privacy preservation to expect from those few changes might also be quite low. Therefore, the minimal requirement for privacy preservation, to change and/or replace words, has been fulfilled far better by DP-only than by PII-only.

However, there is one exception, where PII-only did not work that badly regarding privacy preservation. In the ATIS corpus, we see that in general a lot more words have been replaced by PII-only than in the other corpora. This is due to the fact that there are many easy-to-detect and therefore easy-to-replace PIIs in ATIS. Locations, dates and times can be detected quite well and ATIS is full of locations, dates and times. In SNIPS and TA, there are in general fewer of these easy-to-detect PII and additionally, the often uncommon sentence structures in SNIPS and TA make it harder to detect them. Therefore, PII-only was able to detect and therefore replace more PIIs in the ATIS corpus than in the SNIPS and TA corpora.

Nevertheless, there were also a noticeable number of examples in which PII-only failed in the ATIS corpus. For example, the original sentence "what flights from indianapolis to memphis" has been changed to "what flights from <LOCATION> to memphis" by PII-only. Obviously, "memphis" has not been recognized as a location. There are more examples like this. While one could try to further improve the PII-removal, as discussed before, there is no way to know how well privacy is preserved if you do not either have data in which all PII are labeled or manually check all texts.

All in all, we see that the performance of PII-only regarding privacy preservation is very domain specific. In general, PII-only replaces fewer words than DP-only. Furthermore, with DP-only one can set the upper bound for the probability of a privacy leakage, while with PII-only you do not have any guarantees.

7 Conclusion and future work

In this work, we explored the effects of applying different privacy-preserving rewriting methods on textual data used for crowdsourcing. We compared PII-removal and DP-rewriting as well as a combination of both regarding utility and privacy.

PII-removal turned out to be a simple-to-implement approach that affects the utility least. However, there are no privacy guarantees given.

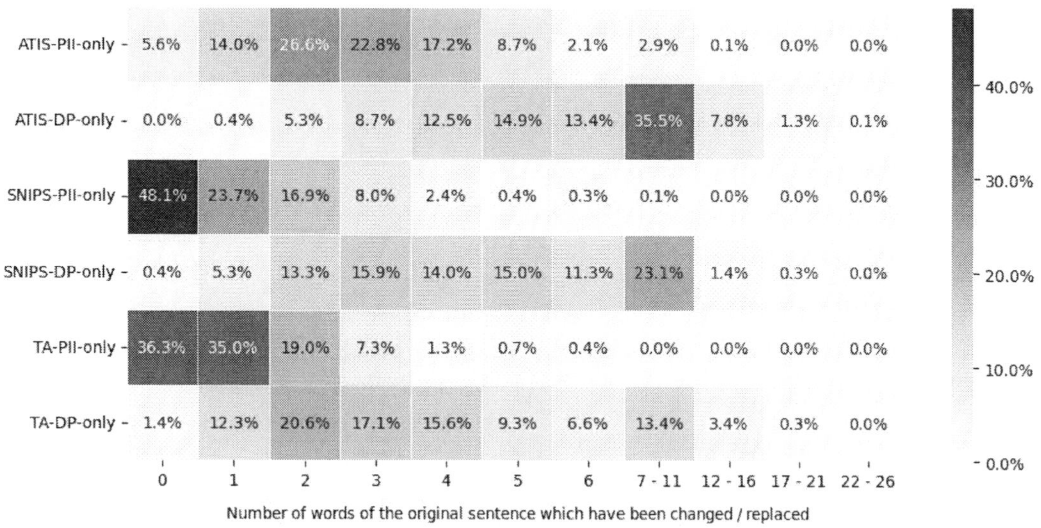

	0	1	2	3	4	5	6	7 - 11	12 - 16	17 - 21	22 - 26
ATIS-PII-only	5.6%	14.0%	26.6%	22.8%	17.2%	8.7%	2.1%	2.9%	0.1%	0.0%	0.0%
ATIS-DP-only	0.0%	0.4%	5.3%	8.7%	12.5%	14.9%	13.4%	35.5%	7.8%	1.3%	0.1%
SNIPS-PII-only	48.1%	23.7%	16.9%	8.0%	2.4%	0.4%	0.3%	0.1%	0.0%	0.0%	0.0%
SNIPS-DP-only	0.4%	5.3%	13.3%	15.9%	14.0%	15.0%	11.3%	23.1%	1.4%	0.3%	0.0%
TA-PII-only	36.3%	35.0%	19.0%	7.3%	1.3%	0.7%	0.4%	0.0%	0.0%	0.0%	0.0%
TA-DP-only	1.4%	12.3%	20.6%	17.1%	15.6%	9.3%	6.6%	13.4%	3.4%	0.3%	0.0%

Figure 3: Distribution of the number of data points by the number of words from the original sentence that have been changed / replaced. E.g. 48.0% in SNIPS-PII-only and 0 means that for 48.0% of the data points of the SNIPS corpus the PII-only version contains the same words as the original sentence. Attention: look at the x-axis closely. There is a single column for each of the values from zero to six. Starting at value seven, we summed up the fractions for five values per column.

DP-rewriting decreases the utility while at the same time giving privacy guarantees and decreasing the risk of privacy leakages. The utility decrease is highly dependent on the type of task and data. Nevertheless, even when applying high ϵ-values for DP rewriting to ensure utility, the privacy of the persons whose data we use can be protected better than with only removing PII.

Therefore, based on our findings, we can give the following recommendations when using DP-rewriting. First, it is important to ensure that the pretraining data has an appropriate size based on the corpus and task. The higher the similarity between classes as well as the diversity in sentence structures and wording of the corpus is, the more pretraining data is needed. Second, pretraining data should in the best case be balanced. This decreases the probability that class differences are not removed. And third, the texts to be rewritten should be as short as possible. Shorter original texts lead to a lower utility loss in the DP-rewriting step in our experiments.

For deciding between DP-rewriting and PII-removal, the properties of the data as well as the needed level of privacy should be taken into consideration. In some cases, DP-rewriting can not be used, because the utility loss would be too high. If both approaches seem possible, DP-rewriting should be preferred if privacy guarantees are needed. If privacy, however, plays only a subordinate role and utility is more important, PII-removal might be the better choice, especially if the privacy risk can mainly be traced back to easy-to-detect PIIs.

Future work should focus on overcoming the current shortcomings of current DP text rewriting approaches, namely the need to use very high values for ϵ which results in very low privacy guarantees.

Limitations and ethical impact

Regarding the corpora, important limitations are that we only requested annotations for three corpora of which at least two had quite simple tasks. With only three corpora there is not that much diversity in the selected corpora so that generalizing our results to other corpora is harder. Therefore, we originally aimed to experiment with more corpora. However, DP-rewriting did not work well enough for half of the originally chosen corpora, therefore we needed to exclude them. While the low number of corpora was one problem, another problem was that the selected corpora and their corresponding tasks were mostly quite simple. We were able to identify a very small set of what we called indicator words for ATIS and SNIPS and a larger set of indicator words for TripAdvisor. Probably, automatic labeling dependent on these indicator words might have already worked quite well. We suggest to carry out the discovery of indicator words with a structured approach in future work, e.g. using chi-squared tests.

Apart from the used corpora, also the used rewriting methods cause some limitations. First, we needed to use very high ϵ-values for DP-rewriting in order to guarantee some basic utility. However, these high ϵ-values might not guarantee sufficient privacy in most scenarios. Second, also PII-removal causes some limitations. PII-removal is very domain dependent. Therefore, transferring our results to other domains is difficult. Furthermore, PII-removal did not work that well for SNIPS and TripAdvisor, since in these corpora PII were harder to identify. Therefore, there were many cases where PII-removal just resulted in copying the input text which resulted in zero privacy.

Acknowledgements

This project was partly supported by the National Research Center for Applied Cybersecurity ATHENE and by the PrivaLingo research grant (Hessisches Ministerium des Innern und für Sport). The independent research group TrustHLT is supported by the Hessian Ministry of Higher Education, Research, Science and the Arts.

References

Haohan Bo, Steven H. H. Ding, Benjamin C. M. Fung, and Farkhund Iqbal. 2021. ER-AE: Differentially Private Text Generation for Authorship Anonymization. In *Proceedings of the 2021 Conference of the North American Chapter of the Association for Computational Linguistics: Human Language Technologies*, pages 3997–4007, Online. Association for Computational Linguistics.

Centers for Medicare & Medicaid Services. 1996. The health insurance portability and accountability act of 1996 (HIPAA). Online at http://www.cms.hhs.gov/hipaa/.

Alice Coucke, Alaa Saade, Adrien Ball, Théodore Bluche, Alexandre Caulier, David Leroy, Clément Doumouro, Thibault Gisselbrecht, Francesco Caltagirone, Thibaut Lavril, Maël Primet, and Joseph Dureau. 2018. Snips Voice Platform: An embedded Spoken Language Understanding system for private-by-design voice interfaces. *arXiv:1805.10190 [cs]*.

Cynthia Dwork and Aaron Roth. 2014. The Algorithmic Foundations of Differential Privacy. *Foundations and Trends® in Theoretical Computer Science*, 9(3–4):211–407.

Elisabeth Eder, Ulrike Krieg-Holz, and Udo Hahn. 2020. CodE alltag 2.0 - A pseudonymized german-language email corpus. In *Proceedings of the 12th Language Resources and Evaluation Conference, LREC 2020, Marseille, France, May 11-16, 2020*, pages 4466–4477. European Language Resources Association.

European Commission. 2016. Regulation (EU) 2016/679 of the European Parliament and of the Council of 27 April 2016 on the protection of natural persons with regard to the processing of personal data and on the free movement of such data, and repealing Directive 95/46/EC (General Data Protection Regulation) (Text with EEA relevance).

Suyu Ge, Fangzhao Wu, Chuhan Wu, Tao Qi, Yongfeng Huang, and Xing Xie. 2020. FedNER: Privacy-preserving medical named entity recognition with federated learning. *CoRR*, abs/2003.09288.

Matthew Honnibal, Ines Montani, Sofie Van Landeghem, and Adriane Boyd. 2020. spaCy: Industrial-strength natural language processing in python, 2020.

Dirk Hovy, Taylor Berg-Kirkpatrick, Ashish Vaswani, and Eduard H. Hovy. 2013. Learning whom to trust with MACE. In *Human Language Technologies: Conference of the North American Chapter of the Association of Computational Linguistics, Proceedings, June 9-14, 2013, Westin Peachtree Plaza Hotel, Atlanta, Georgia, USA*, pages 1120–1130. The Association for Computational Linguistics.

Clayton J. Hutto and Eric Gilbert. 2014. VADER: A parsimonious rule-based model for sentiment analysis of social media text. In *Proceedings of the Eighth International Conference on Weblogs and Social Media, ICWSM 2014, Ann Arbor, Michigan, USA, June 1-4, 2014*. The AAAI Press.

Timour Igamberdiev, Thomas Arnold, and Ivan Habernal. 2022. DP-rewrite: Towards reproducibility and transparency in differentially private text rewriting. In *Proceedings of the 29th International Conference on Computational Linguistics*, pages 2927–2933, Gyeongju, Republic of Korea. International Committee on Computational Linguistics.

Satyapriya Krishna, Rahul Gupta, and Christophe Dupuy. 2021. ADePT: Auto-encoder based Differentially Private Text Transformation. In *Proceedings of the 16th Conference of the European Chapter of the Association for Computational Linguistics: Main Volume, EACL 2021, Online, April 19 - 23, 2021*, pages 2435–2439. Association for Computational Linguistics.

Jiwei Li, Myle Ott, and Claire Cardie. 2013. Identifying manipulated offerings on review portals. In *Proceedings of the 2013 Conference on Empirical Methods in Natural Language Processing*, pages 1933–1942, Seattle, Washington, USA. Association for Computational Linguistics.

Ninareh Mehrabi, Thamme Gowda, Fred Morstatter, Nanyun Peng, and Aram Galstyan. 2020. Man is to person as woman is to location: Measuring gender bias in named entity recognition. In *Proceedings of the 31st ACM Conference on Hypertext and Social Media*, HT '20, page 231–232, New York, NY, USA. Association for Computing Machinery.

Shubhanshu Mishra, Sijun He, and Luca Belli. 2020. Assessing demographic bias in named entity recognition. *CoRR*, abs/2008.03415.

Arvind Narayanan, Hristo Paskov, Neil Zhenqiang Gong, John Bethencourt, Emil Stefanov, Eui Chul Richard Shin, and Dawn Song. 2012. On the feasibility of internet-scale author identification. In *2012 IEEE Symposium on Security and Privacy*, pages 300–314.

Ildikó Pilán, Pierre Lison, Lilja Øvrelid, Anthi Papadopoulou, David Sánchez, and Montserrat Batet. 2022. The Text Anonymization Benchmark (TAB): A Dedicated Corpus and Evaluation Framework for Text Anonymization. *Computational Linguistics*, 48(4):1053–1101.

Gokhan Tur, Dilek Hakkani-Tur, and Larry Heck. 2010. What is left to be understood in ATIS? In *2010 IEEE Spoken Language Technology Workshop*, pages 19–24, Berkeley, CA, USA. IEEE.

A Used Indicator Words

For ATIS and SNIPS, we used a manually curated list of indicator words. These words indicate that a text belongs to the target class. All used indicator words / phrases can be seen in Table 9.

Corpus	target class indicator words
ATIS	airfare, cheapest, cost, fare, fares, how much, price
SNIPS	add, playlist

Table 9: Used target class indicator words for ATIS and SNIPS.

For TripAdvisor, the absence of negatively connoted words indicated that a review was positive. We used the lexicon of VADER (Hutto and Gilbert, 2014) to determine negatively connoted words. We only included words where the sentiment was clear. Therefore, we excluded all words where adding or subtracting the doubled standard deviation from the polarity value would change the polarity.

B Wordclouds

To illustrate the differences between target and non-target class, we created wordclouds containing the 25 most common non-stopwords per class (see Figures 4, 5, 6). For this, we used the PII-only version of the datasets, because then e.g. locations were summarized by "location" and the wordclouds are easier to grasp.

Figure 4: Wordcloud for the 25 most common non-stopword words per class of the PII-only version of SNIPS

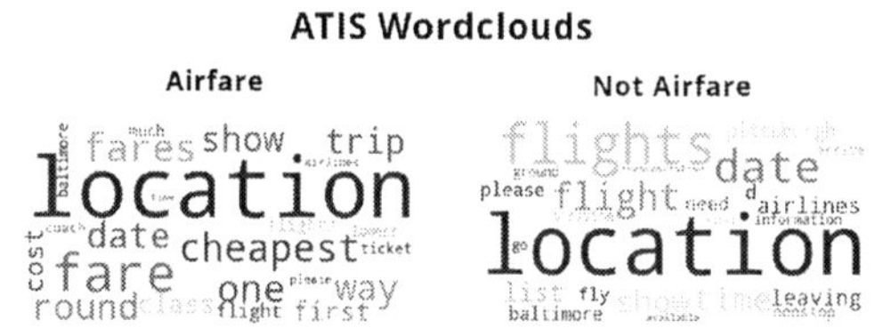

Figure 5: Wordcloud for the 25 most common non-stopword words per class of the PII-only version of ATIS

Figure 6: Wordcloud for the 25 most common non-stopword words per class of the PII-only version of TA

C Example HIT

Read each of the following hotel review titles and decide if the corresponding review is Positive or **Not Positive**. Please be aware that the review titles may contain grammatical errors. As long as they are comprehensible, please ignore grammatical mistakes. Furthermore, the review titles might contain placeholders like <location>, <date>, etc., please understand them as if a real location, date, etc. would have been named instead.

Guidelines:

- Mark a review title as Positive if it is reviewing the hotel in a positive way (e.g. "*very nice hotel*")
- Mark a review title as Positive if the review title is positive, but the hotel is not explicitly mentioned (e.g. "*had a great time*")
- Mark a review title as **Not Positive** if it is negative or neutral about the hotel (e.g. "*would not recommend*")
- Mark a review title as **Not Positive** if it is undistinguishable if a review is positive or not (e .g "*my wife and I spent several days at the hotel*")
- Please make sure that your personal opinion about the topic does not affect your decision

After marking all ten sentences, press the submit button to finish this HIT.

Sentence	Positive	**Not Positive**
a very bad experience	○	○
good location - with dirty hotel stay staff heading heading typical bon leaving fruit a.m. a.m.	○	○
simply stay stay any comfort . comfort comfort of service of price a restaurants	○	○
exceptional hotel & staff	○	○
best place in a silver bar , , , bar . a.m. entrust entrust entrust mansions mansions entrust	○	○
stay reason i cancelled	○	○
a wonderful central 5 5 star hotel	○	○
the magnolia pacific lax	○	○
wonderful chicago hotel ! loved it to	○	○
decription with hotwire	○	○

Feedback on this HIT is highly appreciated.

Submit

Figure 7: Screenshot of an example HIT. This HIT is filled with DP-only data of the TA corpus.

Extending an Event-type Ontology: Adding Verbs and Classes Using Fine-tuned LLMs Suggestions

Jana Straková and **Eva Fučíková** and **Jan Hajič** and **Zdeňka Urešová**
Institute of Formal and Applied Linguistics, Faculty of Mathematics and Physics
Charles University, Prague, Czech Republic
{strakova,fucikova,hajic,uresova}@ufal.mff.cuni.cz

Abstract

In this project, we have investigated the use of advanced machine learning methods, specifically fine-tuned large language models, for pre-annotating data for a lexical extension task, namely adding descriptive words (verbs) to an existing (but incomplete, as of yet) ontology of event types. Several research questions have been focused on, from the investigation of a possible heuristics to provide at least hints to annotators which verbs to include and which are outside the current version of the ontology, to the possible use of the automatic scores to help the annotators to be more efficient in finding a threshold for identifying verbs that cannot be assigned to any existing class and therefore they are to be used as seeds for a new class. We have also carefully examined the correlation of the automatic scores with the human annotation. While the correlation turned out to be strong, its influence on the annotation proper is modest due to its near linearity, even though the mere fact of such pre-annotation leads to relatively short annotation times.

1 Introduction

Annotation of highly-dimensional, voluminous data is expensive, time-consuming and in addition, in case of deep-niche domains, depending on expertly trained specialists, such as linguists or medical experts. Therefore it may be advantageous to organize, prioritize and provide suggestions to guide further annotation efforts efficiently. Especially in a situation with a rich, constantly growing set of classes, such as it is the case with ontologies.

Specifically, given an already partially labeled set of examples with yet unfinished set of classes, classifier based on large language models (LLMs) can be leveraged to navigate the landscape of possible annotations.

Our showcase is an event-type ontology, the SynSemClass 4.0 (Uresova et al., 2022), populated with synonymous verbs denoting events or states. The set of events is currently dynamically evolving and encompasses classes in English, Czech, German and Spanish, so far limited to verbs.

As any ontological resource is never complete, we have investigated various methods to facilitate efficient extension of such ontologies in two ways: adding classes for greater coverage on new texts, and adding verbs to existing classes to allow for more accurate human understanding of the classes in the ontology for a particular form of the given class expression.

We suggest to achieve these by

1. examining examples with consistently low class affiliation scores across a large corpus as potential candidates for new classes;

2. on the other side of the spectrum, examining high-certainty decisions of a supervised classifier to locate highly-affiliated lemmas to a particular class, corresponding to "low-hanging fruit" for a quick manual review and confirmation of the inclusion of the lemma into the suggested class.

In all cases, classifier prediction serves as guidance and the annotators are briefed to consider the suggestions as election votes. The final decision is always the annotator's, who can accept or dismiss the suggestions.

The organization of this paper is as follows: Sect. 2 introduces the SynSemClass v4 ontology and the current state of annotations. Sect. 3 describes the fine-tuned LLM classifier used to generate the annotation suggestions. Sect. 4 describes the manual annotations post-processing. Results are presented in Sect. 5 and discussed in Section 6. Finally, we conclude in Sect. 7.

We release the source code at `https://github.com/strakova/synsemclass_ml`.

Proceedings of the 17th Linguistic Annotation Workshop (LAW-XVII), pages 85–95
July 13, 2023 ©2023 Association for Computational Linguistics

2 The Ontology

In our experiments, we have used the Czech part of the SynSemClass 4.0[1] (Uresova et al., 2022) in which contextually-based synonymous verbs in various languages are classified into multilingual synonym classes according to the semantic and syntactic properties they display. There is no specific model or lexicographic theory behind building the database. However, from the linguistic point of view, the notion of synonymy used is based on the "loose" definition of synonymy by Lyons and Jackson (Lyons, 1968; Jackson, 1988), or alternatively and very closely, on both "near-synonyms" and "partial synonyms" as defined by Lyons (Lyons, 1995; Cruse, 2000) or "plesionyms" as defined by Cruse (Cruse, 1986).[2]

From the ontological point of view, the classes are meant to reflect different event types (concepts) and collect various information about the possible forms of expression of the event type in language.

The following main basic features are distinguished in SynSemClass (Fig. 1) (Uresova et al., 2022):

- The **name of each multilingual class** stands for a single concept (e.g., of *accelerating*)[3] and corresponds to the verb that represents the prototypical sense in each of the languages included: class member (CM) *abuse* for English, *zneužívat* for Czech, and *missbrauchen* for German. So far, SynSemClass focuses on verbal synonyms since they carry the key syntactic-semantic information for language understanding.[4]

- Each class is also provided with a brief language-dependent general **class definition**, which characterizes the meaning, or concept

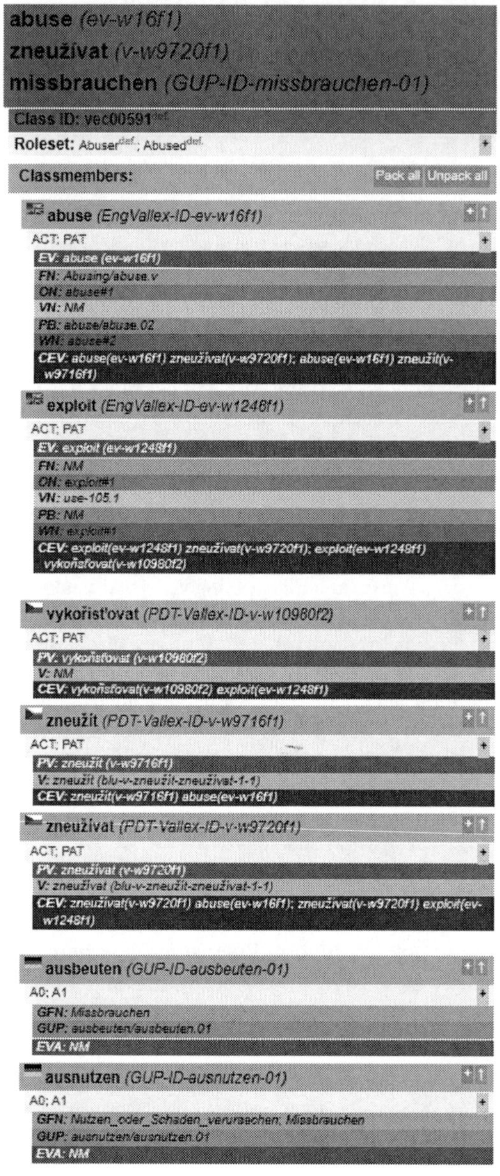

Figure 1: SynSemClass example entry as presented on its public access website, Class ID: vec00591 (simplified)

[1] https://lindat.mff.cuni.cz/repository/xmlui/handle/11234/1-4746

[2] The "loose" definition of synonymy covers synonyms that fulfil some of the conditions stipulated for synonymy in the strictest sense but not all and does not work with the "absolute" synonymy covering the total identity of meaning. The "partial synonymy" is defined (Lyons, 1995) as a relationship holding between two lexemes that satisfy the criterion of identity of meaning, but do not meet all the conditions of absolute synonymy. The "near-synonymy" (Lyons, 1995) and "plesionyms" (Cruse, 1986) is defined as "expressions that are more or less similar, but not identical, in meaning".

[3] This is different from the commonly used term of "semantic classes of verbs" as represented, for example, in VerbNet, where the class is defined much more broadly – such as for all verbs of movement.

[4] As described in detail in (Urešová et al., 2019, 2018a,c,b).

of the class, i.e. the meaning of all synonymous verbs contained in it. The class is viewed as a substitute for an ontology unit representing a single concept, similar to the treatment of WordNet synsets in (McCrae et al., 2014).

- For each class, SynSemClass also provides a fixed set (called **"Roleset"** (RS)) of defined "situational participants" (called "semantic roles" (SR)) that are common for all the members (the individual verb senses) of a particular class. The RS is mapped to the valency frame of the individual synonymous verbs securing for each synonymous verb to be characterized both meaning-wise (SR) and structurally (valency arguments). For example, the class `vec00591` *abuse*, as concept of "abusing", has two semantic roles, `Abuser` and `Abused` (Fig. 1). Every role in SynSemClass is provided with a brief language-dependent general **role definition** as well as every class. While the SRs resemble FrameNet's "Frame Elements" (and sometimes borrow their names from there), it should be pointed out that there is one fundamental difference: the SRs used in SynSemClass aim at being defined across the ontology, and not per class (as they would be if we follow the "per frame" approach used in FrameNet).

- Each individual language-dependent synonymous verb included in a given class is called **Class Member** and for each new CM to be added, it must be possible, in the prototypical case, to create a mapping between its syntactic arguments and the roles in that class' RoleSet; see the example in our web-based lexicon (Fig. 1).[5] Each CM of one class is denoted by a verb lemma and the valency frame ID which, roughly speaking, represents the particular verb sense.

- Each CM is further linked to one, or more existing online lexical resources for each language to support, e.g., comparative studies, or any other possible research in the community. In SynSemClass (SSC), there exist **links** to e.g., Vallex[6] for Czech, FrameNet[7] and VerbNet[8] for English, E-VALBU[9] for German, AnCora[10] for Spanish. Each Class Member is exemplified by instances of real texts (and their translations to English) extracted from translated or parallel corpora. Specifically, data is extracted from the Prague Czech-English Dependency Corpus (PCEDT)[11] for Czech-English, from the Paracrawl corpus[12] for German-English and from the XSRL dataset[13] for Spanish-English.

SynSemClass 4.0 includes 1200 classes (885 active after merging or deleting) with 8169 Class Members. All classes are annotated in Czech and English, 60 of them have also German annotation. Spanish is not included in the web version but is under construction (Fernández-Alcaina et al., 2023).

3 Generating Annotation Suggestions with Fine-tuned LLM Classifier

3.1 Data

The Czech part of the SynSemClass ontology[14] yielded 12045 example sentences with 3313 unique verbs (lemmas) manually annotated in 965 classes.[15] We have split the data randomly in proportion 80/10/10 in a stratified train/dev/test split,[16] resulting in 9635/1205/1205 train/dev/test examples.

Our input is a list of 3389 completely new, unseen verbs (lemmas) and our motivation is to differentiate:

- verbs consistently poorly classified as class members of any of the existing classes, i.e., possible candidates for establishing new classes,

[5]The public web version is available at `https://lindat.cz/services/SynSemClass40/SynSemClass40.html`

[6]`https://hdl.handle.net/11234/1-3524`

[7]`https://framenet.icsi.berkeley.edu/fndrupal/`

[8]`https://uvi.colorado.edu/andhttp://verbs.colorado.edu/verbnet/index.html`

[9]`https://grammis.ids-mannheim.de/verbvalenz`

[10]`http://clic.ub.edu/corpus/es/ancoraverb_es`

[11]`https://ufal.mff.cuni.cz/pcedt2.0/en/index.html`

[12]`https://opus.nlpl.eu/ParaCrawl.php`

[13]`https://catalog.ldc.upenn.edu/LDC2021T09`

[14]SynSemClass 4.0 with additions annotated since the last v4.0 release.

[15]We considered only active (not merged, not deleted) classes in the current state of SynSemClass (SSC) annotated since v4.0 release, and naturally, only those classes which are represented with at least one example sentence (to be used as LLM input).

[16]Stratified means forcing the distribution of the target variable, in our case the classes, to be equal among the train/dev/test split.

- verbs highly affiliate to some of the existing classes, i.e., possible candidates for adding them as one of the verbs characterizing an existing class.

To obtain the classification score for each lemma-class pair, we used a large raw corpus of written Czech, the SYN v4 (Křen et al., 2016; Hnátková et al., 2014).[17] Specifically, we used the first 2.753.494 sentences of the corpus, which amounts to exactly 100-th of all its sentences, as classifying the corpus in its entirety (275.349.474 sentences) is above our GPU computation means. The classification took 20 hours on a single NVIDIA A100 GPU with 4 CPU threads.

3.2 Model

Classification tasks on a finalized set of target variables are usually modeled as a probability distribution over K targets (possible outcomes). However, we find ourselves in an untypical situation in which the output target set is not closed yet, which requires a different perspective. If we model the problem as multi-class probability distribution, we will face an out-of-distribution problem concerning verbs which do not belong to any of the classes. We therefore model the problem as K independent binary classifiers, one for each class, of which each predicts the probability of the input belonging to the particular class in question, much like a multi-label problem. Technically, this equals to replacing the output softmax activaction function with the sigmoid activation function and accommodating the loss function accordingly, from sparse categorical cross entropy to sparse binary (focal) cross entropy,[18] while the weights are estimated jointly by fine-tuning one shared large language model.

3.3 Training

Our classifier is a fine-tuned RemBERT (Chung et al., 2021), a rebalanced 559M-parameter mBERT,[19] with sigmoid activation function on the output layer and sparse binary focal cross entropy ($\gamma = 2.0$) to model the target class probabilities independently (see also previous Section 3.2). We trained our model using the Adam optimizer (Kingma and Ba, 2015) with defaults β's and with a batch size of 10. The model was fine-tuned on a single NVIDA A100 GPU, using linear warm-up in the first training epoch (6.66% training steps) from 0 to peak learning rate $1 \cdot 10^{-5}$ and then decaying with a cosine decay schedule (Loshchilov and Hutter, 2017). The model was trained for 15 epochs and we used dropout with probability 0.5. The hyperparameters were tuned on the development set; the model achieved development set accuracy 78.67% and test set accuracy 79.17%.

3.4 Related Work

We are not aware of a similar work using LLMs to classify words (and specifically, verbs) into synonym classes to enrich an existing ontology or lexicon. There are works building such resources from scratch, starting from (Brown et al., 1992) the model and its statistical, unsupervised class hierarchy building algorithm.

The ASFALDA project ("Analyzing Semantics with Frames: Annotation, Lexicon, Discourse and Automation")[20] aims at projecting English FrameNet frames to French also using machine learning but it is a recently started project and there are no published results yet.

The Predicate Matrix project (Lopez de Lacalle et al., 2016) aims at creating a resource similar to SynSemClass, by using similar resources that SynSemClass links to. The entries created automatically are not manually checked (for the most part) and we are not aware of publications describing if there were specific experiments on the comparison of the automatically created entries vs. human annotation.

There is also work on using DNNs (LSTMs specifically) to model lexical ambiguity (Aina et al., 2019), which is relevant for our task, but the method is not related to another existing ontological or lexical resource for training and/or fine/tuning the ML part of the system.

[17] `http://hdl.handle.net/11234/1-1846`

[18] "Focal" stands for focal loss (Lin et al., 2018), which addresses class imbalances in training data by encouraging learning on the sparse set of hard examples (the rare positives in our case, because only one of hundreds of classes is correct) and discouraging learning from a vast majority of easy (negative) examples.

[19] Although BERT (110M parameters) and RemBERT ($\sim$0.5B parameters) are technically considered large language models (LLMs), they certainly rank among the modest language models w.r.t. number of parameters. Quite precisely, they belong to the masked language models (MLMs) family. Our method can however be used with any fine-tuned LLM.

[20] `https://anr.fr/Project-ANR-12-CORD-0023`

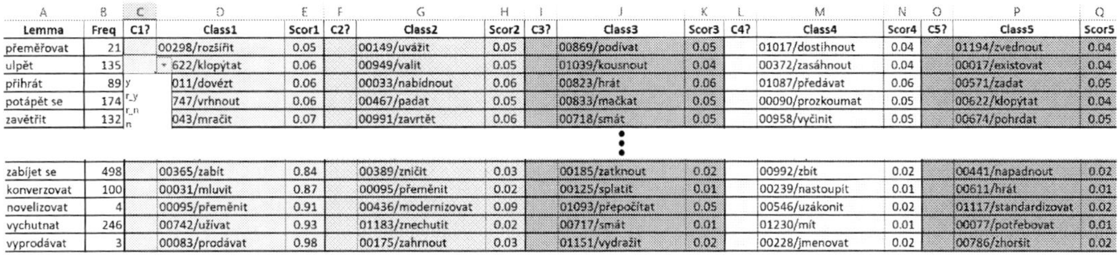

Lemma	Freq	C1?	Class1	Scor1	C2?	Class2	Scor2	C3?	Class3	Scor3	C4?	Class4	Scor4	C5?	Class5	Scor5
přeměřovat	21		00298/rozšířit	0.05		00149/uvážit	0.05		00869/podívat	0.05		01017/dostihnout	0.04		01194/zvednout	0.04
ulpět	135		622/klopýtat	0.06		00949/valit	0.05		01039/kousnout	0.04		00372/zasáhnout	0.04		00017/existovat	0.04
přihrát	89	y	011/dovézt	0.06		00033/nabídnout	0.06		00823/hrát	0.06		01087/předávat	0.06		00571/zadat	0.05
potápět se	174	r_y	747/vrhnout	0.06		00467/padat	0.05		00833/mačkat	0.05		00090/prozkoumat	0.05		00622/klopýtat	0.04
zavětřit	132	r_n n	043/mračit	0.07		00991/zavrtět	0.06		00718/smát	0.05		00958/vyčinit	0.05		00674/pohrdat	0.05
⋮																
zabíjet se	498		00365/zabít	0.84		00389/zničit	0.03		00185/zatknout	0.02		00992/zbít	0.02		00441/napadnout	0.02
konverzovat	100		00031/mluvit	0.87		00095/přeměnit	0.02		00125/splatit	0.01		00239/nastoupit	0.01		00611/hrát	0.01
novelizovat	4		00095/přeměnit	0.91		00436/modernizovat	0.09		01093/přepočítat	0.05		00546/uzákonit	0.02		01117/standardizovat	0.02
vychutnat	246		00742/užívat	0.93		01183/znechutit	0.02		00717/smát	0.01		01230/mít	0.01		00077/potřebovat	0.01
vyprodávat	3		00083/prodávat	0.98		00175/zahrnout	0.03		01151/vydražit	0.02		00228/jmenovat	0.02		00786/zhoršit	0.02

Figure 2: Preprocessed data with 5 suggested classes per lemma, first and last five lines, as presented to the annotators in an Excel spreadsheet (the version with scores shown; cursor (in column C, line 3, 2nd data line) shows the annotation choices)

4 Post-processing with Manual Annotations

4.1 Input Data Preparation

In the output of the automatic classifier, each lemma has been associated with ten highest-scoring classes in which the lemma can potentially be inserted as a class member. The score is thus assigned to each lemma-class pair. These scores are numbers between 0 and 1, but it is not a probability but really just a "score" or a "weight." The smaller the score, the less is the used LLM sure that the verb lemma belongs to the class, and vice versa - the higher the score, the more convinced it is to be added to the class.

The data as received from the classifier (3073 lemmas, with 10 class suggestions and scores for each of them) have been converted to an Excel spreadsheet to be presented to the annotators as follows:

1. For each lemma (line in the resulting file), the first five classes suggested by the classifier with the highest scores as assigned by the classifier have been kept;

2. two disjunct sets of lemmas and their class membership suggestions, with 100 lemmas each, have been randomly selected from the 3073 lemmas scored by the classifier;

3. the two sets (called Set1 and Set2) have been converted to an Excel spreadsheet, keeping frequency information for the lemma, the five highest-scoring class membership suggestions, and the associated scores with each class;

4. in front of each class suggestion, an extra column has been inserted with the four-way list of decisions the annotators will have to make;

5. colors have been used to group all the information pertaining to one lemma-class pair and the decision requested;

6. for each class suggested, a web link has been inserted in its spreadsheet cell, to allow the annotator to get to the class definition and contents (which is available on the web as shown in Fig. 1) by a single click.

Then, each set has been duplicated and in the copy, the scores have been deleted. The four files have then been renamed to contain the annotator abbreviation and the order number (1 for the version without scores, 2 for the version with scores (see Fig. 2), i.e., in a cross-named way for the Set1 and Set2; see Table 1).

Annotator:	A1	A2
1st batch (no scores shown)	Set1	Set2
2nd batch (scores shown)	Set2	Set1

Table 1: Order and Assignment of Data to Annotators

4.2 Experiment Design

The Excel spreadsheets as described in the previous section (Sect. 4.1) have been sent to two annotators in two batches: first, both received the file with five suggestions for each lemma, but no scores. Each thus had 500 decisions to make (100 lemmas × 5 classifier suggestions per lemma) on a four-point scale, 0-3, denoting how strongly they recommend to include the lemma in the suggested class. The "no" decision corresponds to 0, "rather_no" to 1, "rather_yes" to 2, and "yes" to 3. These responses have been provided in the Excel spreadsheet as a fixed list, in order to avoid typos. In the second batch, the annotators received the other 100 lemmas, this time with scores denoting the classifier's view on the strength of the class membership recommendation, for the five classes presented.

In total, there were thus 200 lemmas manually classified twice (by the two annotators), with the classifier scores shown only for half of them to each annotator. No annotator annotated any lemma twice, and they worked independently without consulting each other. The annotators, native speakers of Czech, have been previously trained on the same task (with data coming from a different preprocessing method), so no additional training has been performed. Their pay has been based on hours worked, approx. $8/hour amounting to about 170% of the legal minimal salary valid in 2023 in the Czech Republic.

The order and cross-assignment of the data to the annotators allowed us to measure interannotator agreement and the correlation between the annotators decisions (averaged) and the automatic classifier recommendations. Also, we could compare the speed of annotation with and without the additional clue, namely, the scores suggested by the automatic classifier.

5 Results

This section describes the results obtained as described in Sect. 3 and Sect. 4. For the discussion of the various outputs, see Sect. 6.

5.1 Human Annotation Statistics and IAA

There were 1000 pairs of Czech verb and suggested class in two sets (Set1 and Set2, see Sect. 4.1). The two annotators, A1 and A2, had to decide whether the verb could be a member of the class. Annotators could set 4 values: "yes," "rather_yes," "rather_no" or "no,". Agreement was calculated for only two values, Y and N, to which the four detailed levels of annotation have been mapped in a natural way (specifically, "rather_no" has been mapped to "N" and "rather_yes" to "Y"). The (dis)agreement figures have been counted based on each individual decision as made by the two annotators. The resulting counts are shown in the Tab. 2 and agreement rate and Cohen's κ value in the Tab. 3.

5.2 Human Annotation Time

The annotators have been asked to record the time it took them to annotate the data. Each Set entailed 500 decisions, which took slightly over three hours on average. The detailed breakdown is shown in Tab. 4.

A1\A2	Y	N	Total
Y	129=66+63	43=15+28	172=81+91
N	122=57+65	706=362+444	828=419+409
Total	251=123+128	749=377+372	1000=500+500

Table 2: Annotation statistics: counts shown for the 1000 annotation decisions (500 from Set1, 500 from Set2). Mappings used: y $\rightarrow$ Y, r_y $\rightarrow$ Y, r_n $\rightarrow$ N, n $\rightarrow$ N. Counts are presented in the cells as Total-xy=Set1-xy+Set2-xy, where $x, y \in \{\text{Y, N}\}$.

	IAA	Cohen's κ
All	0.83	0.51
Set1	0.86	0.56
Set2	0.81	0.46

Table 3: Inter-annotator agreement and Cohen's κ between annotators, for the 500 decisions each annotated by both annotators, with the scaled values mapped to Y/N only.

	Batch 1 (no scores)	Batch 2 (with scores)
A1	192	174
A2	210	210
Average	201	192

Table 4: Time of annotation by annotators A1 and A2, in minutes. Batch 1 is Set1 and Set2 without showing the scores assigned by the automatic classifier, Batch 2 shows the scores.

5.3 Correlation between the Scores of the Automatic Classifier and the Human Annotation

To find if there is a relationship between the automatic scores and manually annotated data, we used the Pearson's correlation (Pearson's r) coefficient. Automatic scores and human annotations were found to be moderately correlated ($r(998) = .44$, $p < .001$). A Spearman's correlation was also run to determine the relationship between 1000 automatic scores and human annotations. There was weak to moderate monotonic correlation between automatic scores and human annotations ($\rho = .39$, $n = 1000$, $p < .001$).

We visualize the correlation between the automatic scores assigned to the lemma-class pairs and annotation decisions in Fig. 3; human scores correspond to the annotation scale (3 - yes, 2 - rather_yes, 1 - rather_no and 0 - no) and automatic scores are bucketed (interval size: 0.05) and annotation decisions averaged in each bucket, effectively smoothing out the curve by reducing variance. The Pearson correlation between scores and human

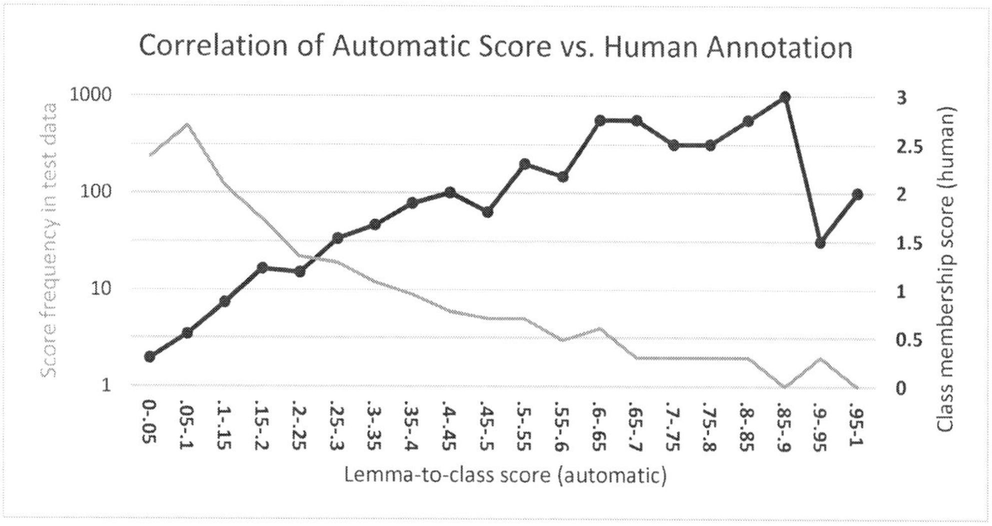

Figure 3: Correlation between the automatic scores assigned to the lemma-class pairs and annotation decisions; human scores correspond to the annotation scale (3 - yes, 2 - rather_yes, 1 - rather_no and 0 - no) and automatic scores are bucketed (interval size: 0.05) and annotation decisions averaged in each bucket. The grey line shows the size of each bucket on a logarithmic scale.

annotations averaged per bucket is $r(18) = .79$ ($p < .001$) and Spearman's ranked correlation is $\rho = .76$ ($n = 20$, $p < .001$).

6 Discussion of Results

It is well known that trained annotators often create high-quality data, needed for many NLP applications, although their services are generally expensive.The experiment described here was designed to answer several questions:

- What is the usual inter-annotator agreement for the human assignment of verbs to classes, using pre-annotated data?
- Can a heuristics be defined to indicate which pre-assigned lemma-class pairs the annotators can trust and to what extent?
- Does the scoring mechanism, which provides scores for each of the lemma-class relation strength, make the annotation more efficient?
- Is the automatic classifier for computing the relation strength between an unknown lemma and an existing class(es), as described in Sect. 3, in any way correlated with the human decisions made by experienced annotators?

As seen from Sect. 5.1 (Tab. 3), the inter-annotator agreement is relatively high (0.83 on average over the two Sets), but the Cohen's kappa κ is low (0.51 on average over the same two Sets annotated). However, the low kappa is caused by the highly skewed distribution of the decisions,[21] the most of which lead to the rejection of the assignment of the lemma to the suggested class, caused mainly by the selection of a fixed number of five suggestions per lemma regardless of the score computed by the classifier. It would be possible - by using more pairs of annotators - to optimally select the number of suggested classes (i.e., most probably between 1 and 5), but it would only be relevant for the current number of classes in the ontology. As the ontology grows, the number of rejections will be different and the optimal number of classes might change.

For the size of the ontology on which it has been tested, the threshold separating the Yes/No decision (with the highest uncertainty being around the average of 0-3, i.e., 1.5) seems to be around 0.3 (see Fig. 3). However, due to the linearity of the correlation (which by itself is a positive result for the classifier–see below), it would still be necessary to provide careful manual inspection results on both sides of the threshold. The same holds for setting any thresholds at the low or high ends of the classifier score scale. In terms of annotation efficiency (providing scores to the annotators vs.

[21] Almost 4:1 - the average number of (mapped) "No" decisions is 788,5 out of 1000.

not providing them), the result is largely negative. A small speedup has been observed only for A1, with A2 consuming the same time for both Sets. The absolute time as recorded by the annotators per lemma (i.e., 5 times the single decisions time, which was $366 \times 60 \div 1000 \approx 22$ sec. for A1 and $420 \div 1000 \approx 25$ sec. for A2) is about two minutes. This is in fact a positive finding which means that the whole set of pre-classified lemmas, as processed by the classifier (3073 lemmas) would be finished within approx. 6000 minutes (100 hours) per annotator, i.e., within 200 hours with double annotation, plus adjudication time.

Finally, the correlation between the automatic classifier and the human annotation is very strong. Of course, the bucketing to the 0.05 interval improves the correlation (see Sect. 5.3), but in any case, it seems that the classifier is able to assign the score denoting the strength of affiliation of the unknown lemma to a class with high correlation to the human annotation decisions.

7 Conclusions and Future Work

As discussed in the previous section (Sect. 6), the strongest result achieved in this study is the correlation between the classifier scoring buckets and the human decisions (Fig. 3, Sect. 5.3). While the scores themselves, when presented to the annotators, do not seem to bring higher efficiency, the selection of the classes and their presentation to the annotators (Sect. 3, Sect. 4.1) result in a reasonable time for the annotation of several thousand previously unseen (unassigned lemmas) to the ontology. Finally, there is no strong heuristics (for the score thresholds) that would allow to assign any unseen words to existing classes automatically – a human post-inspection and annotation is needed across the whole (or almost whole) range of scores as produced by the classifier, given the linear correlation.

In the future, we plan to repeat the experiment for a larger ontology (i.e., test the effort needed for sustainable development and maintenance for such an event-type ontology when it reaches high coverage), possibly with larger LMs or with some additional fine tuning given the large(r) coverage at such future time.

Limitations

We advocate for a moderate and restrained usage of automatic guiding methods and we must advise caution to take the automatic output with a grain of salt, both qualitatively and quantitatively. First, the classifier predictions can fall far from gold labels and should not be considered as such. Second, although measures have been taken to mitigate the out-of-distribution classification problem, one should be aware of the fact that by the very nature of the problem, which is annotation of completely new, possibly out-of-distribution data, the classification predictions are not to be trusted indiscriminately and should subsequently be approved by the annotators. The annotators should be instructed to consider the suggestions as election votes. Furthermore, we should refrain from overly automating the entire annotation process so as to achieve high alignment with the machine learning suggestions, which might lead to trivial and unimaginative annotations from the linguistic perspective. Finally, exhausting the informativeness of the pre-trained (albeit fine-tuned) model might prevent further learning from the annotated data.

Another limitation of the results, or the interpretation of the results, is the fact that the model is trained on an actual state of the ontology. It means that in fact the classifier would have to be retrained after adding a single new class or even a new lemma to an existing class; while in practice it would be OK to process several lemmas at once, it is still a limitation given the non-negligible training and prediction time (20 hours on a single GPU) which cannot be parallelized (see Sect. 3).

In addition, the correlation might decrease and the thresholds shift as the size (and thus coverage) by the ontology grows, since the unseen lemmas will be increasingly rare, with possibly less data available in the LM to reliably estimate the scores. Conversely, for ontologies with much smaller coverage (e.g., for ontologies the development of which has just started) the same shifts in correlation and thresholds are likely.

Finally, the whole experiment has been performed on Czech due to the lower coverage of the ontology than for English, and also in order to explore a morphologically rich language with a high form-to-lemma ratio. Results for other languages might differ.

Ethics Statement

The human subjects used in this study have been experienced, trained annotators who have been in personal contact with the authors, and who have been recruited by a call specifically suited for the experiment and study presented here. The call has been sent to all trained annotators already working with the authors, and volunteers have been asked to respond, on a first-come first-chosen basis. The pay has corresponded to the standard pay for similar annotation tasks taking also the relatively short notice into consideration (for the numbers, see Sect. 4.2). Both annotators were males; this is a possible shortcoming, but there were no female volunteers and from the previous cooperation (with a mixed team of female and male annotators), no differences in the annotation results have been observed.

No personal information has been among the lemmas extracted and used for the preselection. The data for the LLM might have contained it, but it would not show because the experiment and the ontology is currently limited to common verbs which do not describe any personal names or other personal information.

Acknowledgements

The work described herein has been supported by the Grant Agency of the Czech Republic under the EXPRO program as project "LUSyD" (project No. GX20-16819X) and uses resources hosted by the LINDAT/CLARIAH-CZ Research Infrastructure (projects LM2018101 and LM2023062, supported by the Ministry of Education, Youth and Sports of the Czech Republic).

We would like to thank the annotators Petr Kujal and Tomáš Razím for their valuable work and invaluable input, as well as the three anonymous reviewers for their insightful comments.

References

Laura Aina, Kristina Gulordava, and Gemma Boleda. 2019. Putting words in context: LSTM language models and lexical ambiguity. In *Proceedings of the 57th Annual Meeting of the Association for Computational Linguistics*, pages 3342–3348, Florence, Italy. Association for Computational Linguistics.

Peter F. Brown, Vincent J. Della Pietra, Peter V. deSouza, Jenifer C. Lai, and Robert L. Mercer. 1992. Class-based *n*-gram models of natural language. *Computational Linguistics*, 18(4):467–480.

Hyung Won Chung, Thibault Fevry, Henry Tsai, Melvin Johnson, and Sebastian Ruder. 2021. Rethinking embedding coupling in pre-trained language models. In *International Conference on Learning Representations*.

Alan Cruse. 2000. *Meaning in Language. An Introduction to Semantics and Pragmatics*. Oxford University Press. Oxford, UK.

D.Alan Cruse. 1986. *Lexical Semantics*. Cambridge University Press, UK.

Cristina Fernández-Alcaina, Eva Fučíková, and Zdeňka Urešová. 2023. Spanish verbal synonyms in the synsemclass ontology. In *Proceedings of the 21st International Workshop on Treebanks and Linguistic Theories*, pages 10–20, Washington, D.C., USA. Association for Computational Linguistics, Association for Computational Linguistics.

Milena Hnátková, Michal Křen, Pavel Procházka, and Hana Skoumalová. 2014. The SYN-series corpora of written Czech. In *Proceedings of the Ninth International Conference on Language Resources and Evaluation (LREC'14)*, pages 160–164, Reykjavik, Iceland. European Language Resources Association (ELRA).

Howard Jackson. 1988. *Words and Their Meaning*. Routledge.

Diederik P. Kingma and Jimmy Ba. 2015. Adam: A method for stochastic optimization. In *ICLR (Poster), CoRR abs/1412.6980*.

Michal Křen, Václav Cvrček, Tomáš Čapka, Anna Čermáková, Milena Hnátková, Lucie Chlumská, Tomáš Jelínek, Dominika Kováříková, Vladimír Petkevič, Pavel Procházka, Hana Skoumalová, Michal Škrabal, Petr Truneček, Pavel Vondřička, and Adrian Zasina. 2016. SYN v4: large corpus of written czech. LINDAT/CLARIAH-CZ digital library at the Institute of Formal and Applied Linguistics (ÚFAL), Faculty of Mathematics and Physics, Charles University.

Tsung-Yi Lin, Priyal Goyal, Ross Girshick, Kaiming He, and Piotr Dollar. 2018. Focal loss for dense object detection. *IEEE Transactions on Pattern Analysis and Machine Intelligence*, PP:1–1.

Maddalen Lopez de Lacalle, Egoitz Laparra, Itziar Aldabe, and German Rigau. 2016. A multilingual predicate matrix. In *Proceedings of the Tenth International Conference on Language Resources and Evaluation (LREC'16)*, pages 2662–2668, Portorož, Slovenia. European Language Resources Association (ELRA).

Ilya Loshchilov and Frank Hutter. 2017. SGDR: Stochastic gradient descent with warm restarts. In *International Conference on Learning Representations*.

John Lyons. 1968. *Introduction to Theoretical Linguistics*. Cambridge University Press.

John Lyons. 1995. *Linguistic Semantics*. Cambridge University Press.

John P. McCrae, Christiane Fellbaum, and Philipp Cimiano. 2014. Publishing and Linking WordNet using lemon and RDF. In *Proceedings of the 3rd Workshop on Linked Data in Linguistics, colocated with LREC 2014*, Reykjavik, Iceland.

Zdeňka Urešová, Eva Fučíková, Eva Hajičová, and Jan Hajič. 2018a. Creating a Verb Synonym Lexicon Based on a Parallel Corpus. In *Proceedings of the 11th International Conference on Language Resources and Evaluation (LREC'18)*, Miyazaki, Japan. European Language Resources Association (ELRA).

Zdeňka Urešová, Eva Fučíková, Eva Hajičová, and Jan Hajič. 2018b. A Cross-lingual synonym classes lexicon. *Prace Filologiczne*, LXXII:405–418.

Zdeňka Urešová, Eva Fučíková, Eva Hajičová, and Jan Hajič. 2018c. Defining verbal synonyms: between syntax and semantics. In *Proceedings of the 17th International Workshop on Treebanks and Linguistic Theories (TLT 2018), Vol. 155*, Linköping Electronic Conference Proceedings, pages 75–90, Linköping, Sweden. Universitetet i Oslo, Linköping University Electronic Press.

Zdeňka Urešová, Eva Fučíková, Eva Hajičová, and Jan Hajič. 2019. Meaning and Semantic Roles in CzEngClass Lexicon. *Jazykovedný časopis / Journal of Linguistics*, 70(2):403–411.

Zdenka Uresova, Karolina Zaczynska, Peter Bourgonje, Eva Fučíková, Georg Rehm, and Jan Hajic. 2022. Making a semantic event-type ontology multilingual. In *Proceedings of the Thirteenth Language Resources and Evaluation Conference*, pages 1332–1343, Marseille, France. European Language Resources Association.

Appendices

Classifier and Annotation Results

We are providing Supplemental material with the raw classifier file and the human annotation results. The open-source code and the data itself are provided at GitHub (`https://github.com/strakova/synsemclass_ml`). Here, technical description of the supplemental material is provided on top of what has been mentioned in the paper.

Classifier output

The raw output of the classifier, with the 3073 previously unseen (unassigned) lemmas and their classification scores to 10 closest classes, is attached in the Supplemental material file (file `all_buckets_2753494.txt`).

The file contents is structured as follows (each lemma and classifier scores are on a single line):

```
lemma freq-in-data max-score suggested-class-1 score-class-1 ... suggested-class-10 score-class-10
```

where

`lemma`
  is the lemma which has been classified to all the available classes in SynSemClass

`freq-in-data`
  is the frequency of the lemma in the dataset used for building the LM

`max-score`
  is the maximum score (score of the first class in the list)

`suggested-class-n`
  is the ID and name (& Czech sense ID) of the n-th best class assigned to the `lemma` by the classifier

`score-class-n`
  is the score assigned to the (`lemma,suggested-class-n`) pair.

Annotation Results

The annotation results are presented as four Excel Spreadsheets, named `law-Am-n.xlsx`, where `m` is the annotator ID and `n` is the batch number (i.e., the lemmas and classes are identical for `A1-1` and `A2-2` and for `A1-2` and `A2-1`, except for the presence of scores and differing also of course in the assigned `y/r_y/r_n/n` labels by the annotators).

Each Excel file has 100 content lines (100 lemmas and 5 best classes for each as classified by the pre-annotation tool):

`Lemma`
  is the lemma being classified

`Freq`
  is the (informative-only) frequency of the lemma in the training text

`Cn?`
  is the column where the annotators recorded their decisions

`Classn`
  is the ID of the class (clickable)

`Scorn`
  is the score of the lemma-class affiliation by the classifier (in ...-2.xlsx files only)

`AnnotatorComment`
  is an optional annotator's comment.

Temporal and Second Language Influence on Intra-Annotator Agreement and Stability in Hate Speech Labelling

Gavin Abercrombie
Heriot-Watt University
g.abercrombie@hw.ac.uk

Dirk Hovy
Bocconi University
dirk.hovy@unibocconi.it

Vinodkumar Prabhakaran
Google Research
vinodkpg@google.com

Abstract

Much work in natural language processing (NLP) relies on human annotation. The majority of this implicitly assumes that annotator's labels are temporally stable, although the reality is that human judgements are rarely consistent over time.

As a subjective annotation task, hate speech labels depend on annotator's emotional and moral reactions to the language used to convey the message. Studies in Cognitive Science reveal a 'foreign language effect', whereby people take differing moral positions and perceive offensive phrases to be weaker in their second languages. Does this affect annotations as well?

We conduct an experiment to investigate the impacts of (1) time and (2) different language conditions (English and German) on measurements of intra-annotator agreement in a hate speech labelling task. While we do not observe the expected lower stability in the different language condition, we find that overall agreement is significantly lower than is implicitly assumed in annotation tasks, which has important implications for dataset reproducibility in NLP.

1 Introduction

While *inter*-annotator agreement is commonly used in natural language processing (NLP) research to measure annotation *reliability* (how well annotators agree with each other) (Carletta, 1996), *intra*-annotator agreement (the extent to which individuals provide the same responses for the same prompts when asked repeatedly) is rarely reported (Abercrombie et al., 2023).

However, measurements of intra-annotator agreement are essential for NLP datasets as they indicate the consistency of each human annotator and thus the stability of the data they generate (Teufel et al., 1999). Intra-annotator measures can be used to control the quality of the annotation process (e.g. Akhbardeh et al., 2021; Cao et al., 2022; Hengchen and Tahmasebi, 2021) or to assess the difficulty and subjectivity of a particular task (Abercrombie et al., 2023). The field's continuing failure to measure and report intra-annotator agreement, though, suggests that it is implicitly assumed (by omission) that annotators' responses are 100% stable—even when this is intuitively and empirically not the case. In fact, there is widespread evidence from Psychology that the same people often make wildly inconsistent judgments depending on seemingly unrelated factors such as mood, time of day, the weather, or even how well their preferred sports team is performing (Kahneman et al., 2021). Here, we consider the following two aspects:

Time: There is some evidence that annotator inconsistency increases as a function of time (Kiritchenko and Mohammad, 2017; Li et al., 2010). However, in the majority of cases in which intra-annotator agreement *is* reported, repeat annotations are collected in the same session that annotators label the items in the first instance (Abercrombie et al., 2023). In those circumstances, annotators' responses are likely influenced by the recency effects of priming on memory (Vriezen et al., 1995). In this study, we therefore re-examine annotators after substantial temporal intervals of between two and eight weeks.

Language: The kind of language to annotate is likely to affect annotations. Annotating or producing abusive language, such as hateful speech, can be understood as "morally motivated behavior[s] grounded in people's moral values and perceptions of moral violations" (Hoover et al., 2019). However, there is evidence that people take different moral positions when presented with dilemmas in their first or second languages—the '*foreign language effect*' (Costa et al., 2019; Stankovic et al., 2022).

Furthermore, Dewaele (2004) shows that bilingual people perceive the emotional force of swearwords and taboo words to be weaker in their second

Proceedings of the 17th Linguistic Annotation Workshop (LAW-XVII), pages 96–103
July 13, 2023 ©2023 Association for Computational Linguistics

languages, suggesting that they may judge toxic language differently when observed in different languages. We can therefore expect annotators to respond differently to text examples from hateful language datasets that feature moral issues and toxic slurs in their first (L1) or second language (L2). In this work, we investigate the stability of labels produced by bilingual annotators in response to near-identical (i.e., carefully translated) examples presented in both English and German.

We ask the following **Research questions**:

R1: Are annotators' responses **stable over time** when labelling hateful language?

R2: Is label stability lower when repeated annotation items are presented **in a different language** than in the same language?

2 Bilingual hateful speech data

We use the `XHate999` corpus (Glavaš et al., 2020), the test set of which consists of (999) abusive and non-abusive texts that have been translated from English to five other target languages. Translations were made by experts with an emphasis on maintaining the level and nuance of abuse, hatefulness, and aggression present in the texts. We use the English and German language versions of the '*Gao*' hatefulness subset (Gao and Huang, 2017) (the data is originally sourced from three separate datasets). We chose German as it is the most widely-spoken of the target languages, which we expect to expediate annotator recruitment. We chose the '*Gao*' subset as we judged the domain or language and topics of the other two to be somewhat esoteric for primarily Europe-based annotators: Wulczyn et al. (2017) consists of disputes on the content of Wikipedia pages among their authors; and Kumar et al. (2018) is comprised of Hindi-English political discussions. While many examples from the *Gao* subset concern specific events, we expected the subject matter (e.g. the #BlackLivesMatter movement, Israel-Palestine conflict) to be more well-known internationally. The test set comprises 99 items.[1]

3 Experimental Setup

We recruited 30 billingual German (L1) and English (L2) speaking annotators from the Prolific crowdsourcing platform,[2] chosen for its capacity to facilitate longitudinal studies, ethical participant payment policies, and data quality (Peer et al., 2022). We presented the particpants with 96 examples from the test data: 48 in English and 48 in German. With these, we interspersed four items taken from HATECHECK (Röttger et al., 2021), which we used as attention check questions (Abbey and Meloy, 2017), as they were designed to be clearcut examples of hateful language.

We use a 'descriptive dataset paradigm' (Rottger et al., 2022), with annotators provided with minimal instructions to encourage the emergence of subjective perspectives. As such, annotators were presented with the original definition of hateful language from Gao and Huang (2017):

> *We define hateful speech to be language which explicitly or implicitly threatens or demeans a person or a group based upon a facet of their identity such as gender, ethnicity, or sexual orientation.*

We also provided one example each of hateful and non-hateful items taken from the three unused test set items. In order to maintain concentration and to regularly provide the option of withdrawing participation, we split the task into 20 pages with five items to be annotated on each. The instructions, definition, and examples were repeated on each page, and are available in Appendix A.

We made the task available to all German-speakers on the platform that are also fluent in English, as managed by Prolific's in-built participant filtering functions. Based on the findings of Kiritchenko and Mohammad (2017) and Li et al. (2010), we then waited two weeks before opening a second round of the task to the same annotators, filtering by their Prolific identification codes. Here, the annotators were presented with a further four attention check items and the 96 items from the test set. Again, half of these were in English and half in German. 50% were presented in the same language as in round one, and 50% in the alternative language. To control for order-effect bias, we split participants into two groups, and presented the items to each in a different order, also shuffling within-item response options (*hateful/not hateful*).

Following the principles of *perspectivist* data practices (Abercrombie et al. (2022); Cabitza et al. (2023)) and the recommendations of Prabhakaran et al. (2021), full set of collected labels is available at `https://github.com/`

[1]Available at `https://github.com/codogogo/xhate/tree/main/test/en`

[2]`https://www.prolific.co/`

GavinAbercrombie/XHateStability. For reproducibility, we include the question item order and full instructions. We also provide a full data statement and annotator demographic information in Appendix B.

4 Analysis

Of the 28 participants that completed both rounds of annotation, 22 labelled all attention check items in agreement with the original HATECHECK labels, and we report results for these annotators only.[3]

4.1 Reliability

To evaluate reliability, we report Fleiss' *kappa*, which can account for multiple annotators to show overall agreement, as well as average pair-wised Cohen's *kappa* and raw percentage agreement for completeness. We also evaluate agreement between the labels most commonly assigned by our participants (majority vote) with the original labels collected by Gao and Huang (2017).

	Billingual participants			**Majority vote *v.* Original labels**	
	Fleiss	Cohen	%	Cohen	%
All	0.28	0.29	64.2	0.44	71.7
EN	0.29	0.29	64.6	0.48	74.0
DE	0.27	0.27	63.4	0.40	68.9

Table 1: Reliability as measured by inter-annotator agreement (Fleiss' and Cohen's κ and raw percentage agreement). Cohen's κ and % are calculated pairwise.

As shown in Table 1, the participants do not agree with each other to a high degree. *Kappa* scores for agreement between them are below 0.3, suggesting that the task is highly subjective.

Aggregating their responses by majority vote and comparing to the original labels, produces similarly modest agreement ($\kappa < 0.5$). This somewhat calls into question the reliability of the original *Gao* labels, on which the authors reported almost perfect agreement between two annotators. All agreement measurements are poorer still on the German examples, which also casts some doubt on the feasability/validity of translating text and keeping the labels applied to items annotated in a different language, as was the case for XHate999.

[3]Although, agreement scores are, in fact, comparable when including all annotators, to ensure quality, we do not include those that did not pass all attention checks.

4.2 Stability

As we argue in section 1, most dataset developers implicitly assume annotator consistency to be 100% stable. We therefore use raw percentage agreement as the primary metric for stability and examine deviations from full agreement. For completeness, we also report Cohen's *kappa* (Table 2).

		κ	%
All items		0.49	74.5
Same language	All	0.44	72.3
	EN	0.43	71.6
	DE	0.45	72.9
Different language	All	0.53	76.9
	EN→DE	0.54	77.2
	DE→EN	0.53	76.6

Table 2: Stability as measured by intra-annotator agreement (Cohen's κ and raw percentage agreement).

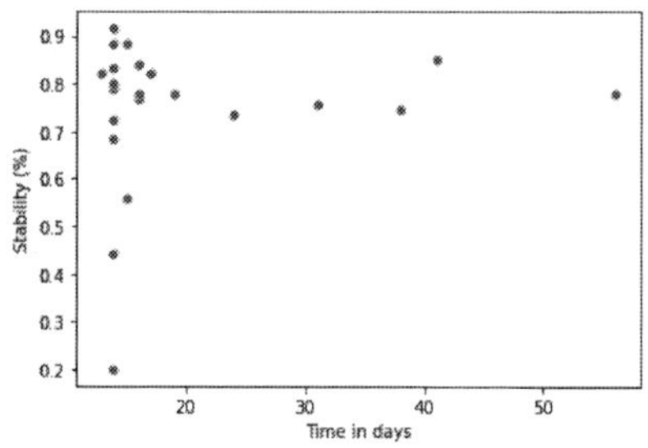

Figure 1: Stability of individual annotators over time measured by raw percentage intra annotator agreement.

Overall stability over time At under 75% and $\kappa = 0.49$, stability is low overall.[4] This is considerably worse than the only reported intra-annotator agreement we are aware of on a similar task: $\kappa = 0.89$ on abusive language detection (Cercas Curry et al., 2021), where those annotations were made by experts under higher levels of supervision.

Consistency varies considerably among the annotators ($max = 91.6\%$, $min = 20.0\%$, $\mu = 74.5\%$, $\sigma = 15.7\%$), with even the most consistent falling considerably below 100%. After the minimum two week interval, we do not see a pattern of further deterioration in intra-annotator agreement, as shown (from limited datapoints) in Figure 1. This lends further support to the findings of Kiritchenko and Mohammad (2017) and Li et al. (2010), that this interval may be sufficient for re-annotation.

[4]Stability of the majority vote on each item is somewhat more stable: $\kappa = 0.77$, 88.4%

Feature	Examples	Prevalence (%)	Reliability	Stability
Length in tokens (normalized [0, 1])	—	100.0	−0.02	−0.05
Different language	—	50.0	n/a	0.03
Identity terms	*feminists, Juden*	37.9	0.06	0.07
Named entities	*Africa, Hillary*	33.7	0.00	0.03
Nature terms	*alligator, Lagune*	21.1	0.01	0.04
Offensive terms	*Blödmann, scumbags*	12.6	0.00	0.03
Political terms	*feminists, Liberalismus*	32.6	0.03	−0.01
Quote	—	11.6	0.06	0.03
Original label = *hateful*	—	41.4	0.00	0.00

Table 3: Regression coefficients for hand-crafted features with example terms and their prevalence in the data by percentage of text examples they feature in. The dependent variables are *reliability* and *stability*.

Language effect We do not see the expected difference between items re-annotated in the different conditions. Indeed, stability is actually slightly higher in the different language condition. However, this effect is not uniform across the participants, with around a third (8 of the 22) exhibiting more consistency for the same language condition.

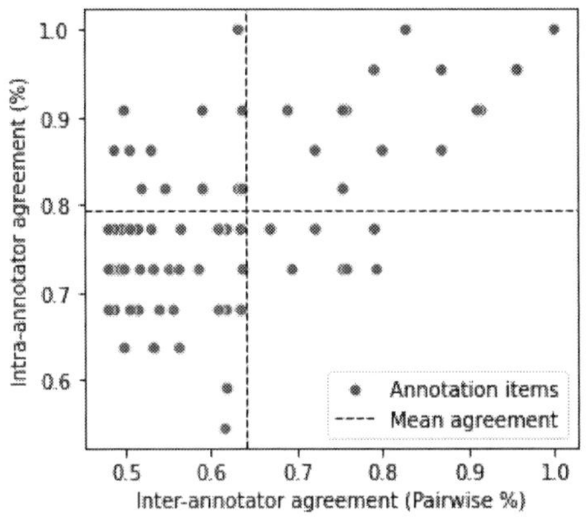

Figure 2: Inter- and intra-annotator agreement by-item.

4.3 By-item agreement

Intuitively, some texts are more straightforward than others to label. We would therefore expect to see variation in intra- (and inter-) annotator agreement between annotation items, and this is indeed the case. Pearson's r for the correlation between raw inter- and intra-annotator agreement is 0.62, indicating a fairly strong, but not perfect relationship between reliability and stability. Following Abercrombie et al. (2023), we can interpret the items furthest towards the top-right of Figure 2 as *straightforward*, those near the top-left as *subjective*, and those in the bottom-left as *ambiguous/difficult*.

To investigate which factors contribute to stability and reliability in this data, we manually labelled each item with a set of hand-crafted features designed to capture the linguistic and world knowledge that intuitively seem necessary to infer whether these texts are hateful. These include the ratio variable *length* in tokens, as well as binary variables based on: the original label assigned to the item; inclusion of quotations; and presence of certain unigram tokens (such as identity terms) in the text. We ran regression analyses on these features with the by-item inter- and intra-annotator agreement scores as the dependent variables.

Table 3 shows the coefficients of each hand-crafted feature for both reliability and stability. None of the features are strongly indicative of either, although several, such as *identity terms* and *text length* do have slightly larger coefficients (positive or negative) than the different language condition. Ultimately, the data sample is not large enough to surface the feature patterns indicative of the ambiguities that provoke annotator disagreements and inconsistencies.

5 Conclusion

While attention has been paid to noise in linguistic annotations caused by factors such as subjectivity and ambiguity (e.g. Aroyo and Welty, 2015; Basile et al., 2021; Prabhakaran et al., 2021), and the level and quality of annotator attention (e.g. Hovy et al., 2013; Klie et al., 2023), this study represents an initial foray into a hitherto understudied aspect of the human labeling work that most NLP research and systems are built upon: intra-annotator agreement and label stability. For this hateful language annotation task, we find that label stability is far lower than common practise implicitly implies (**R1**).

In this study, presenting the items for re-annotation in a different language does not lead to lower stability overall (**R2**), with L1 German speakers no less consistent—and often more so—than when re-annotating items in the same language. We suspect that our data sample of 96 items is too small to disentangle any L2 effects from other factors that may affect label stability. However, we see lower agreement overall (inter- and intra-) on the German language items, suggesting that the translation process adds some ambiguity. Future work should investigate the linguistic and cultural factors that influence annotators' judgments more closely and—on a larger set of items.

Despite the limitations of our study, we have shown that annotator stability, along with reliability, is necessary for the repeatability and reproducibility of annotation studies (Teufel et al., 1999). We therefore recommend that researchers and practitioners measure and report *intra-* (as well as *inter-*) annotator agreement scores for the labeled NLP datasets they create. The fact that this measure is still rarely reported adds to the emerging reproducibility issues in the field (Belz et al., 2023).

Ethical Considerations

We received approval to conduct these experiments from the institutional review board (IRB) of Heriot-Watt University (ref. 2022-3336-7139).

As annotators were exposed to potentially upsetting language, we took the following mitigation measures:

- Participants were warned about the content (1) before accepting the task on the recruitment platform, (2) in the Information Sheet provided at the start of the task, and (3) in the Consent Form where they acknowledged the potential risks.
- Participants were required to give their consent to participation.
- They were able to leave the study at any time on the understanding that they would be paid for any completed work.
- The task was kept short (all participants completed each round in under 30 minutes) to avoid lengthy exposure to upsetting material.

Following the advice of Shmueli et al. (2021) we paid participants at a rate that was above both the living wage in our jurisdiction and Prolific's current recommendation of at least £9.00 GBP/$12.00 USD.

Acknowledgements

Gavin Abercrombie was supported by the EPSRC projects 'Gender Bias in Conversational AI' (EP/T023767/1) and 'Equally Safe Online' (EP/W025493/1). His visit to Bocconi University was funded by a Scottish Informatics and Computer Science Alliance (SICSA) PECE travel grant. Dirk Hovy received funding from the European Research Council (ERC) under the European Union's Horizon 2020 research and innovation program (grant agreement No. 949944, INTEGRATOR), and by Fondazione Cariplo (grant No. 2020-4288, MONICA). He is a member of the MilaNLP group and the Data and Marketing Insights Unit of the Bocconi Institute for Data Science and Analysis. This work was also partly funded by Google Research.

The authors would like to thank Erlint Alitsani, Sabrina McCallum, Elisabetta Pique', and Nikolas Vitsakis for their assistance in developing the annotation task, as well as the anonymous annotators. We are also grateful to Verena Rieser and to Lora Aroyo, Aida Davani, Chris Homan, Chris Welty and others at Google for helpful and insightful discussions on this topic, and to the LAW programme committee for their useful feedback.

References

James D. Abbey and Margaret G. Meloy. 2017. Attention by design: Using attention checks to detect inattentive respondents and improve data quality. *Journal of Operations Management*, 53-56:63–70.

Gavin Abercrombie, Valerio Basile, Sara Tonelli, Verena Rieser, and Alexandra Uma, editors. 2022. *Proceedings of the 1st Workshop on Perspectivist Approaches to NLP @LREC2022*. European Language Resources Association, Marseille, France.

Gavin Abercrombie, Verena Rieser, and Dirk Hovy. 2023. Consistency is key: Disentangling label variation in natural language processing with intra-annotator agreement.

Farhad Akhbardeh, Arkady Arkhangorodsky, Magdalena Biesialska, Ondřej Bojar, Rajen Chatterjee, Vishrav Chaudhary, Marta R. Costa-jussa, Cristina España-Bonet, Angela Fan, Christian Federmann, Markus Freitag, Yvette Graham, Roman Grundkiewicz, Barry Haddow, Leonie Harter, Kenneth Heafield, Christopher Homan, Matthias Huck, Kwabena Amponsah-Kaakyire, Jungo Kasai, Daniel Khashabi, Kevin Knight, Tom Kocmi, Philipp Koehn, Nicholas Lourie, Christof Monz, Makoto Morishita, Masaaki Nagata, Ajay Nagesh, Toshiaki

Nakazawa, Matteo Negri, Santanu Pal, Allahsera Auguste Tapo, Marco Turchi, Valentin Vydrin, and Marcos Zampieri. 2021. Findings of the 2021 conference on machine translation (WMT21). In *Proceedings of the Sixth Conference on Machine Translation*, pages 1–88, Online. Association for Computational Linguistics.

Lora Aroyo and Chris Welty. 2015. Truth is a lie: Crowd truth and the seven myths of human annotation. *AI Magazine*, 36(1):15–24.

Valerio Basile, Michael Fell, Tommaso Fornaciari, Dirk Hovy, Silviu Paun, Barbara Plank, Massimo Poesio, and Alexandra Uma. 2021. We need to consider disagreement in evaluation. In *Proceedings of the 1st Workshop on Benchmarking: Past, Present and Future*, pages 15–21, Online. Association for Computational Linguistics.

Anya Belz, Craig Thomson, and Ehud Reiter. 2023. Missing information, unresponsive authors, experimental flaws: The impossibility of assessing the reproducibility of previous human evaluations in NLP. In *The Fourth Workshop on Insights from Negative Results in NLP*, pages 1–10, Dubrovnik, Croatia. Association for Computational Linguistics.

Emily M. Bender and Batya Friedman. 2018. Data statements for natural language processing: Toward mitigating system bias and enabling better science. *Transactions of the Association for Computational Linguistics*, 6:587–604.

Federico Cabitza, , Andrea Campagner, and Valerio Basile. 2023. Toward a perspectivist turn in ground truthing for predictive computing. In *Proceedings of the 37th AAAI Conference on Artificial Intelligence*, Washington DC, USA.

Yang Cao, Anna Sotnikova, Hal Daumé III, Rachel Rudinger, and Linda Zou. 2022. Theory-grounded measurement of U.S. social stereotypes in English language models. In *Proceedings of the 2022 Conference of the North American Chapter of the Association for Computational Linguistics: Human Language Technologies*, pages 1276–1295, Seattle, United States. Association for Computational Linguistics.

Jean Carletta. 1996. Assessing agreement on classification tasks: The kappa statistic. *Computational Linguistics*, 22(2):249–254.

Amanda Cercas Curry, Gavin Abercrombie, and Verena Rieser. 2021. ConvAbuse: Data, analysis, and benchmarks for nuanced abuse detection in conversational AI. In *Proceedings of the 2021 Conference on Empirical Methods in Natural Language Processing*, pages 7388–7403, Online and Punta Cana, Dominican Republic. Association for Computational Linguistics.

Albert Costa, Jon Andoni Duñabeitia, and Boaz Keysar. 2019. Language context and decision-making: Challenges and advances. *Quarterly Journal of Experimental Psychology*, 72(1):1–2. PMID: 30803348.

Jean-Marc Dewaele. 2004. The emotional force of swearwords and taboo words in the speech of multilinguals. *Journal of Multilingual and Multicultural Development*, 25(2-3):204–222.

Lei Gao and Ruihong Huang. 2017. Detecting online hate speech using context aware models. In *Proceedings of the International Conference Recent Advances in Natural Language Processing, RANLP 2017*, pages 260–266, Varna, Bulgaria. INCOMA Ltd.

Goran Glavaš, Mladen Karan, and Ivan Vulić. 2020. XHate-999: Analyzing and detecting abusive language across domains and languages. In *Proceedings of the 28th International Conference on Computational Linguistics*, pages 6350–6365, Barcelona, Spain (Online). International Committee on Computational Linguistics.

Simon Hengchen and Nina Tahmasebi. 2021. SuperSim: a test set for word similarity and relatedness in Swedish. In *Proceedings of the 23rd Nordic Conference on Computational Linguistics (NoDaLiDa)*, pages 268–275, Reykjavik, Iceland (Online). Linköping University Electronic Press, Sweden.

Joseph Hoover, Mohammad Atari, Aida M. Davani, Brendan Kennedy, Gwenyth Portillo-Wightman, Leigh Yeh, Drew Kogon, and Morteza Dehghani. 2019. Bound in hatred: The role of group-based morality in acts of hate.

Dirk Hovy, Taylor Berg-Kirkpatrick, Ashish Vaswani, and Eduard Hovy. 2013. Learning whom to trust with MACE. In *Proceedings of the 2013 Conference of the North American Chapter of the Association for Computational Linguistics: Human Language Technologies*, pages 1120–1130, Atlanta, Georgia. Association for Computational Linguistics.

D. Kahneman, O. Sibony, and C.R. Sunstein. 2021. *Noise*. Harper Collins Publishers.

Svetlana Kiritchenko and Saif Mohammad. 2017. Best-worst scaling more reliable than rating scales: A case study on sentiment intensity annotation. In *Proceedings of the 55th Annual Meeting of the Association for Computational Linguistics (Volume 2: Short Papers)*, pages 465–470, Vancouver, Canada. Association for Computational Linguistics.

Jan-Christoph Klie, Bonnie Webber, and Iryna Gurevych. 2023. Annotation Error Detection: Analyzing the Past and Present for a More Coherent Future. *Computational Linguistics*, 49(1):157–198.

Ritesh Kumar, Aishwarya N. Reganti, Akshit Bhatia, and Tushar Maheshwari. 2018. Aggression-annotated corpus of Hindi-English code-mixed data. In *Proceedings of the Eleventh International Conference on Language Resources and Evaluation (LREC 2018)*, Miyazaki, Japan. European Language Resources Association (ELRA).

Xuansong Li, Niyu Ge, Stephen Grimes, Stephanie M. Strassel, and Kazuaki Maeda. 2010. Enriching word alignment with linguistic tags. In *Proceedings of the Seventh International Conference on Language Resources and Evaluation (LREC'10)*, Valletta, Malta. European Language Resources Association (ELRA).

Eyal Peer, David Rothschild, Andrew Gordon, Zak Evernden, and Ekaterina Damer. 2022. Data quality of platforms and panels for online behavioral research. *Behavior Research Methods*, 54.

Vinodkumar Prabhakaran, Aida Mostafazadeh Davani, and Mark Diaz. 2021. On releasing annotator-level labels and information in datasets. In *Proceedings of The Joint 15th Linguistic Annotation Workshop (LAW) and 3rd Designing Meaning Representations (DMR) Workshop*, pages 133–138, Punta Cana, Dominican Republic. Association for Computational Linguistics.

Paul Rottger, Bertie Vidgen, Dirk Hovy, and Janet Pierrehumbert. 2022. Two contrasting data annotation paradigms for subjective NLP tasks. In *Proceedings of the 2022 Conference of the North American Chapter of the Association for Computational Linguistics: Human Language Technologies*, pages 175–190, Seattle, United States. Association for Computational Linguistics.

Paul Röttger, Bertie Vidgen, Dong Nguyen, Zeerak Waseem, Helen Margetts, and Janet Pierrehumbert. 2021. HateCheck: Functional tests for hate speech detection models. In *Proceedings of the 59th Annual Meeting of the Association for Computational Linguistics and the 11th International Joint Conference on Natural Language Processing (Volume 1: Long Papers)*, pages 41–58, Online. Association for Computational Linguistics.

Boaz Shmueli, Jan Fell, Soumya Ray, and Lun-Wei Ku. 2021. Beyond fair pay: Ethical implications of NLP crowdsourcing. In *Proceedings of the 2021 Conference of the North American Chapter of the Association for Computational Linguistics: Human Language Technologies*, pages 3758–3769, Online. Association for Computational Linguistics.

Michelle Stankovic, Britta Biedermann, and Takeshi Hamamura. 2022. Not all bilinguals are the same: A meta-analysis of the moral foreign language effect. *Brain and Language*, 227:105082.

Simone Teufel, Jean Carletta, and Marc Moens. 1999. An annotation scheme for discourse-level argumentation in research articles. In *Ninth Conference of the European Chapter of the Association for Computational Linguistics*, pages 110–117, Bergen, Norway. Association for Computational Linguistics.

Ellen R. Vriezen, Morris Moscovitch, and Sandy A. Bellos. 1995. Priming effects in semantic classification tasks. *Journal of Experimental Psychology: Learning, Memory, and Cognition*, 21(4).

Ellery Wulczyn, Nithum Thain, and Lucas Dixon. 2017. Ex machina: Personal attacks seen at scale. In *Proceedings of the 26th International Conference on World Wide Web*, WWW '17, page 1391–1399, Republic and Canton of Geneva, CHE. International World Wide Web Conferences Steering Committee.

A Annotator guidelines

The following guidelines were provided to annotators at the beginning of the task, and the definition and examples were repeated at the top of each page of five items. To avoid reprinting potentially offensive text, here we provide the row numbers of the examples from `XHate999-EN-Gao-test`.[5]

Instructions

We define hateful speech to be the language which explicitly or implicitly threatens or demeans a person or a group based upon a facet of their identity such as gender, ethnicity, or sexual orientation.

Read the following 100 posts, which are written in either English or German.

Do you think that they are **Hateful** or **Not hateful**?

If you're not sure, select the option that seems most likely to you.

Examples:

`EN-Gao-test row 100.`
Hateful

`EN-Gao-test row 95.`
Not hateful

B Data statement

We provide a data statement, as recommended by Bender and Friedman (2018).

[5] Available at `https://github.com/codogogo/xhate/blob/main/test/en/XHate999-EN-Gao-test.txt`

Curation rationale Textual data is from the '*GAO*' subset of `XHate999`, selected for the reasons highlighted in section 2. For further details of the original data collection process, see Gao and Huang (2017). For information on the translations, see Glavaš et al. (2020).

Language variety: `en-US`, `de-DE`. Predominantly US English, as written in comments on the Fox News website. Translated to German by editing automatic outputs of Google Translate. Translators were 'expert' L1 speakers of German who were also fluent in English.

Author demographics: Unknown.

Annotator demographics: The original Gao and Huang (2017) labels were produced by 'two native English speakers', with no further information provided. Annotator demographics for the bilingual labelling are as follows.

- Age: $18 - 70$, $\mu = 33.1$, $\sigma = 12.9$
- Gender: Female: 12 (55%); Male: 10 (45%)
- Ethnicity: White: 19 (86%), Mixed: 3 (14%)
- Native language: German (`de`) 100%
- Socio-economic status:
  - Employment: N/A: 7, Full-Time: 10, Not in paid work: 4, Part-Time: 3, Other: 2
  - Student: Yes: 9, No: 8, N/A: 5
- Training in relevant disciplines: Unknown

Text production situation:

- Time and place: unknown.
- Modality: written, spontaneous, asynchronous interaction.
- Intended audience: other website users.

Text characteristics Comments on articles on the Fox News website. The articles appear to concern events in the United States of America and the wider world in c.2016: Black Lives Matter protests, the Israel-Palestine conflict, and the death of a child at Disney World feature prominently.

Provenance: Data statements were not provided with the original datasets.

BenCoref: A Multi-Domain Dataset of Nominal Phrases and Pronominal Reference Annotations

Shadman Rohan[1], Mojammel Hossain[1], Mohammad Mamun Or Rashid[2], Nabeel Mohammed[1]

[1]North South University [2]Jahangirnagar University

shadman.rohan, mojammel.hossain, nabeel.mohammed@northsouth.edu

mamunbd@juniv.edu

Abstract

Coreference Resolution is a well studied problem in NLP. While widely studied for English and other resource-rich languages, research on coreference resolution in Bengali largely remains unexplored due to the absence of relevant datasets. Bengali, being a low-resource language, exhibits greater morphological richness compared to English. In this article, we introduce a new dataset, BenCoref, comprising coreference annotations for Bengali texts gathered from four distinct domains. This relatively small dataset contains 5200 mention annotations forming 502 mention clusters within 48,569 tokens. We describe the process of creating this dataset and report performance of multiple models trained using BenCoref. We expect that our work provides some valuable insights on the variations in coreference phenomena across several domains in Bengali and encourages the development of additional resources for Bengali. Furthermore, we found poor crosslingual performance at zero-shot setting from English, highlighting the need for more language-specific resources for this task. The dataset is available at [1].

Bengali:

[[তার]$_3$ এক বোনপোকে]$_2$ নিয়ে সেই বাড়ীতে থাকে। [সাধুকে]$_1$ দেখে [বুড়ী]$_3$ [তার]$_3$ হাতের কাজ ফেলে উঠে এল। তারপর নমস্কার করে আসন এনে দিল। [সাধু]$_1$ বসে [বুড়ীর]$_3$ সঙ্গে নানা রকম আলাপ করতে লাগলেন। [[তার]$_3$ [বোনপো]$_2$ এসে [জডিগের]$_4$ সঙ্গে গল্প জুড়ে দিল। [জডিগ]$_4$ একবার করে কথা বলেছিল আর [সাধুর]$_1$ দিকে চাইছিল।

English:

[She]$_3$ resides in the house alongside [[her]$_3$ nephew]$_2$. Upon seeing [the saint]$_1$, [the elderly woman]$_3$ abandoned [her]$_3$ work. [She]$_3$ offered [him]$_1$ a warm greeting and provided a chair. [The saint]$_1$ engaged in conversation with [the woman]$_3$. Meanwhile, [[her]$_1$ nephew]$_2$ began gossiping with [Jodig]$_4$. As [Jodig]$_4$ conversed, [he]$_4$ couldn't help but stare at [the saint]$_1$.

Figure 1: BenCoref annotations with color-coded Coreference chains.

1 Introduction

Coreference resolution is the task of identifying all references to the same entity in a document. This task originally started as a sub-task of information extraction. The Message Understanding Conferences (Grishman and Sundheim, 1996) first introduced three tasks, collectively referred to as SemEval, designed to measure the deeper understanding of any information extraction (IE) system. One of these three tasks proposed in the event was coreferencial noun phrase identification.

The Automatic Content Extraction (ACE) Program (Doddington et al., 2004) was the first major initiative that created a large dataset with entity, event and relation annotations. This project revealed some major complexities behind creating such dataset. Some of the significant challenges reported by the annotators include the coreference of generic entities, use of metonymy, characterization of Geo-Political Entity, distinguishing certain complex relations, and recognizing implicit vs. explicit relations.

Since then coreference resolution, anaphoric & cataphoric relation identification, event reference detection has been studied widely. As a result, large datasets like ACE (Doddington et al., 2004), Ontonotes (Pradhan et al., 2012), WikiCoref (Ghaddar and Langlais, 2016), and LitBank (Bamman et al., 2020) were made public. Some datasets, like ACE (Doddington et al., 2004), and Ontonotes, expanded this task beyond English to include more languages, like Arabic, and Chinese.

This coreference resolution task has shown potential in improving many downstream NLP tasks

[1]codes used to generate the results along with data is available at: https://github.com/ShadmanRohan/BenCoref

Proceedings of the 17th Linguistic Annotation Workshop (LAW-XVII), pages 104–117
July 13, 2023 ©2023 Association for Computational Linguistics

like machine translation (Miculicich Werlen and Popescu-Belis, 2017; Ohtani et al., 2019), literary analysis (Bamman et al., 2014), question anwering (Morton, 1999), text summarization (Steinberger et al., 2007), etc. However, Bengali, despite being a popular lanaguage, has seen very little work is this direction due to lack of public datasets.

Figure 1 shows a sample from our dataset with each color representing an unique entity. The main contributions of this work are:

- We introduce a new Bengali coreference annotated dataset, consisting of 48,569 tokens collected from four diverse domains. Our dataset creation process is shared along with the annotators' guidelines, which we believe is the first of its kind for Bengali coreference annotation.

- We characterize the behaviour and distribution of nominal and pronominal coreference mentions across the four domains with necessary statistics. Furthermore, we report the performance of an end-to-end neural coreference resolution system that was solely built using our data.

- We empirically demonstrate the necessity for more language-specific datasets, particularly for low-resource languages, by comparing our results with zero-shot cross-lingual learning from English.

1.1 Related Datasets

To the best of our knowledge, no coreference dataset in Bengali exists. Most of the works related to Bengali (Sikdar et al., 2013; Senapati and Garain, 2013; Sikdar et al., 2015) uses data from ICON2011 shared task which was never publicly shared.

Most of the major coreference datasets are in English. OntoNotes (Pradhan et al., 2012) is a well-annotated and large dataset with over 1.6M words. This dataset does not contain any singleton mention. Later, LitBank (Bamman et al., 2020) was published that is almost 10 times larger than OntoNotes (12.3M words).

2 Challenges in Bengali

One of the main challenges we faced was the absence of preexisting coreference annotation guidelines tailored for the Bengali language. To overcome this obstacle, we adapted the OntoNotes coreference annotation guideline to suit our objectives. This highlighted several distinctive linguistic characteristics of Bengali, such as zero anaphora, non-anaphoric pronouns, and case-marking, that needs to be carefully considered when preforming co-reference annotation in Bengali. Each of this is discussed with more details and examples in Figure 9 in the Appendix.

Moreover, we discovered that existing annotation software is ill-equipped to manage Bengali text, occasionally leading to inaccurate rendering and unstable character display. This underscores the importance of advancing normalization techniques and standardization of Bengali digital representation.

3 Data Domain Description

The Bengali language can be braoadly categorized into two primary literary dialects, namely "Shadhubhasha" and "Choltibhasha." "Shadhubhasha" was commonly used by Bangla writers and individuals in the 19th and early 20th centuries, while "Choltibhasha" is currently the more prevalent and colloquial dialect. This dataset contains both domains of Bengali text, with story and novel texts sourced from copyright-free books of the 19th and 20th centuries, and biography and descriptive texts obtained from modern sources, primarily in "Choltibhasha." A brief description of each domain is given below:

3.1 Biography

A biography presents a comprehensive account of an individual's life, character, accomplishments, and works, spanning from birth to death or the present time. Although the number of references per document in biographical texts is comparable to other genres, they primarily focus on a single subject throughout the entire narrative. Additionally, the dialect employed in biographies in BenCoref is typically "Choltibhasha."

3.2 Descriptive

By descriptive text we refer to wikipedia-like articles. They cover a broad range of subjects that span various fields, such as technology, professions, travel, economics, and numerous related subtopics. These comprehensive texts try to accurately portray and convey holistic information about real-world objects or experiences.

3.3 Story

BenCoref is primarily composed of short stories, each with a word count of 1000 words or less, which was an arbitrary decision. These stories typically feature 3-4 characters on average. The language used in the stories varies, with some being exclusively in "Shadhubhasha," while others use a mix of "Shadhubhasha" and "Choltibhasha."

3.4 Novel

The Bengali novels in our dataset typically consist of more than 1200 words and feature an average of over 5 characters. These novels primarily employ "Shadhubhasha". The next segment discusses the coreference behaviour across each domain in more detail.

4 Domain Specific Coreference Behaviour Characterization

In this section, some statistics is presented to better understand the coreference phenomenon across each domain. Each coreference cluster may refer to different type of entities, like an object, people, location or event. An arbitrary design choice was made to not explicitly mark the type of entity.

We start by analyzing the mean and standard deviation between mentions across the domains. Table 1 shows that biographies and novels exhibit a low standard deviation but have noticeably different mean distance between mentions. On the other hand, stories and descriptive texts fall in the middle, exhibiting a similar coreference distribution. For mentions that span more than one token, only the first token was used for calculation.

Categories	Mean	Std. Dev
Novel	29.17	3.70
Story	24.10	8.46
Biography	15.67	3.81
Descriptive	22.35	5.42

Table 1: Mean and Std. Deviation of distance between mentions in each domain.

The majority of texts in BenCoref belong to the stories domain, while the biography domain has the smallest contribution. The distribution of mentions, clusters, and tokens across the categories in BenCoref is presented in Figure 4.

Figure 2 depicts the distribution of cluster size across each domain. The cluster size refers to the total number of mentions in each coreference chain. It is worth noting that singletons were not annotated in BenCoref. The story domain has the highest number of coreference chains with two mentions only. Since the story domain contributes the most data to the dataset, this may be a contributing factor to its high frequency in each cluster size. Besides story, the descriptive domain also seems to have more larger coreference chains.

Figure 3 compares the spread of coreference chains in each domain, where the spread refers to the token-level distance between the beginning and end of a coreference chain. A general trend can be observed that as the size of the coreference chain increases, its corresponding frequency decreases in each domain.

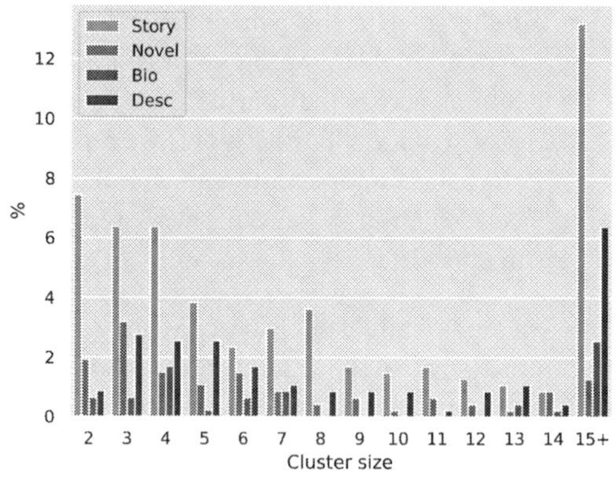

Figure 2: Cluster size comparison between Story, Novel, Biography and wiki-like Descriptive domain.

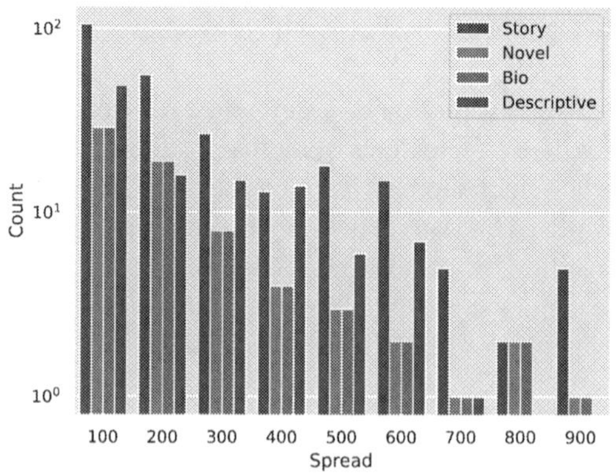

Figure 3: Spread in BenCoref across each domain. The spread is measured by the token level distance between the first and last mention of an entity.

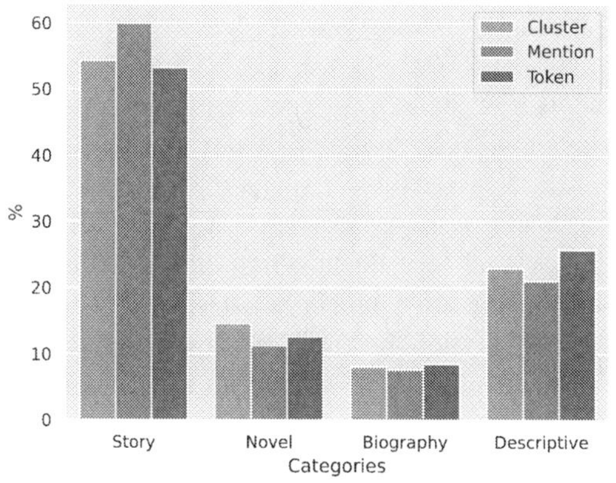

Figure 4: (Right) Distribution of Clusters, Mentions, and Tokens across the categories.

An additional "index.csv" file is included with in the dataset, which serves as an index to all the documents included, organized by title and author. A partial view of this file is presented in Appendix Figure 6.

5 Methodology

We used BnWikiSource[2] and Banglapedia(Islam et al., 2003) as sources of copyright-free Bengali text for our dataset. Banglapedia was used for biographies and wiki-like descriptive texts. The dataset creation process is discussed in detail in the following paragraphs.

5.1 Annotation Phase

The WebAnno annotator (Eckart de Castilho et al., 2016) was the chosen tool for annotation. To accommodate WebAnno's limited capacity to work with large texts, the articles were partitioned according to the Table 2. Each partition ends in a complete sentence and any incomplete portion of a sentence were moved to the next fragment. The partition size was chosen arbitrarily to reduce the number of data fragments. In Appendix Figure 5, a screenshot of the WebAnno interface used during this phase is displayed. A post annotation sample is provided in Figure 7 in Appendix from the Biography domain.

Since there is no existing guideline for coreference annotation, the annotators were initially instructed to annotate the noun phrases and its coreferences, which were predominantly pronouns. The primary noun phrase references were tagged as "entity" and their corresponding coreferences were

[2]https://bn.wikipedia.org

Tokens	Partitions
<699	1
<1000	2
>1000	3

Table 2: Documents with greater than 699 tokens and less than 1000 tokens were divided into 2 parts and the ones with more than 1000 tokens were divided into 3.

tagged as "ref". While determining what forms an entity is an important linguistic problem, it is not the primary challenge we are trying to address in our work. Annotators were free to mark any token or span that they considered an entity. After the annotation phase was completed, the data was exported and the character-level annotations were converted to token-level annotations. For every exceptional cases encountered, a new rule was established and enforced during further annotation of the dataset. The rules are further discussed in the next section.

5.2 Annotation Strategy/Guideline

This coreference annotation guide (refer to A in the Appendix) was prepared concurrently with the annotation phase to ensure consistency throughout the annotation process. We mirrored the overall structure of the OntoNotes annotation guidelines, tailoring them to our specific use case.

Initially, we did not impose any specific restrictions on the definition of an entity during the annotation process. The annotators were instructed to annotate any span they deemed as an entity. However, this approach resulted in an annotator bias, with a strong focus on nominal and pronominal mentions. Subsequently, we made the decision to prioritize and concentrate solely on these types of mentions.

Furthermore, as part of our design decision, we chose to not tag singleton mentions. Consequently, any singletons were removed during the post-annotation processing phase.

5.3 Annotation Criteria:

The general rule used for annotation is to annotate mentions in any form, including nested mentions or those referring to multiple entities. The characterization of mention and coreference link types was conducted after annotating the entire dataset. Annotating coreference link types was kept optional due to the significant training required for the task. This strategy was followed the accelerate the annotation process.

The rules with corresponding examples are illustrated in a more detailed manner in Figure 10 in the Appendix. Furthermore, the coreference link types have been categorized into two groups, namely identical and apposite, and they have been discussed in detail in 11 and 12 in the Appendix. However, the task of annotating coreference link types is currently pending and will be addressed in future work.

While this guideline is incomplete and limited in scope, it can play an impotant role in encouraging the next generation of coreference datasets in Bengali. The OntoNotes coreference guideline(gui, 2007) is currently in its 7th edition which is a strong indication that the first attempt on making a such guideline would be imperfect and will require further revisions. It may take several iterations before we can have a robust guideline for coreference annotation in Bengali.

5.4 Inter-Annotator Agreement

The OntoNotes strategy was roughly employed to assess interannotator agreement in this work. Specifically, two annotators independently annotated the documents, and only in cases of disagreement, a third annotator was consulted to arrive at a final decision. These ultimate annotations were deemed as the gold standard annotations.

Based on the adjudicated version as the ground truth, the individual annotations in our dataset achieved an average MUC score of 78.3 on the combined dataset. while the combined inter-annotator MUC score was 67.6.

However, it is important to acknowledge that the process of resolving disagreements was not adequately documented and will be addressed in greater detail in future endeavors.

6 Experiments

We took an end-to-end neural network based modeling approach. The following section discusses the algorithm, followed by the experimental setup, evaluation strategy and analysis of results.

We used the 300-dimensional Fasttext and Glove embeddings (Grave et al., 2018) as words representations. To generate contexual representations the embeddings were passed through a bi-directional LSTM (Hochreiter and Schmidhuber, 1997) for some experiments and a variation of the popular transformer-based (Vaswani et al., 2017) pretrained model, BERT(Devlin et al., 2019), for other experiments. For the task of coreference resolution, the contextual representations from these base models were passed on to a span ranking model-head, originally proposed in (Lee et al., 2018). For the crosslingual experiment, a multilingual BERT was finetuned on the OntoNotes dataset.

For hyperparameter optimization, we tuned the maximum number of words in a span(s), maximum number of antecedents per span(a), and coref layer depth(CL).

6.1 Experimental Setup

The data was separated into train and dev set on a ratio of 95% by 5%. An additional test set was carefully prepared, completely disjoint from the train and dev set, that contains 37 documents. An overview of the dataset given in Table 3

	categories	documents	mentions	clusters
train + dev	biography	17	421	38
	descriptive	36	1157	108
	novel	13	601	78
	story	56	3021	278
test	biography	10	303	22
	descriptive	9	290	33
	novel	3	191	15
	story	15	697	53

Table 3: Dataset distribution

For evaluating our system, we used the CONLL-2012 official evaluation scripts which calculates four metrics: Identification of Mentions, MUC, B3 and CEAF. The following section analyzes the performance of our model.

6.2 Results and Analysis

category	model	parameters	pre.	rec.	f1
biography	c2f+Glove	s=30, a=50, CL=2	93.83	65.34	77.04
	c2f+Fasttext	s=20, a=50, CL=2	96.51	64.02	76.98
	BERT-base	s=30, a=50, CL=2	94.22	86.13	90.00
	M-BERT(Zero-Shot)	s=30, a=50, CL=2	7.14	4.62	5.61
story	c2f+Glove	s=30, a=50, CL=2	73.78	58.96	65.55
	c2f+Fasttext	s=20, a=50, CL=2	74.80	54.08	62.78
	BERT-base	s=30, a=50, CL=2	83.91	65.85	73.79
	M-BERT(Zero-Shot)	s=30, a=50, CL=2	7.40	3.73	4.96
novel	c2f+Glove	s=30, a=50, CL=2	78.00	40.83	53.60
	c2f+Fasttext	s=20, a=50, CL=2	87.50	43.97	58.53
	BERT-base	s=30, a=50, CL=2	85.41	64.39	73.43
	M-BERT(Zero-Shot)	s=30, a=50, CL=2	8.51	4.18	5.61
descriptive	c2f+Glove	s=30, a=50, CL=2	66.39	27.93	39.32
	c2f+Fasttext	s=20, a=50, CL=2	72.16	24.13	36.17
	BERT-base	s=30, a=50, CL=2	82.95	50.34	62.66
	M-BERT(Zero-Shot)	s=30, a=50, CL=2	7.47	5.51	6.34

Table 4: Identification of mentions

			B^3			MUC			$CEAF_{\phi 4}$			Avg		
category		parameters	Pre.	Rec.	F1	Pre.	Rec.	F1	Pre.	Rec.	f1	Pre.	Rec.	F1
biography	c2f + Glove	s=30, a=50, CL=2	84.52	44.74	58.51	92.26	64.41	76.05	55.33	40.24	46.60	77.37	49.80	60.39
	c2f + Fasttext	s=20, a=50, CL=2	89.09	43.99	58.90	95.74	64.05	76.75	61.24	36.19	45.49	82.02	48.08	60.38
	BERT-base	s=30, a=50, CL=2	85.37	73.59	79.04	93.79	86.12	89.79	57.48	49.64	53.27	78.88	69.78	74.03
	M-BERT(Zero-Shot)	s=30, a=50, CL=2	4.28	0.25	0.46	0.67	0.35	0.46	1.22	2.93	1.72	2.06	1.18	0.88
story	c2f + Glove	s=30, a=50, CL=2	46.92	23.95	31.72	63.41	44.40	52.23	20.24	36.99	26.16	43.52	35.11	36.70
	c2f + Fasttext	s=20, a=50, CL=2	47.31	22.80	30.77	65.23	42.54	51.50	23.49	34.02	27.79	45.34	33.12	36.69
	BERT-base	s=30, a=50, CL=2	54.64	31.62	40.06	74.46	53.88	62.52	28.80	40.23	33.57	52.63	41.91	45.38
	M-BERT(Zero-Shot)	s=30, a=50, CL=2	2.32	0.25	0.45	1.42	0.62	0.86	2.00	2.59	2.26	1.91	1.15	1.19
novel	c2f + Glove	s=30, a=50, CL=2	49.87	7.98	13.77	59.45	25.00	35.20	16.37	26.61	20.27	41.90	19.86	23.08
	c2f + Fasttext	s=20, a=50, CL=2	60.30	10.45	17.82	72.72	31.81	44.26	23.36	27.74	25.37	52.13	23.33	29.15
	BERT-base	s=30, a=50, CL=2	43.55	33.93	38.14	71.31	52.27	60.32	34.98	32.80	33.85	49.95	39.67	44.10
	M-BERT(Zero-Shot)	s=30, a=50, CL=2	3.54	0.25	0.47	2.66	1.13	1.59	1.90	2.49	2.15	2.70	1.29	1.40
descriptive	c2f + Glove	s=30, a=50, CL=2	48.33	11.91	19.12	58.24	20.62	30.45	31.16	26.83	28.83	45.91	19.79	26.13
	c2f + Fasttext	s=20, a=50, CL=2	58.32	9.74	16.70	66.66	18.67	29.17	29.98	20.81	24.57	51.65	16.41	23.48
	BERT-base	s=30, a=50, CL=2	62.81	26.88	37.65	76.62	45.91	57.42	46.12	28.18	34.99	61.85	33.66	43.35
	M-BERT(Zero-Shot)	s=30, a=50, CL=2	2.01	0.56	0.88	1.16	0.77	0.93	2.30	3.00	2.60	1.82	1.44	1.47

Table 5: Performance on test data. The main evaluation metric is the average F1 score of MUC, B^3, and $CEAF_{\phi 4}$. The best scores are highlighted.

The performance of the model was reasonable given the size of our dataset. As neural networks tend to achieve optimal performance with larger datasets, we hypothesize that our results could be enhanced by expanding our dataset. The model demonstrated good performance in identifying individual mentions, as evidenced by the scores presented in Table 4. However, we observed a decrease in performance during the second phase of clustering the mentions, as shown in Table 5. This highlights the challenge of accurately identifying coreference clusters, particularly in languages with complex sentence structures and a high degree of lexical ambiguity. Further innovation is needed to address these challenges and improve the overall performance of coreference resolution models.

Upon closer inspection one recurring problem was discovered. The model failed to do basic common sense reasoning on long coreference clusters, often breaking it up into several clusters. As demonstrated in Figure 8 in Appendix, the model failed to merge clusters 0 and 1, which should have been a single cluster.

Furthermore, it can be observed that the coreference resolution model performs significantly better on the biography domain as compared to other domains. The relatively low mean and standard deviation of the distance between mentions reported in Table 1 may have contributed to this result. However, despite forming the major portion of the dataset, the story domain did not show any significant improvement. The high standard deviation in distance between mentions reported in Table 1 for the story domain may have contributed to this lack of improvement. Qualitative analysis is needed to investigate the underlying causes of this performance gap.

The zero-shot crosslingual experiment demostrated that coreference knowledge doesn't easily transfer through multilingual training. This clearly demonstrates the need for language specific datasets. Some studies (Novák and Žabokrtský, 2014) report developing projection techniques to improve crosslingual coreference resolution. There maybe scope for further work in this direction.

7 Conclusion

This paper presented BenCoref, the first publicly available dataset of coreference annotations in Bengali. The creation process and annotation guidelines were described in detail to facilitate future work in this area. We then used the dataset to develop an end-to-end coreference resolution system and reported its performance across different domains. Our findings indicate that a lower mean and standard deviation of token-distance between mentions may lead to better results, but further experiments on other datasets are needed to confirm this hypothesis. We also observed a higher tendency for breakage in longer coreference chains.

Our zero-shot cross-lingual experiment demonstrated that coreference knowledge does not easily transfer through multilingual training, highlighting the importance of language-specific datasets. While some studies (Novák and Žabokrtský, 2014) have reported success in developing projection techniques to improve cross-lingual coreference resolution, further research is required to explore this area.

Acknowledgements

We would like to express our sincere gratitude to everyone who contributed to this research. We would also like to thank our colleagues and collaborators for their valuable insights and feedback throughout the project. We are especially grateful to our annotators for their hard work and dedication to ensure the quality of this dataset. We also appreciate the feedback and suggestions from the anonymous reviewers, which helped to improve the quality of this manuscript. No financial assistance was provided by any organization for the completion of this project.

References

2007. *Ontonotes English Coreference Guidelines.*

David Bamman, Olivia Lewke, and Anya Mansoor. 2020. An annotated dataset of coreference in English literature. In *Proceedings of the 12th Language Resources and Evaluation Conference*, pages 44–54, Marseille, France. European Language Resources Association.

David Bamman, Ted Underwood, and Noah A. Smith. 2014. A Bayesian mixed effects model of literary character. In *Proceedings of the 52nd Annual Meeting of the Association for Computational Linguistics (Volume 1: Long Papers)*, pages 370–379, Baltimore, Maryland. Association for Computational Linguistics.

Jacob Devlin, Ming-Wei Chang, Kenton Lee, and Kristina Toutanova. 2019. BERT: Pre-training of deep bidirectional transformers for language understanding. In *Proceedings of the 2019 Conference of the North American Chapter of the Association for Computational Linguistics: Human Language Technologies, Volume 1 (Long and Short Papers)*, pages 4171–4186, Minneapolis, Minnesota. Association for Computational Linguistics.

George Doddington, Alexis Mitchell, Mark Przybocki, Lance Ramshaw, Stephanie Strassel, and Ralph Weischedel. 2004. The automatic content extraction (ACE) program – tasks, data, and evaluation. In *Proceedings of the Fourth International Conference on Language Resources and Evaluation (LREC'04)*, Lisbon, Portugal. European Language Resources Association (ELRA).

Richard Eckart de Castilho, Éva Mújdricza-Maydt, Seid Muhie Yimam, Silvana Hartmann, Iryna Gurevych, Anette Frank, and Chris Biemann. 2016. A web-based tool for the integrated annotation of semantic and syntactic structures. In *Proceedings of the Workshop on Language Technology Resources and Tools for Digital Humanities (LT4DH)*, pages 76–84, Osaka, Japan. The COLING 2016 Organizing Committee.

Abbas Ghaddar and Philippe Langlais. 2016. Wikicoref: An english coreference-annotated corpus of wikipedia articles. In *Proceedings of the Tenth International Conference on Language Resources and Evaluation (LREC'16)*, pages 136–142.

Edouard Grave, Piotr Bojanowski, Prakhar Gupta, Armand Joulin, and Tomas Mikolov. 2018. Learning word vectors for 157 languages. In *Proceedings of the International Conference on Language Resources and Evaluation (LREC 2018).*

Ralph Grishman and Beth M Sundheim. 1996. Message understanding conference-6: A brief history. In *COLING 1996 Volume 1: The 16th International Conference on Computational Linguistics.*

Sepp Hochreiter and Jürgen Schmidhuber. 1997. Lstm can solve hard long time lag problems. *Advances in neural information processing systems*, pages 473–479.

Sirajul Islam et al. 2003. Banglapedia. *National Encyclopedia, Asiatic Society of Bangladesh, Dhaka.*

Kenton Lee, Luheng He, and Luke Zettlemoyer. 2018. Higher-order coreference resolution with coarse-to-fine inference. In *Proceedings of the 2018 Conference of the North American Chapter of the Association for Computational Linguistics: Human Language Technologies, Volume 2 (Short Papers)*, pages 687–692, New Orleans, Louisiana. Association for Computational Linguistics.

Lesly Miculicich Werlen and Andrei Popescu-Belis. 2017. Using coreference links to improve spanish-to-english machine translation. Technical report, Idiap.

Thomas S Morton. 1999. Using coreference for question answering. In *Coreference and Its Applications.*

Michal Novák and Zdeněk Žabokrtský. 2014. Cross-lingual coreference resolution of pronouns. In *Proceedings of COLING 2014, the 25th International Conference on Computational Linguistics: Technical Papers*, pages 14–24.

Takumi Ohtani, Hidetaka Kamigaito, Masaaki Nagata, and Manabu Okumura. 2019. Context-aware neural machine translation with coreference information. In *Proceedings of the Fourth Workshop on Discourse in Machine Translation (DiscoMT 2019)*, pages 45–50.

Sameer Pradhan, Alessandro Moschitti, Nianwen Xue, Olga Uryupina, and Yuchen Zhang. 2012. Conll-2012 shared task: Modeling multilingual unrestricted coreference in ontonotes. In *Joint Conference on EMNLP and CoNLL-Shared Task*, pages 1–40.

Apurbalal Senapati and Utpal Garain. 2013. Guitar-based pronominal anaphora resolution in bengali. In *Proceedings of the 51st Annual Meeting of the Association for Computational Linguistics (Volume 2: Short Papers)*, pages 126–130.

Utpal Kumar Sikdar, Asif Ekbal, Sriparna Saha, Olga Uryupina, and Massimo Poesio. 2013. Adapting a state-of-the-art anaphora resolution system for resource-poor language. In *Proceedings of the Sixth International Joint Conference on Natural Language Processing*, pages 815–821.

Utpal Kumar Sikdar, Asif Ekbal, Sriparna Saha, Olga Uryupina, and Massimo Poesio. 2015. Differential evolution-based feature selection technique for anaphora resolution. *Soft Computing*, 19(8):2149–2161.

Josef Steinberger, Massimo Poesio, Mijail A Kabadjov, and Karel Ježek. 2007. Two uses of anaphora resolution in summarization. *Information Processing & Management*, 43(6):1663–1680.

Ashish Vaswani, Noam Shazeer, Niki Parmar, Jakob Uszkoreit, Llion Jones, Aidan N Gomez, Łukasz Kaiser, and Illia Polosukhin. 2017. Attention is all you need. In *Advances in neural information processing systems*, pages 5998–6008.

A Appendices

			B^3			MUC			$CEAF_{\phi 4}$			Avg		
Category		Parameters	Pre.	Rec.	F1	Pre.	Rec.	F1	Pre.	Rec.	F1	Pre.	Rec.	F1
	c2f + Fasttext	s=30, a=250, CL=2	93.43	45.94	61.59	97.88	65.83	78.72	65.62	41.76	51.04	85.64	51.18	63.78
Biography	c2f + Fasttext	s=20, a=50, CL=3	91.63	45.20	60.54	96.84	65.48	78.13	65.87	41.92	51.23	84.78	50.87	63.30
	c2f + Fasttext	s=10, a=50, CL=3	90.98	47.81	62.68	96.92	67.25	79.41	77.44	42.24	54.66	88.54	52.44	65.58
	c2f + Fasttext	s=30, a=250, CL=2	48.07	22.95	31.07	65.78	38.81	48.82	21.98	33.73	26.62	45.28	31.83	35.50
Story	c2f + Fasttext	s=20, a=50, CL=3	53.08	21.70	30.81	67.02	38.50	48.91	22.17	34.02	26.84	47.42	31.41	35.52
	c2f + Fasttext	s=10, a=50, CL=3	53.82	19.35	28.47	66.76	34.62	45.60	21.92	34.77	26.89	47.50	29.58	33.65
	c2f + Fasttext	s=30, a=250, CL=2	47.06	7.32	12.67	61.03	26.70	37.15	16.04	23.06	18.92	41.38	19.03	22.91
Novel	c2f + Fasttext	s=20, a=50, CL=3	65.10	8.54	15.10	71.42	25.56	37.65	24.96	28.08	26.42	53.83	20.73	26.39
	c2f + Fasttext	s=10, a=50, CL=3	57.71	5.82	10.57	63.79	21.02	31.62	17.03	23.42	19.72	46.18	16.75	20.64
	c2f + Fasttext	s=30, a=250, CL=2	56.43	9.88	16.82	61.84	18.28	28.22	25.72	20.01	22.51	48.00	16.06	22.52
Descriptive	c2f + Fasttext	s=20, a=50, CL=3	53.78	7.64	13.37	58.92	12.84	21.08	28.76	19.17	23.01	47.15	13.22	19.15
	c2f + Fasttext	s=10, a=50, CL=3	52.41	7.46	13.06	58.06	14.00	22.57	24.47	19.03	21.41	44.98	13.50	19.01

Table 2: Some additional results on the Model's performance.

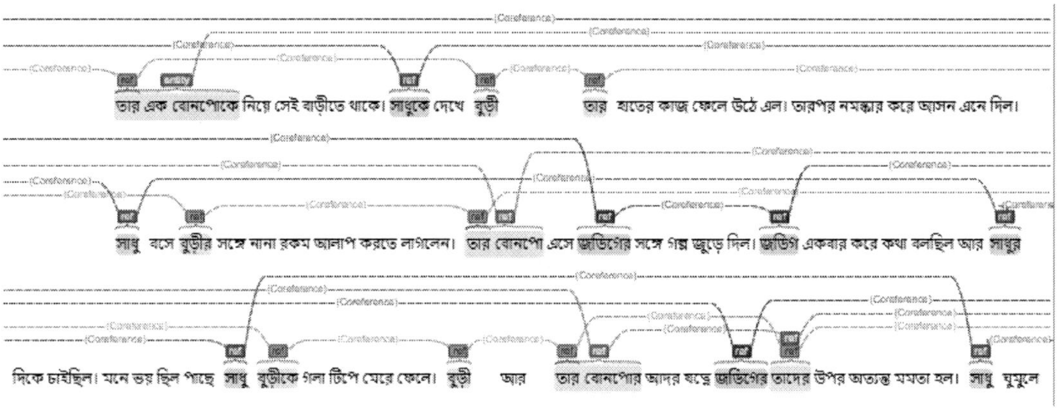

Figure 5: A screenshot from WebAnno(Eckart de Castilho et al., 2016) during annotation phase. In this example, the highlighted words are marked as mentions and same color indicate the mentions belong to the same cluster. A colored line joins the highlighted words creating a chain forming a single cluster.

	Title	Author Name	Ids	Type
0	অবরোধ-বাসিনী	বেগম রোকেয়া সাখাওয়াত হোসেন	doc_067 to 090	Story
1	কিশোরদের মন	দক্ষিণারঞ্জন মিত্র মজুমদার	doc_054 to 063	Novel
2	মায়াবাঁশী	রবীন্দ্রনাথ মৈত্র	doc_091 to 096	Story
3	টুনটুনির বই	উপেন্দ্রকিশোর রায়চৌধুরী	doc_097 to 117	Story
4	বীরবলের হালখাতা/আমরা ও তোমরা	প্রমথ চৌধুরী	doc_119	Story
...	...	...	...	...
56	টুসু উৎসব	বাংলাপিডিয়া	doc_049	Descriptive
57	খোজা	বাংলাপিডিয়া	doc_050	Descriptive
58	একাদশী	বাংলাপিডিয়া	doc_051	Descriptive
59	ঈদুল ফিত্‌র	বাংলাপিডিয়া	doc_052	Descriptive
60	গায়ে হলুদ	বাংলাপিডিয়া	doc_053	Descriptive

Figure 6: The supplementary datafile index.csv contains an index to all the datapoints

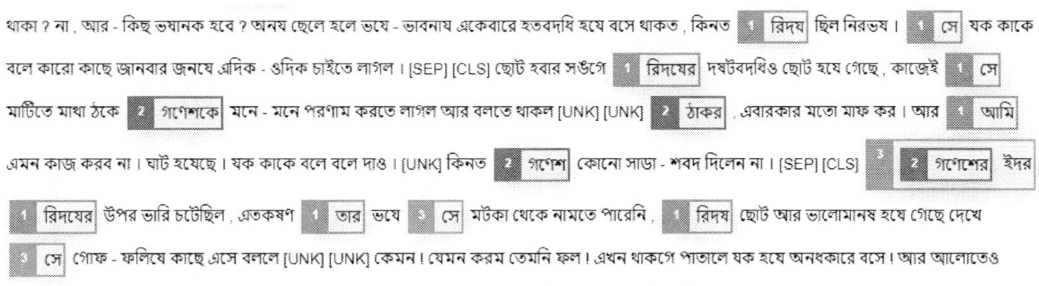

Figure 7: Biography document

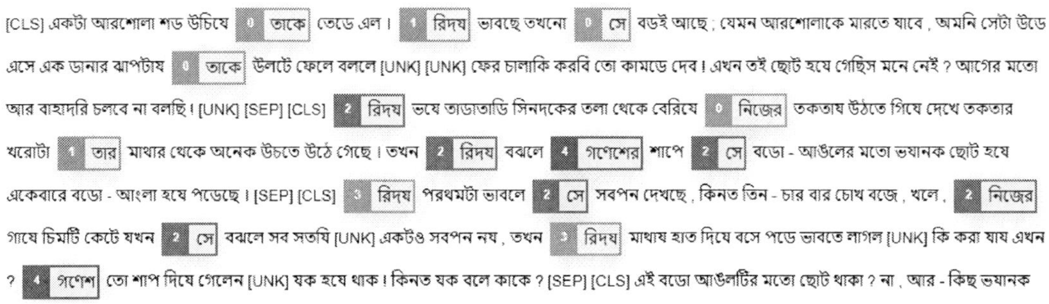

Figure 8: BERT-base model's prediction on a biography document

Category		Parameters	Pre.	Rec.	F1
Biography	c2f+Fasttext	s=30, a=250, CL=2	98.52	66.00	79.05
	c2f+Fasttext	s=20, a=50, CL=3	97.54	65.67	78.50
	c2f+Fasttext	s=10, a=50, CL=3	98.52	66.00	79.05
Story	c2f+Fasttext	s=30, a=250, CL=2	74.20	49.92	59.69
	c2f+Fasttext	s=20, a=50, CL=3	75.16	49.49	59.68
	c2f+Fasttext	s=10, a=50, CL=3	76.52	46.77	58.05
Novel	c2f+Fasttext	s=30, a=250, CL=2	79.00	41.36	54.29
	c2f+Fasttext	s=20, a=50, CL=3	90.12	38.21	53.67
	c2f+Fasttext	s=10, a=50, CL=3	83.75	35.07	49.44
Descriptive	c2f+Fasttext	s=30, a=250, CL=2	74.03	26.55	39.08
	c2f+Fasttext	s=20, a=50, CL=3	70.00	19.31	30.27
	c2f+Fasttext	s=10, a=50, CL=3	68.88	21.37	32.63

Table 7: Additional identification of mention results

Special Considerations in Bengali from Linguistic Perspective

Zero Anaphora: Include implied referents that are not explicitly mentioned in the text. Bangla, like many other South Asian languages, frequently uses zero anaphora, where the subject or object of a sentence is left implicit.
For example, in the sentence "ভাত খাব।" (will eat rice). Here, the subject (who wants to eat) is not explicitly mentioned in the text. This is an example of zero anaphora.

Other common zero anaphora types in Bengali include *Possessive and Reflexive Drop.*
Possessive Drop occurs when the possessive pronoun or possessive marker is omitted, and the possession is understood from the context. Example: "মায়ের কাছে গিয়েছি।" (Went to my mother.) - The possessive pronoun 'আমার' (my) is dropped, but it is understood that the speaker went to their own mother.

Reflexive Drop happens when the reflexive pronoun is dropped, and the reflexive action is understood from the context. Example: "খেলছি।" (I am Playing.) - The reflexive pronoun 'আমি' (I am) is dropped, but it is implied that the subject is performing the action on themselves.

Non-Anaphoric Pronouns: Some pronouns in Bengali are inherently non-anaphoric, meaning they rarely behave as anaphoric. These pronouns should not be considered as mentions for coreference.

When considering the sentence "সে নিজের কাজটা করতে পারে।" (He can do his own work.), the reflexive pronoun "নিজের" (own) is non-anaphoric, as it refers to the subject "সে" (he) and emphasizes that he can perform his own work.

Case Marking: Bengali has a rich system of case markers that indicate grammatical relations, which may differ from English. Rules for coreference resolution in English may not directly account for the impact of case markers on coreferential expressions in Bengali.
For example:

> মানুষটি ধরেছে বাঘ। (The person has caught the tiger.)
> মানুষ ধরেছে বাঘটি। (The tiger has caught the person.)
> পুলিশ মারে ডাকাতকে। (The police apprehend the robber.)
> পুলিশকে মারে ডাকাত। (The robber apprehend the police.)
> মানুষ ধরে বাঘ।
> পুলিশ মারে ডাকাত।
> However, these are valid sentences in Bengali as well, but they do not clarify the relationship between the entities involved.

Thus, the proper use of case markers in Bengali helps to disambiguate the roles and actions of the different entities involved. However, it is also possible to write valid sentences with ambiguity in Bengali by omitting the use of case markers.

Figure 9: This highlights few key considerations when annotating coreference in Bengali.

BenCoref Co-reference Annotation Guideline

0. General Policy

- Tag mentions according to rules defined in section 1
- Annotating the Coreference Link Types is optional
- Nested Mentions are annotated separately for each mention
    - Example: "রিয়া, যিনি আমার বন্ধুর বোন, আমার বাড়িতে এসেছে।"(Riya, who is my friend's sister, has come to my house.)
      In this sentence, the mention of "আমার" (my), "আমার বন্ধুর" (my friend's) is nested within the mention of "আমার বন্ধুর বোন" (my friend's sister). Tag them all within each mention.
- Multiple Reference: Mentions that refers to multiple chains are annotated multiple times for each chain.
    - Example: "রহিম স্কুলে যায় করিমের সাথে এবং মাঠে খেলে আব্দুলের সাথে। রহিম তার বন্ধুদের সাথেই সময় কাটাতে পছন্দ করে।" (Rahim goes to school with Karim and plays on the field with Abdul. Rahim enjoys spending time with his friends.)
      In this example, the mention "রহিম" (Rahim) refers to two different chains: going to school with Karim and playing on the field with Abdul. To capture these multiple references, the mention "রহিম" would be annotated separately for each chain.

1. Identifying Mentions:

- ***Noun Phrases***: Include all noun phrases that refer to entities, events, or abstract concepts. This includes proper nouns, common nouns, and pronouns.
    - Example: "রহিম বাজারে গেল।" (*Rahim* went to the market.)Here, "রহিম" (Rahim) and "বাজার" (market) are noun phrases that can be considered as mentions.

- ***Pronouns***: Include all pronouns that refer to entities, events, or abstract concepts. This includes personal, demonstrative, and interrogative pronouns.
    - Example: "সে বাজারে গেল।" (He went to the market.) Here, "সে" (he) is a pronoun that can be considered as a mention.

- ***Verbs***: Include verbs that imply the existence of a certain entity or event.
  For example, in the sentence "অর্থনীতি তাৎপর্যপূর্ণভাবে বৃদ্ধি পায়। তবে আমরা যদি এই বৃদ্ধি বজায় রাখতে না পারি শিগগিরই এটি হ্রাস পাবে।" (Economics thrives when it grows consistently. However, if we cannot sustain this growth, it will deteriorate quickly.) Here, "বৃদ্ধি" (thrives) is a verb that implies the existence of an event (playing).
  This "Verb" category of mentions is not included in BenCoref. We expect to include this in future.

2. Coreference Link Types:

- ***Identical***: Link mentions that refer to the exact same entity.
    - Example: "রহিম বাজারে গেল। সে ফল কিনল।" (Rahim went to the market. He bought fruits.) Here, "রহিম" (Rahim) and "সে" (he) refer to the exact same entity.
- ***Appositive***: Link mentions that refer to the same entity, but one mention provides additional information about the entity.
    - Example: "রাম, আমার বন্ধু, বাজারে গেল।" (Ram, my friend, went to the market.) Here, "রাম" (Ram) and "আমার বন্ধু" (my friend) refer to the same entity, but "আমার বন্ধু" (my friend) provides additional information about "রাম" (Ram).

Figure 10: BenCoref Annotation Guideline with examples.

Identical References

- ***Predicate Nominative***: Link a noun phrase and a verb or adjective that refer to the same entity.

  For example, in "সোহেল হচ্ছে কর্মঠ।" (Sohel is hardworking.), the noun phrase "সোহেল" (Sohel) is linked to the adjective "কর্মঠ" (hardworking) through the copular verb "হচ্ছে" (is). Both the noun phrase and the adjective refer to the same entity, Sohel being hardworking.

- ***Relative Pronoun***: Link a relative pronoun to a noun phrase in a relative clause.

  For example, in the sentence "রহিম, যিনি বাজারে গেল, আমার বন্ধু।" (Rahim, who went to the market, is my friend.), "রহিম" (Rahim) and "যিনি" (who) refer to the same entity. The relative pronoun "যিনি" (who) refers back to the noun phrase "রহিম" (Rahim), indicating that Rahim is the person who went to the market. This construction allows you to provide additional information about the noun Rahim within the sentence.

- ***Part-Whole***: This type of link occurs when one mention is a part of another mention.

  For example, in the sentence "রাহিমের হাত ভালো নয়।" (Rahim's hand is not good.), "রাহিমের হাত" (Rahim's hand) and "রহিম" (Rahim) would be linked as part-whole.

- ***Event*:** This type of link occurs when two or more mentions refer to the same event or occurrence.

  For example, in the sentence "বিয়েটা সুন্দর হয়েছিল। সেই অনুষ্ঠান আমার মনে আছে।" (The wedding was beautiful. I remember that event.), "বিয়েটা" (The wedding) and "সেই অনুষ্ঠান" (that event) refer to the same event, so they would be linked as event coreference.

- ***Set-Member***: This type of link occurs when one mention is a member of a set referred to by another mention.

  For example: "ছাত্ররা খেলাঘরে গেল। রামও ছিল।" (The students went to the playground. Ram was also there.), "রাম" (Ram) is a member of the set "ছাত্ররা" (The students), so they would be linked as set-member.

- ***Bridging***: This type of link occurs when one mention infers or implies the existence of another mention.

  For example, in the sentence "রাম একটি বাড়ি কিনল। ছাদটা সবুজ ছিল।" (Ram bought a house. The roof was green.), "ছাদটা" (The roof) infers the existence of "একটি বাড়ি" (a house), so they can be linked as bridging.

- ***Metonymy***: This type of link occurs when one mention is used to refer to another related mention.

  For example, in the sentence "বাংলাদেশ ক্রিকেট দল প্রস্তুত। বাংলাদেশ ক্রিকেট খেলতে চায়।" (Bangladesh cricket team is ready. Bangladesh wants to play cricket.), "বাংলাদেশ" (Bangladesh) is used to refer to “বাংলাদেশ ক্রিকেট দল”(Bangladesh cricket team), so they would be linked as metonymy.

Figure 11: Identical Reference Types

Appositive References

- **Role Appositive**: This type of link occurs when one mention describes the role or occupation of another mention.

  Example: "রহিম, একজন ডাক্তার, আমার বন্ধু।" (Rahim, a doctor, is my friend.). Here, "রহিম" (Rahim) and "একজন ডাক্তার" (a doctor) refer to the same person, so they would be linked as role appositive.

- **Descriptive Appositive**: This type of appositive provides descriptive information about the noun it is referring to.

  Example: "আমার বন্ধু, রহিম, আসছে।" (My friend, Rahim, is coming.) In this example, the appositive "রহিম" (Rahim) provides descriptive information about the noun "আমার বন্ধু" (my friend).

- **Identifying Appositive**: Identifying appositives are used to provide specific identifying information about a noun, such as its name or title.

  Example: "বাংলাদেশের প্রধানমন্ত্রী, শেখ হাসিনা, সংসদে উপস্থিত ছিলেন।" (Sheikh Hasina, the Prime Minister of Bangladesh, was present in the Parliament.) In this sentence, the appositive "শেখ হাসিনা" (Sheikh Hasina) provides the specific identifying information about the noun phrase "বাংলাদেশের প্রধানমন্ত্রী" (the Prime Minister of Bangladesh).

- **Occupational Appositive**: Occupational appositives provide information about the occupation or profession of a person.

  Example: "আমার বাবা, একজন ডাক্তার, প্রায়শই বাইকে কাজ করেন।" (My father, a doctor, mostly travels by bike.) In this sentence, the appositive "একজন ডাক্তার" (a doctor) provides information about the occupation of the noun phrase "আমার বাবা" (my father).

- **Qualifying Appositive**: Qualifying appositives provide additional qualifying information or characteristics about a noun phrase.

  Example: "তার ছেলে, সুন্দর গলার অধিকারী, গান গায়।" (Her son, a beautiful-voiced boy, sings songs.) In this example, the appositive "সুন্দর গলার অধিকারী" (a beautiful-voiced boy) provides qualifying information about the noun phrase "তার ছেলে" (her son).

- **Geographic Appositive**: Geographic appositives provide information about a specific location or place associated with the noun phrase.

  Example: "বগুড়া জেলা, বাংলাদেশের উত্তর-পশ্চিমাঞ্চলের একটি প্রশাসনিক অঞ্চল, পরিচিত হয় শিক্ষা নগরী হিসেবে।" (Bogra District, an administrative region in the north-western region of Bangladesh, is known as a renowned educational city.) In this sentence, the appositive "বাংলাদেশের উত্তর-পশ্চিমাঞ্চলের একটি প্রশাসনিক অঞ্চল" (an administrative region in the north-western region of Bangladesh) provides geographic information about the noun phrase "বগুড়া জেলা" (Bogra District).

Figure 12: Appositive Reference Types

Annotators-in-the-loop: Testing a Novel Annotation Procedure on Italian Case Law

Emma Zanoli[1], Matilde Barbini[1], Davide Riva[2], Sergio Picascia[2], Emanuela Furiosi[3], Stefano D'Ancona[3], and Cristiano Chesi[1]

[1]IUSS Pavia - School for Advanced Studies, NETS Lab
[2]Università degli Studi di Milano, Department of Computer Science
[3]IUSS Pavia - School for Advanced Studies
{emma.zanoli, matilde.barbini, emanuela.furiosi, stefano.dancona, cristiano.chesi}@iusspavia.it
{sergio.picascia, davide.riva1}@unimi.it

Abstract

The availability of annotated legal corpora is crucial for a number of tasks, such as legal search, legal information retrieval, and predictive justice. Annotation is mostly assumed to be a straightforward task: as long as the annotation scheme is well defined and the guidelines are clear, annotators are expected to agree on the labels. This is not always the case, especially in legal annotation, which can be extremely difficult even for expert annotators. We propose a legal annotation procedure that takes into account annotator certainty and improves it through negotiation. We also collect annotator feedback and show that our approach contributes to a positive annotation environment. Our work invites reflection on often neglected ethical concerns regarding legal annotation.

1 Introduction

Despite the success of self-supervised deep learning approaches (Jaiswal et al., 2021), accurate human annotation remains essential for NLP research, and it is no different for its applications to the legal domain. The increasing availability of corpora of legal documents has given a tremendous boost to legal NLP (Zhong et al., 2020), but this comes with serious ethical implications given the potential uses of systems trained on the annotated data (see Tsarapatsanis and Aletras (2021) for a brief overview). Legal annotation is a complex task, where even expert annotators may fail to come to straightforward conclusions (Wyner et al., 2013). This warrants particular reflection on the definition of legal annotation guidelines and on making sure they are appropriate and consistently agreed upon among annotators (Santosuosso and Pinotti, 2020).

To address the aforementioned issues, we present an annotation procedure that involves a group of legal experts in the very process of creating and negotiating the annotation guidelines. We also anonymously collect annotators' feedback and show that our procedure makes them more certain of and satisfied with their work. We believe this to be an important step towards a better treatment of annotators in the field of legal NLP.

The Italian legal system is currently undergoing significant changes in an effort to digitally transform and overall improve legal processes at all levels. At this stage, gathering high quality data is crucial to make sure that any downstream applications do not perpetuate errors and biases. The annotation procedure we describe is a preliminary step in the framework of the *Next Generation UPP* (*NGUPP*) project, funded by the Italian Ministry of Justice, and aimed at improving the efficiency of the judicial system in Italy. Specifically, we intend to empower judges with advanced information management tools to facilitate the drafting of court judgements. Such a tool would be used both retroactively, for legal search of case law, and proactively, for the creation of new judgments.

The paper is organized as follows. In Section 2 we discuss the relevant literature. In Section 3 we present the experimental design. Section 4 presents the annotation procedure. Section 5 is dedicated to the discussion of the results. Finally, in Section 6 we provide concluding remarks and ideas for future developments.

2 Related work

Corpora of legal texts are increasingly available and accessible. This is especially true of legislation (Chalkidis et al., 2019; Váradi et al., 2020), but it also applies to court judgments (Grover et al., 2004; Poudyal et al., 2020; Feng et al., 2022; Kapoor et al., 2022) and other types of legal texts (e.g. con-

The paper was jointly conceived by the authors. However, Section 4.1 was written by Emanuela Furiosi and Section 4.2 was written by Stefano D'Ancona.

Proceedings of the 17th Linguistic Annotation Workshop (LAW-XVII), pages 118–128
July 13, 2023 ©2023 Association for Computational Linguistics

tracts, Funaki et al., 2020). There have already been several annotation efforts in the legal domain (Wyner, 2010; Duan et al., 2019; Glaser et al., 2021a; Kalamkar et al., 2022), with a particular interest towards arguments (see Zhang et al., 2022 for an overview).

While some types of annotation are relatively straightforward, obtaining consistent and accurate annotations in law is extremely challenging (Walker, 2016). Nonetheless, legal annotation tasks often leverage law students as domain experts (Wyner et al., 2013; Chalkidis et al., 2017; Soavi et al., 2022; Correia et al., 2022; Kalamkar et al., 2022). We invite caution in using this approach due to a) ethical concerns on adequate annotator compensation and b) difficulty in ascertaining their domain expertise.

Legal annotation tasks may entail another potentially problematic aspect. It is not uncommon to involve a small group of annotators who initially annotate the same text, which is subsequently revised by a more expert annotator tasked with solving any discrepancies (Wyner et al., 2013; Poudyal et al., 2020; Galli et al., 2022). Although this is a widely accepted method used to obtain gold standard annotations in the legal domain, we will not be using this technique; rather, we embrace the line of research that sees variation in human annotation as something that may naturally arise due to, e.g., ambiguity, uncertainty of the annotator, genuine disagreement, or simply the fact that multiple options are correct (Plank, 2022). Specifically, we follow Basile et al. (2021), who argue that "removing the disagreement might lead to better evaluation scores, but it fundamentally hides the true nature of the task we are trying to solve".

To address the aforementioned issues, we propose an annotation procedure that promotes guideline negotiation. Previous work on legal annotation has featured modifications of annotation guidelines over time, either in a top-down manner or within small groups (Teruel et al., 2018; Correia et al., 2022; Galli et al., 2022). Lee et al. (2022) experiment with collaborative guideline creation among pairs of annotators, albeit not in the legal domain. They show that negotiation leads to improved annotator agreement within the pair, but the performance decreases dramatically among annotators of different pairs. Our group of annotators was not split into pairs for the negotiation; we are not aware of previous work that frames legal annotation as a peer-to-peer negotiation process among an entire group of legal professionals.

In an effort to contribute to a positive annotation environment, we collect feedback from the annotators. Following Nedoluzhko and Mírovský (2013) and Andresen et al. (2020), we collect measures of annotator certainty, checking whether they improve after the negotiation process. We also collect data on the overall satisfaction of the annotators.

The dataset we obtain from our annotation will be used for the development of text segmentation models. Segmenting court judgments into relevant sections can improve legal search and information retrieval; this has already been investigated by Savelka and Ashley (2018), Aumiller et al. (2021) and Glaser et al. (2021b). Licari and Comandè (2022) segment Italian civil judgements with simple regular expressions for bench-marking purposes.

We operate in the Italian legal context, which has been amply explored in previous literature (Lenci et al., 2009; Venturi, 2013; Tagarelli and Simeri, 2021; Galli et al., 2022). However, our proposed annotation procedure is language-agnostic.

3 Experimental design

This section describes our experimental design, aimed at developing an annotation procedure for the legal domain. We briefly present the dataset, the task, the annotators, the annotation tool, and the agreement metrics.

3.1 Dataset

The dataset consists of 50 Italian case law judgments, retrieved from 12 different Courts. The documents all concern first degree civil law judgments regarding the matter of unfair competition.

The selected case law judgments were available in PDF files, from which text was extracted using the Python implementation of `MuPDF`, an open source software framework for viewing and converting PDFs. The documents are very heterogeneous in terms of length: the number of tokens ranges from 1,368 for the smallest document, to more than 8,000 for the largest one, with a mean length of 4,387 tokens and a standard deviation of 1,798.

3.2 Annotation task

Given the collection of documents described in 3.1, the annotators were required to perform a "structural annotation", i.e. to recognize the distinct sections that compose the structure of a court judgement. Thus, the task was to identify sections and sub-sections (text segmentation) and to label those segments (segment labeling).

The annotators were presented with text in free form; they had to underline the segments of interest and assign a label to them choosing from a predefined set. This set of labels (called the "annotation scheme") and its development are described in depth in Section 4. The annotation is aimed at creating a dataset for legal text segmentation. The general expectation was that the entire text would be segmented and labeled (i.e. with no gaps between different sections), although this was not made explicit in the annotation guidelines.

The annotators were given the possibility to review and change their own annotations over time, provided that such modifications were made independently from other annotators.

3.3 Annotators

The annotation task was carried out by 9 law professionals, all of whom have relevant experience as both academics and practitioners: all but one of them hold a PhD and they are all licensed lawyers, having passed the Italian bar exam. While seniority varies on an individual basis (years of professional experience: min 3, max 23), they all have significant expertise in either civil law (4 annotators), criminal law (1 annotator), or a mix of different areas (4 annotators). As such, they are all familiar with Italian legal language and did not require ad hoc linguistic training. However, none of them had ever annotated before. For this reason, three law professionals with prior annotation experience were consulted for an initial draft of the annotation guidelines, but they did not perform the actual annotation task.

The annotators were asked to fill out a feedback questionnaire after the annotation process (see 5.4).

3.4 Annotation tool

Technical constraints and privacy issues prompted us to use proprietary annotation software. We use the Ellogon language engineering platform (Ntogramatzis et al., 2022), since it supports the task as defined in 3.2. The platform had to be customized to introduce the annotation labels of interest.

3.5 Agreement metrics

We evaluate agreement among annotators (Inter-Annotator Agreement, IAA) in order to provide a quantitative assessment of (1) the complexity of the annotation task, and (2) the homogeneity of the results. The annotation was carried out and analysed in the absence of a gold standard; we consider appropriate annotations to be an incrementally realised goal rather than a given (see also 5.3).

IAA has to account for 3 factors: a) presence of labels; b) alignment of annotated segments; c) agreement of labels assigned to segments. In order to cover all of these characteristics, we employ the γ coefficient (Mathet et al., 2015). It is computed as the average of all local disagreements, referred to as disorders, between units from different annotators:

$$\forall s \in c, \gamma = 1 - \frac{\delta(s)}{\delta_e(c)} \tag{1}$$

with $\delta(s)$ being the disorder of the annotation set s and $\delta_e(c)$ being the expected disorder of the corpus c. Maximum agreement is represented by $\gamma = 1$, while $\gamma < 0$ corresponds to the worst case, where annotator agreement is worse than annotating at random. Following this methodology, units of annotation are aligned to minimize the overall disorder. We compute γ scores not only for each document, but also for each label defined in the annotation scheme in order to identify the most and the least disputed structural segments.

Finally, since annotators had the possibility of going back to the documents assigned to them and review their own annotations, we store periodic dumps of the annotation database and estimate self-agreement, i.e. the extent to which annotators maintain the segments and labels they had already selected. To this aim, we introduce the metric δ, calculated as:

$$\delta = \frac{1}{T}\sum_{t=2}^{T}\frac{1}{|K|}\sum_{k\in K}\frac{|S_k^{(t-1)} \cap S_k^{(t)}|}{|S_k^{(t-1)}|} \tag{2}$$

where T is the total number of periodic dumps of the annotation database, K is the label set, and S_k^{τ} is the set of segments labelled with k at time τ. Notice that δ takes into account only the intersection of segment sets at consecutive times, and $\delta \in [0; 1]$.

4 Annotation scheme

In this section we summarize the development of the annotation scheme: first, we describe the initial scheme as designed by a restricted pool of experts; then, we recount its subsequent negotiation; finally, we report the resulting annotation scheme.

4.1 Initial development of the annotation scheme

The initial structural annotation scheme was developed through a reflection carried out by a small group of legal experts with specific and complementary expertise in both legal practice and in the digitization of justice. Specifically, these were: a university professor, former judge at the Court of Appeal of Milan; two legal professionals with previous annotation experience; and a researcher who also has around 7 years of experience as a lawyer and who is among the 9 annotators who carried out the annotation task.

The annotation experts involved had previously worked on complex structural annotation schemes. By contrast, it was unanimously decided to keep the structural annotation scheme simple, for two reasons. First, the structural segmentation was, at least initially, primarily aimed at distinguishing the reasoning part of the judgment from the other sections. Second, the more basic structural analysis was to be complemented and enriched by a further layer of more detailed argumentative annotation.

The initial annotation scheme featured 5 sections, specifically:

- the section **"Corte e parti"** included the indication of the **court**, the panel of **judges**, and the **parties** in the trial (i.e., the plaintiffs, the defendants, and any intervening third parties);
- the section **"Antefatto"** included **background information**, specifically on a) the proceedings of the trial, and b) the reconstruction of the facts involved in the case;
- the section **"Domande"** identified the **claims and arguments** brought forward by the parties (i.e., claims made by the plaintiff(s) and any counterclaims made by the defendant(s)). Each claim would be labelled individually;
- the section **"Motivazione"** identified the part of the judgment in which the **reasoning** for the decision of an individual claim is explained. Each line of reasoning would be labelled individually;
- the section **"Decisione"** identified the **final decision(s)** on each individual claim. If there are multiple decisions, each would be labelled individually.

In the presence of multiple claims, lines of reasoning and decisions, they would be numbered to link the three elements to one another.

The content of Italian court judgments is regulated by Article 132, c. 2 of the Italian Civil Procedure Code (CPC), which stipulates that each judgment *"must contain: 1) an indication of the judge who pronounced it; 2) an indication of the parties and their attorneys; 3) the conclusions of the prosecutor and those of the parties; 4) a concise statement of the reasons of fact and law of the judgment; 5) the ruling, the date of the deliberation and the signature of the judge."* Nonetheless, the exact outline and structure of the judgments may vary in practice (e.g. some judges may wish to add section headings to structure their decisions, while others may not; some may provide this information into clearly separated sections, while others may not; etc.). The initial annotation scheme was thus developed taking into consideration not only the structure of the judgments as currently regulated by the CPC, but also as applied in practice by judges.

As one can see, the sections of this initial scheme, while encompassing the essential elements of the judgment outlined in the CPC, are not exactly overlapping. Specifically, the contents of items (1) and (2) are grouped in the "Corte e parti" section; the contents of item (3) can be found in the "Domande" section, the contents of item (4) correspond to the "Motivazione" section, and the contents of item (5) correspond to the "Decisione" section. Additionally, the annotation scheme includes the "Antefatto" section[1]. Previous experimentation with legal search models revealed that they would sometimes retrieve judgments based on content which was presented as background information in the case, even when the expected outcome would relate to the reasoning section. This segmentation was thus meant to aid the models in excluding potentially irrelevant information by focusing on specific sections.

[1]This element was actually mandatory in a previous version of the CPC, but it has not been since 2009; in practice, a lot of judges still use it.

Please note that, at the time this annotation scheme was devised, the technical specifics of how the annotation would be carried out had not yet been defined.

4.2 Negotiation of the annotation scheme

The initial annotation scheme was modified through three meetings involving the entire group of annotators. The need for discussion and negotiation first became evident upon starting to apply the initial annotation guidelines within the constraints of the provided annotation tool. Specifically, there was an interest in mapping the overarching structural relationships between claims, reasoning and final decisions.

It was decided that individual claims, lines of reasoning and decisions would be considered sub-sections of more broadly defined sections. Furthermore, it was noted that the annotations of sub-sections could benefit from the definition of "chains" of reasoning, practically consisting of pairwise relationships between a claim, the reasoning on it, and the corresponding final decision.

After extensive discussion, it was further specified in the guidelines that the aforementioned "chains" should simply reflect lines of reasoning, without specifications on the nature of the reasoning itself (e.g. premise vs. conclusion, support vs. contrast). It was concluded that these would be left for a further layer of argumentative annotation, to be performed at a later time. This integration of the guidelines was considered necessary to prevent annotators from labeling text segments based on an "argumentative" and not a "structural" evaluation of their content.

Another point that required a collaborative discussion was related to the distinction between reasoning and decision. As previously mentioned, Italian court judgements are required to feature a specific section, at the very end, where the main decisions of the case are summarized: it is the so-called "Dispositivo" (final ruling), typically placed after the heading PQM, which translates to "For These Reasons". However, judges often "anticipate" their own decision within the body of the reasoning, as it may come naturally to conclude a given line of thought. The annotators thus concluded that within the "reasoning" section there could be "decision" sub-sections attributed to specific text segments.

4.3 The resulting annotation scheme

As a result of the collaborative (re)negotiation of earlier annotation schemes, the annotators came to agree on a set of guidelines, which were then used to annotate the dataset. We call these guidelines the "resulting annotation scheme", summarized in Table 1.

This annotation scheme is meant to segment Italian court judgements of civil proceedings at two levels: sections and sub-sections. The sections correspond to the ones presented in 4.1. Sub-sections are possible for the last three sections. These are meant to distinguish between different claims (e.g. `<dom1>`, `<dom2>`), different lines of reasoning (e.g. `<mot1>`, `<mot2>`), and different decisions (e.g. `<dec1>`, `<dec2>`). The sub-sections can be put in relationships of the type (`<dom>`,`<mot>`) or (`<mot>`,`<dec>`) if a motivation for decision `<dec>` on claim `<dom>` is explicit in the document, otherwise a (`<dom>`,`<dec>`) relation could be specified.

5 Analysis and discussion of the results

The results of our work include the annotation scheme as well as the output of the annotation activity. We evaluate Inter-Annotator Agreement from both a quantitative and qualitative perspective and we report annotator feedback.

5.1 Appraising the resulting annotation scheme

Given the somewhat unusual nature of our procedure, does the resulting annotation scheme reflect what we might expect?

Considering the provisions of the Italian CPC (see 4.1), it is not surprising that a similar 5-part subdivision can be found in other works on Italian legal NLP (Galli et al., 2022; Licari and Comandè, 2022). Contrary to what one may expect, though, Italian judgments often do not conform to a strict standard, with some sections (<ANT> and <MOT-SEZ>) being presented in different orders or not being clearly distinguished from one another. Text segmentation of Italian judgements is therefore not a trivial task, which motivates the need for text segmentation models to be carefully evaluated.

The scheme is also comparable to other works in the literature that have, within a variety of legal contexts, outlined a structural segmentation of court judgements (see e.g. Wyner et al., 2013 for the UK, Poudyal et al., 2020 for the European Court of Human Rights, Glaser et al., 2021b for Germany).

Sections	Sub-sections	Italian	Explanation
<COR>		Corte e parti	Court, judicial panel, parties
<ANT>		Antefatto	Background information
<DOMSEZ>	<dom1>,<dom2>,...	Domande	Claim(s) and argumentation of the parties
<MOTSEZ>	<mot1>,<mot2>,...	Motivazione	Reason(s) for the final decision(s)
<DECSEZ>	<dec1>,<dec2>,...	Decisione	Final decision(s)

Table 1: The resulting annotation scheme for Italian court judgements of civil proceedings.

5.2 Annotator agreement

We report the results obtained for the metrics introduced in 3.5.

Before computing the agreement metrics, some cleaning operations were applied to the section annotation results. In particular, since sections are meant to be as contiguous as possible, quasi-consecutive segments with the same label were merged into a single segment. For practical purposes, segments within a distance of 25 characters from one another were considered quasi-consecutive. Duplicates and quasi-duplicates (i.e. segments that share at least 90% of another segment underlined later) were deleted, since they likely result from technical difficulties with the annotation tool. Finally, documents with partial annotations (i.e. with segments labelled with less than half of the labels in the annotation scheme) are not considered in the agreement evaluation. This is motivated by the expectation that each document contains at least one segment fulfilling each function, and does not undermine the results, resulting in the exclusion of only 3 documents for the section annotation and 6 documents for the subsection annotation.

Table 2 reports the γ score statistics for both sections and sub-sections. High standard deviation suggests that some documents were more complex to annotate than others.

	Segments per doc.	Mean γ	Std.Dev. γ	Max. γ
Sections	9.92	0.635	0.225	0.996
Sub-sections	13.79	0.483	0.260	0.995

Table 2: Average per-document number of annotated segments and γ score statistics over retained documents. Notice $\gamma < 0$ on a document if the annotation agreement is worse than the null case of random annotations, whereas $\gamma = 1$ on a document if annotations perfectly agree.

As the table shows, the number of labeled segments in each document exceeds the cardinality of the label set, which indicates that the sections tend to be discontinuous and sparse inside the document. Indeed, Figure 1 shows that both in a document with well-aligned and in another document with poorly aligned annotations, some sections are interrupted by others and re-appear later in the text.

Figure 2 shows the confidence intervals of γ scores for each section type, indicating that some sections are more difficult to locate than others. While the <COR> section is usually located at the beginning and is therefore widely agreed upon, the location of the <ANT> section varies depending on the judge and the specific case. Agreement on the <DECSEZ> section is among the lowest. As discussed in 4.2, although the final decisions typically conclude the judgement, anticipations of the decisions can be found in previous sections, leading to interpretative differences as to what constitutes a final decision. Although we do not have a baseline we can compare our results against, our findings are consistent with those reported by Wyner et al. (2013).

To gain a deeper understanding of the causes for disagreement, we calculated how frequent it was for the annotators to label the same segment differently, i.e. the categorial dissimilarity d_{cat} between aligned annotators units. As expected, the label pairs (a, b) that showed the highest disagreement, i.e. the highest number of segments that were annotated with a by one annotator and with b by another annotator, were (<ANT>, <DOMSEZ>) and (<MOTSEZ>, <DECSEZ>).

Figure 3 shows the confidence intervals for γ scores for each subsection type. Agreement drops significantly for these more fine-grained labels. <dec> segments are the ones that raise the highest disagreement, while segments of the other two types are comparable in terms of agreement. The higher numerosity of <dec> segments likely plays a role in their higher variability.

To calculate the metric we introduce, namely self-agreement over time, we made 4 dumps of the database, one before each negotiation meeting

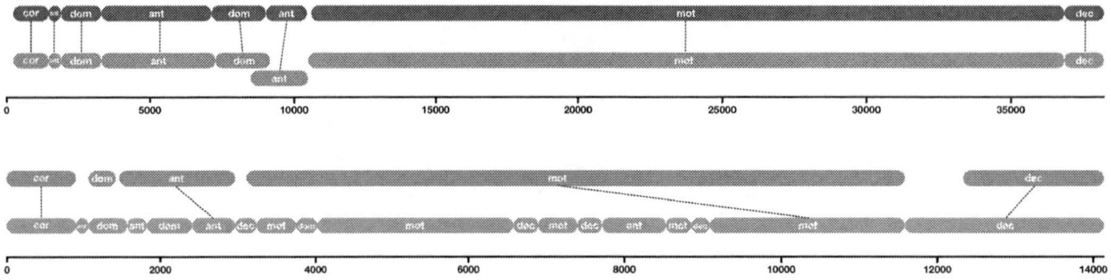

Figure 1: Example of alignment (top image) and misalignment (bottom image) of segments selected and labelled by two annotators for two documents. The horizontal axis represents the position of characters in the document.

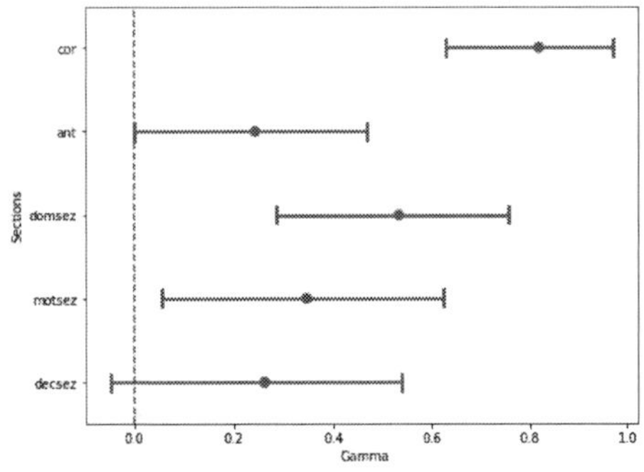

Figure 2: γ score mean and 95% confidence interval for each section label.

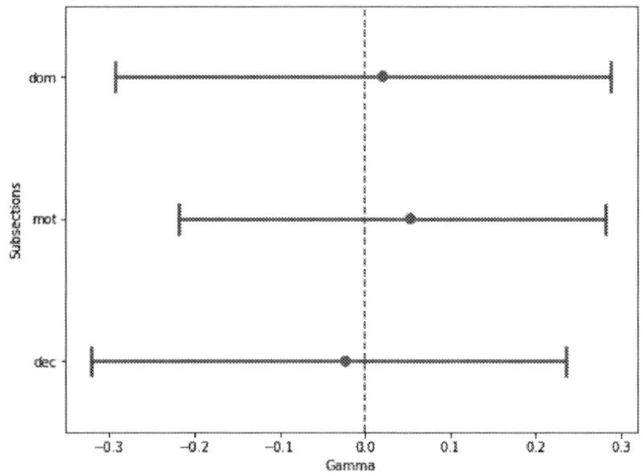

Figure 3: γ score mean and 95% confidence interval for each subsection label.

and one at the end of the annotation process. We found an average δ of 0.963, with a standard deviation of 0.151, which indicates that few changes were made to annotations over time. In particular, the mean δ reveals that few changes occurred as a consequence of the meetings, but its standard deviation suggests some annotators made much more extensive modifications than others.

5.3 Qualitative analysis of annotator disagreement

While agreement metrics are important in the evaluation of annotation, the investigation of disagreement can reveal important considerations which can greatly improve the annotation process (Lee et al., 2022; Plank, 2022). This section presents a brief but illustrative qualitative analysis of some outputs of the annotation: the aim is to highlight where the agreement between the annotators proved to be weak, leading us to reflect on what might be the primary causes of the disagreements.

From a legal standpoint, unfair competition is a rather complex matter and the judgments tend to exhibit a convoluted structure, with the judges having to address a large number of claims brought forward by the parties. This complexity is certainly a challenge for the annotators, who need to deduce and combine non-trivial information to arrive at the label (Malik et al., 2022). As reported in 5.2, the label pairs that exhibited a higher level of disagreement between annotators were (<ANT>, <DOMSEZ>) and (<MOTSEZ>, <DECSEZ>). We now review an example for each label pair.

Background information may be presented and evaluated throughout the entire judgement; an annotator might therefore be uncertain as to which label to apply. For example, the facts of the case can contribute to the argumentation of the reasoning section (see Figure 6 in the Appendix). Additionally, the judge may reference the claims of the parties in their summary of the facts (see Figure 4). Given the ambiguity, Annotator 1 (left) decided to remark the presence of the claims (<DOMSEZ>, in green), while Annotator 2 (right) chose to label the entire section as background information (<ANT>, in purple).

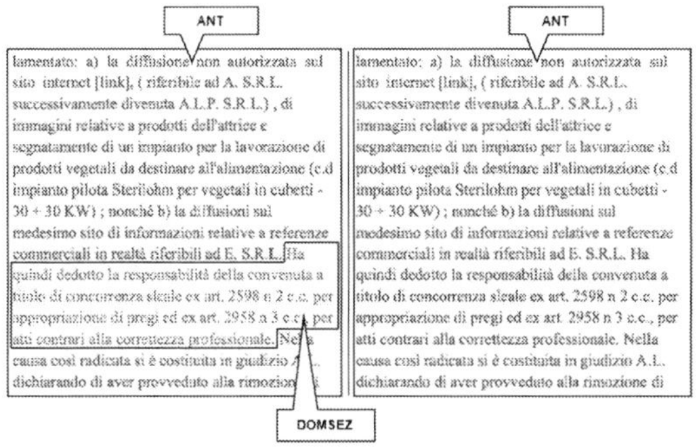

Figure 4: Excerpt showing disagreement between two annotators (<ANT> - purple, <DOMSEZ> - green).

In addition to the inherent difficulty of the subject matter, there is potential ambiguity in the annotation guidelines: as can be seen from Figure 5, Annotator 1 (left) identified parts of the decision (in orange) also within the section containing the legal reasoning (in blue), whereas Annotator 2 (right) labeled the entire segment as legal reasoning (see Figure 7 in the Appendix for another example). Although the negotiation meetings featured extensive discussion on the use of the <DECSEZ> and <dec> labels, some ambiguity remains, leading annotators to different interpretations.

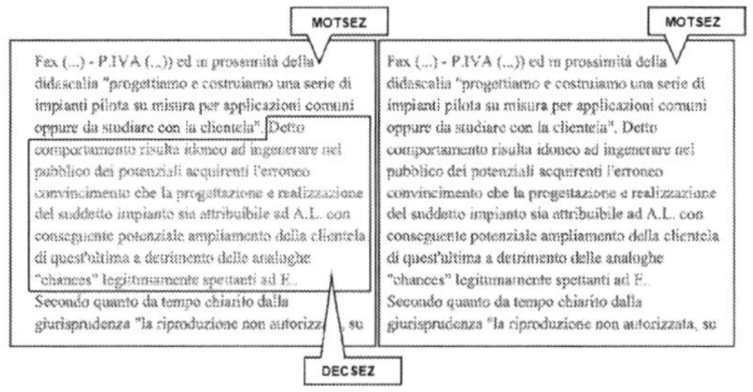

Figure 5: Excerpt showing disagreement between two annotators (<MOTSEZ> - blue, <DECSEZ> - orange).

It is evident that <MOTSEZ> is a complex section whose content interacts with other sections through complex textual realizations; as such, it is difficult to annotate in an unanimous fashion. Let us reiterate that we do not intend to conflate this complexity into an aggregated "ground truth"; rather, we are actively experimenting with methods that can capture and appreciate interpretative differences.

5.4 Annotator feedback

As we have extensively discussed, the annotators were encouraged to (re)negotiate the annotation scheme and guidelines over several meetings. Given the difficulty of legal annotation, we believe this to be crucial in making annotators feel supported. Not only did we believe that this process would improve annotator certainty (Nedoluzhko and Mírovský, 2013; Andresen et al., 2020), but we also hoped it would help annotators be satisfied with their work. To measure this, we asked the annotators to fill out a questionnaire to provide anonymous feedback on the annotation process. Based on the feedback we gathered, it appears that annotator certainty increased slightly after the meetings (35%). Additionally, all respondents but one[2]: a) express satisfaction with the work they have done; b) report that the meetings facilitated a more thorough comprehension of the annotation process; c) indicate that the meetings were instrumental in revisiting guidelines that were not sufficiently clear or appropriate.

6 Conclusion and Future Work

This paper introduces a novel annotation procedure based on the active participation of an entire group of domain experts in the process of creating and negotiating the annotation guidelines. An interdisciplinary research team, involving experts from the legal, linguistic and computer science fields, has actively collaborated in order to address the common issues faced in the annotation of legal documents. The result of this procedure is an annotation scheme tailored to Italian case law judgments, which provides a unifying structure to integrate the sections mandated by the law and the ones used in practice by judges. We consider these to be preliminary results in the ongoing development of a reliable procedure that will be extended in future work. We are currently experimenting with the annotation of more fine-grained phenomena: the structure outlined by our annotation scheme serves as the basis for the annotation of legal arguments. Since the work presented here is still ongoing, we are unable to release the annotated dataset and the annotation guidelines at present; however, the annotation scheme is presented in Table 1 and its development is documented in Section 4.

Our project comes at a crucial time in the process of re-thinking how the judicial system works

[2]In the questionnaire these were presented as statements that the annotators could either agree, partially agree, or disagree with. The same individual disagreed with all of them; regrettably, since the feedback is anonymous, we can not reach out to them directly to understand what may have gone wrong.

in Italy. The work of law professionals is changing due to the introduction of increasingly sophisticated technological tools. The annotations we collect will be used to build corpora that represent the structure and argumentation of Italian court judgments. Leveraging segmented case law judgments can improve both keyword-based and semantic-based search of legal precedents. We are actively experimenting with different techniques, including few-shot learning, that can leverage this data to improve the efficiency of legal search. The long-term goal is to integrate these tools into a document builder that supports Italian judges in the drafting of court judgments.

The annotation of a small set of 50 judgments was used to elaborate, apply and evaluate a novel annotation procedure, capable of taking into account the nuances that the legal subject matter brings, especially when applied to complex cases, while also allowing domain experts to be adequately valued in their specific expertise. Discussions on the ethics of legal NLP abound, with emphasis on the data and its potentially harmful uses. While crucial, these discussions would benefit from further reflection on how the data is being annotated. We hope that our results can inspire researchers and practitioners to carefully consider these issues in future work.

Ethics Statement

Our work is meant to inspire reflection on the treatment of annotators in the field of legal NLP. Specifically: a) we make it a point of involving legal professionals, not law students; b) the annotators involved in the project won a public selection competition to participate in a project aimed at the digitalization of the Italian judicial system; c) the annotators are all hired to work on the project and receive adequate pay; d) we make sure that their specific expertise is valued by involving them in the creation and negotiation of the annotation guidelines; e) we take measures to track whether they are happy with the work they are doing.

Limitations

Although our annotation procedure envisions a negotiation process among an entire group of legal experts, due to time constraints each document was eventually annotated by either 2 or 3 annotators. Having the entire group annotate every document might have yielded more interesting and fruitful discussions for the negotiation process and allowed for a deeper analysis of annotator (dis)agreement. We also have to point out that several annotators lamented technical difficulties in using the annotation tool (due to the limitations of the tool itself); this may have severely impacted annotation quality. We wish to address these limitations in future work.

Acknowledgements

This work is supported by the Next Generation UPP project (May 2022 - September 2023) within the PON program of the Italian Ministry of Justice. We are thankful to Amedeo Santosuosso for generously sharing his valuable expertise to the benefit of this project: he has been a long-time advocate for the creation of a document builder that supports Italian judges in the drafting of court judgments; he also contributed to the initial draft of the annotation guidelines presented here. We would also like to thank the anonymous reviewers for their insightful comments.

References

Melanie Andresen, Michael Vauth, and Heike Zinsmeister. 2020. Modeling ambiguity with many annotators and self-assessments of annotator certainty. In *Proceedings of the 14th Linguistic Annotation Workshop*, pages 48–59, Barcelona, Spain. Association for Computational Linguistics.

Dennis Aumiller, Satya Almasian, Sebastian Lackner, and Michael Gertz. 2021. Structural text segmentation of legal documents. In *Proceedings of the Eighteenth International Conference on Artificial Intelligence and Law*, ICAIL '21, page 2–11, New York, NY, USA. Association for Computing Machinery.

Valerio Basile, Michael Fell, Tommaso Fornaciari, Dirk Hovy, Silviu Paun, Barbara Plank, Massimo Poesio, and Alexandra Uma. 2021. We need to consider disagreement in evaluation. In *Proceedings of the 1st Workshop on Benchmarking: Past, Present and Future*, pages 15–21, Online. Association for Computational Linguistics.

Ilias Chalkidis, Ion Androutsopoulos, and Achilleas Michos. 2017. Extracting contract elements. In *Proceedings of the 16th edition of the International Conference on Articial Intelligence and Law*. ACM.

Ilias Chalkidis, Emmanouil Fergadiotis, Prodromos Malakasiotis, and Ion Androutsopoulos. 2019. Large-scale multi-label text classification on EU legislation. In *Proceedings of the 57th Annual Meeting of the Association for Computational Linguistics*, pages 6314–6322, Florence, Italy. Association for Computational Linguistics.

Fernando A Correia, Alexandre AA Almeida, José Luiz Nunes, Kaline G Santos, Ivar A Hartmann, Felipe A Silva, and Hélio Lopes. 2022. Fine-grained legal entity annotation: A case study on the brazilian supreme court. *Information Processing & Management*, 59(1):102794.

Xingyi Duan, Baoxin Wang, Ziyue Wang, Wentao Ma, Yiming Cui, Dayong Wu, Shijin Wang, Ting Liu, Tianxiang Huo, Zhen Hu, Heng Wang, and Zhiyuan Liu. 2019. Cjrc: A reliable human-annotated benchmark dataset for chinese judicial reading comprehension. In *Chinese Computational Linguistics*, pages 439–451, Cham. Springer International Publishing.

Yi Feng, Chuanyi Li, and Vincent Ng. 2022. Legal judgment prediction: A survey of the state of the art. In *Proceedings of the Thirty-First International Joint Conference on Artificial Intelligence, IJCAI-22*, pages 5461–5469.

Ruka Funaki, Yusuke Nagata, Kohei Suenaga, and Shinsuke Mori. 2020. A contract corpus for recognizing rights and obligations. In *Proceedings of the Twelfth Language Resources and Evaluation Conference*, pages 2045–2053, Marseille, France. European Language Resources Association.

Federico Galli, Giulia Grundler, Alessia Fidelangeli, Andrea Galassi, Francesca Lagioia, Elena Palmieri, Federico Ruggeri, Giovanni Sartor, and Paolo Torroni. 2022. Predicting outcomes of italian vat decisions 1. In *Legal Knowledge and Information Systems*, pages 188–193. IOS Press.

Ingo Glaser, Sebastian Moser, and Florian Matthes. 2021a. Generation of legal norm chains: Extracting the most relevant norms from court rulings. In *Frontiers in Artificial Intelligence and Applications*. IOS Press.

Ingo Glaser, Sebastian Moser, and Florian Matthes. 2021b. Improving legal information retrieval: Metadata extraction and segmentation of german court rulings. In *Proceedings of the 13th International Joint Conference on Knowledge Discovery, Knowledge Engineering and Knowledge Management*. SCITEPRESS - Science and Technology Publications.

Claire Grover, Ben Hachey, and Ian Hughson. 2004. The HOLJ corpus. supporting summarisation of legal texts. In *Proceedings of the 5th International Workshop on Linguistically Interpreted Corpora*, pages 47–54, Geneva, Switzerland. COLING.

Ashish Jaiswal, Ashwin Ramesh Babu, Mohammad Zaki Zadeh, Debapriya Banerjee, and Fillia Makedon. 2021. A survey on contrastive self-supervised learning. *Technologies*, 9(1).

Prathamesh Kalamkar, Aman Tiwari, Astha Agarwal, Saurabh Karn, Smita Gupta, Vivek Raghavan, and Ashutosh Modi. 2022. Corpus for automatic structuring of legal documents. In *Proceedings of the Thirteenth Language Resources and Evaluation Conference*, pages 4420–4429, Marseille, France. European Language Resources Association.

Arnav Kapoor, Mudit Dhawan, Anmol Goel, Arjun T H, Akshala Bhatnagar, Vibhu Agrawal, Amul Agrawal, Arnab Bhattacharya, Ponnurangam Kumaraguru, and Ashutosh Modi. 2022. HLDC: Hindi legal documents corpus. In *Findings of the Association for Computational Linguistics: ACL 2022*, pages 3521–3536, Dublin, Ireland. Association for Computational Linguistics.

Seunggun Lee, Alexandra DeLucia, Ryan Guan, Rubing Li, Nikita Nangia, Shalaka Vaidya, Lining Zhang, Zijun Yuan, Praneeth Ganedi, Britney Ngaw, et al. 2022. Common law annotations: Investigating the stability of dialog annotations. In *The Tenth AAAI Conference on Human Computation and Crowdsourcing*. Association for the Advancement of Artificial Intelligence.

Alessandro Lenci, Simonetta Montemagni, Vito Pirrelli, and Giulia Venturi. 2009. Ontology learning from italian legal texts. In *Law, Ontologies and the Semantic Web*, pages 75–94. IOS Press.

Daniele Licari and Giovanni Comandè. 2022. Italian-legal-bert: A pre-trained transformer language model for italian law. In *EKAW'22: Companion Proceedings of the 23rd International Conference on Knowledge Engineering and Knowledge Management*.

Vijit Malik, Rishabh Sanjay, Shouvik Kumar Guha, Angshuman Hazarika, Shubham Nigam, Arnab Bhattacharya, and Ashutosh Modi. 2022. Semantic segmentation of legal documents via rhetorical roles. In *Proceedings of the Natural Legal Language Processing Workshop 2022*, pages 153–171, Abu Dhabi, United Arab Emirates (Hybrid). Association for Computational Linguistics.

Yann Mathet, Antoine Widlöcher, and Jean-Philippe Métivier. 2015. The unified and holistic method gamma (γ) for inter-annotator agreement measure and alignment. *Computational Linguistics*, 41(3):437–479.

Anna Nedoluzhko and Jiří Mírovský. 2013. Annotators' certainty and disagreements in coreference and bridging annotation in Prague dependency treebank. In *Proceedings of the Second International Conference on Dependency Linguistics (DepLing 2013)*, pages 236–243, Prague, Czech Republic. Charles University in Prague, Matfyzpress, Prague, Czech Republic.

Alexandros Fotios Ntogramatzis, Anna Gradou, Georgios Petasis, and Marko Kokol. 2022. The ellogon web annotation tool: Annotating moral values and arguments. In *Proceedings of the Thirteenth Language Resources and Evaluation Conference*, pages 3442–3450, Marseille, France. European Language Resources Association.

Barbara Plank. 2022. The "problem" of human label variation: On ground truth in data, modeling and evaluation. In *Proceedings of the 2022 Conference on Empirical Methods in Natural Language Processing*, pages 10671–10682, Abu Dhabi, United Arab Emirates. Association for Computational Linguistics.

Prakash Poudyal, Jaromir Savelka, Aagje Ieven, Marie Francine Moens, Teresa Goncalves, and Paulo Quaresma. 2020. ECHR: Legal corpus for argument mining. In *Proceedings of the 7th Workshop on Argument Mining*, pages 67–75, Online. Association for Computational Linguistics.

Amedeo Santosuosso and Giulia Pinotti. 2020. Bottleneck or crossroad? problems of legal sources annotation and some theoretical thoughts. *Stats*, 3(3):376–395.

Jaromir Savelka and Kevin D Ashley. 2018. Segmenting us court decisions into functional and issue specific parts. In *JURIX*, pages 111–120.

Michele Soavi, Nicola Zeni, John Mylopoulos, and Luisa Mich. 2022. Semantic annotation of legal contracts with ContrattoA. *Informatics*, 9(4):72.

Andrea Tagarelli and Andrea Simeri. 2021. Unsupervised law article mining based on deep pre-trained language representation models with application to the italian civil code. *Artificial Intelligence and Law*, pages 1–57.

Milagro Teruel, Cristian Cardellino, Fernando Cardellino, Laura Alonso Alemany, and Serena Villata. 2018. Increasing argument annotation reproducibility by using inter-annotator agreement to improve guidelines. In *Proceedings of the Eleventh International Conference on Language Resources and Evaluation (LREC 2018)*, Miyazaki, Japan. European Language Resources Association (ELRA).

Dimitrios Tsarapatsanis and Nikolaos Aletras. 2021. On the ethical limits of natural language processing on legal text. In *Findings of the Association for Computational Linguistics: ACL-IJCNLP 2021*, pages 3590–3599, Online. Association for Computational Linguistics.

Tamás Váradi, Svetla Koeva, Martin Yamalov, Marko Tadić, Bálint Sass, Bartłomiej Nitoń, Maciej Ogrodniczuk, Piotr Pęzik, Verginica Barbu Mititelu, Radu Ion, Elena Irimia, Maria Mitrofan, Vasile Păiș, Dan Tufiș, Radovan Garabík, Simon Krek, Andraz Repar, Matjaž Rihtar, and Janez Brank. 2020. The MARCELL legislative corpus. In *Proceedings of the Twelfth Language Resources and Evaluation Conference*, pages 3761–3768, Marseille, France. European Language Resources Association.

Giulia Venturi. 2013. Investigating legal language peculiarities across different types of italian legal texts: an nlp-based approach. In *Bridging the Gap (s) between Language and the Law. Proceedings of the 3rd European Conference of the International Association of Forensic Linguistics*, pages 138–156.

Vern R Walker. 2016. The need for annotated corpora from legal documents, and for (human) protocols for creating them: the attribution problem.

Adam Z Wyner. 2010. Towards annotating and extracting textual legal case elements. *Informatica e Diritto: special issue on legal ontologies and artificial intelligent techniques*, 19(1-2):9–18.

Adam Z Wyner, Wim Peters, and Daniel Katz. 2013. A case study on legal case annotation. In *JURIX*, pages 165–174.

Gechuan Zhang, Paul Nulty, and David Lillis. 2022. A decade of legal argumentation mining: Datasets and approaches. In *Natural Language Processing and Information Systems*, pages 240–252, Cham. Springer International Publishing.

Haoxi Zhong, Chaojun Xiao, Cunchao Tu, Tianyang Zhang, Zhiyuan Liu, and Maosong Sun. 2020. How does NLP benefit legal system: A summary of legal artificial intelligence. In *Proceedings of the 58th Annual Meeting of the Association for Computational Linguistics*, pages 5218–5230, Online. Association for Computational Linguistics.

A Appendix: additional examples

Additional examples of annotator disagreement, discussed in 5.3.

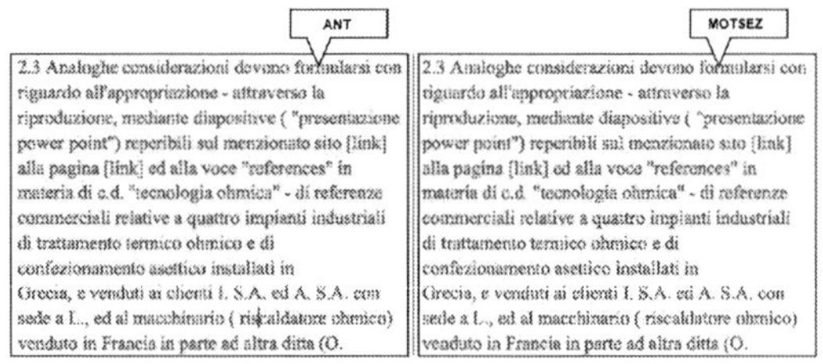

Figure 6: Excerpt showing disagreement between two annotators (<ANT> - purple, <MOTSEZ> - blue)

.

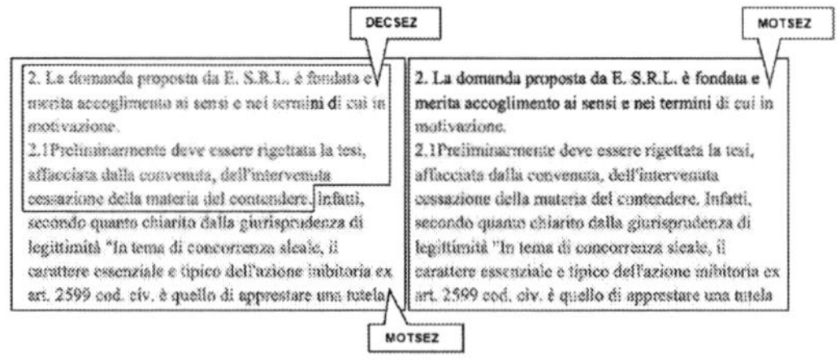

Figure 7: Excerpt showing disagreement between two annotators (<MOTSEZ> - blue, <DECSEZ> - orange). The unlabeled segments (in black) are an example of the quasi-consecutive segments referenced in 5.2, which were likely caused by technical difficulties with the annotation tool.

Annotating Decomposition in Time: Three Approaches for *Again*

Martin Kopf and **Remus Gergel**
Saarland University
{martin.kopf, remus.gergel}@uni-saarland.de

Abstract

This paper reports on a three-part series of original methods geared towards producing semantic annotations for the decompositional marker *again*. The three methods are (i) exhaustive expert annotation based on a comprehensive set of guidelines, (ii) extension of expert annotation by predicting presuppositions with a Multinomial Naïve Bayes classifier in the context of a meta-analysis to optimize feature selection and (iii) quality-controlled crowdsourcing with ensuing evaluation and KMeans clustering of annotation vectors.

1 Introduction

The goal of this paper is to present a series of three original methods in the context of, and first hands-on results for, ascertaining theoretically relevant ambiguities in readings of historical data on decomposition. Decompositional adverbs (e.g., *again* and its relatives in many languages) have attracted attention not only in the context of formal analyses (say, structural vs. lexicalist) since they are insightful, if not uncontroversial, in their own right. They also touch on the representation of events, presuppositions, and more generally the way the structural and the meaning components of particular languages are to be related (cf. Rapp and Stechow, 1999; Beck, 2005; Zwarts, 2019; Ausensi et al., 2021, among many others). Moreover, recent inquiries into diachronic formal semantics have crucially shown that diachronic data can not only receive motivated theoretical analyses but are also able to elucidate synchronic debates that could not be solved otherwise thus far (Beck and Gergel, 2015; Degano and Aloni, 2022). However, major practical issues with much needed diachronic data are the costly process of extraction w.r.t. high-quality data, their reliable annotation, stronger validation (than, say, the intuitions of individual researchers), and, when possible, partially automatic amplification/replication. The structure of this paper is as follows: In section 2, we start off with a discussion of the English adverb *again* and its main readings – as relevant to the discussion at hand. Next, we discuss the three methods for producing semantic annotations for *again*: In section 3, we go into detail regarding the procedure behind exhaustively annotating its various readings with a team of expert annotators based on syntactically parsed diachronic corpora of English (ranging throughout recorded history, from Old to Modern English; our concrete focus here lies 'only' on the last two to four centuries). The first slice of this semantic annotation, i.e., all 1,901 uses of *again* in the Penn Parsed Corpus of Modern British English (2nd ed., 'PPCMBE2', cf. Kroch et al., 2016), is ready to be shared with the community along with a tool to be merged with users' own instances of the PPCMBE2. The second method discussed in this paper (section 4) seeks to tap into the semantically enriched data and extend the expert annotation: We discuss the performance of a Multinomial Naïve Bayes classifier in predicting the main readings of *again* in PPCMBE2. We do so in the context of a meta-analysis exploring the best-performing feature combinations based on a set of 16 different features of three different major types (features based on our semantic annotation, structural features drawn from the pre-existing syntactic parsing, and 'naïve' features based on the textual surface). We cover the third and final approach in section 5. It reports on what we call an 'informed crowdsourcing experiment', which we designed to explore crowd aptitude for providing nuanced semantic annotations on diachronic data – natural language data for which our ('informed') crowd workers can have no actual native speaker intuitions whatsoever (as the bearers of truly native intuition are dead). Here we report on the performance of KMeans clustering of the crowdsourcing data when compared to our gold standard of expert annotations. We close with a general discussion in section 6.

Proceedings of the 17th Linguistic Annotation Workshop (LAW-XVII), pages 129–135
July 13, 2023 ©2023 Association for Computational Linguistics

2 *Again* and its readings

The natural language phenomenon at the core of all annotation tasks discussed here is the English adverb *again* and its well-documented ambiguity. Consider the example corpus data (1) and (2):

(1) i. [A]ll the plants then must be examined, (token 345)
[...]
ii. and those which are planted in pots, should in the following year's bloom be **again examined** (349)
(FALLOWFIELD-1791-2,34.349, '*Gardening Calendar*')

(2) i. He sat really lost in thought for the first few minutes; (token 565)
[...]
ii. He [Mr. Knightley] hesitated, (618)
iii. got up. (619)
[...]
iv. and he **sat down again**; (633)
(AUSTEN-1815-2,169.633, '*Emma*')

The adverb *again* in (1) has a repetitive reading ('*rep*'): An event of the same kind (*examining plants*) is presupposed. The *again* in (2) has a restitutive/counterdirectional readings ('*res/ct*'), i.e., the *again* here does not presuppose a *sitting-down* event by *Mr. Knightley* but an event in the opposite direction. This presupposition is satisfied in (2-iii) where *[he] got up*. The result state of the *sitting-down* event restores a state that held at a time prior to reference time. Note, that in (2) we could naturally assume that Mr. Knightly must have sat down at some point prior to the reference time for (2-iv). In fact, we can infer as much from the context (2-i) but it is never asserted in the prior contexts. Thus, in the domain of relevant times (as far as available in the context) we don't find the repetitive presupposition satisfied in the context. While the result state is overtly spelled out in (2-iv), this need not always be the case for *res/ct* uses, cf. (3) where *again* – on a decompositional analysis – has access to the result state of its predicate:

(3) a. [T]ake them [the trees] up in the fall of the year, give the roots and heads a pruning, (token 391f)
b. and **plant** them **again** [...] (393)
(COBBETT-1838-2,156.393, '*English Gardener*')

These two main readings, *rep* (1) and *res/ct* (2)-(3), are the most frequent ones in the data discussed here and in line with the literature (cf. Gergel and Beck, 2015). A third relevant reading of *again* are discourse-marker uses, which have a discourse organizing function rather than operating on predicates ('*dm*'). Other smaller readings of again exist in the historical data but are not reported here for the sake of brevity (labeled '*other*' in the discussion below).

3 Expert annotation of *again* and its various readings in PPCMBE2

3.1 Method

Based on presupposition (PSP) satisfaction in the linguistic context, our multi-annotator team (i) classified any use of *again* according to its reading, (ii) marked the main verb of the *again*-predicate ('target verb'), and (iii) marked the main verb of the antecedent satisfying a relevant PSP. Other categories were marked in absence of a verb (e.g., *Rain again [...]* cf. RUSKIN-1882-2,3,1019.286). Contextual material was still marked as antecedent – and additionally labeled with an 'inference'-tag – if it 'only' allowed the inference of a relevant PSP but did not constitute a perfect antecedent in a narrow sense. Early stages of the annotation process were marked by iterative cycles of ongoing annotation work informing our annotation guidelines and vice versa. In later stages, our annotators worked on the basis of a detailed multi-page set of annotation guidelines. A crucial point, on a macro level, was to have a robust set of rules to yield uniform decisions for known uses of *again* and to allow for sensitivity for unknown/deviant uses of *again* while remaining general enough to capture the various types of predicates *again* can operate on. On a micro level, our annotation guidelines needed to be able to handle the intricacies in the linguistic representation of event structure not only of *again* events but especially the interaction with (competing) potential antecedent events. Every single use of *again* received (at least) two independent annotations by trained annotators. Disagreements after the first round of annotations were cleared up by repeated reviews and finally consolidated by either a third annotator or by a team consensus.

3.2 Results

To illustrate: Based on our expert annotations, we get the diachronic picture in Table 1 and Figure 1 for Late ModEng (L1-L6), i.e., the PPCMBE2 corpus. These two simplified graphs represent the entire set of 1,901 uses of *again* from the period and show the relative frequency of the two major readings 'repetitive' (*rep*) and 'restitutive/counterdirectional' (*res/ct*), as well as discourse marker uses (*dm*), and the above mentioned fourth class (*other*) (containing minor other readings and low-frequency occurrences of unresolvable ambiguity/unclear cases). In particular, the overall decrease of *res/ct* readings clarifies and certifies previous accounts on the diachronic development of *again* w.r.t. its two major readings (Beck et al., 2009; Gergel and Beck, 2015), which had been done on disparate corpora (i) (solely) based on correspondence and (ii) lacking the 18th century (currently the most general unified corpus is used, from which Tab. 1 is an example).

subperiod	*rep*	*res/ct*	*dm*	*other*
L1, 1700-1734	50.6	42.7	4.5	2.2
L2, 1735-1769	51.2	43.1	2.4	3.4
L3, 1770-1804	59.7	33.1	5.3	2.0
L4, 1805-1839	58.0	33.9	5.3	2.8
L5, 1840-1874	64.1	24.7	10.3	0.8
L6, 1875-1910	60.7	25.0	12.6	1.7

Table 1: Frequency of readings over time in %

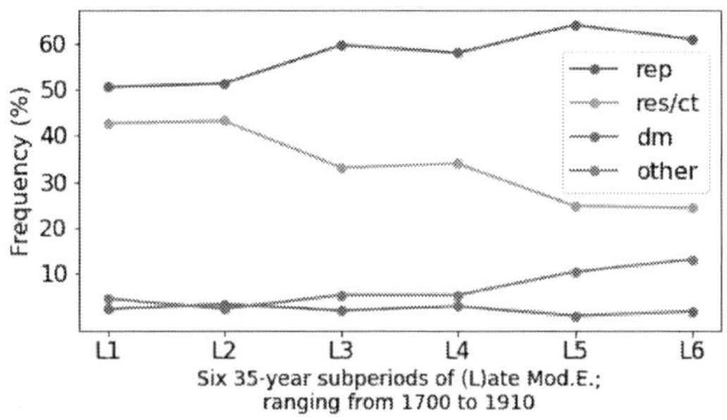

Figure 1: Frequency of readings over time in %

4 Classifying *again*s with a Multinomial Naïve Bayes classifier

4.1 Methods

Based on the expert annotations introduced in section 3 together with a variety of features, we carried out a meta-analysis to find the most promising features in predicting readings of *again* with a Naïve Bayes classifier. We reduced our data set of 1,901 annotations to the 1,722 uses that represent either *rep* (64.4%) or *res/ct* (35.6%) uses of *again*. For these 1,722 *again*s, we collected 16 different features of three major distinct types: (i) "Naïve" features that can be drawn from the linear surface of the text material, (ii) annotational features as per our semantic annotation (but crucially not including the classes of readings, i.e. the dependent variable), and (iii) structural features rooted in the pre-existing syntactic parsing of the data. These features we modeled as count vectors in separate feature matrices for which we computed all possible feature combinations. Over each of the resulting 65,535 different combinations of features, we ran 10 train-test-cycles of a Multinomial Naïve Bayes classifier (with a repeated and randomized 4:1 split between training and testing data for validation) as pretests and 100 train-test-cycles if the pretest gave an accuracy above 77.5%[1]. (Pedregosa et al., 2011; Pustejovsky and Stubbs, 2012)

4.2 Results

We achieve an average accuracy of up to 81.46% in classifying uses of *again* as either *rep* or *res/ct* (based on 100 cycles, standard deviation=2.18%). A set of core features is involved in most feature combinations that achieve average accuracies of 81% or higher: 1. antecedent verb, 2. target verb, 3. distance between antecedent material and *again*, 4. distance between *again* and target verb (also encodes precedence by including negative values), 5. word forms/unigrams in the *again*-clause (as delimited in the syntactic parse). For the average accuracy to go beyond 81% varying other features – often to the exclusion of one another – need to be included. The average accuracy of only the listed features (1.-5.) combined is 80.67% (based on 100 train-test cycles, std.=2.13%). Fig. 2 shows the average accuracies by the number of features. What this also shows is that an abundance of features seems to stunt the classifier and, while improving accuracy overall, also put a cap on it. For the 43 different feature combinations that achieve 81% or higher (purple line in Figs. 2 and 3), the average number of features is 8.58. Another important observation: If we remove all annotational features (especially those pertaining to antecedent material) and rely only on e.g. 3 features that can be gleaned from this corpus data with relative ease (from the preexisting part-of-speech and syntactic annotations): 1. target verb, 2. distance between target verb and *again*, and 3. the object language items

[1] The pretesting was necessary as a measure to reduce computational load. The threshold of 77.5% was informed by previous (shorter) runs in an attempt to strike a balance between expected computational load and desired robustness in the upper range of obtained average accuracies.

in the *again*-clause – with each having a single-feature accuracy of 73.7%, 63.2%, and 74.6%, respectively, – we get an average accuracy of 78.3% (std. 1,93% over 100 train-test cycles). The reported accuracies can be considered a promising first result and, especially since the classifier we used here is insensitive to order (e.g., word order) or weight of features, a result that might be improved upon, e.g. by expanding to *again*-clause bigrams.

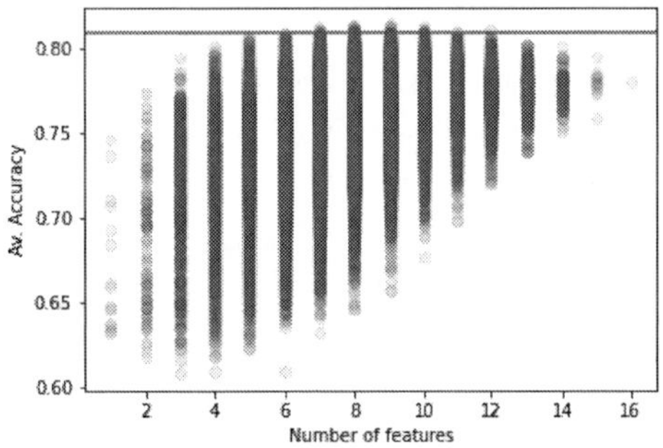

Figure 2: Average accuracy by number of features for 65,535 feature combinations; based on 10 or 100 train-test cycles respectively

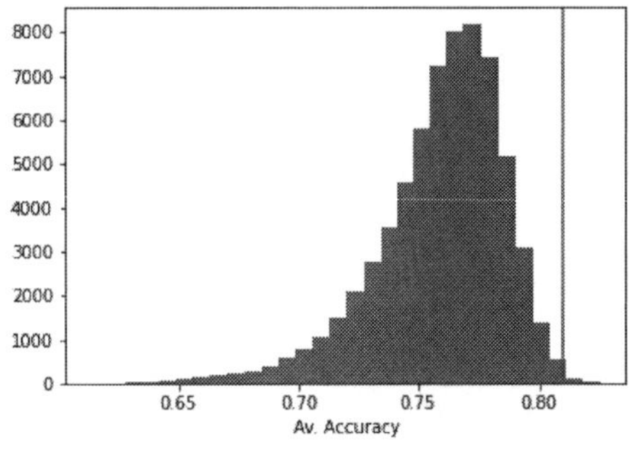

Figure 3: Distribution average accuracy for 65,535 feature combinations; based on 10 or 100 train-test cycles respectively

5 Informed crowdsourcing pilot

5.1 Methods

For this approach we recruited students as crowd workers from two consecutive lectures at the English department at Saarland University. The motivation for this course of action was owing to the intricate nature of the annotation task, i.e., heavily context-dependent semantic annotations on historical language data (with potential antecedent material at varying distances to the PSP trigger – at times significantly greater than, for instance, pronoun reference resolution tasks). Therefore, we needed to be able to communicate with our crowd members in order to quickly respond to uncertainties. We characterize the students who participated as 'informed crowd' because, on the one hand, they were not mere speakers of English providing intuitions but, on the other hand, they were not fully-trained as expert annotators. As students enrolled in an English program, our workers' depths of formal commitment to linguistics is varied: To a large degree, their backgrounds include teachers in training, which means that English is one out of at least two subjects. In other cases, their English studies include a strong emphasis on literary and cultural studies. In next to none of the cases were the student crowd workers formally trained experts. Judging from participants' place of birth – 83.6% out of the 128 participants who submitted annotations for this pilot study were born in Germany – they are overwhelmingly native speakers of German. In order to generate a return of investment for our students/crowd workers' contributions, the lectures were drafted so that the crowdsourcing experiment would complement the lectures well. The first was a history-of-English lecture, the second a contrasting-grammars lecture. Both lectures featured a discussion of the diachrony and the semantics of *again* along with an exploration of the guiding research questions and, thus, a connection to the ongoing annotations tasks. Our crowd workers were given a heavily stripped and condensed version of our annotation guidelines, a practice data set, regular tutorial sessions and a recorded tutorial (i.e. a 'how-to video'). We distributed individualized data sets, each containing five uses of again on a weekly basis directly to students' inboxes (to minimize the possibility for teamwork). To avoid scarcity in the crowd-provided annotations, we only used a subset of the PPCMBE and the PPCEME (Kroch et al., 2004) data, i.e., 328 *agains*. Submissions were handled with the assignment functionality of our home institution's online learning platform. Each student had to perform and submit a minimum of three sets of annotations over the course of a semester as part of their minimum grading requirement. An important note here is that submissions were graded exclusively based on formal criteria of the annotation scheme and not on any notion of 'correctness/incorrectness' of annotations as such (e.g., relative to a gold standard or the rest of the crowd). After the elicitation phase which yielded 3,319 valid annotations, we prepared the crowd-provided data for analysis by vectorizing the crowdsourced annotations. For a toy example of this conversion, consider Table 2 (pre-) and Table 3 (post-conversion). Moreover, see Table 4 where the sums of the toy data point vectors are combined into the unit vector u1 (along with another toy unit vector u2):

data point	factor	unit	annotator	...
dp1	lev_1	u1	a9	...
dp1	lev_1	u1	a2	...
dp3	lev_2	u1	a4	...
dp4	lev_3	u1	a7	...
...	...	...	...	...

Table 2: Annotations as levels

data point	lev_1	lev_2	lev_3	unit	annotator	...
dp1	1	0	0	u1	a9	...
dp1	1	0	0	u1	a2	...
dp3	0	1	0	u1	a4	...
dp4	0	0	1	u1	a7	...
...	...	...	...	...	...	...

Table 3: Annotations as one-hot vectors

data points	lev_1	lev_2	lev_3	unit	...
dp1 – dp4	2	1	1	u1	...
dp5 – dp9	1	2	2	u2	...
...	...	...	...	...	...

Table 4: Unit vectors as total of one-hot vectors

5.2 Results

We tested three different approaches for eliciting a 'crowd winner' and evaluating the crowd annotations in contrast to our gold standard provided by our team of expert annotators. The first was a simple majority vote approach[2] – with lev_1 coming out as the winner for unit u1 in the toy example in Tab. 4. In the second approach, we adjusted the bare data point vectors by crowd quality metrics ("CrowdTruth"; cf. Aroyo and Welty, 2013a,b, 2015; Dumitrache et al., 2018). Similar to simple majority vote, the highest value for a unit vector yielded the 'crowd winner'. The third approach was also based on crowd quality adjusted annotation vectors but relied on a KMeans algorithm for unsupervised classification of unit vectors (Pedregosa et al., 2011). We chose the number of clusters ('K') with the 'within-cluster-sum-of-squares' heuristic (WCSS, 'elbow method'; cf. Fig. 4).

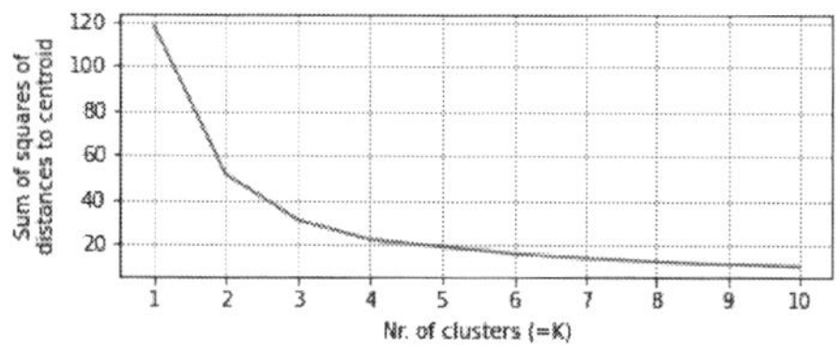

Figure 4: Within Cluster Variation by Ks

Out of the three different approaches, KMeans clustering proved to yield the highest accuracy rates. The detailed results are given in Table 5 where the rows show the gold-standard based readings (*other* were excluded in this pilot). The absolute numbers ('N') represent the number of *agains* available respectively per class and/or period. The corresponding percentages report the accuracies of the KMeans clustering. In addition to per-period, per-century, and overall accuracies, we report Cohen's Kappa in the bottom row. We get high accuracies for the repetitive readings ('*rep*') consistently throughout all periods. The lowest percentage accuracy we get for the restitutive/counterdirectional *agains* ('*res/ct*') – especially in the older data (75.0%). It is predominantly the *res/ct*-reading that is responsible for a decreased overall accuracy of older data.

	17th c.		18th c.		19th c.		all	
	N	%	N	%	N	%	N	%
rep	51	94.1	56	87.5	69	88.4	176	89.8
res/ct	56	75.0	36	80.6	29	89.7	121	80.2
dm	1	100.0	8	87.5	11	90.9	20	90.0
all	112	81.2	102	83.8	114	87.3	328	84.1
C's κ	112	0.65	102	0.7	114	0.73	328	0.7

Table 5: GS units (N) & CS-acc. (%), KMnCl.

Table 6 reports a confusion matrix and shows where the crowd inaccuracies lie. For instance, while Tab. 5 shows that 80.2% out of 121 *res/ct agains* were correctly identified as such (by the crowd and KMeans clustering), Tab. 6 reports on the comple-

[2] In order to avoid ties (u2 in Tab. 4), all data point vectors were adjusted for meta-features of the respective data point:

- $\texttt{experience}_{dp}$ stands for the experience the worker had when providing the data point at hand (ranging from 0 to 11),
- $\texttt{average evaluation}_{dp}$ stands for the average evaluation (i.e. the point system for grading purposes) a student received for the submission of the data set the data point originates from (from 0.0 to 1.0),
- $\texttt{semester progress}_{dp}$ stands for how far into the semester (i.e. ordinal number of weekly data roll-outs) the data point was produced (from 1 to 12), and
- $\texttt{motivation}_{dp}$ gives the total number of data sets the worker submitted who provided the data point at hand (from 2 to 12).

The features were ranked based on our intuition for respective relevance and scaled to such small weights that they could not tip the scale over the number of available crowd votes:

$$\begin{aligned} &(1+(10^{-3} &* \; &\texttt{experience}_{dp})) \; * \\ &(1+(10^{-6} &* \; &\texttt{average evaluation}_{dp})) \; * \\ &(1+(10^{-9} &* \; &\texttt{semester progress}_{dp})) \; * \\ &(1+(10^{-12} &* \; &\texttt{motivation}_{dp})) \\ & &= \; &\texttt{tie breaker}_{dp} \end{aligned}$$

mentary 19.8% inaccurate cases. 23 of these were classified as *repetitive* and only one as *discourse marker* ('*dm*'). The ratio of true to false hits for the two main readings (*rep* vs. *res/ct*) is 9.3:1 for the *rep*-data (gold standard) and 4.2:1 for the *res/ct* data. Thus, if the goal is to reduce costly workload for expert annotators, a review of crowdsourced annotations ought to focus on the data that comes out as *res/ct* since it is here that we find a higher confusion rate (97:17 in contrast to 158:25, true to false positives, respectively).

	CS-*rep*	CS-*res/ct*	CS-*dm*
GS-*rep*	158	17	1
GS-*res/ct*	23	97	1
GS-*dm*	2	0	18

Table 6: Confusion matrix, crowd sourcing by gold std.

The strategy to focus on *res/ct* data for an expert review of crowd sourced data is also supported by the distribution of unit quality scores. Unit quality scores (UQS) are computed for each unit (= use of *again*): We calculated it as the average of all pairwise cosine similarities for all possible distinct worker$_i$ and worker$_j$ pairings (such that worker$_i$ $\neq$ worker$_j$) (Aroyo and Welty, 2013a,b, 2015; Dumitrache et al., 2018). Interpreting the UQS as a measure of crowd confidence, we conclude that the crowd decisions for true *rep*-readings came about with higher confidence than the true *res/ct*-readings, cf. top-left vs. bottom-left subplots in Fig. 5. Thus, focusing on the crowd-provided *res/ct*-labels in a review by expert annotators would also increase robustness of the annotated data in the 'right places'.

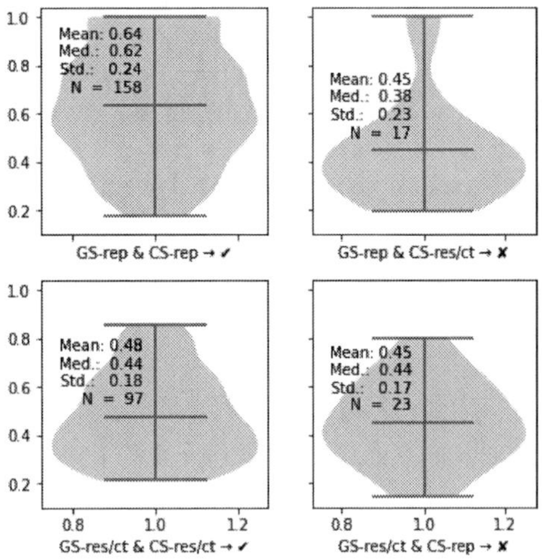

Figure 5: Unit Quality Score (UQS) for GS-CS matches & mismatches; as kernel density plots

6 Conclusion

At the current state of the technical possibilities explored and as far as the natural language phenomenon at hand is concerned, a gold standard cannot be substituted wholesale by either machine learning-based predictions or experimental data. The first upshot is that the gold standard itself must be as solid as possible (we sketched our detailed approach above, and we are open to constantly improving it). At the same time, we think that our two additional case studies are quite telling even if their performance was expectedly lower. The significance of such extensions is obvious when it comes to the annotation of larger amounts of data (be it for decompositional markers or other annotational tasks; of course, for low-frequency phenomena, the use of larger corpora or alternative methods becomes a necessity). The feature-based approach (section 4) then becomes relevant, also for cases in which the syntactic annotation is missing such as the EEBO type of corpora in our object-language English. In such a case, some of the syntactic features we have used in our approximations can be translated, e.g., in terms of precedence (an instance of again that precedes its modifying predicate is typically also higher in structure etc.). Overall, however, we believe that the human approach, i.e., the type of informed crowdsourcing we have utilized, is the most promising variant of annotational support when one strives to cover more data than one's team can handle or for gaining more certainty empirically. The straightforward advantage is that the relatedness in the languages at hand can be used even if the 'nativeness' of the actual participants is not available. Some of our results have indicated that more distant periods in time do not necessarily become worse in the annotational performance. On a conceptual level, there is also initial evidence from independent areas of semantic change (cf. Gergel et al., 2021, 2023) that speakers adapt astonishingly well in simulated situations of change. Finally, even if certain targeted readings are comparatively low performing, one can still place a crowdsourcing approach at the start of an annotation pipeline. By validating crowd annotations with a gold standard for a subset of the data, one can learn which data (i) needs a closer review, (ii) which data needs less attention in a review, and (iii) which data could benefit from a thorough review due to inherent indecisiveness of the crowd.

Acknowledgements

We thank our expert annotators – especially Mohammad Ablli, Maryam Rajestari and Dana Rebar – and our students for their participation in this work, which has been funded by the German Research Foundation through the project Decomposing Decomposition in Time awarded to Remus Gergel.

References

Lora Aroyo and Chris Welty. 2013a. Crowd truth: Harnessing disagreement in crowdsourcing a relation extraction gold standard. In *Web Science 2013*, New York: Association for Computing Machinery.

Lora Aroyo and Chris Welty. 2013b. Measuring crowd truth for medical relation extraction. In *Semantics for Big Data: Papers from the AAAI Fall Symposium*, AAAI Technical Report FS-13-04, Palo Alto, CA.

Lora Aroyo and Chris Welty. 2015. Truth is a lie: Crowd truth and the seven myths of human annotation. *AI Magazine*, 36(1):15–24.

Josep Ausensi, Jianrong Yu, and Ryan Walter Smith. 2021. Agent entailments and the division of labor between functional structure and roots. *Glossa: A journal of General Linguistics*, 6(1):53.

Sigrid Beck. 2005. There and back again: A semantic analysis. *Journal of Semantics*, 22:3–51.

Sigrid Beck, Polina Berezovskaya, and Katja Pflugfelder. 2009. The use of *again* in 19th-century English versus Present-Day English. *Syntax*, 12(3):193–214.

Sigrid Beck and Remus Gergel. 2015. The diachronic semantics of English *again*. *Natural Language Semantics*, 23(3):157–203.

Marco Degano and Maria Aloni. 2022. Indefinite and free choice: When the past matters. *Natural Language and Linguistic Theory*, 40:447–484.

Anca Dumitrache, Inel Oana, Lora Aroyo, Benjamin Timmermans, and Chris Welty. 2018. Crowdtruth 2.0: Quality metrics for crowdsourcing with disagreement.

Remus Gergel and Sigrid Beck. 2015. Early Modern English *again*: a corpus study and semantic analysis. *English Language and Linguistics*, 19(1):27–47.

Remus Gergel, Martin Kopf, and Maike Puhl. 2021. Simulating semantic change: a methodological note. In *Proceedings of Experiments in Linguistic Meaning (ELM)*, pages 184–196, University of Pennsylvania: LSA.

Remus Gergel, Maike Puhl, Simon Dampfhofer, and Edgar Onea. 2023. The rise and particularly fall of presuppositions: Evidence from duality in universals. In *Proceedings of Proceedings of Experiments in Linguistic Meaning (ELM) 2*, pages 72–82, University of Pennsylvania: LSA.

Anthony Kroch, Beatrice Santorini, and Lauren Delfs. 2004. *The Penn-Helsinki Parsed Corpus of Early Modern English (PPCEME)*, first edition. Department of Linguistics, University of Pennsylvania. Release 3.

Anthony Kroch, Beatrice Santorini, and Ariel Diertani. 2016. *The Penn Parsed Corpus of Modern British English (PPCMBE2)*, second edition. Department of Linguistics, University of Pennsylvania. Release 1.

Fabian Pedregosa, Gaël Varoquaux, Alexandre Gramfort, Vincent Michel, Bertrand Thirion, Olivier Grisel, Mathieu Blondel, Peter Prettenhofer, Ron Weiss, Vincent Dubourg, Jake Vanderplas, Alexandre Passos, David Cournapeau, Matthieu Brucher, Matthieu Perrot, and Édouard Duchesnay. 2011. Scikit-learn: Machine learning in Python. *Journal of Machine Learning Research*, 12:2825–2830.

James Pustejovsky and Amber Stubbs. 2012. *Natural Language Annotation for Machine Learning*. O'Reilly, Sebastopol, CA.

Irene Rapp and Arnim von Stechow. 1999. *Fast* 'almost' and the visibility parameter for functional adverbs. *Journal of Semantics*, 16:149–204.

Joost Zwarts. 2019. From 'back' to 'again' in Dutch: The structure of the 're' domain. *Journal of Semantics*, 36:211–240.

How Good is the Model in Model-in-the-loop Event Coreference Resolution Annotation?

Shafiuddin Rehan Ahmed[1] **Abhijnan Nath**[2] **Michael Regan**[3]
Adam Pollins[1] **Nikhil Krishnaswamy**[2] **James H. Martin**[1]

[1]University of Colorado, Boulder, CO, USA [3]University of Washington, Seattle, WA, USA
[2]Colorado State University, Fort Collins, CO, USA

{shah7567,james.martin,adpo0729}@colorado.edu
{abhijnan.nath,nkrishna}@colostate.edu, mregan@cs.washington.edu

Abstract

Annotating cross-document event coreference links is a time-consuming and cognitively demanding task that can compromise annotation quality and efficiency. To address this, we propose a model-in-the-loop annotation approach for event coreference resolution, where a machine learning model suggests likely corefering event pairs only. We evaluate the effectiveness of this approach by first simulating the annotation process and then, using a novel annotator-centric Recall-Annotation effort trade-off metric, we compare the results of various underlying models and datasets. We finally present a method for obtaining 97% recall while substantially reducing the workload required by a fully manual annotation process.

1 Introduction

Event Coreference Resolution (ECR) is the task of identifying mentions of the same event either within or across documents. Consider the following excerpts from three related documents:

e_1: 55 year old star will $replace_{m_1}$ Matt Smith, who announced in June that he was leaving the sci-fi show.

e_2: Matt Smith, 26, will make his debut in 2010, $replacing_{m_2}$ David Tennant, who leaves at the end of this year.

e_3: Peter Capaldi $takes\ over_{m_3}$ Doctor Who... Peter Capaldi $stepped\ into_{m_4}$ Matt Smith's soon to be vacant Doctor Who shoes.

e_1, e_2, and e_3 are example sentences from three documents where the event mentions are highlighted and sub-scripted by their respective identifiers (m_1 through m_4). The task of ECR is to automatically form the two clusters $\{m_1, m_3, m_4\}$, and $\{m_2\}$. We refer to any pair between the mentions of a cluster, e.g., (m_1, m_3) as an ECR link. Any pair formed across two clusters, e.g., (m_1, m_2) is referred to as non-ECR link.

Annotating ECR links can be challenging due to the large volume of mention pairs that must be compared. The annotating task becomes increasingly time-consuming as the number of events in the corpus increases. As a result, this task requires a lot of mental effort from the annotator and can lead to poor quality annotations (Song et al., 2018; Wright-Bettner et al., 2019). Indeed, an annotator has to examine multiple documents simultaneously often relying on memory to identify all the links which can be an error-prone process.

To reduce the cognitive burden of annotating ECR links, annotation tools can provide integrated model-in-the-loop for sampling likely coreferent mention pairs (Pianta et al., 2008; Yimam et al., 2014; Klie et al., 2018). These systems typically store a knowledge base (KB) of annotated documents and then use this KB to suggest relevant candidates. The annotator can then inspect the candidates and choose a coreferent event if present.

The model's querying and ranking operations are typically driven by machine learning (ML) systems that are trained either actively (Pianta et al., 2008; Klie et al., 2018; Bornstein et al., 2020; Yuan et al., 2022) or by using batches of annotations (Yimam et al., 2014). While there have been advances in suggestion-based annotations, there is little to no work in evaluating the effectiveness of these systems, particularly in the use case of ECR. Specifically, both the overall coverage, or recall, of the annotation process as well as the degree of annotator effort needed depend on the performance of the model. In order to address this shortcoming, we offer the following contributions:

1. We introduce a method of model-in-the-loop annotations for ECR[1].
2. We compare three existing methods for ECR (differing widely in their computational costs), by adapting them as the underlying ML mod-

[1]repo: github.com/ahmeshaf/model_in_coref

Proceedings of the 17th Linguistic Annotation Workshop (LAW-XVII), pages 136–145
July 13, 2023 ©2023 Association for Computational Linguistics

els governing the annotations.

3. We introduce a novel methodology for assessing the workflow by simulating the annotations and then evaluating an annotator-centric Recall-Annotation effort tradeoff.

2 Related Work

Previous work for ECR is largely based on modeling the probability of coreference between mention pairs. These models are built on supervised classifiers trained using features extracted from the pairs. Most recent work uses a transformer-based language model (LM) like BERT (Devlin et al., 2018; Liu et al., 2019) to generate joint representations of mention pairs, a method known as cross-encoding. The cross-encoder is fine-tuned using a coreference scoring objective (Barhom et al., 2019; Cattan et al., 2020; Meged et al., 2020; Zeng et al., 2020; Yu et al., 2020; Caciularu et al., 2021). These methods use scores generated from the scorer to then agglomeratively cluster coreferent events.

Over the years, a number of metrics have been proposed to evaluate ECR (Vilain et al., 1995; Bagga and Baldwin, 1998; Luo, 2005; Recasens and Hovy, 2011; Luo et al., 2014; Pradhan et al., 2014). An ECR system is evaluated using these metrics to determine how effectively it can find event clusters (recall) and how cleanly separated the clusters are (precision). From the perspective of annotation, it may only be necessary to focus on the system's recall or its effectiveness in finding ECR links. However, an annotator might still want to know how much effort is required to identify these links in a corpus to estimate their budget. In the remainder of the paper, we attempt to answer this question by first quantifying annotation effort and analyzing its relation with recall of the system.

We use the Event Coreference Bank Plus (ECB+; Cybulska and Vossen (2014)) and the Gun Violence Corpus (GVC; Vossen et al. (2018)) for our experiments. The ECB+ is a common choice for assessing ECR, as well as the experimental setup of Cybulska and Vossen (2015) and gold topic clustering of documents and gold mention annotations for both training and testing[2]. On the other hand, the GVC offers a more challenging set of exclusively event-specific coreference decisions that require resolving gun violence-related events.

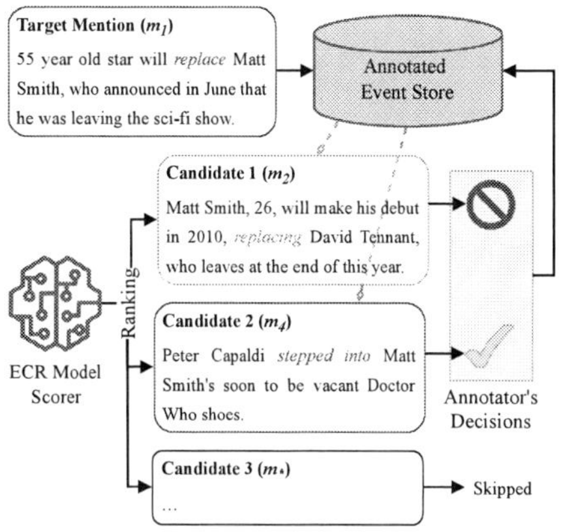

Figure 1: For the target mention (m_1), the Annotated Event Cluster store presents three potential coreferent candidates (m_2, m_4 and m_*). The ranking module (an ECR scorer) then ranks them based on their semantic similarity to m_1. The annotator reviews each candidate one-at-a-time and makes decisions on coreference. m_* is skipped after finding m_4 as coreferent. The cluster store is then updated based on these decisions.

3 Annotation Methodology

We implement an iterative model-in-the-loop methodology[3] for annotating ECR links in a corpus containing annotated event triggers. This approach has two main components - (1) the storage and retrieval of annotated event clusters, which are then compared with each new target event, and (2), an ML model that ranks and prunes the sampled candidate clusters by evaluating their semantic similarity to the target mention.

As illustrated in Figure 1, our annotation workflow queries the Annotated Event Store for the target event (m_1), retrieving three potential coreferring candidates (m_2, m_*, and m_4). The ranking module then evaluates these candidates based on their lexical and semantic similarities to m_1. The annotator then compares each candidate to the target and determines if they are coreferent. Upon finding a coreferent candidate, the target is merged into the coreferent cluster, and any remaining option(s) (m_*) are skipped.

3.1 Ranking

We investigate three separate methods to drive the ranking of candidates distinguished by their computational cost. We use these methods to generate the average pair-wise coreference scores between mentions of the candidate and target events, then

[2]The ECB+ test set has 1,780 event mentions with 5K ECR links among 100K pairwise mentions, while the GVC test set has 1,008 mentions with 2K ECR links in 20K pairs. Full statistics in Table 1 in Appendix A

[3]Utilizing the prodi.gy annotation tool. See Appendix D

use these scores to rank candidates. We use a single RTX 3090 (24 GB) for running our experiments.

Cross-encoder (CDLM): In this method, we use the fine-tuned cross-encoder ECR system of Caciularu et al. (2021) to generate pairwise mention scores[4]. Their state of the art system uses a modified Longformer (Beltagy et al., 2020) as the underlying LM to generate document-level representations of the mention pairs (detailed in §B.1). More specifically, we generate a unified representation (Eq. 1) of the mention pair (m_i, m_j) by concatenating the pooled output of the transformer ($\mathrm{E}_{\mathrm{CLS}}$), the outputs of the individual event triggers (E_{m_i}, E_{m_j}), and their element-wise product. Thereafter, pairwise-wise scores are generated for each mention-pair after passing the above representations through a Multi-Layer Perceptron (mlp) (Eq. 2) that was trained using the gold-standard labels for supervision.

$$\mathtt{LF}(m_i, m_j) = \langle \mathrm{E}_{\mathrm{CLS}}, \mathrm{E}_{m_i}, \mathrm{E}_{m_j}, \mathrm{E}_{m_i} \odot \mathrm{E}_{m_j} \rangle \quad (1)$$

$$\mathtt{CDLM}(m_i, m_j) = \mathtt{mlp}(\mathtt{LF}(m_i, m_j)) \quad (2)$$

BERTScore (BERT): (Zhang et al., 2019) BERTScore (BS) is a NLP metric that measures pairwise text similarity by exploiting pretrained BERT models. It calculates cosine similarity of token embeddings with inverse document frequency weights to rate token importance and aggregates them into precision, recall, and F1 scores. This method emphasizes semantically significant tokens, resulting in a more accurate similarity score (details in §B.2).

$$\mathrm{S}_{\mathrm{bert}}(m) = \langle t_m, \text{[SEP]}, S_m \rangle \quad (3)$$

$$\begin{aligned}\mathtt{BERT}(m_i, m_j) &= \lambda\, \mathtt{BS}(t_{m_i}, t_{m_j}) \\ &+ (1-\lambda)\, \mathtt{BS}(\mathrm{S}_{\mathrm{bert}}(m_i), \mathrm{S}_{\mathrm{bert}}(m_j))\end{aligned} \quad (4)$$

To calculate the BERTScore between the mentions, we first construct a combined sentence ($\mathrm{S}_{\mathrm{bert}}(m)$; Shi and Lin (2019)) for a mention (m) by concatenating the mention text (t_m) and its corresponding sentence (S_m), as depicted in Equation 3. Subsequently, we compute the BS for each mention pair using $\mathrm{S}_{\mathrm{bert}}(m)$ and t_m separately, then extract the F1 from each. We then take the weighted average of the two scores as shown in Equation 4 as our ranking metric. This process, carried out using the $\mathtt{distilbert-base-uncased}$ (Sanh et al., 2019) model, requires approximately seven seconds to complete on each test set.

Lemma Similarity (Lemma): The lemma[5] similarity method emulates the annotation process carried out by human annotators when determining coreference based on keyword comparisons between two mentions. To estimate this similarity, we compute the token overlap (Jaccard similarity; JS) between the triggers and sentences containing the respective mentions and take a weighted average of the two similarities (like Eq 4) as shown in Eq 5[6].

$$\begin{aligned}\mathtt{Lemma}(m_i, m_j) &= \lambda\, \mathtt{JS}(t_{m_i}, t_{m_j}) \\ &+ (1-\lambda)\, \mathtt{JS}(S_{m_i}, S_{m_j})\end{aligned} \quad (5)$$

No Ranking (Random): For our baseline approach, we employ a method that directly picks the candidate-mention pairs through random sampling and without ranking, providing a reference point for evaluating the effectiveness of the above three ranking techniques.

3.2 Pruning

To control the comparisons between candidate and target events, we restrict our selection to the top-k ranked candidates. To refine our analysis, we employ non-integer k values, allowing for the inclusion of an additional candidate with a probability equal to the decimal part of k. We vary the values of k from 2 to 20 on increments of 0.5 and then investigate its relation to recall and effort in §4.

3.3 Simulation

To evaluate the ranking methods, we conduct annotation simulations on the events in the ECB+ and GVC development and test sets. These simulations follow the same annotation methodology of retrieving and ranking candidate events for each target but utilize ground-truth for clustering. By executing simulations on different ranking methods and analyzing their performance, we effectively isolate and assess each approach.

4 Evaluation Methodology

We evaluate the performance of the model-in-the-loop annotation with the ranking methods through simulation on two aspects: (1) how well it finds the coreferent links, and (2) how much effort it would take to annotate the links using the ranking method.

[4] This method is compute-intensive since the transformer's encoding process scales quadratically with the number of mentions. Using the trained weights, running inference on the two test sets for our experiments takes approximately forty minutes to calculate the similarities of all the mention pairs. The weights are provided by Caciularu et al. (2021) here.

[5] We use spaCy 3.4 en_core_web_md lemmatizer

[6] λ is a hyper-parameter to control the weightage of the trigger and sentence similarities in Equations 4 and 5, which we tune using the development set. See Appendix C.

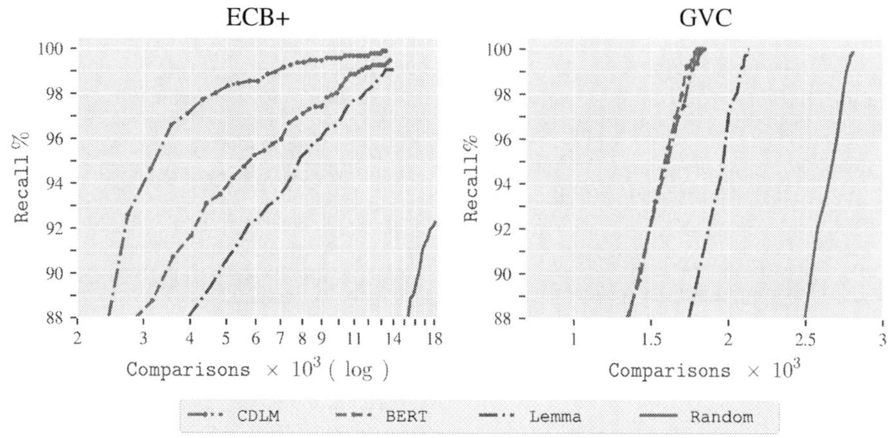

Figure 2: `Recall` and `Comparisons` achieved upon varying the k for each ranking method in the ECR annotation simulation. The three methods result in significantly fewer comparisons than the no-ranking `Random` baseline.

4.1 Recall-Annotation Effort Tradeoff

`Recall`: The recall metric evaluates the percentage of ECR links that are correctly identified by the suggestion model. It is calculated as the ratio of the number of times the true coreferent candidate is among the suggested candidates. The recall error is introduced when the coreferent candidate is erroneously removed based on the top-k value[7].

`Comparisons`: A unit effort represents the comparison between a candidate and target mentions that an annotator would have to make in the annotation process. We count the sampled candidates for each target and stop counting when the coreferent candidate is found. For example, the number of comparisons for the target m_1, in Figure 1, is 2 (m_2 and m_4). We count this number for each target event and present the sum as `Comparisons`.

4.2 Analysis and Discussion

We present an analysis of the various ranking methods employed in our study, highlighting the performance and viability of each approach. We employ the ranking methods on the test sets of ECB+ and GVC. Then, estimate the `Recall` and `Comparisons` measures for different k values, and collate them into the plots as shown in Figure 2.

Performance Comparison: The performance improvement of `CDLM` over `BERT` and `BERT` over `Lemma` can be quantified by examining the graph for the ECB+ and GVC datasets. For example, when targeting a 95% recall for the ECB+ corpus, `CDLM` provides an almost 100 percent improvement over `BERT` reducing the number of comparisons to almost half of the latter. However, both `CDLM` and `BERT` outperform `Lemma` by a significant margin while being drastically better than the `Random` baseline (See Fig. 2). Interestingly, for GVC, the performance gap between `CDLM` and `BERT` is quite close, both needing at least three-fourths as many comparisons as the `Lemma` and crucially outperforming the `Random` baseline. `CDLM`'s inconsistent performance on GVC suggests that a corpus-fine-tuned model such as itself is more effective when applied to a dataset similar to the one it was trained on.

Efficiency and Generalizability of `BERT`: `BERT` offers a compelling advantage in terms of efficiency, as it can be run on low-compute settings. Moreover, `BERT` exhibits greater generalizability out-of-the-box when comparing its performance on both the ECB+ and GVC datasets. This makes it an attractive option for ECR annotation task especially when compute resources are limited or when working with diverse corpora.

5 Conclusion

We introduced a model-in-the-loop annotation method for annotating ECR links. We compared three ranking models through a novel evaluation methodology that answers key questions regarding the quality of the model in the annotation loop (namely, recall and effort). Overall, our analysis demonstrates the viability of the models, with `CDLM` exhibiting the best performance on the ECB+ dataset, followed by `BERT` and `Lemma`. The choice of ranking method depends on the specific use case, dataset, and resource constraints, but all three methods offer valuable solutions for different scenarios.

[7]Note that recall is always 100% if no candidates are ever pruned.

Limitations

It is important to note that the approaches presented in this paper have several constraints. Firstly, the methods presented are restricted to English language only, as `Lemma` necessitates a lemmatizer and, `BERT` and `CDLM` rely on models trained exclusively on English corpora. Secondly, the utilization of the `CDLM` model demands at least a single GPU, posing potential accessibility issues. Thirdly, ECR annotation is susceptible to errors and severe disagreements amongst annotators, which could entail multiple iterations before achieving a gold-standard quality. Lastly, the generated corpora may be biased to the model used during the annotation process, particularly for smaller values of k.

Ethics Statement

We use publicly-available datasets, meaning any bias or offensive content in those datasets risks being reflected in our results. By its nature, the Gun Violence Corpus contains violent content that may be troubling for some.

Acknowledgements

We would like to express our sincere gratitude to the anonymous reviewers whose insightful comments and constructive feedback helped to greatly improve the quality of this paper. We gratefully acknowledge the support of U.S. Defense Advanced Research Projects Agency (DARPA) FA8750-18-2-0016-AIDA – RAMFIS: Representations of vectors and Abstract Meanings For Information Synthesis. Any opinions, findings, conclusions, or recommendations expressed in this material are those of the authors and do not necessarily reflect the views of DARPA or the U.S. government. We would also like to thank ExplosionAI GmbH for partly funding this work. Finally, we extend our thanks to the BoulderNLP group and the SIGNAL Lab at Colorado State for their valuable input and collaboration throughout the development of this work.

References

Amit Bagga and Breck Baldwin. 1998. Algorithms for scoring coreference chains. In *In The First International Conference on Language Resources and Evaluation Workshop on Linguistics Coreference*, pages 563–566.

Shany Barhom, Vered Shwartz, Alon Eirew, Michael Bugert, Nils Reimers, and Ido Dagan. 2019. Revisiting joint modeling of cross-document entity and event coreference resolution. In *Proceedings of the 57th Annual Meeting of the Association for Computational Linguistics*, pages 4179–4189, Florence, Italy. Association for Computational Linguistics.

Iz Beltagy, Matthew E. Peters, and Arman Cohan. 2020. Longformer: The long-document transformer.

Ari Bornstein, Arie Cattan, and Ido Dagan. 2020. CoRefi: A crowd sourcing suite for coreference annotation. In *Proceedings of the 2020 Conference on Empirical Methods in Natural Language Processing: System Demonstrations*, pages 205–215, Online. Association for Computational Linguistics.

Avi Caciularu, Arman Cohan, Iz Beltagy, Matthew Peters, Arie Cattan, and Ido Dagan. 2021. CDLM: Cross-document language modeling. In *Findings of the Association for Computational Linguistics: EMNLP 2021*, pages 2648–2662, Punta Cana, Dominican Republic. Association for Computational Linguistics.

Arie Cattan, Alon Eirew, Gabriel Stanovsky, Mandar Joshi, and Ido Dagan. 2020. Streamlining cross-document coreference resolution: Evaluation and modeling.

Agata Cybulska and Piek Vossen. 2014. Using a sledgehammer to crack a nut? lexical diversity and event coreference resolution. In *Proceedings of the Ninth International Conference on Language Resources and Evaluation, LREC 2014, Reykjavik, Iceland, May 26-31, 2014*, pages 4545–4552. European Language Resources Association (ELRA).

Agata Cybulska and Piek Vossen. 2015. Translating granularity of event slots into features for event coreference resolution. In *Proceedings of the The 3rd Workshop on EVENTS: Definition, Detection, Coreference, and Representation*, pages 1–10, Denver, Colorado. Association for Computational Linguistics.

Jacob Devlin, Ming-Wei Chang, Kenton Lee, and Kristina Toutanova. 2018. BERT: pre-training of deep bidirectional transformers for language understanding. *CoRR*, abs/1810.04805.

Jan-Christoph Klie, Michael Bugert, Beto Boullosa, Richard Eckart de Castilho, and Iryna Gurevych. 2018. The INCEpTION platform: Machine-assisted and knowledge-oriented interactive annotation. In *Proceedings of the 27th International Conference on Computational Linguistics: System Demonstrations*, pages 5–9, Santa Fe, New Mexico. Association for Computational Linguistics.

Yinhan Liu, Myle Ott, Naman Goyal, Jingfei Du, Mandar Joshi, Danqi Chen, Omer Levy, Mike Lewis, Luke Zettlemoyer, and Veselin Stoyanov. 2019. Roberta: A robustly optimized bert pretraining approach.

Xiaoqiang Luo. 2005. On coreference resolution performance metrics. In *Proceedings of the Conference on*

Human Language Technology and Empirical Methods in Natural Language Processing, HLT '05, page 25–32, USA. Association for Computational Linguistics.

Xiaoqiang Luo, Sameer Pradhan, Marta Recasens, and Eduard Hovy. 2014. An extension of BLANC to system mentions. In *Proceedings of the 52nd Annual Meeting of the Association for Computational Linguistics (Volume 2: Short Papers)*, pages 24–29, Baltimore, Maryland. Association for Computational Linguistics.

Yehudit Meged, Avi Caciularu, Vered Shwartz, and Ido Dagan. 2020. Paraphrasing vs coreferring: Two sides of the same coin. In *Findings of the Association for Computational Linguistics: EMNLP 2020*, pages 4897–4907, Online. Association for Computational Linguistics.

Emanuele Pianta, Christian Girardi, and Roberto Zanoli. 2008. The TextPro tool suite. In *Proceedings of the Sixth International Conference on Language Resources and Evaluation (LREC'08)*, Marrakech, Morocco. European Language Resources Association (ELRA).

Sameer Pradhan, Xiaoqiang Luo, Marta Recasens, Eduard Hovy, Vincent Ng, and Michael Strube. 2014. Scoring coreference partitions of predicted mentions: A reference implementation. In *Proceedings of the 52nd Annual Meeting of the Association for Computational Linguistics (Volume 2: Short Papers)*, pages 30–35, Baltimore, Maryland. Association for Computational Linguistics.

M. Recasens and Eduard Hovy. 2011. Blanc: Implementing the rand index for coreference evaluation. *Natural Language Engineering*, 17:485 – 510.

Victor Sanh, Lysandre Debut, Julien Chaumond, and Thomas Wolf. 2019. Distilbert, a distilled version of bert: smaller, faster, cheaper and lighter. *ArXiv*, abs/1910.01108.

Peng Shi and Jimmy Lin. 2019. Simple bert models for relation extraction and semantic role labeling. *arXiv preprint arXiv:1904.05255*.

Zhiyi Song, Ann Bies, Justin Mott, Xuansong Li, Stephanie Strassel, and Christopher Caruso. 2018. Cross-document, cross-language event coreference annotation using event hoppers. In *Proceedings of the Eleventh International Conference on Language Resources and Evaluation (LREC 2018)*, Miyazaki, Japan. European Language Resources Association (ELRA).

Marc Vilain, John Burger, John Aberdeen, Dennis Connolly, and Lynette Hirschman. 1995. A model-theoretic coreference scoring scheme. In *Proceedings of the 6th Conference on Message Understanding*, MUC6 '95, page 45–52, USA. Association for Computational Linguistics.

Piek Vossen, Filip Ilievski, Marten Postma, and Roxane Segers. 2018. Don't annotate, but validate: A data-to-text method for capturing event data. In *Proceedings of the Eleventh International Conference on Language Resources and Evaluation (LREC 2018)*.

Kristin Wright-Bettner, Martha Palmer, Guergana Savova, Piet de Groen, and Timothy Miller. 2019. Cross-document coreference: An approach to capturing coreference without context. In *Proceedings of the Tenth International Workshop on Health Text Mining and Information Analysis (LOUHI 2019)*, pages 1–10, Hong Kong. Association for Computational Linguistics.

Seid Muhie Yimam, Chris Biemann, Richard Eckart de Castilho, and Iryna Gurevych. 2014. Automatic annotation suggestions and custom annotation layers in WebAnno. In *Proceedings of 52nd Annual Meeting of the Association for Computational Linguistics: System Demonstrations*, pages 91–96, Baltimore, Maryland. Association for Computational Linguistics.

Xiaodong Yu, Wenpeng Yin, and Dan Roth. 2020. Paired representation learning for event and entity coreference.

Michelle Yuan, Patrick Xia, Chandler May, Benjamin Van Durme, and Jordan Boyd-Graber. 2022. Adapting coreference resolution models through active learning. In *Proceedings of the 60th Annual Meeting of the Association for Computational Linguistics (Volume 1: Long Papers)*, pages 7533–7549, Dublin, Ireland. Association for Computational Linguistics.

Yutao Zeng, Xiaolong Jin, Saiping Guan, Jiafeng Guo, and Xueqi Cheng. 2020. Event coreference resolution with their paraphrases and argument-aware embeddings. In *Proceedings of the 28th International Conference on Computational Linguistics*, pages 3084–3094, Barcelona, Spain (Online). International Committee on Computational Linguistics.

Tianyi Zhang, Varsha Kishore, Felix Wu, Kilian Q Weinberger, and Yoav Artzi. 2019. Bertscore: Evaluating text generation with bert. *arXiv preprint arXiv:1904.09675*.

A ECB+ Corpus Event Statistics

Table 1 contains the detailed statistics for both the ECB+ and the GVC corpora.

B Model Details

B.1 CDLM

The CDLM model, based on the Longformer architecture, cleverly uses a combination of global and local attention for event trigger words and the rest of the document containing those events respectively. More specifically, the Longformer's increased input capacity of 4096 tokens is utilized

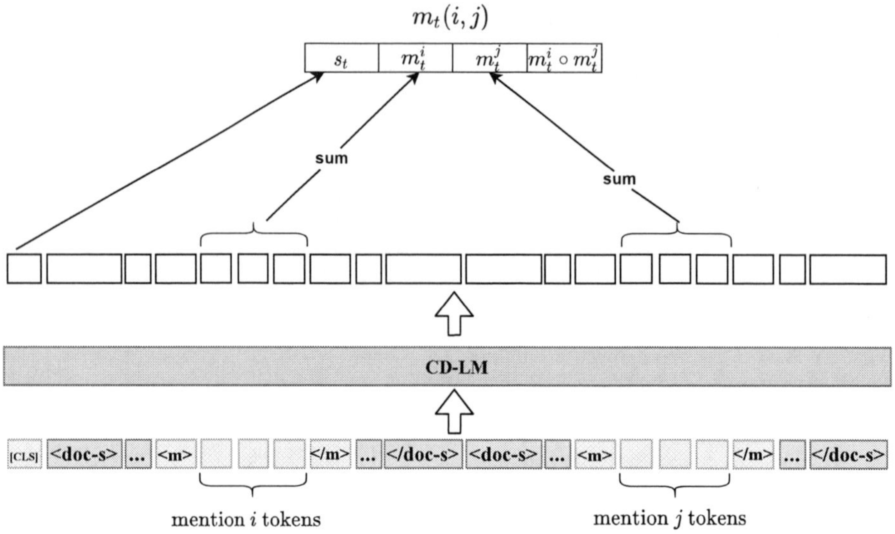

Figure 3: Illustration of Cross-encoding with CDLM from Caciularu et al. (2021).

	ECB+			GVC		
	Train	Dev	Test	Train	Dev	Test
T/ST	25	8	10	170	37	34
D	594	196	206	358	78	74
M	3808	1245	1780	5313	977	1008
C	1464	409	805	991	228	194
S	1053	280	623	252	70	43
P	300K	100K	180K	100K	20K	20K
P_+	15K	6K	6.5K	24K	3.7K	4.1K

Table 1: ECB+ and GVC Corpus statistics for event mentions. T/ST = topics/sub-topics, D = documents, M = event mentions, C = clusters, S = singletons. P = unique mention pairs by topic. P_+ = mention pairs that are coreferent.

to encode much longer documents at finetuning that are usually seen in coreference corpora like the ECB+. As seen in Fig. 3, apart from the document-separator tokens like <doc-s> and <doc-s/> that help contextualize each document in a pair, it adds two special tokens (<m> and </m>) to the model vocabulary while pretraining to achieve a greater level of contextualization of a document pair while attending to the event triggers globally at finetuning. Apart from the event-trigger words, the finetuned CDLM model also applies the global attention mechanism on the [CLS] token resulting in a more refined embedding for that document pair while maintaining linearity in the transformer's self-attention.

B.2 BERTScore

BERT-Score is an easy-to-use, low-compute scoring metric that can be used to evaluate NLP tasks that require semantic-similarity matching. This task-agnostic metric uses a base language model like BERT to generate token embeddings and leverages the entire sub-word tokenized reference and candidate sentences (x and $\hat{x}$ in Fig. 4) to calculate the pairwise cosine similarity between the sentence pair. It uses a combination of a greedy-matching subroutine to maximize the similarity scores while

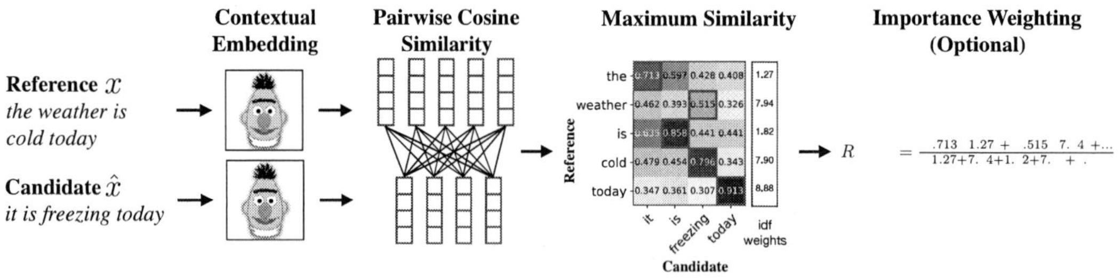

Figure 4: Illustration of the Recall Measure of BERTScore from Zhang et al. (2019).

normalizing the generated scores based on the IDF (Inverse Document Frequency) of the sub-tokens thereby resulting in more human-readable scores. The latter weighting parameter takes care of rare-word occurrences in sentence pairs that are usually more indicative of how semantically similar such pairs are. In our experiments, we use the `distilbert − base − uncased` model to get the pairwise coreference scores, consistent with our goal of deploying an annotation workflow suitable for resource-constrained settings. Such lighter and 'distilled' encoders allow us to optimize resources at inference with minimal loss in performance.

C λ Hyper-parameter Tuning

We employ the evaluation methodology detailed in §4 to determine the optimal value of λ (the weight for trigger similarity and sentence similarity) for both `BERT` and `Lemma` approaches. By conducting incremental annotation simulations on the development sets of ECB+ and GVC, we assess λ values ranging from 0 to 1. The recall-effort curve is plotted for each λ value, as shown in Figure 5, allowing us to identify the one that consistently achieves the highest recall with the fewest comparisons. Remarkably, the optimal value for both methods is found to be 0.7, and this value remains consistent across the two datasets and approaches.

D Annotation Interface using Prodigy

Figure 6 illustrates the interface design of the annotation methodology on the popular model-in-the-loop annotation tool - Prodigy (prodi.gy). We use this tool for the simplicity it offers in plugging in the various ranking methods we explained. The recipe for plugging it in to the tool along with other experiment code: `github.com/ahmeshaf/model_in_coref`.

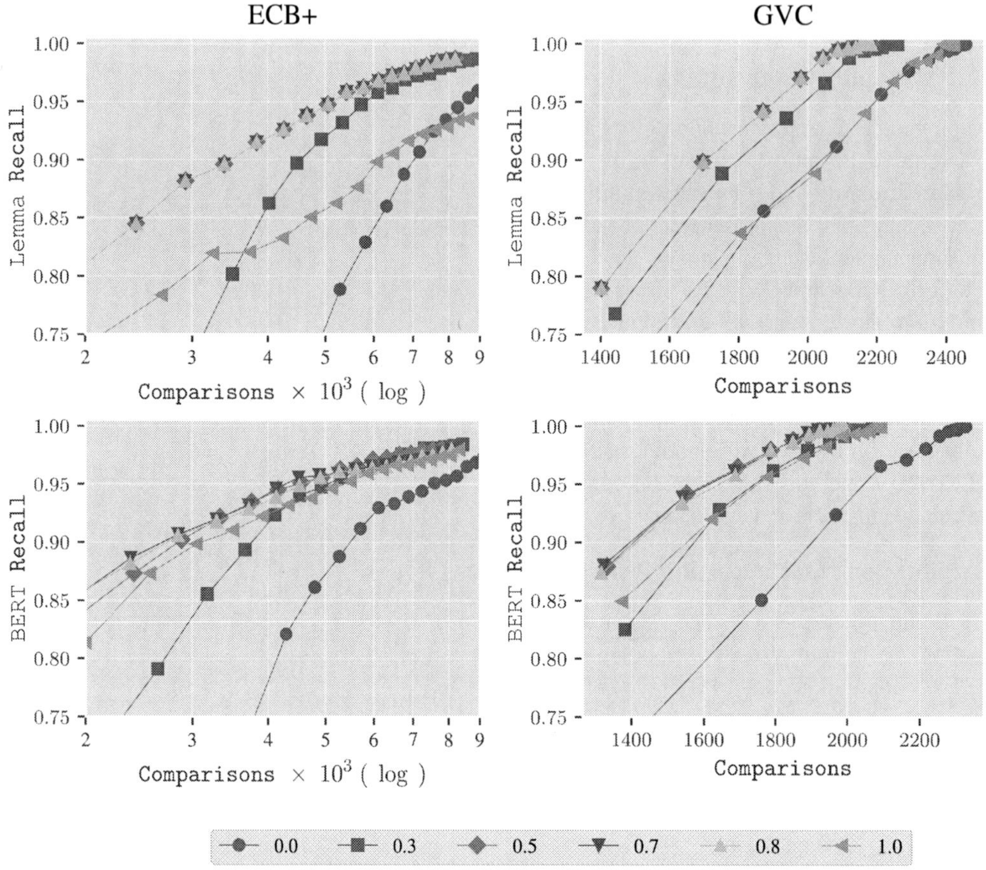

Figure 5: Trigger and Sentence Similarity weight (λ) Hyper-parameter tuning on the development sets of ECB+ and GVC. We deduce $\lambda = 0.7$ is optimal for both methods for both datasets.

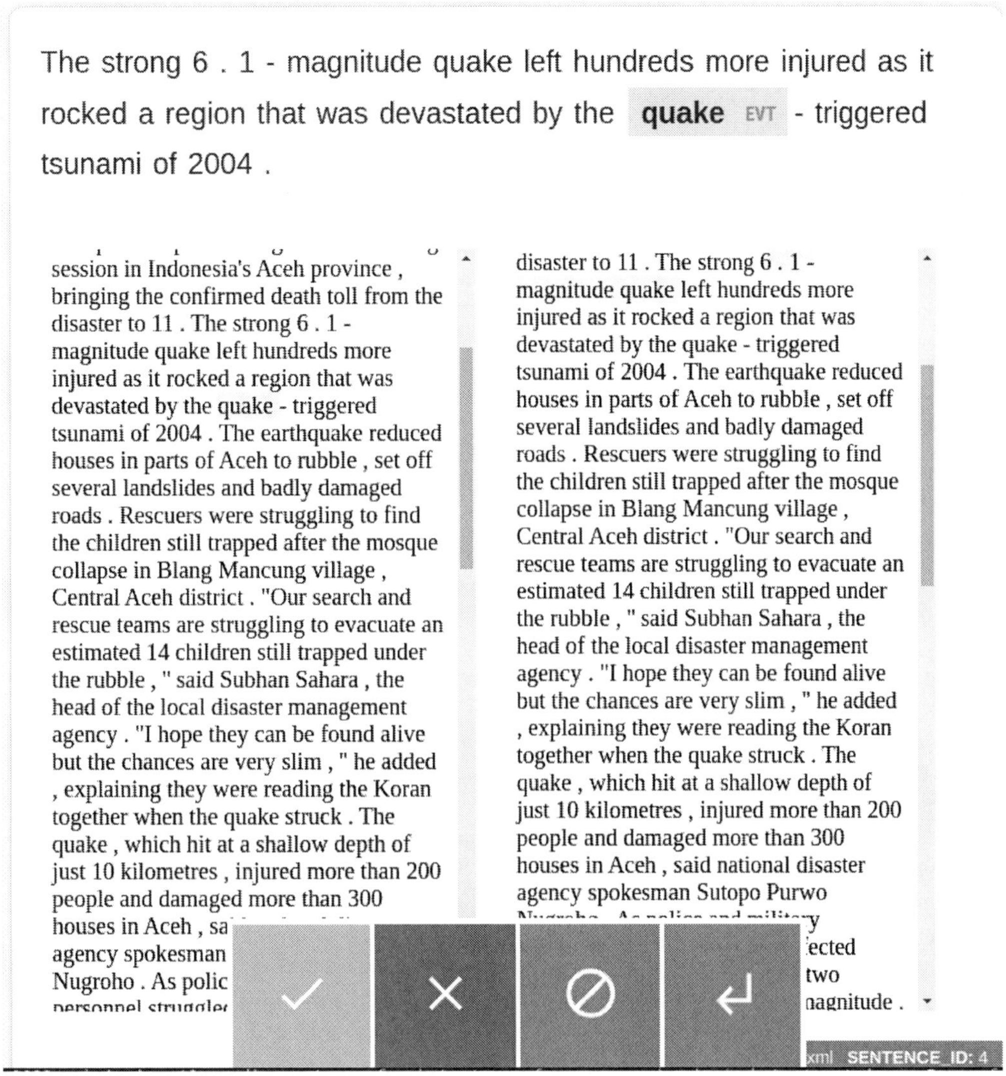

Figure 6: The model-in-the-loop ECR annotation using the Prodigy Annotation Tool. The target event is on the left and the Candidate cluster is on the right.

Pragmatic Annotation of Articles Related to Police Brutality

Tess Feyen and **Alda Mari**
Institut Jean Nicod
ENS-PSL/CNRS/EHESS

Paul Portner
Georgetown University

Abstract

The annotation task we elaborated aims at describing the contextual factors that influence the appearance and interpretation of moral predicates, in newspaper articles on police brutality, in French and in English. The paper provides a brief review of the literature on moral predicates and their relation with context. The paper also describes the elaboration of the corpus and the ontology. Our hypothesis is that the use of moral adjectives and their appearance in context could change depending on the political orientation of the journal. We elaborated an annotation task to investigate the precise contexts discussed in articles on police brutality. The paper concludes by describing the study and the annotation task in details.

1 Introduction

The use of moral predicates in natural language is a topic of interest for linguists, as it sheds light on the complex interplay between language, ethics, and society. The annotation task proposed in this paper studies the use of moral predicates in newspaper articles in French and in English discussing police brutality, with a focus on the contextual factors that influence their appearance and interpretation. Indeed, our broader research goal is to determine whether the use of moral adjectives and their appearance in context changes depending on the political orientation of the journal.

To achieve this goal, we elaborated a pragmatic annotation on a corpus of newspaper articles on the George Floyd and Adama Traoré cases, published between May 2020 and August 2020, from a variety of newspapers across the political spectrum. A basic contextual ontology that has been elaborated specifically for this study, that takes into account various actors involved in events surrounding police brutality.

We will start by making a brief review of the literature on moral predicates, their relation with context, and pragmatic annotation. Then we'll describe the elaboration of the ontology, and some preliminary results that lead us to decisions for the annotation task. Finally, we'll describe the study and annotation task in details. We currently don't have the results of this annotation, as the participants are still annotating at this time.

2 Background of the study and some assumptions

Moral predicates (like *good, wrong*) gained more popularity in the last years (Faroldi and Ruiz, 2017; Ruiz and Stojanovic, 2019; Stojanovic, 2019; Soria Ruiz and Faroldi, 2022), and linguists often compared them to predicates of personal taste (like *tasty, fun*) (i.a. Lasersohn, 2005) and to aesthetic predicates (like *beautiful, elegant*) (i.a. McNally and Stojanovic, 2014). Indeed, moral predicates show similar patterns to predicates of personal taste (PPTs) in that they express a subjective judgment. Faultless disagreement appears when two speakers disagree on a subjective matter. It is the type of disagreement that two people can have over liking pork belly or not for example ; no one is right or wrong, they just have different tastes.

Indeed, a statement made about taste cannot be countered by stating the speaker's experience is false. For that reason, and similarly to PPTs, moral predicates are very sensitive to the context they are in ; they react to the experience the speaker is discussing[1]. To our knowledge, only one corpus study was done on moral predicates (Stojanovic and McNally, 2022), precisely on the type of subjectivity moral predicates capture. Kaiser and Rudin (2020) argue in their article that the strength of faultless disagreements changes when taste predicates are used in the context of widely-held opinions. Indeed, faultless disagreement isn't a binary phenomenon, but a gradient one, that depends on the object of

[1]They are also often called "experiential predicates" (see i.a. Stojanovic, 2019; Willer and Kennedy, 2022).

Proceedings of the 17th Linguistic Annotation Workshop (LAW-XVII), pages 146–153
July 13, 2023 ©2023 Association for Computational Linguistics

predication (and not just on the predicate itself). We can then make the hypothesis that moral predicates are also sensitive to a change of context, and that this could have implications for the subjectivity they express. The lack in current knowledge on the use of moral predicates in context, and the assumption that context can influence their understanding all together were the first issues that brought us to investigate this topic.

Theses consideration in mind brought us to the field of pragmatics, specifically at the intersection of what Yule (1996) calls "speaker meaning" and "contextual meaning". Indeed, what the speaker is thinking before uttering a sentence, and how the context can influence this thought is especially vague when it comes to moral predicates. For PPTs like *tasty*, we assume the speaker is talking about her own experience relating to some dish. However, expressing that pizza for example is tasty is less surprising than doing it for spinach or snails (see again Kaiser and Rudin, 2020). Context then has to remain the same if we want to analyze the behavior of moral predicates. What differentiates the use of *right* from the use of *good*? Are *just* and *right* more likely to be used in contexts where justice is mentioned, as one could infer intuitively? Are moral adjectives used when the context is clear, or when it is shifting from one topic to another? Our goal with this annotation task isn't as broad as analyzing the specific subjectivity expressed in moral predicates or giving a semantic analysis of the meaning of such predicates[2]. Instead, understanding precisely what is being discussed in these articles will allow us to understand the contexts in which moral predicates are more likely to be used. This annotation task is to be considered as the first step towards this analysis. It will help us provide a better understanding of the context itself, in order to make hypothesis on the behavior of moral predicates in articles on police brutality.

3 Elaboration of the ontology and some preliminary results

3.1 Corpus data

To provide an analysis of moral predicates in context, we chose to gather articles discussing the similar contexts – the George Floyd case for the American news sources, and the Adama Traoré case for the French news sources. We did choose news sources bearing diverging political view points to offer a wide range of contexts: for example, we picked Jacobin for their left-orientation and Breitbart for their right-orientation for this study[3].

We started with a very large corpus, composed of every article mentioning George Floyd (US) or Adama Traoré (FR) between the day each of them passed away (May 2020 for George Floyd and July 2016 for Adama Traoré) and September 1st 2021. However, we realized that some articles had no real mention to either case, and were only using the names of the victim once. Preventing this problem was possible if we focused on the time period surrounding the protests that came after the death of George Floyd. Indeed, Adama Traoré died in 2016 but the case gained in popularity in France after the BLM protests emerged throughout the United States. To compare the articles containing sentences using moral predicates and articles containing sentences that don't (see Rayson and Garside, 2000), we decided to gather articles between May 2020 and August 2020[4], and picked for each article containing a moral predicate an article that's doesn't and is close in time – published the day before or after when possible. We made sure that the same number of articles from each sources was gathered.

3.2 Basic ontology

Now that all the data is gathered, we started discussing how to narrow down contexts surrounding police brutality. The core of our needs for annotating these articles is to precise our understanding of the broad context "police brutality". Understanding the context precisely isn't linked to the "side" the

[2]One reviewer noted the polysemy of moral predicates, and the difficulty to distinguish moral predicates from non-moral predicates. For clarity, here is the list of moral predicates we are interested in in this study : *fair, unfair, just, unjust, good, bad, right, wrong, correct, incorrect* and their French equivalents : *équitable, inéquitable, juste, injuste, bien, mal, bon, mauvais, correct, incorrect*. We are also working on a semantic analysis of these predicates, but this is beyond the scope of this paper.

[3]We are hoping that this preliminary annotation task will be useful for further investigation of bias in reporting. We did not automatically predict the political orientation of these newspapers beforehand (see i.a. Kulkarni et al.; Baly et al.) and simply chose newspapers known to have a specific political orientation. We are not excluding using automation in the future, and comparing it to our results.

[4]This is the time period that concentrates the most of the protests, both in France and in the United States.

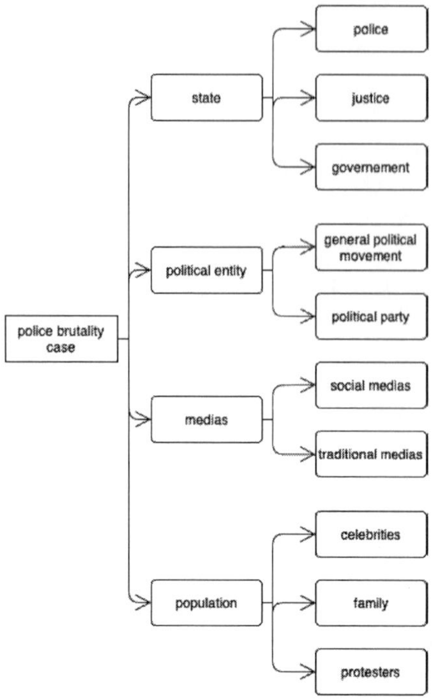

Figure 1: Simple ontology of police brutality

article was taking – pro- or against BLM for example –, as we didn't want our annotators to have to provide their own opinion. We read approximately 50% of articles that were published during the time period we agreed on, and noted various events that were recurrently mentioned[5].

It appeared that out of the police brutality case, other recurrent circumstances resulted in both the French and the American data : tributes from the family, protests, and mentions of trial. In terms of who was talked about though, the policemen involved were, without a real surprise, the actors that were the most mentioned. We sensed a difference between the events related to the state as an entity, and the events related to the population as a whole. However, we sometimes encountered elements that weren't completely understandable either as state or as population : social media entities like Twitter, or specific political parties that weren't discussed as elected officials. Indeed, what we wanted to focus on in this ontology is what is "being talked about", not who is talking. As such, an elected official, like a governor for example, can be discussed specifically for his views as a Republican, not in his quality as a governor. Our goal with this ontology was to see if it would both lead to an understanding of what type of event is mostly discussed by the different news papers, and if any moral predicate was more used in one context or the other.

3.3 Some tests and modification

To see if our ontology would be able to give an insight into the semantics of the moral predicates, we annotated 30 sentences containing moral predicates from each newspapers – like *right*, *good* or *correct*–, following the first level of the ontology. These preliminary results showed that Breitbart used 8 times the moral predicate *right* to discuss contexts related to the State (like police or justice system), whereas the New York Times mostly used *good* in those contexts. Jacobin and the New York Times however, used *right* when discussing the population as a whole. We realized that the broad categories State and Population weren't precise enough for our purpose, simply because it gathered together the justice system and the police, or the family of the victim and protesters, when those entities had very different events associated to them : the policemen involved are, in the context of police brutality, the ones being judged, but in some articles the justice system itself was criticized. We wanted to show this contrast, and ended up with the ontology in Figure 1.

4 Annotation task

This is a description of the annotation task our participants are currently accomplishing. Each sentence will be annotated twice : once by a member of the research team, and once by a recruited participant. We currently cannot present a measure of the inter-annotator agreement, as the task is still in progress. However, we are aware of the subjectivity of the task : even though the guidelines focus on the context surrounding each sentence and doesn't ask from the annotator to express a personal opinion on the topic itself, the perceived importance of the topic discussed can still vary from one person to the other.

4.1 Elaboration of the task

The annotation task was based off of the second level of our ontology, to ensure a more precise annotation, as we understood the first level to be too broad. We used Qualtrics as our software for

[5]We didn't use Latent Semantic Analysis (i.a. Deerwester et al.; Landauer et al.) for this specific task, but are hoping to in the future when we will look at documents discussing a larger variety of topics. We thank reviewers for their very constructive comments that will guide our next steps.

this task[6], specifically the matrix table survey type.

Each sentence from each article was separated using NLTK, and placed in the rows of the matrix table. The categories are appearing on the horizontal axis of the table, and the participant has to tick the correct box, according to the annotation guidelines (see Appendix A). We choose to divide the articles in sentences to ensure great precision. We wanted to observe the moment were the context shifted from one category to the other.

To transfer each article to Qualtrics, we used Python to convert them to the Advanced Text format of Qualtrics. The Advanced Text format is a simple way to import data into Qualtrics without having to import every single article by hand and add each category by hand as well.

Every set of articles was randomly assigned to participants, to ensure that they would get a similar amount of article containing moral predicates and not containing moral predicates. The participants were not aware we were precisely focusing on moral predicates. Each article was double-annotated by a participant and by a member of the research team.

4.2 Task and participants recruitment

The task itself was to associate each sentence from each article to a category from the ontology[7]. We found participants by putting an ad on the university list-serv. We recruited 5 participants for the English data, and 1 participant for the French one. Indeed, the French corpus is much smaller than the American one. Participants recruited for the American data have to annotate 294 articles in total, whereas the French participant has to annotate 136 articles. We had to immensely lower the amount of articles given to each participants, as they progressed with the annotation task slower than anticipated. We gave every single participant the annotation guidelines when sending them the survey link, but also had an individual Zoom meeting to review these guidelines, answer any question, and review the consent form. This meeting took place before any data collection.

Before starting the annotation task, each participant had to consent to the study. To do so, they were presented with the consent form, and had to tick a box to consent. They were not asked to provide their name, signature, or any other identifying data. Indeed, this annotation task is anonymous, and each participant was provided with an anonymous Qualtrics link as well. At no point during the study were the participants told the research was done on moral predicates. This was done to ensure they wouldn't treat sentences containing moral predicates differently than sentences that don't include them. The participants also don't know the newspaper the article was taken from, nor the date it was published.

After the consent form, they were introduced to the annotation guidelines we explained to them during the Zoom. They had to pass a quick test to make sure those guidelines were understood properly before starting the annotation. The test was composed of five multiple choice questions. Each question had between one and three sentences taken from articles that had to be annotated. To make the task easier, only 5 out of 11 categories were presented as a possible answer. The participant had to click on the correct one in order to pass the test. If one category was wrongly chosen, the participant had to choose again until they chose the right one. Then, they were able to move on to the proper annotation task.

As we stated earlier, the articles are randomized. However, the sentences themselves are not. The sentences of the articles had to be shown as they appear in the article, in order to provide the proper context.

4.3 Examples

To explain the task in further details, let's look at some examples of expected annotation in sentences containing moral predicates. We put emphasis on the moral predicates by making them bold.

(1) Americans have watched protests dedicated to ending **unjust** violence mutate into riots that inflict **unjust** violence themselves.[8]
PROTESTS

[6]This was done to ensure meeting university requirements and provide a better user experience for our participants, the website being optimized for survey responses.

[7]As such, this task is very similar to the early stage of an basic entity linking task, where sentences are associated with the knowledge base of the context categories. However, sentences discussing police brutality were classified as a category of the ontology whether they contained a mention the actual name of the category or not. For example, sentences classified as "Family" didn't always include the word "family". This task is different from named-entity recognition in that regard (i.a. Marrero et al.).

[8]"McConnell: Can't 'Deafen' Ourselves to Pain of Black Americans, Riots Inflicting 'Unjust Violence Themselves'", 06/01/2020, Ian Hanchett for Breitbart News.

In (1), the topic of discussing is the protests, and even if the authors used the word "riot", which is biased in comparison to a more neutral word like "protest", the event in question is still the protests following the George Floyd murder. We tried our best to make the ontology categories insensitive to the expressed bias. The classification as "Protest" is here preferable.

(2) Right now, defunding the police is not a radical demand. That is **good** government. The idea of funding public services and making sure that people have their needs met — that's just **good** government. [9]
GOVERNMENT

In (2), the author does not focus on "defund the police" as a claim made by protesters (it would have been classified as "Protest") or a specific political group (that would be "General political movement"). She also does not insist on the repercussions such a policy could have for law enforcement as a whole (that would be "Police"). Instead, she qualify this as "good governement", and a policy that could benefit the population. As such, this whole paragraph should be classified as "Government".

5 Conclusion

The aim of this paper was to describe the elaboration of a pragmatic annotation task, that takes into account the specifics of the police brutality context. Our hypotheses is that moral predicates could potentially be a marker of biases in newspapers articles. Currently, we know very little about the behavior of moral predicates in context, since only one corpus study involving them has been conducted. To allow for an understanding of the variety of topics surrounding police brutality, we elaborated a ontology based on the Adama Traoré and the George Floyd cases. Our goal is to investigate how moral predicates behave in discussion of these similar contexts, to compare them with one another and crosslinguistically, as well as to see if one (or more) sub-context of police brutality is more likely to involve moral predicates. By proposing an annotation task to precise the context of police brutality itself, and by choosing articles containing moral predicates and articles that don't, we are hoping to answer these questions.

We are aware that this work is still at its early stage, but are looking forward to get feedback on this primary study, in hopes of perfecting it in the future.

Limitations

Despite the contributions this study might bring, there are several limitations that must be acknowledged.

- Scope of the study: We focused solely on police brutality and did not consider other contexts that could bring interesting uses of moral predicates in the media.
- Sentiment analysis: The link between sentiment analysis and moral predicates hasn't, to our knowledge, been studied as such. We don't make any claim about the polarity of moral predicates in this study, and focus on associations between predicates and the context they are used in, regardless of the tone they are conveying. We hope we would be able to in the future.
- Cultural differences, issues in comparison: As we collected data from different news sources in French and English, finding accurate equivalences between the two languages was challenging, making a perfect comparison impossible. Furthermore, The French and American contexts differ significantly, including differences in public opinion on cases of police brutality. For instance, the death of George Floyd shocked a majority of Americans, whereas it took four years for the French media to bring Adama Traoré's case to the center of public attention.
- Limited data and generalization: Our study relies on the analysis of 430 articles in both languages (294 in English, 136 in French). The inclusion of more data could potentially strengthen our findings. Moreover, only one case of police brutality per country was annotated, when a larger set of similar circumstances from different time periods would have helped us sketch a more precise picture of police brutality as a whole.
- Translating difficulty: Some moral predicates, such as *right* and *just*, do not have a precise

[9]"Police Are Not Designed to Solve the Problems People Are Facing", 06/12/2020, An interview with Rossana Rodriguez-Sanchez. Jeanette Taylor for Jacobin.

equivalent and are both translated in French by *juste*. Similarly, the French language has two possible translations for *good* namely *bon* and *bien*. If the semantics of these terms isn't the purpose of this paper, we are aware that these potential differences in meaning could have an impact on their use in context. We are also working on a semantic description.

Ethics Statement

When elaborating this study, we took into consideration the following elements :

- Informed consent: We made sure to elaborate a consent form stating the goals of the study and the precise actions the participant will have to accomplish in order to finish it. The consent form also included information about the risks and benefits of participating in this research. Indeed, some articles are describing the violent interaction the victim had with the police, and mention systemic racism. We disclosed that some articles were taken from extremely conservatives news sources and could make an apology of white supremacy as well. A full review of the consent form was done beforehand with the participants to answer any potential questions they might have.

- Confidentiality: At no point during the study were the participants asked to disclose any information, whether name, age, gender, occupation, or any other potentially identifying data. We used the Qualtrics survey software's anonymous link, and did not include any identifiable question in the survey itself.

- Participants welfare: Participants were told that they could withdraw from the study at any time, without any consequences, and that the choice to participate or not was their own.

- Ethical review: This study was approved by the Institutional Review Board of our university before any data collection began. The members of this research team were asked to pursue an ethics training before being able to submit the study protocol.

References

Ramy Baly, Giovanni Da San Martino, James Glass, and Preslav Nakov. We can detect your bias: Predicting the political ideology of news articles. In *Proceedings of the 2020 Conference on Empirical Methods in Natural Language Processing (EMNLP)*, pages 4982–4991. Association for Computational Linguistics.

Scott Deerwester, Susan T. Dumais, George W. Furnas, Thomas K. Landauer, and Richard Harshman. Indexing by latent semantic analysis. *Journal of the American Society for Information Science*, 41(6):391–407.

Federico L. G. Faroldi and Andrés Soria Ruiz. 2017. The scale structure of moral adjectives. *Studia Semiotyczne*, 31(2):161–178.

Elsi Kaiser and Deniz Rudin. 2020. When faultless disagreement is not so faultless: What widely-held opinions can tell us about subjective adjectives. *Proceedings of the Linguistic Society of America*, 5(1):698–707. Number: 1.

Christopher Kennedy and Malte Willer. 2016. Subjective attitudes and counterstance contingency. *Semantics and Linguistic Theory*, 26(0):913–933. Number: 0.

Vivek Kulkarni, Junting Ye, Steve Skiena, and William Yang Wang. Multi-view models for political ideology detection of news articles. In *Proceedings of the 2018 Conference on Empirical Methods in Natural Language Processing*, pages 3518–3527. Association for Computational Linguistics.

Thomas K Landauer, Peter W. Foltz, and Darrell Laham. An introduction to latent semantic analysis. *Discourse Processes*, 25(2):259–284.

Peter Lasersohn. 2005. Context dependence, disagreement, and predicates of personal taste*. *Linguistics and Philosophy*, 28(6):643–686.

Geoffrey Leech. 1993. Corpus annotation schemes. *Literary and Linguistic Computing*, 8(4):275–281.

Teresa Marques. 2015. Disagreeing in context. *Frontiers. Psychology.*, 6.

Mónica Marrero, Julián Urbano, Sonia Sánchez-Cuadrado, Jorge Morato, and Juan Miguel Gómez-Berbís. Named entity recognition: Fallacies, challenges and opportunities. *Computer Standards & Interfaces*, 35(5):482–489.

Louise McNally and Isidora Stojanovic. 2014. Aesthetic adjectives. In James Young, editor, *The Semantics of Aesthetic Judgment*. Oxford University Press.

Paul Rayson and Roger Garside. 2000. Comparing corpora using frequency profiling. In *The Workshop on Comparing Corpora*, pages 1–6, Hong Kong, China. Association for Computational Linguistics.

Andrés Soria Ruiz and Isidora Stojanovic. 2019. On linguistic evidence for expressivism. *Royal Institute of Philosophy Supplements*, 86:155–180. Publisher: Cambridge University Press.

Andrés Soria Ruiz and Federico L.G. Faroldi. 2022. Moral adjectives, judge-dependency and holistic multidimensionality. *Inquiry*, 65(7):887–916. Publisher: Routledge _eprint: https://doi.org/10.1080/0020174X.2020.1855241.

Tamina Stephenson. 2007. Judge dependence, epistemic modals, and predicates of personal taste. *Linguistics and Philosophy*, 30(4):487–525. Publisher: Springer.

Isidora Stojanovic. 2019. Disagreements about taste vs. disagreements about moral issues. *American Philosophical Quarterly*, 56(1):29–41. Publisher: University of Illinois Press.

Isidora Stojanovic and Louise Mcnally. 2022. Are Moral Predicates Subjective? A Corpus Study. In David Bordonaba, editor, *Experimental philosophy of language: perspectives, methods and prospects*. Springer.

Malte Willer and Christopher Kennedy. 2022. Assertion, expression, experience. *Inquiry*, 65(7):821–857. Publisher: Routledge _eprint: https://doi.org/10.1080/0020174X.2020.1850338.

George Yule. 1996. *Pragmatics*. OUP Oxford. Google-Books-ID: E2SA8ao0yMAC.

A Annotation guidelines

What follow is the annotation guidelines that were given to the participants.

There are 11 categories total. Each of them represents something that can be associated with police brutality in context. Our goal is to have a more fine understanding of the contexts mentioning police brutality.

Here is the list of all categories :

- Justice ; mentions of judges, justice decisions, trials, testimonies from witnesses, autopsy results...
- Police ; mentions of policemen involved or of the police institution as a whole, statements from the lawyers of the policemen involved and of police unions...
- Government ; mentions of statements from government and elected officials, changes in state policing...
- Political party ; mentions of a specific political party like the Republicans or the Democrats, or one of their elected officials, mentions of their political stances...
- General political movement ; mentions of a vague political movement, like "the Left", or "populists" and their political stances. Also includes vague mentions of communities coming together, outside of protests.
- Social medias ; mentions of social medias such as Twitter or Facebook, and their uses.
- Traditional medias ; mentions of traditional medias such as TV, radio, newspaper, and their uses, mentions of journalists.
- Celebrities ; mentions of any type of celebrity, whether it is to support BLM or not.
- Protests ; mentions of any type of protesters or protests, whether they support BLM or not, descriptions of protest violence and discourse.
- Family ; mentions of the victim's family or the victim themselves, victim's family statements, and statements from the lawyer of the family. Also includes direct descriptions of the victim himself and tributes.
- Other ; everything that cannot be related to any of these categories.

For each sentence, your goal will be to associate it with one of these categories. Sometimes, it's easy to see how to classify the sentence, but it also can get tricky.

(3) The trial of Mr. Chauvin, charged in the death of George Floyd, will resume on Monday.

For example, in the sentence (3), the policeman involved in in Floyd's murder is mentioned, but the main topic of the sentence is the trial. As such, this sentence should be classified as Justice and not Police. It is a statement made about the trial timeline.

(4) Players have spoken at protest marches, and leagues have bankrolled new social-justice efforts.

In (4), one could wonder if the "players" in question are to be understood as Protests or as Other, since they are attending protest marches, and don't seem to fit another category. Actually, the "players" in question are MLB top players, in the context of this article. They represent a celebrity, and should be classified as such. Each sentence of each article will be presented in order, meaning that the article won't have all of its sentences randomized. The reason for this choice is for sentences like (4), since they can only be properly understood in context. Sometimes a specific sentence does not mention a category, but this sentence is included in the context of another category, like (5):

(5) "This is tough.
First of all, I have to say my heart and my prayers go out to the family of George Floyd.
What we see in this video is devastating and it's senseless."

In this quote, the general context is to be classified as Family. Even though "This is tough" is not in itself related to the family of the victim, the sentence was said in a context discussing about Floyd's family. Please try your best to see the big picture of the article, and not to just focus on each individual sentence.

Moreover, even though we tried our best to make this survey perfect, it's possible that some lines are wrongly separated (in the case of tweets containing images for example). In that case, please classify those sentences in the same way you would have the whole tweet. In (6) to (9), the same tweet was separated in 4 lines. This tweet should be classified as Protests, meaning each line has to be classified as Protests, not just (7) and (8).

(6) Decent amount of riot cops showing up.

(7) Thankfully Still no sign of any violence.

(8) "#SanAntonioprotest
pic.twitter.com/S1vMELh6cl

(9) — / (@PropheticLaw) May 31, 2020

If you feel like two categories are mentioned - that may happen often! -, please focus on the global context surrounding the sentence and the main category that could fit this context.

Another thing worth mentioning : the correct category is not defined by the speaker, but by the content of the sentence. For example, if the sentence you're annotating contains a quote from Donald Trump, former president of the United States, talking about the police, it has to be classified as Police and not as Government. What matters is what the sentence is about, not the person expressing it.

The category Other can be used - like its name suggests - when no other category seem to fit the sentence. However, we will ask that you try your best to associate the sentences you see with one of the 10 other categories. The Other category was mostly created for sentences that don't relate at all to police brutality, for example for mentions of the COVID-19 pandemic. Indeed, some articles mention both police brutality and other topics. This category is made for those cases.

The RST Continuity Corpus

Debopam Das
Åbo Akademi University
Tehtaankatu 2
20500 Turku, Finland
debopam.das@abo.fi

Markus Egg
Humboldt-Universität zu Berlin
Unter den Linden 6
10099 Berlin, Germany
markus.egg@hu-berlin.de

Abstract

We present the RST Continuity Corpus (RST-CC), a corpus of discourse relations annotated for continuity dimensions. Continuity or discontinuity (maintaining or shifting deictic centres across discourse segments) is an important property of discourse relations, but the two are correlated in greatly varying ways. To analyse this correlation, the relations in the RST-CC are annotated using operationalised versions of Givón's (1993) continuity dimensions. We also report on the inter-annotator agreement, and discuss recurrent annotation issues. First results show substantial variation of continuity dimensions within and across relation types.

1 Introduction

In this paper, we present the RST Continuity Corpus (RST-CC), the first corpus of discourse relations annotated for a wide range of continuity dimensions (e.g., *time*, *space*, *reference*, or *perspective*). These dimensions describe different ways in which a deictic centre can be maintained or updated during a discourse. The corpus contains 1,009 relations from five major relation types, which are a subset of the RST Discourse Treebank (Carlson et al., 2002). In the RST-CC, relations are annotated with respect to Givón's (1993, ch. 13) seven continuity dimensions. The relations are furthermore annotated for additional features such as *polarity* (positive or negative relation) and *context* (intra- vs. inter-sentential relation).

The paper is structured as follows: Section 2 outlines previous work on continuity and discourse relations. In Section 3, we describe the composition of the RST-CC, its general format, and the selected relations. Section 4 elaborates on the selected continuity dimensions and their operationalisation into distinctive features. Additional features of annotation are described in Section 5. Section 6 reports on the inter-annotator agreement study, and Section 7 discusses recurrent annotation issues. We present first results in Section 8, and conclude with an outlook on the next steps of our work.

2 Theoretical background

2.1 The notion of continuity

Continuity emerges in multi-segment discourse when the deictic centre remains constant along a situational dimension across segments; e.g., the events or situations described in two segments occur at the same time or share their protagonists. The deictic centre is the point of reference with respect to which context-dependent expressions are evalutated, it is often but not always determined by the speaker.

In contrast, changes along these dimensions, e.g., when a new segment refers to a situation set in an earlier time (like in a flashback) or introduces a new protagonist, result in discontinuity. Continuity is monitored during text processing in that readers maintain or update their frame of reference for dimensions like time, space, character, or causation (Zwaan et al., 1995; Zwaan and Singer, 2003).

We define continuity in terms of thematic coherence (Givón, 1993), which distinguishes seven continuity dimensions or 'coherence strands'. Maintaining or shifting deictic centres on these dimensions between discourse segments determines the extent of thematic coherence (continuity) or disruption (discontinuity). The seven dimensions are *time*, *space*, *reference*, *action*, *perspective*, *modality*, and *speech act*. The first four dimensions are more concrete and local, the others, more abstract and global, as visualised in Table 1.

The grouping of dimensions is based on effect; consider (1)-(2) from Givón (1993). In (1), a change in the temporal continuity across the two clauses causes a local break, but does not necessarily terminate a larger coherent sequence of clauses in the text. In contrast, a change in one of the global dimensions amounts to a stronger break, which can

Proceedings of the 17th Linguistic Annotation Workshop (LAW-XVII), pages 154–165
July 13, 2023 ©2023 Association for Computational Linguistics

local	time
	space
	reference
	action
global	perspective
	modality
	speech act

Table 1: Givón's coherence strands

terminate such a sequence of clauses. There is such a break in (2), because it exhibits discontinuity in perspective between the two sentences (viewpoint of the author vs. the one of the protagonist).

(1) She flew in at midnight and left the next day.

(2) She came in and sat on the bed. She was tired, she thought.

We base our annotation on these continuity dimensions, as they offer a comprehensive range of continuity dimensions. Also, the framework locates continuity at the level of clauses or sequences of clauses and the way they are linked, which is exactly where discourse relations are situated.

2.2 Discourse relations and continuity

Continuity is a crucial feature of discourse (or coherence) relations, which introduce a semantic or pragmatic link (e.g., additive, causal, or adversative) between two discourse segments. The relations exhibit continuity or discontinuity across the discourse segments they link. For example, the clauses in (3)[1] are linked by a CONSEQUENCE relation, the situation presented in the first clause being the consequence of the event in the second clause.

(3) [The Indian stock markets have been on a five-year high, with dips and corrections,] [since Prime Minister Rajiv Gandhi started liberalizing industry.]

The situation in the first clause of (3) temporally follows the event in the second clause. This backward temporal shift introduces discontinuity along the temporal dimension. Also, the segments have no common discourse referents, which amounts to referential discontinuity. In contrast, there is no spatial shift across the segments, neither is there a perspective change because both segments can be attributed to the same source (the author). So, the relation is continuous for space and perspective.

[1]All examples are from the RST Discourse Treebank (Carlson et al., 2002) unless specified otherwise.

2.3 Previous work

Previous work models the relation between continuity and discourse relations in different ways. Sometimes, continuity is treated as a binary feature, and discourse relations, or even whole groups of such relations, are summarily classified as continuous or discontinuous. For instance, Murray (1997) considers CAUSAL relations continuous, and Zufferey and Gygax (2016) regard CONTRASTIVE relations as discontinuous. Asr and Demberg (2012) classify discourse relations in the Penn Discourse Treebank (Prasad et al., 2008) for continuity and discontinuity. They group relations like RESULT, INSTANTIATION, and LIST as continuous and relations like PRAGMATIC CONTRAST, CONTRA-EXPECTATION, or TEMPORAL relations as discontinuous, but leave the CONDITIONAL relations underspecified with respect to continuity.

Other work classifies discourse relations as configurations of individual continuity dimensions (e.g., time, space, or reference). Fetzer (2018) describes relations with a set of continuity dimensions ('particularized features'), which include temporal and referential continuity, but also continuity of action. Relations are distinguished in terms of the presence or absence of continuity along specific dimensions. For example, CONTINUATION relations are characterised as continuous for dimensions of time, reference, topic, aspect, and lexical coherence, while CONTRAST relations display discontinuity on at least one of these dimensions.

In sum, there is as yet no unanimously accepted classification of discourse relations for continuity. What is more, even individual relations can be continuous and discontinuous on different dimensions simultaneously. For example, CAUSAL relations, which are generally deemed to be continuous, can simultaneously exhibit continuity for the temporal dimension, but discontinuity for the reference dimension, as in (4).

(4) [As some securities mature and the proceeds are reinvested,] [the problems ought to ease.]

At the same time, CONTRAST relations, usually regarded as discontinuous, can show the same configuration (continuity for time, not for reference):

(5) [The gasoline picture may improve this quarter,] [but chemicals are likely to remain weak.]

Such cases raise the fundamental question of whether relation types in their entirety can be classified with respect to continuity.

For some dimensions it is even debated whether they introduce continuity or discontinuity in the first place. For example, temporal progression in narration is often cited as indicative of continuity since it represents the expected flow of events (Zwaan, 1996; Zufferey and Gygax, 2016). However, such transitions, particularly when signalled by a temporal connective like *then*, have also been taken to indicate discontinuity (Segal et al., 1991). Asr and Demberg (2012) even regard synchronous temporal relations as discontinuous because they are often used to introduce new events.

The lack of unanimity across approaches and corpus examples like (4) and (5) suggest re-examining the relationship of continuity and discourse relations in detail, i.e., on the level of individual tokens of the relations. For each continuity dimension of a token, continuity must be determined separately.

Since there is as yet no resource for this research question, we compiled the RST-CC, whose format will be described in the next section.

3 The RST Continuity Corpus

The RST-CC comprises relations from the RST Discourse Treebank or RST-DT (Carlson et al., 2002). The RST-DT contains 385 newspaper texts annotated for over 20,000 relations according to Rhetorical Structure Theory or RST (Mann and Thompson, 1988). In RST, relations link a more and a less central discourse unit (nucleus and satellite), or two equally central units (nuclei). Linking is recursive, which models discourse as a tree structure. Elementary discourse units (EDUs) in RST are typically clauses; there may be sub-clausal EDUs units, however (especially in the RST-DT). Fig. 1 illustrates an RST analysis for (6), in which the segments A and B are collectively connected to C by a REASON relation. Text in square brackets represents discourse units; in Fig. 1, arrows go from satellites to nuclei.

(6) [[The U.S. Coast Guard closed six miles of the Houston Ship Channel,]^{A} [where about 150 companies have operations,]^{B}] [because the thick, black smoke obscured the area.]^{C}

The RST-CC includes five relation types: CAUSAL, CONTRASTIVE, CONDITIONAL, ELABORATION, and TEMPORAL. This selection is motivated by previous classifications, which categorise, for example, CAUSAL and ELABORATION relations as continuous (Murray, 1997), CONTRASTIVE relations as discontinuous (Zufferey and Gygax, 2016), TEMPORAL relations as one or the other (Hopper, 1979), and CONDITIONAL relations as underspecified with respect to continuity (Asr and Demberg, 2012).

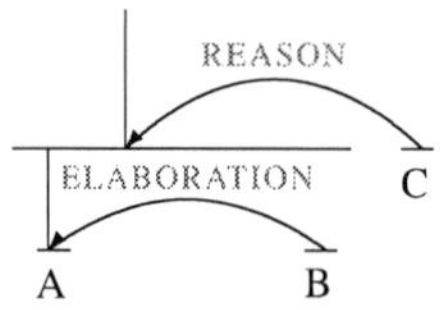

Figure 1: Graphical representation of an RST analysis

The relations are also classified in terms of the Cognitive approach to Coherence Relations or CCR (Sanders et al., 1992, 2021), using features such as polarity (positive or negative)[2] and basic operation (implicational or additive, i.e., causal or non-causal). For instance, ELABORATION relations are positive and additive, whereas CONTRASTIVE relations are negative. Table 2 summarises these classifications.

In the RST-CC, the relation types are subdivided according to the RST-DT relation taxonomy (Carlson and Marcu, 2001); e.g., the CONTRASTIVE type includes the subtypes ANTITHESIS, CONCESSION, and CONTRAST. Table 6 in the Appendix offers a detailed account of the relation types, their member subtypes, and their key features.

<table>
<tr><th>Relation type</th><th>Predicted continuity</th><th>Polarity</th><th>Basic operation</th></tr>
<tr><td>CAUSAL</td><td>continuous</td><td>positive</td><td>implicational</td></tr>
<tr><td rowspan="2">CONTRASTIVE</td><td rowspan="2">discontinuous</td><td rowspan="2">negative</td><td>additive</td></tr>
<tr><td>implicational</td></tr>
<tr><td rowspan="2">CONDITIONAL</td><td rowspan="2">not specified</td><td>positive</td><td rowspan="2">implicational</td></tr>
<tr><td>negative</td></tr>
<tr><td>ELABORATION</td><td>continuous</td><td>positive</td><td>additive</td></tr>
<tr><td rowspan="2">TEMPORAL</td><td>continuous</td><td rowspan="2">positive</td><td rowspan="2">additive</td></tr>
<tr><td>discontinuous</td></tr>
</table>

Table 2: Relation types and their features

In our continuity corpus, we strove to strike a balance between the distribution of the different relation types and that of their subtypes, which turned out to be challenging at times. First, some subtypes have only very few relation tokens, such as ELABORATION-PROCESS-STEP (3 tokens) and INVERTED-SEQUENCE (12 tokens). Second, for

[2]Negative relations introduce a negation operator in their definition, e.g., OTHERWISE (see the Appendix, Table 6).

certain relation types the distribution of the subtypes in the RST-DT corpus was extremely uneven. For example, in the CONDITIONAL relation type, the subtype CONDITION ranges over 200 tokens, whereas the other subtypes such as CONTINGENCY and OTHERWISE have fewer than 30 tokens.

For an optimal representation of the relation variety, we collected all instances of the infrequent subtypes, further balancing out their low counts by including a higher number of tokens of the more frequent subtypes of the same type[3]. In the end, we collected 1,009 relations with 276 CAUSAL, 156 CONTRASTIVE, 172 CONDITIONAL, 179 ELABORATION, and 226 TEMPORAL relations. (For the distribution of the subtypes in our corpus, see Table 7 in the Appendix).

Each relation was independently annotated by the two authors for the seven continuity dimensions. Any differences were subsequently adjudicated before including the relation in the corpus.

4 Operationalising continuity dimensions

To annotate the relations in the RST-CC according to Givón's (1993) seven continuity dimensions, we operationalised them into distinctive features[4].

4.1 Time

We model temporal continuity using Evers-Vermeul et al.'s (2017) classification of temporality. For a sequence of discourse segments, they distinguish non-temporal, synchronous, and sequential constellations, and divide the latter into chronological and anti-chronological. (7) and (8) exhibit synchronous and anti-chronological constellations, respectively.

(7) [The Ministry of Education is nothing but a cartel for licensed teachers,] [and certainly does not act on behalf of students.]
[relation: CAUSE-RESULT; time: synchronous]

(8) [Monsanto Co., too, is expected to continue reporting higher profit,] [even though its sales of crop chemicals were hurt in the latest quarter by drought in northern Europe and the western U.S.]
[relation: CONCESSION; time: anti-chronological]

<table>
<tr><th colspan="3">Evers-Vermeul et al.</th><th>Our features</th></tr>
<tr><td colspan="3">Non-temporal
[-TIME]</td><td rowspan="3">continuity</td></tr>
<tr><td rowspan="3">Temporal
[+TIME]</td><td colspan="2">Synchronous
[+SIMULTANEOUS]</td></tr>
<tr><td rowspan="2">Sequential
[-SIMULTANEOUS]</td><td>Chronological
[+PRIOR]</td></tr>
<tr><td>Anti-chronological
[-PRIOR]</td><td>discontinuity</td></tr>
</table>

Table 3: Operationalisation of the temporal dimension

We assume that anti-chronological pairs of discourse segments introduce temporal discontinuity. All other constellations are classified as continuous; see Table 3. According to this classification, (7) emerges as continuous, and (8) as discontinuous.

4.2 Space

We consider a relation spatially continuous if the events or situations in the discourse segments are non-spatial, as in (9), or situated in the same place. In spatially discontinuous relations, location shifts in between segments, as in (10).

(9) [Passenger car prices jumped 3.8% in September,] [after climbing 0.5% in August and declining in the late spring and summer.]
[relation: TEMPORAL-AFTER; space: no change]

(10) [investment will be more likely to flow toward the other European economies] [and "the U.K. will be less prepared for the single market."]
[relation: CONSEQUENCE; space: change]

4.3 Reference

We express referential continuity in terms of Centering Theory or CT (Grosz et al., 1995). CT determines for each segment a central discourse referent ('backward-looking centre'), which can be continued or updated between segments, and occupy different positions on a salience hierarchy for all referents of a segment. This gives rise to four types of transition between segments: *continue*, *retain*, *smooth shift*, and *rough shift*. Poesio et al. (2004) add the types *establishment*, *zero*, and *null*, for the initialisation, termination, or lack of anaphoric reference across segments.

[3]We found some potentially misclassified relation tokens in the RST-DT, especially within the CONDITIONAL relation type. Our corpus does not contain such tokens, however.

[4]The features are summarised in Table 8 in the Appendix.

We classify a discourse relation as referentially continuous if the transition between its segments involves some kind of shared referent, like *the Soviets* in (11). Thus, *continue*, *retain*, *smooth shift*, *rough shift*, and *establish* transitions are considered as continuous. In contrast, *zero* and *null* transitions emerge as discontinuous, as in (12), where reference to the Aetna company is discontinued in the second segment.

(11) It's not enough! [If the Soviets want to be believed,] [they need to start telling the truth about more than the totally obvious.]
[relation: CONDITION; reference: *establish*]

(12) In a few instances, Aetna knew [it would probably be shelling out big bucks] [even before a client called or faxed in a claim]
[relation: TEMPORAL-BEFORE; reference: *zero*]

4.4 Action

We operationalise action continuity in terms of *script theory* (Schank and Abelson, 1975; Modi et al., 2016), which postulates that part of our knowledge is organised in 'scripts' or stereotypical descriptions of routine activities like having a meal in a restaurant or visiting a doctor. This operationalisation makes it possible to support inter-annotator agreement by falling back on existing script data collections like the one of Regneri et al. (2010) or InScript (Modi et al., 2016).

We examine whether the actions or events in the discourse segments can be considered part of a script, so that there is a logical *flow* from one action or event to another. If yes, the relation is considered continuous, as in (13); otherwise, we classify it as discontinuous, as in (14).

(13) [A substantial warming would melt some of the Earth's polar ice caps,] [raising the level of the oceans]
[relation: SEQUENCE; action: flow]

(14) [Mercedes officials said they expect flat sales next year] [even though they see the U.S. luxury-car market expanding slightly.]
[relation: CONCESSION; action: no flow]

4.5 Perspective

We distinguish three types of perspective (Pander Maat, 1998): *objective*, *author* (in the form of comments), and *other* (quotations). We consider a discourse relation continuous on the perspective dimension if its two segments share the same perspective, as in (15), otherwise, we classify the relation as discontinuous, as in (16).

(15) ["Climate varies drastically due to natural causes," said Mr. Thompson.] [But he said ice samples from Peru, Greenland and Antarctica all show substantial signs of warming.]
[relation: CONTRAST; perspective: no change]

(16) ["The earnings were fine and above expectations," said Michael W. Blumstein, an analyst at First Boston Corp.] [Nevertheless, Salomon's stock fell $1.125 yesterday to close at $23.25 a share in New York Stock Exchange composite trading.]
[relation: CONTRAST; perspective: change]

4.6 Modality

Modality is predominantly introduced by modal verbs, but also by modal adverbials and verbs like *probably* and *doubt*, respectively. Modal expressions describe what the world would be like according to a 'modal source', e.g., wishes, obligations (including laws), or expectations (for a formalisation, see Kratzer 2001).

Discontinuity in modality amounts to a shift of the reality or possible world dimension of the deictic centre. For instance, in (18) below, the modal dimension shifts from the real world (in which Temple-Inland is not expanding) to the world according to Mr. Palmero, in which the company is capable of future debt reduction. If both arguments of a discourse relation are non-modal or if they are modal with respect to the same modal source, we classify the relation as continuous, as in (17); otherwise, as discontinuous, like in (18).

(17) [Cineplex traded on the New York Stock Exchange at $11.25 a share, up $1.125,] [before trading was halted.]
[relation: TEMPORAL-BEFORE; modality: no change]

(18) Mr. Palmero recommends Temple-Inland, explaining [that it is "virtually the sole major paper company not undergoing a major capacity expansion"] [and thus should be able to lower long-term debt substantially next year.]
[relation: CAUSE-RESULT; modality: change]

4.7 Speech act

Discourse segments can be declarative clauses, questions, or imperatives. When sentence mood changes in between segments, Givón (1993) assumes discontinuity along the speech act dimension.[5] Thus, relations count as discontinuous if only one of the segments is declarative, as in (19).

(19) [The next time you hear a Member of Congress moan about the deficit,] [consider what Congress did Friday.]
[relation: CONTINGENCY; speech act: change]

The only exception are rhetorical questions, which we classified as statements (declaratives) in our analysis in spite of their syntactic guise, because they are interpreted as statements. For instance, the second discourse unit of (20) introduces the claim that no one will pay high prices for racehorse anymore:

(20) [If bluebloods won't pay high prices for racehorses anymore,] [who will?]
[relation: CONDITION; speech act: no change]

5 Additional features

Features that potentially influence the relationship between discourse relations and continuity are also annotated in the RST-CC. We include the CCR features *polarity* (see Section 3) and *order of segments*. The latter applies to implicational (CAUSAL and CONDITIONAL) relations only: The order is basic if the cause or antecedent segment precedes the result or consequent segment (Sanders et al., 1992); the reverse order indicates a non-basic relation.

[5]This overlaps with but is not identical to speech act relations (Sweetser, 1990), a subset of pragmatic relations, which link one argument to the speech act expressed in the other one.

The relations are annotated for two more features: *nuclearity* (which specifies the segment pair as nucleus-satellite, nucleus-nucleus, or satellite-nucleus, according to RST) and *context* (whether the relation occurs intra- or inter-sententially). The annotation scheme for the additional features is summarised in Table 9 in the Appendix.

For illustration, we provide an example of the RST-CC annotation (for seven continuity dimensions and also for four additional features) in Table 10 in the Appendix.

6 Reliability of annotation

To assess the quality of our annotation, we conducted an annotation experiment. For the seven continuity dimensions, we independently annotated a selection of 240 relations, which are not part of the RST-CC, but represent the five relation types of the corpus. Agreement was substantial according to Cohen's kappa (Landis and Koch, 1977) for the four dimensions *time*, *reference*, *perspective*, and *modality*, as shown in Table 4. For the remaining dimensions, prevalence prevented the calculation of meaningful κ-values. The agreement scores are 97.07% for *space*, 95.82% for *action*, and 98.74% for *speech act*.[6]

time	reference	perspective	modality
0.72	0.69	0.70	0.76

Table 4: Inter-annotator agreement on four dimensions

To annotate the *action* dimension, we had to consult external encyclopaedic sources, since there were no script data available for the events described in the corpus data. However, our results show that for specialised domains like the economic topics featured in many articles of the RST-CC, external sources can greatly contribute to safeguarding inter-rater agreement.

The scores reported for *time* and *reference* measure agreement on the binary distinction between continuous and discontinuous relations, as described in Section 4. However, we also calculated scores for more fine-grained classifications.

For *reference*, our annotation of the entire sevenfold classification of Centering Theory also yielded

[6]Prevalence refers to the ratio between the cardinalities of the classes that emerged in the classification. High prevalence leads to high chance agreement. And, since the idea of the kappa statistic is to abstract away from chance agreement, it returns very low kappa values for highly unbalanced samples, even if inter-rater agreement is very high.

substantial agreement ($\kappa = 0.62$). The confusion matrices reveal that agreement is especially high for the preservation, the termination, and the lack of reference continuity (*continue*, *zero*, and *null*, respectively). We interpret this result as confirming the usefulness of Centering Theory for practical annotation initiatives.

For *time*, we annotated a more fine-grained classification into non-temporal/synchronous, chronological, and anti-chronological constellations. Agreement on this classification was only moderate ($\kappa = 0.49$). Subsequent evaluation showed that the problematic distinction was the one between synchronous and chronological, in particular, for implicational relations. The choice of the values for temporal continuity varied over whether the consequent (or result) starts simultaneously with the antecedent (cause) or whether the latter follows the former. The issue is illustrated in (21), for which one annotator assumed that the junk market getting its biggest jolt (cause) is synchronous with it going into a tailspin (consequence), whereas the other one understood a chronological order in that the tailspin began after the jolt.

(21) [The fragile market received its biggest jolt last month from Campeau Corp...] [At that point, the junk market went into a tailspin...] [Relation: CONSEQUENCE; time: ?]

Subsequent discussion of these decisions revealed that the forced choice between the two possible temporal constellations introduced considerable arbitrariness, which was reflected in low agreement. Consequently, one should avoid forcing a choice in these cases by subsuming the two constellations in the underspecified statement that the consequence does not precede the antecedent. We conclude that such examples pose a severe challenge for approaches to temporal continuity that, unlike ours, regard chronological (as opposed to synchronous) order as non-continuous.

For *perspective*, the high agreement was supported by the fact that newspaper text indicates the sources of direct or indirect quotes very clearly. The disagreements mainly involved distinguishing reported facts from any kind of comment or conclusion drawn from them. For other text types, we envisage that the identification of perspectives must take into account additional linguistic evidence, e.g., in the case of free indirect discourse (Eckardt, 2014).

7 Recurrent annotation issues

This section presents recurring issues for our annotation which make choosing the correct label for a specific continuity dimension challenging.

7.1 *Perspective* annotation for implicit attribution

In newspaper texts, quotes and reported speech are not always indicated (or attributed to their sources) explicitly. This typically happens when a whole series of statements of one single speaker is reported: Some of the statements are presented as a direct quote (*X said, "..."*) or as reported speech (*X said that...*), while the others are not marked explicitly. This is illustrated by (22) [= (18)], where the first segment is a direct quote with attribution to the speaker, while the second one is unmarked, although they both belong to the same statement (made by Mr. Palmero). Accordingly, there is no change of perspective for the relation.

(22) Mr. Palmero recommends Temple-Inland, explaining [that it is "virtually the sole major paper company not undergoing a major capacity expansion,"] [and thus should be able to lower long-term debt substantially next year.] [relation: CAUSE-RESULT, perspective: no change]

However, in certain instances it is unclear whether a segment is attributed to a source or not, e.g., in (23), the last segment might be due to Guy Witman or to the author of the article. In this case, even the context of the whole article does not provide a definitive clue to answer this question:

(23) [[Still, today's highest-yielding money funds may beat CDs over the next year even if rates fall,] says Guy Witman, an editor of the Bond Market Advisor newsletter in Atlanta.] [That's because top-yielding funds currently offer yields almost $1\frac{1}{2}$ percentage points above the average CD yield.] [relation: EXPLANATION-ARGUMENTATIVE, perspective: ?]

7.2 Annotating *modality*

In annotating *modality*, we encountered the problem of indirect speech transforming future-tense auxiliaries into conditional forms, without introducing modality. For instance, *would* in (24) merely expresses the future tense as it is part of the indirect speech introduced by the matrix clause *he said*:

(24) He said [construction wouldn't resume] [until market conditions warrant it.]
(relation: CONDITION, modality: no change)

This disambiguation is especially difficult when the scope of the indirect speech is not clear or if the context does not suffice to distinguish between equally plausible readings, as in (25):

(25) [Sears expected] [that the pricing program wouldn't have any effect on revenue].
(relation: ATTRIBUTION, modality: ?)

Another issue is the scope of modality. The scope of a modal expression might extend over both segments, which entails continuity along the modal dimension, e.g., in (26):

(26) ... a quarterly dividend of 76 cents, [which would be received] [before the February option expires]
(relation: TEMPORAL-BEFORE, modality: no change)

(26) involves no change of modality, because *would* scopes over both segments. This is reflected in its interpretation as the possibility of receiving a dividend before the expiration of an option.

8 First results

We provide the distribution of continuous relations (proportions in percentages) for five relation types with respect to the seven continuity dimensions in Table 5, with the highest and lowest scores for a dimension in bold font.

We found that some continuity dimensions show uniformity across relation types. Relations of all types are found to be overwhelmingly continuous (> 98%) for the dimensions *space* and *speech act*, and almost never continuous (< 2%) for *action*[7]. We believe that this is due to our data: In particular, the non-narrative character of our data is responsible for the low degree of *action* continuity and for the high degree of *space* continuity. In addition, there are very few questions and imperatives in our newspaper data, which explains the overall continuity for *speech act*. Due to these limitations of our corpus, we believe that the uniformity we found for the *space*, *speech act*, and *action* dimensions does not suggest that these dimensions are less important for continuity in discourse relations; instead, they might become distinctive if material from other registers is investigated.

For the dimensions *time*, *reference*, *perspective*, and *modality*, however, there is considerable difference between the relation types, as summarised in Table 5. In addition, we found that the relation types are not homogeneously continuous or discontinuous, but can be simultaneously more continuous for some dimensions but less continuous or even predominantly discontinuous for other dimensions. In particular, CONTRASTIVE relations are the least continuous for *reference* and *perspective*, but highly continuous for *time*. CONDITIONAL relations are the most continuous for *perspective*, and the least continuous for *modality*. TEMPORAL relations are the least continuous for *time*, but the most continuous for *reference* and *modality*. What is more, continuity is not uniform even for a single dimension of one of these relations; e.g., only 82.61% (and not 100%) of the CAUSAL relations are continuous for time.

Continuity scores for *reference* are consistently lower for two reasons: There are many small discourse segments in the RST-DT, which reduces the chance of finding a shared referent across the segments. This is illustrated by (27), where the target relation, CONSEQUENCE-N, holds between segments A (the single word 'lost') and B.

(27) [Mr. Lagnado said] [that] [although retailers probably won't ever recover sales] [lost]^{A} [because of the California quake and Hurricane Hugo,]^{B} [they could see some benefits later on.]

Since neither of the two segments has a background-looking centre (Cb), referential continuity of the relation is calculated as *null*, which amounts to discontinuity. Moreover, we did not consider eventive and propositional referents in the analysis. However, as long as we compare only reference scores across the relation types (or subtypes), this will not affect our results.

[7]However, even these dimensions exhibit 100% continuity or discontinuity for a specific relation type only rarely: ELABORATION is 100% continuous for *space*, CONTRASTIVE, 0.00% for *action*, and 100% for *speech act*.

Relation	Time	Reference	Perspective	Modality	Space	Action	Speech act
CAUSAL	82.61	30.79	85.87	80.79	97.46	2.54	99.64
CONDITIONAL	81.98	35.47	**93.61**	**61.63**	98.84	**5.81**	**98.26**
CONTRASTIVE	91.67	**23.72**	**67.31**	77.56	98.08	**0.00**	**100**
ELABORATION	**93.85**	34.64	78.21	85.47	**100**	0.56	99.44
TEMPORAL	**74.34**	**38.50**	90.27	**92.92**	**97.35**	0.88	98.67
mean	84.04	32.90	83.94	80.57	98.23	1.98	99.21

Table 5: Continuity scores across relation types

The correlations between relation types and continuity along a specific dimension are significant at $p < .001$ ($p < .05$ for *reference*) for all dimensions except *space* and *speech act*.

9 Conclusions and outlook

We presented the RST Continuity Corpus (RST-CC), which comprises five major types of discourse relations annotated for a wide array of continuity dimensions and additional features. We envisage two applications of the corpus. First, the RST-CC will contribute to a more precise characterisation of discourse relations, providing a systematic, detailed, and reliable resource for examining the relationship between continuity (dimensions) and discourse relations. In addition, the corpus can also be used to test hypotheses about correlations between continuity dimensions and discourse relations. For example, CONTRASTIVE relations often present information about different (though comparable) items or information from different sources, and one can test whether this would lead to low scores for *reference* and *perspective* continuity.

Second, the corpus, in conjunction with parallel resources like the RST Signalling Corpus (Das et al., 2015), will contribute to the study of discourse signalling, e.g., to explore the *continuity hypothesis* (Murray, 1997), which entails that discontinuous discourse relations are harder to process, and hence, their processing should be facilitated by more explicit signalling.

Furthermore, it is an important research question whether continuity in discourse relations patterns uniformly or differently across genres or languages. For further work in this field, the development of the RST-CC could be a model for similar resources for different genres and different languages (other than news texts in English, as in the RST-CC).

Finally, we believe that our decompositional approach towards continuity would support further in-depth analyses of discourse relations. The varying effect of different continuity dimensions on discourse relations, for instance, would help resolving incongruities found in the study of discourse processing (why certain discourse relations are processed quicker and remembered better than others).

For a broader empirical basis for such investigations, we will extend the RST-CC, adding more instances of the relation types covered so far, but also including additional relation types like BACKGROUND, COMPARISON, EVALUATION, and EXPLANATION. The final version of the RST-CC will be published via the Linguistic Data Consortium.

References

Fatemeh Asr and Vera Demberg. 2012. Measuring the strength of linguistic cues for discourse relations. In *Proc. Workshop on Advances in Discourse Analysis and its Computational Aspects*, pages 33–42.

Lynn Carlson and Daniel Marcu. 2001. Discourse Tagging Manual. ISI Technical Report ISI-TR-545, USC.

Lynn Carlson, Daniel Marcu, and Mary Ellen Okurowski. 2002. RST Discourse Treebank, LDC2002T07.

Debopam Das, Maite Taboada, and Paul McFetridge. 2015. RST Signalling Corpus, LDC2015T10.

Regine Eckardt. 2014. *The semantics of free indirect discourse: How texts allow us to mind-read and eavesdrop*. Brill, Leiden.

Jacqueline Evers-Vermeul, Jet Hoek, and Merel Scholman. 2017. On Temporality in Discourse Annotation. *Dialogue & Discourse*, 8(2):1–20.

Anita Fetzer. 2018. The encoding and signalling of discourse relations in argumentative discourse. In M. de los Ángeles Gómez González and J. L. Mackenzie, editors, *The Construction of Discourse as Verbal Interaction*, page 13–44. John Benjamins.

Talmy Givón. 1993. *English Grammar: A function-based introduction*, volume 2. John Benjamins.

Barbara Grosz, Aravind Joshi, and Scott Weinstein. 1995. Centering: A Framework for Modelling the Local Coherence of Discourse. *Computational Linguistics*, 21(2):203–225.

Paul Hopper. 1979. Aspect and foregrounding in discourse. In Talmy Givón, editor, *Syntax and semantics, Vol. 12. Discourse and syntax*, page 213–241. Academic Press, New York.

Angelika Kratzer. 2001. Modality. In Arnim v. Stechow and Dieter Wunderlich, editors, *Semantics*, page 639–650. Mouton, Berlin.

Richard Landis and Gary Koch. 1977. The measurement of observer agreement for categorical data. *Biometrics*, 33:159–174.

William Mann and Sandra Thompson. 1988. Rhetorical Structure Theory: Towards a Functional Theory of Text Organization. *Text*, 8:243–281.

Ashutosh Modi, Tatjana Anikina, Simon Ostermann, and Manfred Pinkal. 2016. InScript: Narrative texts annotated with script information. In *Proceedings of LREC 2016*.

John Murray. 1997. Connectives and narrative text: The role of continuity. *Memory and Cognition*, 25(2):227–236.

Henk Pander Maat. 1998. Classifying negative coherence relations on the basis of linguistic evidence. *Journal of Pragmatics*, 30:177–204.

Massimo Poesio, Rosemary Stevenson, Barbara Di Eugenio, and Janet Hitzeman. 2004. Centering: A Parametric Theory and Its Instantiations. *Computational Linguistics*, 30(3):309–363.

Rashmi Prasad, Nikhil Dinesh, Alan Lee, Eleni Miltsakaki, Livio Robaldo, Aravind Joshi, and Bonnie Webber. 2008. The Penn Discourse Treebank 2.0. In *Proceedings of the 6th International Conference on Language Resources and Evaluation (LREC)*, pages 2961–2968, Marrakech, Morocco.

Michaela Regneri, Alexander Koller, and Manfred Pinkal. 2010. Learning script knowledge with web experiments. In *Proceedings of the 48th Annual Meeting of the ACL*, page 979–988.

Ted Sanders, Wilbert Spooren, and Leo Noordman. 1992. Toward a taxonomy of coherence relations. *Discourse Processes*, 15:1–35.

Ted J.M. Sanders, Vera Demberg, Jet Hoek, C.J. Scholman, Merel, Fatemeh Torabi Asr, Sandrine Zufferey, and Jacqueline Evers-Vermeul. 2021. Unifying dimensions in coherence relations: How various annotation frameworks are related. *Corpus Linguistics and Linguistic Theory*, 17(1):1–71.

Roger Schank and Robert Abelson. 1975. Scripts, Plans, and Knowledge. In *Proceedings of the 4th IJCAI*, page 151–157. Morgan Kaufmann Publishers Inc.

Erwin Segal, Judith Duchan, and Paula Scott. 1991. The role of interclausal connectives in narrative structuring: Evidence from adults' interpretations of simple stories. *Discourse Processes*, 14(1):27–54.

Eve Sweetser. 1990. *From Etymology to Pragmatics: The Mind-Body Metaphor in Semantic Structure and Semantic Change.* Cambridge University Press, Cambridge.

Sandrine Zufferey and Pascal Gygax. 2016. The Role of Perspective Shifts for Processing and Translating Discourse Relations. *Discourse Processes*, 53(7):532–555.

Rolf Zwaan. 1996. Processing Narrative Time Shifts. *Journal of Experimental Psychology: Learning, Memory and Cognition*, 22(5):1196–1207.

Rolf Zwaan, Mark Langston, and Arthur Graesser. 1995. The construction of situation models in narrative comprehension: An event-indexing model. *Psychological Science*, 6(5):292–297.

Rolf Zwaan and Murray Singer. 2003. Text Comprehension. In A. Graesser, M. Gernsbacher, and S. Goldman, editors, *Handbook of Discourse Processes*, pages 83–121. Erlbaum.

A Appendix

Dimension	Value	(Dis)continuous?
time	non-temporal	continuous
	synchronous	
	chronological	
	anti-chronological	discontinuous
space	no change	continuous
	change	discontinuous
reference	continue	continuous
	retain	
	smooth shift	
	rough shift	
	establish	
	zero	discontinuous
	null	
action	flow	continuous
	no flow	discontinuous
perspective	no change	continuous
	change	discontinuous
modality	no change	continuous
	change	discontinuous
speech act	no change	continuous
	change	discontinuous

Table 8: Continuity dimensions and their values

add. feature	value
polarity	positive
	negative
order of segments	basic
	non-basic
nuclearity	S-N
	N-S
	N-N
context	intra-sentential
	inter-sentential

Table 9: Additional features and their values

Relation type	Relation subtype	Definition: key feature(s)
CAUSAL	CAUSE	Nucleus (N) is the cause; Satellite (S) is the result.
	RESULT	N is the result; S is the cause.
	CAUSE-RESULT (multinuclear)	Cause and result are equally important.
	CONSEQUENCE-S	Weaker version of CAUSE; N is the cause; S is the consequence.
	CONSEQUENCE-N	Weaker version of RESULT; N is the consequence; S is the cause.
	CONSEQUENCE (multinuclear)	Weaker version of CAUSE-RESULT; cause and consequence are equally important.
CONTRASTIVE	ANTITHESIS	N and S stand in contrast with each other.
	CONTRAST (multinuclear)	Two equally important units stand in contrast with each other.
	CONCESSION	The contrast arises due to a violated expectation between N and S.
CONDITIONAL	CONDITION	The consequent holds if the antecedent holds.
	CONTINGENCY	In any context, the consequent holds if the antecedent holds.
	HYPOTHETICAL	Like CONDITION, in addition, the antecedent is assumed to be true.
	OTHERWISE (mostly multinuclear)	The consequent does not hold if the antecedent does.
ELABORATION	ELABORATION-ADDITIONAL	S provides additional information about N.
	ELABORATION-GENERAL-SPECIFIC	S provides specific information about N.
	ELABORATION-OBJECT-ATTRIBUTE	S is an embedded clause/NP modifying an object/entity representing N.
	ELABORATION-PART-WHOLE	S specifies or elaborates on a part of N.
	ELABORATION-PROCESS-STEP	S enumerates the steps for carrying out a process introduced by N.
	ELABORATION-SET-MEMBER	N introduces a set/list of information; S elaborates on one (or more) member of the set/list
	EXAMPLE	S provides an example for the information in N.
	DEFINITION	S provides a definition of N.
TEMPORAL	TEMPORAL-BEFORE	The situation in N occurs before or leading up to the situation in S.
	TEMPORAL-AFTER	The situation in N occurs after the situation in S.
	TEMPORAL-SAME-TIME	The situations in N and S occur at approximately the same time.
	SEQUENCE	A multinuclear list of events presented in chronological order.
	INVERTED-SEQUENCE	A multinuclear list of events presented in reverse chronological order.

Table 6: Relation types, relation subtypes, and their key features

Relation type	Relation subtype	#	#
CAUSAL	CAUSE	43	276
	RESULT	52	
	CAUSE-RESULT (multinuclear)	52	
	CONSEQUENCE-S	52	
	CONSEQUENCE-N	52	
	CONSEQUENCE (multinuclear)	25	
CONTRASTIVE	ANTITHESIS	52	156
	CONCESSION	52	
	CONTRAST (multinuclear)	52	
CONDITIONAL	CONDITION	108	172
	CONTINGENCY	27	
	HYPOTHETICAL	22	
	OTHERWISE (predominantly multinuclear)	15	
ELABORATION	ELABORATION-ADDITIONAL	44	179
	ELABORATION-GENERAL-SPECIFIC	22	
	ELABORATION-OBJECT-ATTRIBUTE	22	
	ELABORATION-PART-WHOLE	22	
	ELABORATION-PROCESS-STEP	3	
	ELABORATION-SET-MEMBER	22	
	EXAMPLE	22	
	DEFINITION	22	
TEMPORAL	TEMPORAL-BEFORE	35	226
	TEMPORAL-AFTER	57	
	TEMPORAL-SAME-TIME	56	
	SEQUENCE	66	
	INVERTED-SEQUENCE	12	
total			1009

Table 7: Distribution of relations types and subtypes

Relation to be annotated: To be sure, [big investors might put away their checkbooks in a hurry] [if stocks open sharply lower today] [relation: CONDITION]			
Dimension	**Value**	**Explanation**	**Continuity**
time	change	The consequent or protasis (first segment) precedes the antecedent or apodosis (second segment).	discontinuous
space	no change	The segments have no spatial markers; hence, the relation is non-spatial.	continuous
reference	null	None of the segments has a backward-looking centre (Cb).	discontinuous
action	no flow	The transition of the segments does not represent part of a script (a stereotypical situation or routine activity).	discontinuous
perspective	no change	Both segments bear the perspective of the writer.	continuous
modality	change	The first segment uses the modal verb 'might' while the second one uses none.	discontinuous
speech act	no change	Both segments are declarative sentences.	continuous
add. feature	**value**		
polarity	positive		
order of segments	non-basic (consequent-antecedent)		
nuclearity	N-S		
context	intra-sentential		

Table 10: Example of RST-CC annotation

GENTLE: A Genre-Diverse Multilayer Challenge Set for English NLP and Linguistic Evaluation

Tatsuya Aoyama, Shabnam Behzad, Luke Gessler, Lauren Levine, Jessica Lin, Yang Janet Liu, Siyao Peng, Yilun Zhu, Amir Zeldes
Corpling Lab
Georgetown University
{ta571, sb1796, lg876, lel76, yl1290, yl879, sp1184, yz565, az364}@georgetown.edu

Abstract

We present GENTLE, a new mixed-genre English challenge corpus totaling 17K tokens and consisting of 8 unusual text types for out-of-domain evaluation: dictionary entries, esports commentaries, legal documents, medical notes, poetry, mathematical proofs, syllabuses, and threat letters. GENTLE is manually annotated for a variety of popular NLP tasks, including syntactic dependency parsing, entity recognition, coreference resolution, and discourse parsing. We evaluate state-of-the-art NLP systems on GENTLE and find severe degradation for at least some genres in their performance on all tasks, which indicates GENTLE's utility as an evaluation dataset for NLP systems.

1 Introduction

In the past several years, there have been great advances in NLP system performance on various tasks. However, many of these tasks are still evaluated on in-domain data, i.e. held-out data taken from the same domain as the system's training data. While this methodology is sound, it often overstates systems' ability to perform in real-world settings, where out-of-domain (OOD) data can lead to significant degradation (Plank, 2016; Joshi et al., 2018), even when target data comes from a similar domain (Nayak et al., 2020). For this reason, it is essential to have evaluation datasets with diverse text types, which can give a more accurate picture of systems' capabilities on OOD data, especially for domains that are distant from commonly studied domains or underrepresented in existing training datasets.

In this paper, we present GENTLE (**GEN**re **T**ests for **L**inguistic **E**valuation), a small but "extreme" open-access dataset that can be used for OOD evaluation of popular NLP tasks in English, as well as for linguistic analysis of less studied genres. The NLP tasks considered here include morphosyntactic tagging and dependency parsing according to Universal Dependencies (UD, de Marneffe et al. 2021), nested named and non-named entity recognition (NNER), coreference resolution, entity linking (Wikification), and hierarchical discourse parsing in the framework of Rhetorical Structure Theory (RST, Mann and Thompson 1988).[1] Our data comes from eight genres explicitly selected to represent unusual and diverse data types not currently included in the English Universal Dependencies corpora: dictionary entries, transcripts of live esports commentary, legal documents, medical notes, poetry, mathematical proofs, course syllabuses, and threat letters.

GENTLE enables us to answer various questions, including how well state-of-the-art (SOTA) models can parse OOD data and whether or not OOD genres are equally difficult for all NLP tasks. Apart from NLP performance, we can also see whether the annotation tasks in our challenge genres are difficult for humans and how the difficulties that arise in individual genres in GENTLE differ from those in existing datasets.

The rest of this paper is structured as follows: Section 2 presents some related work on OOD testing. Section 3 presents an overview of the corpus, while Section 4 compares the genres in the corpus in detail. Section 5 evaluates human agreement and NLP system performance on our data for each task, compared to more standard UD English data. Section 6 offers our conclusions. Our corpus is available at `https://github.com/gucorpling/gentle`.

2 Related Work

Previous work has focused on the importance of genre diversity and OOD evaluation for many of the NLP tasks included in GENTLE, supporting the general conclusion that NLP system performance tends to degrade on OOD data.

In coreference resolution, Moosavi and Strube

[1]The corpus is also openly released as part of the Universal Dependencies 2.12 version available at `https://github.com/UniversalDependencies/UD_English-GUM`.

Proceedings of the 17th Linguistic Annotation Workshop (LAW-XVII), pages 166–178
July 13, 2023 ©2023 Association for Computational Linguistics

(2017) and Zhu et al. (2021) point out that existing models mainly rely on lexical features (e.g. word embeddings) and may face the problem of overfitting because of the large overlap of vocabulary between training and testing data. Apart from overfitting, low recall resulting from domain discrepancy is another major problem for named entity recognition (NER, Augenstein et al. 2017).

Despite a recent surge in approaches for discourse-level tasks, there is still room for improvement in this area, especially for OOD data (Atwell et al., 2021). Liu and Zeldes (2023) investigate the impact of genre diversity in training data composition for RST discourse parsing, the task of recursively identifying relations between propositions. They show that diverse data is essential for stable and generalizable models for this task.

Similarly to the present work, Kanerva and Ginter (2022) conduct an OOD evaluation of Finnish dependency parsing, including constructing a relatively "extreme" OOD treebank, including 5 distinct genres (web documents, clinical, online discussions, tweets, and poetry).[2] Their experiments indicate that syntactic parsing performance degrades severely on OOD data, particularly on the LAS (labeled attachment score) metric.

Data diversity is thus crucial for a range of NLP tasks, but the lack of diverse data available hampers training and evaluation. Previous corpus construction efforts cover a wide range of English genres, for example, 5 genres in the English Web Treebank (EWT, Silveira et al. 2014) for syntactic annotations, and 6 in OntoNotes (Weischedel et al., 2012) for NER and coreference as well. However, both datasets lack nested, non-named entities, entity linking (Wikification), and discourse parsing.

More recently, the UD English GUM corpus (Georgetown University Multilayer corpus, Zeldes 2017), with data from 12 genres (academic articles, biographies, conversation transcripts, works of fiction, Reddit posts, how-to-guides, interviews, news articles, political speeches, textbook excerpts, Wikivoyage travel guides, and YouTube vlog transcripts), covers all of the annotations examined in this paper, and raises the expectation of being a possibly good training set for OOD targets, due to its diverse content. Experiments in this paper will therefore use our newly annotated OOD GENTLE corpus to evaluate SOTA models trained on the already diverse GUM corpus and compare their performance on both datasets.

3 GENTLE

The GENTLE corpus is constructed as an OOD evaluation dataset, modeled on the test set for the English GUM corpus. Table 1 gives an overview of partitions in GUM (v9.0) compared to GENTLE.

dataset	genres	docs	tokens
$\text{GUM}_{\text{train}}$	12	165	160,700
GUM_{dev}	12	24	21,409
GUM_{test}	12	24	21,770
GENTLE	8	26	17,797

Table 1: GUM Partitions vs. GENTLE.

GENTLE forms an extension to the GUM test set with 8 more genres, for a total of 20 diverse text types to test on. Although the amount of data in GENTLE is small, the data follows GUM's scheme and is richly annotated on many layers, containing over 250K key-value annotations connected by complex annotation graphs. For treebanking, the annotations include gold-standard layers for Universal Dependencies morphosyntax, such as XPOS (Penn Treebank) tags, lemmas, and basic dependencies. In addition, automatically-derived morphological features, enhanced dependencies and UPOS tags are obtained using the DepEdit library (Peng and Zeldes, 2018) with the same scripts that produce these layers for the GUM corpus.

For NNER and coreference resolution, the data includes nested, named and non-named entity annotations. These employ the same scheme used in GUM, with 10 entity types, 6-way information status annotations, coreference and bridging links (9 edge types from GUM, including split antecedents, discourse deixis, etc., see `https://gucorpling.org/gum/`). GUM-style entity linking (wikification, Lin and Zeldes 2021) is also provided, with an automatically produced alternate version of the entity/coreference annotations matching the OntoNotes scheme (Weischedel et al. 2012; see Zhu et al. 2021 for details). The data also includes complete hierarchical discourse trees in Rhetorical Structure Theory (RST, Mann and Thompson 1988), following the same scheme as GUM.

Annotation was conducted by the authors of this paper during several hackathon-style annotation sessions. Although varying in expertise on each task, every annotator had previous experience annotating every layer of annotation described

[2] `https://github.com/UniversalDependencies/UD_Finnish-OOD/`

above. For annotation tools, morphosyntactic layers (XPOS tags, lemmas, and basic dependencies), entity layers (entity and coreference), and discourse layers (EDU segmentation and discourse relation) were annotated on Arborator (Gerdes, 2013) and Midas Loop (Gessler et al., 2022), GitDox (Zhang and Zeldes, 2017), and rstWeb (Zeldes, 2016), respectively. We also double annotated a portion of the corpus to measure human agreement, which will be further described in §5.

In choosing data, we attempted to select challenging types of spoken and written open-access materials that are maximally different from those already found in GUM (cf. §2). Texts were selected for each genre from a single source, making sure that (1) the total number of tokens falls between 2k and 2.5k tokens per genre; (2) at least 2 texts are selected to better represent the genre (as mean can only be calculated with 2 or more documents per genre). While the texts were selected randomly for most genres, the texts for some genres were manually selected. For instance, since poetry texts can be extremely short, the documents for this genre were chosen to be varied in length, as to limit the number of documents needed to reach the target token range. Table 2 gives the genre composition and sources for each data type in GENTLE.[3]

genre	docs	tokens	source
`dictionary`	3	2,423	Wiktionary
`esports`	2	2,149	YouTube
`legal`	2	2,288	Wikisource / CUAD[4]
`medical`	4	2,164	MTSamples
`poetry`	5	2,090	Wikisource
`proof`	3	2,106	Proofwiki
`syllabus`	2	2,431	GitHub
`threat`	5	2,146	casetext
total	26	17,797	

Table 2: Corpus Contents of GENTLE.

The chosen data is broad not only in domain, including medical, legal, and other technical areas, but also in medium (online linked resources such as Wiktionary data, spontaneous spoken esports commentary, and threat letters) and communicative intent (e.g. poetry, syllabuses, and mathematical proofs). These genres can also be challenging for both humans and NLP models, as they diverge in various ways from standard training data and materials that guidelines are based on for each task.

genre	slen	pass	n/v	ttr	oov	sglt
GUM	20.16	.07	2.36	.4	–	.29
GUM_{news}	22.52	.12	3.34	.45	–	.28
dictionary	10.98	.1	3.65	.39	.11	**.49**
esports	21.07	.01	1.48	.36	.08	.24
legal	21.58	.04	3.33	.36	.17	.33
medical	11.21	.15	4.31	.46	.22	.32
poetry	17.7	.01	1.59	**.53**	.11	.25
proof	15.63	**.18**	5.14	.25	**.24**	.13
syllabus	7.65	.12	**5.34**	.43	**.24**	.38
threat	**24.25**	.02	1.3	.49	.05	.28

Table 3: Average sentence length (`slen`), passive ratio (`pass`), noun/verb ratio (`n/v`), type-token ratio (`ttr`), out-of-vocabulary ratio (`oov`), and singleton ratio (`sglt`).

Before approaching a technical evaluation of how well humans can annotate these materials (inter-annotator agreement) and how NLP models score on them for each task, in the next section, we explore how the materials differ from genres in GUM descriptively, in text content and annotations.

4 Variation across Genres

4.1 Summary Statistics

Because the materials in GUM and GENTLE cover a vast range of text types, a quantitative view of variation in the data can provide a useful starting point in understanding what makes each genre unique. Although we could also devote as much attention to GUM genres, for space reasons, we will focus here on how each GENTLE genre is distinct from GUM and other genres (for more on GUM genres, see Zeldes and Simonson 2016).

Table 3 gives an overview of some commonly used descriptive metrics to compare GENTLE genres to the GUM corpus average, as well as the score for GUM's `news` genre, which can be taken as a stand-in for the standard language typically found in reference corpora, e.g. the Wall Street Journal (Marcus et al., 1993). The lowest and highest numbers in each metric are colored in red and blue.

Most genres in GENTLE have substantially shorter sentences (**slen**) than the GUM average, with `syllabus` having the lowest mean of 7.65 tokens, largely due to frequent bulleted or numbered lists of course topics, which are noun phrase fragments (e.g. *Week 3 - JavaScript Fundamentals*). The only genre with substantially above average sentence length is `threat`, in which long and sometimes rambling justifications or elaborate

[3]Please refer to Appendix A for detailed information on the contents of each genre.

[4]The **C**ontract **U**nderstanding **A**tticus **D**ataset (CUAD) v1 from the The Atticus Project (Hendrycks et al., 2021): `https://www.atticusprojectai.org/`

	UPOS		dependency relations		entity types		discourse relations	
GUM	PROPN	↓-25.13	dep	↓-20.93	org.	↓-19.50	joint	↓-8.89
GUM_{news}	PROPN	↑41.41	flat	↑21.74	org.	↑30.60	attrib.	↑12.14
dictionary	X	↑21.16	punct	↑20.37	abstract	↑17.05	org.	↑5.72
esports	ADV	↑5.91	parataxis	↑16.68	event	↑9.94	eval.	↑6.82
legal	X	↑18.37	dep	↑17.20	org.	↑12.62	context	↓-3.69
medical	NOUN	↑11.59	nummod	↑7.88	substance	↑11.02	joint	↑12.86
poetry	PROPN	↓-7.07	compound	↓-5.68	animal	↑17.84	mode	↑5.50
proof	SYM	↑56.27	dep	↑10.92	abstract	↑39.23	explan.	↑8.46
syllabus	X	↑54.48	dep	↑46.31	abstract	↑25.69	joint	↑18.23
threat	PRON	↑13.17	punct	↓-6.98	person	↑12.91	explan.	↑6.43

Table 4: Strongest Standardized χ^2 Residual Label in 4 Layers for each Genre.

consequences are often added to main sentences.

Passivization (**pass**) is rare overall, except for medical texts (double the GUM average) and math proofs (even more), in which volitional agents are often suppressed (in the former, someone was *diagnosed* but we do not know by whom; in the latter, a variable *can be assigned*, etc.).

Noun/verb ratio (**n/v**) and type-token ratio (**ttr**) reveal that `syllabus` has a rich and mainly nominal vocabulary (lists of skills or topics, primarily nouns/compounds). Though rich in **ttr**, `threat` is more verbal. `poetry` has the highest **ttr**, partly because some poetic constraints discourage repetition (e.g. alliteration and rhyming, where duplication is avoided). In contrast, `proof` has the lowest **ttr** since some terms are used repeatedly (e.g., *vertex* is repeated ten times in one proof about vertices).

The out-of-vocabulary (**oov**) rate shows the percentage of tokens in each genre that is not attested in GUM, which can be expected to correlate with NLP tool degradation. `proof`, `syllabus` and `medical` have extremely high rates (nearly 25% of tokens are never seen in GUM), while `threat` and `esports` have less alarming rates of 5–8%.

Finally, the proportion of singleton mentions (**sglt**, entities referred to just once in a text) shows that `proof` documents have repetitive vocabularies and repeatedly refer to the same entity. This is because once a member or a class of possible items has been introduced, its properties are discussed in detail (e.g., after defining *Let DE be a rational straight line*, we may continue discussing the line DE). By contrast, `dictionary` documents use many arbitrary entities in example sentences that are never mentioned again (in an example sentence for *school*, we find *Harvard University is a famous American post-secondary school*, but *Harvard* is then never mentioned again). These genre disparities and unique environments can be expected to interfere with prior probabilities learned by NLP models, and, as we will see below, also with human annotation agreement.

4.2 Label Distributions

To give a quick overview of which labels deviate from their expected frequency in each genre, Table 4 gives standardized chi-square residuals in a contingency table of labels versus genres. A positive residual means that a label is used more frequently than expected based on its overall frequency, and a negative residual means the opposite – that a label is used less frequently than expected. Here we give only the strongest deviation associated with each genre in each of four annotation layers (for the complete tables of residuals, see Appendix B).

The deviation with the absolute highest score in the parts-of-speech (UPOS) is the unsurprising frequency of the tag `SYM` in math proofs, used for many mathematical symbols. The second highest is the tag `X` in `syllabus`, used to tag bullet point markers and also used frequently in `legal` documents. Other tag deviations include the lack of proper nouns in `poetry`, dense use of punctuation in dictionary entries, and the prevalence of common nouns in the medical data (a lack of pronouns mirrors this, see Table 7 in Appendix B).

Dependencies show some parallel phenomena (`punct` in `dictionary`, `dep` in `legal` and `syllabus`, which is used to attach bullet points), but also reveal lack of punctuation in threat letters. The prevalence of `parataxis` in `esports` to narrate chains of events as they unfold is also noteworthy, as in (1), and the use of numerical quantities in medical texts, often used for medication dosages as in (2). The `poetry` genre shows a negative deviation in avoiding nominal compounds, which are more typically a property of technical texts in English, e.g. in nested noun-noun compounds found in `medical` notes, as in (3).

(1) *Jović scoring, van de Beek and Ibrahimovic coming on 3-1 ...*

(2) *Prilosec 20 mg b.i.d.*

(3) *white blood cell count*

Residuals of entity types also expose differences compared to GUM genres and `news` in particular, which distinguishes itself by frequently mentioning `organization` entities. `proof` is the most extreme in favoring the `abstract` type (in fact, over 96% of mentions in `proof` are `abstract`), while `threat` focuses on people. `medical` is unique with its preponderance of `substance` entities, primarily medications, while `esports` disproportionately uses the `event` type. One result in the table is an artifact of one specific document, and the small corpus size: `animal` in `poetry` is due entirely to the inclusion of Edgar Alan Poe's "The Raven".

Finally, discourse relations reveal the prevalence of coordinated lists annotated in the relation class JOINT in `syllabus` (topics, assignments, weeks in the course, etc.) and `medical` (symptoms, vital statistics, medications; all mainly the relation subtype JOINT-LIST); `esports` unsurprisingly favors EVALUATION to convey positive or negative impressions of players, and `poetry` is unique in favoring MODE relations, primarily due to the relation subtype MODE-MANNER, which is used in adverbial manner adjuncts or parataxis, as in (4)–(5). `legal` shows a negative tendency to avoid CONTEXT relations, which include background and spatio-temporal contextual information, both of which are less needed in a highly specialized and professional text in which context is often a given and statements apply in general.

(4) *I sat divining, [with my head at ease]*$_{\text{MANNER}}$

(5) *[We slowly drove]*$_{\text{MANNER}}$ *He knew no haste*

4.3 Proximity across Genres

The metrics in §4.2 reveal differences among GENTLE genres compared to GUM. But needless to say, there are also many similarities between the GENTLE and GUM genres. To describe proximity across genres, we utilize the features in Table 3 and the full residual tables for the four annotation layers in Appendix B to build a cluster dendrogram of GENTLE and GUM genres.

Because labels occupy different numerical ranges and have diverse tag set sizes (only 10 entity types but 34 coarse dependency labels), we scale the data by transforming it into z-scores, and then reduce the dimensionality of each table of residuals to five columns using Principal Component Analysis (PCA). In other words, while the original table of entity residuals has one row per genre and ten columns for the entity types (Table 9 in the Appendix) and contains chi-square residuals, the transformed table is based on a z-scaled version of the same table, which is reduced to having only 5 total columns using PCA. This affords each annotation layer as much space as the five features in Table 3 (excluding OOV rate, which is inapplicable to GUM data), for a total of 25 features per genre (the five scaled metrics without OOV, and five features each for POS, dependencies, entities, and discourse relations).

Because we are interested in concord/discord between genres across layers and do not necessarily care if z-scores are more or less extreme for a particular annotation layer, we use ordinal Kendall correlations between values of each dimension to compute the distance metric between genres, thereby avoiding single features with large values dominating the clustering. In the ordinal clustering, genres are closer if their ranks for multiple features are ordered more similarly—e.g., if they are ranked first and second in type-token ratio and singletons, then those two genres display positive concord along those features. We apply single linkage clustering to produce the dendrogram in Figure 1.[5]

As the figure shows, several of the GENTLE genres (in red) form outliers and cluster apart from genres in GUM (in blue). This suggests, on the one hand, they are substantially distinct and, therefore, valuable additions to already available genres in GUM. On the other hand, they may be challenging to handle for models trained on GUM. This is especially true for genres like `proof` on the left side of the plot, which forms the most distinct outlier, in a top-level cluster of its own, and quite distant vertically from other genres. We can also see `legal` quite distant from its nearest neighbors,

[5]An anonymous reviewer has inquired whether we attempted other clustering procedures: the answer is yes—the decision to use ordinal clustering resulted from the observation that single annotation layers had outsize influence for some genres, such as SYM tags in `proof`; single linkage is both a default choice, and works well to cluster pairs of near genres as dendrogram leaves.

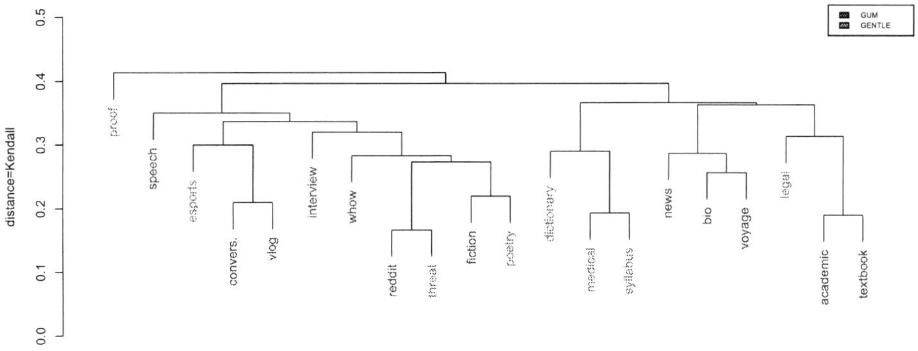

Figure 1: Cluster Dendrogram for GUM and GENTLE Genres.

GUM's `academic` and `textbook`, which are near each other. Three GENTLE genres, `dictionary`, `medical`, and `syllabus` form a sub-cluster, with the latter two being relatively similar, possibly due to both genres being dominated by bulleted lists comprised of noun phrases, i.e., sentences fragments.

In the middle, `poetry` is the closest to GUM's `fiction`, perhaps partly due to long sentences, extensive vocabulary, and verb-dominated morphosyntax. `threat` clusters with GUM's `reddit` genre, perhaps because both are relatively argumentative genres, often written in first-person, and include many interjections and swearwords (see Behzad and Zeldes 2020 for similar and additional observations on Reddit data). `esports` is somewhat far from its nearest neighbors, the informal spoken genres `conversation` and `vlog` which intuitively share features and cluster together; the latter also comes from the same source and modality as `esports`, since both were collected from YouTube. GUM's more informative expository genres also cluster together plausibly, with biographies (`bio`) and travel guides (`voyage`) grouped together after the split with `news`.

5 Evaluation

To understand how challenging GENTLE data is for both NLP models and humans, we evaluate representative systems on each task using the entire corpus and conduct an inter-annotator agreement (IAA) experiment by double annotating 10% of the data. Table 5 reports Cohen's Kappa (κ) and task-specific scores where applicable, taking the gold standard release data as a reference, compared to a second human's annotation. The double annotations were done without additional validation checks; in other words, the final gold data, subjected to stringent validations by the official UD validator and validation scripts from the English GUM repository, can be expected to be more consistent and reliable. Double annotated data comes from document initial "snippets" in each genre since non-initial sections may be incoherent for layers such as coreference. Each snippet was around 200-250 tokens in length, amounting to 1,838 tokens in total ($\approx$10.34% of the entire corpus).

However, it is also true that NLP accuracy in document-initial positions diverges from overall accuracy since documents are systematically non-homogeneous. For example, `dictionary` entry beginnings are much harder to parse since they contain technical notation, foreign language etymologies, and more, while later sections typically include grammatically simple usage example sentences. Therefore, we report NLP accuracy on the double annotated snippets compared to human scores in Table 5, separately from the overall performances on the GENTLE corpus in Table 6. For each setting, we report scores by genre, for the entire corpus (micro-average), and the averaged per-genre score (macro-average). All NLP models were trained on the GUM v9 train partition and tested on the established GUM v9 test set and GENTLE. Additionally, we include genre-specific numbers for GUM's `news` section, which can be taken to represent the most commonly used evaluation data type in most NLP tasks.

Tokenization, Tagging, Lemmatization, and Dependency Parsing We use the widely employed Stanza package (Qi et al., 2020) to evaluate gold-

Tasks	Metrics	MICRO	MACRO	dictionary	esports	legal	medical	poetry	proof	syllabus	threat
					Human Agreement on Snippets						
POS Tagging (XPOS)	Acc	95.38	95.37	94.69	**98.25**	93.48	94.81	97.85	95.67	93.86	94.37
	κ	94.98	94.78	95.38	**98.00**	93.46	94.49	97.29	94.38	92.08	92.94
Lemmatization	Acc	96.90	96.89	92.92	**99.56**	95.22	96.54	97.42	98.70	95.61	99.13
	κ	96.86	96.82	92.65	**99.55**	95.12	96.47	97.36	98.66	95.56	99.11
Dependency Parsing	UAS	88.79	88.77	77.88	85.53	90.00	88.74	90.13	88.74	93.86	**95.24**
	LAS	84.66	84.63	73.01	81.58	83.48	87.01	88.41	83.55	89.47	**90.48**
Entity Recognition (untyped)	P	89.47	89.25	93.24	92.54	91.94	79.71	78.08	**96.19**	86.36	95.71
	R	85.27	84.84	81.18	92.54	79.17	77.46	82.61	**97.12**	84.44	83.75
	F	87.32	86.88	86.79	92.54	85.07	78.57	80.28	**96.65**	85.39	89.33
Entity Recognition (typed)	P	81.91	81.35	90.54	70.15	90.32	73.91	76.71	**96.19**	73.86	78.57
	R	78.06	77.32	78.82	70.15	77.78	71.83	81.16	**97.12**	72.22	68.75
	F	79.94	79.19	84.28	70.15	83.58	72.86	78.87	**96.65**	73.03	73.33
Coreference Resolution	MUC	70.46	66.01	47.05	**94.44**	72.22	60.86	62.06	70.58	38.09	82.75
	B^3	77.63	77.21	83.50	**90.29**	75.31	65.65	62.97	84.74	76.38	78.87
	$CEAF_{\phi 4}$	72.25	70.55	84.43	**86.38**	69.30	63.55	48.10	74.50	73.46	64.70
	Avg. F	73.45	71.26	71.66	**90.37**	72.28	63.35	57.71	76.61	62.64	75.44
					NLP Performance on Snippets						
XPOS	Acc	92.56	92.55	86.73	97.66	95.36	97.55	**97.71**	77.63	93.27	94.52
Lemmatization	Acc	96.32	96.33	97.64	**99.56**	97.10	96.25	92.56	94.81	94.44	98.27
Dependency Parsing	UAS	80.69	80.65	65.34	85.23	87.83	87.01	**90.41**	54.69	85.09	89.61
	LAS	76.22	76.18	59.00	79.39	82.75	83.41	**87.55**	50.65	81.14	85.57
Entity Recognition (typed)	P	75.63	75.14	72.22	70.42	66.89	74.86	72.80	**84.91**	78.42	80.60
	R	70.01	69.81	60.61	64.88	61.72	71.21	69.80	73.33	71.40	**78.26**
	F	72.71	72.34	65.91	67.53	64.20	72.98	71.27	**82.67**	74.74	79.41
Coreference Resolution	MUC	65.66	54.86	0.00	**83.72**	30.30	80.95	74.62	52.30	42.85	74.15
	B^3	41.25	36.72	4.49	54.27	22.78	38.73	56.33	26.45	29.47	**61.23**
	$CEAF_{\phi 4}$	17.72	18.31	1.80	22.00	20.95	6.82	**36.13**	14.32	15.79	28.67
	Avg. F	41.54	36.63	2.10	53.33	24.68	42.17	**55.69**	31.02	29.37	54.68

Table 5: Human Performance and Corresponding NLP Performance on GENTLE Snippets for 5 NLP Tasks. The highest scoring ('easiest') GENTLE genres are highlighted in **blue**, and the lowest scoring are in red.

tokenized texts in Table 5 allowing comparisons with human agreements, as well as end-to-end from plain text in Table 6 to also evaluate tokenization. Tokenization degrades in the end-to-end scenario for all GENTLE genres except for threat. Tokenization is error-prone in syllabus and legal due to the abundance of bulleted and numbered nominal phrases and abbreviations. XPOS tagging degrades nearly 10 points on GENTLE and scores the lowest on proof and syllabus due to mathematical symbols (e.g. $\leq$, $\in$, x, y) and genre-specific terminologies (e.g. TAs, TBD). Micro-averaged lemmatization performance drops nearly 6 points to 92.38 and parsing by 15 points to a LAS of 72.38, again worst for proof and syllabus.

While these results may be somewhat shocking, human performance is also imperfect, with XPOS and lemmatization accuracy in the mid-90s, less than 3 points above Stanza for tagging, and neck-and-neck for lemmatization, and with human LAS at 84.66, about 8 points above Stanza on average. To illustrate why humans disagree on syntax especially in technical genres, we offer a brief example of parsing a legal case law designation for '410 U.S. 113' in Figure 2. '410 U.S.' is a volume of US Supreme Court cases, including case '113' (Roe v. Wade) – one annotator (in black) analyzes '113' (the case) as the head, which is modified by the name of the volume that includes it, while the other treats the volume as the head, with a numerical modifier attached as dep, similar to how GUM annotates cases like 'Page 5.' Without good intuitions about Supreme Court case nomenclature and very clear guidelines, any chance of perfect agreement is hampered by a myriad of such cases.

On the other hand, some potentially difficult genres, such as esports, turned out to have high human agreement for tokenization, tagging and lemmatization, despite well known challenges in annotating User Generated Content (UGC, see Sanguinetti et al. 2022).

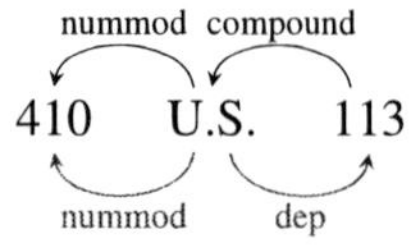

Figure 2: Annotation Disagreement for *410 U.S. 113*.

Tasks	Metrics	GUM_{test}	$GUM_{test\text{-}news}$	GENTLE (MICRO)	GENTLE (MACRO)	dictionary	esports	legal	medical	poetry	proof	syllabus	threat
Tokenization	F	**99.61**	99.67	97.29	97.46	98.12	99.52	95.55	97.73	99.59	97.98	91.46	**99.69**
POS Tagging (XPOS)	Acc	**97.46**	**97.85**	88.34	88.56	90.74	**95.89**	89.71	92.93	91.51	78.76	75.22	93.74
Lemmatization	Acc	**98.13**	**98.52**	92.38	92.64	95.53	**98.29**	91.72	93.01	95.51	91.06	79.74	96.23
Dependency Parsing	UAS	**89.49**	**89.68**	76.71	77.01	75.39	83.99	77.23	81.15	76.74	71.23	63.99	**86.37**
	LAS	**87.21**	**87.45**	72.38	72.65	70.78	78.84	73.95	77.64	71.70	65.58	59.94	**82.77**
Entity Recognition (typed)	P	**77.14**	65.01	75.63	75.10	72.22	70.42	66.56	74.86	72.80	**84.91**	78.42	80.60
	R	**76.24**	72.69	70.01	69.77	60.61	64.88	61.41	71.21	69.80	**80.56**	71.40	78.26
	F	**76.88**	68.64	72.71	72.30	65.91	67.53	63.88	72.98	71.27	**82.67**	74.74	79.41
Coreference Resolution	MUC	**76.38**	59.67	60.89	55.98	9.30	67.84	59.14	70.13	70.92	48.95	41.09	**80.48**
	B^3	**64.71**	53.97	33.37	33.91	14.74	45.49	31.07	32.78	43.98	29.08	20.88	**53.29**
	$CEAF_{\phi4}$	**57.15**	**53.06**	9.75	11.18	4.91	**17.48**	9.22	7.06	15.10	13.48	7.78	14.38
	Avg. F	**66.08**	55.57	34.67	33.69	9.65	43.60	33.14	36.66	43.33	30.50	23.25	**49.38**
RST EDU Segmentation (Gold)	P	**96.43**	**95.68**	93.90	93.21	**97.58**	95.71	90.07	**97.58**	91.30	88.81	94.35	93.62
	R	**95.85**	**97.17**	93.17	92.07	95.48	87.01	96.11	96.58	88.06	87.89	**98.04**	92.69
	F	**96.14**	**96.42**	93.53	92.60	96.52	91.16	92.99	**97.07**	89.66	88.35	96.16	93.16
RST EDU Segmentation (Trankit)	P	**93.63**	**92.91**	89.90	90.17	95.48	94.37	85.29	**97.92**	87.46	87.41	80.48	92.98
	R	**93.48**	**96.46**	86.78	87.79	86.24	87.01	92.23	**96.58**	85.48	88.93	73.48	92.36
	F	**93.55**	**94.65**	88.31	88.89	90.62	90.54	88.62	**97.24**	86.46	88.16	76.82	92.67
RST Parsing	S	**70.07**	**71.89**	62.15	62.83	59.31	55.77	**72.72**	65.51	59.78	69.11	57.13	63.29
	N	**56.90**	**60.61**	47.63	48.05	47.47	40.41	**59.79**	50.35	40.87	55.25	44.18	46.06
	R	**49.57**	**56.40**	37.64	38.16	30.52	29.30	**51.48**	46.88	30.93	41.73	40.17	34.23

Table 6: End-to-End NLP Performance on All Tasks on Full Plain Texts (averaged over 3 runs). Top and bottom scoring GENTLE genres are marked in **blue** and red (GUM scores are nearly always higher, in **bold**).

Entity Recognition and Coreference Resolution For NNER, we evaluate a SOTA neural system (seq2set, Tan et al. 2021). In both full GENTLE and snippets, we consider plain text with gold tokenization as input and use precision, recall and F1 to evaluate. In Table 6, F1 drops over 4 points on average, and over 13 points on legal. Inspection reveals most errors involve malpredicted spans, especially when deciding entity boundaries with PP attachment, apposition, or coordination. For example, in *[Proto-Germanic *nēhwist ("[nearest]*$_2$*, [closest]*$_3$*")]*$_1$, span 2 (blue) and span 3 (orange) are appositions providing additional information for the word *nēhwist* and span 1 (red) as a whole forms a non-named entity span, but neither of them are correctly predicted by the model. proof outperforms GUM because mathematical variables, which are frequent in proof, are easier to identify compared with other types of entities. We also observe this in Table 5, where IAA is the highest for proof. Note that IAA for typed and untyped entities are identical; this is because most entities in proof, e.g. mathematical variables, are *abstract*.

The coreference resolution task uses MTL-coref (*under review*), a new SOTA model for the GUM benchmark which is trained with singletons and other entity-level information. We use the F1-measure of MUC, B^3, $CEAF_{\phi4}$, and the average CoNLL score as evaluation metrics. Table 6 reveals that the model performs substantially worse on GENTLE, with nearly 32 points degradation. Genre-wise analysis reveals that dictionary, which has few pronouns, performs worst, while threat, rich in pronouns, scores best in GENTLE. This shows that the model struggles more with complex NPs (with possible PP attachments) and proper nouns but can more easily identify coreference chains involving pronouns (and especially the easy pronouns 'I' and 'you' in threat letters). For instance, in GENTLE_epsorts_fortnite, the model incorrectly clusters *[Kreo]*$_1$ ... *[him]*$_1$ ... *[Maufin]*$_1$, a chain including multiple names unseen during training.

RST Segmentation and Parsing We evaluate GENTLE on two RST tasks: elementary discourse unit (EDU) segmentation and RST parsing. For EDU segmentation, we use DisCoDisCo (Gessler et al., 2021), the winning system in the 2021 DISRPT shared task on segmentation. We evaluate EDU segmentation under two conditions: 'Gold', where the full, human-provided UD parses for GENTLE documents are provided to the system; and 'Trankit', where with the sole exception of tokenization (which remains human-provided), all UD parse information is provided by Trankit's (Nguyen et al., 2021) default English model.

For RST parsing, we use the best setting from the bottom-up neural parser by Guz and Carenini (2020), SpanBERT-NoCoref, which obtained the SOTA performance on GUM as of v8 (Liu and Zeldes, 2023) using the original Parseval procedure on binary trees, following Morey et al. (2017). We evaluate using gold discourse units for simplicity and comparability with previous work.

Unsurprisingly, GENTLE contains challenging materials even with gold discourse units: overall, the best-performing genre is `legal` while the worst-performing genre is `esports`. By examining dependency conversions of gold vs. predicted trees following Li et al. (2014), we found that the model was only able to correctly identify the Central Discourse Unit in 6 out of 26 documents (23.1%) in GENTLE. The top 2 most difficult relation classes are TOPIC and EXPLANATION, both of which tend to lack explicit and unambiguous cues such as discourse markers, and may require an understanding over multiple EDUs.

6 Conclusion

We have introduced GENTLE, a new, genre-diverse, richly-annotated test corpus for English. While this new resource is relatively small, the challenging genres included in the corpus are diverse not only in topic, but also in terms of medium and communicative intent. The 8 genres have considerably distinct characteristics reflected in metrics and label distributions for individual annotation layers. These genres also differ substantially from the 12 genres in the GUM reference corpus. As such, GENTLE serves as an important complement to GUM's test set, and can provide valuable insights into NLP systems' ability to perform on OOD data.

We found in evaluations that system performance generally degraded on GENTLE compared to GUM, corroborating prior findings that NLP systems degrade on OOD data. However, degradation was not uniform, and different genres presented differing degrees of difficulty for different NLP tasks. For dependency parsing, the steepest degradation was in `syllabus` and `proof`, while entity recognition saw particularly poor performance in `legal` and `dictionary`, and RST parsing performed lowest on `esports`, `dictionary` and `poetry`. It is thus necessary to have a wide variety of genres available for evaluation if one aims for a holistic understanding of the capabilities and limitations of an NLP system.

Moreover, it is worth noting that the annotation tasks for our challenge genres were not just difficult for the NLP systems, but for our human annotators as well. Our IAA experiments showed that human annotation generally outperformed the NLP systems in terms of accuracy. However, some genres stood out as being particularly difficult for humans, such as `dictionary`, which suggests that it would be beneficial to develop additional annotation guidelines targeting difficult cases that arise from genre-specific phenomena.

With the introduction of GENTLE and the results from the above evaluation experiments, we hope to encourage the use of genre-diverse test corpora for NLP benchmarks. This will allow researchers to obtain realistic measures of how NLP systems will perform on OOD data, which is frequently the use case of interest in real-world applications of NLP technologies.

Limitations

Our corpus is designed to serve as a challenge set, and is limited in size: each of the 8 genres ranges from 2k to 2.5k tokens, totaling around 18k tokens. Given the amount of work necessary for multilayer annotations, building a larger challenge set was not deemed realistic with the limited resources available for this project, and is left for future work.

Additionally, the evaluation of inter-annotator agreement is limited to a small amount of data, since double annotating the amount of annotation layers involved is costly. In particular, the evaluation is limited by the use of a common gold tokenization standard to facilitate reporting commonly used scores (Cohen's Kappa, tagging accuracy, NNER F1, etc.), which do not reflect cascading errors due to tokenization disagreements. Additionally, we did not perform double annotation experiments for RST discourse parsing, as these would require annotating entire documents in each genre, which would exceed the amount of data we were able to have annotated for this evaluation.

References

Mitchell Abrams. 2019. Uncovering the genre of threatening texts: A multilayered corpus study. Master's thesis, Georgetown University.

Katherine Atwell, Junyi Jessy Li, and Malihe Alikhani. 2021. Where are we in discourse relation recognition? In *Proceedings of the 22nd Annual Meeting of the Special Interest Group on Discourse and Dialogue*, pages 314–325, Singapore and Online. Association for Computational Linguistics.

Isabelle Augenstein, Leon Derczynski, and Kalina Bontcheva. 2017. Generalisation in named entity recognition: A quantitative analysis. *Computer Speech & Language*, 44:61–83.

Shabnam Behzad and Amir Zeldes. 2020. A cross-genre ensemble approach to robust Reddit part of speech tagging. In *Proceedings of the 12th Web as Corpus Workshop*, pages 50–56, Marseille, France. European Language Resources Association.

Marie-Catherine de Marneffe, Christopher D. Manning, Joakim Nivre, and Daniel Zeman. 2021. Universal Dependencies. *Computational Linguistics*, 47(2):255–308.

Kim Gerdes. 2013. Collaborative dependency annotation. In *Proceedings of the Second International Conference on Dependency Linguistics (DepLing 2013)*, pages 88–97, Prague, Czech Republic. Charles University in Prague, Matfyzpress, Prague, Czech Republic.

Luke Gessler, Shabnam Behzad, Yang Janet Liu, Siyao Peng, Yilun Zhu, and Amir Zeldes. 2021. DisCoDisCo at the DISRPT2021 shared task: A system for discourse segmentation, classification, and connective detection. In *Proceedings of the 2nd Shared Task on Discourse Relation Parsing and Treebanking (DISRPT 2021)*, pages 51–62, Punta Cana, Dominican Republic. Association for Computational Linguistics.

Luke Gessler, Lauren Levine, and Amir Zeldes. 2022. Midas loop: A prioritized human-in-the-loop annotation for large scale multilayer data. In *Proceedings of the 16th Linguistic Annotation Workshop (LAW-XVI) within LREC2022*, pages 103–110, Marseille, France. European Language Resources Association.

Grigorii Guz and Giuseppe Carenini. 2020. Coreference for discourse parsing: A neural approach. In *Proceedings of the First Workshop on Computational Approaches to Discourse*, pages 160–167, Online. Association for Computational Linguistics.

Dan Hendrycks, Collin Burns, Anya Chen, and Spencer Ball. 2021. CUAD: An Expert-Annotated NLP Dataset for Legal Contract Review. *NeurIPS*.

Vidur Joshi, Matthew Peters, and Mark Hopkins. 2018. Extending a parser to distant domains using a few dozen partially annotated examples. In *Proceedings of the 56th Annual Meeting of the Association for Computational Linguistics (Volume 1: Long Papers)*, pages 1190–1199, Melbourne, Australia. Association for Computational Linguistics.

Jenna Kanerva and Filip Ginter. 2022. Out-of-domain evaluation of Finnish dependency parsing. In *Proceedings of the Thirteenth Language Resources and Evaluation Conference*, pages 1114–1124, Marseille, France. European Language Resources Association.

Sujian Li, Liang Wang, Ziqiang Cao, and Wenjie Li. 2014. Text-level discourse dependency parsing. In *Proceedings of the 52nd Annual Meeting of the Association for Computational Linguistics (Volume 1: Long Papers)*, pages 25–35, Baltimore, Maryland. Association for Computational Linguistics.

Jessica Lin and Amir Zeldes. 2021. WikiGUM: Exhaustive entity linking for wikification in 12 genres. In *Proceedings of the Joint 15th Linguistic Annotation Workshop (LAW) and 3rd Designing Meaning Representations (DMR) Workshop*, pages 170–175, Punta Cana, Dominican Republic. Association for Computational Linguistics.

Yang Janet Liu and Amir Zeldes. 2023. Why can't discourse parsing generalize? A thorough investigation of the impact of data diversity. In *Proceedings of the 17th Conference of the European Chapter of the Association for Computational Linguistics*, pages 3104–3122, Dubrovnik, Croatia. Association for Computational Linguistics.

William C. Mann and Sandra A. Thompson. 1988. Rhetorical Structure Theory: Toward a functional theory of text organization. *Text*, 8(3):243–281.

Mitchell P. Marcus, Beatrice Santorini, and Mary Ann Marcinkiewicz. 1993. Building a large annotated corpus of English: The Penn Treebank. *Special Issue on Using Large Corpora, Computational Linguistics*, 19(2):313–330.

Nafise Sadat Moosavi and Michael Strube. 2017. Lexical features in coreference resolution: To be used with caution. In *Proceedings of the 55th Annual Meeting of the Association for Computational Linguistics (Volume 2: Short Papers)*, pages 14–19, Vancouver, Canada. Association for Computational Linguistics.

Mathieu Morey, Philippe Muller, and Nicholas Asher. 2017. How much progress have we made on RST discourse parsing? a replication study of recent results on the RST-DT. In *Proceedings of the 2017 Conference on Empirical Methods in Natural Language Processing*, pages 1319–1324, Copenhagen, Denmark. Association for Computational Linguistics.

Anmol Nayak, Hariprasad Timmapathini, Karthikeyan Ponnalagu, and Vijendran Gopalan Venkoparao. 2020. Domain adaptation challenges of BERT in tokenization and sub-word representations of out-of-vocabulary words. In *Proceedings of the First Workshop on Insights from Negative Results in NLP*, pages 1–5, Online. Association for Computational Linguistics.

Minh Van Nguyen, Viet Dac Lai, Amir Pouran Ben Veyseh, and Thien Huu Nguyen. 2021. Trankit: A light-weight transformer-based toolkit for multilingual natural language processing. In *Proceedings of the 16th Conference of the European Chapter of the Association for Computational Linguistics: System Demonstrations*, pages 80–90, Online. Association for Computational Linguistics.

Siyao Peng and Amir Zeldes. 2018. All roads lead to UD: Converting Stanford and Penn parses to English Universal Dependencies with multilayer annotations. In *Proceedings of the Joint Workshop on Linguistic*

Annotation, Multiword Expressions and Constructions (LAW-MWE-CxG-2018), pages 167–177, Santa Fe, New Mexico, USA. Association for Computational Linguistics.

Barbara Plank. 2016. What to do about non-standard (or non-canonical) language in NLP. *KONVENS 2016 Invited Talk.*

Peng Qi, Yuhao Zhang, Yuhui Zhang, Jason Bolton, and Christopher D. Manning. 2020. Stanza: A python natural language processing toolkit for many human languages. In *Proceedings of the 58th Annual Meeting of the Association for Computational Linguistics: System Demonstrations*, pages 101–108, Online. Association for Computational Linguistics.

Manuela Sanguinetti, Lauren Cassidy, Cristina Bosco, Özlem Çetinoğlu, Alessandra Teresa Cignarella, Teresa Lynn, Ines Rehbein, Josef Ruppenhofer, Djamé Seddah, and Amir Zeldes. 2022. Treebanking user-generated content: A UD based overview of guidelines, corpora and unified recommendations. *Language Resources and Evaluation*, 57:493–544.

Natalia Silveira, Timothy Dozat, Marie-Catherine de Marneffe, Samuel Bowman, Miriam Connor, John Bauer, and Chris Manning. 2014. A gold standard dependency corpus for English. In *Proceedings of the Ninth International Conference on Language Resources and Evaluation (LREC'14)*, pages 2897–2904, Reykjavik, Iceland. European Language Resources Association (ELRA).

Zeqi Tan, Yongliang Shen, Shuai Zhang, Weiming Lu, and Yueting Zhuang. 2021. A sequence-to-set network for nested named entity recognition. In *Proceedings of the Thirtieth International Joint Conference on Artificial Intelligence, IJCAI-21*, pages 3936–3942. International Joint Conferences on Artificial Intelligence Organization. Main Track.

Ralph Weischedel, Sameer Pradhan, Lance Ramshaw, Jeff Kaufman, Michelle Franchini, Mohammed El-Bachouti, Nianwen Xue, Martha Palmer, Jena D. Hwang, Claire Bonial, Jinho Choi, Aous Mansouri, Maha Foster, Abdel aati Hawwary, Mitchell Marcus, Ann Taylor, Craig Greenberg, Eduard Hovy, Robert Belvin, and Ann Houston. 2012. OntoNotes release 5.0. Technical report, Linguistic Data Consortium, Philadelphia.

Amir Zeldes. 2016. rstWeb - a browser-based annotation interface for Rhetorical Structure Theory and discourse relations. In *Proceedings of the 2016 Conference of the North American Chapter of the Association for Computational Linguistics: Demonstrations*, pages 1–5, San Diego, California. Association for Computational Linguistics.

Amir Zeldes. 2017. The GUM Corpus: Creating Multilayer Resources in the Classroom. *Language Resources and Evaluation*, 51(3):581–612.

Amir Zeldes and Dan Simonson. 2016. Different flavors of GUM: Evaluating genre and sentence type effects on multilayer corpus annotation quality. In *Proceedings of the 10th Linguistic Annotation Workshop held in conjunction with ACL 2016 (LAW-X 2016)*, pages 68–78, Berlin, Germany. Association for Computational Linguistics.

Shuo Zhang and Amir Zeldes. 2017. GitDOX: A linked version controlled online XML editor for manuscript transcription. In *Proceedings of FLAIRS 2017*, pages 619–623, Marco Island, FL.

Yilun Zhu, Sameer Pradhan, and Amir Zeldes. 2021. OntoGUM: Evaluating contextualized SOTA coreference resolution on 12 more genres. In *Proceedings of the 59th Annual Meeting of the Association for Computational Linguistics and the 11th International Joint Conference on Natural Language Processing (Volume 2: Short Papers)*, pages 461–467, Online. Association for Computational Linguistics.

A Genre Descriptions

GENTLE comprises 8 genres, with each having 2 to 5 individual documents—cf. Table 2. They are as follows:

- **`dictionary`** – entries for a single English word from Wiktionary (`https://en.wiktionary.org`). GENTLE includes documents for the words *next*, *trust*, and *school*.
- **`esports`** – transcripts of a YouTube video clip containing esport commentary. GENTLE includes two documents: one featuring Fortnite, and the other featuring FIFA 20.
- **`legal`** – segments of legal text from the United States. Of the two documents, one is a portion of the Supreme Court opinion for Roe v. Wade (1973) from Wikisource (`https://en.wikisource.org`), and the other is a portion of a contract, extracted from the **C**ontract **U**nderstanding **A**tticus **D**ataset (CUAD) v1 from the The Atticus Project (Hendrycks et al., 2021).
- **`medical`** – snippets of a Subjective, Objective, Assessment and Plan (SOAP) note. A SOAP note is a common kind of text used by medical professionals to document a patient's medical visits and history. The notes are taken from MTSamples (`https://mtsamples.com`).
- **`poetry`** – poems taken from Wikisource (`https://en.wikisource.org/wiki/Portal:Poetry`). The poems come from 3 different authors and are of varying lengths.
- **`proof`** – mathematical proofs taken from ProofWiki (`https://proofwiki.org`).
- **`syllabus`** – syllabuses taken from course materials posted publicly on GitHub.
- **`threat`** – threat letters recorded in publicly available United States court proceedings. Accessed through casetext (`https://casetext.com/cases`; see also Abrams 2019 for some analysis of these texts).

B Full Label Residual Tables

The following tables give complete standardized Pearson residuals for label distributions in each GENTLE genre, along with comparisons to GUM as a whole and GUM news in particular. Tables 7–10 give numbers for UPOS, dependency, entity, and RST coarse labels respectively.

	ADJ	ADP	ADV	AUX	CCONJ	DET	INTJ	NOUN	NUM	PART	PRON	PROPN	PUNCT	SCONJ	SYM	VERB	X
GUM	-0.5	-2.1	11.3	8.7	2.3	1.8	13.3	-15.1	-5.2	3.9	20.8	-25.1	-0.2	4.1	-14.6	6.6	-22.6
GUM$_{news}$	-1.3	5.9	-11.5	-6.2	-4.8	4.9	-11.5	5.7	4.6	-1.1	-21.7	41.4	-5.4	-3.3	-1.9	-3.3	-6.6
dictionary	7.9	-1.2	-5.9	-7.2	-0.4	-5.2	-2.9	4.4	-5.0	-0.6	-8.6	-4.9	20.4	-4.6	-2.1	-6.1	21.2
esports	-3.3	-1.1	5.9	2.1	-1.9	-0.6	0.4	-5.2	1.8	4.7	3.7	1.4	-4.1	-1.5	-1.3	4.2	-2.1
legal	0.3	0.0	-4.7	-5.5	3.0	3.2	-4.1	4.7	2.6	0.4	-9.5	3.9	0.8	0.0	4.9	-3.1	18.4
medical	7.6	0.0	-5.3	-0.4	0.0	-5.0	-4.0	11.6	5.4	-4.2	-2.6	-6.9	1.0	-3.3	-0.4	-4.8	8.9
poetry	-2.6	-1.4	5.0	-4.5	2.7	2.1	-2.8	-1.6	-5.3	-4.5	5.5	-7.1	5.5	0.9	-1.9	1.9	-2.2
proof	-1.0	0.4	0.5	0.3	-1.2	-4.7	-3.9	14.5	1.8	-5.8	-9.0	-8.1	0.9	3.7	56.3	-6.4	-2.3
syllabus	-1.4	-3.1	-6.6	-5.1	2.5	-6.4	-2.5	13.6	7.3	-4.5	-10.4	11.2	-3.4	-3.3	5.4	-5.3	54.5
threat	-2.5	-1.3	0.8	5.5	-0.5	-2.2	1.6	-2.6	-2.1	3.3	13.2	-7.4	-7.0	2.5	-1.7	4.5	-0.9

Table 7: Residuals for UPOS Labels by Genre.

	acl	advcl	advmod	amod	appos	aux	case	cc	ccomp	compound	conj	cop	csubj	dep	det	discourse	dislocated	expl
GUM	1.3	4.3	12.2	-1.9	-12.8	4.7	-4.3	2.3	-1.2	-16.1	-2.2	7.8	3.8	-20.9	1.4	9.9	-2.9	4.3
GUM$_{news}$	-0.6	-2.6	-11.7	3.5	7.5	-2.1	9.6	-5.1	4.9	20.3	-4.5	-7.1	-3.1	-2.5	5.3	-9.3	-1.4	-4.0
dictionary	-1.6	-4.4	-6.3	2.1	7.0	-5.2	-2.4	-0.5	-4.1	-2.2	9.7	-4.7	-1.7	5.6	-5.1	-3.1	-0.3	-2.4
esports	-1.5	0.9	4.7	-3.9	-2.3	2.3	-3.0	-2.4	-0.5	-0.4	-0.3	0.5	-1.3	-2.2	-0.7	2.1	9.2	-1.2
legal	4.2	-1.3	-4.4	1.4	3.6	-4.1	1.8	2.7	-2.7	3.4	1.8	-3.4	-1.4	17.2	3.3	-3.4	-0.2	-1.7
medical	-3.8	-4.3	-5.9	7.7	-1.3	0.4	0.2	0.1	-1.8	1.9	3.5	-0.9	-1.6	7.7	-4.7	-3.3	-0.2	-1.2
poetry	1.9	1.5	3.8	-2.8	-2.0	-4.3	-1.6	2.5	1.3	-5.7	-0.3	-1.8	-0.7	-3.6	2.2	-1.9	1.7	-0.7
proof	-1.2	-0.3	-0.1	-3.0	3.6	-3.2	1.6	0.5	1.6	-6.1	3.1	4.6	2.6	10.9	-5.2	-3.3	3.0	3.9
syllabus	-3.6	-2.9	-7.7	-0.5	19.8	-2.8	-3.5	2.7	-3.8	16.6	1.7	-4.5	-1.7	46.3	-6.5	-2.0	-0.3	-2.4
threat	2.5	2.4	3.0	-3.6	-2.8	5.9	-2.2	-0.7	2.2	-2.8	-0.0	1.0	0.4	-1.9	-2.1	3.3	1.7	0.5

(a) Part 1.

	fixed	flat	goeswith	iobj	list	mark	nmod	nsubj	nummod	obj	obl	orphan	parataxis	punct	reparandum	root	vocative	xcomp
GUM	0.0	-9.7	-2.7	0.6	1.8	5.0	-4.0	8.4	-7.2	4.6	-2.2	-0.1	-4.1	-0.1	5.5	-2.7	1.8	4.9
GUM$_{news}$	1.1	21.7	-0.5	-0.6	-1.6	-4.2	7.3	-4.2	4.2	-4.0	3.6	-0.8	-6.5	-5.4	-5.7	-6.8	-2.4	-4.8
dictionary	-0.3	-4.5	0.5	-1.7	-0.4	-2.2	-3.1	-9.8	-2.9	-5.3	-1.7	-0.0	18.4	20.4	-2.0	7.3	-0.3	-3.9
esports	1.5	-2.4	1.7	1.5	-0.3	3.9	-5.6	2.4	3.5	1.0	1.8	-0.4	16.7	-4.1	5.8	-1.5	-0.2	5.2
legal	-0.2	-1.6	0.6	-1.1	-0.3	-0.9	3.5	-6.6	0.6	-0.3	-1.5	-0.5	-2.0	0.8	-1.9	-2.4	-0.7	-2.6
medical	-1.2	-3.8	0.6	-1.5	-0.3	-3.8	3.4	-2.1	7.9	-2.6	0.5	2.2	-1.3	0.9	-1.8	6.7	-0.7	-1.8
poetry	-0.7	-2.8	0.6	1.6	-0.3	-2.2	-0.6	0.8	-2.2	0.1	0.5	-0.4	1.4	5.5	-0.1	0.1	1.7	-0.8
proof	-0.3	-4.5	0.6	-1.5	-0.3	0.0	2.7	1.4	-1.2	-1.2	2.1	0.1	-2.3	0.9	-1.8	1.3	-0.6	-1.1
syllabus	-0.3	1.1	0.5	-1.7	-0.4	-4.3	-3.1	-9.1	8.5	-1.9	-2.9	1.9	-0.5	-3.5	-1.7	16.4	-0.7	-3.9
threat	-1.5	-3.3	6.0	4.0	-0.3	2.6	-1.3	4.6	0.9	4.2	0.4	-0.4	1.1	-7.0	-1.6	-1.1	1.6	4.1

(b) Part 2.

Table 8: Residuals for Deprel Labels by Genre.

	abstract	animal	event	object	organization	person	place	plant	substance	time
GUM	-13.8	3.5	-3.1	6.4	-19.5	13.4	8.7	6.4	4.2	-2.3
GUM$_{news}$	-15.2	-7.7	7.2	0.5	30.6	-6.7	3.9	-2.2	-0.3	5.7
dictionary	17.1	5.0	-4.9	-5.9	6.6	-10.1	-6.1	-2.4	-3.6	0.4
esports	-9.3	-2.6	9.9	0.1	-0.5	7.8	-2.4	-2.0	-3.0	-0.7
legal	9.8	-2.7	1.9	-6.7	12.6	-8.0	-4.5	-2.1	-3.9	0.2
medical	4.4	-0.4	2.8	6.2	-6.1	-4.8	-7.8	-2.3	11.0	-0.2
poetry	-3.6	17.8	-4.3	1.5	-5.4	4.2	1.3	-0.8	-1.9	-1.4
proof	39.2	-3.0	-7.0	-7.7	-6.4	-16.5	-9.2	-2.4	-4.3	-6.7
syllabus	25.7	-3.4	-2.5	-8.6	-4.7	-12.1	-7.3	-2.7	-4.7	4.6
threat	-4.1	-2.2	-1.6	-1.0	-2.9	12.9	-2.9	-2.1	-3.7	-3.2

Table 9: Residuals for Entity Labels by Genre.

	adversative	attribution	causal	context	contingency	elaboration	evaluation	explanation	joint	mode	organization	purpose	restatement	same	topic
GUM	5.9	-3.7	2.6	0.6	1.3	-2.2	5.7	2.6	-8.9	1.9	-2.4	1.8	4.1	-0.8	7.7
GUM$_{news}$	-3.6	12.1	2.1	3.6	-1.8	5.3	-4.4	-6.0	-2.7	-2.1	-4.6	2.2	-3.5	1.4	-5.2
dictionary	-3.6	-5.4	-4.3	1.0	-2.3	2.6	-4.0	0.6	3.2	-1.8	5.7	-2.5	0.1	3.8	-2.6
esports	0.3	-1.2	-0.2	1.5	-1.6	-3.2	6.8	-1.2	1.3	-0.2	-0.8	0.9	0.3	-0.3	-1.4
legal	-2.5	-3.6	-2.3	-3.7	0.3	3.1	-3.0	0.9	2.3	-1.4	2.1	1.5	0.2	2.9	-1.9
medical	-1.6	-2.2	-2.4	-3.6	-1.5	-4.2	-3.2	-3.5	12.9	-1.4	9.1	-2.5	-1.9	-3.3	-2.0
poetry	2.4	1.7	2.7	0.3	-2.2	-0.3	-0.1	-1.9	-3.1	5.5	-3.0	-2.3	2.7	2.5	0.0
proof	-4.2	1.6	-2.1	2.4	4.2	-1.4	-3.0	8.5	-0.0	0.4	2.7	-2.5	-2.3	-3.0	-2.0
syllabus	-3.3	-5.1	-4.3	-5.5	-0.5	-0.7	-4.1	-4.0	18.2	-1.8	4.3	-2.7	-3.5	-2.0	-2.6
threat	1.2	1.1	0.5	-2.2	4.1	-0.8	2.4	6.4	-1.3	-0.5	-2.9	-0.3	-1.3	-1.5	-2.0

Table 10: Residuals for RST Relation Classes by Genre.

A Pilot Study on Annotation Interfaces for Summary Comparisons

Sian Gooding **Lucas Werner** **Victor Cărbune**
Google Research
{sgooding|lucaswerner|vcarbune}@google.com

Abstract

The task of summarisation is notoriously difficult to evaluate, with agreement even between expert raters unlikely to be perfect. One technique for summary evaluation relies on collecting comparison data by presenting annotators with generated summaries and tasking them with selecting the best one. This paradigm is currently being exploited in reinforcement learning using human feedback, whereby a reward function is trained using pairwise choice data. Comparisons are an easier way to elicit human feedback for summarisation, however, such decisions can be bottle necked by the usability of the annotator interface. In this paper, we present the results of a pilot study exploring how the user interface impacts annotator agreement when judging summary quality.

1 Introduction

As language models become more powerful, training and evaluation are increasingly limited by the data and metrics used for a particular task (Stiennon et al., 2020). Human evaluation has traditionally been used in the field of summarisation as a gold standard when assessing the quality of model outputs and for corroborating automated evaluation techniques. However, ensuring high quality evaluation with human annotators is difficult due to the subjective and task-dependent paradigm of summarisation. As model refinement will increasingly rely on human feedback it is important to consider how to best elicit high quality signal from human annotators.

One technique to judge the quality of summaries is the use of human preferences via comparison or ranking. Such rankings can also be used to improve summary quality by training models in a reinforcement learning paradigm. For instance, Stiennon et al. (2020) show that human preference data can be used to improve the capability of large language models (LLMs) for summarisation via a technique referred to as Reinforcement Learning from Human Feedback (RLHF). However, human feedback does not always provide a gold standard for summarisation when the task is not clearly defined. It has been established that linguistically trained, expert raters, provide the gold standard in summarisation evaluation and the reliability of non-experts has been repeatedly questioned (Lloret et al., 2018). For instance, it has been found that crowd workers should not be used to evaluate summary quality because of a non-correlation with experts (Gillick and Liu, 2010; Fabbri et al., 2021). Furthermore, even for expert annotations mediation meetings are necessary to assure reliability (Iskender et al., 2021). In short, evaluating the quality of a summary is not an easy or straightforward task.

The use of RLHF to train LLMs is becoming increasingly common. However, training a model from human feedback relies on the collection of data via user interfaces for the chosen task. Increasingly then, natural language processing applications are heavily influenced by the human computer interaction that takes place when collecting preference data. Recent work in RLHF for summarisation overlooks how critical the user interface is in this process, with little to no discussion of the design decisions made.

In this paper, we present the findings from a pilot study introducing a novel user interface for summary comparisons. We document how the introduction of the new interface impacts annotator engagement as well as investigate the following research questions:

- **RQ1:** Does the annotator agreement for the task of summary comparison change based on the user-interface and task conceptualisation?

- **RQ2:** Does allowing the highlighting of tokens improve the agreement of summary comparisons?

Proceedings of the 17th Linguistic Annotation Workshop (LAW-XVII), pages 179–187
July 13, 2023 ©2023 Association for Computational Linguistics

2 Background

It is widely understood that machine learning systems are limited by the quality of the labelled training data (Gooding et al., 2019). One approach to improving the performance of such systems is to treat the human labeller(s) as a source of noise (Frénay and Verleysen, 2014) who can be modelled statistically (Yan et al., 2010) in order to more accurately identify an underlying ground truth. Noise estimation can be improved if multiple labels are obtained for each item in the training set in order to model inconsistency (Ipeirotis et al., 2014), or if a distribution of label values can be used as a basis for rejecting outliers (Brodley and Friedl, 1999). More recent approaches have relied on probabilistic methods for training deep classifiers under input-dependent label noise (Collier et al., 2021).

However, these approaches focus on dealing with noise post-annotation, whereas it is known that the quality and clarity of the user interface itself, as well as the task formulation has large implications for the annotator agreement. For instance, several of the human factors can be addressed through the use of pairwise comparison, where labellers make relative judgments to compare training items, rather that attempting to characterize each item independently against an abstract conceptual category, for which they are expected to have a stable definition and associated membership criteria. In the context of labelling, comparative judgments are used to compare how well the training items correspond to the required concept. Carterette et al. (2008) demonstrate that this method can facilitate judgments for information retrieval applications. Comparative judgments have also been used in gamified labelling (Bennett et al., 2009), where cooperating players reduce the set of alternative items until agreement is reached.

Recent work has looked into the application of comparative judgments to labelling as opposed to assignment of categorical values or scores on a scale (Simpson et al., 2019; Yang and Chen, 2011; Kingsley and Brown, 2010). Simpson et al. (2019) note that comparative judgments are suitable for abstract linguistic properties, whose nature can cause inconsistencies in the assigned numerical scores.

2.1 Agreement in summarisation

Text summarisation is the process of generating short, fluent, and factually accurate summaries of longer documents. As with most natural language generation tasks, evaluation of generated summarisation is difficult, with automated metrics often falling short. Human evaluation on summarisation has been broadly classified into two types: intrinsic and extrinsic (Jones and Galliers, 1995; Belz and Reiter, 2006; Steinberger and Jezek, 2009). In intrinsic evaluation, the summarisation quality is measured based on the resulting summary itself without considering the source. Generally, it has been carried out as a pair comparison task (generated output to expert summaries) or using absolute scales without showing a reference summary. Extrinsic evaluation, also known as task-based evaluation, aims to measure the summary's impact using a task based on the source document (Mani, 2001). (Reiter and Belz, 2009) have argued that the extrinsic evaluation is more useful than intrinsic because the summarization systems are developed to satisfy the information need from the source text in a condensed way, but van der Lee et al. (2021) have reported that only 3% of summarisation papers employ extrinsic evaluation. Extrinsic evaluation is important because it is rooted in the fundamental application of summarisation models. Across papers, guidelines provided to annotators on what constitutes a good summary have a high degree of variation. For instance, Howcroft et al. (2020) found over 200 variations in terminology when analysing annotator guidelines.

2.2 Summary Comparisons for RLHF

Stiennon et al. (2020) show that human preference data can be used to improve summary quality by training the model to optimise for human preferences instead of using coarse proxies like ROUGE. This is achieved via RLHF whereby a large dataset of human preferences between generated summaries is collected, and a reward model trained using this data. The annotations collected are from researchers (experts) and human annotations with the agreement rate between researchers ranging from about 65% on the most difficult comparisons, to approximately 80% on the easiest comparisons (comparing a high-temperature sample from a supervised baseline to the human reference summary). For cases where annotators discussed the comparisons with each other the agreement reached 95%. The paper states that: substantial noise comes from comparisons being quite difficult and subjective. In the entire corpus, labellers agree with each other 72% of the time. Using the modal

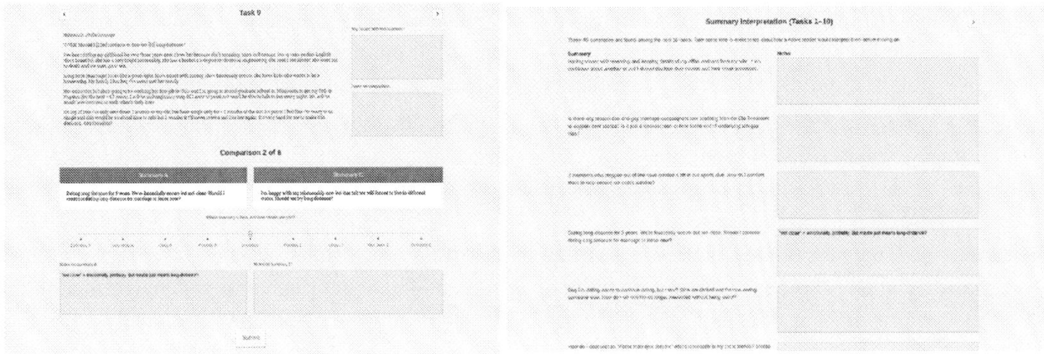

Figure 1: Stiennon et al. (2020) user interface to collect preference data from annotators (left) and interface to collect interpretations of summaries on (right)

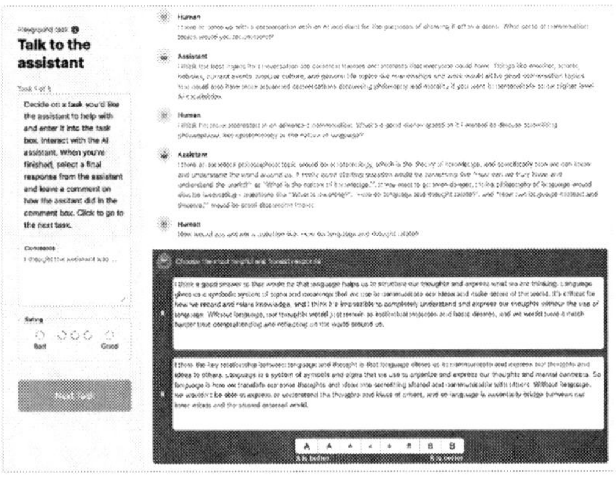

Figure 2: Bai et al. (2022) conversational interface for annotators to select helpful LLM responses

output from 3 labellers can increase this agreement rate from 72% to 77%. However, this is not used as the work prioritises label throughput with summaries receiving on average 1 annotation. Figure 1 shows the interface used by annotators to collect the preference data. The main focus of this work was to prove the efficacy of RLHF for summarisation, as such there is little discussion on how the user interface was designed or how this may be impacting the engagement or agreement of raters for this task.

Finally, Bai et al. (2022) apply preference modelling and reinforcement learning from human feedback (RLHF) to fine tune language models to act as ‘helpful and harmless assistants’. They explicitly outline summarisation as an example of a helpful task. They state that they found poor average agreement between researchers from Anthropic[1] and crowd sourced data and found that author-rater agreement wasn’t a good guide for assessing overall conversation quality. Similarly to the work by Stiennon et al. (2020), the discussion of the interface, shown in Figure 2, is limited.

Both works are valuable in setting the groundwork for RLHF as a technique for LLM task alignment. However, the annotator agreement is a factor which is highlighted as unstable for differing tasks and settings in both papers. We argue that the design and usability of the interfaces used should be considered as a much more critical component in the paradigm of RLHF research.

3 Experimental Design

Our study compares the use of a baseline interface for summary comparisons with an novel interface designed in conversation with annotators. We investigate how the use of the new interface impacts both annotator engagement and agreement using specially trained annotators for the task of summary comparison.

3.1 Methodology

The study relies on two experimental settings: in the baseline setup, annotators are tasked with selecting the best summary from a set of 5 generated summaries using a standard interface. The summary selections include generations from a range of LLMs as well as human-written gold standard summaries. Further details on summary generation are provided in § 3.3. Prior to the study, annotators have worked with the initial interface for 6 months. In the second setting, annotators are asked to select the top n summaries in a ranked order, where n can be chosen by the annotator. Annotators interact with a novel user interface which has

[1]https://www.anthropic.com/

been designed in conversation with annotators to improve readability and aid in annotation judgements. We collect annotations for 500 documents (in each UI setting). Every document and set of summaries are annotated 3 times in total.

3.2 Annotators

As emphasised, the task of judging summary quality is non-trivial and the best results are attained using judgements from trained annotators. In our experiments, we use a team of 6 in-house annotators who have been trained on the task of judging summary quality. Annotators are paid at a daily rate, irrespective of their throughput, to incentivise high quality judgements. Annotator demographic information is included in Table 1. All annotators have worked on the task of summary evaluation for a minimum of 6 months prior to the study.

3.3 Data

The datasets provided to the annotators consisted of two batches containing 500 samples each. Each batch contains articles which have been scraped from the web. Summaries for these datasets were produced by fine-tuning the following language models: LaMDA (150B), Pegasus (500M) and FlanT5 XXL. All models used in this study were Transformer Encoder models with six layers and LSTM Decoders with two layers, containing approximately 27 million parameters, resulting in a file size of around 35MB. These small models are designed to run on-device and the data used to fine-tune the models for the task of summarisation were between 1-10K gold standard summaries.

3.4 Interface design

Annotators had been working with the baseline interface (interface 1) for 6 months prior to the study. To understand which features may improve the annotation experience we conduct a qualitative interview to identify pain points. Feedback from annotators was then used to design a novel interface which addressed the following two issues; (1) the readability of text and (2) the ability to highlight tokens in either the original or in the generated summaries to identify overlap more quickly.

Figure 3 shows screenshots of the baseline and updated interface. As demonstrated in the screenshot, the highlight interface allows for the selection of words within the original text and corresponding summaries. If a token is selected, all instances of the token will be highlighted to emphasise the overlap of summaries with the original. Annotators can select and de-select as many tokens as they want, an analysis of this behaviour is presented in Section 4.1.1.

4 Results

The following results section presents the findings related to annotator behavior and agreement in the decision-making tasks. The initial analysis focuses on measuring the time taken by annotators to make decisions in two task settings. Additionally, we examine annotators' engagement with the highlighting tool in the second interface, assessing the overlap between annotators and the tool's usage patterns. Lastly, we evaluate the level of agreement among annotators when selecting the best summary in both scenarios. These results provide insights into annotator decision-making processes, tool engagement, and the consensus achieved, contributing to a better understanding of the task dynamics and effectiveness in each setting.

4.1 Annotator engagement

The time taken for annotators to perform both tasks is recorded for each set of summaries presented. Figure 4 shows a plot of the time distributions normalised by the length of the texts and summaries for each interface. Interface 1 represents the original interface used by annotators and 2 is the highlight interface. Both time distributions are binned into 200 buckets and the density of occurrences for each bucket is plotted.

The task presented to annotators in the highlight interface is more cognitively demanding as annotators can select n best summaries instead of the best one. This is reflected in the proportion of time taken to perform the task as the histogram shows that the task takes longer to perform by annotators. There is a larger spread of time taken for annotators using the highlight interface which may be due to a lack of familiarity with the new set-up. However, from analysing the highlight behaviour of annotators we can see that the extent to which users are interacting with the highlighting tool differs greatly and this will contribute to a larger spread of times.

4.1.1 Token selection

Figure 5 presents histograms showing the varying degrees of engagement exhibited by annotators in response to the annotation task, as determined by the number of selected tokens. The histograms

Proficiency		Education		Age range		Hours reading English per week	
Native	1/6	Graduate	5/6	18 - 24	3/6	0 - 5	1/6
Near native	0/6	Undergraduate	1/6	25 - 34	3/6	5 - 10	2/6
Advanced	5/6	High School	0/6	35 - 44	0/6	10 - 15	1/6
Intermediate	0/6	Vocational Training	0/6	45 - 54	0/6	15 - 20	0/6
Beginner	0/6	No formal education	0/6	55+	0/6	20 +	2/6

Table 1: Background statistics for annotators in study

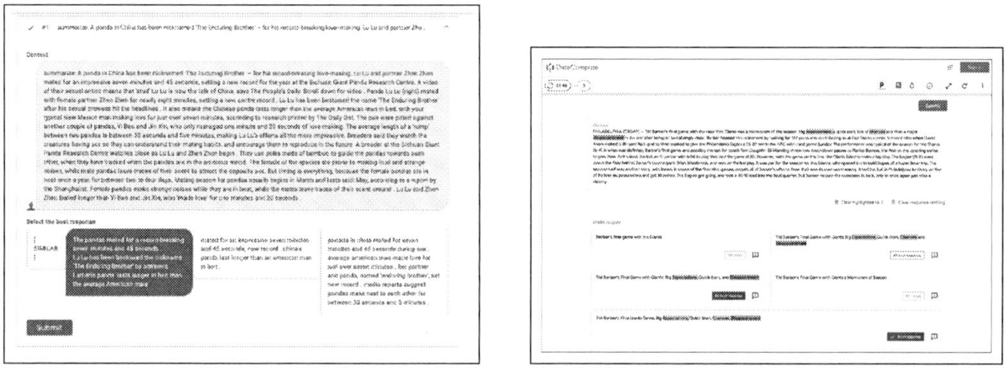

(a) Interface 1: baseline

(b) Interface 2: highlight interface

Figure 3: Screenshots of the annotation interfaces – the baseline interface is presented on the left and the highlight interface on the right.

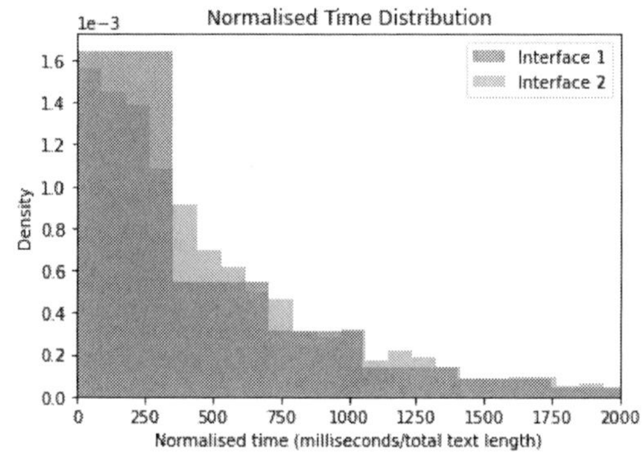

Figure 4: Histogram showing the time distribution for annotators to complete labelling using both interfaces.

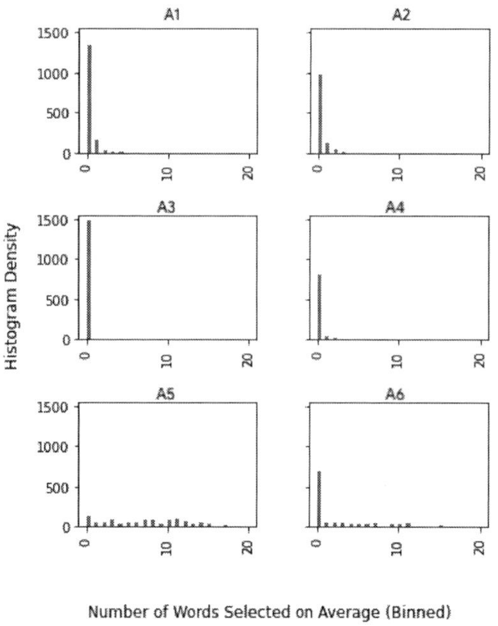

Figure 5: Histograms displaying the number of highlighted words for each annotation, labeled by annotator ID.

depict the average number of highlighted words per annotator and reveal discrepancies in uptake among individuals. This data provides an insight into the highlighting practices of annotators. We see that the adoption varies, with one annotator (A3) not selecting any tokens during annotation compared with annotator (A5) who selects 509 tokens. The total tokens highlighted by all 6 annotators was 1836.

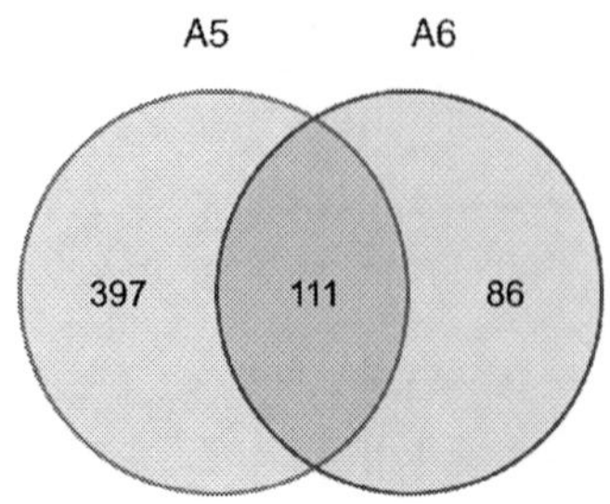

Figure 6: Venn diagram illustrating agreement between two most active annotators when selecting tokens for shared documents.

Token selection agreement Due to the variation in highlighting engagement we identify the two annotators who were most active in their use of the highlighting tool, as demonstrated in the bottom two histograms of Figure 5. To examine their degree of highlighting agreement in the annotation process, we focused on the subset of documents that were highlighted by both annotators, and investigated the crude overlap in terms of the tokens that were selected. The resulting venn diagram, shown in Figure 6, provides a visual representation of the extent of overlap between the two annotators' selected tokens for the 71 documents annotated by both.

Annotator A5 highlights a larger number of words in total than annotator A6. The overlap between their highlighted words was 22% of annotator A5's total and 56% of annotator A6's total. Of the words selected by both annotators for the shared documents 63% were nouns. It is worth noting that a more comprehensive analysis of token agreement will require a longer-term study, as annotator adoption of the highlighting tool is expected to increase over time.

4.2 Token selection

Using the total 1836 tokens selected across annotators, we find that there is a statistically significant correlation ($p < 0.01$) in the number of times a token is selected and the number of occurrences of that token in the original article. The total proportion of nouns selected is 64% which implies that the search of noun specific content words is most useful when considering whether generated summaries are high quality.

4.2.1 Annotator agreement

Table 2 shows the results of the pairwise Kappa agreement for annotators in both interface settings. The first interface yields a higher overall agreement compared to the second and the values range from 0.36 to 0.74 with an average of 0.59, while the values for the second setting range from 0.32 to 0.65 with an average of 0.46. These results show that there was higher inter-annotator agreement for interface 1 than for interface 2. In general, whilst there were some pairs of annotators who agreed more strongly than others for both interfaces, the results indicate that there is some variability in the inter-annotator agreement. Further efforts are needed to increase the consistency of annotations for the task, especially for Interface 2.

We posit that the lower annotator agreement in the second setting is for two reasons. Firstly, annotators are much less familiar with the new interface as this is the first experience they have with labelling via the new tool. Additionally, the new task requires a higher cognitive load as it involves selecting the best set of n summaries, as opposed to a single best summary. We found a substantial drop in the average agreement for annotators in the second setting, which raises questions about the stability of annotation and the complexity of the task. While this not the expected result, it provides an opportunity to investigate the task further. We plan to conduct a longitudinal study to examine whether annotator agreement improves with experience. Our preliminary results from this study are encouraging, showing that agreement increases as annotators become more familiar with the tool (an average kappa of 0.52 for the last 100 annotations in interface 2).

The highlight interface has an advantage in that it is designed to capture a more comprehensive range of behavioural information during the annotation process. One such behaviour is the frequency with which annotators change their top choice of summary. This is particularly useful when judging the difficulty of the decision, as it indicates the level of uncertainty for annotators. We investigate whether the level of agreement among annotators differs significantly based on the number of times they reselect their top choice in the highlight annotation interface. To do this we calculate significance using Satterthwaite's method (Kuznetsova et al., 2017), applied to a mixed-effects model that treats participants and the specific annotation task as crossed

	Annotator	A1	A2	A3	A4	A5	A6	Avg
Interface 1	A1	1.00	0.73	0.36	0.71	0.74	0.58	0.62
	A2	0.73	1.00	0.34	0.61	0.61	0.64	0.59
	A3	0.36	0.34	1.00	0.59	0.43	0.49	0.44
	A4	0.71	0.61	0.59	1.00	0.63	0.60	0.63
	A5	0.74	0.61	0.43	0.63	1.00	0.49	0.58
	A6	0.58	0.64	0.49	0.60	0.49	1.00	0.56
Interface 2	A1	1.00	0.45	0.52	0.39	0.44	0.32	0.42
	A2	0.45	1.00	0.45	0.42	0.65	0.38	0.47
	A3	0.52	0.45	1.00	0.42	0.48	0.45	0.46
	A4	0.39	0.42	0.42	1.00	0.36	0.40	0.40
	A5	0.44	0.65	0.48	0.36	1.00	0.45	0.48
	A6	0.32	0.38	0.45	0.40	0.45	1.00	0.40

Table 2: Kappa agreement between annotators for interface 1 (baseline) and interface 2 (highlight): results show a higher degree of agreement for annotators when using interface 1

random effects.[2] We find that there is a statistically significant relationship between the agreement of annotators and the frequency of changes made during the annotation process. This finding suggests that there are inherent indicators of annotator uncertainty in their behaviour prior to making a final decision.

5 Discussion

After receiving written feedback from annotators following the adoption of the new user interface, it was noted that all annotators stated the highlighting feature was useful. However, when analysing annotator behaviours not all annotators are using the tool. This presents an interesting issue of misaligned incentives, where annotators may feel the need to praise the new interface to maintain their employment status, even if they don't actually find it useful. While it's beneficial to have a consistent pool of annotators for engagement purposes, it's challenging to eliminate the power dynamic that arises from employing them directly. Therefore, performing an interaction-based analysis is valuable as it shows the true nature of tool adoption by annotators. It is possible that the lack of adoption among some annotators is due to unfamiliarity rather than a lack of utility, which may change over time.

In the second setting, we observed a reduction in annotator agreement compared to the first setting, which we attribute to both the change in interface and the new annotation task. Rather than selecting a single best summary, annotators were now allowed to choose multiple summaries, which increased the cognitive load. To determine if the decrease in agreement was due to the interface design or the increased cognitive load, we plan to conduct further experiments while controlling for the task. We also observed that annotator agreement tends to increase with greater exposure to the new interface, which suggests that familiarity with the tool is an important factor to consider.

The new interface has a significant advantage in that it enables us to use annotation behaviour to gain a better understanding of the task of summary comparison. For instance, we have observed that annotators who use the highlight option tend to prefer nouns as their preferred token type to search for. Furthermore, we have found that the stability of annotator choices during annotation (i.e. the frequency of deselecting an option) is a reliable indicator of annotator uncertainty and is strongly correlated with the level of agreement among annotators. These behaviours are statistically significant and can be used to predict the likelihood of achieving high agreement.

6 Limitations and Future Work

The authors would like to emphasise that this paper presents an initial pilot study aimed at documenting the process of updating an internal annotation tool. Our main contribution lies in emphasizing the

[2] Using R formula notation, the model is: $agreement \sim uncertainty + (1|participant) + (1|task)$. Tests were performed using the lme4 and lmerTest R packages by Bates et al. (2014).

influence of task conceptualization and interface design on annotator agreement. Additionally, we draw attention to the significant impact of the interface used for annotating summaries in the current human feedback reinforcement learning paradigm, which is often overlooked.

While there is a distinction between binary selection of the best summary and n-ary ranking, it is still the case that both scenarios involve selecting a preferred top candidate. Therefore, the substantial difference in agreement rates raises questions about the stability of the task and how the experimental setting can affect annotators' perception of summary quality, even among experienced and trained individuals. It is important to acknowledge that due to the variations in experiment settings and interfaces between the two task formats, it is difficult to draw definitive conclusions about the primary factor impacting annotator agreement. However, as an initial exploratory pilot study, our focus was primarily on assessing the tool's robustness and comparing the relative times taken in the different scenarios as well as measuring the annotator's usage of the new tool.

In future work, we will investigate how annotator behaviors can provide insights into the task difficulty and likelihood of agreement. This will involve analysing the interactions with the new interface, such as the time taken to complete the task, the frequency of selecting tokens, and the number of summary selections. By gaining a better understanding of the cognitive processes involved in annotation and how they affect annotator agreement, we can improve the development of annotation tools and methodologies for more accurate reward models.

7 Conclusion

The results of this pilot study emphasise how subtle variations in an annotation task can impact annotator agreement. Even highly experienced annotators can experience fluctuations in agreement as a result of interface changes. To aid in the annotation of summary comparison, we developed a new interface that allows tokens to be selected and displayed across resulting summaries and observed patterns in the types of tokens highlighted by annotators. Moving forward, we plan to conduct additional studies to explore the use of implicit interaction signals in predicting annotator agreement.

References

Yuntao Bai, Andy Jones, Kamal Ndousse, Amanda Askell, Anna Chen, Nova DasSarma, Dawn Drain, Stanislav Fort, Deep Ganguli, Tom Henighan, Nicholas Joseph, Saurav Kadavath, Jackson Kernion, Tom Conerly, Sheer El-Showk, Nelson Elhage, Zac Hatfield-Dodds, Danny Hernandez, Tristan Hume, Scott Johnston, Shauna Kravec, Liane Lovitt, Neel Nanda, Catherine Olsson, Dario Amodei, Tom Brown, Jack Clark, Sam McCandlish, Chris Olah, Ben Mann, and Jared Kaplan. 2022. Training a helpful and harmless assistant with reinforcement learning from human feedback.

Douglas Bates, Martin Mächler, Ben Bolker, and Steve Walker. 2014. Fitting linear mixed-effects models using lme4. *arXiv preprint arXiv:1406.5823*.

Anja Belz and Ehud Reiter. 2006. Comparing automatic and human evaluation of nlg systems. In *11th conference of the european chapter of the association for computational linguistics*, pages 313–320.

Paul N. Bennett, David Maxwell Chickering, and Anton Mityagin. 2009. Learning consensus opinion: mining data from a labeling game. In *Proceedings of the 18th international conference on World wide web*, pages 121–130. ACM.

Carla E. Brodley and Mark A. Friedl. 1999. Identifying mislabeled training data. *Journal of Artificial Intelligence Research*, pages 131–167.

Ben Carterette, Paul N. Bennett, David Maxwell Chickering, and Susan T. Dumais. 2008. Here or there preference judgments for relevance. *Lecture Notes in Computer Science (including subseries Lecture Notes in Artificial Intelligence and Lecture Notes in Bioinformatics)*, 4956 LNCS:16–27.

Mark Collier, Basil Mustafa, Efi Kokiopoulou, Rodolphe Jenatton, and Jesse Berent. 2021. Correlated input-dependent label noise in large-scale image classification. In *Proceedings of the IEEE/CVF Conference on Computer Vision and Pattern Recognition*, pages 1551–1560.

Alexander R Fabbri, Wojciech Kryściński, Bryan McCann, Caiming Xiong, Richard Socher, and Dragomir Radev. 2021. Summeval: Re-evaluating summarization evaluation. *Transactions of the Association for Computational Linguistics*, 9:391–409.

Benoit Frénay and Michel Verleysen. 2014. Classification in the presence of label noise: a survey. *IEEE Transactions on Neural Networks and Learning Systems*, 25(5):845–869.

Dan Gillick and Yang Liu. 2010. Non-expert evaluation of summarization systems is risky. In *Proceedings of the NAACL HLT 2010 Workshop on Creating Speech and Language Data with Amazon's Mechanical Turk*, pages 148–151.

Sian Gooding, Ekaterina Kochmar, Advait Sarkar, and Alan Blackwell. 2019. Comparative judgments are more consistent than binary classification for labelling word complexity. In *Proceedings of the 13th Linguistic Annotation Workshop*, pages 208–214, Florence, Italy. Association for Computational Linguistics.

David Howcroft, Anya Belz, Miruna Clinciu, Dimitra Gkatzia, Sadid A Hasan, Saad Mahamood, Simon Mille, Emiel Van Miltenburg, Sashank Santhanam, and Verena Rieser. 2020. Twenty years of confusion in human evaluation: Nlg needs evaluation sheets and standardised definition. Association for Computational Linguistics (ACL).

Panagiotis G. Ipeirotis, Foster Provost, Victor S. Sheng, and Jing Wang. 2014. Repeated labeling using multiple noisy labelers. *Data Mining and Knowledge Discovery*, 28(2):402–441.

Neslihan Iskender, Tim Polzehl, and Sebastian Möller. 2021. Reliability of human evaluation for text summarization: Lessons learned and challenges ahead. In *Proceedings of the Workshop on Human Evaluation of NLP Systems (HumEval)*, pages 86–96, Online. Association for Computational Linguistics.

Karen Sparck Jones and Julia R Galliers. 1995. Evaluating natural language processing systems: An analysis and review.

David C. Kingsley and Thomas C. Brown. 2010. Preference Uncertainty, Preference Learning, and Paired Comparison Experiments. *Land Economic*, 86:530–544.

Alexandra Kuznetsova, Per B Brockhoff, Rune HB Christensen, et al. 2017. lmertest package: tests in linear mixed effects models. *Journal of statistical software*, 82(13):1–26.

Elena Lloret, Laura Plaza, and Ahmet Aker. 2018. The challenging task of summary evaluation: an overview. *Language Resources and Evaluation*, 52:101–148.

Inderjeet Mani. 2001. Automatic summarization. *Automatic Summarization*, pages 1–298.

Ehud Reiter and Anja Belz. 2009. An investigation into the validity of some metrics for automatically evaluating natural language generation systems. *Computational Linguistics*, 35(4):529–558.

Edwin Simpson, Erik-Lân Do Dinh, Tristan Miller, and Iryna Gurevych. 2019. Predicting Humorousness and Metaphor Novelty with Gaussian Process Preference Learning. In *Proceedings of the 57th Annual Meeting of the Association for Computational Linguistics (ACL 2019)*. Association for Computational Linguistics.

Josef Steinberger and Karel Jezek. 2009. Evaluation measures for text summarization. *Computing and Informatics*, 28(2):251.

Nisan Stiennon, Long Ouyang, Jeff Wu, Daniel M. Ziegler, Ryan Lowe, Chelsea Voss, Alec Radford, Dario Amodei, and Paul F. Christiano. 2020. Learning to summarize from human feedback. *CoRR*, abs/2009.01325.

Chris van der Lee, Albert Gatt, Emiel van Miltenburg, and Emiel Krahmer. 2021. Human evaluation of automatically generated text: Current trends and best practice guidelines. *Computer Speech & Language*, 67:101151.

Yan Yan, Rómer Rosales, Glenn Fung, Mark Schmidt, Gerardo Hermosillo, Luca Bogoni, Linda Moy, and Jennifer G. Dy. 2010. Modeling annotator expertise: Learning when everybody knows a bit of something. In *International conference on artificial intelligence and statistics*, pages 932 – 939.

Yi-Hsuan Yang and Homer H. Chen. 2011. Ranking-Based Emotion Recognition for Music Organization and Retrieval. *IEEE Transactions on Audio, Speech, and Language Processing*, 19:762–774.

A Question Answering Benchmark Database for Hungarian

Attila Novák and **Borbála Novák**
Pázmány Péter Catholic University, Faculty of Information Technology and Bionics
Práter u. 50/a, 1083 Budapest, Hungary
`{surname.firstname}@itk.ppke.hu`

Tamás Zombori and **Gergő Szabó** and **Zsolt Szántó** and **Richárd Farkas**
University of Szeged, Institute of Informatics
Árpád tér 2, 6720 Szeged, Hungary
`ztamas2000@gmail.com {gszabo,szantozs,rfarkas}@inf.u-szeged.hu`

Abstract

Within the research presented in this article, we created a new question answering benchmark database for Hungarian called MILQA. When creating the dataset, we basically followed the principles of the English SQuAD 2.0, however, like in some more recent English question answering datasets, we introduced a number of innovations beyond SQuAD: e.g., yes/no-questions, list-like answers consisting of several text spans, long answers, questions requiring calculation and other question types where you cannot simply copy the answer from the text. For all these non-extractive question types, the pragmatically adequate form of the answer was also added to make the training of generative models possible.

We implemented and evaluated a set of baseline retrieval and answer span extraction models on the dataset. BM25 performed better than any vector-based solution for retrieval. Cross-lingual transfer from English significantly improved span extraction models. [1]

1 Introduction

In this research, our goal was to create a Hungarian question answering dataset that enables the training of Hungarian question answering systems and the automatic evaluation of their performance. In the paper we first review existing systems and resources, then describe the annotation procedure we followed and features of the dataset, closed by the presentation and evaluation of baseline retrieval and extractive answer span extraction models trained and tested on the dataset.

[1]The dataset and trained models can be found on GitHub and the Hugging Face Model Hub searching for the term MILQA.

2 Background

Early question answering databases were either very small in size or did not contain questions in the form of grammatical interrogative sentences, but they consisted of so-called cloze-type "questions": these are declarative sentences, a part of which is masked and this part must be filled in based on the text. The latter resources were machine-generated, so they were easy to create, but the sentences containing the masked part do not resemble real questions at all.

One of the most important milestones in the series of databases used for training question answering systems was the English SQuAD database (Stanford Question Answering Dataset) (Rajpurkar et al., 2016) created at Stanford University. This is a much larger database than the previous ones, containing more than 108,000 question-answer pairs in its first version, which was later further supplemented with questions that could not be answered based on the given text passage (151,000 questions, (Rajpurkar et al., 2018)) in the second version. The publicly available training and tuning set contains 143,000 (93,000 answerable and 50,000 unanswerable) questions. In addition to its size, this resource can be considered a breakthrough because, on the one hand, unlike previous resources containing cloze-type questions (e.g. CNN/Daily Mail (Hermann et al., 2015)), it actually contained well-formed questions and on the other hand, it was not built of multiple-choice questions (e.g. MCTest (Richardson et al., 2013) or WikiQA (Yang et al., 2015)). Furthermore, it gave a huge boost to the development of question answering systems.

Among question answering datasets and systems, we can distinguish extractive and generative approaches. In the case of the former, the answer is simply a highlighted part of the text (as if we

Proceedings of the 17th Linguistic Annotation Workshop (LAW-XVII), pages 188–198
July 13, 2023 ©2023 Association for Computational Linguistics

were working with a text highlighter, this is what SQuAD is like), and in the case of the latter, the answer is actually formulated in well-formed human language (e.g. MS MARCO (Nguyen et al., 2016), NarrativeQA (Kočiský et al., 2018)). In addition, some of the QA databases contain questions that require the execution of multi-step inference chains to arrive at an answer (multi-hop/multi-step QA tasks). This not only means a greater complexity of the underlying logical derivation, but this type of task can also go beyond the level of individual documents or text fragments, if the given question can only be answered by combining the information contained in several different documents or text fragments (e.g. HotpotQA (Yang et al., 2018), NarrativeQA (Kočiský et al., 2018)).

In the case of the multi-step question answering tasks and SQuAD, it was the task of the annotators to formulate questions based on given texts. Companies operating large search engines, however, created resources in which relevant documents were collected based on frequent questions entered into the search engine, and the annotators selected or formulated the answers using these results. Natural Questions (NQ, Kwiatkowski et al. (2019)) based on questions entered into the Google search engine belongs to the former extractive type. In NQ, the documents used as context were Wikipedia articles, similar to SQuAD. The MS MARCO QnA dataset based on Microsoft Bing queries belongs to the latter abstractive/generative type (Nguyen et al., 2016). Resources based on existing quiz and literacy question sets were also created using similar web query techniques (e.g. TriviaQA (Joshi et al., 2017)).

Perhaps one of the sources of SQuAD's popularity was that it assumes a relatively simplistic model, according to which a single coherent span of text can be selected as an answer for each answerable question, which greatly simplifies the implementation of SQuAD-based systems. This restriction can be implemented well if the annotators are instructed to ask only questions that can be answered in this manner. However, in the case of a non-negligible part of real-life questions, the answer is some kind of list, the elements of which do not necessarily occupy a single contiguous span of the text. In such cases, a single span including all relevant answers may contain a significant amount of text that is irrelevant to the answer. For example, in the Natural Questions dataset based on real questions, the answer is not a single span for 6.9% of the questions. In the case of SQuAD, the context of the questions (the part of the text in which the answer to the question must be found) has a relatively limited length: between 150 and 4000 characters, with an average of 740 characters, which also limits the complexity of the task.

Yes-no questions naturally occur in datasets similar to NQ (Natural Questions: 2.5%) that originate from actually asked questions. Typically, the answer to these questions is not a selected part of the text, but a (usually probable, not clear) yes/no answer follows from a relevant part of the text. There are also datasets specifically containing only yes-no questions (e.g. BoolQ (Clark et al., 2019), also based on Wikipedia, AmazonYesNo (Dzendzik et al., 2019), based on texts related to Amazon product reviews, or the biomedical PubMedQA based on article abstracts (Jin et al., 2019)). At the same time, BoolQ and AmazonYesNo show significant overlap with the yes-no questions in NaturalQuestions and AmazonQA (Gupta et al., 2019) databases (in the case of Amazon resources, there is essentially a subset relationship).

In biomedical question sets of "natural origin", similarly to NQ, the proportion of "non-SQuAD-compatible" questions is often much higher than previously mentioned in relation to the NQ database. For example, in the case of the Clinical Questions Collection (CQC) data set (D'Alessandro et al., 2004; Ely et al., 1997, 1999) containing questions formulated by actual practicing doctors during their daily professional activities and the PubMed Query Log Dataset (Herskovic et al., 2007) composed of questions formulated by PubMed users in a single day, the proportion of yes-no questions is 28.1%, and that of list-type answers is 21.9% (Yoon et al., 2022).

In addition to the lack of list-type answers and the scarcity of yes-no questions, another problem with extractive datasets arises from the fact that questions about a given text often do not use the same words that appeared in the original context. During the compilation of SQuAD, annotators were encouraged to paraphrase the part of the question anchored to the context when formulating the questions, and not simply copy it. This in itself is not necessarily a serious problem for neural models based on current pre-trained language models, since these usually have sufficiently abstract internal semantic representations to often avoid that

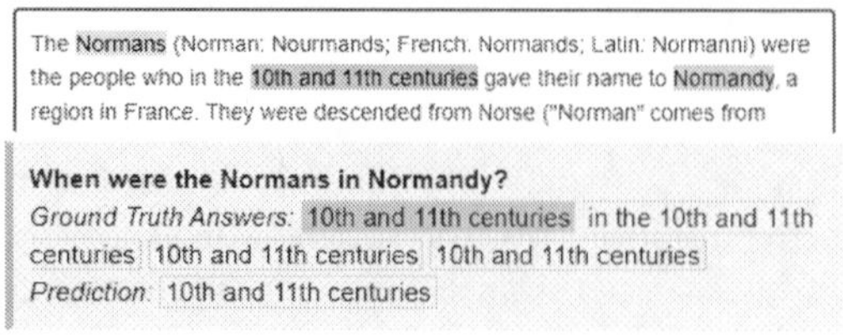

Figure 1: In SQuAD, relevant prepositions are usually not included in the answer

paraphrases confuse them. However, if we use a verb in the question different from the one in the original context, then this often involves a different argument frame, which means that the given expression should often appear in the answer in a form different from that in the original text. In the case of SQuAD, the solution to this problem was that prepositions were not made part of the answer, but only the minimal lexical content (annotators were instructed to do so, see Fig. 1.).

In the case of English, an essentially isolating language, this solves the above problem in most cases, but at the price that the answer of the system is often not formulated in a pragmatically appropriate form (the latter would include the preposition). In the case of languages, where case is marked morphologically, this solution obviously does not work. In such cases an extractive QA system will definitely give an inadequate answer, because it returns the answer with the original case appearing in the text. At the same time, this does not represent a real problem if the answer is presented as highlighted text in context, since in this case the user does not feel that the machine "answered in a strange manner", but rather that it "highlighted the answer correctly in the text". If, however, the answer is presented as an answer, then it is definitely necessary to move on and use a generative model.

We illustrate the problem with an example in Hungarian. In the context of *Péternek az idegeire ment a zaj.* 'The noise got on Peter's nerves.' (here *Péter* 'Peter' is in the dative case), the adequate short answer to the question *Kit idegesített a zaj?* 'Who was annoyed by the noise?' would be *Pétert* (in accusative), but this cannot be extracted in this form from the original context. Here, the complete sentence would be an adequate (but not minimal) answer to the question. However, this is often not the case, especially when the original context contains the answer in a derived form. In the context *A Duna Európa második leghosszabb folyama az oroszországi Volga után.* 'The Danube is the second-longest river in Europe, after the Volga in Russia.', the adequate answer to the question *Melyik országban található Európa leghosszabb folyama?* 'In which country is the longest river in Europe?' would be *Oroszországban* 'In Russia' (inessive of *Oroszország*). The word form *oroszországi* in the original context is an adjective derived from the name of the country (and as such, it is decapitalized). Here, the original sentence would not be an adequate answer, either.

There are some additional question types: question-answer pairs that require counting, the execution of some arithmetic operations, or comparison *(how many, how much, which is the most... etc.),* which are not a problem even for people with minimal education, but the models must be specially prepared to perform such tasks in order to prevent the machine from failing miserably. The DROP (Dua et al., 2019) question-answer database primarily focuses on such questions.

Some resources approach the problem of answering questions in the context of a dialogue. The questions are often ambiguous or incomplete, and additional information is needed to answer them. Data sets such as ShARC (Saeidi et al., 2018) aim at modeling such situations. Training the groundbreaking ChatGPT model of OpenAI required extensive dialog modeling resources as well as further human-in-the-loop annotation for reinforcement learning.

2.1 Non English resources

All the previously mentioned question answering databases (and countless others) are in English. At the same time, the presented methods have been adapted to many other languages, and multilingual question answering datasets have also been created.

Relatively many and large datasets in Chinese have been created. The best known is DuReader (He et al., 2018) based on Baidu searches and Baidu Zhidao, a Chinese question-and-answer platform.

Based on the SQuAD approach, French (FQuAD 2.0, Heinrich et al. 2022, almost 80000 questions), Korean (KorQuAD 2.0, Youngmin Kim 2020, 100000 questions), Russian (SberQuAD, Efimov et al. 2020) and German (GermanQuAD, Möller et al. 2021, approx. 14000 questions) resources have also been created. XQuAD (Artetxe et al., 2019) contains translations of 1190 question-answer pairs related to 240 paragraphs from the

SQuAD 1.1 tuning set (dev. set) by professional translators in 10 languages.

The MLQA benchmark database covering six other languages in addition to English (Lewis et al. (2020); about 12,000 question-answer pairs for English and 5-6 thousand question-answer pairs for the other languages), is built around quasi-equivalent Wikipedia sentences to which the questions were translated from English by translators. SQuAD has been machine-translated into several languages (e.g., Korean, Hindi, Japanese, Spanish, Czech, French, and the languages included in the MLQA dataset).

11 typologically diverse languages are covered by the TyDi QA dataset (Clark et al. (2020); a total of 200,000 question-answer pairs), which is also based on Wikipedia. The questions were formulated based on the introductory section of the articles only, but you could ask anything related to the topic. Thus, most of the questions formulated in TyDi QA do not have an answer, but where there is, the method guarantees that the question is formulated differently than the answer.

3 A new Hungarian question answering benchmark dataset

Within the research presented in this paper, we created the first publicly available extractive question answering benchmark dataset in Hungarian. When creating the database, we largely followed the principles of SQuAD 2.0, however, similar to some of the more recent English Q&A databases (Natural Questions, MS MARCO, DROP) mentioned in section 2, we introduced a number of new question-answer types, which contain more difficult but more realistic tasks.

Similarly to SQuAD 2.0, the corpus is characterized by the following: **a)** high-quality Wikipedia articles serve as context for the questions, **b)** factual (not opinion-type) questions are included, **c)** also contains questions that are not answered in the given text, **d)** in the original text, we marked the shortest possible answer to the given question (if any), **e)** when formulating the questions, we paraphrased the original text, so in most cases the answer cannot be found using a lexical search, **f)** the questions can be interpreted not only in the context of the given text, but also as independent questions (e.g. they do not contain unanchored pronouns).

Compared to SQuAD, we introduced the following innovations (special question types are explicitly marked in the database): **a)** There may be more than one short answer to the given question in the given text (list type answer, approx. 8.5% of the answered questions). **b)** In addition to the short answer, we also gave a long answer, which includes all the relevant information necessary to answer the question (min. 1 clause, often several sentences). **c)** It contains yes-no questions (about 9%). Here, in addition to the long answer containing the essential circumstances, an explicit yes/no answer is also specified (or the lack of a clear binary answer is indicated). **d)** The unanswerable questions (about 28.3% of the questions) are relevant questions related to the given topic, not questions generated by substitution from questions having an answer. **e)** There are also questions that can only be answered after performing counting or arithmetic operations (similarly to the DROP database). Calculations involve counting of listed elements, calculation of dates, durations and other quantities with simple arithmetic operations. **f)** Some of the unanswerable questions are tricky questions, where people would easily infer an answer from the text based on wrong default assumptions. These cases were marked separately, and the assumed answer was also indicated. **g)** If the expression in the text does not correspond to the form in which the given question should be answered (e.g. the original case ending is not appropriate), the annotators have provided the form of the answer appropriate in the context of the question.

3.1 Creation of the corpus

In order to create the data set that forms the basis of the database, we selected articles from the Hungarian Wikipedia marked as featured or high quality articles, and sorted them based on their page visit counts between the beginning of 2016 and the end of 2021. From this list, the annotators selected the articles to be annotated based on their personal interests in order to avoid that the annotation task become unpleasant or boring to them. They were also encouraged to abandon and report articles they found low quality or uninteresting and to move on to a new task. We used the first section of each article and, in addition, a maximum of 10 randomly selected sections of at least 500 characters. Similarly to SQuAD, the units were paragraphs, but paragraphs shorter than 500 characters were combined, and we omitted those longer than approximately

1200 characters (text sections of this size could be clearly displayed on the annotation interface).

The annotation interface was created by customizing version 1.4 of the Label Studio open source web annotation platform. It was a relatively complex task to make the interface suitable for asking questions, marking the corresponding answers, and marking special question and answer types in a intuitive manner, but we managed to create a relatively easy-to-use user interface and workflow for the annotators. (Figure 2.).

Questions were added as text markup by the annotators. Answerable questions were numbered. We used the span annotation feature of Label Studio, usually used to do named entity annotation, to mark the long/short answers. Questions and answers were matched on the basis of the question number. List answers were marked as a set of spans referring to the same question number. As overlapping spans marking answers to different questions could easily clutter the annotation interface, shortcuts could be used to make answer spans belonging to other questions invisible. The answers could be marked as yes/no/arithmetic/non-extractive/wrong (for tricky unanswerable questions), and an explicit non-extractive answer was entered for arithmetic and non-extractive questions.

The annotation system provided the annotators with continuous statistics on the progress, and they could also invoke the display of all questions and extracted short and long answers belonging to the given context to check that the answers were marked as intended. The annotation was made by five annotators. Apart from the more problematic cases that were later re-edited, the time required for the work can be estimated well based on the editing time stored by Label Studio: it took roughly 85 seconds per question to formulate the questions and mark the long and short answer spans and the eventual reformulation of the answer if necessary.

A part of the corpus containing 2391 questions (including 1751 answerable questions) consisting of 36 articles (roughly 10% of the corpus) was separated for a test/tuning set, and two independent annotations were made for this part. The annotation work, which did not require writing questions, progressed faster: it took an average of 46 seconds to mark the long and short answers.

Type	number	ratio
There is an answer	**16992**	71,67%
. Yes-no	1621	9,20%
. . Yes	859	52,99%
. . No	638	39,36%
. . Uncertain	124	7,65%
. Not an extractive answer	4452	26,20%
. Arithmetics	427	2,51%
. List	1455	8,56%
. Not SQuAD-compatible	5203	30,62%
No answer	**6716**	28,33%
. Tricky no answer	629	9,37%
Sum	**23708**	100

Table 1: Distribution of question and answer types in the dataset. For subtypes, the ratio column indicates the ratio within the given main type.

3.2 Features of the corpus

The database contains a total of 23,700 (17,000 answerable and 6,700 unanswerable) questions. Questions were created for 142 Wikipedia articles. In Table 1, we have summarized the occurrence of special question and answer types in the corpus.

9.20% of the questions are yes-no questions. In the case of 7.65% of these, there is no clear yes/no answer, but the text reflects that the opinions on the given question are diverse, the results are mixed, or there is uncertainty. At the same time, this is not the same as the case of unanswerable questions, where the text does not answer the question at all: here the text explicitly reveals that the world is not black and white from the point of view of the given question. In the case of yes-no questions, the span annotation is relevant in the sense that the answer follows from the marked spans. The yes-no question type is not SQuAD-incompatible in itself: the original SQuAD also contains yes-no questions, which were all formulated in a way that a nice extractive answer could be given to them. What is new here is that the annotation includes an explicit marking for this type of questions and whether the answer is yes or no. About 9% of unanswerable questions are yes-no questions.

The annotation environment and specification allowed annotators to work free from the usual restrictions in SQuAD (i.e. that the answer should be exactly a single span in the text). This resulted in more than 30% of the questions that have an answer in the text being not SQuAD compatible. 26.2% of the (answered) questions are not extrac-

Figure 2: The annotation interface for the corpus is based on Label Studio

tive: the natural form of the answer to the given question would be different from what is in the text (e.g. the given expression would need to have a different case ending to be an adequate answer to the question). To answer 2.51% of the questions, some calculations need to be performed (similarly to those in the DROP database; the answer cannot be copied from the text for these either, so they are included in the former 26.2%). And for 8.56% of the questions, SQuAD's "single contiguous answer span" assumption is not fulfilled (this set also partially overlaps with cases where the form needs to be modified to be adequate).

9.37% of unanswerable questions are tricky. For these, one tends to derive an answer based on some rule-of-thumb assumptions (even by doing calculations), the result of which could easily prove to be wrong. For example, in a particular paragraph of the Normandy landings article, from the fact that the fleet units participating in the landings had three commanders, one might infer that there were three fleet units; in fact, there were only two, and there was a commander-in-chief.

As for question words, the most common questions ask about the subject (>17%), dates/times (>10%), reasons (>8%), quantities (>7%) and places ($\sim$ 7%).

4 Models and performance

We created and evaluated a number of document retrieval and reader (answer span extraction) models using the dataset. For document retrieval, we evaluated both traditional lexical and various vector-based retrieval models. For span extraction, we finetuned both a monolingual Hungarian model and multilingual models. We also tested to what extent cross-lingual transfer from English can be applied to this specific task.

4.1 Document retrieval models

The first model we applied for document retrieval was a BM25-based solution (Robertson and Zaragoza, 2009) using Elasticsearch. BM25 (Best Matching 25) is a simple and effective ranking function widely used in information retrieval systems. It takes into account term frequency, document length and inverse document frequency to calculate the score representing the relevance of a document to a query. Our first experiment concerned the question to what extent traditional preprocessing steps like lemmatization or part-of-speech-based term filtering can improve retrieval performance. We expected some improvement, because Hungarian is a morphologically rich language. We performed preprocessing using components of the HuSpaCy library (Orosz et al., 2022; Szabó et al., 2023). In this experiment, we tested the accuracy of selecting the exact paragraph corresponding to answerable questions from all paragraphs in the dataset. The results are shown in Table 2. We have found that applying lemmatization and a simple PoS-based filter to eliminate wh-words improves retrieval per-

Preprocessing	R@1	R@3	R@4	R@5	R@10	R@300	MRR@300	@300-w-time
Base	0.438	0.595	0.627	0.655	0.729	0.896	0.538	466.17 s
PoS	0.448	0.603	0.636	0.665	0.741	0.878	0.547	262.25 s
Lemma	0.647	0.807	0.835	0.858	0.908	0.984	0.740	505.53 s
PoSLemma	0.656	0.814	0.844	0.866	0.916	0.984	0.748	385.31 s

Table 2: Evaluation of the effect of preprocessing on BM25 retrieval performance. Evaluated on all answerable questions and the corresponding paragraph from a pool of all paragraphs. R@1..300: Recall/match with a cutoff at position 1 ... 300. MRR@300: Mean Reciprocal Rank (with retrieval cutoff at 300 documents). Lemma: applying lemmatization. PoS: applying a simple PoS-based filter to eliminate wh-words from the query.

formance significantly.

In the follow-up retrieval experiments, all query results in which the gold answer was present *exactly* in the form given in the dataset, was accepted as a valid hit. First, we tested how performance (recall/MRR) of the retrieval model depends on the document entity type stored in the database. The results are shown in Table 3. Results in the upper half of the table are for configurations where only articles covered in the dataset were added to the document pool. In the configurations shown in bottom half of the table, we increased the size of the document pool 30 fold by adding further 4927 randomly selected Wikipedia articles.

We also evaluated sentence-transformer-based embedding and dense passage retrieval (DPR) models for context retrieval (on the base in-dataset-passages-only pool). There is no such model specifically trained for Hungarian, so we tested an English model trained specifically on QA datasets (multi-qa-mpnet-base-dot-v1) and multilingual models (which were trained on semantic similarity/paraphrase rather than QA tasks). We also tested a multilingual DPR model (it is a pair of encoders; one for the question and another for the context: dpr-(question/ctx)_encoder-bert-base-multilingual). We used the retrieval engines implemented in Haystack (Deepset GmbH, 2022). We compared the results with Haystack's BM25 implementation, which differs from our own in that it does not involve lemmatization. The results are shown in Table 4.

All embedding-based models performed significantly worse than the simple and fast BM25 model. Of the vector-based models, multilingual models covering Hungarian finetuned on paraphrase databases performed best. The DPR model had the weakest performance in spite of being both multilingual and specifically trained for QA passage retrieval. The English-only QA-trained *mpnet* model performed significantly better than the multilingual paraphrase-based *distiluse-bmc-v1* model (USE: Universal Sentence Encoder), which does not cover Hungarian, either.

4.2 Reader models

In our experiments concerning reader models, we finetuned baseline answer span extraction models. Here we used only the unproblematic SQuAD-compatible questions in the dataset (i.e. where the extracted answers need not be reformulated to be adequate and arithmetic reasoning is not needed.) There was one exception to this: we created two versions of each model variant that differed in how multispan answers were handled. In one version, individual spans were handled in the training and test set as if they were independent question answer pairs. In another version, questions with multispan answers were omitted from both the training and the test set. The *with multispan* and *no multispan* columns of Table. 5 on model evaluation correspond to these model versions. The models do not currently properly handle multispan answers, because they consider the most likely span only. As an orthogonal dimension, we created and evaluated models on short and long answers. The long answers task is easier: only the clauses relevant to the question need to be identified rather without focusing on the actual answer.

We finetuned models from scratch from the Hungarian BERT base model huBERT (Nemeskey, 2021) on the short and long answers in the dataset (hubert-base-T in Table. 5). The model turned out to be undertrained for the short answer task. So we experimented with knowledge transfer from SQuAD 2.0. We tested one model finetuned from huBERT on a machine translated version of SQuAD 2.0 (huBert-squadv2[2]), and two XLM-RoBERTa-based models finetuned by Deepset di-

[2] https://huggingface.co/mcsabai/huBert-fine-tuned-hungarian-squadv2

	R@1	R@3	R@4	R@5	R@10	R@300	MRR@300	@300-w-time
In-dataset articles only								
Base	0.662	0.816	0.846	0.868	0.919	0.984	0.753	453.48 s
Paragraphs	0.475	0.621	0.651	0.675	0.736	0.872	0.567	502.12 s
Sections	0.577	0.741	0.772	0.791	0.837	0.896	0.671	839.22 s
Articles	0.824	0.879	0.885	0.888	0.896	-	-	-
In-dataset + 4927 random articles								
Paragraphs	0.412	0.562	0.593	0.618	0.682	0.860	0.506	486.17 s
Sections	0.485	0.664	0.704	0.729	0.792	0.891	0.593	708.12 s
Articles	0.617	0.733	0.754	0.768	0.804	0.904	0.686	20188.95 s

Table 3: Retrieval performance wrt. document entity types in the document pool. Evaluated on all answerable questions. The rows represent the configuration of document entities in the database. Base: In-dataset paragraphs only. Paragraphs: all paragraphs of all Wiki articles in the pool. Sections: all sections of articles. Articles: all full articles. R@1..300: Recall/match with a cutoff at position 1 ... 300. MRR@300: Mean Reciprocal Rank (with retrieval cutoff at 300 documents).

Model	Lang/training	R@10	MRR@10
haystack BM25		**0.817**	**0.626**
multi-qa-mpnet-base-dot-v1	English only QA	0.483	0.285
paraphrase-multilingual-MiniLM-L12-v2	multiling. paraphrase	0.566	0.315
distiluse-base-multilingual-cased-v1	15 lang USE	0.299	0.150
distiluse-base-multilingual-cased-v2	50+ lang USE	**0.589**	**0.326**
dpr-encoder-bert-base-multilingual	m-BERT-based DPR	0.281	0.123

Table 4: Evaluation of vector-based retrieval models on the base in-dataset-passages-only pool. BM25 far outperformed all of them. The best model performance is in bold.

rectly on SQuAD 2.0 (xlmr-(base/large)-squad2[3]). Zero-shot performance of these models is shown in the zero-shot section of Table 5. As these models were not trained to identify long answers, they unsurprisingly perform poorly on that task (with the exception of question types where short answers tend to be full clauses, like *why* questions). Also xlmR-base-squad2 performed worse than huBert-squadv2 across the board in spite of the fact that xlmR-base is more resource-hungry (in part due to its extensive multilingual token dictionary and the corresponding embeddings), so we did not include xlmR-base-squad2 in the further finetuning experiments. On the other hand, all these models performed better on the short answer task than hubert-base-T finetuned from scratch.

In the next round, we finetuned huBert-squadv2 and xlmR-large-squad2 on our train data . The models perform much better than huBert-base-T. One surprising result, however, is that while F_1 scores consistently improved, exact match scores worsened compared to the short answer span zero-shot models. We need to investigate why this happened. xlmR-large-squad2-T performs best in this group. On the other hand, this model is much more resource hungry than the monolingual BERT-base-sized models.

Finally, we turned to the Retro-Reader model type, which involves a cascade of sketchy and intensive reader models (Zhang et al., 2021). The training and evaluation of these models is in progress, but preliminary results presented in Table 5 show that they outperform all other models on the short answer task. On the other hand, training these models requires about twice as much computation as the vanilla single transformer models as they are combination of two models. Inference also requires twice as much computation and memory.

5 Conclusions

We presented a new QA benchmark database in Hungarian, that in several aspects, goes beyond SQuAD-type datasets: it is not limited to single contiguous short extractive answer spans, contains yes/no questions, non-contiguous multispan short answers, long answers, questions requiring arith-

[3] `https://huggingface.co/deepset/xlm-roberta-large-squad2`

model	short answers				long answers			
	with multispan		no multispan		with multispan		no multispan	
	F_1	EM	F_1	EM	F_1	EM	F_1	EM
Zero-shot models								
huBert-squadv2	0.595	0.473	0.653	0.538	*0.331*	*0.170*	*0.332*	*0.171*
xlmR-base-squad2	0.553	0.442	0.612	0.507	0.323	0.182	0.325	0.183
xlmR-large-squad2	0.646	0.516	0.712	0.591	0.372	0.204	0.373	0.205
Transformers QA models finetuned on the train set								
huBert-base-T	0.439	0.258	0.486	0.304	0.701	0.383	0.706	0.388
huBert-squadv2-T	0.659	0.404	0.737	0.469	0.742	0.423	0.747	0.429
xlmR-large-squad2-T	0.686	0.439	0.768	0.512	0.766	0.436	0.772	0.441
Retro-Reader QA models finetuned on the train set								
hubert-base-RR	0.675	0.555						
huBert-squadv2-RR	0.702	0.572						
xlmR-large-squad2-RR	**0.724**	**0.623**						

Table 5: Performance of extractive reader models on short and long answer spans with and without multispan answers.

metic reasoning, and other questions where the answer cannot be simply copied from the text. The annotation was created using a customized Label-Studio-based annotation platform. The annotators were encouraged to get actively involved in selecting the texts to be annotated and to abandon annotation of uninteresting or low quality texts in order to make the annotation task less boring and demotivating. We also trained and evaluated baseline models for document retrieval and reader models for answer span extraction. Cross-lingual knowledge transfer naturally facilitated by multilingual transformer models was found to be beneficial for the quality of the trained models.

Limitations

In light of the near human-like lingustic performance of the groundbreaking ChatGPT model that has attracted unprecedented public attention, one can't help feeling extremely humble about the importance of the work presented in this paper on a basically extractive QA dataset in a niche agglutinating language (even if it contains annotation that can be used for training generative models capable of handling questions that cannot be answered adequately in an extractive manner). On the other hand, while we obviously do not have the resources needed to train, finetune or even run the sort of large language models that have the chance of replicating ChatGPT's behavior, models that can more-or-less decently handle the much less resource-intensive task of extracting and displaying relevant answers from stored documents in a language not too much interesting for big tech companies can be trained and run even on hardware available in our modestly equipped academic environment. Not to mention that this approach also inherently avoids the most imminent and difficult-to-handle problem of large generative models that they tend to hallucinate seemingly very convincing non-facts and to generate toxic content.

The resource is also very limited in extent compared to similar English resources both concerning size and the number of parallel annotations. In our baseline model training experiments, we have not tackled the problem of multispan answers, questions requiring counting or arithmetic reasoning, and we have not trained generative models to handle questions that cannot be answered adequately in an extractive manner.

Acknowledgements

This research was implemented with support provided by grant FK 125217 of the National Research, Development and Innovation Office of Hungary financed under the FK 17 funding scheme, and by the Ministry of Innovation and Technology NRDI Office and subsequently the European Union project RRF-2.3.1-21-2022-00004 within the framework of the Artificial Intelligence National Laboratory Program.

References

Mikel Artetxe, Sebastian Ruder, and Dani Yogatama. 2019. On the cross-lingual transferability of monolingual representations. *CoRR*, abs/1910.11856.

Christopher Clark, Kenton Lee, Ming-Wei Chang, Tom Kwiatkowski, Michael Collins, and Kristina Toutanova. 2019. BoolQ: Exploring the surprising difficulty of natural yes/no questions. In *Proceedings of the 2019 Conference of the North American Chapter of the Association for Computational Linguistics: Human Language Technologies, Volume 1 (Long and Short Papers)*, pages 2924–2936, Minneapolis, Minnesota. Association for Computational Linguistics.

Jonathan H. Clark, Eunsol Choi, Michael Collins, Dan Garrette, Tom Kwiatkowski, Vitaly Nikolaev, and Jennimaria Palomaki. 2020. TyDi QA: A benchmark for information-seeking question answering in typologically diverse languages. *Transactions of the Association for Computational Linguistics*, 8:454–470.

Deepset GmbH. 2022. Haystack. Computer software.

Dheeru Dua, Yizhong Wang, Pradeep Dasigi, Gabriel Stanovsky, Sameer Singh, and Matt Gardner. 2019. DROP: A reading comprehension benchmark requiring discrete reasoning over paragraphs. In *Proceedings of the 2019 Conference of the North American Chapter of the Association for Computational Linguistics: Human Language Technologies, Volume 1 (Long and Short Papers)*, pages 2368–2378, Minneapolis, Minnesota. Association for Computational Linguistics.

Daria Dzendzik, Carl Vogel, and Jennifer Foster. 2019. Is it dish washer safe? Automatically answering "yes/no" questions using customer reviews. In *Proceedings of the 2019 Conference of the North American Chapter of the Association for Computational Linguistics: Student Research Workshop*, pages 1–6, Minneapolis, Minnesota. Association for Computational Linguistics.

Donna M D'Alessandro, Clarence D Kreiter, and Michael W Peterson. 2004. An evaluation of information-seeking behaviors of general pediatricians. *Pediatrics*, 113(1):64–69.

Pavel Efimov, Andrey Chertok, Leonid Boytsov, and Pavel Braslavski. 2020. SberQuAD – Russian reading comprehension dataset: Description and analysis. In *Experimental IR Meets Multilinguality, Multimodality, and Interaction*, pages 3–15, Cham. Springer International Publishing.

John W Ely, Jerome A Osheroff, Mark H Ebell, George R Bergus, Barcey T Levy, M Lee Chambliss, and Eric R Evans. 1999. Analysis of questions asked by family doctors regarding patient care. *Bmj*, 319(7206):358–361.

John W Ely, Jerome A Osheroff, Kristi J Ferguson, M Lee Chambliss, Daniel C Vinson, and Joyce L Moore. 1997. Lifelong self-directed learning using a computer database of clinical questions. *Journal of family practice*, 45(5):382–390.

Mansi Gupta, Nitish Kulkarni, Raghuveer Chanda, Anirudha Rayasam, and Zachary C. Lipton. 2019. AmazonQA: A review-based question answering task. In *Proceedings of the Twenty-Eighth International Joint Conference on Artificial Intelligence, IJCAI-19*, pages 4996–5002. International Joint Conferences on Artificial Intelligence Organization.

Wei He, Kai Liu, Jing Liu, Yajuan Lyu, Shiqi Zhao, Xinyan Xiao, Yuan Liu, Yizhong Wang, Hua Wu, Qiaoqiao She, Xuan Liu, Tian Wu, and Haifeng Wang. 2018. DuReader: a Chinese machine reading comprehension dataset from real-world applications. In *Proceedings of the Workshop on Machine Reading for Question Answering*, pages 37–46, Melbourne, Australia. Association for Computational Linguistics.

Quentin Heinrich, Gautier Viaud, and Wacim Belblidia. 2022. FQuAD2.0: French question answering and learning when you don't know. In *Proceedings of the Thirteenth Language Resources and Evaluation Conference*, pages 2205–2214, Marseille, France. European Language Resources Association.

Karl Moritz Hermann, Tomás Kociský, Edward Grefenstette, Lasse Espeholt, Will Kay, Mustafa Suleyman, and Phil Blunsom. 2015. Teaching machines to read and comprehend. In *Advances in Neural Information Processing Systems*, pages 1693–1701.

Jorge R Herskovic, Len Y Tanaka, William Hersh, and Elmer V Bernstam. 2007. A day in the life of PubMed: analysis of a typical day's query log. *Journal of the American Medical Informatics Association*, 14(2):212–220.

Qiao Jin, Bhuwan Dhingra, Zhengping Liu, William Cohen, and Xinghua Lu. 2019. PubMedQA: A dataset for biomedical research question answering. In *Proceedings of the 2019 Conference on Empirical Methods in Natural Language Processing and the 9th International Joint Conference on Natural Language Processing (EMNLP-IJCNLP)*, pages 2567–2577, Hong Kong, China. Association for Computational Linguistics.

Mandar Joshi, Eunsol Choi, Daniel Weld, and Luke Zettlemoyer. 2017. TriviaQA: A large scale distantly supervised challenge dataset for reading comprehension. In *Proceedings of the 55th Annual Meeting of the Association for Computational Linguistics (Volume 1: Long Papers)*, pages 1601–1611, Vancouver, Canada. Association for Computational Linguistics.

Tomáš Kočiský, Jonathan Schwarz, Phil Blunsom, Chris Dyer, Karl Moritz Hermann, Gábor Melis, and Edward Grefenstette. 2018. The NarrativeQA reading comprehension challenge. *Transactions of the Association for Computational Linguistics*, 6:317–328.

Tom Kwiatkowski, Jennimaria Palomaki, Olivia Redfield, Michael Collins, Ankur Parikh, Chris Alberti,

Danielle Epstein, Illia Polosukhin, Jacob Devlin, Kenton Lee, Kristina Toutanova, Llion Jones, Matthew Kelcey, Ming-Wei Chang, Andrew M. Dai, Jakob Uszkoreit, Quoc Le, and Slav Petrov. 2019. Natural Questions: A benchmark for question answering research. *Transactions of the Association for Computational Linguistics*, 7:452–466.

Patrick Lewis, Barlas Oguz, Ruty Rinott, Sebastian Riedel, and Holger Schwenk. 2020. MLQA: Evaluating cross-lingual extractive question answering. In *Proceedings of the 58th Annual Meeting of the Association for Computational Linguistics*, pages 7315–7330, Online. Association for Computational Linguistics.

Timo Möller, Julian Risch, and Malte Pietsch. 2021. GermanQuAD and GermanDPR: Improving non-English question answering and passage retrieval. In *Proceedings of the 3rd Workshop on Machine Reading for Question Answering*, pages 42–50, Punta Cana, Dominican Republic. Association for Computational Linguistics.

Dávid Márk Nemeskey. 2021. Introducing huBERT. In *XVII. Magyar Számítógépes Nyelvészeti Konferencia*, pages 3–14, Szeged. Szegedi Tudományegyetem, Informatikai Intézet.

Tri Nguyen, Mir Rosenberg, Xia Song, Jianfeng Gao, Saurabh Tiwary, Rangan Majumder, and Li Deng. 2016. MS MARCO: A human generated machine reading comprehension dataset. In *Proceedings of the Workshop on Cognitive Computation: Integrating neural and symbolic approaches 2016 co-located with the 30th Annual Conference on Neural Information Processing Systems (NIPS 2016), Barcelona, Spain, December 9, 2016*, volume 1773 of *CEUR Workshop Proceedings*. CEUR-WS.org.

György Orosz, Zsolt Szántó, Péter Berkecz, Gergő Szabó, and Richárd Farkas. 2022. HuSpaCy: An Industrial-strength Hungarian Natural Language Processing Toolkit. In *XVIII. Magyar Számítógépes Nyelvészeti Konferencia*, pages 59–73, Szeged. Szegedi Tudományegyetem, Informatikai Intézet.

Pranav Rajpurkar, Robin Jia, and Percy Liang. 2018. Know what you don't know: Unanswerable questions for SQuAD. In *Proceedings of the 56th Annual Meeting of the Association for Computational Linguistics (Volume 2: Short Papers)*, pages 784–789, Melbourne, Australia. Association for Computational Linguistics.

Pranav Rajpurkar, Jian Zhang, Konstantin Lopyrev, and Percy Liang. 2016. SQuAD: 100,000+ questions for machine comprehension of text. In *Proceedings of the 2016 Conference on Empirical Methods in Natural Language Processing*, pages 2383–2392, Austin, Texas. Association for Computational Linguistics.

Matthew Richardson, Christopher J.C. Burges, and Erin Renshaw. 2013. MCTest: A challenge dataset for the open-domain machine comprehension of text. In *Proceedings of the 2013 Conference on Empirical Methods in Natural Language Processing*, pages 193–203, Seattle, Washington, USA. Association for Computational Linguistics.

Stephen Robertson and Hugo Zaragoza. 2009. The probabilistic relevance framework: BM25 and beyond. *Foundations and Trends in Information Retrieval*, 3:333–389.

Marzieh Saeidi, Max Bartolo, Patrick Lewis, Sameer Singh, Tim Rocktäschel, Mike Sheldon, Guillaume Bouchard, and Sebastian Riedel. 2018. Interpretation of natural language rules in conversational machine reading. In *Proceedings of the 2018 Conference on Empirical Methods in Natural Language Processing*, pages 2087–2097, Brussels, Belgium. Association for Computational Linguistics.

Gergő Szabó, György Orosz, Zsolt Szántó, Péter Berkecz, and Richárd Farkas. 2023. Transformer-alapú HuSpaCy előelemző láncok [Transformer-based HuSpaCy pipelines]. In *XIX. Magyar Számítógépes Nyelvészeti Konferencia*, pages 305–317, Szeged. Szegedi Tudományegyetem, Informatikai Intézet.

Yi Yang, Wen-tau Yih, and Christopher Meek. 2015. WikiQA: A challenge dataset for open-domain question answering. In *Proceedings of the 2015 Conference on Empirical Methods in Natural Language Processing*, pages 2013–2018, Lisbon, Portugal. Association for Computational Linguistics.

Zhilin Yang, Peng Qi, Saizheng Zhang, Yoshua Bengio, William Cohen, Ruslan Salakhutdinov, and Christopher D. Manning. 2018. HotpotQA: A dataset for diverse, explainable multi-hop question answering. In *Proceedings of the 2018 Conference on Empirical Methods in Natural Language Processing*, pages 2369–2380, Brussels, Belgium. Association for Computational Linguistics.

Wonjin Yoon, Richard Jackson, Aron Lagerberg, and Jaewoo Kang. 2022. Sequence tagging for biomedical extractive question answering. *Bioinformatics*, 38(15):3794–3801.

Seungyoung Lim;Hyunjeong Lee;Soyoon Park;Myungji Kim Youngmin Kim. 2020. KorQuAD 2.0: Korean QA Dataset for Web Document Machine Comprehension. *Journal of KIISE*, 47:577–586.

Zhuosheng Zhang, Junjie Yang, and Hai Zhao. 2021. Retrospective reader for machine reading comprehension. In *Proceedings of the AAAI Conference on Artificial Intelligence*, volume 35, pages 14506–14514.

No Strong Feelings One Way or Another: Re-operationalizing Neutrality in Natural Language Inference

Animesh Nighojkar, Antonio Laverghetta Jr., and **John Licato**
Advancing Machine and Human Reasoning (AMHR) Lab
University of South Florida
{anighojkar, alaverghett, licato} @usf.edu

Abstract

Natural Language Inference (NLI) has been a cornerstone task in evaluating language models' inferential reasoning capabilities. However, the standard three-way classification scheme used in NLI has well-known shortcomings in evaluating models' ability to capture the nuances of natural human reasoning. In this paper, we argue that the operationalization of the *neutral* label in current NLI datasets has low validity, is interpreted inconsistently, and that at least one important sense of neutrality is often ignored. We uncover the detrimental impact of these shortcomings, which in some cases leads to annotation datasets that actually *decrease* performance on downstream tasks. We compare approaches of handling annotator disagreement and identify flaws in a recent NLI dataset that designs an annotator study based on a problematic operationalization. Our findings highlight the need for a more refined evaluation framework for NLI, and we hope to spark further discussion and action in the NLP community.

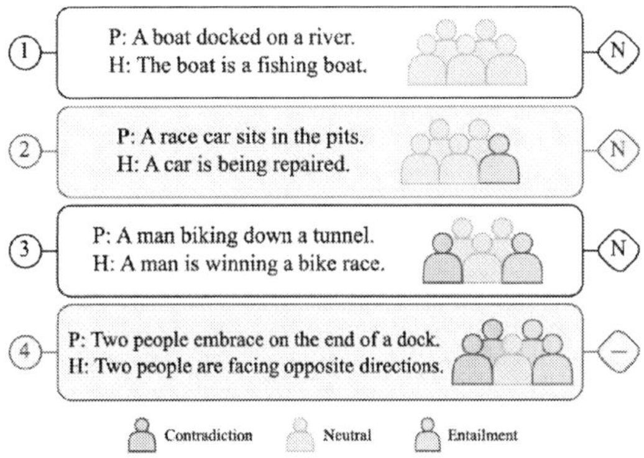

Figure 1: Selected NLI items from SNLI with annotations (shown by colors). The diamonds on the right show the gold label for these items in SNLI; note item 4 is marked '-' and is not assigned a gold label (hence it is ignored). We argue that items with all four annotation distributions should be considered neutral, but that there should be at least two sub-types of neutral.

1 Introduction

With the rise of large language models like GPT-3 (Brown et al., 2020), PaLM (Chowdhery et al., 2022), and GPT-4,[1] it has become increasingly necessary to evaluate their language understanding and reasoning abilities. One influential task in this regard is natural language inference (NLI) (MacCartney and Manning, 2009, 2014), which is used to examine the inferential and commonsense reasoning skills of language models (Jeretic et al., 2020). NLI requires a model to determine the relationship between a statement, known as the *premise* P, and another statement, called the *hypothesis* H, by classifying it as *entailment* (H must be true given P), *contradiction* (H must be false given P), or *neutral* (H can or cannot be true given P).[2] NLI is crucial because it involves comprehending the logical properties of sentences, which is arguably a core capability of human reasoning and an important skill for language models to possess.

Solving NLI requires the ability to perform textual inference between any two sentences (and in some cases, between any two arbitrarily long texts), making it a versatile framework for developing and evaluating reasoning benchmarks. Many NLP tasks, like question answering (Demszky et al., 2018), dialog systems (Gong et al., 2018), machine translation (Poliak et al., 2018), identifying biased or misleading statements (Nie et al., 2019), fake news detection (Yang et al., 2019), paraphrase detection (Nighojkar and Licato, 2021a,b), and fact verification (Thorne et al., 2018), require understanding and reasoning about the meaning of text and can be re-framed as NLI

[1] `https://openai.com/research/gpt-4`

[2] Recognizing textual entailment (RTE) (Dagan et al., 2006), a variant of NLI, only considers entailment and non-entailment.

Proceedings of the 17th Linguistic Annotation Workshop (LAW-XVII), pages 199–210
July 13, 2023

problems. NLI provides a broad framework for studying and alleviating logical inconsistencies in a language model's reasoning (Poliak, 2020; Mitchell et al., 2022) including explanation-based maieutic prompting (Jung et al., 2022), that uses NLI to evaluate individual links in a reasoning chain.

Most NLI datasets (Bowman et al., 2015; Williams et al., 2018; Nie et al., 2020a; Chen et al., 2020) utilize crowdsourcing to either generate NLI items or gather labels for pre-existing items. While this approach has advanced research on textual entailment, we believe that current NLI datasets, both established and recent, have overlooked important issues in their annotation design that hinder their validity as measures of textual entailment. Although the effects of different crowdsourcing schemes for NLI dataset development has been studied (Bowman and Dahl, 2021; Parrish et al., 2021), we focus on a specific issue: the operationalization of *neutral*. Neutral items usually have the lowest levels of annotator agreement (Nie et al., 2020b), and we contend that this disagreement has been handled improperly in previous work, contributing to the ongoing debate about how to handle disagreement in NLI (Palomaki et al., 2018; Pavlick and Kwiatkowski, 2019; Bowman et al., 2015; Williams et al., 2018). Instructions provided to annotators for labeling items as neutral are often ambiguous and inconsistent between datasets, with phrases like "neither" (Nie et al., 2020a) or "might be correct" (Bowman et al., 2015; Williams et al., 2018).

We believe these problems can be addressed by reconsidering the prevailing operationalization of neutral and replacing it with one which embraces disagreement. Although we are not the first to argue for the importance of properly incorporating disagreement (Palomaki et al., 2018; Pavlick and Kwiatkowski, 2019; Basile et al., 2021; Plank, 2022; Rottger et al., 2022; Uma et al., 2022b), we identify specific problems introduced by ignoring disagreement (for example, by dropping examples with low agreement entirely), and offer new evidence supporting its adoption grounded in the psychometric concept of *construct validity*. Consider the items shown in Figure 1, sourced from the SNLI dataset (Bowman et al., 2015). A general consensus on the gold label is reached by the annotators in the first three items, but the fourth item exhibits a high degree of disagreement. While the first three items are labeled neutral in SNLI and used to train models, the fourth is labeled with a special '-' class, indicating an irresolvable level of disagreement, and hence it is removed from training data (Bowman et al., 2015). This practice (also used by Williams et al.) effectively treats disagreement as an undesirable product of NLI data collection—a *linguistic annotation artifact* to be considered as noise rather than signal. But what is the source of this disagreement? Should item 4 in Figure 1 be ignored, or is it simply a different form of neutrality? We argue that item 4 should be considered a different sense of neutral than the one represented by item 1, because two interpretations are possible: (1) the individuals in the embrace may be facing in opposite directions, resembling a conventional embrace, and (2) one individual may be embracing the other from behind, thereby causing them to face the same direction. This ambiguity in how to interpret such items leads to two irreconcilable types of neutrals; items can be either *true* neutrals (item 1 in Figure 1), or they can be neutral as a result of *conflicting* interpretations (item 4).

Main contributions. In this paper, we address the aforementioned issues with neutrality in three ways:

1. We propose a new operationalization of neutral based on inter-annotator agreement, which we argue better captures two distinct senses of neutrality (true neutral and conflicting neutral) often conflated in NLI.

2. We compare our operationalization with a 4-way classification scheme based on annotator disagreement suggested by Jiang and de Marneffe (2019); Zhang and de Marneffe (2021); Jiang and de Marneffe (2022) and find that our operationalization has better construct validity, as using it to train models for NLI leads to better downstream performance.

3. We show that known limitations of at least one published NLI dataset (UNLI) are a direct consequence of its adopting an operationalization that did not embrace disagreement, instead opting to aggregate NLI annotations on a continuous scale. We analyze its methodological flaws, and make recommendations to avoid similar problems in future work.

2 Related Work

NLI is widely used for assessing language models' inferential capabilities, in part due to its generality and versatility. Many datasets, like SNLI (Bowman et al., 2015), MultiNLI (Williams et al., 2018), Adversarial NLI (ANLI) (Nie et al., 2020a), and WA-NLI (Liu et al., 2022) have been developed to evaluate a model's ability to reason through entailment relationships across a wide variety of contexts. Other datasets focus on specific domain knowledge (Holzenberger et al., 2020; Koreeda and Manning, 2021; Yin et al., 2021; Khan et al., 2022; Yang, 2022) or require knowledge of non-English languages (Conneau et al., 2018; Araujo et al., 2022).

In most NLI datasets, only one label per item is deemed correct, and models are tasked with determining the most plausible of three possible labels. However, there is a growing need for NLI tasks to handle a broader range of relationships and make finer-grained distinctions between them. Researchers are shifting their focus towards finer-grained annotations (Chen et al., 2020; Gantt et al., 2020; Meissner et al., 2021), as classical NLI tasks are not well-equipped to handle disagreement between annotators (Zhang et al., 2021; Zhang and de Marneffe, 2021; Jiang and de Marneffe, 2022; Wang et al., 2022). Recent research has also focused on assessing models' performance on *ambiguous* NLI items, where humans may disagree on the correct label. ChaosNLI (Nie et al., 2020b) was developed to study such ambiguities by gathering 100 human annotations on items from a subset of SNLI and MultiNLI, where only 3/5 of annotators agreed on the correct label. They found that models struggled to perform above random chance on items with low inter-annotator agreement and were unable to replicate the annotator label distribution (Zhou et al., 2022). Since most of the low agreement items are neutral (Nie et al., 2020b), we believe a possible reason for this poor performance is the conflation of true and conflicting neutrals as a single category (Section 4).

Zhou et al. (2022); Meissner et al. (2021) build on ChaosNLI and test language models' ability to recover the original annotator label distribution. However, the best results are still below estimated human performance. To solve ambiguous NLI items, Wang et al. (2022) argue that models need to be well-calibrated (i.e., their predicted probability distribution must correctly match the annotator distribution), and they show that label smoothing or temperature scaling can achieve competitive performance without direct training on the label distribution, though it should be noted that other work has found mixed success with using either of these approaches to address ambiguity in NLI (Uma et al., 2022a). According to Pavlick and Kwiatkowski (2019), annotator disagreements are *irresolvable* even when the number of annotators and context are both increased. Such items should not be ignored since the disagreement cannot be always attributed to noise. They argue that handling disagreements should be left to the ones using the models trained on these datasets. Similar to Zhou et al. (2022), Pavlick and Kwiatkowski (2019) also show that NLI models trained to predict one label cannot capture the human annotation distribution.

Despite calls in the literature for annotator disagreement to be accommodated rather than ignored, how this should be done has been the subject of much study. The earliest attempts from SNLI and MultiNLI simply assigned a '–' label to cases that had sufficiently low agreement, indicating that they should not be used for training (Bowman et al., 2015; Williams et al., 2018). More recent work has tried to incorporate low agreement items as a fourth *disagreement* class, a practice that began with Jiang and de Marneffe (2019) and was later used by Zhang and de Marneffe (2021); Jiang and de Marneffe (2022). We examine this practice in Section 3 and demonstrate that simply using a *catch-all* category for disagreement is not as effective as our operationalization for neutral items.

Another line of research has explored changing the annotation schema to use a continuous scale, rather than a discrete one, in the hope that this type of scale will better capture the subtleties of reasoning over ambiguity and lead to less disagreement. Chen et al. (2020) introduce *uncertain natural language inference* (UNLI), where annotators indicate the likelihood of a hypothesis being true given a premise. While models trained on UNLI can closely predict human estimations, later work has found that fine-tuning on UNLI can hurt downstream performance (Meissner et al., 2021), suggesting a serious flaw in the UNLI dataset. We analyze further issues with UNLI in Section 5.

In a recent study, Kalouli et al. (2023) propose

a new interpretation of neutral based on the concept of *strictness*. They argue that, under "strict interpretation", the pair *P: The woman is cutting a tomato. H: The woman is slicing a tomato/* would be considered neutral as she could be cutting squares, but it could be considered an entailment pair if the interpretation is not so strict. Their operationalization of neutral based on the concept of *strictness* lacks clarity due to the absence of a precise, understandable definition of *strictness*. In effect, it simply shifts the problem of understanding what makes a pair of sentences neutral to understanding what makes their relationship "strictly logical" (a term they use to define strict interpretation, without further elaboration).[3]

3 Empirical evaluation of 'disagreement' as a fourth class

The classification scheme that uses a fourth 'disagreement' label for low-agreement items (Jiang and de Marneffe, 2019; Zhang and de Marneffe, 2021; Jiang and de Marneffe, 2022) conflates all three NLI labels in doing so. To explore this possibility, we conduct an empirical study to compare this disagreement-based scheme with other 4-way classification schemes. We define the *level of agreement* (**A**) between annotators on NLI items as:

$$\mathbf{A} = \frac{\textit{number of votes for the majority label}}{\textit{total number of votes}} \quad (1)$$

We also explore two agreement threshold t values (0.8, and 1),[4] which is the cutoff-value of **A** below which items are considered to have "low agreement." Note that Jiang and de Marneffe (2019) choose $t = 0.8$ but do not provide an explanation for choosing it. We train ALBERT-base (Lan et al., 2019), DistilBERT-base-uncased (Sanh et al., 2019), Electra-base (Clark et al., 2020), DeBERTa-v3-base (He et al., 2020), and RoBERTa-base (Liu et al., 2019) to show that these results are not specific to just a few models. We are limited to using SNLI and MultiNLI because they are the only NLI datasets that report individual annotations in sufficient quantity to finetune transformer language models. We trained each model for 5 epochs and tested their performance on a held out, stratified, evaluation set.[5]. We use only the base versions of these models because our objective here is not to train the best models, but to examine and compare classification schemes. Models are being used in this experiment only to compare the *separability* of all classes for each of these classification schemes:

- **Con:** Entailment, Neutral, $\uparrow$ Contradiction, $\downarrow$ Contradiction [6]
- **Dis:** Entailment, Neutral, Contradiction, Disagreement
- **Ent:** $\uparrow$ Entailment, $\downarrow$ Entailment, Neutral, Contradiction
- **Neu:** Entailment, $\uparrow$ Neutral, $\downarrow$ Neutral, Contradiction

Better F_1 scores would suggest the model could better differentiate between the classes of the given classification scheme, and thus the scheme has better *ecological validity*.[7]

Results are shown in Figure 2. We find that using a fourth 'disagreement' label leads to the worst results consistently. These results suggest that having a catch-all 'disagreement' label does not provide enough information to help models successfully reason over ambiguous items. Note that unlike the other three schemes, **Dis** classifies all low-agreement items as 'disagreement', thus making the other three schemes more imbalanced than **Dis**. For instance, **Con** classifies only low-agreement contradiction items as the fourth class and low-agreement neutral and entailment items are classified as their respective majority labels. Lowest F_1 score on **Dis** (the most balanced classification scheme) is perhaps even more informative than it would have been if the schemes were equally balanced. Any of the other three schemes consistently leads to better

[3]Note that the strict conditional $\Box(p \rightarrow h)$ was famously introduced by Lewis (1912) as a formalization of the indicative conditional. However, this does not appear to be the sense of "strict" meant by Kalouli et al. (2023).

[4]Because SNLI and MultiNLI have at most 5 annotations, and the majority label is always taken as the gold label, 0.4 is the smallest possible **A** that can be used. Since all items at that agreement are marked as - in both the datasets, $t = 0.6$ cannot be used for **Ent** and **Con**. Also, $t = 0.6$ will give us same items for all four classes in **Dis** as well as **Neu**, making their comparison at that threshold meaningless.

[5]Github code will be released upon publication.

[6]$\uparrow$ and $\downarrow$ denote high and low annotator agreement respectively.

[7]Ecological validity examines whether the results of a study can be generalized to real-life settings (Egger et al., 2008).

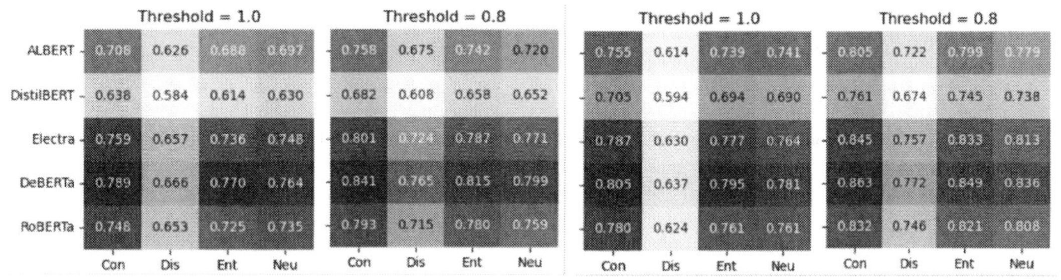

(a) MultiNLI (b) SNLI

Figure 2: Heatmaps of F_1 scores on different 4-way classification schemes (x-axis) for different language models (y-axis). Darker boxes indicate better performance. Models consistently under-perform on the disagreement-based classification scheme (**Dis**) proposed by Jiang and de Marneffe (2019); Zhang and de Marneffe (2021); Jiang and de Marneffe (2022), indicating that a catch-all disagreement label does not provide enough information to models to reason over ambiguous items.

performance, regardless of model or threshold used, and thus has better construct validity (Bleidorn and Hopwood, 2019; Zhai et al., 2021) than the classification scheme based on disagreement.

4 Operationalizing Neutral

In NLI, the neutral label is used for situations where the relationship between the premise and hypothesis is ambiguous or there is insufficient information to determine the relationship. Neutral is often considered a catch-all for relationships that do not fall under entailment or contradiction. The definition of neutral is typically provided to crowd-source workers as "neither" (Nie et al., 2020a) or "might be correct" (Bowman et al., 2015; Williams et al., 2018).

But is a classification of neutral simply a default assumption that always means neither entailment nor contradiction can be definitively determined, or can it be a positive claim that a different type of relationship holds between the sentences? A closer look at the data obtained from NLI datasets suggests that neutrality is more complex than it may initially seem. According to Nie et al. (2020b), neutral items in many NLI datasets exhibit the lowest agreement levels. The most frequent label below an agreement level of $\mathbf{A} = 0.8$ for both the SNLI and MultiNLI subsets is neutral, while it is the least frequent label at a perfect agreement level. This lack of agreement motivates our focus on neutral particularly, as it is consistently the most problematic label to annotate. The empirical study in Section 3 also shows that a neutral-based classification scheme has a better separability than a disagreement-based classification scheme.

There are at least two senses in which the relationship between two sentences can be said to be neutral, which become clear if we imagine two possible justifications that an individual NLI annotator may provide for why they selected the label neutral: (1) *True Neutral:* The annotator cannot find any sufficiently strong reasons (using whichever standard of strength they determine appropriate) to satisfy either entailment or contradiction; or (2) *Conflicting Neutral:* The annotator finds strong reasons to support *both* entailment and contradiction.

It is a central position of this paper that these two interpretations of the neutral label are irreconcilable and should not be confused with each other. Attempting to conflate the two, e.g. by assuming that neutrality is simply the mid-point on a continuous scale between the two extremes of entailment and contradiction, will and has led to significant reductions in quality of data collections and their resulting benchmark datasets (see §5).

No existing NLI dataset, to our knowledge, asks or encourages annotators to explain whether their reasons for selecting neutral are in line with true or conflicting neutral as we have defined them above. For the present work, then, we present evidence for the discriminant validity of true and conflicting neutral (i.e., that they refer to two distinct constructs that can and should be measured separately Campbell and Fiske (1959)) by assuming that they will be *approximately reflected in the distribution* of individual annotations on a single NLI item—in other words, conflicting neutral items will tend to have annotation distributions resembling item

Dataset	Mean Length (T)	Mean Length (C)	Reading Ease (T)	Reading Ease (C)
$*$ SNLI dev + test	109.6	118.2	84.0	82.8
SNLI train	102.8	111.3	84.8	83.6
$*$ MultiNLI matched + mismatched	172.0	183.0	67.0	65.2
MultiNLI train	163.8	186.0	68.7	64.4
ANLI R3 dev	389.0	372.7	67.9	65.3
ANLI R3 test	382.4	392.7	69.8	66.1
ANLI R3 train	369.3	377.3	66.3	64.6
WA-NLI test	147.3	147.6	77.4	77.4
WA-NLI train	147.5	148.6	77.1	77.0

Table 1: Comparison of true (T) and conflicting (C) neutrals. Smaller values for reading ease indicate harder-to-read items. We use our trained model to estimate **A** for the datasets that do not release individual annotations and the ones that do are marked with a "$*$". Cases where our hypothesis was NOT confirmed are underlined and in brown.

4 in Figure 1, whereas true neutrals will tend to match item 1. Results in Section 3 show that indeed such a classification scheme does a much better job of separating the four classes for models than a scheme that conflates all three labels.

True vs. Conflicting Neutral: Surface-level Differences We perform an exploratory analysis to identify potential reasons why annotators may disagree on some 'neutral' items, to better motivate our operationalization of 'neutral'. Drawing from Pavlick and Kwiatkowski (2019), who found that disagreement increases as more context is given, we investigate whether ambiguity in NLI items arises due to increased complexity, leading to difficulties in accurately interpreting them. We measure this complexity using two metrics: mean length of the item in terms of number of characters (after the premise and hypothesis are joined with a space), and Flesch Reading Ease (Flesch, 1948), a commonly-used measure of text readability. Our findings, shown in Table 1, reveal that true neutral items are shorter and easier to read than conflicting neutral items. However, the observed difference in complexity between the two forms of neutrals is marginal and inconclusive. These results suggest that at least superficial qualitative differences exist between different types of neutrals, but more extensive research is needed to clarify the extent of these differences.

5 An Analysis of UNLI

We have argued that a carefully grounded operationalization of the neutral label is crucial for ensuring the reliability (performance should be free from random error) and validity of NLI. To demonstrate the issues that can arise if this caution is not taken, we next analyze a recent NLI dataset — Uncertain NLI (UNLI) (Chen et al., 2020). The UNLI dataset, when used for fine-tuning, appears to actually harm downstream performance (Meissner et al., 2021; Zhou et al., 2022; Wang et al., 2022). UNLI attempts to enhance NLI by converting the categorical labels for some SNLI items to a continuous scale. Participants were instructed to rate the likelihood of a given hypothesis being entailed by a given premise using an ungraduated slider, ranging from 0 (labeled as "impossible") to 1 (labeled as "very likely") and were shown the probability they were assigning to the *premise-hypothesis* pair in real time.

According to Chen et al. (2020), the probabilistic nature of NLI (Glickman et al., 2005) suggests that not all contradictions or entailments are equally strong.[8] Thus, UNLI was developed with the intention of capturing subtler distinctions in *entailment strength* using a continuous scale. This dataset has over 60K items from SNLI, annotated by humans. For each premise-hypothesis pair, two annotations were collected, and in cases where the first two annotators differed by 20% or more, a third annotator was consulted. However, the dataset only reports the averaged scores, which makes it impossible to assess the degree of agreement or correlation between the two annotators or even identify examples where a third annotator was needed. Thus, reported values near 0.5 (which we might take to be the equivalent of *neutral* items) fundamentally conflate items where both annotators chose the midpoint on the slider with items where each annotator chose one of the extremities.

The assumption that one continuous scale can capture even the three categories in standard NLI (entailment, contradiction, and neutral) is

[8]The view that NLI is inherently probabilistic, or that natural inference can be best modeled with probability, is not universally held, e.g. (Bringsjord, 2008).

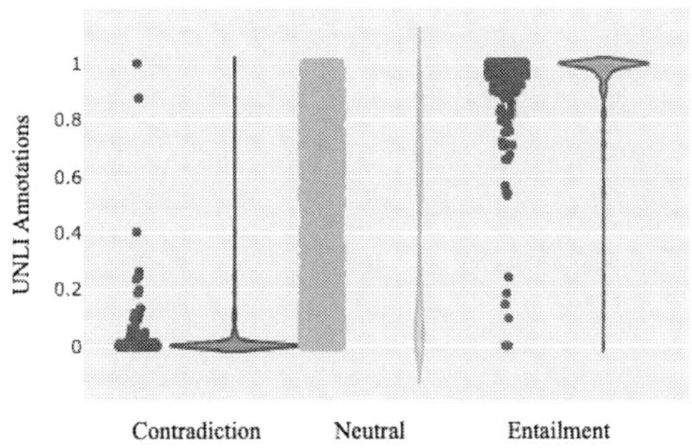

Figure 3: Figure 1 from Chen et al. (2020) redrawn on a linear scale. Note the two distinct bulges in the violin plot for neutral items, suggesting that annotators were confused about whether neutral items should be placed near 0 or middle of the slider.

a strong one (already shown to be problematic in (Pavlick and Kwiatkowski, 2019)), which is typically glossed over by presuming that entailment lies at the higher end of the spectrum, contradiction at the other end, and neutral somewhere in the middle. But no such instruction to interpret the scale this way was provided to annotators. Indeed, as we will show, annotators appeared to be confused as to whether an absence of entailment meant that the slider should be at the '0' position, or in the middle.

In their attempt to obtain subjective probabilities for premise-hypothesis pairs, the authors used a scale with 10K steps with a scaled logistic transformation ($f(x) = \sigma(\beta(x - 5000))$) to convert the values on the scale into probabilities between 0 and 1. They do not report the chosen value of β and do not specify whether the scores were averaged before or after applying the function, which is crucial information as both would yield different results. Because raw values of x are not provided, and we do not know whether scaling is performed before or after averaging, we are unable to recover the chosen values of β.

The scale Chen et al. (2020) used was based on EASL (Sakaguchi and Van Durme, 2018), an approach developed to collect scalar ratings in NLP tasks.[9] They then modified the EASL scale by utilizing the aforementioned logistic transformation, which they argued would allow for more nuanced values near both extremes. Notably, the source of the anchor points used on the scale (i.e., "impossible" and "very likely") is not explicitly stated by Chen et al. (2020), although it is possible they were obtained from JOCI (Zhang et al., 2017), a dataset created for studying ordinal commonsense reasoning that uses the same anchor points for opposite ends of the scale.[10]

In effect, their logistic transformation compresses the extreme ends of the scale, so that the graphic they display (Figure 1 in Chen et al. (2020)), at first glance, appears as if the NLI items labeled as contradiction, neutral, and entailment occupy roughly equal space across the continuum of values. Figure 3 instead depicts the distribution of averaged human responses collected by Chen et al. (2020) on a linear scale.[11] It is clear to observe in Figure 3 that while entailment and contradiction annotations are distinctly separated and skewed heavily towards the extreme opposite ends of the scale, annotations for neutral *span the entire range from 0 to 1*. The origin of this discrepancy is unclear, but based on the instructions given to them, it may be that annotators were unsure where to place neutral on the scale. Supporting this hypothesis is the bulge near 0 on the violin plot for neutral in Figure 3, which suggests that annotators chose 0 for both neutral and contradiction items. This information is obscured by the logistically transformed graph displayed by Chen et al. (2020).

Table 2 highlights some examples from UNLI that demonstrate the poor alignment of its annotations with SNLI annotation distributions. From Figure 3, the reliability of the scale for neutral annotations is notably poor, with annotations spanning the entire range of the scale. This suggests that neutral annotations lack internal consistency, an important measure of reliability (Rust and Golombok, 2014), because annotators do not label the NLI items in a consistent fashion even when the label remains constant.

Measurement issues are not uncommon in other fields that routinely run human studies, including psychological and educational mesurement. Development of annotation schemes in these fields often involves careful consideration of the item

[9]This scale was not validated for NLI by Sakaguchi and Van Durme (2018) and the tasks they evaluated it for — like evaluating quality of machine translations, or the frequency of words in language — differ significantly from NLI.

[10]This is further supported by the fact that Chen et al. (2020) cite Zhang et al. (2017) as a previous attempt to model likelihood judgments in NLI, which is also the aim of UNLI.

[11]Many of the properties of the scale we address here were unclear from reading the original figure in Chen et al. (2020), necessitating the redrawing.

Premise	Hypothesis	SNLI Annotations	UNLI score
A woman with a blue jacket around her waist is sitting on the ledge of some stone ruins resting.	A man sits on a ledge.	$4C-0N-1E$	0.88
A lady is standing up holding a lamp that is turned on.	She is lighting a dark room.	$2C-2N-1E$	0.78
A singer wearing a leather jacket performs on stage with dramatic lighting behind him.	A singer is on American idol.	$1C-4N-0E$	0.01
A small boy wearing a blue shirt plays in the kiddie pool.	Boy cooling off during the summer.	$1C-4N-0E$	0.89

Table 2: Items from UNLI along with their individual annotations from SNLI.

format, including the rating scale, to ensure that it effectively measures the construct of interest (Bandalos, 2018). This can be achieved through qualitative analysis, such as cognitive interviews and focus groups, where items are administered to test takers and feedback is collected to ensure that the scale is understood and completed accurately, among other things (Miller et al., 2014). However, in the development of UNLI, Chen et al. (2020) did not report using such procedures. Moreover, common practices in measurement research were missing from UNLI, such as reporting how bad-faith responses were identified and filtered out, using attention-check items (except the qualifying test, whose results are not provided as part of the dataset), employing a sufficienlty large sample size of annotators, and providing individual annotations and relevant information about the annotators like their recruitment and compensation. These omissions make precise scientific replication impossible, and raise concerns about the validity of UNLI as a measure of (and benchmark for) NLI, while also providing a plausible explanation for why prior research yielded poor results when using UNLI for fine-tuning.

6 Conclusion

In this paper, we examined the operationalization of neutral in NLI datasets. Our analysis revealed that previous attempts to handle ambiguity in NLI based on neutrality have significant issues with their validity as annotation strategies for NLI. We proposed a new operationalization of neutral into *true neutral* and *conflicting neutral*. Although instances of these forms of neutral are present in most popular NLI datasets, they have been conflated into one neutral label, limiting our ability to measure ambiguity in NLI effectively. We showed that this approach of casting NLI to a 4-way classification task is better than the disagreement-based classification scheme used in previous work. We used UNLI as a case study to highlight measurement and annotation issues that should be avoided in the future.

Of the many factors that make science successful, two of the most important are the ability to make carefully designed measurements, and replicability. The first of these cannot be met when measurements of constructs are made in ways that significantly compromise their validity and reliability. And replicability is made impossible when papers are published in reputable venues reporting unclear collection details, having important parameter choices omitted, and with datasets reporting summary statistics in place of crucially important data. A significant roadblock of the work we reported in this paper was the lack of availability of individual annotations in widely-adopted NLI benchmarks, even when there seems to be no public benefit in leaving out such information. It is our hope that the present work will encourage our fellow AI researchers to more highly value such considerations.

Limitations

We approximated the operationalization of the two senses of neutrality using annotator agreement. Perhaps a better basis for operationalizing the two senses of neutrality could be found in the reasons behind the annotators choosing the neutral label. Since no NLI datasets ask annotators to explain their choice and release those responses, we will try to analyze this in the future.

We presented a surface-level syntactic analysis of the differences between the two types of neutrals, but semantic differences should also be analyzed. Intuitively, semantic differences might give us a better understanding of these two types, but further study is needed to verify this.

Though we focus on UNLI as a case study to back up our claims, further analysis on a broader range of NLI datasets (and possible extensions to tasks beyond NLI) should also be conducted.

References

Vladimir Araujo, Andrés Carvallo, Souvik Kundu, José Cañete, Marcelo Mendoza, Robert E. Mercer, Felipe Bravo-Marquez, Marie-Francine Moens, and Alvaro Soto. 2022. Evaluation benchmarks for Spanish sentence representations. In *Proceedings of the Thirteenth Language Resources and Evaluation Conference*, pages 6024–6034, Marseille, France. European Language Resources Association.

Deborah L. Bandalos. 2018. *Measurement theory and applications for the social sciences*. Methodology in the Social Sciences. The Guilford Press, New York, New York ;.

Valerio Basile, Michael Fell, Tommaso Fornaciari, Dirk Hovy, Silviu Paun, Barbara Plank, Massimo Poesio, and Alexandra Uma. 2021. We need to consider disagreement in evaluation. In *Proceedings of the 1st Workshop on Benchmarking: Past, Present and Future*, pages 15–21, Online. Association for Computational Linguistics.

Wiebke Bleidorn and Christopher James Hopwood. 2019. Using machine learning to advance personality assessment and theory. *Personality and Social Psychology Review*, 23(2):190–203.

Samuel R. Bowman, Gabor Angeli, Christopher Potts, and Christopher D. Manning. 2015. A large annotated corpus for learning natural language inference. In *Proceedings of the 2015 Conference on Empirical Methods in Natural Language Processing*, pages 632–642, Lisbon, Portugal. Association for Computational Linguistics.

Samuel R. Bowman and George Dahl. 2021. What will it take to fix benchmarking in natural language understanding? In *Proceedings of the 2021 Conference of the North American Chapter of the Association for Computational Linguistics: Human Language Technologies*, pages 4843–4855, Online. Association for Computational Linguistics.

Selmer Bringsjord. 2008. The logicist manifesto: At long last let logic-based artificial intelligence become a field unto itself. *Journal of Applied Logic*, 6(4):502–525. The Philosophy of Computer Science.

Tom Brown, Benjamin Mann, Nick Ryder, Melanie Subbiah, Jared D Kaplan, Prafulla Dhariwal, Arvind Neelakantan, Pranav Shyam, Girish Sastry, Amanda Askell, et al. 2020. Language models are few-shot learners. *Advances in neural information processing systems*, 33:1877–1901.

Donald T Campbell and Donald W Fiske. 1959. Convergent and discriminant validation by the multitrait-multimethod matrix. *Psychological bulletin*, 56(2):81.

Tongfei Chen, Zhengping Jiang, Adam Poliak, Keisuke Sakaguchi, and Benjamin Van Durme. 2020. Uncertain natural language inference. In *Proceedings of the 58th Annual Meeting of the Association for Computational Linguistics*, pages 8772–8779, Online. Association for Computational Linguistics.

Aakanksha Chowdhery, Sharan Narang, Jacob Devlin, Maarten Bosma, Gaurav Mishra, Adam Roberts, Paul Barham, Hyung Won Chung, Charles Sutton, Sebastian Gehrmann, Parker Schuh, Kensen Shi, Sasha Tsvyashchenko, Joshua Maynez, Abhishek Rao, Parker Barnes, Yi Tay, Noam Shazeer, Vinodkumar Prabhakaran, Emily Reif, Nan Du, Ben Hutchinson, Reiner Pope, James Bradbury, Jacob Austin, Michael Isard, Guy Gur-Ari, Pengcheng Yin, Toju Duke, Anselm Levskaya, Sanjay Ghemawat, Sunipa Dev, Henryk Michalewski, Xavier Garcia, Vedant Misra, Kevin Robinson, Liam Fedus, Denny Zhou, Daphne Ippolito, David Luan, Hyeontaek Lim, Barret Zoph, Alexander Spiridonov, Ryan Sepassi, David Dohan, Shivani Agrawal, Mark Omernick, Andrew M. Dai, Thanumalayan Sankaranarayana Pillai, Marie Pellat, Aitor Lewkowycz, Erica Moreira, Rewon Child, Oleksandr Polozov, Katherine Lee, Zongwei Zhou, Xuezhi Wang, Brennan Saeta, Mark Diaz, Orhan Firat, Michele Catasta, Jason Wei, Kathy Meier-Hellstern, Douglas Eck, Jeff Dean, Slav Petrov, and Noah Fiedel. 2022. Palm: Scaling language modeling with pathways. *arxiv:2204.02311*.

Kevin Clark, Thang Luong, Quoc V. Le, and Christopher Manning. 2020. Electra: Pre-training text encoders as discriminators rather than generators. In *ICLR*.

Alexis Conneau, Ruty Rinott, Guillaume Lample, Adina Williams, Samuel Bowman, Holger Schwenk, and Veselin Stoyanov. 2018. XNLI: Evaluating cross-lingual sentence representations. In *Proceedings of the 2018 Conference on Empirical Methods in Natural Language Processing*, pages 2475–2485, Brussels, Belgium. Association for Computational Linguistics.

Ido Dagan, Oren Glickman, and Bernardo Magnini. 2006. The pascal recognising textual entailment challenge. In *Machine Learning Challenges. Evaluating Predictive Uncertainty, Visual Object Classification, and Recognising Tectual Entailment: First PASCAL Machine Learning Challenges Workshop, MLCW 2005, Southampton, UK, April 11-13, 2005, Revised Selected Papers*, pages 177–190. Springer.

Dorottya Demszky, Kelvin Guu, and Percy Liang. 2018. Transforming question answering datasets into natural language inference datasets. *arXiv preprint arXiv:1809.02922*.

Matthias Egger, George Davey Smith, and Douglas Altman. 2008. *Systematic reviews in health care: meta-analysis in context*. John Wiley & Sons.

Rudolph Flesch. 1948. A new readability yardstick. *Journal of Applied Psychology*, 32(3):221–233.

William Gantt, Benjamin Kane, and Aaron Steven White. 2020. Natural language inference with mixed effects. In *Proceedings of the Ninth Joint Conference on Lexical and Computational Semantics*, pages 81–87, Barcelona, Spain (Online). Association for Computational Linguistics.

Oren Glickman, Ido Dagan, and Moshe Koppel. 2005. A probabilistic classification approach for lexical textual entailment. In *AAAI*, pages 1050–1055. Pittsburgh, PA.

Yichen Gong, Heng Luo, and Jian Zhang. 2018. Natural language inference over interaction space. *arXiv preprint arXiv:1709.04348v2*.

Pengcheng He, Xiaodong Liu, Jianfeng Gao, and Weizhu Chen. 2020. Deberta: Decoding-enhanced bert with disentangled attention. *arXiv preprint arXiv:2006.03654*.

Nils Holzenberger, Andrew Blair-Stanek, and Benjamin Van Durme. 2020. A dataset for statutory reasoning in tax law entailment and question answering.

Paloma Jeretic, Alex Warstadt, Suvrat Bhooshan, and Adina Williams. 2020. Are natural language inference models IMPPRESsive? Learning IMPlicature and PRESupposition. In *Proceedings of the 58th Annual Meeting of the Association for Computational Linguistics*, pages 8690–8705, Online. Association for Computational Linguistics.

Nan-Jiang Jiang and Marie-Catherine de Marneffe. 2022. Investigating Reasons for Disagreement in Natural Language Inference. *Transactions of the Association for Computational Linguistics*, 10:1357–1374.

Nanjiang Jiang and Marie-Catherine de Marneffe. 2019. Evaluating BERT for natural language inference: A case study on the CommitmentBank. In *Proceedings of the 2019 Conference on Empirical Methods in Natural Language Processing and the 9th International Joint Conference on Natural Language Processing (EMNLP-IJCNLP)*, pages 6086–6091, Hong Kong, China. Association for Computational Linguistics.

Jaehun Jung, Lianhui Qin, Sean Welleck, Faeze Brahman, Chandra Bhagavatula, Ronan Le Bras, and Yejin Choi. 2022. Maieutic prompting: Logically consistent reasoning with recursive explanations. *arXiv preprint arXiv:2205.11822*.

Aikaterini-Lida Kalouli, Hai Hu, Alexander F Webb, Lawrence S Moss, and Valeria de Paiva. 2023. Curing the sick and other nli maladies. *Computational Linguistics*, page 1–45.

Kashif Khan, Ruizhe Wang, and Pascal Poupart. 2022. WatClaimCheck: A new dataset for claim entailment and inference. In *Proceedings of the 60th Annual Meeting of the Association for Computational Linguistics (Volume 1: Long Papers)*, pages 1293–1304, Dublin, Ireland. Association for Computational Linguistics.

Yuta Koreeda and Christopher Manning. 2021. ContractNLI: A dataset for document-level natural language inference for contracts. In *Findings of the Association for Computational Linguistics: EMNLP 2021*, pages 1907–1919, Punta Cana, Dominican Republic. Association for Computational Linguistics.

Zhenzhong Lan, Mingda Chen, Sebastian Goodman, Kevin Gimpel, Piyush Sharma, and Radu Soricut. 2019. Albert: A lite bert for self-supervised learning of language representations. *arXiv preprint arXiv:1909.11942*.

C. I. Lewis. 1912. Implication and the algebra of logic. *Mind*, 21(84):522–531.

Alisa Liu, Swabha Swayamdipta, Noah A. Smith, and Yejin Choi. 2022. WANLI: Worker and AI collaboration for natural language inference dataset creation. In *Findings of the Association for Computational Linguistics: EMNLP 2022*, pages 6826–6847, Abu Dhabi, United Arab Emirates. Association for Computational Linguistics.

Yinhan Liu, Myle Ott, Naman Goyal, Jingfei Du, Mandar Joshi, Danqi Chen, Omer Levy, Mike Lewis, Luke Zettlemoyer, and Veselin Stoyanov. 2019. Roberta: A robustly optimized bert pretraining approach.

Bill MacCartney and Christopher D Manning. 2009. An extended model of natural logic. In *Proceedings of the eight international conference on computational semantics*, pages 140–156.

Bill MacCartney and Christopher D. Manning. 2014. *Natural Logic and Natural Language Inference*, pages 129–147. Springer Netherlands, Dordrecht.

Johannes Mario Meissner, Napat Thumwanit, Saku Sugawara, and Akiko Aizawa. 2021. Embracing ambiguity: Shifting the training target of NLI models. In *Proceedings of the 59th Annual Meeting of the Association for Computational Linguistics and the 11th International Joint Conference on Natural Language Processing (Volume 2: Short Papers)*, pages 862–869, Online. Association for Computational Linguistics.

Kristen Miller, Valerie Chepp, Stephanie Willson, and Jose-Luis Padilla. 2014. *Cognitive interviewing methodology*. Wiley Series in Survey Methodology. Hoboken, New Jersey.

Eric Mitchell, Joseph Noh, Siyan Li, Will Armstrong, Ananth Agarwal, Patrick Liu, Chelsea Finn, and Christopher Manning. 2022. Enhancing self-consistency and performance of pre-trained language models through natural language inference. In *Proceedings of the 2022 Conference on Empirical Methods in Natural Language Processing*, pages 1754–1768, Abu Dhabi, United Arab Emirates. Association for Computational Linguistics.

Yixin Nie, Haonan Chen, and Mohit Bansal. 2019. Combining fact extraction and verification with neural semantic matching networks. In *Proceedings of the Thirty-Third AAAI Conference on Artificial Intelligence and Thirty-First Innovative Applications of Artificial Intelligence Conference and Ninth AAAI Symposium on Educational Advances in Artificial Intelligence*, AAAI'19/IAAI'19/EAAI'19. AAAI Press.

Yixin Nie, Adina Williams, Emily Dinan, Mohit Bansal, Jason Weston, and Douwe Kiela. 2020a. Adversarial NLI: A new benchmark for natural language understanding. In *Proceedings of the 58th Annual Meeting of the Association for Computational Linguistics*, pages 4885–4901, Online. Association for Computational Linguistics.

Yixin Nie, Xiang Zhou, and Mohit Bansal. 2020b. What can we learn from collective human opinions on natural language inference data? In *Proceedings of the 2020 Conference on Empirical Methods in Natural Language Processing (EMNLP)*, pages 9131–9143, Online. Association for Computational Linguistics.

Animesh Nighojkar and John Licato. 2021a. Improving paraphrase detection with the adversarial paraphrasing task. In *Proceedings of the 59th Annual Meeting of the Association for Computational Linguistics and the 11th International Joint Conference on Natural Language Processing (Volume 1: Long Papers)*, pages 7106–7116, Online. Association for Computational Linguistics.

Animesh Nighojkar and John Licato. 2021b. Mutual implication as a measure of textual equivalence. *The International FLAIRS Conference Proceedings*, 34.

Jennimaria Palomaki, Olivia Rhinehart, and Michael Tseng. 2018. A case for a range of acceptable annotations. In *Workshop on Subjectivity, Ambiguity and Disagreement in Crowdsourcing*.

Alicia Parrish, William Huang, Omar Agha, Soo-Hwan Lee, Nikita Nangia, Alex Warstadt, Karmanya Aggarwal, Emily Allaway, Tal Linzen, and Samuel R Bowman. 2021. Does putting a linguist in the loop improve nlu data collection? *arXiv preprint arXiv:2104.07179*.

Ellie Pavlick and Tom Kwiatkowski. 2019. Inherent disagreements in human textual inferences. *Transactions of the Association for Computational Linguistics*, 7:677–694.

Barbara Plank. 2022. The "problem" of human label variation: On ground truth in data, modeling and evaluation. In *Proceedings of the 2022 Conference on Empirical Methods in Natural Language Processing*, pages 10671–10682, Abu Dhabi, United Arab Emirates. Association for Computational Linguistics.

Adam Poliak. 2020. A survey on recognizing textual entailment as an NLP evaluation. In *Proceedings of the First Workshop on Evaluation and Comparison of NLP Systems*, pages 92–109, Online. Association for Computational Linguistics.

Adam Poliak, Yonatan Belinkov, James Glass, and Benjamin Van Durme. 2018. On the evaluation of semantic phenomena in neural machine translation using natural language inference. In *Proceedings of the 2018 Conference of the North American Chapter of the Association for Computational Linguistics: Human Language Technologies, Volume 2 (Short Papers)*, pages 513–523, New Orleans, Louisiana. Association for Computational Linguistics.

Paul Rottger, Bertie Vidgen, Dirk Hovy, and Janet Pierrehumbert. 2022. Two contrasting data annotation paradigms for subjective NLP tasks. In *Proceedings of the 2022 Conference of the North American Chapter of the Association for Computational Linguistics: Human Language Technologies*, pages 175–190, Seattle, United States. Association for Computational Linguistics.

John Rust and Susan Golombok. 2014. *Modern psychometrics: The science of psychological assessment*. Routledge.

Keisuke Sakaguchi and Benjamin Van Durme. 2018. Efficient online scalar annotation with bounded support. In *Proceedings of the 56th Annual Meeting of the Association for Computational Linguistics (Volume 1: Long Papers)*, pages 208–218, Melbourne, Australia. Association for Computational Linguistics.

Victor Sanh, Lysandre Debut, Julien Chaumond, and Thomas Wolf. 2019. Distilbert, a distilled version of bert: smaller, faster, cheaper and lighter. *arXiv preprint arXiv:1910.01108*.

James Thorne, Andreas Vlachos, Christos Christodoulopoulos, and Arpit Mittal. 2018. FEVER: a large-scale dataset for fact extraction and VERification. In *Proceedings of the 2018 Conference of the North American Chapter of the Association for Computational Linguistics: Human Language Technologies, Volume 1 (Long Papers)*, pages 809–819, New Orleans, Louisiana. Association for Computational Linguistics.

Alexandra Uma, Dina Almanea, and Massimo Poesio. 2022a. Scaling and disagreements: Bias, noise, and ambiguity. *Frontiers in Artificial Intelligence*, 5.

Alexandra N. Uma, Tommaso Fornaciari, Dirk Hovy, Silviu Paun, Barbara Plank, and Massimo Poesio. 2022b. Learning from disagreement: A survey. *J. Artif. Int. Res.*, 72:1385–1470.

Yuxia Wang, Minghan Wang, Yimeng Chen, Shimin Tao, Jiaxin Guo, Chang Su, Min Zhang, and Hao Yang. 2022. Capture human disagreement distributions by calibrated networks for natural language inference. In *Findings of the Association for Computational Linguistics: ACL 2022*, pages 1524–1535, Dublin, Ireland. Association for Computational Linguistics.

Adina Williams, Nikita Nangia, and Samuel Bowman. 2018. A broad-coverage challenge corpus for sentence understanding through inference. In *Proceedings of the 2018 Conference of the North American Chapter of the Association for Computational Linguistics: Human Language Technologies, Volume 1 (Long Papers)*, pages 1112–1122, New Orleans, Louisiana. Association for Computational Linguistics.

Kai-Chou Yang, Timothy Niven, and Hung-Yu Kao. 2019. Fake news detection as natural language inference. *arXiv preprint arXiv:1907.07347*.

Zhanye Yang. 2022. Legalnli: natural language inference for legal compliance inspection. In *International Conference on Advanced Algorithms and Neural Networks (AANN 2022)*, volume 12285, pages 144–150. SPIE.

Wenpeng Yin, Dragomir Radev, and Caiming Xiong. 2021. DocNLI: A large-scale dataset for document-level natural language inference. In *Findings of the Association for Computational Linguistics: ACL-IJCNLP 2021*, pages 4913–4922, Online. Association for Computational Linguistics.

Xiaoming Zhai, Joseph Krajcik, and James W Pellegrino. 2021. On the validity of machine learning-based next generation science assessments: A validity inferential network. *Journal of Science Education and Technology*, 30:298–312.

Sheng Zhang, Rachel Rudinger, Kevin Duh, and Benjamin Van Durme. 2017. Ordinal common-sense inference. *Transactions of the Association for Computational Linguistics*, 5:379–395.

Shujian Zhang, Chengyue Gong, and Eunsol Choi. 2021. Capturing label distribution: A case study in nli. *arXiv preprint arXiv:2102.06859*.

Xinliang Frederick Zhang and Marie-Catherine de Marneffe. 2021. Identifying inherent disagreement in natural language inference. In *Proceedings of the 2021 Conference of the North American Chapter of the Association for Computational Linguistics: Human Language Technologies*, pages 4908–4915, Online. Association for Computational Linguistics.

Xiang Zhou, Yixin Nie, and Mohit Bansal. 2022. Distributed NLI: Learning to predict human opinion distributions for language reasoning. In *Findings of the Association for Computational Linguistics: ACL 2022*, pages 972–987, Dublin, Ireland. Association for Computational Linguistics.

UMR-Writer 2.0: Incorporating a New Keyboard Interface and Workflow into UMR-Writer

Sijia Ge [1*], Jin Zhao [2*], Kristin Wright-Bettner[1], Skatje Myers[1]
Nianwen Xue[2], Martha Palmer[1]
[1] University of Colorado at Boulder
[2] Brandeis University
{sijia.ge,kristin.wrightbettner,skatje.myers,
martha.palmer}@colorado.edu
{jinzhao,xuen}@brandeis.edu

Abstract

UMR-Writer is a web-based tool for annotating semantic graphs for the Uniform Meaning Representation (UMR) scheme. UMR is a graph-based semantic representation that can be applied cross-linguistically for deep semantic analysis of text. In this work, we implemented a new keyboard interface for UMR-Writer 2.0, which adds to the original click-based interface to support faster annotation for more experienced annotators. The new interface also addresses some issues with the original click-based interface. Additionally, we demonstrate an efficient workflow for annotation project management in UMR-Writer 2.0, which has been applied to many projects.

1 Introduction

UMR-Writer (Zhao et al., 2021) is a web-based application used for annotating Uniform Meaning Representation (UMR). UMR is a graph-based, cross-linguistically applicable semantic representation designed to support interpretable natural language applications that require deep semantic analysis (Gysel et al., 2021; Bonn et al., 2023). It captures the meaning of natural language sentences and documents in a structured, human- and machine-readable format (Figure A1 shows a complete UMR graph).

UMR is an extension of Abstract Meaning Representation (AMR, Banarescu et al., 2013) and enriches the AMR semantic scheme to cover additional linguistic categories such as aspect (Donatelli et al., 2018; Van Gysel et al., 2019), and scope (Pustejovsky et al., 2019) in sentence-level annotation. UMR also supports document-level annotation for temporal relations (Yao et al., 2020), modality (Vigus et al., 2019), and coreference (O'Gorman et al., 2018). Moreover, UMR is also a universal multi-language semantic scheme that can be used to annotate low-resource languages such as Arapaho, Kukama, and Secoya, etc (Van Gysel et al., 2021; Vigus et al., 2020).

As graphs, UMR can be serialized into triples (parent concept node, relation, child concept node). Parent and child nodes can be abstract concepts, lexicalized concepts, or attribute values. Relations can be roles or other types of semantic relations. UMR-Writer originally has a click-based interface for annotators to construct UMR triples at the sentence level. An example is shown in Figure 1, which requires five steps for annotating the concept "*free*" in the sentence "*Edmund Pope tasted freedom today for the first time in more than eight months*". Annotators could 1) select a parent concept node "*taste*" by clicking the node; 2) select the child concept node "*free*" by selecting a span from the raw text; 3) look up senses by clicking the "lexicalized concept" box. Then, by hovering the cursor, annotators could 4) view the frame information and choose the correct concept sense, and finally 5) choose the correct relation (here, "*ARG1*", proto-patient) from the corresponding drop-down menus.

This approach creates several issues during annotation. Firstly, many annotators have extensive experience in annotating AMR with the AMR editor (Hermjakob, 2013). It uses a keyboard interface to annotate AMR graphs by entering editing commands. Therefore, annotators who are accustomed to the AMR editor may prefer to keep the keyboard interface instead of learning how to annotate in a click-based interface from scratch. Secondly, the multiple complicated drop-down menus in the click-based interface often confuse and overwhelm annotators. Annotators need to move the mouse back and forth between multiple drop-down menus and the sentence itself in order to add just one node to the graph, in addition to simultaneously paying attention to the sentence-level UMR graph, as shown in Figure 1. This impacts the annotation

*These authors contributed equally to this work.

Proceedings of the 17th Linguistic Annotation Workshop (LAW-XVII), pages 211–219
July 13, 2023 ©2023 Association for Computational Linguistics

efficiency and quality. Finally, some concepts are non-sequential in some languages, and it is tricky to select multiple non-sequential spans with a mouse.

To address these issues, we implemented a keyboard interface in UMR-Writer 2.0 (§3). The new interface was developed using Flask, JavaScript/Jquery, HTML/CSS, and PostgreSQL. It is specifically designed for sentence-level annotation and coexists with the original click-based interface, allowing annotators to choose their preferred approach. The interface for document-level annotation remains unchanged. Besides the annotation procedure, in terms of the workflow set-up, users also reported that managing annotation data for multiple corpora becomes difficult with the increasing size of the annotation. Thus this paper also introduces an efficient workflow for project management (§4), and other features for UMR-Writer 2.0 [1].

2 Related Tools

AMR editor is an easily accessible web-based annotation tool for AMR with comprehensive functionalities (Hermjakob, 2013). It is a command-based tool where annotators can enter short editing commands to annotate AMR graphs. Besides the basic function of building AMR graphs, it offers many useful features such as copy and paste of partial graphs, searching, and administrative support. Many features of the keyboard interface in this paper are inspired by the AMR editor. However, the AMR editor does not support document-level annotation and languages other than English.

There are other annotation tools available, such as Anafora (Chen and Styler, 2013) and BRAT (Stenetorp et al., 2012). Anafora is a web-based text annotation tool that is lightweight, flexible, easy to use, and capable of annotating with a variety of schemas. BRAT offers visualization for annotators to intuitively figure out the relations across text annotations. However, neither of these annotation tools is compatible with the UMR scheme and annotation requirements because they cannot annotate the concepts in the form of word lemmas, concatenated words, or abstract concepts that do not correspond to any specific word tokens in the source text. Like Anafora and BRAT, UMR-Writer can be modified to extend its usage to other graph-based formalisms besides UMR in theory, making it a versatile annotation tool. These modifications include customizing the relations and concept types to meet the requirements of various annotation tasks.

3 The Keyboard Interface of UMR-Writer 2.0

We first overview the layout of the new keyboard interface, then introduce the annotation methods and related functionalities.

3.1 Layout

Compared with the original click-based interface of UMR-Writer shown in Figure 1, the keyboard interface removes the drop-down menus on the right since annotators no longer need to interact with them. Instead, annotators enter the editing commands. To input commands, we added an input box under the raw text.

In the click-based interface, there is insufficient space to directly display the frame information, requiring annotators to hover the cursor over the predicate's sense to view the frame. In the new keyboard interface, we leverage the space created by removing the drop-down menus to display the frame information directly to annotators. The overall layout is shown in Figure 2. Annotators can primarily focus on the left-most area of the interface, which includes the raw text, editing command, and the generated UMR graph. This reduces the need for excessive eye and mouse movements associated with the click-based interface.

3.2 UMR Input Methods

To construct UMR graphs, we adopt the same "typing" method as the AMR editor for annotation but use an index-based style command (Li et al., 2016). The tool assigns a "superscript" to each token to signify its 1-based indexing position in the raw text. Annotators add an "x" before the index to refer to the token in the raw text. For example:

```
Edmund¹ Pope² tasted³ freedom⁴
today⁵ for⁶ the⁷ first⁸ time⁹ in¹⁰
more¹¹ than¹² eight¹³ months¹⁴
```

In this example, the first token "*Edmund*" is "x1", the second token "*Pope*" is "x2", and so on. The tool keeps track of tokens entered by the annotator and queries the lemmas from the database to obtain the corresponding concepts. It then displays the corresponding PropBank-style frame (Palmer

[1] UMR-Writer can access via the link: http://umr-tool.cs.brandeis.edu/.

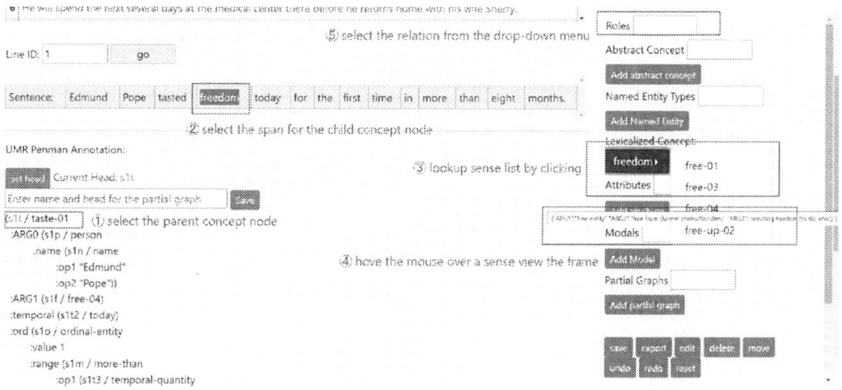

Figure 1: The click-based interface

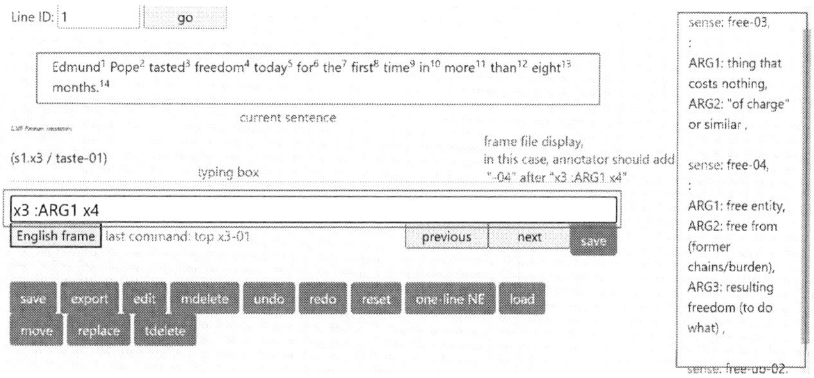

Figure 2: The keyboard interface

et al., 2005; Pradhan et al., 2022) information in the area to the right of the annotator. If annotators need to choose the correct sense from the current predicate's frame, they only have to attach the sense number with a dash marker following the index, such as "`x3-01`". This represents the first sense of the concept "*taste*" and indicates that it is the third token in the raw text. Annotators can input commands such as "`x3 :ARG1 x4-04`" shown in Figure 2 for annotating concept "*free*". This represents the fourth sense of the concept, which is the fourth token "*freedom*" in the text, acting as the "*ARG1*" (proto-patient) of its parent node, the concept "*taste*" (the sense number only needs to be specified once). The tool will then add a node to the UMR graph. When annotating abstract concepts such as named entities, annotators can enter a command such as "`x3 :ARG0 person x1_x2`" by attaching the abstract concept label before the index.

Additionally, such an approach using index-based command is applicable to situations where a concept is composed of multiple tokens or parts of a token resulting from segmentation errors or other reasons. In particular, it addresses the issue that a concept may consist of several non-sequential tokens such as the phenomenon of "Ionization of Pseudo-V-O Compounds" in Chinese (Chao, 1968), e.g.,[2]

(1) 我[1] 先[2] 给[3] 你[4] 提[5] 个[6] 醒[7]
1SG first give 2SG **warn** CLS **reminder**

'I'll first give you a reminder.'

In this case, the fifth token and the seventh token should be considered as a whole compound "提醒" (make aware), but other grammatical elements, such as the noun classifier, can be freely inserted into the middle, making the word look like a V-O construction, even though it makes no sense to interpret the two tokens separately. It can be tricky to select multiple non-sequential spans with a mouse, but annotators can enter commands like "`x5_x7`" to represent the concept consisting of the fifth and the seventh tokens.

[2] 1SG = first person singular, 2SG = second person singular, CLS = noun classifier.

The tool does not adopt the method used in the AMR editor that requires typing the concept directly for three reasons:

1. It can be difficult to record the alignment information, which is crucial for UMR annotation. Explicitly representing the correspondence between word tokens in the sentence and the concepts/relations in the UMR graph is useful for automatic parsing.
2. Entering a concept creates a higher probability of accidental typos compared with entering an index.
3. Annotators may need to frequently switch input method editors (IME) for languages such as Chinese and Arabic that are not based on an alphabet writing system to input commands.

Along with input commands, we also change variables represented in PENMAN (Kasper, 1989; Goodman, 2020) notation for concepts in UMR graphs. Each concept is associated with a variable that uniquely identifies a graph node. Variables serve as "shorthand" references for concepts, for example:

t / taste-01

"`t`" is the variable represented in PENMAN notation for the concept "*taste*". It uses the initials of the concept and a ascending number to distinguish between concept nodes with the same initial in AMR. The click-based interface follows the same convention but adds a sentence number to form strings such as "`s2t`" for document-level annotation ("`s2`" represents the second sentence).

In the keyboard interface, we concatenate the index after the auto-generated sentence number to form variables such as "`s2x3`" instead of taking the initials of concepts. This is because using the initials as variables is not feasible for languages that do not have an alphabet-based writing system. Additionally, initials-based variables cannot differentiate abstract concepts from lexicalized concepts. In the keyboard interface, each abstract concept is assigned a variable with an index that exceeds the total number of tokens in the sentence, and it is marked as an abstract concept with the prefix "`ac`" instead of the prefix "`x`" used for lexicalized concepts. For example, in the previous sentence "*Edmund Pope tasted freedom today for the first time in more than eight months*", the phrase "*eight months*" corresponds to an abstract concept "*temporal-quantity*", and since the number of tokens in this example is 14, we can assign the variable "`s2ac15`" to the "*temporal-quantity*" concept. Moreover, while the index of a token in a text is fixed, initial-based variables can vary based on the annotation order for concepts with the same initials. If we use the index as the input command to annotate a concept and then later on adopt initial-based variables, it would result in inconsistency. The index-based variables also encode alignment information.

The above changes in the keyboard interface make the annotation process more efficient, reducing five steps required in the click-based interface (Figure 1) to a single command (Figure 2) for adding a node in UMR graphs.

3.3 Other Functionalities for Editing UMR Graphs

We have implemented additional functionalities that go beyond adding a single concept node. For example, annotators can edit UMR graphs and they can delete an incorrect partial graph by clicking on its parent concept node. This action will delete both the parent node and its descendant nodes. Annotators can also move a partial graph to a different location instead of deleting and recreating it. In addition, annotators can use the new "redo" and "undo" buttons to recover from mistakes and track their editing progress. Furthermore, they can name and save partial graphs for future use, or copy-and-paste a partial graph directly from another annotation when constructing a new graph.

Overall, these additional functionalities enhance efficiency and flexibility, making the annotation process more convenient and effective.

4 Annotation as Projects

The annotation process can become messy and disorganized if an annotator works on multiple corpora. To address this issue, we have introduced the "project" concept in UMR-Writer 2.0.

Each project folder contains two sub-folders for storing completed annotations submitted by annotators: The first sub-folder is called "Quality Control" (QC), which stores the final version of each annotation file, and the second sub-folder is called "Double Annotated" (DA), which preserves multiple copies of the same file annotated by different annotators.

To manage the annotation projects effectively, we have created an administrative permission hierarchy. The hierarchy of administrative permissions

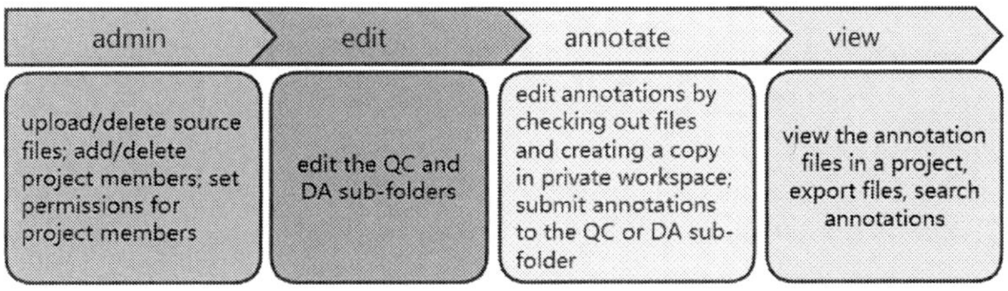

Figure 3: Permission hierarchy

and the descriptions for each are shown in Figure 3. The permission level decreases sequentially from left to right. The permission on the left side by default has all permissions on the right side. Thus, users with the "annotate" permission have the "view" permission. Similarly, users with the "edit" permission also have both the "view" and the "annotate" permissions, and so on. Same-level permission can be issued to multiple users except for "admin", which belongs to the owner of the project only.

Moreover, we have established an efficient workflow for each project:

- Each user can create project folders with the "admin" permission. "Admin" adds members to the project, assigns permissions, and uploads files into project folders. The annotation files can be exported files including UMR graphs, or just raw text.
- Anyone can view the original annotation files. Members with the "annotate" permission or higher can check out files and independently edit annotations without impacting other members in the project who have checked out the same files.
- If multiple users check out the same file, they should submit their annotations into the "DA" folder[3] after completing their work. Members with the "edit" or "admin" permission can decide which annotation should be put into the final "QC" folder by deleting the rest. If a file is checked out by only one member, the member can directly upload it to the "QC" folder. Members with the "edit" or "admin" permission can delete files with poor quality.

This workflow has been successfully applied to many projects such as the THYME corpus (Albright et al., 2013), and the Arabic UMR corpus.

Furthermore, UMR-Writer 2.0 provides a search functionality that allows users to search for annotations based on strings, concepts, or triples. Users can also specify whose annotations they want to query by entering user names. Each user has the option to choose the visibility of their project using a slider bar. The annotations in the project are publicly searchable by any user if the slider bar is checked. Annotation managers can leverage the search functionality to check annotations for beginner annotators during the training process.

5 Conclusion

UMR-Writer is a significant annotation tool for Uniform Meaning Representation. This paper introduces a new keyboard interface that constructs UMR graphs by entering index-based commands. This increases efficiency and guarantees higher accuracy of annotations. The new interface also solves the existing issues within the original click-based interface for the tool such as non-sequential tokens as concepts and variable inconsistencies across languages. The keyboard interface is especially welcomed by annotators who annotated with the AMR editor. Moreover, we introduce an annotation project workflow that can manage annotation projects efficiently.

Limitations

Raw text can sometimes be incorrectly segmented, especially in languages like Chinese which often have propagated segmentation errors due to the absence of explicit word boundaries and ambiguity caused by multi-character words with shared components. Annotators currently correct segmentation errors by using an underscore "_" to concatenate or splice tokens. However, this can be inconvenient, as annotators need to use this approach every time they edit concatenated/sliced concepts or add an edge between other concepts. In the future, we plan to allow annotators to manually correct segmentation errors by deleting or adding a space in the raw

[3] One file can be checked out by multiple users rather than just "double" annotated.

text.

Although the click-based interface supports low-resource languages well, we have not extensively experimented on many low-resource languages using the keyboard interface. Currently, for morphologically-complex languages, annotators need to manually count the index of a character in the token. Below is an example of Arapaho[4]:

(2) ceesisnoo'oebiicitiit
ceesis-noo'oe-**biicitii**-t

IC.begin-around-bead.s.t.-3S

'She is starting to bead around it.'

Here "*biicitii* " ("bead s.t.") is a concept. To select the token representing the concept, we need to input "`x1_13:20`" to represent "*biicitii*", where "`x1`" represents the token "*ceesisnoo'oebiicitiit*" as the entire sentence is a single token, "`_13:20`" represents the substring "*biicitii*" spanning from the thirteenth to the twentieth character in the token. Many low-resource languages such as Arapaho lack the lexical frame, thus we define frameworks for both non-lexicalized and lexicalized annotation of predicates and semantic roles (Gysel et al., 2021). For non-lexicalized UMR predicates, the role annotation is based on a general inventory of core participant roles given in Table A1. We are expanding the lexical frame coverage and constructing the predicate-specific definitions on the fly. The lexical entries should be mapped to the non-lexicalized roles in Table A1. We are also working on simplifying the process of selecting tokens by combining span selection with a mouse.

In the keyboard interface, the index-based variable system assigns different variables to within-sentence co-reference entities due to their distinct token alignments. Previously, we marked within-sentence co-reference using re-entrancy with the same variable. In the keyboard interface, it is necessary to identify and mark the two variables representing the co-referenced entities.

The identification of event-related concepts is crucial for annotating participant roles, as well as aspect and modality annotations. Currently, we do not include such a feature to detect eventive concepts. We plan to develop a system capable of detecting eventive concepts and providing auto-complete reminders to assist annotators in fully annotating the UMR graph. This approach aims to prevent any necessary annotations (such as the aspect of the eventive concept) from being omitted during the annotation process.

[4]IC = initial change, 3S = third person singular.

We also plan to refactor our code into a JavaScript framework, such as React.js, in a future version release. Additionally, we plan to make some improvements and changes to streamline the user experience, such as adjusting the visualization of the document-level annotation and implementing auto-completion of commands. Finally, we are currently working on mapping the named entities hierarchy in UMR to the ontology hierarchy in Wikidata.

Ethics Statement

We did not identify any potential ethical issues with the annotation tool.

Acknowledgements

This work is supported by grants from the CNS Division of National Science Foundation (Awards no: NSF_2213805, NSF_2213804, NSF_IIS 1764048, NSF_1763926 RI) entitled "Building a Broad Infrastructure for Uniform Meaning Representation" and "Developing a Uniform Meaning Representation for Natural Language Processing", respectively. We also gratefully acknowledge the support of NIH: 5R01LM010090-09, THYME-3, Temporal Relation Discovery for Clinical Text, (sub from Harvard Children's). Any opinions, findings, and conclusions or recommendations expressed in this material are those of the authors and do not necessarily reflect the views of NSF, NIH, or the U.S. government. We extend our thanks to Jie Cao and Kathryn Conger for their valuable suggestions on the paper revision.

References

Daniel Albright, Arrick Lanfranchi, Anwen Fredriksen, IV Styler, William F, Colin Warner, Jena D Hwang, Jinho D Choi, Dmitriy Dligach, Rodney D Nielsen, James Martin, Wayne Ward, Martha Palmer, and Guergana K Savova. 2013. Towards comprehensive syntactic and semantic annotations of the clinical narrative. *Journal of the American Medical Informatics Association*, 20(5):922–930.

Laura Banarescu, Claire Bonial, Shu Cai, Madalina Georgescu, Kira Griffitt, Ulf Hermjakob, Kevin Knight, Philipp Koehn, Martha Palmer, and Nathan Schneider. 2013. Abstract Meaning Representation for sembanking. In *Proceedings of the 7th Linguistic Annotation Workshop and Interoperability with Discourse*, pages 178–186, Sofia, Bulgaria. Association for Computational Linguistics.

Julia Bonn, Skatje Myers, Jens E. L. Van Gysel, Lukas Denk, Meagan Vigus, Jin Zhao, Andrew Cowell, William Croft, Jan Hajič, James H. Martin, Alexis Palmer, Martha Palmer, James Pustejovsky, Zdenka Urešová, Rosa Vallejos, and Nianwen Xue. 2023. Mapping AMR to UMR: Resources for adapting existing corpora for cross-lingual compatibility. In *Proceedings of the 21st International Workshop on Treebanks and Linguistic Theories (TLT, GURT/SyntaxFest 2023)*, pages 74–95, Washington, D.C. Association for Computational Linguistics.

Yuen Ren Chao. 1968. *A grammar of spoken Chinese / by Yuen Ren Chao*. University of California Press Berkeley.

Wei-Te Chen and Will Styler. 2013. Anafora: A web-based general purpose annotation tool. In *Proceedings of the 2013 NAACL HLT Demonstration Session*, pages 14–19, Atlanta, Georgia. Association for Computational Linguistics.

Lucia Donatelli, Michael Regan, William Croft, and Nathan Schneider. 2018. Annotation of tense and aspect semantics for sentential AMR. In *Proceedings of the Joint Workshop on Linguistic Annotation, Multiword Expressions and Constructions (LAW-MWE-CxG-2018)*, pages 96–108, Santa Fe, New Mexico, USA. Association for Computational Linguistics.

Michael Wayne Goodman. 2020. Penman: An open-source library and tool for AMR graphs. In *Proceedings of the 58th Annual Meeting of the Association for Computational Linguistics: System Demonstrations*, pages 312–319, Online. Association for Computational Linguistics.

Jens Van Gysel, Meagan Vigus, Jayeol Chun, Kenneth Lai, Sarah Moeller, Jiarui Yao, Timothy J. O'Gorman, Andrew Cowell, W. Bruce Croft, Chu-Ren Huang, Jan Hajic, James H. Martin, Stephan Oepen, Martha Palmer, James Pustejovsky, Rosa Vallejos, and Nianwen Xue. 2021. Designing a uniform meaning representation for natural language processing. *KI - Künstliche Intelligenz*, 35:343 – 360.

Ulf Hermjakob. 2013. Amr editor: A tool to build abstract meaning representations. *USC Information Sciences Institute, Tech. Rep.*

Robert T. Kasper. 1989. A flexible interface for linking applications to Penman's sentence generator. In *Speech and Natural Language: Proceedings of a Workshop Held at Philadelphia, Pennsylvania, February 21-23, 1989.*

Bin Li, Yuan Wen, Weiguang Qu, Lijun Bu, and Nianwen Xue. 2016. Annotating the little prince with Chinese AMRs. In *Proceedings of the 10th Linguistic Annotation Workshop held in conjunction with ACL 2016 (LAW-X 2016)*, pages 7–15, Berlin, Germany. Association for Computational Linguistics.

Tim O'Gorman, Michael Regan, Kira Griffitt, Ulf Hermjakob, Kevin Knight, and Martha Palmer. 2018. AMR beyond the sentence: the multi-sentence AMR corpus. In *Proceedings of the 27th International Conference on Computational Linguistics*, pages 3693–3702, Santa Fe, New Mexico, USA. Association for Computational Linguistics.

Martha Palmer, Daniel Gildea, and Paul Kingsbury. 2005. The Proposition Bank: An annotated corpus of semantic roles. *Computational Linguistics*, 31(1):71–106.

Sameer Pradhan, Julia Bonn, Skatje Myers, Kathryn Conger, Tim O'gorman, James Gung, Kristin Wright-bettner, and Martha Palmer. 2022. PropBank comes of Age—Larger, smarter, and more diverse. In *Proceedings of the 11th Joint Conference on Lexical and Computational Semantics*, pages 278–288, Seattle, Washington. Association for Computational Linguistics.

James Pustejovsky, Ken Lai, and Nianwen Xue. 2019. Modeling quantification and scope in Abstract Meaning Representations. In *Proceedings of the First International Workshop on Designing Meaning Representations*, pages 28–33, Florence, Italy. Association for Computational Linguistics.

Pontus Stenetorp, Sampo Pyysalo, Goran Topić, Tomoko Ohta, Sophia Ananiadou, and Jun'ichi Tsujii. 2012. brat: a web-based tool for NLP-assisted text annotation. In *Proceedings of the Demonstrations at the 13th Conference of the European Chapter of the Association for Computational Linguistics*, pages 102–107, Avignon, France. Association for Computational Linguistics.

Jens E. L. Van Gysel, Meagan Vigus, Lukas Denk, Andrew Cowell, Rosa Vallejos, Tim O'Gorman, and William Croft. 2021. Theoretical and practical issues in the semantic annotation of four indigenous languages. In *Proceedings of the Joint 15th Linguistic Annotation Workshop (LAW) and 3rd Designing Meaning Representations (DMR) Workshop*, pages 12–22, Punta Cana, Dominican Republic. Association for Computational Linguistics.

Jens E. L. Van Gysel, Meagan Vigus, Pavlina Kalm, Sook-kyung Lee, Michael Regan, and William Croft. 2019. Cross-linguistic semantic annotation: Reconciling the language-specific and the universal. In *Proceedings of the First International Workshop on Designing Meaning Representations*, pages 1–14, Florence, Italy. Association for Computational Linguistics.

Meagan Vigus, Jens E. L. Van Gysel, and William Croft. 2019. A dependency structure annotation for modality. In *Proceedings of the First International Workshop on Designing Meaning Representations*, pages 182–198, Florence, Italy. Association for Computational Linguistics.

Meagan Vigus, Jens E. L. Van Gysel, Tim O'Gorman, Andrew Cowell, Rosa Vallejos, and William Croft. 2020. Cross-lingual annotation: a road map for low-

and no-resource languages. In *Proceedings of the Second International Workshop on Designing Meaning Representations*, pages 30–40, Barcelona Spain (online). Association for Computational Linguistics.

Jiarui Yao, Haoling Qiu, Bonan Min, and Nianwen Xue. 2020. Annotating Temporal Dependency Graphs via Crowdsourcing. In *Proceedings of the 2020 Conference on Empirical Methods in Natural Language Processing (EMNLP)*, pages 5368–5380, Online. Association for Computational Linguistics.

Jin Zhao, Nianwen Xue, Jens Van Gysel, and Jinho D. Choi. 2021. UMR-writer: A web application for annotating uniform meaning representations. In *Proceedings of the 2021 Conference on Empirical Methods in Natural Language Processing: System Demonstrations*, pages 160–167, Online and Punta Cana, Dominican Republic. Association for Computational Linguistics.

A Appendix

Figure A1 is a UMR graph example borrowed from Zhao et al. (2021). It includes three sentences:

1. "Edmund Pope tasted freedom today for the first time in more than eight months."
2. "Pope was convicted on spying charges and sentenced to 20 years in a Russian prison."
3. "He denied any wrongdoing."

Each sentence is represented as a Directed Acyclic Graph (DAG), and multiple sentences can be connected to form a more complex graph at the document level.

Table A1 presents a general inventory of non-lexical core participant roles for low-resources languages.

Figure A2 is an example of project management (the "DA" folder is not shown here).

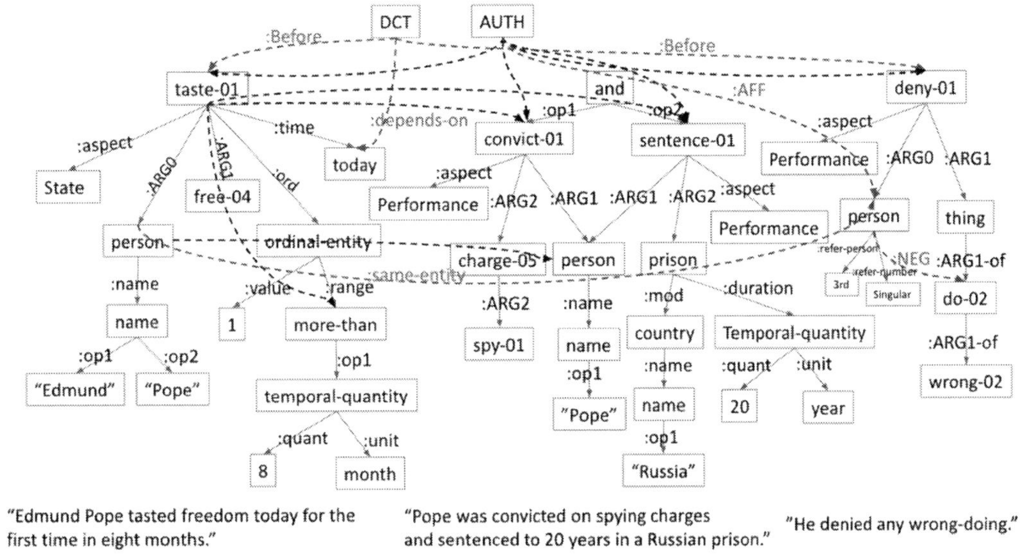

Figure A1: An example of UMR

Central roles	Actor, Undergoer, Theme, Recipient, Force, Causer, Experiencer, Stimulus
Peripheral roles	Instrument, Companion, Material/Source, Place, Start, Goal, Affectee
Roles for entities and events	Cause, Manner, Reason, Purpose, Temporal, Extent

Table A1: UMR non-lexical roles

Figure A2: Project management page

Unified Syntactic Annotation of English in the CGEL Framework

Brett Reynolds
Humber College
brett.reynolds@humber.ca

Aryaman Arora
Georgetown University
aa2190@georgetown.edu

Nathan Schneider
Georgetown University
nathan.schneider@georgetown.edu

Abstract

We investigate whether the *Cambridge Grammar of the English Language* (2002) and its extensive descriptions work well as a corpus annotation scheme. We develop annotation guidelines and in the process outline some interesting linguistic uncertainties that we had to resolve. To test the applicability of CGEL to real-world corpora, we conduct an interannotator study on sentences from the English Web Treebank, showing that consistent annotation of even complex syntactic phenomena like gapping using the CGEL formalism is feasible. Why introduce yet another formalism for English syntax? We argue that CGEL is attractive due to its exhaustive analysis of English syntactic phenomena, its labeling of both constituents and functions, and its accessibility. We look towards expanding CGELBank and augmenting it with automatic conversions from existing treebanks in the future.

1 Introduction

Ask a linguist about a detail of English grammar, and chances are they will reach for the *Cambridge Grammar of the English Language* (CGEL; Huddleston and Pullum, 2002). The product of the labors of two editors and 13 other chapter authors over more than a decade, CGEL is the most recent comprehensive reference grammar of English, describing nearly every syntactic facet of present-day Standard English in its 1700+ pages (Culicover, 2004). As but one example, a section[1] is devoted to the form and function of sentences like the first sentence of this paragraph, where the part before *and* is grammatically imperative but interpreted as a condition, and the part after *and* is interpreted as a consequence. CGEL is a gold mine for such idiosyncrasies that a sharp-eyed English student (or linguist, or treebanker) might want to look up, in bottom-up fashion. It is also a systematic top-down survey of the building blocks of the language—in this respect, aided by a lucid companion textbook (SIEG2; Huddleston et al., 2021).

In a review for *Computational Linguistics*, Brew (2003) argued that CGEL is a descriptive reference that echos precise formal thinking about grammatical structures; and as such, it holds considerable relevance for computational linguistics, supplementing formal grammars and treebanks like the venerable Penn Treebank (PTB; Marcus et al., 1994). Brew exhorts: "it should become a routine part of the training of future grammar writers and treebank annotators that they absorb as much as is feasible of this grammar". It has certainly had an impact, for example, on the Universal Dependencies project (UD; Nivre et al., 2016, 2020; de Marneffe et al., 2021), whose annotation guidelines cite CGEL many times in discussing particular phenomena[2] (though the UD trees themselves, for reasons of lexicalism and panlingualism, diverge significantly from the representations given in CGEL).

We ask: **What would it take to develop an annotation scheme based on CGEL?** If CGEL's attention to terminological precision and rigor is as strong as Brew suggests, it should not be nearly as difficult as mounting an effort of a completely new annotation framework. Most substantive questions of grammatical analysis should be addressed by CGEL, leaving only minor points to flesh out for treebanking. On the other hand, because CGEL was not designed for annotation, and therefore not tested systematically on corpora, perhaps it has substantial holes, regularly missing constructions that occur in real data.

To answer this question, we bootstrap an annotation manual and small set of sentences based on the

[1] "Imperatives interpreted as conditionals" (pp. 937–939)

[2] References to CGEL can be found, for example, at https://universaldependencies.org/u/overview/complex-syntax.html (regarding content clauses and secondary predicates) and https://universaldependencies.org/u/overview/specific-syntax.html (regarding comparative constructions).

Proceedings of the 17th Linguistic Annotation Workshop (LAW-XVII), pages 220–234
July 13, 2023

descriptions from CGEL. We examine what blanks in the CGEL specifications need to be filled in to realize full-sentence trees in our data—both qualitatively (through working sentence-by-sentence) and quantitatively (by conducting an interannotator agreement study).

What practical benefits hinge on the answer to this question? We are cognizant that substantial English treebanks already exist—constituency treebanks following the Penn Treebank standard, dependency treebanks, and others (§2). Thus, we do not anticipate a significant amount of from-scratch annotation in the CGEL framework. Yet we see practical benefits of the CGEL style of description, perhaps induced automatically as a new "view" of gold PTB trees. First, **exhaustiveness**: CGEL trees systematize *both constituent categories and functions in a unified framework*, whereas mainstream approaches for English prioritize either constituent structure (like PTB) or dependency structure (like UD). And second, **accessibility**: the trees would be consistent with human-readable descriptions and linguistic argumentation in the CGEL and SIEG2 texts, allowing users of a treebank (or parser) to look up the constructions in question.[3]

Through developing guidelines and annotating data, we find that CGEL offers a powerful foundation for treebanking, though there are points where further specification is needed. Our small but growing treebank—which we call **CGELBank**—and accompanying code for validation and measuring interannotator agreement are available at `https://github.com/nert-nlp/cgel/`. We also publish our annotation manual, which stands at about 75 pages (mostly of example trees): Reynolds et al. (2023).

2 Related Work

Even considering just English, there have been many formalisms deployed for syntactic annotation. A sample is given in Table 1. Each formalism makes different theoretical claims (e.g., is deep structure distinct from surface structure?) which bring computational tradeoffs (e.g. complexity vs. parsing efficiency). Many, beginning with

[3]PTB has an extensive annotation manual (Bies et al., 1995), but that serves a different purpose from a reference grammar: an annotation manual is a set of policies for an expert reader, not a complete presentation of syntactic phenomena or a defense of design decisions. Moreover, the terminology in the PTB manual draws heavily from particular syntactic theories like Government and Binding, whereas CGEL employs more general descriptive terminology.

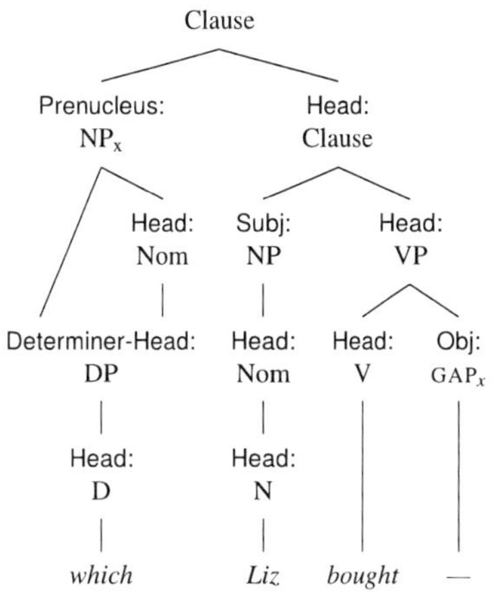

Figure 1: CGEL-style tree for the interrogative clause in *I wonder which Liz bought.*

PTB, have been used to annotate the Wall Street Journal corpus (WSJ; Marcus et al., 1993). CGEL shares ideas with many treebanks, such as constituency structure (PTB, TAG, etc.), labelled dependency relations (SD, UD, etc.), gapping (PTB), among other features.

A corpus that likewise integrates constituent categories and functions in a single tree is the TIGER treebank for German (Brants et al., 2004).

3 The CGEL Framework

An example parse in the CGEL framework appears in Figure 1.[4] Its building blocks are constituents, each of which receives a *category* indicating the type of unit it is and a *function* (notated with a colon) indicating its grammatical relation within the higher constituent. The constituent structure is a hierarchical bracketing of the sentence, which is projective with respect to the order of words in the sentence. Terminals consist of lexical items (omitting punctuation) as well as *gaps* used to handle constructions with noncanonical word order.

Categories. CGEL posits a distributionally-defined set of **lexical** categories, on which basis we developed a part-of-speech tagset with 11 tags: N (noun), N_{pro} (pronoun), V (verb), V_{aux} (auxiliary verb), P (preposition), D (determinative),[5] Adj (adjective), Adv (adverb), Sdr (subordinator), Coordinator, and Int (interjection). (See

[4]See Appendix C for more examples and a comparison with PTB.

[5]In CGEL, *determinative* is a lexical category whereas *determiner* is a function within an NP. A determinative heads

	Framework	Representative Citations
Constituency		
PTB	Penn Treebank	(Marcus et al., 1994; Bies et al., 2012; Pradhan et al., 2013)
TAG	Tree-Adjoining Grammar	(Chen and Vijay-Shanker, 2000)
MG	Minimalist Grammars	(Torr, 2018)
RRG	Role and Reference Grammar	(Bladier et al., 2018)
Dependency		
SD	Stanford Dependencies	(de Marneffe et al., 2006)
UD	Universal Dependencies	(Nivre et al., 2016)
SUD	Surface Universal Dependencies	(Gerdes et al., 2018)
FGD	Functional Generative Description	(Čmejrek et al., 2005)
Constraint-Based		
LFG	Lexical-Functional Grammar	(Sulger et al., 2013)
HPSG	Head-Driven Phrase Structure Grammar	(Oepen et al., 2002; Miyao et al., 2004; Flickinger et al., 2012)
Categorial		
CCG	Combinatory Categorial Grammar	(Hockenmaier and Steedman, 2007)

Table 1: A sample of grammatical frameworks that have been applied to English corpora.

(Reynolds et al., 2022) for further details and comparison to PTB/UD tagsets, especially regarding P and D.) Pronouns and proper nouns are a subset of nouns, though we have created a distinct tag for pronouns; auxiliary verbs are a subset of verbs. All of these categories except subordinator and coordinator project higher-level **phrasal** constituents, e.g. N ← Nom (nominal) ← NP (noun phrase). The basic phrasal categories are: Nom, NP, VP, Clause (the various subtypes of which are unmarked here except $\text{Clause}_{\text{rel}}$ for relative clauses), PP, DP, AdjP, AdvP, and IntP. Phrases are typically binary- or unary-branching, but *n*-ary branches are also possible. There is also a non-phrasal constituent category: Coordination, which may have ternary branching or higher.

Functions. Each constituent has a function indicating its syntactic role in the higher constituent. A *phrasal* constituent is headed, i.e. it has exactly one child in Head function along with zero or more dependents. Coordination constituents are the main exception: there is no head, and each element (conjunct) in the coordination receives a function of Coordinate. Figure 2 illustrates the main CGEL functions, organized into a hierarchy. Note that CGEL contrasts adjuncts (Mod, Supplement) with complements (Comp and subtypes, including Subj, Obj, PredComp, and others). Other dependent functions include Determiner (Det) function in an NP, and Marker for grammatical words that mark but do not head a phrase, notably coordinators and subordinators.

a determinative phrase (DP), not to be confused with the notion of a *determiner phrase* in generative grammar (Abney, 1987).

Gaps. CGEL employs gap constituents and coindexation, as in Figure 1, to handle unbounded dependency constructions (UDCs) and other constructions that deviate from the canonical declarative order, showing where there is a clear structural gap. Nevertheless "the account is quite informal" (R. Huddleston, personal communication). To make it more formal, we have restricted the use of gaps to UDCs, subject-auxiliary inversion (SAI), and pre- and post-posing of complements. We also use gaps for adjunct fronting when it triggers SAI (e.g., *Only once had I – seen it –*). Subject–dependent inversion (SDI) is a double-gapped construction with a subject gap and a complement gap in the VP (e.g., *Here – is – Jim*). All subject-relatives have a gap, as do delayed right constituent coordination and end-attachment coordination. Coindexation is used with and only with a gap. Every gap must be coindexed with exactly one overt constituent (and possibly other gaps). There are no gaps for ellipsis.

Fusion. Certain constructions are analyzed with *fusion of functions*, in which a constituent participates in two different higher constituents (Payne et al., 2007; Pullum and Rogers, 2008). This is shown in Figure 1 for the NP *which*, short for something like "which items": the DP is taken to fulfill both the Determiner function in the NP and the Head in its Nominal. Other constructions where CGEL employs fusion of functions include compound determinatives (e.g. *someone*), other determinatives or adjectives as NP heads (*the **rich**, the **tallest**, those **three***[6]), and fused (a.k.a. free or head-

[6]Elazar and Goldberg (2019) offer an NLP approach to reasoning about numeric fused heads.

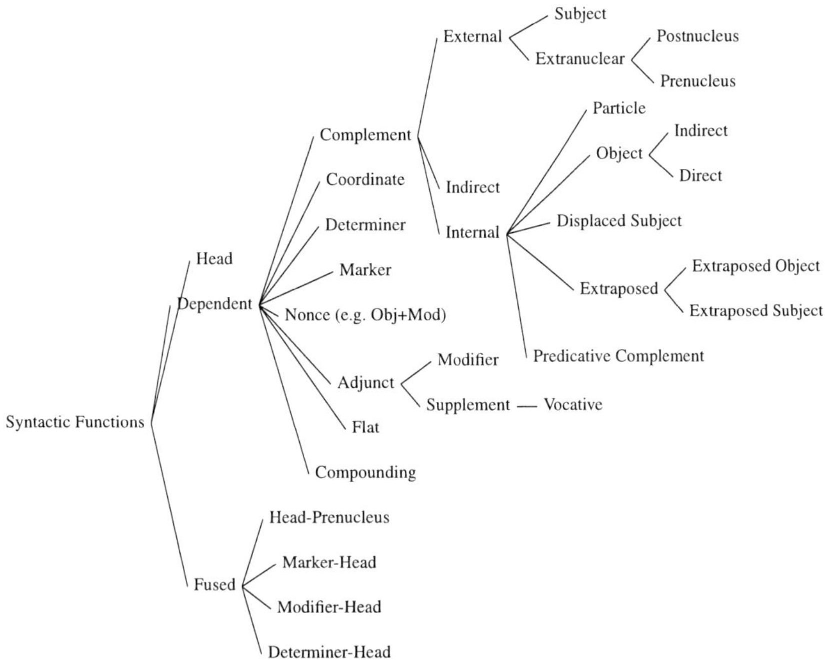

Figure 2: Hierarchy of functions. The ones annotated directly in the data are the leaves plus Complement (Comp), Object (Obj), and Supplement. The distinction between direct and indirect objects is made only in double object constructions.

less) relative constructions (***whatever** you want*). The hyphenated notation such as Determiner-Head indicates its dual function. Thus, technically the parse is a graph rather than a tree. However, the longer of the two incoming edges can be inferred deterministically based on the Determiner-Head label and the rest of the structure. For computational purposes, then, we can omit the longer edge wherever there is fusion of functions, maintaining the tree property, and automatically add it in postprocessing for visualization. We therefore refer to CGEL-style parses as trees.

4 Towards CGELBank

Despite its detail and richness, in 1700+ pages, CGEL includes just 40 trees, and on some points is inexplicit. Annotating naturally occurring sentences (§5) brought many of these ambiguities to the fore. Here we identify questions we faced and the decisions we made.

4.1 Categorizing individual lexemes

Creating part-of-speech (POS) tagsets and defining tag boundaries have been contentious in treebanking (Atwell, 2008). CGEL's guidance in this area is extensive but dispersed, and lists of closed-category items are inexhaustive. For CGELBank, we compiled mentions of lexemes and their categories from CGEL and applied CGEL principles to classify numerous unmentioned lexemes.[7] Examples include the determinative *said* (e.g., *as in said contract*), the coordinator *slash* (e.g., *Dear God slash Allah slash Buddha slash Zeus*), and the preposition *o'clock* (Pullum and Reynolds, 2013).

4.2 Simplifying and un-simplifying

CGEL uses various subtypes of head within clause structure (Nucleus, Predicate, Predicator); we collapse these to Head. CGEL sometimes removes intermediate unary nodes, such as eliminating Head:Nom between Head:N and its projected NP. We consistently include these nodes.

4.3 Gaps

CGEL posits gaps in tree structures for prenucleus position constituents, but is inconsistent in indicating them. We explicitly indicate a gap in most cases and outline our decisions for unclear cases.

Subject gaps. For open interrogatives such as (1a) and (1b), CGEL's position is unclear. Given

[7]Conducted since 2006 in consultation with Huddleston and Pullum, recorded in Simple English Wiktionary.

ambiguity, we follow the standard position that a gap exists (e.g. Maling, 2000; Bies et al., 1995) in questioned or relativized subject clauses.

(1) a. What did she tell you?
    b. Who told you that?

Adjunct gaps. Adjuncts may appear in various locations, with some not appearing clause finally. We decided against including a gap, except in relative and open interrogative clauses where CGEL marks a gap.

Phrasal genitives. In NPs ending in a gap, we attach *'s* to the gap, as in *a guy I know _'s house*.

Coordination and comparatives. CGEL's Gapped Coordination refers to ellipsis, not gaps. CGELBank does not include gaps in tree structure for coordination and comparatives.

4.4 Branching & tree structure

In CGEL, some rare phenomena are not explicitly depicted in tree form due to the limited number of actual syntax trees in the text. Also, unary nodes (e.g. N → Nom → NP) are inconsistently indicated due to space considerations. In general, we sought to ensure that tree structure was consistent and thus had to make some decisions on how to treat phenomena such as coordination, complementation, etc.

Lexical Projection Principle. Outside of morphologically derived expressions, and excepting coordinators and subordinators, **a lexical node almost always projects a phrase of the corresponding category**. Thus, every N must serve as head within a Nom; every V must head a VP; every Adj must head an AdjP; and so forth. The one exception is that subject-auxiliary inversion targets auxiliaries specifically (rather than the VP they would project in normal position), so if the constituent in Prenucleus function consists of a single unmodified V_{aux}, it will not project a VP there.

Coordinates & markers. A coordi**nation** is a non-headed construction with coordi**nates** as children (CGEL p. 1278). Therefore, coordi**nates** in coordinations are neither heads nor dependents. Consider, though, the following coordination *the guests and indeed his family too* (p. 1278), reproduced here as Figure 3.

Unlike coordinations, NPs like *and indeed his family too* are headed constructions in CGEL. The NP has two modifiers: *indeed* and *too*, which, like all modifiers, are dependents requiring a head sibling. But if the *his family* is not a head but a coordinate as labeled, then this NP is headless, an internal contradiction in CGEL.

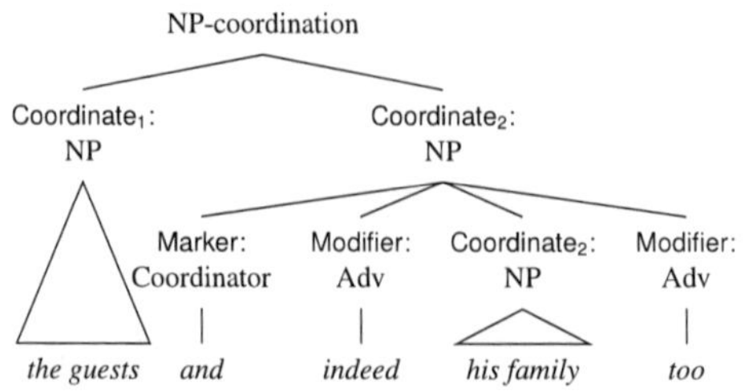

Figure 3: CGEL flat coordination—rejected in CGELBank, where *indeed his family too* is an NP serving as the Head of the second coordinate.

Markers[8] are siblings of heads when they are subordinators (see (9) on p. 954 and (51) on p. 1187), so a marker is a dependent. This, however, is incompatible with the analysis in Figure 3 (p. 1277).

To resolve these inconsistencies, the NP *his family* in Figure 3 must be a head and not a coordinate. We generalize from this to the principle that, contra Figure 3, a coordinate is never the child of a non-coordination, and a marker is always a dependent with a sibling head.

Indirect complements. Indirect complements, such as in *enough time to complete the work*, are licensed by a dependent in the phrase. We construct a superordinate phrase of the head type and branch the indirect complement from that. When the complement is further delayed, we do the same for nearest possible parent phrase.

Verbless clauses. CGEL's treatment of verbless clauses (VlCs) is incompatible with its general treatment of clauses. VlCs have no verb and no VP, so they must not be clauses in the syntactic sense that CGEL implies. We treat certain PPs as having two complements, analogous to complex transitive verbs, and PPs like *while happy* as taking predicative complements. Supplement VlCs are analyzed as headless nonce constructions.

Names. CGEL claims that the syntactic structure of proper names mostly conforms to the rules for ordinary NPs, but it also notes that there is no convincing evidence for treating one element as head in personal names. We treat proper names, along

[8]Though CGEL uses "marker" both non-technically (e.g., marker of distinctively informal style), and technically as a function term, we discuss only the latter.

Split	Trees	Tokens	Nodes	Ann.
EWT	100	1,864	5,110	2
Twitter	65	824	2,316	2
EWT-trial	27	500	1,365	1
Twitter-trial	10	257	727	1
Pilot	5	61	174	1 + 2
IAA	50	642	1,747	1 + 2
Total	257	4,148	11,439	

Table 2: Overall statistics about the treebank and its splits. *Nodes* is the sum of the count of all constituents and gaps in each tree, including tokens. *Ann.* indicates the annotators involved.

with chemical compounds, as single lexical items, analyzing multiple tokens using the Flat relation.

5 Annotation Process

What began as a pet project to make CGEL-style trees for interesting sentences found in the wild eventually became a corpus-building effort, with two linguists interested in the CGEL framework (the first and third authors) serving as annotators. To date, this has resulted in over 200 trees of naturally occurring sentences—some handpicked, others sampled at random from a corpus. Statistics for **CGELBank** are presented in Tables 2 and 3.

CGELBank trees were drawn from multiple sources, and were annotated in four phases.

1. **Twitter**: Exploratory annotation of real-world sentences taken from Twitter by Annotator 2 resulted in this set of 65 trees. At this point, there were no agreed-upon guidelines for CGEL annotation and the project was largely informal.
2. **EWT**: A set of 100 sentences sampled from the English Web Treebank (Bies et al., 2012) was annotated by Annotator 2 and simultaneously the guidelines were composed in discussion with Annotator 1. To maintain consistency with the guidelines, both the EWT and Twitter treebanks were validated and iteratively corrected.
3. **EWT-trial, Twitter-trial**: Once the guidelines and validation script were mostly complete, and as the browser-based annotation workflow was under development, the two annotators used it to make 37 more trees (27 from additional EWT sentences, 10 from Twitter and other sources). These trees were singly annotated and validated but not adjudicated.
4. **IAA** and **Pilot**: For an interannotator study, both annotators independently annotated and then adjudicated a pilot set of 5 trees and then a larger set of 50 trees. These were also drawn from EWT.

```
# sent_id = which-liz-bought
# text = which Liz bought.
# sent = which Liz bought --
(Clause
   :Prenucleus (x / NP
      :Head (Nom
         :Det-Head (DP
            :Head (D :t "which"))))
   :Head (Clause
      :Subj (NP
         :Head (Nom
            :Head (N :t "Liz")))
      :Head (VP
         :Head (V :t "brought" :l "bring" :p ".")
         :Obj (x / GAP))))
```

Figure 4: Illustration of the `.cgel` data format for the clause from Figure 1. Note that the bracketed notation forms a proper tree: the reentrancy of the fused determiner-head is automatically added post hoc. The verb lemma is included as it differs from its inflected form. Features on nodes are extensible: for example, CGELBank uses `:p` for punctuation, `:note` to offer commentary on a construction (with CGEL page references), and `:correct` to indicate corrections to typos. Finer-grained morphosyntactic information (inflectional features, clause types, etc.) may be added in the future.

The initial 165 Twitter and EWT sentences were annotated in LaTeX using the `forest` package and converted into the `.cgel` format using an ad hoc Python script. Later annotation was done with a customized version[9] of Active DOP, a browser-based graphical treebanking tool (van Cranenburgh, 2018). Active DOP incorporates disco-dop (van Cranenburgh et al., 2016), an active learning parser, which considerably sped up annotation. We trained disco-dop on the 202 trees created prior to the start of the IAA pilot. As input to the Active DOP tool, EWT sentences were preannotated with POS tags and gaps heuristically derived from gold UD and PTB trees; the tagging was then manually edited in a text editor.[10] For the 50 IAA sentences, after trees were exported to the `.cgel` format, adjudication was performed cooperatively between the two annotators using a text editor with a file comparison mode.

Each split is stored in a separate file in the `.cgel` data format illustrated in Figure 4. This combines the sentence metadata style from the CONLL-U format[11] with trees in a bracketed format adapted

[9] `https://github.com/nschneid/activedop`

[10] At present, Active DOP does not support editing of tokenization or gap positions in the browser interface. This should be added in the future to make the tool more usable.

[11] Described in the UD docs.

POS		Nonlexical Category		Function	
1091	N	1701	Nom	6817	Head
537	P	1400	NP	935	Mod
535	V	1196	VP	630	Comp
470	D	927	Clause	627	Obj
404	N_{pro}	558	PP	457	Det
338	V_{aux}	470	DP	453	Subj
267	Adj	300	AdjP	320	Coordinate
199	Adv	201	AdvP	299	Marker
156	Coordinator	156	Coordination	142	PredComp
143	Sdr	141	$Clause_{rel}$	133	Supplement
8	Int	9	NP+PP	111	Flat
		8	IntP	79	Det-Head
		5	NP+Clause	72	Prenucleus
		3	NP+AdvP	19	Postnucleus
		3	AdjP+PP	12	Particle
155	*GAP*	1	NP+AdjP	11	$Comp_{ind}$

Table 3: Counts in CGELBank of lexical categories (POS tags), nonlexical categories, and grammatical functions. Special phrasal categories for coordination and some functions are not listed due to low frequency.

from PENMAN notation (Kasper, 1989). CGELBank includes a Python API for working with this format, including a script to export it to LaTeX for visualization (with any reentrancies due to fusion of functions).

During the initial phases of development, it became clear that certain structural properties (like the number of Nom layers in a complex NP) were sources of annotator inconsistency. We therefore developed a **validator**, a script to check structural properties for obvious errors (e.g., misspelled labels; phrases with no Head) as well as less obvious errors (a category occurring in an unusual position in the tree; an unnecessary level of nesting of a phrase; a Modifier forming a ternary-branching structure; invalid coindexation of a gap; improper structure of Coordinates in coordination). Some of the validation rules are conservative and need to be broadened as new data is encountered; but flagging them is an opportunity for the annotator to check for an error or inconsistency. In our experience, the rules (implemented in 500 lines of Python) often find small problems that might otherwise have gone undetected. We quantify the impact of the validator in the next section.

6 Interannotator Study

To test the consistency of our CGEL annotation guidelines, we conducted an interannotator study. As a pilot, five sentences sampled from the English Web Treebank (Bies et al., 2012) were annotated independently by the first and third authors. After adjudicating annotation disagreements and adapting to the annotation tool, we sampled 50 new sentences from EWT for the interannotator study. The annotators independently annotated the new set and then jointly adjudicated disagreements.

6.1 Evaluation Metric

A variety of measures for interannotator agreement on constituency syntax annotation exist in the literature. The standard metric is Parseval (Black et al., 1991), which computes precision and recall of the token spans that each constituent corresponds to. One problem with the usual implementation of Parseval is that it ignores hierarchy when comparing unary nodes (i.e. multiple constituents share the same token span).[12] Furthermore, there is no obviously correct way to compare trees with non-identical leaves using Parseval—which can be caused by disagreement on tokenization (e.g. on hyphenated terms) or the existence/placement of gaps, both of which we encountered in our study.

To be able to compare trees with unary nodes and potentially nonidentical tokenized strings, we turn to **Tree Edit Distance** (TED), which has been pointed out as an alternative to Parseval's reliance on token spans (Emms, 2008). TED defines a correspondence between trees via insertion, deletion (which promotes children), and substitution of nodes—it can be thought of as an extension of Levenshtein distance from strings to trees.[13] Like Levenshtein distance, TED is solved with dynamic programming; we adapt Zhang and Shasha's (1989) algorithm, with details in Appendix A. We compute microaveraged precision and recall scores based on the three types of edit costs, editing the gold tree to produce the predicted tree: deletions contribute to recall error, insertions to precision error, and substitution cost is split equally between the two. We then compute F_1 from precision and recall, which is equivalent to the *TreeDice* metric of Emms (2008) (as explained in Appendix A).

Score types. We report several scores using TED, based on different criteria for scoring candidate node alignments (matches/substitutions). In increasing order of strictness:

[12] For example, consider one tree with unary nodes $\{A,B,C\}$ and another with $\{A,C,B\}$, all corresponding to the same token span. Parseval will report both precision and recall to be 100%, which is too lenient for our purposes since the order of unary nodes matters in CGEL.

[13] If the tree is viewed as a bracketed string, structural operations insert or delete a pair of brackets and the associated node label.

Metric	1~2	1~adj	2~adj
unlab	94.8	98.1	96.0
flex	93.9	97.6	95.5
strict	91.6	96.0	94.2
gap	87.2	100.0	87.2
full-tree	18.0	54.0	32.0

Table 4: Results of the 50-sentence interannotator agreement study after the validation script. Scores are all microaveraged F1, except for `full-tree` which is the percentage of trees that are identical. See Table 2, "IAA" row for statistics of the adjudicated data.

- `unlab`: Unlabelled constituents. This metric examines the tree structure alone.
- **`flex`: Labelled with function, category, and (for lexical nodes) token string, with partial credit for a node that differs in some of these respects.** For each of these components, a mismatch incurs a cost of 0.25; together these comprise the node substitution cost. An exact match has cost 0. We consider `flex` to be the main metric as it is most nuanced and should therefore induce the most accurate alignment between the two trees.
- `strict`: Labelled with all components, and no partial credit: the substitution cost is 1 for any two nodes that are not fully identical.

For gaps, the category is `GAP` and the token string is empty. Gaps are coindexed to an antecedent; this is factored into the scores by checking, after running the TED algorithm, whether two otherwise matched gaps have "the same" (aligned) antecedents. If not, the gap is not considered a full match (the `flex` penalty is 0.25).

Other metrics are:

- `gap`: F1 score of gaps per the alignment induced by the `flex` metric.
- `full-tree`: Proportion of trees that match exactly.

6.2 Results

Agreement scores between the two annotators as well as between the unadjudicated and the final adjudicated trees are reported in Table 4.[14] For all metrics, agreement F1 exceeds 90%. In particular, the `flex` metric shows an interannotator agreement F1 of 93.9%. Therefore, we are confident that, with reference to our guidelines, the CGEL formalism can be applied to the annotation of real-world text in a consistent manner.

[14]Full output of the scorer on the 50 IAA sentences is provided at: `https://github.com/nert-nlp/cgel/blob/b95309f6c2ada885728b80a21b6d576bd85a20c9/datasets/iaa/iaa.out`

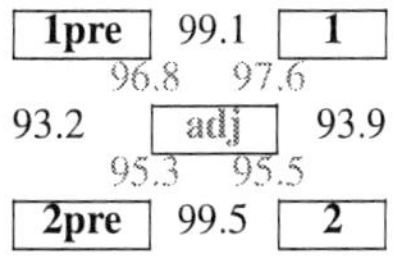

Table 5: Agreement F1 scores on 50 IAA sentences via the `flex` metric before and after validation and adjudication. **1pre** denotes the trees from annotator 1 prior to running the validation script. **1** indicates annotator 1's final trees after revisions to address warnings from the validation script. **adj** denotes the final adjudicated trees. (Exact tree match scores appear in Appendix B.)

Operation	Cost	Unit Cost
insertion	98.00	1.00
deletion	82.00	1.00
substitution	31.75	
category	11.00	0.25
function	18.75	0.25
lexeme	2.00	0.25
gap ant.	0.00	0.25

Table 6: Costs by error type for the **1~2** interannotator comparison with the `flex` metric (sum across 50 trees). E.g., 75 nodes were identified as substitutions with a different function; each of these incurs a cost of 0.25, hence 18.75 function cost. A single substitution can involve a mixture of multiple subtypes whose costs would be added together. The gap antecedent error subtype did not occur in this comparison (gaps either were inserted/deleted or had matching antecedents).

As expected, the `strict` score of 91.6% is lower than the `flex` score, while the `unlab` score (which considers structure only) is higher, at 94.8%.

A breakdown of `flex` costs by edit type appears in Table 6. Among nodes aligned by TED, function disagreements were more numerous than category disagreements (75 vs. 44 occurrences, costing 0.25 each). But many nodes were inserted/deleted, e.g. due to attachment differences.

Zooming in to just gaps, of which there were 21 in the 50 adjudicated trees, we find good (but lower) agreement F1 of 87.2%. A major source of disagreement was a phrase in sentence 5 involving a shared object between 4 coordinated verbs—annotator 1 indicated this with 4 gaps while annotator 2 used none. Still, overall this demonstrates that even complex phenomena described in CGEL can be analysed consistently by trained annotators.

Finally, only 18.0% of trees (`full-tree`) are identical between the two annotators. However, many more of the trees between the annotators and the adjudicated set are identical—54.0% (annotator

1) and 32.0% (annotator 2).

Impact of validator. Output from the validation script was shown to each annotator after their initial pass through the 50 trees.[15] Table 5 shows the impact of the validator by reporting `flex` agreement scores before and after validation. (See also Appendix B for validator effects on exact tree accuracy.) Self-agreement before vs. after validation was 99.1% (A1) and 99.5% (A2). Agreement between the two annotators improved after validation, 93.2% → 93.9%, as the tool helped to identify spurious errors like missing or extra Nom levels in an NP, and categories in implausible functions. Agreement with the final adjudicated data increased measurably as well (A1: 96.8% → 97.6%; A2: 95.3% → 95.5%).

Note that all of the trees in the IAA experiment were created by editing trees proposed by the active learning parser, which at least featured locally well-formed structures—reducing the rate of spurious errors compared to annotation from scratch.

Qualitative findings. Many of the uncertainties and disagreements in the IAA experiment concerned structured names and measurements, including street addresses, age expressions, and temperature expressions. The phrase *over $300* exposed the problem of treating currency symbols in orthographic order, as CGEL assigns the structure [*over 300*] *dollars*, with a complex DP. Consequently, we added a guideline requiring currency expressions to be treebanked in pronunciation order, regardless of orthographic order.

Another recurring difficulty came from compounds that might have been hyphenated, like *flight test* functioning as a verb: should these be treated as one lexeme or two?

The choice of function for certain types of phrases (especially PPs) seems to lie on a continuum between Complement, Modifier, and Supplement. On substitutions, the scoring script reports 18 Comp vs. Mod disagreements and 11 Mod vs. Supplement disagreements. While it may be possible to further clarify the boundaries, it seems that some subjectivity along this continuum is inevitable.

Finally, one IAA sentence contained a fronted partitive PP (of the form *Out of* X *and* Y, *which is the best?*). We could not find an explicit account of partitive fronting in CGEL, and plan to revisit this in future work.

[15] A handful of warnings were false positives, prompting changes to the script.

7 Conclusion

Using the analysis developed in CGEL (Huddleston and Pullum, 2002), we introduced a new expressive and linguistically-informed syntactic formalism to corpus annotation of English, which unifies constituent and dependency information in an accessible format. Creating annotation guidelines confirmed that CGEL was a strong foundation for syntactic analysis, but also revealed some minor points of underspecification for which new policies were necessary. Using our guidelines, we have created trees from naturally occurring sentences in multiple genres, and we conducted an interannotator study. We find high annotator agreement overall and even on the complex phenomenon of gapping. Overall, we are confident that the formalism of CGEL is suitable for consistent annotation of real-world text. In the future, we intend to take advantage of existing resources in other frameworks to obtain CGEL-style trees and parsers on a larger scale and in a wider range of genres.

Acknowledgements

Author contributions: All authors contributed to the scientific direction, writing, and analysis of this work. ▷ *BR:* Initiator of making ad hoc CGEL-style trees (shared via `https://twitter.com/DailySyntaxTree`) that blossomed into this project; annotation and guidelines lead. ▷ *AA:* Design of evaluation metric, scripting including data format reader/tree API, quantitative analysis. ▷ *NS:* Secondary annotator, editing of guidelines; design of data format, design of evaluation metric, scripting including validator, scoring, annotation tool customizations, quantitative analysis.

We thank John Payne, Geoffrey Pullum, and Pairoj Kunanupatham for useful discussion on many linguistic issues that arose in annotation as well as the CGEL formalism in general. We also thank various Twitter users (including Rui P. Chaves and Russell Lee-Goldman) who commented on syntactic analyses posted by Brett Reynolds, as well as anonymous reviewers. This research was supported in part by NSF award IIS-2144881.

References

Steven P. Abney. 1987. *The English noun phrase in its sentential aspect*. PhD thesis, Massachusetts Institute of Technology, Cambridge, MA.

ES Atwell. 2008. Development of tag sets for part-of-speech tagging. In *Corpus Linguistics: An International Handbook*, volume 1, pages 501–526. Walter de Gruyter.

Ann Bies, Mark Ferguson, Karen Katz, Robert MacIntyre, Victoria Tredinnick, Grace Kim, Mary Ann Marcinkiewicz, and Britta Schasberger. 1995. Bracketing guidelines for Treebank II style Penn Treebank project.

Ann Bies, Justin Mott, Colin Warner, and Seth Kulick. 2012. English Web Treebank. Technical Report LDC2012T13, Linguistic Data Consortium, Philadelphia, PA.

E. Black, S. Abney, D. Flickenger, C. Gdaniec, R. Grishman, P. Harrison, D. Hindle, R. Ingria, F. Jelinek, J. Klavans, M. Liberman, M. Marcus, S. Roukos, B. Santorini, and T. Strzalkowski. 1991. A procedure for quantitatively comparing the syntactic coverage of English grammars. In *Speech and Natural Language: Proceedings of a Workshop Held at Pacific Grove, California, February 19-22, 1991*.

Tatiana Bladier, Andreas van Cranenburgh, Kilian Evang, Laura Kallmeyer, Robin Möllemann, and Rainer Osswald. 2018. RRGbank: a Role and Reference Grammar corpus of syntactic structures extracted from the Penn Treebank. In *Proc. of the 17th International Workshop on Treebanks and Linguistic Theories (TLT 2018)*, pages 5–16, Oslo, Norway.

Sabine Brants, Stefanie Dipper, Peter Eisenberg, Silvia Hansen-Schirra, Esther König, Wolfgang Lezius, Christian Rohrer, George Smith, and Hans Uszkoreit. 2004. TIGER: Linguistic interpretation of a German corpus. *Research on Language and Computation*, 2(4):597–620.

Chris Brew. 2003. The Cambridge Grammar of the English Language, Rodney Huddleston and Geoffrey K. Pullum. *Computational Linguistics*, 29(1):144–147.

John Chen and K. Vijay-Shanker. 2000. Automated extraction of TAGs from the Penn Treebank. In *Proceedings of the Sixth International Workshop on Parsing Technologies*, pages 65–76, Trento, Italy. Association for Computational Linguistics.

Martin Čmejrek, Jan Cuřín, Jan Hajič, and Jiří Havelka. 2005. Prague Czech-English Dependency Treebank: resource for structure-based MT. In *Proc. of EAMT*, pages 73–78, Budapest, Hungary.

Peter W. Culicover. 2004. The Cambridge Grammar of the English Language (review). *Language*, 80(1):127–141.

Marie-Catherine de Marneffe, Bill MacCartney, and Christopher D. Manning. 2006. Generating typed dependency parses from phrase structure parses. In *Proc. of LREC*, pages 449–454, Genoa, Italy.

Marie-Catherine de Marneffe, Christopher D. Manning, Joakim Nivre, and Daniel Zeman. 2021. Universal Dependencies. *Computational Linguistics*, 47(2):255–308.

Yanai Elazar and Yoav Goldberg. 2019. Where's my head? Definition, data set, and models for numeric fused-head identification and resolution. *Transactions of the Association for Computational Linguistics*, 7:519–535.

Martin Emms. 2008. Tree distance and some other variants of evalb. In *Proc. of LREC*, Marrakech, Morocco.

Dan Flickinger, Yi Zhang, and Valia Kordoni. 2012. DeepBank. A dynamically annotated treebank of the Wall Street Journal. In *Proc. of the 11th International Workshop on Treebanks and Linguistic Theories*, pages 85–96.

Kim Gerdes, Bruno Guillaume, Sylvain Kahane, and Guy Perrier. 2018. SUD or surface-syntactic Universal Dependencies: An annotation scheme near-isomorphic to UD. In *Proceedings of the Second Workshop on Universal Dependencies (UDW 2018)*, pages 66–74, Brussels, Belgium. Association for Computational Linguistics.

Michael Heilman and Noah A. Smith. 2010. Tree edit models for recognizing textual entailments, paraphrases, and answers to questions. In *Proc. of NAACL-HLT*, pages 1011–1019, Los Angeles, California.

Julia Hockenmaier and Mark Steedman. 2007. CCGbank: A corpus of CCG derivations and dependency structures extracted from the Penn Treebank. *Computational Linguistics*, 33(3):355–396.

Rodney Huddleston and Geoffrey K. Pullum. 2002. *The Cambridge Grammar of the English Language*. Cambridge University Press, Cambridge.

Rodney Huddleston, Geoffrey K. Pullum, and Brett Reynolds. 2021. *A Student's Introduction to English Grammar*, 2nd edition. Cambridge University Press.

Robert T. Kasper. 1989. A flexible interface for linking applications to Penman's sentence generator. In *Speech and Natural Language: Proceedings of a Workshop Held at Philadelphia, Pennsylvania, February 21-23, 1989*.

Wolfgang Maier. 2010. Direct parsing of discontinuous constituents in German. In *Proc. of the NAACL HLT 2010 First Workshop on Statistical Parsing of Morphologically-Rich Languages*, pages 58–66, Los Angeles, CA, USA.

Joan Maling. 2000. A simple argument for subject gaps. In Yosef Grodzinsky, Lewis P. Shapiro, and David Swinney, editors, *Language and the Brain*. Academic Press, San Diego.

Mitchell Marcus, Grace Kim, Mary Ann Marcinkiewicz, Robert MacIntyre, Ann Bies, Mark Ferguson, Karen Katz, and Britta Schasberger. 1994. The Penn Treebank: Annotating predicate argument structure. In *Human Language Technology: Proceedings of a Workshop held at Plainsboro, New Jersey, March 8-11, 1994*.

Mitchell P. Marcus, Beatrice Santorini, and Mary Ann Marcinkiewicz. 1993. Building a large annotated corpus of English: The Penn Treebank. *Computational Linguistics*, 19(2):313–330.

Yusuke Miyao, Takashi Ninomiya, and Jun'ichi Tsujii. 2004. Corpus-oriented grammar development for acquiring a Head-driven Phrase Structure Grammar from the Penn Treebank. In *Proc. of IJCNLP*, Lecture Notes in Computer Science, pages 684–693, Hainan Island, China.

Joakim Nivre, Marie-Catherine de Marneffe, Filip Ginter, Yoav Goldberg, Jan Hajič, Christopher D. Manning, Ryan McDonald, Slav Petrov, Sampo Pyysalo, Natalia Silveira, Reut Tsarfaty, and Daniel Zeman. 2016. Universal Dependencies v1: A multilingual treebank collection. In *Proceedings of the Tenth International Conference on Language Resources and Evaluation (LREC'16)*, pages 1659–1666, Portorož, Slovenia. European Language Resources Association (ELRA).

Joakim Nivre, Marie-Catherine de Marneffe, Filip Ginter, Jan Hajič, Christopher D. Manning, Sampo Pyysalo, Sebastian Schuster, Francis Tyers, and Daniel Zeman. 2020. Universal Dependencies v2: An evergrowing multilingual treebank collection. In *Proc. of LREC*, pages 4027–4036, Marseille, France.

Stephan Oepen, Kristina Toutanova, Stuart Shieber, Christopher Manning, Dan Flickinger, and Thorsten Brants. 2002. The LinGO Redwoods Treebank: Motivation and Preliminary Applications. In *Proc. of COLING*.

Mateusz Pawlik and Nikolaus Augsten. 2011. RTED: A robust algorithm for the tree edit distance. arXiv:1201.0230 [cs.DB].

Mateusz Pawlik and Nikolaus Augsten. 2016. Tree edit distance: Robust and memory-efficient. *Information Systems*, 56:157–173.

John Payne, Rodney Huddleston, and Geoffrey K. Pullum. 2007. Fusion of functions: The syntax of *once, twice* and *thrice*. *Journal of Linguistics*, 43(3):565–603.

Sameer Pradhan, Alessandro Moschitti, Nianwen Xue, Hwee Tou Ng, Anders Björkelund, Olga Uryupina, Yuchen Zhang, and Zhi Zhong. 2013. Towards robust linguistic analysis using OntoNotes. In *Proc. of CoNLL*, pages 143–152, Sofia, Bulgaria.

Geoffrey K. Pullum and Brett Reynolds. 2013. New members of 'closed classes' in English. Manuscript.

Geoffrey K. Pullum and James Rogers. 2008. Expressive power of the syntactic theory implicit in the Cambridge Grammar of the English Language. In *Annual Meeting of the Linguistics Association of Great Britain*. University of Essex.

Vasin Punyakanok, Dan Roth, and Wen-tau Yih. 2004. Mapping dependencies trees: an application to question answering. In *Proc. of the International Symposium on Artificial Intelligence and Mathematics (AIM)*.

Brett Reynolds, Aryaman Arora, and Nathan Schneider. 2022. CGELBank: CGEL as a framework for English syntax annotation. arXiv:2210.00394 [cs.CL].

Brett Reynolds, Nathan Schneider, and Aryaman Arora. 2023. CGELBank annotation manual v1.0. arXiv:2305.17347 [cs.CL].

Milos Simic. 2022. Tree Edit Distance. Baeldung on Computer Science. Accessed 23 April 2023.

Sebastian Sulger, Miriam Butt, Tracy Holloway King, Paul Meurer, Tibor Laczkó, György Rákosi, Cheikh Bamba Dione, Helge Dyvik, Victoria Rosén, Koenraad De Smedt, Agnieszka Patejuk, Özlem Çetinoğlu, I Wayan Arka, and Meladel Mistica. 2013. ParGramBank: The ParGram parallel treebank. In *Proceedings of the 51st Annual Meeting of the Association for Computational Linguistics (Volume 1: Long Papers)*, pages 550–560, Sofia, Bulgaria. Association for Computational Linguistics.

John Torr. 2018. Constraining MGbank: Agreement, L-selection and supertagging in Minimalist Grammars. In *Proceedings of the 56th Annual Meeting of the Association for Computational Linguistics (Volume 1: Long Papers)*, pages 590–600, Melbourne, Australia. Association for Computational Linguistics.

Reut Tsarfaty, Joakim Nivre, and Evelina Andersson. 2011. Evaluating dependency parsing: Robust and heuristics-free cross-annotation evaluation. In *Proceedings of the 2011 Conference on Empirical Methods in Natural Language Processing*, pages 385–396, Edinburgh, Scotland, UK. Association for Computational Linguistics.

Andreas van Cranenburgh. 2018. Active DOP: A constituency treebank annotation tool with online learning. In *Proceedings of the 27th International Conference on Computational Linguistics: System Demonstrations*, pages 38–42, Santa Fe, New Mexico. Association for Computational Linguistics.

Andreas van Cranenburgh, Remko Scha, and Rens Bod. 2016. Data-oriented parsing with discontinuous constituents and function tags. *Journal of Language Modelling*, 4(1):57–111.

Stephen Wan, Mark Dras, Robert Dale, and Cécile Paris. 2006. Using dependency-based features to take the 'para-farce' out of paraphrase. In *Proc. of the 2006 Australasian Language Technology Workshop*, pages 131–138, Sydney, Australia.

Kaizhong Zhang and Dennis Shasha. 1989. Simple fast algorithms for the editing distance between trees and related problems. *SIAM Journal on Computing*, 18(6):1245–1262.

A Tree Edit Distance Details

For our evaluation metrics, we adapted Zhang and Shasha's (1989) TED algorithm as described in the pseudocode of Simic (2022). This is a simple recursive algorithm that compares spans of subforests in both trees, and runs in $O(n^4)$ time with memoization where n is the greater number of nodes of the two trees.[16] More efficient implementations have been proposed since, such as RTED (Pawlik and Augsten, 2011) and AP-TED (Pawlik and Augsten, 2016), but memoized TED was sufficient for our purposes—50 trees could be compared in <10 seconds with a straightforward Python implementation.

An unexpected source of inefficiency we ran into at first was the direction of recursion. If subtrees are recursed into from the rightmost child, the algorithm is an order of magnitude slower than if recursion starts from the leftmost child. Inspection of the memo-table size revealed that leftmost recursion requires much fewer function calls. We think this is because English tends to be a right-branching language, and so recursing beginning from the right increases the possible number of spans to compare between trees.

TED has been used to evaluate parsers in the past, including parsers with discontinuous constituents (Maier, 2010) and dependency parsers (Tsarfaty et al., 2011). It has also been applied or extended for other uses of comparing parse trees, such as measures of paraphrase, entailment, and answers to questions (e.g., Punyakanok et al., 2004; Wan et al., 2006; Heilman and Smith, 2010).

Relation of TED F_1 to TreeDice. Emms (2008) presents *TreeDice*, a TED-based metric for comparing constituency trees. Briefly: TED can be used to obtain the edits required to transform a gold tree into a predicted tree. With G as the size (number of nodes in) the gold tree, T as the size of the predicted tree, D as the number of deletions, I as the number of insertions, and S as the number of substitutions (where a node's label changes), *TreeDice* is given by

[16] Or, more precisely, $O(m^2n^2)$, where m and n are the sizes of the respective trees, as the recurrence is parameterized by a contiguous span of nodes in each tree under postorder traversal.

$$TreeDice = 1 - \frac{D+I+S}{G+T} \tag{1}$$

Using the invariant that $T = G - D + I$, one can substitute $G + I - T$ for D and show that this equals

$$\frac{2T - 2I - S}{G+T} = \frac{2(T - I - \frac{1}{2}S)}{G+T} \tag{2}$$

While Emms (2008) does not explicitly present precision and recall metrics based on TED (only ones based on `evalb` a.k.a. Parseval), we observe that the substitution cost can be split between precision and recall. Defining

$$Prec = \frac{T - I - \frac{1}{2}S}{T} \tag{3}$$

$$Rec = \frac{G - D - \frac{1}{2}S}{G} = \frac{T - I - \frac{1}{2}S}{G} \tag{4}$$

it is easily shown that the F_1 of these is equal to the *TreeDice* score (echoing the correspondence between F_1-score and the Dice coefficient over sets).

$$\begin{aligned}
F_1 &= \frac{2}{Rec^{-1} + Prec^{-1}} && (5)\\
&= 2\left(Rec^{-1} + Prec^{-1}\right)^{-1} && (6)\\
&= 2\left(\frac{G}{T - I - \frac{1}{2}S} + \frac{T}{T - I - \frac{1}{2}S}\right)^{-1} && (7)\\
&= 2\left(\frac{G+T}{T - I - \frac{1}{2}S}\right)^{-1} && (8)\\
&= \frac{2(T - I - \frac{1}{2}S)}{G+T} && (9)\\
F_1 &= TreeDice && (10)
\end{aligned}$$

B Exact tree accuracy

For comparison with the `flex` metric IAA results in Table 5, we also report exact tree accuracy below.

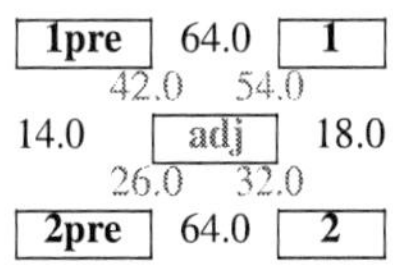

Table 7: Exact tree accuracy scores (i.e. whether trees are identical) on 50 IAA sentences before and after validation and adjudication. **1pre** denotes the trees from annotator 1 prior to running the validation script. **1** indicates annotator 1's final trees after revisions to address warnings from the validation script. **adj** denotes the final adjudicated trees.

C EWT Examples in PTB and CGELBank

Trees in the two styles appear in Figures 5 and 6 for comparison. Further cross-framework comparisons appear in Reynolds et al. (2022, §4).

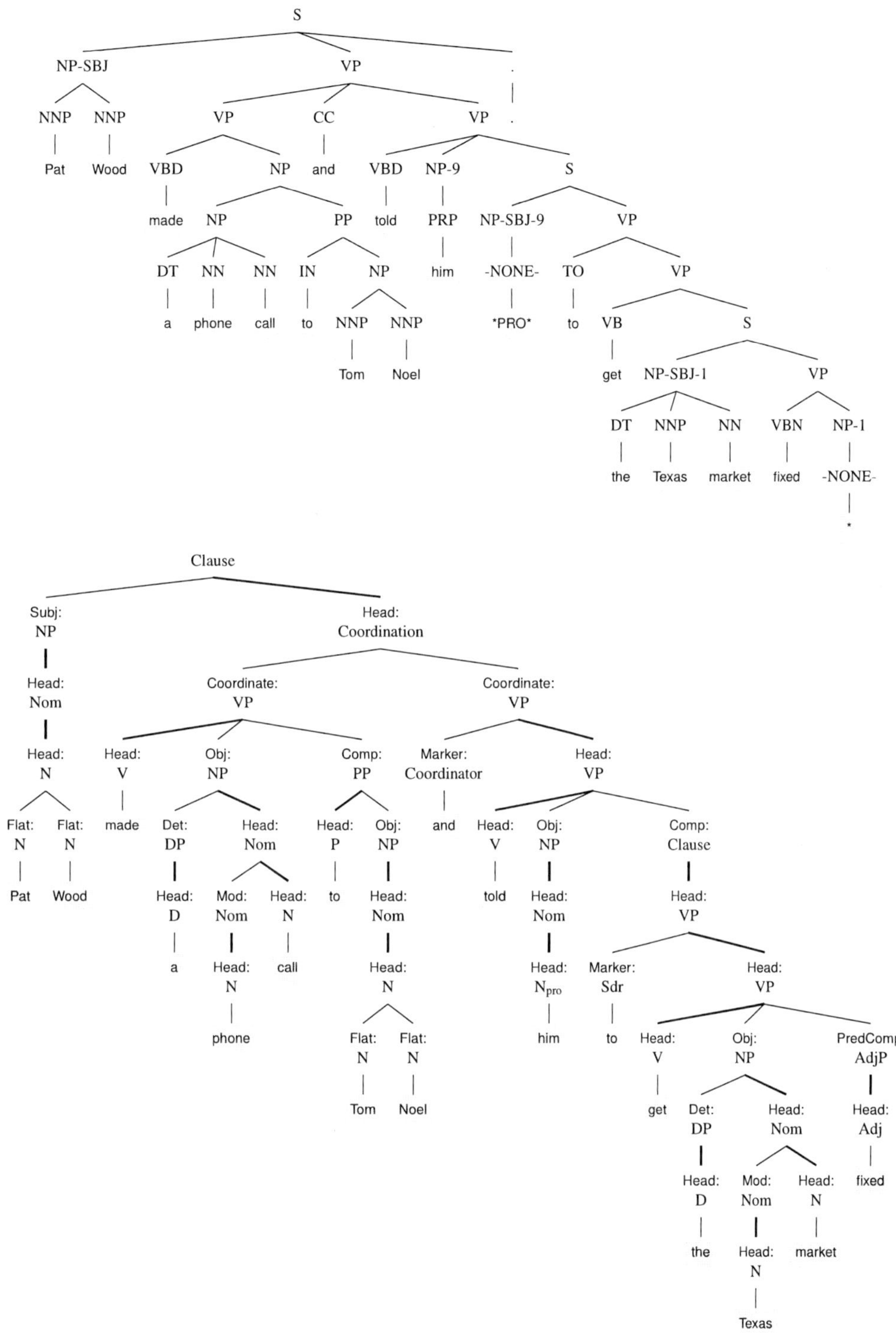

Figure 5: PTB-style and CGELBank trees for an EWT sentence with VP coordination. (Note that NPs are flatter in PTB style, and that control is indicated in PTB style with `*PRO*`, but not in CGELBank.)

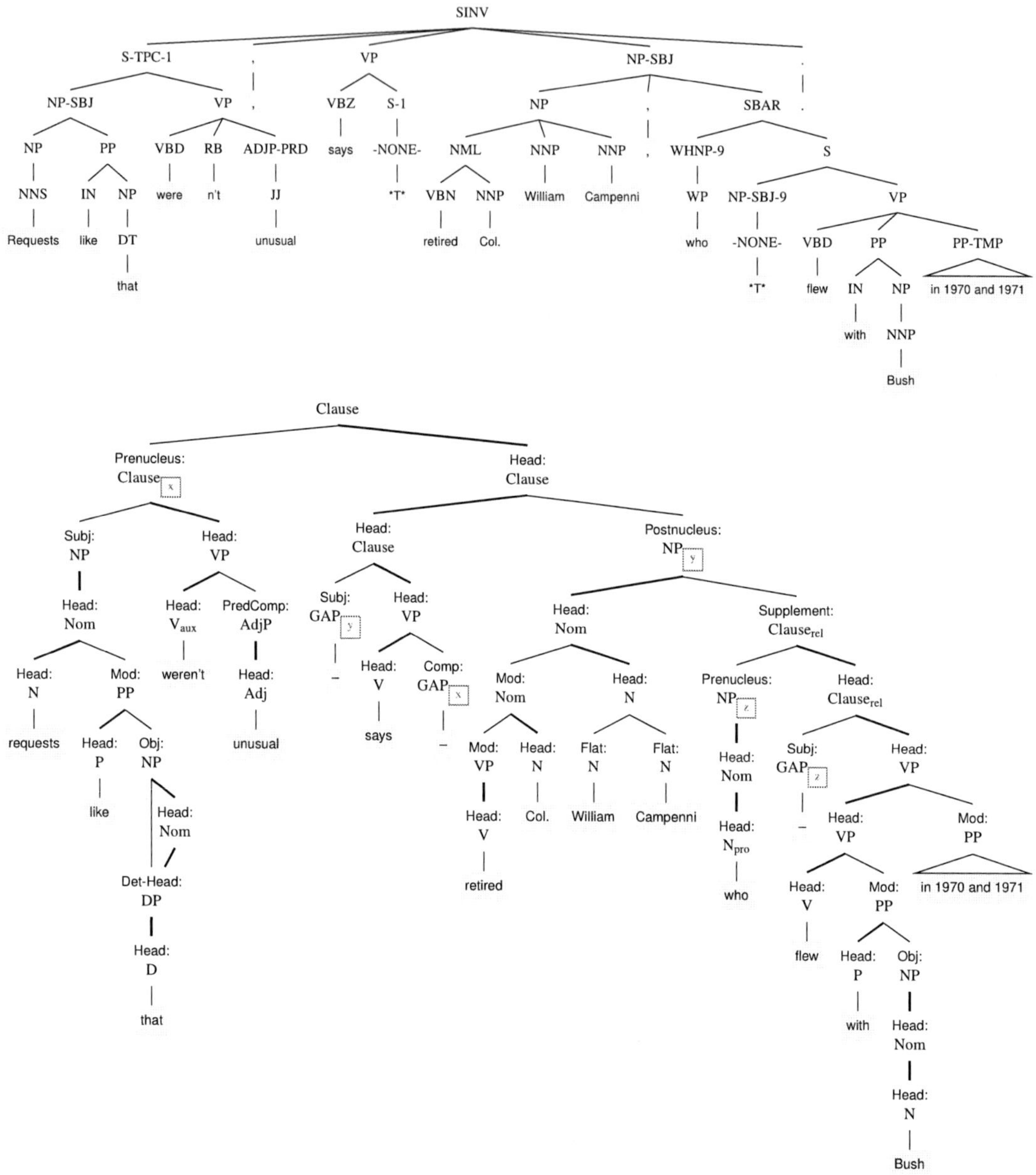

Figure 6: PTB-style and CGELBank trees for an EWT sentence with inversion and a relative clause (part of the tree is collapsed for space). Traces indicated with $*T*$ in PTB generally map to gaps in CGELBank.

Annotating Discursive Roles of Sentences in Patent Descriptions

Lufei Liu[1] and **Xu Sun**[1,2] and **François Veltz**[1] and **Kim Gerdes**[1,3]
[1]Qatent, Paris, France
[2]Université Paris Cité, France
[3]Université Paris-Saclay, Lisn (CNRS), France
{lufei, francois, kim}@qatent.com, xu.sun@etu.u-paris.fr

Abstract

Patent descriptions are a crucial component of patent applications, as they are key to understanding the invention and play a significant role in securing patent grants. While discursive analyses have been undertaken for scientific articles, they have not been as thoroughly explored for patent descriptions, despite the increasing importance of Intellectual Property and the constant rise of the number of patent applications. In this study, we propose an annotation scheme containing 16 classes that allows categorizing each sentence in patent descriptions according to their discursive roles. We publish an experimental human-annotated corpus of 16 patent descriptions and analyze challenges that may be encountered in such work. This work can be base for an automated annotation and thus contribute to enriching linguistic resources in the patent domain.

1 Introduction

Patent applications represent a first step in obtaining exclusive rights over an invention. Analyzing these documents enables inventors to understand technological trends, avoid potential litigation, and assess the competition. The *patent description*, a substantial part of the patent application, provides detailed information about the invention. Although specific segments have to be present in order to have the application accepted, the information can be provided without any pre-imposed order. Patent descriptions should be well organized in order to communicate the invention's technical details, advantages, and scope with more clarity. This, in turn, helps patent examiners to review applications more efficiently, reduces the likelihood of misinterpretation or ambiguity, and increases the chances of obtaining a patent grant with a well-defined scope of protection.

The contributions of our work are as follows:

- Introducing an annotation scheme based on and adapted for the discursive structure of patent descriptions.
- By focusing on patent descriptions, we aim to contribute to a better understanding of these documents' linguistic characteristics and structures, which have received little attention in patent-related research.
- Set a ground for future patent description analysis, for example, develop automatic methods to apply the annotation to large scale patent datasets. This can contribute to the detection of abnormal patent description and study the patent writing style according to different assignees.

2 Related work

The analysis of document structure allows for a deeper understanding of the author's thought process and facilitates the retrieval of specific information within the document. Many previous studies have focused on the analysis of technical documents, particularly scientific papers. For example, (Fisas et al., 2015) created a multi-layered annotated corpus of 40 scientific papers in the domain of Computer Graphics, with each sentence annotated according to its rhetorical role. (Dasigi et al., 2017) created a corpus by manually annotating 75 articles in the domain of intercellular cancer pathways. Each article was divided into clauses which are classified into one of the following categories: Goal, Fact, Result, Hypothesis, Method, Problem, Implication, None. This corpus was used to develop a discourse tagger for claim extraction and evidence fragment detection (Li et al., 2021).

Patent applications are another type of technical document that has garnered researchers' interest. A patent application usually consists of various components, including a title, abstract, description, one or more claims, drawings, and classification information. Current patent text analysis mainly focuses

Proceedings of the 17th Linguistic Annotation Workshop (LAW-XVII), pages 235–243
July 13, 2023

on claims or abstracts to improve claim readability (Ferraro et al., 2014; Okamoto et al., 2017), such as using them to build an engineering knowledge graph (Siddharth et al., 2021; Zuo et al., 2022), or to aid in patent classification models (Lee and Hsiang, 2020). However, the less-structured and much longer patent descriptions, an essential part of understanding patents, receive little attention. To our knowledge, only (Nakamitsu et al., 2022) analyzes the structure of patent descriptions, but they focus solely on four content types: Field, Problem, Solution, and Effect. Nevertheless, patent descriptions contain much richer information, including technical term definitions in context, advantages of the invention, and drawing descriptions. Exploring the structure of patent descriptions can be used to acquire patent writing skills – for humans and machines. Writing a good patent description not only requires an understanding of legal knowledge, but also requires expertise in relevant technical fields. Furthermore, mastering the structure of a patent description enables the extraction of reliable features, which may be useful for patent text modeling, specific to domains, assignees, and legal goals of the patent.

The goal of this study is to apply the discourse structure analysis, a common practice in scientific papers, to the whole patent descriptions while considering their unique writing style. To achieve this, we design an annotation scheme to label each sentence in the description according to its discursive role.

3 Annotation scheme

The patent description is typically divided into several sections. Under the Patent Cooperation Treaty (PCT), the description contains mainly (WIPO, 2022): *Title of invention*, *Technical field*, *Background art*, *Summary of invention*, *Brief description of drawings*, and *Description of embodiments*. The field section specifies the **technical domain** to which the invention belongs. The background section discusses the **prior art** related to the invention, identifies previously encountered **problems**, and explains how the proposed invention may offer solutions to one or more of these issues. The summary section highlights the **key features** and **advantages** of the invention. This is commonly followed by a section that provides a concise overview of the content present in each illustrative drawing, if they are included. Lastly, the Detailed Description section should encompass greater detail of the **claimed** invention by way of **examples (embodiments)**, **describing figures** in detail and **defining** little known or specially formulated technical terms when necessary, to further clarify the structure and functioning of the invention.

Based on the above essential elements recognized in a patent description and with the assistance of a patent attorney, we initially designed a set of 12 labels corresponding to the bold elements above. **key features** and **examples (embodiments)** were combined, represented by the label *Embodiment*, as the invention is usually described by introducing its features. Following this, two annotators collaboratively annotated two patent descriptions and identified a need to distinguish between the *Advantage* and *Problem* labels, to clarify whether these pertain to the invention itself or to existing technologies. In addition, we added the label *Other* for sentences that don't fall into any of the established 14 categories.

This set of 15 labels was applied by two annotators on the first test dataset of 8 patent applications. We noticed that the *Section title* label does not cover all kinds of titles within a patent description, since different applicants may introduce subsections with additional titles according to their writing styles. The annotators found it difficult to decide on the class of non-standard titles: Are they section titles or part of the embodiment?

To remedy this difficulty, a 16th label *Section subtitle* was added following the annotation of the first dataset. This new label also allows for an elementary encoding of the scope of the main sections, whenever they are indicated by section titles. It is this set of 16 labels that has reached consensus and is deemed operational and representative for annotating the discursive role of sentences within patent descriptions.

3.1 Annotation tags

Below is a brief summary of the labels defined for annotating patent descriptions. Additionally, a more detailed annotation guideline has been prepared, offering further explanations, examples, and counterexamples for each label. The guideline was made available to annotators to facilitate their understanding and ensure consistent application of the labeling criteria throughout the annotation process.

3.1.1 Patent title

The title of the patent application.
Example: VEHICLE SPEAKER DISPOSITION STRUCTURE

3.1.2 Section title

The title of each main section of a patent description.
Example: BACKGROUND ART

3.1.3 Section subtitle

The title of sub-sections inside the main sections of a patent description, if any.
Example: Stability studies

3.1.4 Technical field

Sentences determining the technical scope of the invention. These sentences specify to which field the invention relates and are usually carried out in one single paragraph.
Example: This application relates to the field of electronic materials and component technologies, and in particular, to an embedded substrate and a method for manufacturing an embedded substrate.

3.1.5 Reference

Sentences introducing the state-of-the-art or presenting the context to reach the invention, including related patents or publications, previous techniques, or general knowledge.
Example: In Patent Document 1, the acoustic transducer is disposed in the fender located near a front corner of a vehicle cabin, and sound is reproduced from the vicinity of the front corner toward the vehicle cabin.

3.1.6 Reference problem

Sentences stating the disadvantages of prior arts or indicating the technical problem that the invention is designed to solve.
Example: It can be learned that according to the existing embedded component packaging process, laser generated when the drill holes 104 are drilled damage the chip.

3.1.7 Reference advantage

Sentences explaining the advantage or quality of the prior arts or known technologies. In the example below, the first sentence provides context and the second sentence should be tagged as Reference advantage.
Example: In Patent Document 1, the acoustic transducer is disposed in the fender located near a front corner of a vehicle cabin, and sound is reproduced from the vicinity of the front corner toward the vehicle cabin. **By employing such a structure, an improvement in the reproduction efficiency, of high-quality sound including a low range, with a wide range of directivity in a plan view, is expected**.

3.1.8 Embodiment

Sentences describing physical instances or variations of the invention, explaining necessary ways to achieve the desired outcome. These sentences serve to demonstrate the flexibility and applicability of the invention in various contexts. (We keep the original reference numerals such as "104" in the text.)
Example: That is, a metal boss maybe disposed on each pad, and then embedded packaging (including drilling, conductive material filling, conductive layer disposing, and the like) is performed on the chip.

3.1.9 Invention advantage

Sentences providing the advantage, quality, or improvement brought about by the invention.
Example: The technique disclosed herein achieves both an improvement in the reproduction efficiency of the speaker and a reduction in the noise caused in the vehicle body by the sound generated by the speaker.

3.1.10 Invention problem

Sentences highlighting drawbacks or problems that the invention may cause.
Example: In short, since the speaker box 10 needs to have sealing properties in view of improving the reproduction efficiency of the sound including the low range, the drainage performance tends to deteriorate.

3.1.11 Figure description

Some patent applications contain figures which give a visual representation of the invention in the form of drawings, diagrams, or flowcharts. The Figure description tag is assigned to sentences that provide detailed explanations of figures, which usually contain reference numerals of the invention's components. These sentences should allow readers to navigate and understand the various depicted elements.
Example: As seen from Figure 3, for example, in its closed position, the door 20 is received within the recess 10 of the housing base 12 and its lower

face 24 lies generally flush with the lower surface 26 of the lip 14.

3.1.12 Definition

The explanation or clarification of technical terms, which could be a specifically formulated term. Context-specific explanations of which are given within the scope of the patent.
Example: As used herein, the term "cofactor" refers to a non-protein compound that operates in combination with a ketoredutase enzyme.

3.1.13 Rephrased claim

Sentences repeating portions of claims with non-substantive modifications, i.e., without incorporating additional content words that may alter the scope of the claims.
Example: A harness system for a power drive unit is disclosed. In various embodiments, the harness system includes an electrical cable having a first end and a second end, a plurality of cover members positioned along a length of the cable and a spring member positioned adjacent the plurality of cover members along the length of the cable.
original claim: A harness system for a power drive unit, comprising: an electrical cable (580) having a first end and a second end; a plurality of cover members (581) positioned along a length of the electrical cable; and a spring member (582) positioned adjacent the plurality of cover members along the length of the electrical cable.

3.1.14 Juridical template

Standardized phrases or sentences, which can be used regardless of the patent content. They serve specific purposes, such as facilitating transitions between sections of the description, and extend or narrow down the scope of the claims.
Example: The foregoing implementations of the present invention do not constitute a limitation on the protection scope of the present invention.

3.1.15 Technical template

Sentences giving the comprehensive usage of a technical term by providing its closely related synonyms or hyponyms.
Example: The first and the second plastic material may also be selected from a third group comprising a High Density Polyethylene, Low Density Polyethylene, Polyethylene, Terephthalate, Polyvinyl Chloride, Polycarbonate, Polypropylene, Polystyrene, Fluorine Treated, Post Consumer Resin, K-Resin, Bio-plastic, or combinations thereof.

3.1.16 Other

Sentences belonging to none of the previous categories or contains ambiguity. The following example demonstrates a typical OCR problem that has grouped all the elements of a table of contents together. Given that each title appeared in the corresponding subsection, this sequence is considered as *Other* to avoid introducing noise into the data.
Example: I. OverviewII. Description of StepsA. Tissue PreparationB. Distribution of DNA moleculesC. Detection and Quantification1. Digital PCR Methods2. Bead emulsion PCR3. Microfluidic Dilution with PCR4. Single molecule detection and/or sequencingD.

4 Corpus annotation

4.1 Corpus preparation

To build our annotation corpus, we use patent applications published by the European Patent Office (EPO). These patent applications are classified using the Cooperative Patent Classification (CPC) system, which comprises eight domains (Table 1). We randomly selected 2 applications per domain and divided them into two datasets, each containing one document per CPC class. In cases where an application is classified under multiple domains, we only considered the first one (the primary CPC label). The aim of this dataset separation is to verify whether the inter-annotator agreement remains consistent across the two datasets.

We extracted the description section from each patent application, each description is then segmented into sentences before being annotated. We use scispacy[1] combining with special rules to perform sentence splitting. For example, patent claims, which are usually extremely long sentences separated by semicolons, could be copied into description. In order to balance the size of each sentence, semicolons are also considered as ending punctuation. We chose to stay on the sentence level because delving into a finer-grained level would require not only knowledge in linguistics but also expertise in various technical domains. For instance, the following sentence, which we simply classify as being of type *Figure description*, could be broken down into sub-sequences that detail the interaction

[1]https://allenai.github.io/scispacy/

between elements described in the figure: *CPU 16 controls first conveyance section 21 to move conveyance pallet 40 to the loading position, and controls multi-joint robot 24 so that robot-side attachment section 27 grips pallet-side attachment section 42 below conveyance pallet 40 (refer to fig. 8).*

- Controller action: *CPU 16 controls first conveyance section 21*; *and controls multi-joint robot 24*
- Result of the action: *to move conveyance pallet 40 to the loading position*; *so that robot-side attachment section 27 grips pallet-side attachment section 42*
- Location of the action: *below conveyance pallet 40*
- Figure reference: *refer to fig. 8*

As an exploratory study and considering the number of defined labels, we decided to remain at the coarse-grained level. Table 1 shows the number of sentences in each document for both datasets of the corpus.

CPC	dataset 1	dataset 2
Human necessities (A)	393	228
Performing operations; transporting (B)	217	101
Chemistry; metallurgy (C)	349	681
Textiles; paper (D)	307	106
Fixed constructions (E)	364	102
Mechanical engineering; lighting; heating; weapons; blasting engines or pumps (F)	109	245
Physics (G)	224	284
Electricity (H)	193	221
Total (nb tokens)	62203	56886
Average tokens per sentence	*28.9*	*28.9*
Total (nb sentences)	**2156**	**1968**

Table 1: Number of sentences for each domain in the corpus (and the total number of tokens as well as the average tokens per sentence for information).

4.2 Annotation process

In order to measure the consistency across the annotation process, the annotation is conducted in two sessions. For each session, a pair of annotators (with a computational linguists background) independently annotate the same documents. Only one tag is allowed for each sentence. Discussion before the annotation is permitted, in order to allow both annotators to become familiar with the general structure of patent description. During the annotation, discussions are not allowed, instead, annotators have access to the context and any other information necessary for understanding the sentence to be annotated. After the first session, a collective review of the annotation guideline is conducted in order to complete the guideline with newly encountered examples.

4.3 Annotation agreement

We employed the pairwise Cohen's kappa to measure inter-annotator agreement. Table 2 shows the scores for each class within each corpus. As explained in Section 3, the label *Section subtitle* was added after the annotation of the first dataset.

Labels	dataset 1	dataseet 2
Patent title	1.00	1.00
Section title	0.96	1.00
Section subtitle		1.00
Technical field	0.93	0.92
Definition	0.59	0.46
Reference	0.77	0.64
Reference_problem	0.67	0.70
Reference_advantage	0.45	0.11
Rephrased claim	0.76	0.84
Figure description	0.47	0.75
Embodiment	0.47	0.61
Invention_advantage	0.64	0.70
Invention_problem	0.58	0.09
Juridical template	0.70	0.79
Technical template	0.22	0.43
Other	0.19	0.55
kappa	**0.56**	**0.69**

Table 2: IAA for each label in each dataset of the corpus. The Cohen's kappa score for the entire dataset is used instead of the mean of scores for each category due to the imbalanced distribution of labels.

This modification has contributed to the perfect agreement concerning the labels associated with titles. It is worth noting that the agreement is relatively low for some labels, which is due to their imbalanced distribution in the corpus (as shown in Figure 1). The matrices in Figure 1 present the

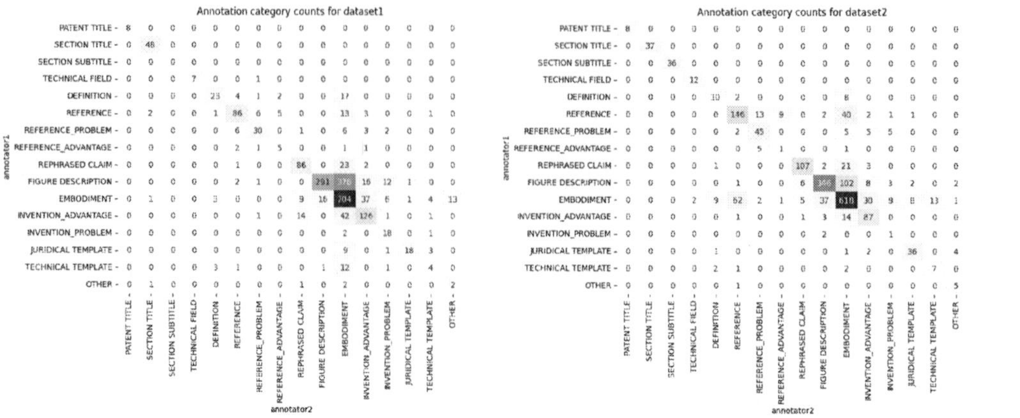

(a) dataset 1

(b) dataset 2

Figure 1: The annotation by class across the two datasets. The matrices show, for each annotator, occurrence of labels assigned by each annotator for each dataset. We can observe that the two datasets are mainly composed of *Rephrased claim, Figure description, Embodiment*, and *Invention advantage*. In the dataset 2, *Reference* also represent a significant portion.

number of labels assigned to each sentence by each annotator. It can be observed that the majority of annotations fall under the categories of Figure description, Embodiment and Rephrased claim, followed by Reference and Invention advantage. This is consistent with the objective of patent description drafting, which aims to explicitly explain the way of carrying out the invention and its novelty compared to prior arts.

Overall, we observe an improvement in the agreement between the two annotation sessions, particularly for *Figure description* and *Embodiment*. The label *Other* denotes sentences that appear ambiguous or do not belong to any class. Few sentences received this label from both annotators, which shows that our label set is comprehensive enough to cover the entirety of sentences in a patent description.

As we can see from IAA score and Figure 1, apart from labels concerning titles, the categories that receive higher agreement are those less dependent on the annotator's interpretation of sentence meanings, such as *Technical field, Rephrased claim*, and *Juridical template*.

Compared to the work of (Nakamitsu et al., 2022), we have expanded the label set with the intention to encompass the entirety of patent description content, rather than merely focusing on specific parts thereof. We attempted to create an exemplary dataset manually, with the objective of identifying relevant labels and establishing a reliable sample for future data augmentation. On the whole, our annotation achieved an IAA score of 0.69 following a revision on the first dataset. This result aligns with the performance of similar annotation work (Fisas et al., 2015), who obtained an IAA score of 0.6567 across eight categories.

However, although we improved the agreement score for some categories, it is worth noting that the level of agreement remains relatively low for some categories, despite post-annotation discussions following the first session. The following section gives examples of pairs of labels that are frequently confused by annotators.

4.4 Disagreement analysis

Based on the annotation results, we noticed that certain pairs of labels are often confused. We attempted to analyze the reason for this confusion.

4.4.1 Reference VS Embodiment

The challenge associated with this pair of labels lies in distinguishing whether the subject of the sentence concerns the prior art or the applicant's invention. The reason is that, in the section describing embodiments of the invention, the description of the invention can be mixed with the explanation of prior art. This is particularly the case for patents in the *Chemistry; metallurgy* domain. In these patents, the disclosure of detailed experimentation is required, which often leads to numerous references when existing components or methods are needed for the experiments. Consequently, the description of the invention example becomes intertwined with that of the prior art, complicating the annotators' comprehension, especially when they lack domain-specific expertise.

Example: Fluorescent nucleotide incorporation by DNA polymerase. As described in the above-referenced PNAS publication by Braslavsky et al., DNA polymerase may be employed to image sequence information in a single DNA template as its complementary strand is synthesized. The nucleotides are inserted sequentially;

In this example, it is challenging to determine whether the sentence underlined is part of the publication cited in the previous sentence or merely a step in the *Fluorescent nucleotide incorporation by DNA polymerase* experiment. We have chosen *Embodiment* as the label for this sentence because the following context explains the experiments related to the invention itself and not the reference.

4.4.2 Reference advantage VS Reference problem

Distinguishing between advantages and problems can be challenging, especially when purely critical or, conversely, commendatory terms are missing.

Example: Furthermore, in regular operation, an auxiliary circuit may be energized and connected to a junction by way of a second current interrupting element. Electrical power can thus be provided from DFIG to auxiliary components, with the electrical power from main power transformer being converted to the appropriate voltage by auxiliary transformer. However, during maintenance operations, the DFIG may be shut down, and the main power circuit may be isolated from the power grid.

In this example, it's difficult to tell if *DFIG may be shut down* and *main power circuit may be isolated* are positive characteristics even though the two preceding sentences have provided context. With the help of the following context, we understood that it indeed represents an advantage, especially it was mentioned that this can help to *reducing the risk of electrocution during maintenance operations*. We thereby decided to annotate it as *Reference advantage*.

4.4.3 Reference problem VS Invention advantage

Sometimes, the information is presented as a dual statement which requires annotators to interpret the context and infer the intended meaning.

Example: This entails the need to exert a high torque by the motor to carry out the movement quickly.

In this example, it can be inferred that the sentence implies a drawback of the current technique. However, in a patent description, such a sentence exists only to indicates that the mentioned problem will be rectified through the invention, thereby expressing an advantage of the latter. To solve the ambiguity, we added a rule to our annotation guideline, explicitly stating that for such dual statements, the sentence will be annotated as *Invention advantage* because the presented problem would be solved by the invention.

4.4.4 Embodiment VS Figure description

Despite the introduction of additional specifications after the first annotation session regarding the distinction between *Embodiment* and *Figure description*, with a particular emphasis on the functional aspect of the former and the visual aspect of the latter, the differentiation remains challenging. This is because the description of an embodiment often refers to components drawn in the figures.

Example: In atmospheric pressure plasma-generating device 10, processing gas composed only of an inert gas is supplied from first connecting passage 130 to reaction chamber 100 through the inside of holders 72 and 74 of holding member 20.

In this example, the technical terms followed by numbers indicate that these are important components of the invention and that they are illustrated in the drawings. However, the sentence only describes how the processing gas is supplied, which is not depicted in the drawings. Considering the process is not shown in the drawings, we decided to label it as *Embodiment* and we clarified that it is possible to refer to drawings attached to the patent applications in case of indecision between *Embodiment* and *Figure description*.

4.4.5 Embodiment VS Invention advantage

Using comparatives when describing an invention may not always clearly indicate an improvement of the invention. The confusion often caused by insufficient technical knowledge in the respective domain.

Example: It is therefore known that the particle size distribution computed using the profile data about the coke 30 shows larger particle size distribution than the actual particle size distribution.

In this example, it's difficult to decide if *larger particle size distribution* is an improvement achieved by *using the profile data about the coke 30*. Thus, in cases where we cannot be certain that the presented feature is an advantage, we annotate it as *Embodiment* in order to avoid introducing errors.

The analysis of disagreement sheds light on the challenges involved in annotating the discursive roles of sentences in patent descriptions, which are not only related to language complexity but also to individual manner of expression.

5 Conclusion

In this paper, we have proposed an annotation scheme adapted to the specific writing style of patent applications. As an exploratory work, we defined a set of 16 labels to categorize each sentence in a patent description according to their discursive roles. The initial results show that such work is feasible, since strong agreement is achieved for most categories. However, challenges remain. Considering the aforementioned difficulties, we propose the following improvement to the future work: allow multi-labeling for ambiguous sentences or consider implementing a multi-layer annotation scheme. In the first level, include classes corresponding only to the five common sections of a patent description, followed by additional specific categories in subsequent layers as necessary.

In conclusion, our annotation work is an ongoing process. We plan to expand our dataset once the relevant labels have been established, and to employ active learning methods to streamline the annotation process. We believe that a such linguistic resource in the patent domain could contribute to enhancing the accuracy of tasks such as patent classification, patent novelty detection, patent information retrieval, and, most central to Qatent, computer-assisted patent drafting.

Limitations

Our sample dataset contains only 16 randomly selected documents, which might not be sufficient to contribute to classification model training. Additionally, our work could benefit from having a lead annotator to supervise the annotation process. This would help reduce the time spent on correcting annotation errors and ensure adherence to the annotation guideline.

Ethics Statement

All data used in this study were collected from publicly available sources, with no infringement of intellectual property rights or privacy.

Acknowledgments

We would like to express our profound thanks to You Zuo for taking the time to read our paper, offering thoughtful comments, and providing enriching ideas. Finally, We are grateful to the anonymous reviewers and for their detailed and helpful feedback.

References

Pradeep Dasigi, Gully Burns, and Anita Waard. 2017. Experiment segmentation in scientific discourse as clause-level structured prediction using recurrent neural networks.

Gabriela Ferraro, Hanna Suominen, and Jaume Nualart. 2014. Segmentation of patent claims for improving their readability. In *Proceedings of the 3rd Workshop on Predicting and Improving Text Readability for Target Reader Populations (PITR)*, pages 66–73, Gothenburg, Sweden. Association for Computational Linguistics.

Beatriz Fisas, Horacio Saggion, and Francesco Ronzano. 2015. On the discoursive structure of computer graphics research papers. In *Proceedings of the 9th Linguistic Annotation Workshop*, pages 42–51, Denver, Colorado, USA. Association for Computational Linguistics.

Jieh-Sheng Lee and Jieh Hsiang. 2020. Patent classification by fine-tuning bert language model. *World Patent Information*, 61:101965.

Xiangci Li, Gully Burns, and Nanyun Peng. 2021. Scientific discourse tagging for evidence extraction. In *Proceedings of the 16th Conference of the European Chapter of the Association for Computational Linguistics: Main Volume*, pages 2550–2562, Online. Association for Computational Linguistics.

Jun Nakamitsu, Satoshi Fukuda, and Hidetsugu Nanba. 2022. Analyzing the structure of u.s. patents using patent families. In *2022 12th International Congress on Advanced Applied Informatics (IIAI-AAI)*, pages 150–153.

Masayuki Okamoto, Zifei Shan, and Ryohei Orihara. 2017. Applying information extraction for patent structure analysis. In *Proceedings of the 40th International ACM SIGIR Conference on Research and Development in Information Retrieval*, SIGIR '17, page 989–992, New York, NY, USA. Association for Computing Machinery.

L. Siddharth, Lucienne T. M. Blessing, Kristin L. Wood, and Jianxi Luo. 2021. Engineering Knowledge Graph From Patent Database. *Journal of Computing and Information Science in Engineering*, 22(2). 021008.

WIPO. 2022. Wipo patent drafting manual, second edition. page 97.

H. Zuo, Y. Yin, and P. Childs. 2022. Patent-kg: Patent knowledge graph extraction for engineering design. *Proceedings of the Design Society*, 2:821–830.

The Effect of Alignment Correction on Cross-Lingual Annotation Projection

Shabnam Behzad*[1], Seth Ebner*[2], Marc Marone[2], Benjamin Van Durme[2], Mahsa Yarmohammadi[2]

[1]Georgetown University,[2]Johns Hopkins University

{seth,mmarone1,vandurme,mahsa}@jhu.edu,
shabnam@cs.georgetown.edu

Abstract

Cross-lingual annotation projection is a practical method for improving performance on low resource structured prediction tasks. An important step in annotation projection is obtaining alignments between the source and target texts, which enables the mapping of annotations across the texts. By manually correcting automatically generated alignments, we examine the impact of alignment quality—automatic, manual, and mixed—on downstream performance for two information extraction tasks and quantify the trade-off between annotation effort and model performance.

1 Introduction

Cross-lingual annotation projection (Yarowsky and Ngai, 2001) involves mapping source annotations to target text through alignments. Recent studies such as Yarmohammadi et al. (2021) and Chen et al. (2022) suggest that word alignment quality substantially impacts downstream performance.

Automatic word alignments are inexpensive to obtain but may be of low quality. On the other side of the alignment quality spectrum (Figure 1) are manual (human-labeled) alignments, which are expensive but accurate. Our goals are to quantify the impact of automatic vs. manual alignments on downstream task performance and to explore the quality spectrum to quantify the trade-off between automatic and manual alignments in terms of downstream performance and cost.

We investigate the alignment quality spectrum on two structured prediction tasks: shallow semantic parsing (BETTER Basic IE[1]) and named entity recognition (NER). In the BETTER IE scenario, we start with a typical fully automatic *translate, align, and project* pipeline, so-called "silver" data creation, and compare with manually labeled data (annotated by two of the authors). For NER, the dataset we use already has annotations in two languages (with gold bitext and gold word alignments).

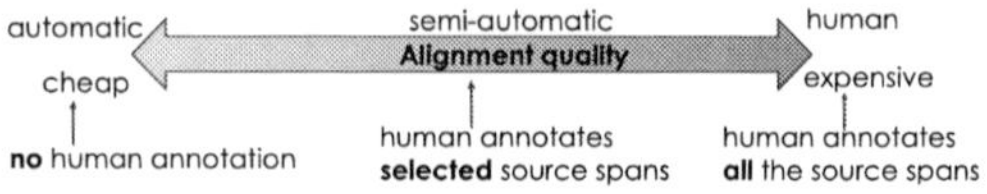

Figure 1: Alignment annotation spectrum. It is often easier to annotate alignments than to train annotators for a complex downstream task. Higher quality alignments improve performance but are more costly.

Rather than manually annotate alignments for every example, which is expensive as shown on the right end of the spectrum in Figure 1, we collect manual annotations on the data for which two alignment methods—silver data creation and an unsupervised embedding-based span alignment tool—point to different target spans (§5). Our contributions are: 1) evidence that manually correcting alignments improves downstream performance, 2) evidence that downstream performance correlates with the amount of manual alignment effort, and 3) analysis on the types of spans that are manually corrected.

2 Related Work

Cross-lingual projection is a method of transferring annotations from a source language to a target language that has often been used to increase performance on the target language (Yarowsky and Ngai, 2001; Yarmohammadi et al., 2021; Chen et al., 2022, *i.a.*), but its utility depends on obtaining reliable alignments between the source and target text. There has been extensive research on supervised and unsupervised alignment at the word, phrase, and sentence levels (Zhang et al., 2016; Jalili Sabet et al., 2020; Nagata et al., 2020; Chousa et al., 2020; Chen et al., 2021; Li et al., 2022, *i.a.*). However, these studies report primarily intrinsic evaluation of alignment quality and leave extrinsic

*Equal contribution

[1]https://ir.nist.gov/better

Proceedings of the 17th Linguistic Annotation Workshop (LAW-XVII), pages 244–251
July 13, 2023 ©2023 Association for Computational Linguistics

	BETTER (%)	NER (%)
Unique source spans	4896	3180
Identical automatic spans	2432 (50%)	1942 (61%)
Candidates for correction	2464 (50%)	1238 (39%)

Table 1: Number of source spans in total and in the candidate subset for correction. Candidates are spans that are non-identical (different or overlapping), based on two automatic alignment results. BETTER candidate spans are shown to humans for re-alignment. NER candidate spans are corrected according to gold alignments from the original resource.

evaluation on downstream tasks underexplored.

Stengel-Eskin et al. (2019) showed that gold alignment data has a greater impact on word alignment performance than the amount of pre-training bitext does, suggesting that the benefits of manually correcting alignments may also extend to the creation of higher-quality projected data.

Our work responds to these lines of prior work by examining the extrinsic downstream impact of our approaches and how the incorporation of different amounts of gold alignment data affects performance. In contrast to prior work on projection, such as Yarmohammadi et al. (2021), our work focuses on the impact of the alignment component of the projection pipeline on the overall effectiveness of cross-lingual projection and explicitly adjusts automatic alignments with manual corrections.

3 Methods

Fully Automatic We consider improving the zero-shot learning scenario where the gold training data is in a different language than the target data we want to evaluate on. For both tasks, we explore multiple setups that include training on gold English data alone (zero-shot) or combined with projected target-language data. Projected data is created by transferring the gold source labels to translated target text via automatically obtained or manually corrected word alignments.

Silver Data Creation To create silver data, we followed the process of Yarmohammadi et al. (2021). First, if there was no gold translation of the source text (as in BETTER), we translated the source text into the target language using a state of the art translation system (Xu et al., 2021). Second, we obtained word alignments between the original and target parallel text using `awesome-align` (Dou and Neubig, 2021), a state of the art contextualized embedding-based word aligner (see Appendix A for further details). Finally, we projected the annotations from the source language to the target language based on the word alignments. For multi-word spans, the target span is a contiguous span containing all aligned words from the same source span.

Unsupervised Span Alignment We implemented a span alignment tool by extending the techniques of SimAlign (Jalili Sabet et al., 2020) to compute similarities between the representations of spans rather than of tokens.[2] We used a frozen pre-trained encoder and did not update any model parameters. We performed a hyperparameter search (Appendix C) to configure an aligner that most frequently produces spans identical to those of `awesome-align`.

Alignment Correction After obtaining "silver spans" from `awesome-align` and "unsupervised spans" from the span aligner, we selected source spans which the two methods aligned to different target spans. Around half the total source spans were selected for re-alignment (Table 1). For BETTER, we asked human annotators to re-align selected spans from scratch. For NER, we simulated manually correcting automatic alignments by retrieving gold alignments from the original manually annotated resource.[3] Further details are given in §5. We refer to data projected after the alignment correction step as *semi-automatic* because it is created from a mix of automatic and manual alignments.

4 Tasks

We investigate the impact of alignment quality using established models, as modeling improvements are outside the scope of this work.

4.1 NER

Data We utilized GALE (Li et al., 2015), which includes word-aligned Chinese and English parallel text. Alignments were obtained from multiple rounds of human annotations. As a part of the OntoNotes corpus (Weischedel et al., 2013), a portion of the Chinese section of GALE was annotated for NER. The gold-aligned NER data consists of 2385, 287, and 189 sentences in the train, dev, and

[2] We considered all spans of up to a certain length, giving a linear number of spans per sentence.

[3] To avoid issues with labeling overlapping spans in the BIO-tagged NER data, we use the gold alignments for the entire sentence rather than for individual spans. In many cases, identical `awesome-align` silver spans and unsupervised spans present in the sentence that should not have been re-aligned closely match the gold-aligned spans anyway.

test splits, respectively. Further human annotation was not necessary for this task because data and annotations were already available in both languages.

Model We used a BERT-based token tagging NER model,[4] which outputs tag probabilities via a softmax on logits from a linear layer on top of a bert-base-multilingual-cased encoder (Devlin et al., 2019). We select the checkpoint from the epoch that achieved the best F1 performance on the gold Chinese dev set. We evaluate our models using micro-averaged F1.

4.2 BETTER

Data The Better Extraction from Text Towards Enhanced Retrieval (BETTER) Program[5] develops methods for event extraction in a target language, given gold annotations only in English. We focus on the "Basic" events level, where the goal is to identify events and their arguments (agents and patients), i.e. shallow semantic parsing, with Farsi as the target language.

Model Our BETTER IE system is based on the Spanfinder model (Xia et al., 2021), consisting of a contextualized encoder and a BiLSTM-CRF span tagger. The model first extracts event anchors and labels them with event types. Conditioned on an anchor span, the model then identifies argument spans (agents and patients). We report the program-defined "combined F1" metric, which is the product of "event match F1" and "argument match F1" based on an alignment of predicted and reference event structures.

Annotation Task We gather alignment corrections through the TASA[6] human annotation interface (Stengel-Eskin et al., 2019). Additional information about the interface is given in Appendix B. 2,464 candidate source spans (training and analysis) occur across 1,012 sentence pairs. Each sentence pair, containing one or more source spans highlighted for alignment, is considered a task. Tasks took 1 minute on average for a total annotation time of ~ 16 hours.

5 Experiments and Results

We compare the performance of models trained on various combinations of gold, silver, and semi-automatic training data. We evaluate the models on the target language test sets: the Chinese gold test set for NER and Farsi semi-automatic analysis set for BETTER.

We also use English training data in two different ways: combined with the target language data ('En +' in Table 2 and Table 3) and as pre-training before we fine-tune on the target data ('En →' in Table 2).

Training Data	Micro-F1 on Gold Zh Test Set
En (zero-shot baseline)	17.6
Gold Zh (upper bound)	74.7
Silver Zh	44.0
Semi-automatic Zh	56.0
Gold projection Zh	58.9
En + Silver Zh	35.1
En + Semi-automatic Zh	51.9
En + Gold projection Zh	60.7
En → Silver Zh	45.5
En → Semi-automatic Zh	53.8
En → Gold projection Zh	51.7

Table 2: NER results on GALE Chinese gold test set. In general, as alignment quality increases, downstream performance increases.

5.1 NER

The results in Table 2 show that by augmenting the source language training data (En) with data in the target language (Zh), zero-shot performance can be much improved. When projection is performed via gold word alignments (Gold projection Zh), there is 15.8% absolute performance degradation compared to when gold Chinese data (Gold Zh) is used for training. Thus, there is some loss in performance when using projected data. Training on alignment-corrected (semi-automatic) data outperforms training on silver Chinese data in all settings. Performance per entity type in a representative experimental setting is shown in Table 5. Overall, performance correlates with the amount of manual effort used in creating the data.

5.2 BETTER

The results in Table 3 show that using projected training data, either by itself or combined with source language (En) training data, outperforms the zero-shot setting. Even though the majority of the semi-automatic spans match the silver spans (see §6.2 for details), replacing the silver data with the semi-automatic data improves the BETTER scores. However, the gain is not as substantial as that for NER. This could be due to the BETTER an-

[4]Adapted from `http://github.com/kamalkraj/BERT-NER` and Stengel-Eskin et al. (2019).

[5]`https://www.iarpa.gov/index.php/research-programs/better`

[6]`https://github.com/hltcoe/tasa`

Train	Test on Semi-automatic Fa
En (zero-shot baseline)	36.9
Silver Fa	40.1
Semi-automatic Fa	40.7
En + Silver Fa	44.8
En + Semi-automatic Fa	45.1

Table 3: BETTER results on semi-automatic Farsi analysis set.

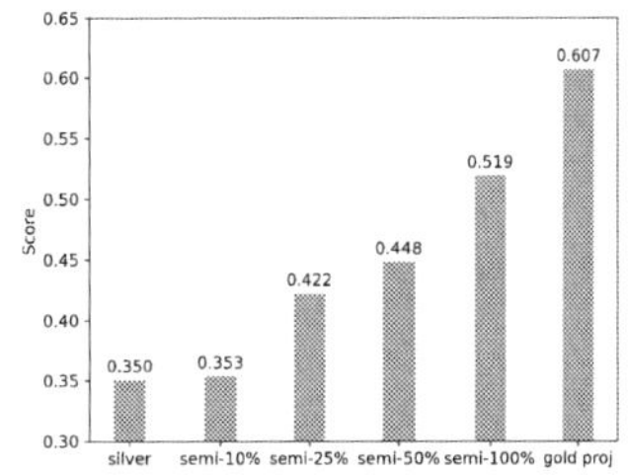

(a) NER: Micro-F1 on gold Chinese test set

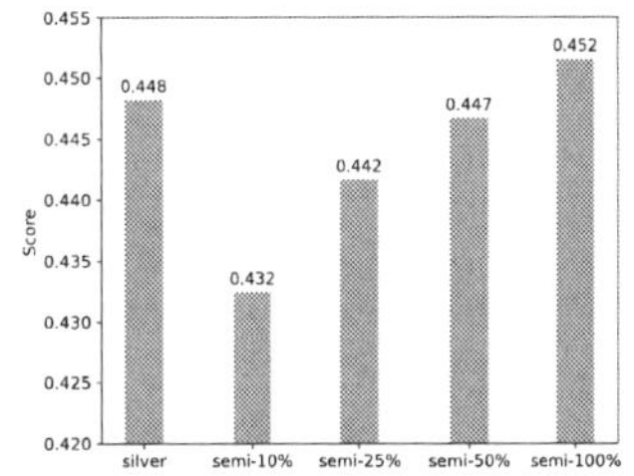

(b) BETTER: Combined F1 on semi-automatic (corrected) Farsi analysis set

Figure 2: Performances for (a) NER and (b) BETTER for systems trained on gold English combined with: automatic (silver), subsampled semi-automatic (semi-x%), or gold projection (gold proj) data.

alysis data being non-gold or the BETTER scorer's sensitivity to small changes in predictions.

6 Analysis

6.1 Annotation Budget Constraints

Annotation budgets constrain how much of the data can be projected along gold alignments. Furthermore, it is cheaper to annotate alignments than to train annotators on a complex task. Note that our annotation task took only ~ 16 hours for all data. We analyze downstream performance as a function of the amount of data correction.

For both NER and BETTER, we subsample 10%, 25%, and 50% of the tasks (sentences) in which the two automatic alignment methods have a disagreement, and then replace their silver alignments with the correct alignments: gold (for NER) and manually corrected (for BETTER). The remaining portion of the data comes from the silver data aligned with `awesome-align` (i.e., semi-10% consists of 10% corrected data and 90% automatic silver data). We do the sampling process 5 times and report the average performance.

The results in Figure 2a show that the performance consistently improves as subsampling percentage increases. In all of the cases where projected Zh is combined with En, either added or fine-tuned, any percentage of manual correction outperforms training on silver Zh only (see Appendix E for the plot for the fine-tuning setting).

Figure 2b shows a similar trend for BETTER. The plots suggest, however, that to outperform training on silver data, more than 50% of the alignments need to be corrected. We hypothesize this is in part due to the evaluation set being non-gold, so correcting the training data shifts away from the distribution of the evaluation data.

6.2 Extent of Alignment Disagreements

Around 86% and 60% of all manually corrected BETTER target spans match, either fully or partially, the automatic silver spans or the automatic unsupervised spans, respectively. We consider two spans to be partially matching or overlapping if the length of the longest consecutive common character sequence is larger than 30% of the length of the longer span. As Table 4 shows, most of the silver and manually annotated spans are identical (73.4%), whereas the unsupervised and manually annotated spans mostly are overlapping (52.4%).

6.3 Alignment Agreement Per Span Type

Table 4 shows that there is no substantial difference between the types of spans that have been categorized as identical, overlapping, or different. The silver and unsupervised span alignment approaches do not seem to do particularly better or worse on event anchors, agents, or patients.

For the NER task we observe that overall, the silver span extraction setup gave better quality spans compared to the unsupervised span alignment approach. See Appendix F for results per entity type.

	Identical Spans				Overlapping Spans				Different Spans			
	Anchor	Agent	Patient	Total (%)	Anchor	Agent	Patient	Total (%)	Anchor	Agent	Patient	Total (%)
Silver	669	679	473	73.4	163	75	73	12.5	117	107	126	14.1
Unsupervised	59	66	64	7.6	470	450	380	52.4	420	345	228	40.0

Table 4: (Dis)agreement of semi-automatic spans with automatic spans in BETTER.

7 Conclusion and Future Work

In this paper, we investigated how much the quality of alignments impacts downstream task performance when annotations are projected from English to another language. Our experimental results show that the utilization of different alignment methodologies, followed by corrections of the disagreements arising from such approaches, can reduce human effort while improving results.

There are several promising avenues for future research in cross-lingual annotation projection. Although this study did not investigate the influence of translation quality on downstream performance (which is the first step of the data projection pipeline), we believe this could yield important findings. Another direction involves the investigation of active learning techniques for prioritizing which alignments to correct.

Limitations

The automatic data creation procedure can introduce errors during both the translation and alignment steps. This study is limited to the errors during the alignment step. Even though we used state of the art machine translation techniques in this work, the translation errors could still affect the quality of the alignments or projected data, especially in silver data creation.

Moreover, we studied only two tasks, NER and BETTER, and considered only two target languages, Chinese and Farsi. Tasks with significantly different structures (e.g., deep parsing) may be affected differently by alignment corrections.

Acknowledgments

We acknowledge support through a fellowship from JHU + Amazon Initiative for Interactive AI (AI2AI). This work was supported in part by IARPA BETTER (#2019-19051600005). The views and conclusions contained in this work are those of the authors and should not be interpreted as necessarily representing the official policies, either expressed or implied, or endorsements of ODNI, IARPA, or the U.S. Government. The U.S. Government is authorized to reproduce and distribute reprints for governmental purposes notwithstanding any copyright annotation therein.

References

Julien Abadji, Pedro Ortiz Suarez, Laurent Romary, and Benoît Sagot. 2022. Towards a cleaner document-oriented multilingual crawled corpus. In *Proceedings of the Thirteenth Language Resources and Evaluation Conference*, pages 4344–4355, Marseille, France. European Language Resources Association.

Chi Chen, Maosong Sun, and Yang Liu. 2021. Mask-align: Self-supervised neural word alignment. In *Proceedings of the 59th Annual Meeting of the Association for Computational Linguistics and the 11th International Joint Conference on Natural Language Processing (Volume 1: Long Papers)*, pages 4781–4791, Online. Association for Computational Linguistics.

Yang Chen, Chao Jiang, Alan Ritter, and Wei Xu. 2022. Frustratingly easy label projection for cross-lingual transfer. *arXiv preprint arXiv:2211.15613*.

Katsuki Chousa, Masaaki Nagata, and Masaaki Nishino. 2020. SpanAlign: Sentence alignment method based on cross-language span prediction and ILP. In *Proceedings of the 28th International Conference on Computational Linguistics*, pages 4750–4761, Barcelona, Spain (Online). International Committee on Computational Linguistics.

Jacob Devlin, Ming-Wei Chang, Kenton Lee, and Kristina Toutanova. 2019. BERT: Pre-training of deep bidirectional transformers for language understanding. In *Proceedings of the 2019 Conference of the North American Chapter of the Association for Computational Linguistics: Human Language Technologies, Volume 1 (Long and Short Papers)*, pages 4171–4186, Minneapolis, Minnesota. Association for Computational Linguistics.

Zi-Yi Dou and Graham Neubig. 2021. Word alignment by fine-tuning embeddings on parallel corpora. In *Proceedings of the 16th Conference of the European Chapter of the Association for Computational Linguistics: Main Volume*, pages 2112–2128, Online. Association for Computational Linguistics.

Masoud Jalili Sabet, Philipp Dufter, François Yvon, and Hinrich Schütze. 2020. SimAlign: High quality word alignments without parallel training data using static and contextualized embeddings. In *Findings of the Association for Computational Linguistics:*

EMNLP 2020, pages 1627–1643, Online. Association for Computational Linguistics.

Diederik P Kingma and Jimmy Ba. 2014. Adam: A method for stochastic optimization. *arXiv preprint arXiv:1412.6980*.

Lei Li, Kai Fan, Hongjia Li, and Chun Yuan. 2022. Structural supervision for word alignment and machine translation. In *Findings of the Association for Computational Linguistics: ACL 2022*, pages 4084–4094, Dublin, Ireland. Association for Computational Linguistics.

Xuansong Li, Stephen Grimes, Stephanie Strassel, Xiaoyi Ma, Nianwen Xue, Mitch Marcus, and Ann Taylor. 2015. Gale chinese-english parallel aligned treebank–training. *Linguistic Data Consortium, Philadelphia, PA*.

Masaaki Nagata, Katsuki Chousa, and Masaaki Nishino. 2020. A supervised word alignment method based on cross-language span prediction using multilingual BERT. In *Proceedings of the 2020 Conference on Empirical Methods in Natural Language Processing (EMNLP)*, pages 555–565, Online. Association for Computational Linguistics.

Elias Stengel-Eskin, Tzu-ray Su, Matt Post, and Benjamin Van Durme. 2019. A discriminative neural model for cross-lingual word alignment. In *Proceedings of the 2019 Conference on Empirical Methods in Natural Language Processing and the 9th International Joint Conference on Natural Language Processing (EMNLP-IJCNLP)*, pages 910–920, Hong Kong, China. Association for Computational Linguistics.

Leila Tavakoli and Heshaam Faili. 2014. Phrase alignments in parallel corpus using bootstrapping approach. *International Journal of Information and Communication Technology*, 6:63–76.

Shubham Toshniwal, Haoyue Shi, Bowen Shi, Lingyu Gao, Karen Livescu, and Kevin Gimpel. 2020. A cross-task analysis of text span representations. In *Proceedings of the 5th Workshop on Representation Learning for NLP*, pages 166–176, Online. Association for Computational Linguistics.

Ralph Weischedel, Martha Palmer, Mitchell Marcus, Eduard Hovy, Sameer Pradhan, Lance Ramshaw, Nianwen Xue, Ann Taylor, Jeff Kaufman, Michelle Franchini, et al. 2013. Ontonotes release 5.0 ldc2013t19. *Linguistic Data Consortium, Philadelphia, PA*, 23.

Patrick Xia, Guanghui Qin, Siddharth Vashishtha, Yunmo Chen, Tongfei Chen, Chandler May, Craig Harman, Kyle Rawlins, Aaron Steven White, and Benjamin Van Durme. 2021. LOME: Large ontology multilingual extraction. In *Proceedings of the 16th Conference of the European Chapter of the Association for Computational Linguistics: System Demonstrations*, pages 149–159, Online. Association for Computational Linguistics.

Haoran Xu, Benjamin Van Durme, and Kenton Murray. 2021. BERT, mBERT, or BiBERT? a study on contextualized embeddings for neural machine translation. In *Proceedings of the 2021 Conference on Empirical Methods in Natural Language Processing*, pages 6663–6675, Online and Punta Cana, Dominican Republic. Association for Computational Linguistics.

Mahsa Yarmohammadi, Shijie Wu, Marc Marone, Haoran Xu, Seth Ebner, Guanghui Qin, Yunmo Chen, Jialiang Guo, Craig Harman, Kenton Murray, Aaron Steven White, Mark Dredze, and Benjamin Van Durme. 2021. Everything is all it takes: A multipronged strategy for zero-shot cross-lingual information extraction. In *Proceedings of the 2021 Conference on Empirical Methods in Natural Language Processing*, pages 1950–1967, Online and Punta Cana, Dominican Republic. Association for Computational Linguistics.

David Yarowsky and Grace Ngai. 2001. Inducing multilingual POS taggers and NP bracketers via robust projection across aligned corpora. In *Second Meeting of the North American Chapter of the Association for Computational Linguistics*.

Dongxu Zhang, Boliang Zhang, Xiaoman Pan, Xiaocheng Feng, Heng Ji, and Weiran Xu. 2016. Bitext name tagging for cross-lingual entity annotation projection. In *Proceedings of COLING 2016, the 26th International Conference on Computational Linguistics: Technical Papers*, pages 461–470, Osaka, Japan. The COLING 2016 Organizing Committee.

A `awesome-align` Hyperparameters

We used `awesome-align` (Dou and Neubig, 2021), a contextualized embedding-based word aligner that extracts word alignments based on token embedding similarities. We fine-tuned the underlying XLM-R encoder on around two million parallel sentences from the OSCAR corpus (Abadji et al., 2022) of English-Farsi and English-Chinese pairs. We further fine-tuned the encoder for BETTER on English-Farsi gold alignments on 1500 sentence pairs by Tavakoli and Faili (2014). We reused empirically-chosen `awesome-align` hyperparameters from prior work for a similar task (Yarmohammadi et al., 2021): softmax normalization with probability thresholding of 0.001, 4 gradient accumulation steps, 1 training epoch with a learning rate of 2×10^{-5}, alignment layer of 16, and masked language modeling ("mlm"), translation language modeling ("tlm"), self-training objective ("so"), and parallel sentence identification ("psi") training objectives. We further fine-tuned the resulting model on the gold word alignments with the same hyperparameters, for 5 training epochs with a learning rate of 10^{-4} and only "so" as the training objective.

B Annotation Interface

In each task, a pair of tokenized sentences, one in English (source) on the top and one in Farsi (target) on the bottom are shown to the user. In each English sentence, there are one or more spans to align, as highlighted in Figure 3. The user needs to annotate the English spans word by word.

C Unsupervised Span Alignment Hyperparameters

We did a random search to find the best hyperparameters for the unsupervised span aligner. We selected the following for NER:

- Span enumeration strategy: full (all spans of length up to maximum width)
- Max target span width: 5 tokens
- Alignment decoding method: greedy (decode alignments in decreasing order of similarity score)
- Allow overlap: true (alignments can contain overlapping spans)
- Span representation: diff-sum (Toshniwal et al., 2020)
- Encoder and layer: bert-base-multilingual-cased (Devlin et al., 2019), layer 7 (0-indexed)
- Coupled: false (encode source and target text separately)

and the following for BETTER:

- Span enumeration strategy: full (all spans of length up to maximum width)
- Max target span width: 4 tokens
- Alignment decoding method: greedy (decode alignments in decreasing order of similarity score)
- Allow overlap: true (alignments can contain overlapping spans)
- Span representation: endpoint (concatenate embeddings of first and last subtokens)
- Encoder and layer: EnFav1.0 (internal bilingual model), layer 15 (0-indexed)
- Coupled: true (encode source and target text as a single sequence)

D NER Model Hyperparameters

- Encoder: bert-base-multilingual-cased (Devlin et al., 2019)
- Max sequence length: 128 WordPieces
- Batch size: 32
- Optimizer: Adam (Kingma and Ba, 2014)
- Learning rate: 5×10^{-5}
- Learning rate linear warmup: 10% of training steps
- Epochs: 25

E Annotation Budget Constraints in Fine-tuning Setting

Figure 4 shows the results of semi-automatic data subsampling experiments for NER when the models are pre-trained on English and fine-tuned on Chinese data. The performance improves with increasing subsampling percentage. However, there is a slight degradation when using the entire semi-automatic data compared to 50%. Gold projection is unexpectedly lower than the semi-50% and semi-100% settings.

Experiments for BETTER in which we train on only Farsi data, not combined with gold English, show inconsistent results. We hypothesize this is due to training and validating on noisy non-gold data. Further investigations of these phenomena are left as future work.

F Alignment Agreement Per Entity Type

The entity types that needed the most correction in both extraction settings were NORP (nationalities or religious or political groups) and PERCENT (percentage, including "%"). PERSON (people, including fictional), MONEY (monetary values, including unit), and WORK-OF-ART (titles of books, songs, etc.) were among the entity types with the highest number of identical spans for both the silver span extraction and unsupervised approaches (Figure 5).

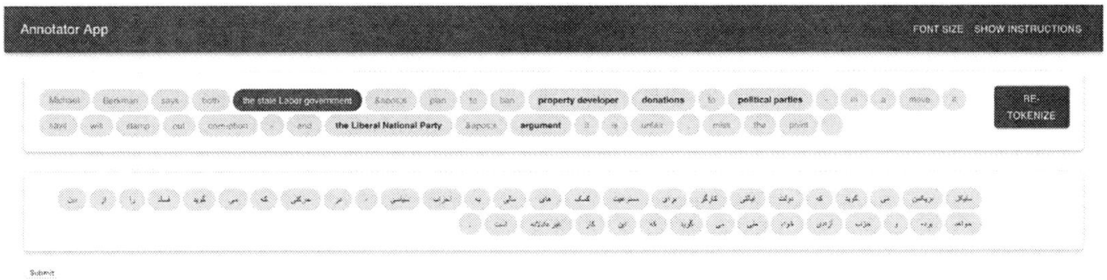

Figure 3: An example of the annotation interface for BETTER.

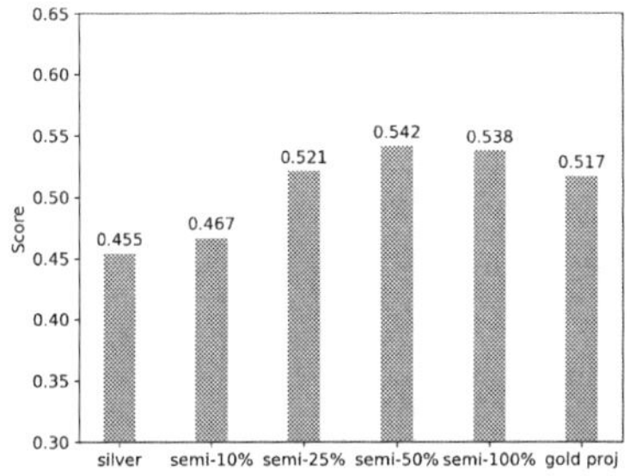

Figure 4: NER Micro-F1 on gold Chinese test set. Models are pre-trained on English data and fine-tuned on projected Chinese data.

Type	# Train	# Test	F1 (%)
GPE	921	41	75.6
CARDINAL	440	17	50.0
DATE	351	24	63.6
ORG	335	32	47.4
NORP	256	17	37.5
PERSON	230	31	51.5
MONEY	139	6	100.0
ORDINAL	107	6	20.0
PERCENT	100	0	NA
LOC	80	9	31.6
FAC	59	7	0.0
QUANTITY	55	3	57.1
EVENT	48	4	50.0
TIME	30	3	66.7
WORK-OF-ART	20	8	0.0
LAW	6	0	NA
LANGUAGE	1	0	NA
PRODUCT	1	1	0.0
Micro-avg	—	—	53.8

Table 5: NER per-type performance on the test set when pre-trained on English data and fine-tuned on semi-automatic projected Chinese data.

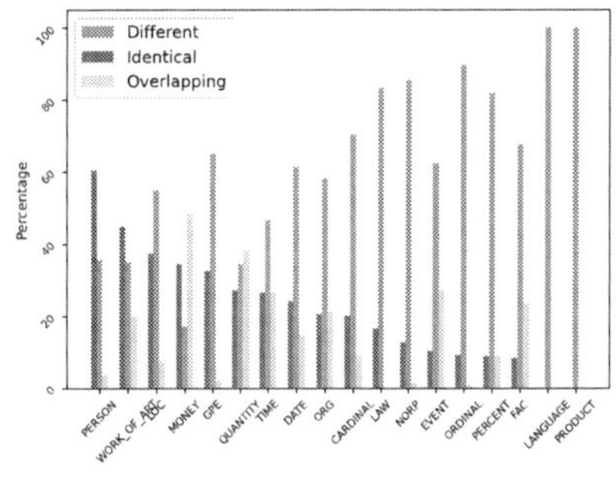

(a) Semi-automatic vs unsupervised spans

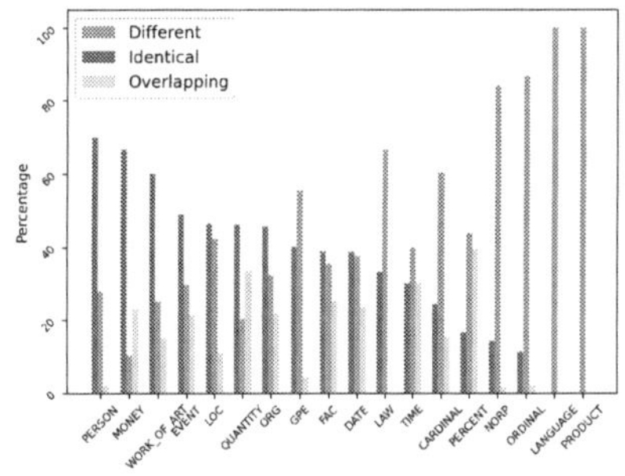

(b) Semi-automatic vs silver spans

Figure 5: Disagreements of semi-automatic spans with automatic spans in NER.

When Do Annotator Demographics Matter? Measuring the Influence of Annotator Demographics with the POPQUORN Dataset

Jiaxin Pei
School of Information
University of Michigan
pedropei@umich.edu

David Jurgens
School of Information
University of Michigan
jurgens@umich.edu

Abstract

Annotators are not fungible. Their demographics, life experiences, and backgrounds all contribute to how they label data. However, NLP has only recently considered how annotator identity might influence their decisions. Here, we present POPQUORN (the **Po**tato-**Pr**olific dataset for **Qu**estion-Answering, **O**ffensiveness, text **R**ewriting and politeness rating with demographic **N**uance). POPQUORN contains 45,000 annotations from 1,484 annotators, drawn from a representative sample regarding sex, age, and race as the US population. Through a series of analyses, we show that annotators' background plays a significant role in their judgments. Further, our work shows that backgrounds not previously considered in NLP (e.g., education), are meaningful and should be considered. Our study suggests that understanding the background of annotators and collecting labels from a demographically balanced pool of crowd workers is important to reduce the bias of datasets. The dataset, annotator background, and annotation interface are available at https://github.com/Jiaxin-Pei/potato-prolific-dataset.

1 Introduction

Supervised machine learning relies heavily on datasets with high-quality annotations and data labeling has long been an integral part of the machine learning pipeline (Roh et al., 2019). While recent large language models show promising performances on many zero-shot and few-shot NLP tasks (Bang et al., 2023), reinforcement learning with human feedback (RLHF), the core technology behind these models also heavily relies on large-scale and high-quality human annotations (Ouyang et al., 2022; Stiennon et al., 2020). Therefore, how to curate high-quality labeled datasets is one of the most important questions for both academia and industry.

Crowdsourcing is actively used as one of the major approaches to collect human labels for various NLP and ML tasks. Early studies on crowdsourcing NLP datasets suggest that crowd workers are able to generate high-quality labels even for relatively difficult tasks and with relatively low costs (Snow et al., 2008). However, other studies also suggest that collecting high-quality annotations from crowdsourcing platforms is challenging and requires rounds of iterations to create a reliable annotation pipeline (Zha et al., 2023).

Annotation quality has typically been measured by proxy through inter-annotator agreement (IAA) metrics like Krippendorff's α (Krippendorff, 2011) or Cohen's κ (Kvålseth, 1989). To attain higher IAA, researchers usually conduct pilot studies or rounds of annotator training to attain higher agreement among annotators. While such a method generally works in settings like part of speech tagging, the use of IAA as a proxy for quality implicitly assumes that the task has real ground truth and disagreements are mistakes. However, annotations for subjective tasks presents a far more challenging setting (Sandri et al., 2023); and as NLP and ML models are more frequently used in social settings where single true answer may not naturally exists, using IAA as the single metric for data quality can be problematic or can even create social harm. For example, Sap et al. (2021) studies how annotators' identity and prior belief affect their ratings on language toxicity and found significant gender and race differences in rating toxic language. Other studies also suggest that disagreement in annotations can also be due to the inherent contextual ambiguity (Jurgens, 2013; Poesio et al., 2019; Pavlick and Kwiatkowski, 2019) which can also be leveraged to improve the model performances (Uma et al., 2021).

Despite multiple studies on annotator background and disagreement, a systematic study on how annotator background influences different

Proceedings of the 17th Linguistic Annotation Workshop (LAW-XVII), pages 252–265
July 13, 2023 ©2023 Association for Computational Linguistics

Task	Description	Data	Total Annotations	Number of Annotators	Instances	Average Labels per Instance
Offensiveness rating	Rate comment offensiveness using a 1-5 scale	Ruddit	13,036	262	1,500	8.7
Reading comprehension	Read a passage and answer a question through highlighting the text	SQuAD	4,576	459	1,000	4.6
Text rewriting / Style transfer	Read an email and revise it to make it sound more polite	Enron	2,346	257	1,429	1.6
Politeness Rating	Rate the politeness of an email using a 1-5 scale	Enron	25,042	506	3,718	6.7
POPQUORN			45,000	1,484	7,647	–

Table 1: POPQUORN contains 45,000 annotations from 1,484 participants from a representative sample regarding sex, age and race. Each annotator is paid $12 per hour as suggested by Prolific. POPQUORN covers four representative NLP tasks.

types of labeling tasks is still missing in the current literature. To address this gap, in this study, we present POPQUORN (the **Po**tato-**Pro**lific dataset for **Qu**estion-Answering, **O**ffensiveness, text **R**ewriting and politeness rating with demographic **N**uance) a large dataset labeled by a US-population representative sample of annotators. POPQUORN contains 45,000 annotations for four diverse NLP tasks: offensiveness detection (classification/regression), questions answering (span identification), politeness style transfer (language generation) and politeness rating (classification/regression). All four tasks are annotated with a total of 1,484 annotators sampled from a representative sample regarding sex, age and race as the US population.

Through our analysis, we find that demographic background is significantly associated with people's ratings and performance on all four tasks—even for a more objective task such as reading comprehension. For example, people with higher levels of education perform better on the question-answering task and Black or African American participants tend to rate the same email as more polite and the same comment as more offensive than other racial groups. Our study suggests that demographic-aware annotation is important for various types of NLP tasks.

Overall our study makes the following four contributions. First, we create and release POPQUORN, a large-scale NLP dataset for four NLP tasks annotated by a representative sample of the US population with respect to sex, age, and race. Second, we analyze the annotations by different groups of annotators and found that various demographic backgrounds is significantly associated with people's rating of offensiveness, politeness as well as their performance on reading comprehension. Third, in comparison with existing annotations from curated workers, we demonstrate that a general sample of Prolific participants can produce high-quality results with minimal filtering, suggesting the platform is a reliable source of quality annotations. All the annotations, annotator background information, and labeling interface are available at `https://github.com/Jiaxin-Pei/potato-prolific-dataset`.

2 Motivation

Individual and group differences are two of the most fundamental components of social sciences (Biggs, 1978). Social and behavioral sciences exist, in part, because of systematic human variations: if everyone were to behave in the same way, there would be no need to build theories and models to understand people's behaviors in different settings. As a special form of human task, data labeling is also subject to such a basic rule: different people may have different perceptions of various information and different performances on various language tasks. In this sense, while NLP researchers try to achieve a higher IAA, disagreement is a natural and integral part of any human annotation task (Leonardelli et al., 2021). Existing studies in this direction generally focus on building models that can learn from human disagreement (Uma et al., 2021) and some recent studies start to look at how annotators' identity and prior belief could affect their ratings in offensive language and hate speech (Sap et al., 2019, 2021). However, most of the existing studies only focus on selected dimensions of identities (e.g., gender) and on certain tasks (e.g., toxic language detection).

Our study aims at providing a systematic examination of how annotators' background affect their perception of and performances on various language tasks. On the annotator side, we use a representative sample that matches the sex, age and race distribution of the US population. On the task side, we try to select tasks that are representative of common NLP tasks and with different degrees of difficulty, creativity, and subjectivity. Following this criterion, we selected four NLP tasks: (1) offensiveness detection, which is a relatively subjective task for classification and regression, (2) question answering, which is an objective task for span identification that is argued to test reading comprehension, (3) email rewriting, which requires creativity for a text generation task, and (4) politeness rating, which is also a subjective task for classification and regression.

3 Task 1: Offensiveness detection

Abusive or offensive language has been one of the most prominent issues on social media (Saha et al., 2023) and many existing studies tried to build datasets and models to detect offensive language (Malmasi and Zampieri, 2017; Yin and Zubiaga, 2021). Despite all the efforts on offensiveness detection, these models and datasets may have their own biases and during the creation of these datasets, annotators may introduce their own biases into their labels (Sap et al., 2019)—possibly marginalizing populations whose views differ from the majority. Indeed, Breitfeller et al. (2019) show that it was necessary to model the disparity between ratings from men and women annotators to identify gender-based microaggressions. However, most of the existing studies do not report the background of the annotators (Vidgen and Derczynski, 2020). Vidgen and Derczynski (2020) reviewed 63 offensiveness datasets and found that only 12 of them report detailed information about annotators.

To understand how annotator backgrounds (e.g. age, sex and race) affect their ratings on offensiveness, we re-annotated 1500 comments sampled from the Ruddit dataset (Hada et al., 2021) using 262 annotators from a representative sample from prolific.co.[1] In this section, we introduce the data sampling process, annotation task design, annotation result and then discuss how annotators' background affect their ratings of offensiveness.

[1]Prolific provides a service to request a sample of annotators with the same distribution of sex, age, and race as the US population using participants self-reported identities. We note that these demographic categories are based on the US Census questions in order to estimate a balanced sample.

3.1 Data and sampling

We use the Ruddit dataset (Hada et al., 2021) which contains 6,000 Reddit comments annotated using best-worst scaling (BWS; Flynn and Marley, 2014). Each comment is associated with an offensiveness score ranging from -1 to 1, computed from the BWS ratings. To select the subset we annotate, we remove comments that are shorter than 4 words or longer than 100 words, comments containing URLs as well as quote comments. Such a process led to 5,658 cleaned comments from the Ruddit dataset. We speculated that annotator background might be most influential in borderline cases, i.e., those not extremely offensive or inoffensive. Therefore, we use bucketed sampling based on the offensiveness score and we sample 10% from (-1, -0.5), 30% from (-0.5, 0), 50% from (0, 0.5) and 20% from (0.5, 1). Figure 1 shows the distribution of offensiveness scores before and after the sampling process. Our sampling process produced a subsample of comments with potentially more balanced offensiveness scores.

3.2 Task design

Each participant is presented with 50 comments and is asked to rate "Consider you read the above comment on Reddit, how offensive do you think it is?" using a 1-5 Likert scale where 1 means "Not offensive at all" and 5 means "Very offensive". Prior to annotating, each participant is shown an explicit warning about potentially seeing offensive content and has to answer a consent question before any comment is presented. When Prolific provides a demographically-representative sample, some information on the participants is provided. However, to ensure participants consent to have this information shared and reported as they themselves identify, we include a demographic and background screening question after the study is finished. Participants are shown an explanation for why demographic information was being asked for and were allowed to select "prefer not to disclose" if they wished.

To validate the annotation procedure, we conducted a pilot study with 8 participants. We used MACE (Hovy et al., 2013) to calculate the annotator competence score and ultimately removed one annotator with a competence score lower than 0.1. The annotators attain moderate IAA (Krippendorff's α=0.35), which is on par with existing studies on offensiveness labeling (Kang and Hovy,

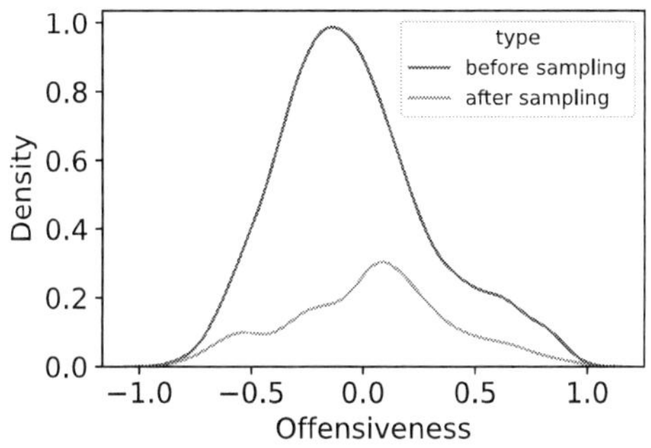

Figure 1: The offensiveness score in the Ruddit data before and in our subset after sampling. Positive scores denote offensive text.

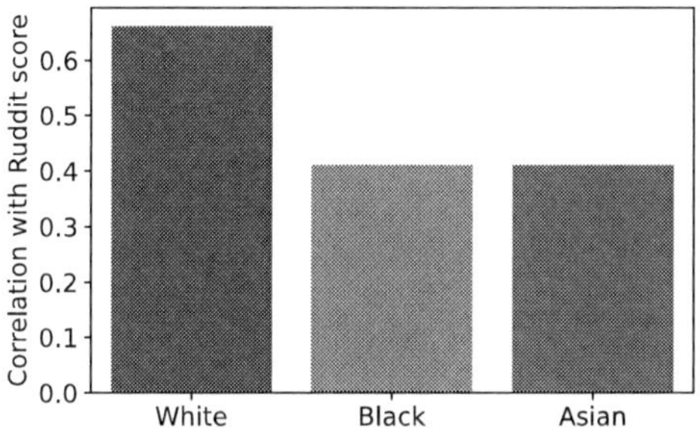

Figure 2: Correlation with the original Ruddit offensiveness score by race. Annotations by White participants have the highest correlation with the Ruddit score, while annotations by Asian and Black participants are significantly less correlated.

2021). We use POTATO (Pei et al., 2022) to set up the annotation website because of its integration with Prolific; Appendix Figure 8 shows the annotation interface.

3.3 Annotation result

The full annotation process collected 13,036 annotations from 262 participants and each comment received 8.7 annotations on average. The medium time of finishing 50 annotations is 13 minutes. Krippendorff's α=0.29, showing moderate to low agreement among annotators. However, the overall correlation between the averaged annotations and the original Ruddit score is 0.67, suggesting that, on average, the judgments largely matched those of the original dataset. Participants were highly open to sharing their demographics, with over 95% filling out the questionnaire.

	Coef.	Std.Err.	z	P> |z|
intercept	1.998	0.048	41.259	0.000
gender: Non-binary	-0.235	0.060	-3.890	0.000
gender: Woman	-0.022	0.020	-1.065	0.287
race: Black or African American	0.184	0.045	4.124	0.000
race: Hispanic or Latino	-0.405	0.078	-5.174	0.000
race: White	-0.104	0.038	-2.758	0.006
age: 25-29	-0.185	0.043	-4.268	0.000
age: 30-34	-0.165	0.041	-4.071	0.000
age: 35-39	-0.142	0.040	-3.525	0.000
age: 40-44	-0.037	0.043	-0.860	0.390
age: 45-49	-0.087	0.044	-1.979	0.048
age: 50-54	-0.141	0.046	-3.077	0.002
age: 54-59	0.001	0.039	0.025	0.980
age: 60-64	0.309	0.050	6.163	0.000
age: >65	0.117	0.042	2.755	0.006
education: College degree	-0.015	0.023	-0.660	0.509
education: Graduate degree	0.052	0.029	1.801	0.072

Table 2: Mixed-effect regression results showing the influence of annotator demographics on their offensiveness rating, controlling for the item being rated. Reference categories are Gender: Men, Race: Asian, Age: 18-25, and Education: High school degree.

3.4 Does annotator background affect offensiveness rating?

To understand the influence of annotator background on offensiveness ratings, we ran a linear mixed-effect model to predict the offensiveness rating with gender, age, race, and educational background, controlling each instance as the random effect. By controlling for each instance, we control for differences in the relative levels of offensiveness between instances, which allows us to study deviations from a mean judgment. Categories that are too rare in the data are removed from the regression (e.g. only 1 annotator chooses the "other" category for education). 16 annotators are dropped from this process.

Gender Do men and women have different ratings for offensiveness? Surprisingly, while some existing studies suggest that men and women may have different ratings of toxic language (Sap et al., 2021), we found no statistically significant difference between men and women. However, participants with non-binary gender identities tend to rate messages as less offensive than those identifying as men and women.

Age People older than 60 tend to perceive higher offensiveness scores than middle-aged participants. It is possible that older people are more sensitive to offensive language and they are less exposed to the language style of Reddit comments. Younger individuals are known to avoid swearing in the presence of older individuals but not among peers

(Fägersten, 2012, p. 111) and that younger individuals tend to use stronger swearing (Gauthier and Guille, 2017), which supports the idea that intergeneration norms may lead to differences in the perception of toxitiy.

Race We found significant racial differences in offensiveness rating: Black participants tend to rate the same comments with significantly more offensiveness than all the other racial groups. In this sense, classifiers trained on data annotated by White people may systematically underestimate the offensiveness of a comment for Black and Asian people.

Education No signficant differences were found with respect to annotator education, though the relatively small effect for those with graduate degrees does approach significance.

3.5 Are Ruddit annotations closer to perceptions of people in certain ethnicity groups?

We calculated the aggregated score of each racial group and calculate the overall correlation with the Ruddit offensiveness score. As shown in Figure 2, scores by White annotators are highly correlated with the Ruddit annotations (Pearson's r=0.66), while the scores by Black, and Asian annotators are only moderately correlated with the Ruddit score (Pearson's $r \approx 0.4$), suggesting that the Ruddit annotations are more likely to have been done by White annotators.

4 Task 2: Question Answering

Question Answering/Reading comprehension is one of the most fundamental tasks of NLP (Rogers et al., 2023) and SQuAD has been actively used by the research community to evaluate the performance of their models on question answering (QA) as a form of reading comprehension (Rajpurkar et al., 2016, 2018). To evaluate crowd workers' ability to complete QA tasks and study whether participants' background is associated with different performances, we build the second task as part of the POPQUORN.

4.1 Data and sampling

We use SQuAD 2.0 (Rajpurkar et al., 2018) as it also contains unanswerable questions and can pose external challenges to the annotators compared with SQuAD 1.0. In SQuAD 2.0, each passage can contain multiple questions. We sample 1000 unique passages and questions from the SQuAD 2.0 dataset. The final sampled dataset contains 695 questions with correct answers and 305 unanswerable questions.

4.2 Annotation task design

We recruit participants from a US-population representative sample (with respect to sex, age, and ethnicity) on Prolific. Each annotator is assigned with 10 passage and question pairs and is paid $12 per hour for their participation. At the end of the study, their demographic information is collected through an after-study survey. Besides the question-answering schema, we also ask participants to self-report the difficulty of their questions as task difficulty might be associated with disagreement (Uma et al., 2021). Appendix Figure 9 shows the annotation interface for this task.

4.3 Annotation result

4,576 annotations are collected from 459 annotators. Each question received 4.6 annotations on average (similar to the SQuAD data where on average 4.8 answers are collected for each question). We use a similar strategy as Rajpurkar et al. (2016) to aggregate the answers for each question: choose the majority answer and use the shorter version if there is a tie. We use the evaluation script provided by SQuAD to calculate the token-level precision, recall and F1 score for each answer. The aggregated answers achieve 0.75 F1, 0.72 precision, and 0.79 recall.

We manually examined a sample of human errors and we found that the crowd workers are mostly able to identify the correct answer but may use a larger span, which leads to higher recall but lower precision. More specifically, we annotated 50 instances where the F1 score is lower than 1 and found that for all these instances, at least one annotator is able to answer it correctly. Moreover, the SQuAD groundtruth is only correct in 12 out of 50 (24%) instances and for 8 instances (16%), the crowdworkers are able to identify the correct answer where the SQuAD groundtruth is incorrect. We found 2 out of 50 (4%) instances that both SQuAD and our crowdworkers didn't answer the question correctly.

What demographic factors influence answer accuracy? To study the connection between demographic background and performance on the read-

	Coef.	Std.Err.	z	P> |z|
Intercept	0.580	0.032	18.238	0.000
gender: Non-binary	0.008	0.036	0.233	0.816
gender: Woman	-0.031	0.013	-2.392	0.017
race: Black or African American	-0.092	0.032	-2.847	0.004
race: Hispanic or Latino	-0.149	0.038	-3.874	0.000
race: White	-0.062	0.028	-2.242	0.025
age: 25-29	0.012	0.029	0.404	0.686
age: 30-34	0.040	0.027	1.491	0.136
age: 35-39	-0.050	0.028	-1.779	0.075
age: 40-44	0.072	0.028	2.567	0.010
age: 45-49	0.079	0.027	2.903	0.004
age: 50-54	0.116	0.029	3.938	0.000
age: 54-59	0.072	0.027	2.697	0.007
age: 60-64	0.002	0.027	0.060	0.952
age: >65	0.008	0.026	0.311	0.756
education: College degree	0.027	0.015	1.824	0.068
education: Graduate degree	0.060	0.018	3.382	0.001

Table 3: Mixed-effect regression results showing the influence of annotator demographics on their performance at question answering (as measured by F1 score), controlling for the item being rated. Reference categories are Gender: Men, Race: Asian, Age: 18-25, and Education: High school degree.

ing comprehension task, we run a mixed effect model as in §3.4 with variables for gender, age, education, and ethnicity as fixed effects and the instance as the random effect. Despite the task being largely objective, accuracy at question answering varied relative to annotator background, as shown in Table 3. The largest effects were seen with race and age variation, with a smaller effect for education. While the root causes of this performance disparity cannot be directly tested from our survey, two notable general trends are worth mentioning.

First, the performance differences mirror known disparities in education and economic opportunities for minorities compared with their White male peers in the US.[2] Multiple studies have shown how structural forces have led to lower levels of reading abilities by race (Dixon-Román et al., 2013; Merolla and Jackson, 2019) and socioeconomic status (Merz et al., 2020).

Second, the trend for age matches known results showing a moderate increase in reading ability with age (Pfost et al., 2014; Locher and Pfost, 2020). Further, Locher and Pfost (2020) also note that individuals in professions that require reading also have better reading comprehension, which we view as a potential contributor to the performance increase seen from annotators with graduate degrees who are more likely to have such professions.

[2]We note that the regression uses the reference category of Asian for race but the relative differences between groups with factors match with expectations.

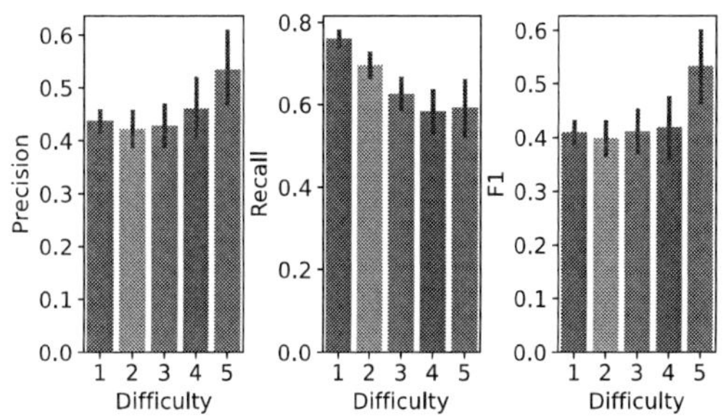

Figure 3: Questions rated with lower difficulty are generally associated with higher Recall. However, when people use the highest difficulty score, people generally perform better as measured by precision, suggesting that people tend to be more selective about their answers when they perceive that the task is difficult.

Is self-reported difficulty associated with participant performance? During the study, participants are also asked to rate "How difficult do you think this question is" on a 1-5 likert scale where 1 means not difficult at all and 5 means very difficult. Figure 3 shows the overall F1, recall and precision score and the difficulty rated by each participant. We found that when people report lower difficulty, their recalls tend to be higher, suggesting that they are better able to identify the potential span of the answer. However, perceived difficulty is also associated with increased precision. Multiple mechanisms might explain this pattern: it is possible that difficult questions require a more specific answer. It is also possible that people may be more cognitively focused to solve the challenge when they perceive the task is more difficult.

5 Task 3: Politeness rewriting

Politeness is one of the most prominent social factors in interpersonal communication (Brown et al., 1987). The NLP community has built computational models for predicting politeness scores and built models to generate polite text in different settings (Danescu-Niculescu-Mizil et al., 2013; Madaan et al., 2020; Porayska-Pomsta and Mellish, 2004). However, few resources exist with human-authored examples of pairs of original and style-transferred texts for politeness. Therefore, to test the crowdworker's ability to generate open-domain text for style-transfer tasks, we recruit participants from Prolific to rewrite emails from the Enron dataset as part of POPQUORN.

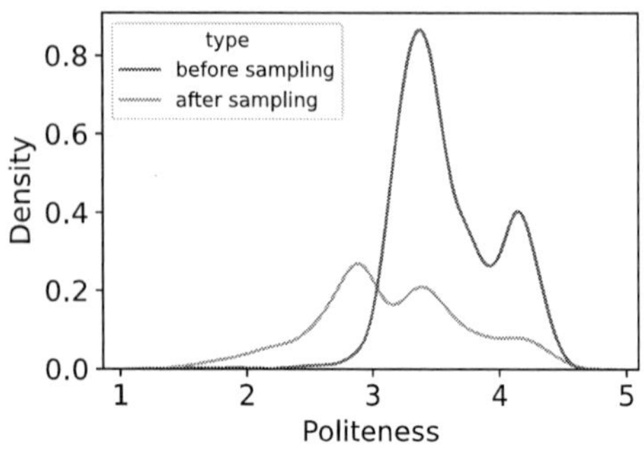

Figure 4: The inferred politeness score of emails in the original Enron dataset and in our subset after sampling. Higher scores indicate higher degrees of politeness.

5.1 Data and samples

We use the Enron email dataset (Shetty and Adibi, 2004) which contains approximately 500,000 emails from senior management executives at the Enron Corporation. We first extract the main body of the emails and then we remove emails that are too long (larger than 100 words), too short (shorter than 8 words), containing URLs, containing more than 10 numbers or were automatically generated by systems. This preprocessing lead to 84,066 remaining emails. We use `politenessr` [3] to infer the politeness score of each email. As most of the emails are relatively polite in the dataset, to draw a more balanced sample for annotation, we use bucket sampling and sample 50% from (1,3), 40% from (3,4), and 10% from (4,5). The final dataset used for annotation contains 1000 emails. Figure 4 shows the distribution of politeness score after bucket sampling. The sampled emails contain more emails with lower inferred politeness scores than the original Enron dataset.

5.2 Annotation task

In the annotation task, each annotator is presented with 10 emails and asked to "rewrite the email to make it sound more polite in a work setting". Appendix Figure 10 shows the annotation interface for this rewriting task. We conduct a pilot study with 18 participants to validate the annotation procedure. The pilot study attained 180 annotations for 150 emails and the average editing distance is 102, suggesting that the annotators are making substantial changes to the original message. Politeness of the revised email increases by 0.53 on average when compared with the original emails, suggesting that the revised emails are much more polite.

[3]The model is accessible at `https://github.com/wujunjie1998/Politenessr` and was trained on politeness data from Danescu-Niculescu-Mizil et al. (2013) and Wang and Jurgens (2018).

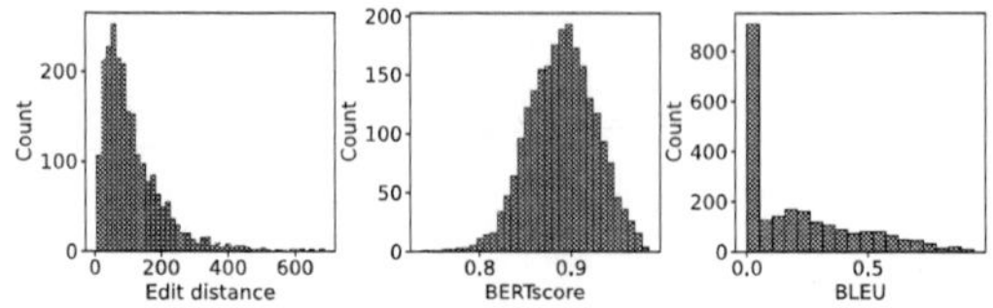

Figure 5: Measures comparing the original and revised emails show that the revisions are still very semantically similar (high BERTScore) but the form of the content has been substantially changed (high edit distance and low BLEU score).

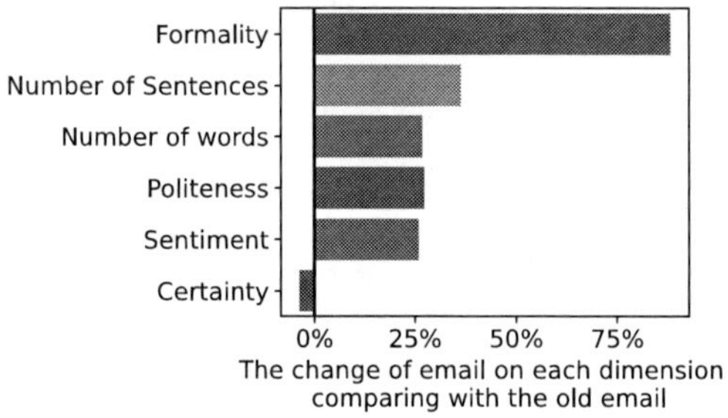

Figure 6: The revised emails have 36% more sentences and 26% more words than the original emails. Moreover, the revised emails are 88% more formal, 27% more polite, 25% more positive, and 3% less certain than the old emails, suggesting that the participants are making substantial changes to make the email more polite.

5.3 Full Annotation Results

The final politeness rewriting dataset contains 2,346 emails written by 257 participants drawn from a US population representative sample (regarding sex, age, and race). In the final dataset, we remove the revised emails if they are shorter than 7 words or if the edit distance is lower than 5 (79 out of 2376 emails are removed). As shown in Figure 6, the overall politeness increase 27% compared with the original emails, suggesting that the rewritten emails are significantly more polite than the original ones. The revised emails are more positive[4], more formal[5] and less certain[6] comparing with the original emails. To achieve these changes, annotators substantially changed the emails, with

[4]`https://huggingface.co/Seethal/sentiment_analysis_generic_dataset`

[5]`https://huggingface.co/s-nlp/roberta-base-formality-ranker`

[6]`https://pypi.org/project/certainty-estimator/` (Pei and Jurgens, 2021)

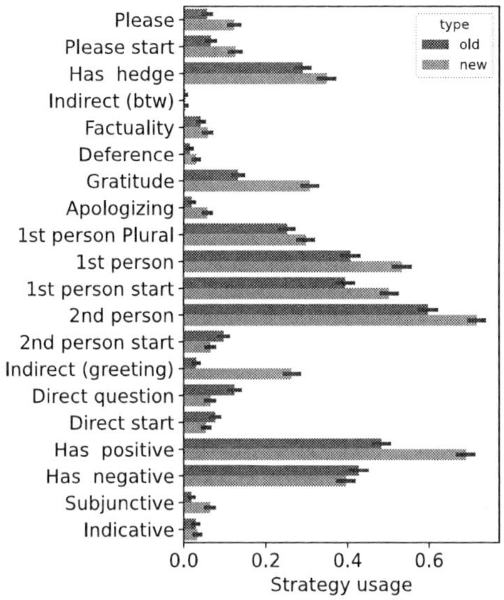

Figure 7: Annotators adopt a wide range of politeness strategies.

an average editing distance of 112; this indicates that changes were mostly not perfunctory, small edits.

Despite these changes to the tone and style of the emails, annotators kept the meaning largely consistent. Figure 5 shows the distribution of edit distance, BERTscore (Zhang et al., 2019) and BLEU, with the latter two being proxies for the interpretation or meaning of the email content. The BERTscore for the emails is generally above 0.8, suggesting that the revised email are able to retain the meaning of the original content. On the other hand, most of the BLEU scores are lower than 0.2, suggesting that the participants are able to make changes to the original content while keeping its meaning.

Did annotators use a diversity of strategies for increasing politeness—or did they just add "please" to every sentence? To further understand changes annotators made to the original emails, we analyzed the politeness strategies using ConvoKit (Chang et al., 2020) and compared the strategies' prevalence in both revised and original emails. As shown in Figure 7, annotators adopt a wide range of politeness strategies (Danescu-Niculescu-Mizil et al., 2013). The usage of "please" in a sentence does increase (as expected), and we see a larger increase in strategies such as expressing gratitude, use of positive words, and indirect greetings. Together, this variation suggests that the revisions capture more natural variation in writing and are not artificial revisions driven by task design or speed incentives.

6 Task 4: Politeness Rating

To validate the email rewriting results from Task 3, we perform a follow-up participant recruitment to rate the politeness of the original and revised emails. As resources on computational modeling of politeness remain rare and the research community heavily relies on the Stanford politeness dataset (Danescu-Niculescu-Mizil et al., 2013), we hope this dataset helps promote future studies on politeness prediction and to understand how people with different backgrounds perceive politeness.

6.1 Annotation setup

We use 1,372 emails from the original Enron dataset and 2,346 emails rewritten by the participants. Annotators are asked to rate "Consider you read this email from a colleague, how polite do you think it is?" using a 1-5 Likert scale where 1 means "not polite at all" and 5 means "Very polite". Each annotator is presented with 50 emails in a random order and on average each email is annotated by 6.7 annotators. Appendix Figure 11 shows the interface of this annotation task. We ran one pilot study with 8 annotators and each annotator is presented with 50 emails. The overall Krippendorff's α is 0.43, suggesting moderate inter-annotator agreement and is reasonable for such a subjective task.

6.2 Full annotations

Our final politeness rating dataset contains 25,042 annotations from 506 annotators. Each email receives 6.7 annotations on average. The overall Krippendorff's α is 0.43, indicating moderate to low inter-annotator agreement. The overall politeness rating is 2.8 and 3.6 for original and revised emails, suggesting that the revised emails are perceived as more polite than the original emails, which correlates with the previous result.

6.3 Does annotator background affect politeness rating?

We ran a linear mixed-effect model to predict the politeness rating with gender, age, race, and education, controlling each instance as the random effect, similar to previous setups. Table 4 shows the regression results.

Gender We found that women rate messages as less polite, though the effect size is relatively small

	Coef.	Std.Err.	z	P> |z|
Intercept	3.167	0.035	89.497	0.000
gender: Non-binary	-0.048	0.042	-1.149	0.250
gender: Woman	-0.042	0.014	-3.116	0.002
race: Black or African American	0.192	0.032	6.105	0.000
race: Hispanic or Latino	0.057	0.036	1.607	0.108
race: White	0.060	0.027	2.212	0.027
age: 25-29	0.291	0.030	9.630	0.000
age: 30-34	0.078	0.028	2.764	0.006
age: 35-39	0.169	0.031	5.376	0.000
age: 40-44	0.137	0.029	4.704	0.000
age: 45-49	0.296	0.031	9.677	0.000
age: 50-54	0.305	0.030	10.275	0.000
age: 54-59	0.198	0.029	6.717	0.000
age: 60-64	0.249	0.029	8.623	0.000
age: >65	0.209	0.028	7.508	0.000
education: College degree	-0.145	0.015	-9.394	0.000
education: Graduate degree	-0.135	0.020	-6.837	0.000

Table 4: Mixed-effect regression results showing the influence of annotator demographics on their politeness ratings, controlling for the item being rated. Reference categories are Gender: Men, Race: Asian, Age: 18-25, and Education: High school degree.

compared with other demographic dimensions.

Age Compared with the youngest segment in our sample (Ages 18-25), all older segments were more likely to give a higher politeness rating.

Race We found significant racial differences in politeness rating. Relative to Asian peers, Black participants rated messages as more polite, with a small positive effect for White peers. No significant result was seen for annotators identifying as Hispanic or Latino. Given known differences in the cultural perceptions of politeness (Troutman, 2010; Brown, 2015; Rodríguez-Arauz et al., 2019), these differences suggest systematic variation in the rating that would otherwise be treated as disagreement, rather than valid, culturally-situated judgments.

Educational Background As shown in Table 4, participants with more education (a graduate or college degree) tend to rate the same email with less politeness than those with a high school degree. Education is strongly correlated with socioeconomic status and with that status typically comes increased social standing. While multiple works have shown how individuals modify their speech with respect to power/status differences between speaker and recipient (e.g., Brown et al., 1987; Wang, 2021), we believe our result offers a valuable new insight to how individuals with different status view the *same* message. Our results suggest that higher-status (more educated) individuals are

7 Discussion

High-quality annotated data has been one of the primary driving factors of NLP and ML. While some studies try to look at improving data quality through analyzing disagreements among annotators, systematic studies of how annotators' background affects crowdsourcing results remain rare. In this paper, we create a new NLP dataset labeled by annotators from a US-representative sample regarding sex, age and race. We re-annotated the Ruddit offensiveness dataset and found that the offensiveness is strongly correlated with annotations by White participants, while the correlation between the Ruddit offensiveness score and annotations by participants from other racial groups are only 0.41, suggesting that the Ruddit dataset might largely reflect the views of White annotators of what content is offensive. As people from other cultures may perceive the same comment with a lower or higher degree of offensiveness, classifiers trained on a dataset annotated by White participants could pose risks for many people. Such an issue becomes increasingly important as both the industry and research community are trying to align the values of LLMs with human beings through instruction tuning.

8 Conclusion

Who annotates your data matters. Across four annotation tasks, we show that an annotator's background influences their decisions, across multiple annotation tasks with different degrees of subjectivity. In more subjective tasks, these differences in decisions are not mistakes but rather valid differences in views. Our results underscore that NLP papers that curate datasets must consider whose voices appear in their datasets, as these ultimately decide whose voice are captured in models trained on the data. Indeed, by comparing our annotations with those from the existing annotated datasets, we show that the existing annotated dataset might be annotated by a demographically-biased group of annotators. To support work in this modeling demographic-aware and socially-responsible NLP, we release POPQUORN with 45,000 annotations on four NLP tasks by nearly 1.5K annotators.

Acknowledgments

We thank Prolific for their generous support to this study. We thank Tom Rodenby, Andrew Gordon and Agrima Seth for their helpful feedback.

Ethical Implications

Collecting background information about annotators can be sensitive and have ethical implications. In our study, we follow best practices when asking about demographic information (Spiel et al., 2019) and always allow participants to choose "Prefer to not disclose" and provide external options for them to self-describe identities. Understanding how different groups of people perceive social information in language and perform different tasks is important when NLP models are applied in more and more social applications. We believe that through carefully designed procedures to collect background information of annotators along with the data annotation, we will be able to build better NLP and ML models that could better serve different groups of people and reduce potential social harm.

References

Yejin Bang, Samuel Cahyawijaya, Nayeon Lee, Wenliang Dai, Dan Su, Bryan Wilie, Holy Lovenia, Ziwei Ji, Tiezheng Yu, Willy Chung, et al. 2023. A multitask, multilingual, multimodal evaluation of chatgpt on reasoning, hallucination, and interactivity. *arXiv preprint arXiv:2302.04023*.

John B Biggs. 1978. Individual and group differences in study processes. *British Journal of Educational Psychology*, 48(3):266–279.

Luke Breitfeller, Emily Ahn, David Jurgens, and Yulia Tsvetkov. 2019. Finding microaggressions in the wild: A case for locating elusive phenomena in social media posts. In *Proceedings of the 2019 conference on empirical methods in natural language processing and the 9th international joint conference on natural language processing (EMNLP-IJCNLP)*, pages 1664–1674.

Penelope Brown. 2015. Politeness and language. In *The International Encyclopedia of the Social and Behavioural Sciences (IESBS),(2nd ed.)*, pages 326–330. Elsevier.

Penelope Brown, Stephen C Levinson, and Stephen C Levinson. 1987. *Politeness: Some universals in language usage*, volume 4. Cambridge university press.

Jonathan P Chang, Caleb Chiam, Liye Fu, Andrew Z Wang, Justine Zhang, and Cristian Danescu-Niculescu-Mizil. 2020. Convokit: A toolkit for the analysis of conversations. *arXiv preprint arXiv:2005.04246*.

Cristian Danescu-Niculescu-Mizil, Moritz Sudhof, Dan Jurafsky, Jure Leskovec, and Christopher Potts. 2013. A computational approach to politeness with application to social factors. In *Proceedings of the 51st Annual Meeting of the Association for Computational Linguistics (Volume 1: Long Papers)*, pages 250–259.

Ezekiel J Dixon-Román, Howard T Everson, and John J McArdle. 2013. Race, poverty and sat scores: Modeling the influences of family income on black and white high school students' sat performance. *Teachers College Record*, 115(4):1–33.

Kristy Beers Fägersten. 2012. *Who's swearing now? The social aspects of conversational swearing*. Cambridge Scholars Publishing.

Terry N Flynn and Anthony AJ Marley. 2014. Best-worst scaling: theory and methods. In *Handbook of choice modelling*, pages 178–201. Edward Elgar Publishing.

Michael Gauthier and Adrien Guille. 2017. Gender and age differences in swearing. *Advances in swearing research: New languages and new contexts*, pages 137–156.

Rishav Hada, Sohi Sudhir, Pushkar Mishra, Helen Yannakoudakis, Saif M Mohammad, and Ekaterina Shutova. 2021. Ruddit: Norms of offensiveness for english reddit comments. *arXiv preprint arXiv:2106.05664*.

Dirk Hovy, Taylor Berg-Kirkpatrick, Ashish Vaswani, and Eduard Hovy. 2013. Learning whom to trust with mace. In *Proceedings of the 2013 Conference of the North American Chapter of the Association for Computational Linguistics: Human Language Technologies*, pages 1120–1130.

David Jurgens. 2013. Embracing ambiguity: A comparison of annotation methodologies for crowdsourcing word sense labels. In *Proceedings of the 2013 Conference of the North American Chapter of the Association for Computational Linguistics: Human Language Technologies*, pages 556–562.

Dongyeop Kang and Eduard Hovy. 2021. Style is not a single variable: Case studies for cross-stylistic language understanding. In *Proceedings of the 59th Annual Meeting of the Association for Computational Linguistics and the 11th International Joint Conference on Natural Language Processing (Volume 1: Long Papers)*, pages 2376–2387.

Klaus Krippendorff. 2011. Computing krippendorff's alpha-reliability.

Tarald O Kvålseth. 1989. Note on cohen's kappa. *Psychological reports*, 65(1):223–226.

Elisa Leonardelli, Stefano Menini, Alessio Palmero Aprosio, Marco Guerini, and Sara Tonelli. 2021. Agreeing to disagree: Annotating offensive language datasets with annotators' disagreement. *arXiv preprint arXiv:2109.13563*.

Franziska Locher and Maximilian Pfost. 2020. The relation between time spent reading and reading comprehension throughout the life course. *Journal of Research in Reading*, 43(1):57–77.

Aman Madaan, Amrith Setlur, Tanmay Parekh, Barnabas Poczos, Graham Neubig, Yiming Yang, Ruslan Salakhutdinov, Alan W Black, and Shrimai Prabhumoye. 2020. Politeness transfer: A tag and generate approach. *arXiv preprint arXiv:2004.14257*.

Shervin Malmasi and Marcos Zampieri. 2017. Detecting hate speech in social media. *arXiv preprint arXiv:1712.06427*.

David M Merolla and Omari Jackson. 2019. Structural racism as the fundamental cause of the academic achievement gap. *Sociology Compass*, 13(6):e12696.

Emily C Merz, Elaine A Maskus, Samantha A Melvin, Xiaofu He, and Kimberly G Noble. 2020. Socioeconomic disparities in language input are associated with children's language-related brain structure and reading skills. *Child development*, 91(3):846–860.

Long Ouyang, Jeffrey Wu, Xu Jiang, Diogo Almeida, Carroll Wainwright, Pamela Mishkin, Chong Zhang, Sandhini Agarwal, Katarina Slama, Alex Ray, et al. 2022. Training language models to follow instructions with human feedback. *Advances in Neural Information Processing Systems*, 35:27730–27744.

Ellie Pavlick and Tom Kwiatkowski. 2019. Inherent disagreements in human textual inferences. *Transactions of the Association for Computational Linguistics*, 7:677–694.

Jiaxin Pei, Aparna Ananthasubramaniam, Xingyao Wang, Naitian Zhou, Jackson Sargent, Apostolos Dedeloudis, and David Jurgens. 2022. Potato: The portable text annotation tool. *arXiv preprint arXiv:2212.08620*.

Jiaxin Pei and David Jurgens. 2021. Measuring sentence-level and aspect-level (un) certainty in science communications. In *Proceedings of the 2021 Conference on Empirical Methods in Natural Language Processing*, pages 9959–10011.

Maximilian Pfost, John Hattie, Tobias Dörfler, and Cordula Artelt. 2014. Individual differences in reading development: A review of 25 years of empirical research on matthew effects in reading. *Review of educational research*, 84(2):203–244.

Massimo Poesio, Jon Chamberlain, Silviu Paun, Juntao Yu, Alexandra Uma, and Udo Kruschwitz. 2019. A crowdsourced corpus of multiple judgments and disagreement on anaphoric interpretation. In *Proceedings of the 2019 Conference of the North American Chapter of the Association for Computational Linguistics: Human Language Technologies, Volume 1 (Long and Short Papers)*, pages 1778–1789.

Kaśka Porayska-Pomsta and Chris Mellish. 2004. Modelling politeness in natural language generation. In *Natural Language Generation: Third International Conference, INLG 2004, Brockenhurst, UK, July 14-16, 2004. Proceedings*, pages 141–150. Springer.

Pranav Rajpurkar, Robin Jia, and Percy Liang. 2018. Know what you don't know: Unanswerable questions for squad. *arXiv preprint arXiv:1806.03822*.

Pranav Rajpurkar, Jian Zhang, Konstantin Lopyrev, and Percy Liang. 2016. Squad: 100,000+ questions for machine comprehension of text. *arXiv preprint arXiv:1606.05250*.

Gloriana Rodríguez-Arauz, Nairán Ramírez-Esparza, Adrián García-Sierra, Elif G Ikizer, and María José Fernández-Gómez. 2019. You go before me, please: Behavioral politeness and interdependent self as markers of simpatía in latinas. *Cultural Diversity and Ethnic Minority Psychology*, 25(3):379.

Anna Rogers, Matt Gardner, and Isabelle Augenstein. 2023. QA dataset explosion: A taxonomy of NLP resources for question answering and reading comprehension. *ACM Computing Surveys*, 55(10):1–45.

Yuji Roh, Geon Heo, and Steven Euijong Whang. 2019. A survey on data collection for machine learning: a big data-ai integration perspective. *IEEE Transactions on Knowledge and Data Engineering*, 33(4):1328–1347.

Punyajoy Saha, Kiran Garimella, Narla Komal Kalyan, Saurabh Kumar Pandey, Pauras Mangesh Meher, Binny Mathew, and Animesh Mukherjee. 2023. On the rise of fear speech in online social media. *Proceedings of the National Academy of Sciences*, 120(11):e2212270120.

Marta Sandri, Elisa Leonardelli, Sara Tonelli, and Elisabetta Ježek. 2023. Why don't you do it right? analysing annotators' disagreement in subjective tasks. In *Proceedings of the 17th Conference of the European Chapter of the Association for Computational Linguistics*, pages 2420–2433.

Maarten Sap, Dallas Card, Saadia Gabriel, Yejin Choi, and Noah A Smith. 2019. The risk of racial bias in hate speech detection. In *Proceedings of the 57th annual meeting of the association for computational linguistics*, pages 1668–1678.

Maarten Sap, Swabha Swayamdipta, Laura Vianna, Xuhui Zhou, Yejin Choi, and Noah A Smith. 2021. Annotators with attitudes: How annotator beliefs and identities bias toxic language detection. *arXiv preprint arXiv:2111.07997*.

Jitesh Shetty and Jafar Adibi. 2004. The enron email dataset database schema and brief statistical report. *Information sciences institute technical report, University of Southern California*, 4(1):120–128.

Rion Snow, Brendan O'connor, Dan Jurafsky, and Andrew Y Ng. 2008. Cheap and fast–but is it good? evaluating non-expert annotations for natural language tasks. In *Proceedings of the 2008 conference on empirical methods in natural language processing*, pages 254–263.

Katta Spiel, Oliver L Haimson, and Danielle Lottridge. 2019. How to do better with gender on surveys: a guide for hci researchers. *Interactions*, 26(4):62–65.

Nisan Stiennon, Long Ouyang, Jeffrey Wu, Daniel Ziegler, Ryan Lowe, Chelsea Voss, Alec Radford, Dario Amodei, and Paul F Christiano. 2020. Learning to summarize with human feedback. *Advances in Neural Information Processing Systems*, 33:3008–3021.

Denise Troutman. 2010. Attitude and its situatedness in linguistic politeness. *Poznań Studies in Contemporary Linguistics*, 46(1):85–109.

Alexandra N Uma, Tommaso Fornaciari, Dirk Hovy, Silviu Paun, Barbara Plank, and Massimo Poesio. 2021. Learning from disagreement: A survey. *Journal of Artificial Intelligence Research*, 72:1385–1470.

Bertie Vidgen and Leon Derczynski. 2020. Directions in abusive language training data, a systematic review: Garbage in, garbage out. *Plos one*, 15(12):e0243300.

Yi Wang. 2021. The price of being polite: politeness, social status, and their joint impacts on community q&a efficiency. *Journal of Computational Social Science*, 4:101–122.

Zijian Wang and David Jurgens. 2018. It's going to be okay: Measuring access to support in online communities. In *Proceedings of the 2018 Conference on Empirical Methods in Natural Language Processing*, pages 33–45.

Wenjie Yin and Arkaitz Zubiaga. 2021. Towards generalisable hate speech detection: a review on obstacles and solutions. *PeerJ Computer Science*, 7:e598.

Daochen Zha, Zaid Pervaiz Bhat, Kwei-Herng Lai, Fan Yang, Zhimeng Jiang, Shaochen Zhong, and Xia Hu. 2023. Data-centric artificial intelligence: A survey. *arXiv preprint arXiv:2303.10158*.

Tianyi Zhang, Varsha Kishore, Felix Wu, Kilian Q Weinberger, and Yoav Artzi. 2019. Bertscore: Evaluating text generation with bert. *arXiv preprint arXiv:1904.09675*.

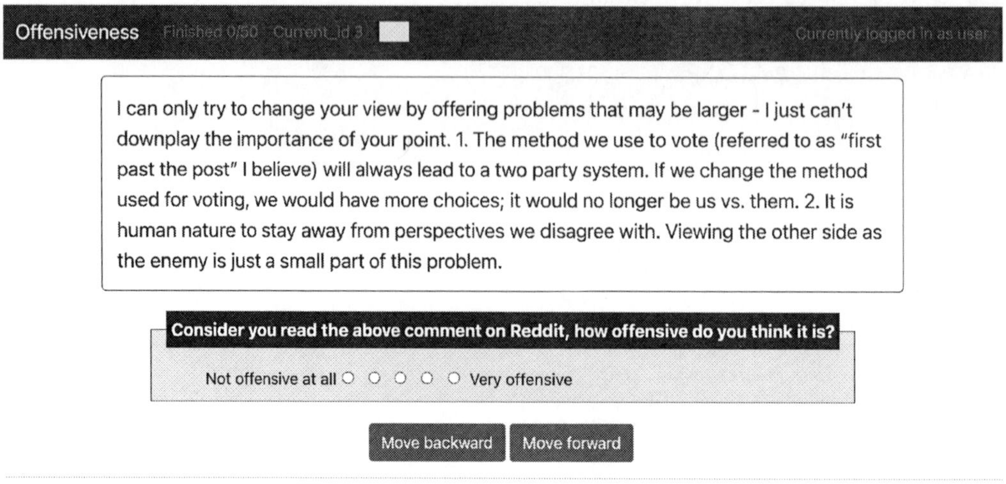

Figure 8: Annotation interface for the offensiveness rating task.

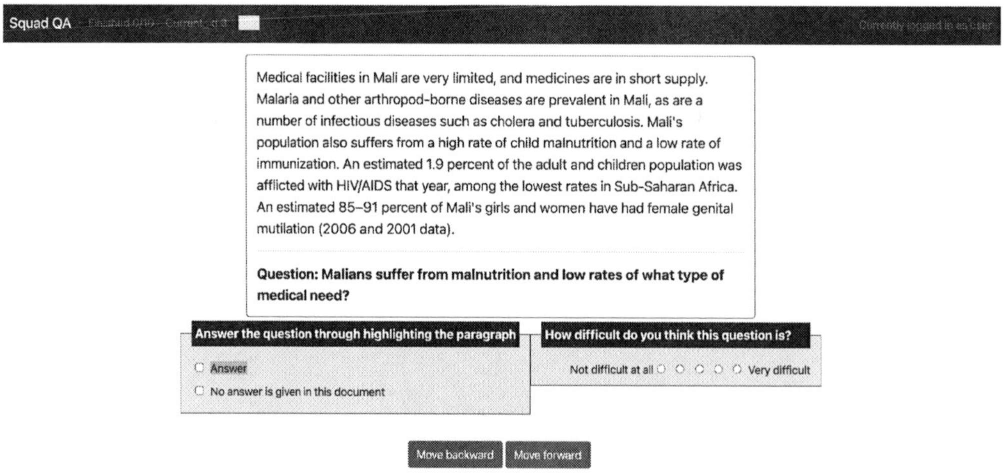

Figure 9: Annotation interface for the SQuAD reading comprehension task

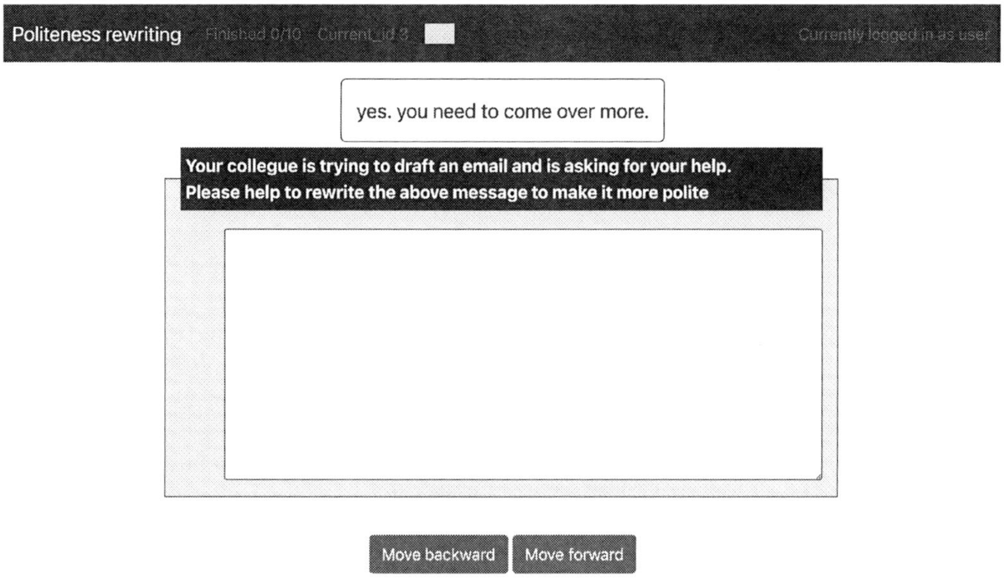

Figure 10: Annotation interface for the email rewriting task

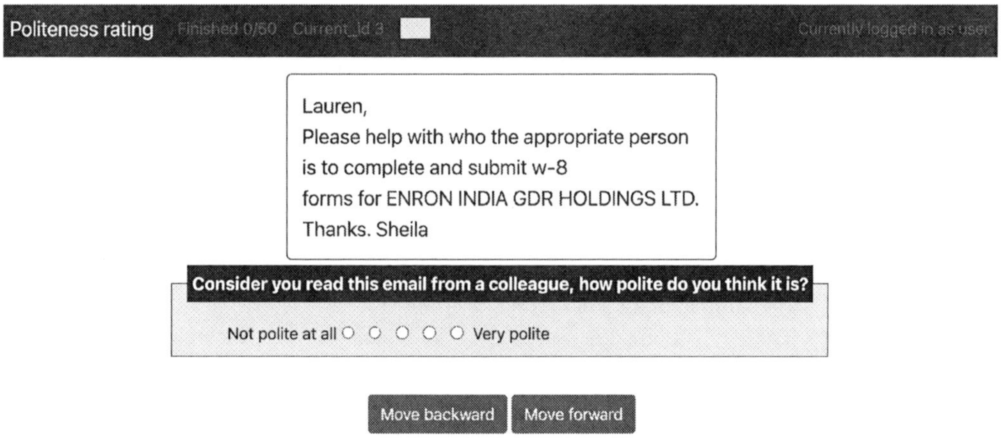

Figure 11: Annotation interface for the politness rating task.

Enriching the NArabizi Treebank: A Multifaceted Approach to Supporting an Under-Resourced Language

Arij Riabi Menel Mahamdi Djamé Seddah
Inria, Paris
{firstname,lastname}@inria.fr

Abstract

In this paper we address the scarcity of annotated data for NArabizi, a Romanized form of North African Arabic used mostly on social media, which poses challenges for Natural Language Processing (NLP). We introduce an enriched version of NArabizi Treebank (Seddah et al., 2020) with three main contributions: the addition of two novel annotation layers (named entity recognition and offensive language detection) and a re-annotation of the tokenization, morpho-syntactic and syntactic layers that ensure annotation consistency. Our experimental results, using different tokenization schemes, showcase the value of our contributions and highlight the impact of working with non-gold tokenization for NER and dependency parsing. To facilitate future research, we make these annotations publicly available. Our enhanced NArabizi Treebank paves the way for creating sophisticated language models and NLP tools for this under-represented language.

1 Introduction

Despite the abundance of rich and diverse dialects worldwide, each possessing distinctive features and characteristics, many of these dialects still lack the necessary resources and support to enable their speakers to access modern technologies in their own language (Joshi et al., 2020). Therefore, it is imperative to undertake endeavors aimed at creating annotated corpora, developing language models, and establishing dictionaries and grammars for low-resource dialects. These efforts are crucial for the preservation and advancement of these dynamic languages, which encapsulate unique cultures, histories, and experiences within their respective communities.

One notable example of such an effort is the Masakhane community, which is dedicated to enhancing natural language processing (NLP) research for African languages through significant initiatives such as MasakhaNER (Adelani et al., 2021). Similar efforts are ongoing for Indonesian languages (Cahyawijaya et al., 2022).

In addition, a long-standing and somewhat unrelated initiative known as the Universal Dependencies project (Nivre et al., 2020) originally aimed to provide a standardized set of syntactic guidelines for a limited number of languages turned out to become the recipient of numerous treebank initiatives for low-resource languages. These initiatives not only adopted the initial guidelines but also expanded upon them to accommodate the unique idiosyncrasies of each language.

In this work, we aim to enhance a pre-existing multi-view treebank devoted to a very low-resource language, namely the North-African Arabic dialect written in Latin script, collected from Algerian sources and denoted as the Narabizi treebank, the first available for this dialect, where Arabizi refers to both the practice of writing Arabic using the Latin alphabet and *N* for the North African dialect (Seddah et al., 2020). Made of noisy user-generated content that exhibits a high level of language variability, its annotations faced many challenges as described by the authors and contained remaining errors (Touileb and Barnes, 2021).

Our work builds on previous efforts to annotate and standardize treebank annotations for low-resource languages to enhance the quality and consistency of linguistic resources (Schluter and van Genabith, 2007; Sade et al., 2018; Türk et al., 2019; Zariquiey et al., 2022).

Following previous research, we consider the impact of refining annotation schemes on downstream tasks. Mille et al. (2012) examine how much a treebank's performance relies on its annotation scheme and whether employing a more linguistically rich scheme would decrease performance. Their findings indicate that using a fine-grained annotation for training a parser does not necessarily improve performance when parsing with a coarse-grained tagset. This observation is relevant to our study as

Proceedings of the 17th Linguistic Annotation Workshop (LAW-XVII), pages 266–278
July 13, 2023 ©2023 Association for Computational Linguistics

we expect refining the treebank could enhance the parsing performance even though the inherent variability of this language, which, tied to its small size treebank, could bring a negative impact on such enhancements.

On the other hand, the experiments conducted by Schluter and van Genabith (2007) demonstrate that using a cleaner and more coherent treebank yields superior results compared to a treebank with a training set five times larger. This observation highlights the significance of high-quality dataset annotations, particularly for smaller datasets. This understanding primarily drives the goal of improving the NArabizi treebank's annotations.

In this context, we propose a heavily revised version of NArabizi treebank (Seddah et al., 2020) that includes two novel annotation layers for Named Entity Recognition (NER) and offensive language detection. One of the goals of this work is also to study the impact of non-gold tokenization on NER, a scenario almost never investigated by the community (Bareket and Tsarfaty, 2021). Our primary contributions are as follows:

- Using error mining tools, we release a new corrected version of the treebank, which leads to improved downstream task performance.
- We show that corrections made to a small size treebank of a highly variable language favorably impacts the performance of NLP models trained on it.
- We augment the treebank by adding NER annotations and offensive language detection, expanding its applicability in various NLP tasks.
- We homogenize tokenization across the dataset, analyze the impact of proper tokenization on UD tasks and NER and conduct a realistic evaluation on predicted tokenization, including NER evaluation.

The enhanced version of the Narabizi Treebank is freely available.[1]

2 Related work

NArabizi The Arabic language exhibits diglossia, where Modern Standard Arabic (MSA) is employed in formal contexts, while dialectal forms are used informally (Habash, 2010). Dialectal forms, which display significant variability across regions and predominantly exist in spoken form, lack standardized spelling when written. Many Arabic speakers employ the Latin script for transcribing their dialects online, using digits and symbols for phonemes not easily mapped to Latin letters (Seddah et al., 2020). This written form, known as Arabizi and its North African variant, NArabizi, often showcases code-switching with French and Amazigh (Amazouz et al., 2017). Textual resources for Arabizi primarily consist of noisy, user-generated content (Foster, 2010; Seddah et al., 2012; Eisenstein, 2013), complicating the creation of supervised models or collection of extensive pre-training datasets. The original NArabizi treebank (Seddah et al., 2020), contains about 1500 sentences. The sentences are randomly sampled from the romanized Algerian dialectal Arabic corpus of Cotterell et al. (2014) and from a small corpus of lyrics from Algerian dialectal Arabic songs popular among the younger generation. This treebank is manually annotated with morpho-syntactic information (parts-of-speech and morphological features), together with glosses and code-switching labels at the word level, as well as sentence-level translations to French. Moreover, this treebank also contains 36% of French tokens. Since its creation, this treebank spawned two derived versions that first added a transliteration to the Arabic script at the word level and sentiment and topic annotation at the sentence level (Touileb and Barnes, 2021). In parallel to our own corrections and annotation work[2], Touileb (2022) extended this work to include a named-entity annotation layer.

Treebanking for User-generated Content Treebanks and annotated corpora have greatly impacted NLP tools, applications, and research in general. Despite the challenges of constructing large and structurally consistent corpora, which requires considerable effort and time, many in the field considered this pursuit valuable and necessary (de Marneffe et al., 2021). However, constructing treebanks for user-generated content is more challenging due to the extensive variation in language usage and style, the prevalence of non-standard spellings and grammar, and the necessity for domain-specific annotations (Sanguinetti et al., 2022). Interest in treebanking user-generated content, such as social media posts and online forum discussions, has risen, and numerous efforts have been undertaken to create treebanks for user-generated content (Foster et al., 2011; Seddah et al., 2012; Sanguinetti

[1] https://gitlab.inria.fr/ariabi/release-narabizi-treebank

[2] Released on November 26th, 2022, the same day as the publication of (Touileb, 2022).

et al., 2018; Rehbein et al., 2019; Sanguinetti et al., 2020).

NER for Dialects and User-generated Content NER is an information extraction task that identifies and categorizes entities at the token level. It is an extensively investigated NLP task with numerous datasets and models for various languages. However, datasets for low-resource languages are rare, and NER datasets for social media platforms such as Twitter predominantly exist for English (Ritter et al., 2011; Derczynski et al., 2016, 2017).

A prominent NER dataset for *lower-than-English* resource languages is the CoNLL 2002 Shared Task dataset (Tjong Kim Sang, 2002), which provides NER annotations for four languages: Dutch, Spanish, Chinese, and Czech. Additionally, the WikiAnn dataset (Pan et al., 2017) includes NER annotations for several low-resource languages. Nevertheless, it is derived from Wikipedia content which is not well-suited for NER tasks involving user-generated content. As mentioned above, Touileb (2022) added a NER annotation for the first version of the NArabizi treebank. However, they did not address the tokenization issues inherent in the dataset and used a different annotation scheme. The following sections delve deeper into the tokenization challenges and the differences between the two datasets.

3 Extending a Low-resource Language treebank

In this section, we outline our methodology for expanding and enhancing the NArabizi treebank. We start by re-annotating tokenization, morpho-syntactic, and syntactic layers to ensure consistency, followed by detailing the annotation guidelines and procedures for NER and Offensive Language detection. We refer to the initial treebank introduced by Seddah et al. (2020) as NArabiziV1 and our extended version as NArabiziV2.

3.1 Maintaining Consistency in Treebank Annotations

We start with an extended clean-up of the NArabiziV1 formatting, which involves reinstating missing part-of-speech tags and rectifying Conllu formatting discrepancies. Then, we embark on general error mining in the lexical and syntactical annotation and correction phase. We implement this stage using semi-automated methods. We do not change the UD tagsets used in the original treebank.

Error Mining We use the UD validator Vr2.11 [3], a tool designed to assess the annotation of treebanks in UD and ensure compliance with the UD specifications. The validator is specifically employed to detect common errors, such as invalid dependency relations, incorrect part-of-speech tags, and inconsistent usage of features like tense and aspect. By leveraging the UD validator, we guarantee that our dataset is syntactically consistent and conforms to the standards established by the UD project. These changes encompass correcting cycle and projectivity issues and removing duplicates.

We also use Errator (Wisniewski, 2018), a data mining tool, to pinpoint inconsistencies in our dataset. It implements the annotation principle presented by Boyd et al. (2008), which suggests that if two identical word sequences have different annotations, one is likely erroneous.

We remove the duplicated sentences when the text field is an exact match and fix duplicated sentence identification for different sentences. We also fixed some problems with the original text, such as Arabic characters encoding and sentence boundaries.

Tokenization We address tokenization concerns to uphold consistency in the NArabizi Treebank annotations. Furthermore, we introduce targeted adjustments to resolve issues related to segmenting specific word classes, including conjunctions, interjections (e.g., "ya"), determiners, and prepositions, especially when adjacent to noun phrases. For example, we segment determiners at the initial vowel ("a" or "e"), as demonstrated in the examples "e ssalam" ("the peace") and "e dounoub" ("the sins"). The lemma field for these terms is aligned with the French translation for the splitting (e.g., "e ssalam" ⇒ "la paix" ("the peace")). For prepositions, we perform splitting at the first letter followed by "i" when possible, as seen in "brabi" ⇒ "b rabi" ("with my god"). We also establish rules for segmenting determiners and proper nouns. When possible, we separate prepositions at the initial letter and "i" and instituted guidelines for segmenting determiners and proper nouns. We implement these alterations for splitting using the Grew graph rewriting tool for NLP (Guillaume, 2021) to improve the consistency and quality of the treebank annotations. Additionally, we fix all the problems mentioned by Touileb and Barnes (2021) regarding the incoherence of the

[3] https://github.com/UniversalDependencies/tools/releases/tag/r2.11

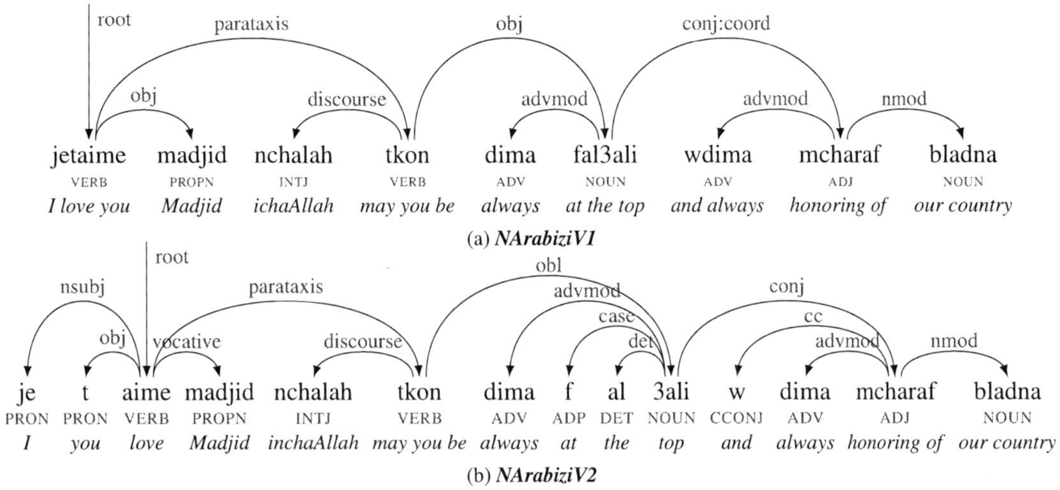

Figure 1: Illustration of an example from the NAarabizi treebank before and after the modifications.

tokenization, wrong translations, and incoherent annotations.

Translation The translation quality is also enhanced; previously, translations were not consistently carried out by Algerian speakers, resulting in local expressions and phrases being frequently misinterpreted, either in a literal manner or, at times, entirely inaccurately. This had implications for lexical and syntactical annotation. For instance, the term "skara" was initially annotated as "on purpose" but was later revised to "taunting". Recognizing that "skara fi" represents a local expression facilitates annotation and promotes corpus harmonization.

Example In Figure 1, we illustrate a parse tree before and after applying several corrections. Tokenization errors in French were rectified ("jetaime" ⇒ "je t aime"), and Arabic prepositions, articles, and conjunctions were separated from the nouns or adverbs they were attached to ("fal3ali" ⇒ "f al 3ali", "wdima" ⇒ "w dima"). We also correct some dependency relations: the previous "obj" relation between the verb "aimer" and the proper noun "madjid" was altered to "vocative".

Interesting Properties The corpus displays several interesting linguistic features, including *parataxis*, *goeswith*, and dislocated structures, characteristic of oral productions and user-generated content. A deeper examination of the root/parataxis ratio and the average parataxis per tree in the corpus, which contains 2066 parataxis for 1287 sentences, shows that the corpus exhibits a high level of juxtaposed clauses resulting from the absence of punctuation. Given the initial data sources (web forums), it is likely that these end of sentences markers were initially present as carriage returns.

As pointed out by Seddah et al. (2020) the corpus also exhibits a high level of spelling variation, reflecting the speakers' diversity in terms of geography and accents. Furthermore, analyzing the number of sentences without a verb and the average number of verbs per sentence shows that NArabizi speakers tend to favor nominalization, as seen in the abundance of ellipses (e.g., "rabbi m3ak" which translates in English to "God bless you").

3.2 Annotation Methodology for NER and Offensive Language Detection

Named Entity Recognition Our NER annotation guidelines are based on the revised tokenization of the NArabizi treebank, which ensures consistency between token-level annotations, an essential aspect of multi-task learning. We use the Inception tool (Klie et al., 2018) for our manual annotation by two native speakers, adhering to the IOB2 Scheme (Tjong Kim Sang and Veenstra, 1999). Each word is labeled with a tag indicating whether it is at the beginning, inside, or outside of a named entity. In case of disagreement between annotators, the multiple annotations were subsequently discussed until agreement was reached, and one annotation was selected to be retained. We extend the FTB NER

(Sagot et al., 2012) French treebank annotations. Our annotation contains the following NE types: PER for real or fictional persons, ORG for organizations, LOC for locations, COMP for companies, and OTH for brands, events, and products.

In cases of ambiguity between products and companies, we adhere to the decision made in the FTB dataset. For person names, we exclude grammatical or contextual words from the mention. We annotate football teams as organizations, and we annotate mentions of "Allah" or "Rabi" as PERderivA. The PERderiv annotation is applied to groups of individuals who originate from or share the same location. Country names are consistently labeled as locations, irrespective of the context. TV channels and ambiguous brand names are annotated as companies, while religious groups are not designated entities. The names of football stadiums are classified under OTH, whereas journal names are identified as organizations.

Table 1 presents the distribution of entities, with a similar distribution observed across both the development and test splits. The most frequent entity type is PERderivA, while the least frequent is COMP.

Type	train	dev	test	Total
PER	371	61	47	479
LOC	358	58	50	466
ORG	200	23	28	251
COMP	6	5	3	14
OTH	44	6	7	57
PERderiv	96	14	13	123
PERderivA	386	57	66	509
Total	1461	224	214	1899

Table 1: Named entity type distribution across train, dev, and test splits.

Type	train	dev	test
nb sentences	1003	139	145
nb tokens	15522	2124	2118
nb unique tokens	6652	1284	1327

Table 2: Statistics of the deduplicated corpus across train, dev, and test splits. The train-dev intersection contains 549 tokens, the train-test intersection contains 551 tokens, and the dev-test intersection contains 266 tokens.

Table 2 displays the number of unique words which can provide information about the language used in the corpus. The fact that the count of unique tokens constitutes nearly half of the total tokens suggests that the language used in the corpus is complex and diverse, with a wide range of vocabulary and expressions. This can make it more challenging for NER algorithms to accurately identify and classify named entities in the corpus.

Touileb (2022) recently introduced NERDz, a version of the NArabizi treebank annotated for NER. As our dataset's annotation labels differ from theirs, we establish a mapping between the two annotation schemes to enable comparisons (cf. see Table 10 in the appendix A). Our schemes also differ in named entities' scope, as we split contracted forms, ours only cover the nominal phrase parts. Regarding nouns, such as "*bled*", which means *country*, some are annotated as entity GPE in NERDz, which is not the case in our dataset. Also, the names of stadiums are annotated as LOC in NERDz while they are considered OTH in our dataset. Similarly, for "*equipe nationale*", which means *national team* is annotated ORG in NERDz, while we do not consider it as an entity, following the FTB NER's guidelines. Added to annotator divergences, this may explain the differences in the count of the entities.

Offensive Language Classification The annotation process for offensive language classification was conducted manually by three annotators with diverse backgrounds. The annotators consisted of two females and one male, each bringing unique expertise to the task. One female annotator is a Ph.D. student in NLP, the other is a Ph.D. student in political sciences, and the male annotator is an engineer with in-depth knowledge of North African football, a prominent topic in the dataset.

The annotators were asked to annotate every sentence as offensive (OFF) or non-offensive (NOT-OFF). Offensive posts included any form of unacceptable language, targeted offense (veiled or direct), insults, threats, profane language, and swear words. To maintain objectivity and minimize potential bias, the annotators were not granted access to the other annotators' work and were not allowed to discuss their annotations with one another. This approach ensured the independence of their judgments, allowing for a more reliable evaluation of the offensive language classification process. For the offensive annotation, the two female annotators did not usually agree with the male annotator as they have different backgrounds and hence different opinions about football-related sentences. The final label is determined through a majority voting process. Additionally, we calculate the average pair-wise Cohen's κ (Cohen, 1960) to highlight how hard this task was. The average κ value is 0.54, indicating a moderate agreement between annotators, common in sentence level annotation for annotators with different backgrounds and topic familiarity (Bobicev and Sokolova, 2017). This disagreement likely stems from the interpretation of terms that can be considered offensive or non-offensive depending on either the dialect or context.

Table 3 presents the distribution of non-offensive and offensive language instances. The dataset features an imbalance between non-offensive and offensive classes, with non-offensive samples being considerably more frequent in each split.

Split	Non-Offensive	Offensive
Train	804	199
Dev	86	53
Test	118	27

Table 3: Offensive language detection distributions across train, dev, and test splits.

4 Dataset Evaluation

We evaluate the NarabiziV2 dataset on UD parsing tasks and NER using standard transfer learning architectures on which we vary the pre-trained language model and the tokenization scenario.

New NArabizi CharacterBert Model Following Riabi et al. (2021), we train a CharacterBERT (El Boukkouri et al., 2020) model, a character-based BERT variant, on a NArabizi new filtered corpus. The authors demonstrate that CharacterBERT achieves significant results when dealing with noisy data while being extremely data efficient.

We improve the initial pre-training dataset used by Riabi et al. (2021) by more stringently filtering non-NArabizi examples from the 99k instances provided by Seddah et al. (2020), as well as incorporating new samples from the CTAB corpus (Amara et al., 2021) and 12k comments extracted from various Facebook and forum posts, mostly in the Tunisian dialect taken from different datasets listed by Younes et al. (2020). This results in a 111k sentence corpus. To exclude non-NArabizi content, we first use a language detection tool (Nakatani, 2010) with a 0.9 confidence threshold to eliminate text in French, English, Hindi, Indonesian, and Russian, which are commonly found in mixed Arabizi data. Following the filtering process, a bootstrap sampling method is adopted to randomly select a subset of the remaining text for manual annotation. This annotated text is then used to train an SVM classifier for NArabizi detection. The final dataset, containing 91k annotated text instances after deduplication, focuses on North African Arabizi text. We make this corpus publicly available.

Sub-word Models We also evaluate the performance of subword-based language models, monolingual and multilingual. For the multilingual subword-based language model, we use mBERT, the multilingual version of BERT (Devlin et al., 2018). It is trained on data from Wikipedia in 104 different languages, including French and Arabic. Muller et al. (2020) demonstrated that such a model could be transferred to NArabizi to some degree. Finally, our monolingual model is DziriBERT (Abdaoui et al., 2021), a monolingual BERT model trained on 1.2M tweets from major and highly-populated Algerian cities scrapped using a set of popular keywords in the Algerian spoken dialect in both Arabic and Latin scripts.

5 Results

5.1 New Results for UD

For our updated version of the treebank, we present results for models trained and tested on NArabiziV2, as shown in Table 4 and highlighted by a red box. These results represent the new state-of-the-art performance for the treebank, and we report findings for three previously used models. The DziriBERT model exhibits the best performance; however, CharacterBERT delivers competitive results while being trained on a mere 7.5% of the data used for training DziriBERT. This observation is consistent with the conclusions drawn by Riabi et al. (2021).

In order to assess the influence of the implemented corrections, we use NArabiziV1 and eliminate duplicate sentences [4]. For this comparison, we focused on the DziriBERT model's performance when trained on either NArabiziV1 or NArabiziV2 and tested on NArabiziV2, as denoted by the blue highlights in Table 4. Training on NArabiziV2 enhances the average scores for UPOS, UAS, and LAS by 3.5 points, illustrating the favorable outcomes of the refinements introduced in the NArabiziV2 dataset. This observation is further substan-

[4]To use the prior version with an equivalent number of sentences, format errors must be rectified (earlier experiments with these sentences excluded them).

Model	Test / Train	*NArabiziV1*			*NArabiziV2*		
		UPOS	UAS	LAS	UPOS	UAS	LAS
mBERT	*NArabiziV1*	$77.42^{\pm 1.52}$	$68.91^{\pm 0.65}$	$56.19^{\pm 0.86}$	$74.59^{\pm 1.42}$	$66.01^{\pm 0.47}$	$53.19^{\pm 0.87}$
DziriBERT	*NArabiziV1*	$83.57^{\pm 0.92}$	$73.97^{\pm 0.72}$	$62.04^{\pm 0.54}$	$80.19^{\pm 0.82}$	$70.28^{\pm 0.83}$	$58.63^{\pm 0.78}$
CharacterBERT	*NArabiziV1*	$76.19^{\pm 2.48}$	$68.78^{\pm 0.36}$	$55.14^{\pm 0.38}$	$73.01^{\pm 2.05}$	$66.10^{\pm 0.48}$	$52.41^{\pm 0.50}$
mBERT	*NArabiziV2*	$74.48^{\pm 0.95}$	$66.03^{\pm 0.35}$	$52.82^{\pm 0.66}$	$79.65^{\pm 0.90}$	$70.56^{\pm 0.32}$	$58.08^{\pm 0.76}$
DziriBERT	*NArabiziV2*	$78.75^{\pm 1.29}$	$70.51^{\pm 0.43}$	$57.51^{\pm 0.67}$	$83.10^{\pm 1.60}$	$74.26^{\pm 0.27}$	$62.66^{\pm 0.52}$
CharacterBERT	*NArabiziV2*	$72.24^{\pm 2.62}$	$65.74^{\pm 0.24}$	$51.86^{\pm 0.51}$	$76.34^{\pm 2.68}$	$69.84^{\pm 0.27}$	$56.27^{\pm 0.54}$

Table 4: Results for UD on test set, DEV set is used for validation (with gold tokenization) (We report average of F1 scores over 5 seeds with the standard deviation)

tiated by examining the performance of CharacterBERT and mBERT, reinforcing the validity of the noted improvements.

A comparative analysis of the results for models trained and tested on NArabiziV1, denoted by the blue box, and those for models trained and tested on NArabiziV2, denoted by the red box, reveals that NArabiziV2 generally yields superior evaluation scores. This observation underlines the impact of the treebank's consistency on the overall performance of the models. When we test on NArabiziV1, the model trained on NArabiziV1 gets better results than the model trained on NArabiziV2. The modifications in tokenization can explain this drop in performance.

5.2 Results for NER and Offensive Language Detection

NER Table 5 presents the results for NER[6]. The CharacterBERT model achieves the highest F1 scores for `LOC` and `OTH` categories, as well as the best performance for `PERderiv` and `PERderivA`. On the other hand, the DziriBERT model outperforms the other models in the `ORG` and `PER` categories. It is important to note that the performance varies significantly across the different categories, reflecting the diverse challenges posed by each entity type. For instance, some categories contain named entities with variations of the same word, such as "Allah"/"Alah"/"Elah", which translates into God for `PERderivA`. Since CharacterBERT uses character-level information, it is more robust to noise, which explains the high performances for those entities.

Offensive Language Detection The imbalance between non-offensive and offensive instances is challenging during the models' training and evaluation. For example, we fail to train mBERT as it only predicts non-offensive labels corresponding to the majority class. This can also be explained by how hard the distinction between offensive and non-offensive content is without context and external knowledge, as explained before. This also raises the question of how relevant is the backgrounds of the annotators for the offensive detection dataset (Basile et al., 2020; Uma et al., 2021; Almanea and Poesio, 2022).

6 Discussion

6.1 Impact of the Pre-training Corpus

In Appendix A, we present the results of all our experiments using the CharacterBERT model trained by Riabi et al. (2021). We observe a heterogeneous improvement in performance, with predominantly better outcomes for our CharacterBERT. We hypothesize that the impact of filtering the training data may not be overly beneficial, possibly due to some smoothing during the training process. Both models' final training data sizes are comparable: 99k for CharacterBERT (Riabi et al., 2021) and 91k for our CharacterBERT. Nevertheless, we believe this new corpus can be a valuable resource for this language.

6.2 Impact of Tokenization

In this section, we investigate the tokenization influence on the enhanced NArabizi Treebank, with a particular emphasis on the homogenization of the tokenization [7] and its subsequent impact on our tasks. We also evaluate the models in a realistic scenario where gold tokenization is unavailable. We use the UDPipe tokenizer (Straka et al., 2016) that employs a Gated Linear Units (GRUs) (Cho

[6] We use Seqeval (Nakayama, 2018) classification report.

[7] We follow the terminology of UD where a tokenizer performs token segmentation (i.e. source tokens).

Model	LOC	ORG	PER	OTH	PERderiv	PERderivA	macro avg
mBERT	82.93 $\pm$ 4.02	66.17 $\pm$ 6.61	61.84 $\pm$ 3.56	25.56 $\pm$ 14.64	57.98 $\pm$ 11.30	95.62 $\pm$ 1.24	65.02 $\pm$ 1.24
DziriBERT	85.84 $\pm$ 3.43	**73.67** $\pm$ 4.03	**73.42** $\pm$ 3.52	26.27 $\pm$ 4.23	57.47 $\pm$ 6.62	94.98 $\pm$ 1.39	68.61 $\pm$ 1.39
CharacterBERT	**87.98** $\pm$ 1.77	70.16 $\pm$ 3.63	69.35 $\pm$ 3.01	**31.27** $\pm$ 9.30	**64.19** $\pm$ 7.03	**96.13** $\pm$ 0.70	**69.85** $\pm$ 0.70

Table 5: NER average of F1 scores over 5 seeds with the standard deviation with gold tokenization[5].

Model	Off	Non-Off	macro avg
mBERT	0.00 $\pm$ 0.00	**89.73** $\pm$ 0.00	44.87 $\pm$ 0.00
DziriBERT	**36.77** $\pm$ 10.88	**84.78** $\pm$ 2.58	60.78 $\pm$ 6.21
CharacterBERT	24.58 $\pm$ 7.44	80.21 $\pm$ 3.66	52.39 $\pm$ 3.18

Table 6: Offensive language detection F1 scores, *off* for offensive and *Non-Off* for non offensive

et al., 2014) artificial neural network for the identification of token and sentence boundaries in plain text. It processes fixed-length segments of Unicode characters and assigns each character to one of three classes: token boundary follows, sentence boundary follows, or no boundary. The tokenizer is trained using the Adam stochastic optimization method, employing randomly shuffled input sentences to ensure effective tokenization across various NLP tasks.

Tokenizer	Prec	Recall	F1
Tokens	97.10 $\pm$ 0.35	95.49 $\pm$ 0.45	96.29 $\pm$ 0.39
Multiwords	79.74 $\pm$ 4.30	33.81 $\pm$ 2.87	47.35 $\pm$ 2.59
Words	92.92 $\pm$ 0.65	88.06 $\pm$ 0.96	90.42 $\pm$ 0.80

Table 7: Tokenization evaluation average scores over 5 folds

We conduct a 5-fold evaluation using the UDPipe tokenizer and assess its performance based on the token-level, multiword, and word-level scores. The results in Table 7 show high scores for the tokens and words F1 scores demonstrate the tokenizer's efficacy in handling various tokens and words, which shows that the tokenization for NArabizi is learnable. We also notice sub-optimal performance regarding multi-words, due to their random occurrence nature.[8].

For our following experiments, we train a tokenizer using the train and dev as held-out and tokenize the test set for evaluation. We do not predict the boundaries of the sentence.

[8]It is important to note that tokens refer to surface tokens (e.g., French "au" counts as one token), while words represent syntactic words ("au" is split into two words, "à" and "le").

Pos-tagging and Dependency Parsing Table 8 presents the results for models trained on the NArabiziV2 training set and tested on both the predicted tokenization and the previous version of tokenization with gold annotations from NArabiziV2. The outcomes for the predicted tokenization indicate that despite having a well-performing tokenizer, as demonstrated in Table 7, there is still a substantial loss in performance when compared to the gold tokenization results, highlighted by the red box in Table 4. Similarly, using the tokenization from NArabiziV1 and gold annotations from NArabiziV2 also exhibits a significant drop in performance. This observation first highlights the impact of the corrections brought to standardize the treebank tokenization and then, given the difference of performance between predicted and gold tokens, calls for the development of morphological-analysers, crucial for Arabic-based dialects, as UD tokenization is indeed a morpho-syntactic process.

Named Entity Recognition Evaluation on Non-Gold Tokenization The conventional evaluation methodology for NER typically assigns entities to distinct token positions. Nevertheless, this method proves inadequate when the token count for evaluation differs from the number of gold tokens, which is almost always the case when processing user-generated content.

As a result, we adopt the evaluation strategy devised by Bareket and Tsarfaty (2021), which associates entities with their forms instead of their indices. This approach yields F1 scores based on strict, exact matches of surface forms for entities, irrespective of the category distinctions, thereby offering a more accurate and reliable evaluation in scenarios with varying token counts. In other words, the gold and predicted NE spans must exhibit an exact match regarding their form, boundaries, and associated entity type.

Table 9 presents the NER scores, considering our three main NE categories: PER, LOC, and ORG. As expected, we observe a decline in performance when evaluating the models using predicted tokenization. The CharacterBERT model exhibits the

Model	*Predicted tokenization*			*NArabiziV1 tokenization*		
	UPOS	UAS	LAS	UPOS	UAS	LAS
mBERT	72.44 $\pm$ 0.87	61.40 $\pm$ 0.29	50.39 $\pm$ 0.64	75.84 $\pm$ 0.92	65.77 $\pm$ 0.40	54.15 $\pm$ 0.68
DziriBERT	76.27 $\pm$ 1.46	65.35 $\pm$ 0.39	55.04 $\pm$ 0.65	79.49 $\pm$ 1.63	70.04 $\pm$ 0.48	59.19 $\pm$ 0.70
CharacterBERT	70.03 $\pm$ 2.10	61.08 $\pm$ 0.18	49.13 $\pm$ 0.42	73.10 $\pm$ 2.33	65.37 $\pm$ 0.22	52.99 $\pm$ 0.50

Table 8: UD results for models trained on NArabiziV2 treebank and tested on test set with predicted tokenization and old tokenization from NArabiziV1

Model	*Gold*	*Predicted*
mBERT	71.79 $\pm$ 2.30	66.76 $\pm$ 1.52
DziriBERT	75.56 $\pm$ 2.13	68.89 $\pm$ 2.64
CharacterBERT	**76.30** $\pm$ 1.29	**70.54** $\pm$ 2.00

Table 9: Comparison of NER scores for PER/ LOC/ ORG entities F1 micro average on predicted tokenization and gold tokenization averaged across five seeds.

best performance on gold and predicted tokenization. Moreover, when evaluated using predicted tokenization, all models demonstrate a similar performance drop. This demonstrates that there is an important gap when evaluating using gold tokenization, which raises the question of how much the current evaluation of NER models reflects the actual model performance in a realistic setting for noisy UGC.

7 Conclusion

In this paper, we present a comprehensive study on the development and refinement of the NArabizi Treebank (Seddah et al., 2020) by improving its annotations, consistency, and tokenization, as well as providing new annotations for NER and offensive language. Our work contributes to the enhancement of the NArabizi Treebank, making it a valuable resource for research on low-resource languages and user-generated content with high variability. We explore the impact of tokenization on the refined NArabizi treebank, employing the UDPipe tokenizer for our evaluation. The results demonstrate the tokenizer's effectiveness in handling various tokens and multiword expressions. Our experiments show that training and testing on the NArabiziv2 improve the UD tasks performances. Furthermore, we show the impact of the tokenization for NER and UD tasks, and we report results using predicted tokenization for evaluation to estimate the models' performance on raw data.

Future research could emphasize expanding the NArabizi Treebank towards other dialects and examining the treebank's potential applications in various NLP tasks. Our dataset is made freely available as part of the new version of the Narabizi Treebank[9]. The next release will additionally contain a set of other sentence translations prepared by a Tunisian speaker. These translations will be interesting for cross-dialect studies, given that the Narabizi corpus is predominantly made of Algerian dialect.

Acknowledgements

We warmly thank the reviewers for their very valuable feedback. This work received funding from the European Union's Horizon 2020 research and innovation programme under grant agreement No. 101021607. We are grateful to Roman Castagné for his valuable feedback and proofreading and wish to gratefully acknowledge the OPAL infrastructure from Université Côte d'Azur for providing resources and support.

References

Amine Abdaoui, Mohamed Berrimi, Mourad Oussalah, and Abdelouahab Moussaoui. 2021. Dziribert: a pre-trained language model for the algerian dialect. *arXiv preprint arXiv:2109.12346*.

David Ifeoluwa Adelani, Jade Abbott, Graham Neubig, Daniel D'souza, Julia Kreutzer, Constantine Lignos, Chester Palen-Michel, Happy Buzaaba, Shruti Rijhwani, Sebastian Ruder, Stephen Mayhew, Israel Abebe Azime, Shamsuddeen H. Muhammad, Chris Chinenye Emezue, Joyce Nakatumba-Nabende, Perez Ogayo, Aremu Anuoluwapo, Catherine Gitau, Derguene Mbaye, Jesujoba Alabi, Seid Muhie Yimam, Tajuddeen Rabiu Gwadabe, Ignatius Ezeani, Rubungo Andre Niyongabo, Jonathan Mukiibi, Verrah Otiende, Iroro Orife, Davis David, Samba Ngom, Tosin Adewumi, Paul Rayson, Mofetoluwa Adeyemi, Gerald Muriuki, Emmanuel Anebi, Chiamaka Chukwuneke, Nkiruka Odu, Eric Peter Wairagala, Samuel Oyerinde, Clemencia Siro, Tobius Saul Bateesa,

[9] `https://gitlab.inria.fr/ariabi/release-narabizi-treebank`

Temilola Oloyede, Yvonne Wambui, Victor Akinode, Deborah Nabagereka, Maurice Katusiime, Ayodele Awokoya, Mouhamadane MBOUP, Dibora Gebreyohannes, Henok Tilaye, Kelechi Nwaike, Degaga Wolde, Abdoulaye Faye, Blessing Sibanda, Orevaoghene Ahia, Bonaventure F. P. Dossou, Kelechi Ogueji, Thierno Ibrahima DIOP, Abdoulaye Diallo, Adewale Akinfaderin, Tendai Marengereke, and Salomey Osei. 2021. MasakhaNER: Named entity recognition for African languages. *Transactions of the Association for Computational Linguistics*, 9:1116–1131.

Dina Almanea and Massimo Poesio. 2022. ArMIS - the Arabic misogyny and sexism corpus with annotator subjective disagreements. In *Proceedings of the Thirteenth Language Resources and Evaluation Conference*, pages 2282–2291, Marseille, France. European Language Resources Association.

Amina Amara, Houcemeddine Turki, Mohamed Ali Hadj Taieb, Mohamed Ben Aouicha, and Kawthar Ellouze. 2021. Ctab: Corpus of tunisian arabizi. This corpus has been developed by the Data Engineering and Semantics Research Unit (DES- Unit), University of Sfax, Tunisia. It has been developed to increase the coverage of Latin Script in the NLP resources for Tunisian. It is included as a part of the Tunisian Arabic Corpus (http://www.tunisiya.org/).

Djegdjiga Amazouz, Martine Adda-Decker, and Lori Lamel. 2017. Addressing code-switching in french/algerian arabic speech. In *Interspeech 2017*, pages 62–66.

Dan Bareket and Reut Tsarfaty. 2021. Neural modeling for named entities and morphology (NEMO2). *Transactions of the Association for Computational Linguistics*, 9:909–928.

Valerio Basile et al. 2020. It's the end of the gold standard as we know it. on the impact of pre-aggregation on the evaluation of highly subjective tasks. In *CEUR WORKSHOP PROCEEDINGS*, volume 2776, pages 31–40. CEUR-WS.

Victoria Bobicev and Marina Sokolova. 2017. Inter-annotator agreement in sentiment analysis: Machine learning perspective. In *Proceedings of the International Conference Recent Advances in Natural Language Processing, RANLP 2017*, pages 97–102, Varna, Bulgaria. INCOMA Ltd.

Adriane Boyd, Markus Dickinson, and W Detmar Meurers. 2008. On detecting errors in dependency treebanks. *Research on Language and Computation*, 6(2):113–137.

Samuel Cahyawijaya, Holy Lovenia, Alham Fikri Aji, Genta Indra Winata, Bryan Wilie, Rahmad Mahendra, Christian Wibisono, Ade Romadhony, Karissa Vincentio, Fajri Koto, Jennifer Santoso, David Moeljadi, Cahya Wirawan, Frederikus Hudi, Ivan Halim Parmonangan, Ika Alfina, Muhammad Satrio Wicaksono, Ilham Firdausi Putra, Samsul Rahmadani, Yulianti Oenang, Ali Akbar Septiandri, James Jaya, Kaustubh D. Dhole, Arie Ardiyanti Suryani, Rifki Afina Putri, Dan Su, Keith Stevens, Made Nindyatama Nityasya, Muhammad Farid Adilazuarda, Ryan Ignatius, Ryandito Diandaru, Tiezheng Yu, Vito Ghifari, Wenliang Dai, Yan Xu, Dyah Damapuspita, Cuk Tho, Ichwanul Muslim Karo Karo, Tirana Noor Fatyanosa, Ziwei Ji, Pascale Fung, Graham Neubig, Timothy Baldwin, Sebastian Ruder, Herry Sujaini, Sakriani Sakti, and Ayu Purwarianti. 2022. Nusacrowd: Open source initiative for indonesian nlp resources.

Kyunghyun Cho, Bart van Merriënboer, Caglar Gulcehre, Dzmitry Bahdanau, Fethi Bougares, Holger Schwenk, and Yoshua Bengio. 2014. Learning phrase representations using RNN encoder–decoder for statistical machine translation. In *Proceedings of the 2014 Conference on Empirical Methods in Natural Language Processing (EMNLP)*, pages 1724–1734, Doha, Qatar. Association for Computational Linguistics.

Jacob Cohen. 1960. A coefficient of agreement for nominal scales. *Educational and Psychological Measurement*, 20(1):37–46.

Ryan Cotterell, Adithya Renduchintala, Naomi Saphra, and Chris Callison-Burch. 2014. An Algerian Arabic-French code-switched corpus. In *Workshop on Free/Open-Source Arabic Corpora and Corpora Processing Tools Workshop Programme*, page 34.

Marie-Catherine de Marneffe, Christopher D. Manning, Joakim Nivre, and Daniel Zeman. 2021. Universal Dependencies. *Computational Linguistics*, 47(2):255–308.

Leon Derczynski, Kalina Bontcheva, and Ian Roberts. 2016. Broad Twitter corpus: A diverse named entity recognition resource. In *Proceedings of COLING 2016, the 26th International Conference on Computational Linguistics: Technical Papers*, pages 1169–1179, Osaka, Japan. The COLING 2016 Organizing Committee.

Leon Derczynski, Eric Nichols, Marieke van Erp, and Nut Limsopatham. 2017. Results of the WNUT2017 shared task on novel and emerging entity recognition. In *Proceedings of the 3rd Workshop on Noisy User-generated Text*, pages 140–147, Copenhagen, Denmark. Association for Computational Linguistics.

Jacob Devlin, Ming-Wei Chang, Kenton Lee, and Kristina Toutanova. 2018. Bert: Pre-training of deep bidirectional transformers for language understanding. *arXiv preprint arXiv:1810.04805*.

Jacob Eisenstein. 2013. What to do about bad language on the internet. In *Proceedings of the 2013 conference of the North American Chapter of the association for computational linguistics: Human language technologies*, pages 359–369.

Hicham El Boukkouri, Olivier Ferret, Thomas Lavergne, Hiroshi Noji, Pierre Zweigenbaum, and Jun'ichi Tsujii. 2020. CharacterBERT: Reconciling ELMo and

BERT for word-level open-vocabulary representations from characters. In *Proceedings of the 28th International Conference on Computational Linguistics*, pages 6903–6915, Barcelona, Spain (Online). International Committee on Computational Linguistics.

Jennifer Foster. 2010. "cba to check the spelling": Investigating parser performance on discussion forum posts. In *Human Language Technologies: The 2010 Annual Conference of the North American Chapter of the Association for Computational Linguistics*, pages 381–384, Los Angeles, California. Association for Computational Linguistics.

Jennifer Foster, Özlem Çetinoğlu, Joachim Wagner, Joseph Le Roux, Joakim Nivre, Deirdre Hogan, and Josef van Genabith. 2011. From news to comment: Resources and benchmarks for parsing the language of web 2.0. In *Proceedings of 5th International Joint Conference on Natural Language Processing*, pages 893–901, Chiang Mai, Thailand. Asian Federation of Natural Language Processing.

Bruno Guillaume. 2021. Graph matching and graph rewriting: Grew tools for corpus exploration, maintenance and conversion. In *Proceedings of the 16th Conference of the European Chapter of the Association for Computational Linguistics: System Demonstrations*, pages 168–175.

Nizar Habash. 2010. *Introduction to Arabic Natural Language Processing*. Morgan and Claypool.

Pratik Joshi, Sebastin Santy, Amar Budhiraja, Kalika Bali, and Monojit Choudhury. 2020. The state and fate of linguistic diversity and inclusion in the NLP world. In *Proceedings of the 58th Annual Meeting of the Association for Computational Linguistics*, pages 6282–6293, Online. Association for Computational Linguistics.

Jan-Christoph Klie, Michael Bugert, Beto Boullosa, Richard Eckart de Castilho, and Iryna Gurevych. 2018. The inception platform: Machine-assisted and knowledge-oriented interactive annotation. In *proceedings of the 27th international conference on computational linguistics: system demonstrations*, pages 5–9.

Simon Mille, Alicia Burga, Gabriela Ferraro, and Leo Wanner. 2012. How does the granularity of an annotation scheme influence dependency parsing performance? In *Proceedings of COLING 2012: Posters*, pages 839–852, Mumbai, India. The COLING 2012 Organizing Committee.

Benjamin Muller, Benoit Sagot, and Djamé Seddah. 2020. Can multilingual language models transfer to an unseen dialect? a case study on north african arabizi. *arXiv preprint arXiv:2005.00318*.

Shuyo Nakatani. 2010. Language detection library for java.

Hiroki Nakayama. 2018. seqeval: A python framework for sequence labeling evaluation. Software available from https://github.com/chakki-works/seqeval.

Joakim Nivre, Marie-Catherine de Marneffe, Filip Ginter, Jan Hajič, Christopher D. Manning, Sampo Pyysalo, Sebastian Schuster, Francis Tyers, and Daniel Zeman. 2020. Universal Dependencies v2: An evergrowing multilingual treebank collection. In *Proceedings of the Twelfth Language Resources and Evaluation Conference*, pages 4034–4043, Marseille, France. European Language Resources Association.

Xiaoman Pan, Boliang Zhang, Jonathan May, Joel Nothman, Kevin Knight, and Heng Ji. 2017. Cross-lingual name tagging and linking for 282 languages. In *Proceedings of the 55th Annual Meeting of the Association for Computational Linguistics (Volume 1: Long Papers)*, pages 1946–1958, Vancouver, Canada. Association for Computational Linguistics.

Ines Rehbein, Josef Ruppenhofer, and Bich-Ngoc Do. 2019. tweeDe – a Universal Dependencies treebank for German tweets. In *Proceedings of the 18th International Workshop on Treebanks and Linguistic Theories (TLT, SyntaxFest 2019)*, pages 100–108, Paris, France. Association for Computational Linguistics.

Arij Riabi, Benoît Sagot, and Djamé Seddah. 2021. Can character-based language models improve downstream task performances in low-resource and noisy language scenarios? In *Proceedings of the Seventh Workshop on Noisy User-generated Text (W-NUT 2021)*, pages 423–436, Online. Association for Computational Linguistics.

Alan Ritter, Sam Clark, Mausam, and Oren Etzioni. 2011. Named entity recognition in tweets: An experimental study. In *Proceedings of the 2011 Conference on Empirical Methods in Natural Language Processing*, pages 1524–1534, Edinburgh, Scotland, UK. Association for Computational Linguistics.

Shoval Sade, Amit Seker, and Reut Tsarfaty. 2018. The Hebrew Universal Dependency treebank: Past present and future. In *Proceedings of the Second Workshop on Universal Dependencies (UDW 2018)*, pages 133–143, Brussels, Belgium. Association for Computational Linguistics.

Benoît Sagot, Marion Richard, and Rosa Stern. 2012. Annotation référentielle du corpus arboré de paris 7 en entités nommées. In *Traitement Automatique des Langues Naturelles (TALN)*, volume 2.

Manuela Sanguinetti, Cristina Bosco, Lauren Cassidy, Özlem Çetinoğlu, Alessandra Teresa Cignarella, Teresa Lynn, Ines Rehbein, Josef Ruppenhofer, Djamé Seddah, and Amir Zeldes. 2020. Treebanking user-generated content: A proposal for a unified representation in Universal Dependencies. In *Proceedings of the Twelfth Language Resources and Evaluation Conference*, pages 5240–5250, Marseille, France. European Language Resources Association.

Manuela Sanguinetti, Cristina Bosco, Lauren Cassidy, Özlem Çetinoğlu, Alessandra Teresa Cignarella, Teresa Lynn, Ines Rehbein, Josef Ruppenhofer, Djamé Seddah, and Amir Zeldes. 2022. Treebanking user-generated content: a ud based overview of guidelines, corpora and unified recommendations. *Language Resources and Evaluation*, pages 1–52.

Manuela Sanguinetti, Cristina Bosco, Alberto Lavelli, Alessandro Mazzei, Oronzo Antonelli, and Fabio Tamburini. 2018. PoSTWITA-UD: an Italian Twitter treebank in Universal Dependencies. In *Proceedings of the Eleventh International Conference on Language Resources and Evaluation (LREC 2018)*, Miyazaki, Japan. European Language Resources Association (ELRA).

Natalie Schluter and Josef van Genabith. 2007. Preparing, restructuring, and augmenting a french treebank: Lexicalised parsers or coherent treebanks?

Djamé Seddah, Farah Essaidi, Amal Fethi, Matthieu Futeral, Benjamin Muller, Pedro Javier Ortiz Suárez, Benoît Sagot, and Abhishek Srivastava. 2020. Building a user-generated content North-African Arabizi treebank: Tackling hell. In *Proceedings of the 58th Annual Meeting of the Association for Computational Linguistics*, pages 1139–1150, Online. Association for Computational Linguistics.

Djamé Seddah, Benoit Sagot, Marie Candito, Virginie Mouilleron, and Vanessa Combet. 2012. The French Social Media Bank: a treebank of noisy user generated content. In *Proceedings of COLING 2012*, pages 2441–2458, Mumbai, India. The COLING 2012 Organizing Committee.

Milan Straka, Jan Hajič, and Jana Straková. 2016. UDPipe: Trainable pipeline for processing CoNLL-U files performing tokenization, morphological analysis, POS tagging and parsing. In *Proceedings of the Tenth International Conference on Language Resources and Evaluation (LREC'16)*, pages 4290–4297, Portorož, Slovenia. European Language Resources Association (ELRA).

Erik F. Tjong Kim Sang. 2002. Introduction to the CoNLL-2002 shared task: Language-independent named entity recognition. In *COLING-02: The 6th Conference on Natural Language Learning 2002 (CoNLL-2002)*.

Erik F. Tjong Kim Sang and Jorn Veenstra. 1999. Representing text chunks. In *Ninth Conference of the European Chapter of the Association for Computational Linguistics*, pages 173–179, Bergen, Norway. Association for Computational Linguistics.

Samia Touileb. 2022. Nerdz: A preliminary dataset of named entities for algerian. In *Proceedings of the 2nd Conference of the Asia-Pacific Chapter of the Association for Computational Linguistics and the 12th International Joint Conference on Natural Language Processing*, pages 95–101.

Samia Touileb and Jeremy Barnes. 2021. The interplay between language similarity and script on a novel multi-layer Algerian dialect corpus. In *Findings of the Association for Computational Linguistics: ACL-IJCNLP 2021*, pages 3700–3712, Online. Association for Computational Linguistics.

Utku Türk, Furkan Atmaca, Şaziye Betül Özateş, Abdullatif Köksal, Balkiz Ozturk Basaran, Tunga Gungor, and Arzucan Özgür. 2019. Turkish treebanking: Unifying and constructing efforts. In *Proceedings of the 13th Linguistic Annotation Workshop*, pages 166–177, Florence, Italy. Association for Computational Linguistics.

Alexandra N Uma, Tommaso Fornaciari, Dirk Hovy, Silviu Paun, Barbara Plank, and Massimo Poesio. 2021. Learning from disagreement: A survey. *Journal of Artificial Intelligence Research*, 72:1385–1470.

Guillaume Wisniewski. 2018. Errator: a tool to help detect annotation errors in the universal dependencies project. In *Proceedings of the Eleventh International Conference on Language Resources and Evaluation (LREC 2018)*.

Jihene Younes, Emna Souissi, Hadhemi Achour, and Ahmed Ferchichi. 2020. Language resources for maghrebi arabic dialects' nlp: a survey. *Language Resources and Evaluation*, 54(4):1079–1142.

Roberto Zariquiey, Claudia Alvarado, Ximena Echevarría, Luisa Gomez, Rosa Gonzales, Mariana Illescas, Sabina Oporto, Frederic Blum, Arturo Oncevay, and Javier Vera. 2022. Building an endangered language resource in the classroom: Universal Dependencies for kakataibo. In *Proceedings of the Thirteenth Language Resources and Evaluation Conference*, pages 3840–3851, Marseille, France. European Language Resources Association.

A Appendix

A.1 Datasets

NERDz		Our dataset	
Entities	Count	Entities	Count
PER	467	PER	479
GPE/LOC	479	LOC	466
ORG	290	ORG/COMP	265

Table 10: Mapping of NER labels in our dataset to the Published NERDz dataset (Touileb, 2022).

A.2 Results with CharacterBERT from (Riabi et al., 2021)

Model	Train \ Test	NArabiziV1 UPOS	NArabiziV1 UAS	NArabiziV1 LAS	NArabiziV2 UPOS	NArabiziV2 UAS	NArabiziV2 LAS
CharacterBERT (Riabi et al., 2021)	*NArabiziV1*	75.33 ± 2.77	67.86 ± 0.95	54.40 ± 0.81	72.33 ± 2.60	65.17 ± 0.79	51.51 ± 1.05
CharacterBERT (Ours)	*NArabiziV1*	**76.19** ± 2.48	**68.78** ± 0.36	**55.14** ± 0.38	**73.01** ± 2.05	**66.10** ± 0.48	**52.41** ± 0.50
CharacterBERT (Riabi et al., 2021)	*NArabiziV2*	**72.46** ± 3.19	65.30 ± 0.50	51.84 ± 0.68	**79.65** ± 0.90	**70.56** ± 0.32	**58.08** ± 0.76
CharacterBERT (Ours)	*NArabiziV2*	72.24 ± 2.62	**65.74** ± 0.24	**51.86** ± 0.51	76.34 ± 2.68	69.84 ± 0.27	56.27 ± 0.54

Table 11: Results for UD on test set, DEV set is used for validation (with gold tokenization) (We report average of F1 scores over 5 seeds with the standard deviation)

Model	LOC	ORG	PER	OTH	PERderiv	PERderivA
CharacterBERT (Riabi et al., 2021)	86.80 ± 2.01	68.53 ± 6.09	65.36 ± 2.74	**45.16** ± 13.60	58.96 ± 10.42	95.00 ± 1.32
CharacterBERT (Ours)	**87.98** ± 1.77	**70.16** ± 3.63	**69.35** ± 3.01	31.27 ± 9.30	**64.19** ± 7.03	**96.13** ± 0.70

Table 12: NER average of F1 scores over 5 seeds with the standard deviation with gold tokenization[10].

Model	Off	Non-Off	macro avg
CharacterBERT (Riabi et al., 2021)	**36.29** ± 5.73	76.49 ± 3.81	**56.39** ± 2.95
CharacterBERT (Ours)	24.58 ± 7.44	**80.21** ± 3.66	52.39 ± 3.18

Table 13: Offensive language detection F1 scores, *off* for offensive and *Non-Off* for non offensive

Author Index